Scientific Computing:
An Introductory Survey

McGraw-Hill Series in Computer Science

SENIOR CONSULTING EDITOR
C. L. Liu, University of Illinois at Urbana-Champaign

CONSULTING EDITOR
Allen B. Tucker, Bowdoin College

Fundamentals of Computing and Programming
Computer Organization and Architecture
Computers in Society/Ethics
Systems and Languages
Theoretical Foundations
Software Engineering and Database
Artificial Intelligence
Networks, Parallel and Distributed Computing
Graphics and Visualization
The MIT Electrical and Computer Science Series

Theoretical Foundations

*Cormen, Leiserson, and Rivest: *Introduction to Algorithms*
Heath: *Scientific Computing: An Introductory Survey*
Kohavi: *Switching and Finite Automata Theory*
Liu: *Introduction to Combinatorial Mathematics*
Liu: *Elements of Discrete Mathematics*
McEliece, Ash, and Ash: *Introduction to Discrete Mathematics*
Martin: *Introduction to Languages and the Theory of Computation*
Rosen: *Discrete Mathematics and Its Applications*
Skeel and Keiper: *Elementary Numerical Computing with Mathematica®*

*Co-published by the MIT Press and The McGraw-Hill Companies, Inc.

Scientific Computing:

An Introductory Survey

Michael T. Heath

University of Illinois at Urbana-Champaign

THE McGRAW-HILL COMPANIES, INC.

New York   St. Louis   San Francisco   Auckland   Bogotá   Caracas
Lisbon   London   Madrid   Mexico City   Milan   Montreal   New Delhi
San Juan   Singapore   Sydney   Tokyo   Toronto

McGraw-Hill

A Division of The **McGraw·Hill** *Companies*

This book was set in Times Roman by Publication Services, Inc.
The editor was Eric M. Munson;
the production supervisor was Denise L. Puryear.
The design manager was Charles A. Carson;
the cover designer was Rafael Hernandez.
Project supervision was done by Publication Services, Inc.
R. R. Donnelley & Sons Company was printer and binder.

SCIENTIFIC COMPUTING:
An Introductory Survey

1 2 3 4 5 6 7 8 9 0 DOC DOC 9 0 9 8 7 6

ISBN 0-07-027684-6

Library of Congress Cataloging-in-Publication Data
Heath, Michael T.
    Scientific computing : an introductory survey / Michael T. Heath.
        p.   cm.
    Includes bibliographical references and index.
    ISBN 0-07-027684-6
    1. Science–Data processing.   2. Numerical analysis–Data
processing.   I. Title.
    Q183.8.H4   1996
    519.4'0285–dc20   96-43722

http://www.mhcollege.com

ABOUT THE AUTHOR

MICHAEL T. HEATH holds three positions at the University of Illinois at Urbana-Champaign: Professor in the Department of Computer Science, Director of the Computational Science and Engineering Program, and Senior Research Scientist at the National Center for Supercomputing Applications (NCSA). He received a B.A. in Mathematics from the University of Kentucky, an M.S. in Mathematics from the University of Tennessee, and a Ph.D. in Computer Science from Stanford University. Before joining the University of Illinois in 1991, he spent a number of years at Oak Ridge National Laboratory, first as Eugene P. Wigner Postdoctoral Fellow and later as Computer Science Group Leader in the Mathematical Sciences Research Section. His research interests are in numerical analysis—particularly numerical linear algebra and optimization—and in parallel computing. He has edited two conference proceedings on hypercube multiprocessors; and he has been an editor of the *SIAM Journal on Scientific Computing, SIAM Review*, and the *International Journal of Supercomputer Applications and High Performance Computing*.

To Mona

CONTENTS

PREFACE

This book presents a broad overview of numerical methods and software for students and professionals in computationally oriented disciplines who need to solve mathematical problems. It is not a traditional numerical analysis text in that it contains relatively little detailed analysis of the computational algorithms presented. Instead, I try to convey a general understanding of the techniques available for solving problems in each major category, including proper problem formulation and interpretation of results, but I advocate the use of professionally written mathematical software for obtaining solutions whenever possible. The book is aimed much more at potential users of mathematical software than at potential creators of such software. I hope to make the reader aware of the relevant issues in selecting appropriate methods and software and using them wisely.

At the University of Illinois, this book is used as the text for a comprehensive, one-semester course on numerical methods that serves three main purposes:

- As a terminal course for senior undergraduates, mainly computer science, mathematics, and engineering majors
- As a breadth course for graduate students in computer science who do *not* intend to specialize in numerical analysis
- As a training course for graduate students in science and engineering who need to use numerical methods and software in their research. It is a core course for the interdisciplinary graduate program in Computational Science and Engineering sponsored by the College of Engineering.

To accommodate this diverse student clientele, the prerequisites for the course and the book have been kept to a minimum: basic familiarity with linear algebra, multivariate calculus, and a smattering of differential equations. No prior familiarity with numerical methods is assumed. The book adopts a fairly sophisticated perspective, however, and the course moves at a rather rapid pace in order to cover all of the material, so a reasonable level of maturity on the part of the student (or reader) is advisable. Beyond the academic setting, I hope that the book will also be useful as a reference for practicing engineers and scientists who may need a quick overview of a given computational problem and the methods and software available for solving it.

Although the book emphasizes the use of mathematical software, unlike some other software-oriented texts it does not provide any software, nor does it concentrate on any specific software packages, libraries, or environments. Instead, for each problem category pointers are provided to specific routines available from publicly accessible repositories, other textbooks, and the major commercial libraries and packages. In many academic and industrial computing environments such software is already installed, and in any case pointers are also provided to public domain software that is freely accessible via the Internet. The computer exercises in the book are not dependent on any specific choice of software or programming language.

The main elements in the organization of the book are as follows:

Chapters. Each chapter of the book covers a major computational problem area. The first half of the book deals primarily with algebraic problems, whereas the second half treats analytic problems involving derivatives and integrals. The first two chapters are fundamental to the remainder of the book, but the subsequent chapters can be covered in various orders according to the instructor's preference. More specifically, the direct interdependence of chapters is as follows:

Chapter	Depends on	Chapter	Depends on	Chapter	Depends on
2	1	6	1–5	10	1, 2, 4, 5, 7–9
3	1, 2	7	1, 2	11	1, 2, 4–10
4	1–3	8	1, 2, 5, 7	12	1, 2, 7
5	1, 2, 4	9	1, 2, 4, 5, 7, 8	13	1

Thus, the main opportunities for moving material around are to cover Chapters 7 and 12 earlier and Chapter 6 later than their appearance in the book. For example, Chapters 3, 7, and 12 all involve some type of data fitting, so it might be desirable to cover them as a unit. As another example, iterative methods for linear systems are covered in Chapter 11 on partial differential equations because that is where the most important motivating examples come from, but much of this material could be covered immediately following direct methods for linear systems in Chapter 2.

The entire book can be covered in one semester by moving at a rapid pace or by omitting a few sections. There is also sufficient material for a more leisurely two-quarter course. A one-quarter course would likely require omitting some chapters. Chapter 13, on random numbers and stochastic simulation, is only peripherally related to the remainder of the book and is an obvious candidate for omission if time runs short (random number generators are used in a number of exercises throughout the book, however).

Examples. Almost every concept and method introduced is illustrated by one or more examples. These examples are meant to supplement the relatively terse general discussion and should be read as an essential part of the text. The examples have been kept as simple as possible (sometimes at the risk of oversimplification) so that the reader can easily follow them. In my experience, a simple example that is thoroughly understood is usually more helpful than a more realistic example that is more difficult to follow.

Software. The lists of available software for each problem category are meant to be reasonably comprehensive. I have not attempted to single out the "best" software available for a given problem, partly because usually no single package is superior in all respects and partly to allow for the varied software availability and choice of programming language that may apply for different readers. All of the recommended software is at least competently written, and some of it is superb.

Exercises. The book contains many exercises, which are divided into three classes:

- *Review questions,* which are short-answer questions designed to test basic conceptual understanding

- *Exercises,* which require somewhat more thought, longer answers, and possibly some hand computation
- *Computer problems,* which require some programming and often involve the use of existing software.

The *review questions* are meant for self-testing on the part of the reader. They include some deliberate repetition to drive home key points and to build confidence in the mastery of the material. The longer *exercises* are meant to be suitable for written homework assignments. Some of these require manual computations with simple examples, whereas others are designed to supply missing details of derivations and proofs omitted from the main text. The latter should be especially useful if the book is used for a more theoretical course. The *computer problems* provide an opportunity for hands-on experience in using the recommended software for solving typical problems in each category. Some of these problems are generic, but others are directly related to specific applications in various scientific and engineering disciplines.

This book provides a fairly comprehensive introduction to scientific computing, but scientific computing is only part of what has become known as *computational science.* Computational science is a relatively new mode of scientific investigation that includes several phases:

1. Development of a mathematical model—often expressed as some type of equation—of a physical phenomenon or system of interest
2. Development of an algorithm to solve the equation numerically
3. Implementation of the algorithm in computer software
4. Numerical simulation of the physical phenomenon using the computer software
5. Representation of the computed results in some comprehensible form, often through graphical visualization
6. Interpretation and validation of the computed results, which may lead to correction or further refinement of the original mathematical model and repetition of the cycle, if necessary

As construed in this book, scientific computing is primarily concerned with phases 2–4: the development, implementation, and use of numerical algorithms and software. Although the other phases are equally as important in the overall process, their detailed study is beyond the scope of this book. A serious study of mathematical modeling would require far more domain-specific knowledge than we assume and far more space than we can accommodate. Fortunately, mathematical modeling is the subject of numerous excellent books, some of a general nature and others focusing on specific individual disciplines. Thus, although numerous concrete applications appear in the exercises, the main discussion treats each major problem type in a very general form. Similarly, the accuracy of computed results is measured with respect to the true solution of a given equation, whereas in practice results should also be validated against the actual physical phenomenon being modeled whenever possible. Learning about scientific computing is an important component in the training of computational scientists and engineers, but there is more to computational science than just numerical methods and software.

Accordingly, this book is intended as only a portion of a well-rounded curriculum in computational science, which should also include additional computer skills—e.g., software design principles, data structures, non-numerical algorithms, performance evaluation and tuning, graphics/visualization, and the software tools associated with all of these—as well as much deeper treatment of specific applications in science and engineering.

The presentation of largely familiar material is inevitably influenced by other treatments one has seen. My initial experience in presenting some of the material in this book was as a graduate teaching assistant at Stanford University using a prepublication draft of the book by Forsythe, Malcolm, and Moler [82]. "FMM" was one of the first software-oriented textbooks on numerical methods, and its spirit is very much reflected in the current book. I later used FMM very successfully in teaching in-house courses for practical-minded scientists and engineers at Oak Ridge National Laboratory, and more recently I have used its successor, by Kahaner, Moler, and Nash [142], in teaching a similar course at the University of Illinois. Readers familiar with those two books will recognize the origin of some aspects of the treatment given here. As far as they go, those two books would be difficult to improve upon; in the present book I have incorporated a significant amount of new material while trying to preserve the spirit of the originals. In addition to these two obvious sources, I have doubtless borrowed many examples and exercises from many other sources over the years, for which I am grateful.

I would like to acknowledge the influence of the mentors who first introduced me to the unexpected charms of numerical computation, Alston Householder and Gene Golub. I am grateful for the feedback I have received from students and instructors who have used the lecture notes from which this book evolved and from numerous reviewers, some anonymous, who read and commented on the manuscript before publication. Specifically, I would like to acknowledge the helpful input of Eric Grosse, Jason Hibbeler, Paul Hovland, Linda Kaufman, Thomas Kerkhoven, Cleve Moler, Padma Raghavan, David Richards, Faisal Saied, Paul Saylor, Robert Skeel, and the following reviewers: Alan George, University of Waterloo; Dianne O'Leary, University of Maryland; James M. Ortega, University of Virginia; John Strikwerda, University of Wisconsin; and Lloyd N. Trefethen, Cornell University. Finally, I deeply appreciate the patience and understanding of my wife, Mona, during the countless hours spent in writing the original lecture notes and then transforming them into this book. With great pleasure and gratitude I dedicate the book to her.

Michael T. Heath

NOTATION

The notation used in this book is rather standard and should require little explanation. We freely use vector and matrix notation, generally using uppercase letters for matrices and lowercase letters for vectors. Lowercase Greek letters usually denote scalars. Iteration and component indices are denoted by subscripts, usually i through n. For example, a vector x and matrix A might have entries x_i and a_{ij}, respectively. On the few occasions when both an iteration index and a component index are needed, the iteration is indicated by a parenthesized superscript, as in $x_i^{(k)}$ to indicate the ith component of the kth vector in a sequence. Otherwise, x_i may denote either the ith component of a vector x or the ith vector in a sequence; the particular meaning should be clear from context.

For simplicity, we will deal primarily with real vectors and matrices, although most of the theory and algorithms we discuss carry over with little or no change to the complex case. The set of real numbers is denoted by $\mathbb{R}$, n-dimensional real Euclidean space by $\mathbb{R}^n$, and the set of real $m \times n$ matrices by $\mathbb{R}^{m \times n}$.

The transpose of a vector or matrix is indicated by a superscript T, and the conjugate transpose by superscript H (for Hermitian). Unless otherwise indicated, all vectors are regarded as column vectors; a row vector is indicated by explicitly transposing a column vector. For typesetting convenience, the components of a column vector are sometimes indicated by transposing the corresponding row vector, as in $x = [x_1 \quad x_2]^T$. The inner product (also known as dot product or scalar product) of two n-vectors x and y is simply a special case of matrix multiplication and thus is denoted by $x^T y$ (or $x^H y$ in the complex case). Similarly, their outer product, which is an $n \times n$ matrix, is denoted by xy^T. The identity matrix of order n is denoted by I_n (or just I if n is clear from context), and its ith column is denoted by e_i. A diagonal matrix with diagonal entries $d_1, \ldots, d_n$ is denoted by $\mathrm{diag}(d_1, \ldots, d_n)$.

The ordinary derivative of a function $f(t)$ of one variable is denoted by df/dt or by $f'(t)$. Partial derivatives of a function of several variables, such as $u(x, y)$, are denoted by $\partial u / \partial x$, for example, or in some contexts by a subscript, as in u_x. Notation for gradient vectors and Jacobian and Hessian matrices will be introduced as needed. All logarithms are natural logarithms (base $e \approx 2.718$) unless another base is explicitly indicated.

The computational cost, or complexity, of numerical algorithms is usually measured by the number of arithmetic operations required. Traditionally, numerical analysts have counted only multiplications (and possibly divisions and square roots), because multiplications were usually significantly more expensive than additions or subtractions and because in most algorithms multiplications tend to be paired with a similar number of additions (for example, in computing the inner product of two vectors). More recently, the difference in cost between additions and multiplications has largely disappeared.[1] Computer vendors and users like to advertise the highest possible performance,

---

[1] Many modern microprocessors can perform a coupled multiplication and addition with a single **multiply-add** instruction.

so it is increasingly common for every arithmetic operation to be counted. Because certain operation counts are so well known using the traditional practice, however, in this book only multiplications are usually counted. To clarify the meaning, the phrase "and a similar number of additions" will be added, or else it will be explicitly stated when both are being counted.

In quantifying operation counts and the accuracy of approximations, we will often use "big-oh" notation to indicate the order of magnitude, or dominant term, of a function. For an operation count, we are interested in the behavior as the size of the problem, say n, becomes large. We say that

$$f(n) = \mathcal{O}(g(n))$$

(read "f is big-oh of g" or "f is of order g") if there is a positive constant C such that

$$|f(n)| \le C|g(n)|$$

for n sufficiently large. For example,

$$2n^3 + 3n^2 + n = \mathcal{O}(n^3)$$

because as n becomes large, the terms of order lower than n^3 become relatively insignificant. For an accuracy estimate, we are interested in the behavior as some quantity h, such as a stepsize or mesh spacing, becomes small. We say that

$$f(h) = \mathcal{O}(g(h))$$

if there is a positive constant C such that

$$|f(h)| \le C|g(h)|$$

for h sufficiently small. For example,

$$\frac{1}{1-h} = 1 + h + h^2 + h^3 + \cdots = 1 + h + \mathcal{O}(h^2)$$

because as h becomes small, the omitted terms beyond h^2 become relatively insignificant. Note that the two definitions are equivalent if $h = 1/n$.

Scientific Computing:
An Introductory Survey

CHAPTER 1

Scientific Computing

1.1 INTRODUCTION

The subject of this book is traditionally called *numerical analysis*. Numerical analysis is concerned with the design and analysis of algorithms for solving mathematical problems that arise in computational science and engineering. For this reason, numerical analysis has more recently become known as *scientific computing*. Numerical analysis is distinguished from most other parts of computer science in that it deals with quantities that are *continuous,* as opposed to discrete. It is concerned with functions and equations whose underlying variables—time, distance, velocity, temperature, density, pressure, stress, and the like—are continuous in nature.

Most of the problems of continuous mathematics (for example, almost any problem involving derivatives, integrals, or nonlinearities) cannot be solved, even in principle, in a finite number of steps and thus must be solved by a (theoretically infinite) iterative process that ultimately converges to a solution. In practice, of course, one does not iterate forever, but only until the answer is approximately correct, "close enough" to the desired result for practical purposes. Thus, one of the most important aspects of scientific computing is finding rapidly convergent iterative algorithms and assessing the accuracy of the resulting approximation. If convergence is sufficiently rapid, even some of the problems that *can* be solved by finite algorithms, such as systems of linear algebraic equations, may in some cases be better solved by iterative methods, as we will see.

Consequently, a second factor that distinguishes numerical analysis is its concern with approximations and their effects. Many solution techniques involve a whole series of approximations of various types. Even the arithmetic used is only approximate, for digital computers cannot represent all real numbers exactly. In addition to having the usual properties of good algorithms, such as efficiency, numerical algorithms should also be as reliable and accurate as possible despite the various approximations made along the way.

1.1.1 General Strategy

In seeking a solution to a given computational problem, a basic general strategy, which occurs throughout this book, is to replace a difficult problem with an easier one that has the same solution, or at least a closely related solution. Examples of this approach include

- Replacing infinite processes with finite processes, such as replacing integrals or infinite series with finite sums, or derivatives with finite difference quotients
- Replacing general matrices with matrices having a simpler form
- Replacing complicated functions with simple functions, such as polynomials
- Replacing nonlinear problems with linear problems
- Replacing differential equations with algebraic equations
- Replacing high-order systems with low-order systems
- Replacing infinite-dimensional spaces with finite-dimensional spaces

For example, to solve a system of nonlinear differential equations, we might first replace it with a system of nonlinear algebraic equations, then replace the nonlinear algebraic system with a linear algebraic system, then replace the matrix of the linear system with one of a special form for which the solution is easy to compute. At each step of this process, we would need to verify that the solution is unchanged, or is at least within some required tolerance of the true solution.

To make this general strategy work for solving a given problem, we must have

- An alternative problem, or class of problems, that is easier to solve
- A transformation of the given problem into a problem of this alternative type that preserves the solution in some sense

Thus, much of our effort will go into identifying suitable problem classes with simple solutions and solution-preserving transformations into those classes.

Ideally, the solution to the transformed problem is identical to that of the original problem, but this is not always possible. In the latter case the solution may only approximate that of the original problem, but the accuracy can usually be made arbitrarily good at the expense of additional work and storage. Thus, primary concerns are estimating the accuracy of such an approximate solution and establishing convergence to the true solution in the limit.

1.2 APPROXIMATIONS IN SCIENTIFIC COMPUTATION

1.2.1 Sources of Approximation

There are many sources of approximation or inexactness in computational science. Some of these occur even before computation begins:

- **Modeling:** Some physical features of the problem or system under study may be simplified or omitted (e.g., friction, viscosity).

- **Empirical measurements:** Laboratory instruments have finite precision. Their accuracy may be further limited by small sample size, or readings obtained may be subject to random noise or systematic bias. For example, even the most careful measurements of important physical constants, such as Newton's gravitational constant or Planck's constant, typically yield values with at most eight or nine significant decimal digits.
- **Previous computations:** Input data may have been produced by a previous step whose results were only approximate.

The approximations just listed are usually beyond our control, but they still play an important role in determining the accuracy that should be expected from a computation. We will focus most of our attention on approximations over which we do have some influence. These systematic approximations that occur *during* computation include

- **Truncation or discretization:** Some features of a mathematical model may be omitted or simplified (e.g., replacing a derivative by a difference quotient or using only a finite number of terms in an infinite series).
- **Rounding:** The computer representation of real numbers and arithmetic operations upon them is generally inexact.

The accuracy of the final results of a computation may reflect a combination of any or all of these approximations, and the resulting perturbations may be amplified or magnified by the nature of the problem being solved or the algorithm being used, or both. The study of the effects of such approximations on the accuracy and stability of numerical algorithms is traditionally called *error analysis*.

EXAMPLE 1.1 APPROXIMATIONS. The surface area of the Earth might be computed using the formula

$$A = 4\pi r^2$$

for the surface area of a sphere of radius r. The use of this formula for the computation involves a number of approximations:

- The Earth is modeled as a sphere, which is an idealization of its true shape.
- The value for the radius, $r \approx 6370$ km, is based on a combination of empirical measurements and previous computations.
- The value for π is given by an infinite limiting process, which must be truncated at some point.
- The numerical values for the input data, as well as the results of the arithmetic operations performed on them, are rounded in a computer.

The accuracy of the computed result depends on all of these approximations.

1.2.2 Data Error and Computational Error

As we have just seen, some errors can be attributed to the input data, whereas others are due to subsequent computational processes. Although this distinction is not always clear-cut (rounding, for example, may affect both the input data and subsequent computational results), it is nevertheless helpful in understanding the overall effects of approximations in numerical computations.

A typical problem can be viewed as the computation of the value of a function, say $f: \mathbb{R} \rightarrow \mathbb{R}$ (most realistic problems are multidimensional, but for now we consider only one dimension for illustration). Denote the true value of the input data by x, so that the desired true result is $f(x)$. Suppose that we must work with inexact input, say $\hat{x}$, and we can compute only an approximation to the function, say $\hat{f}$. Then

$$
\begin{aligned}
\text{Total error} &= \hat{f}(\hat{x}) - f(x) \\
&= (\hat{f}(\hat{x}) - f(\hat{x})) \quad + \quad (f(\hat{x}) - f(x)) \\
&= \text{computational error} + \text{propagated data error}.
\end{aligned}
$$

The first term in the sum is the difference between the exact and approximate functions for the *same* input and hence can be considered pure *computational error*. The second term is the difference between exact function values due to error in the input and thus can be viewed as pure propagated *data error*. Note that the choice of algorithm has no effect on the propagated data error.

1.2.3 Truncation Error and Rounding Error

Similarly, computational error (that is, error made *during* the computation) can be subdivided into truncation (or discretization) error and rounding error:

- *Truncation error* is the difference between the true result (for the actual input) and the result that would be produced by a given algorithm using exact arithmetic. It is due to approximations such as truncating an infinite series, replacing a derivative by a finite difference quotient, replacing an arbitrary function by a polynomial, or terminating an iterative sequence before convergence.
- *Rounding error* is the difference between the result produced by a given algorithm using exact arithmetic and the result produced by the same algorithm using finite-precision, rounded arithmetic. It is due to inexactness in the representation of real numbers and arithmetic operations upon them, which we will consider in detail in Section 1.3.

By definition, then, computational error is simply the sum of truncation error and rounding error.

Although truncation error and rounding error can both play an important role in a given computation, one or the other is usually the dominant factor in the overall computational error. Roughly speaking, rounding error tends to dominate in purely algebraic problems with finite solution algorithms, whereas truncation error tends to dominate in problems involving integrals, derivatives, or nonlinearities, which often require a theoretically infinite solution process.

The distinctions we have made among the different types of errors are important for understanding the behavior of numerical algorithms and the factors affecting their accuracy, but it is usually not necessary, or even possible, to quantify precisely the individual types of errors. Indeed, as we will soon see, it is often advantageous to lump all of the errors together and attribute them to error in the input data.

1.2.4 Absolute Error and Relative Error

The significance of an error is obviously related to the magnitude of the quantity being measured or computed. For example, an error of 1 is much less significant in counting the population of the Earth than in counting the occupants of a phone booth. This motivates the concepts of *absolute error* and *relative error*, which are defined as follows:

$$\text{Absolute error} = \text{approximate value} - \text{true value},$$

$$\text{Relative error} = \frac{\text{absolute error}}{\text{true value}}.$$

Some authors define absolute error to be the absolute value of the foregoing difference, but we will take the absolute value explicitly when only the magnitude of the error is needed.

Relative error can also be expressed as a percentage, which is simply the relative error times 100. Thus, for example, an absolute error of 0.1 relative to a true value of 10 would be a relative error of 0.01, or 1 percent. A completely erroneous approximation would correspond to a relative error of at least 1, or at least 100 percent, meaning that the absolute error is as large as the true value. One interpretation of relative error is that if a quantity $\hat{x}$ has a relative error of about 10^{-t}, the decimal representation of $\hat{x}$ has about t correct significant digits.

Another useful way to express the relationship between absolute and relative error is the following:

$$\text{Approximate value} = (\text{true value}) \times (1 + \text{relative error}).$$

Of course, we do not usually know the true value; if we did, we would not need to bother with approximating it. Thus, we will usually merely *estimate* or *bound* the error rather than compute it exactly, because the true value is unknown. For this same reason, relative error is often taken to be relative to the approximate value rather than to the true value, as in the foregoing definition.

1.2.5 Sensitivity and Conditioning

Difficulties in solving a problem accurately are not always due to an ill-conceived formula or algorithm, but may be inherent in the problem being solved. Even with exact computation, the solution to the problem may be highly sensitive to perturbations in the input data.

A problem is said to be *insensitive*, or *well-conditioned*, if a given relative change in the input data causes a reasonably commensurate relative change in the solution. A problem is said to be *sensitive*, or *ill-conditioned*, if the relative change in the solution can be much larger than that in the input data.

More formally, we define the *condition number* of a problem f at x as

$$\text{Cond} = \frac{|\text{relative change in solution}|}{|\text{relative change in input data}|} = \frac{|[f(\hat{x}) - f(x)]/f(x)|}{|(\hat{x} - x)/x|},$$

where $\hat{x}$ is a point near x. A problem is sensitive, or ill-conditioned, if its condition number is much larger than 1. Anyone who has felt a shower go from freezing to scalding, or vice versa, at the slightest touch of the temperature control has had first-hand experience with a sensitive system.

EXAMPLE 1.2 EVALUATING A FUNCTION. Consider the propagated data error when a function f is evaluated for an approximate input argument $\hat{x} = x + h$ instead of the "true" input value x. We know from calculus that

$$\text{Absolute error} = f(x + h) - f(x) \approx hf'(x),$$

so that

$$\text{Relative error} = \frac{f(x + h) - f(x)}{f(x)} \approx h\frac{f'(x)}{f(x)},$$

and hence

$$\text{Cond} \approx \left| \frac{hf'(x)/f(x)}{h/x} \right| = \left| x\frac{f'(x)}{f(x)} \right|.$$

Thus, the relative error in the function value can be much larger or smaller than that in the input, depending on the properties of the function involved and the particular value of the input. For example, if $f(x) = e^x$, then the absolute error $\approx he^x$, relative error $\approx h$, and cond $\approx |x|$.

EXAMPLE 1.3 SENSITIVITY. Consider the problem of computing values of the cosine function for arguments near $\pi/2$. Let $x \approx \pi/2$ and let h be a small perturbation to x. Then the error in computing $\cos(x + h)$ is given by

$$\text{Absolute error} = \cos(x + h) - \cos(x) \approx -h\sin(x) \approx -h,$$

and hence

$$\text{Relative error} \approx -h\tan(x) \approx \infty.$$

Thus, small changes in x near $\pi/2$ cause large relative changes in $\cos(x)$ regardless of the method for computing it. For example,

$$\cos(1.57079) = 0.63267949 \times 10^{-5},$$

whereas

$$\cos(1.57078) = 1.63267949 \times 10^{-5},$$

so that the relative change in the output, 1.58, is about a quarter of a million times larger than the relative change in the input, 6.37×10^{-6}.

1.2.6 Backward Error Analysis

Analyzing the forward propagation of errors in a computation is often very difficult. Moreover, the worst-case assumptions made at each stage often lead to a very pessimistic bound on the overall error. An alternative approach is *backward error analysis*: Consider the approximate solution obtained to be the exact solution for a modified problem, then ask how large a modification to the original problem is required to give the result actually obtained. In other words, how much data error in the initial input would be required to explain *all* of the error in the final computed result? In terms of backward error analysis, an approximate solution to a given problem is good if it is the exact solution to a "nearby" problem.

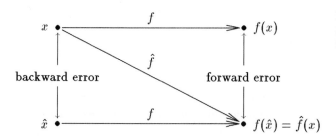

FIGURE 1.1
Schematic diagram of
backward error analysis.

These relationships are illustrated schematically (and not to scale) in Fig. 1.1, where x and f denote the exact input and function, respectively, $\hat{f}$ denotes the approximate function actually computed, and $\hat{x}$ denotes an input value for which the exact function would give this computed result. Note that the equality $f(\hat{x}) = \hat{f}(x)$ is due to the choice of $\hat{x}$; indeed, this requirement *defines* $\hat{x}$.

EXAMPLE 1.4 BACKWARD ERROR ANALYSIS. Suppose we want a simple function for approximating the exponential function $f(x) = e^x$, and we want to examine its accuracy for the argument $x = 1$. We know that the exponential function is given by the infinite series

$$f(x) = e^x = 1 + x + \frac{x^2}{2!} + \frac{x^3}{3!} + \cdots,$$

so we might consider truncating the series after, say, four terms to get the approximation

$$\hat{f}(x) = 1 + x + \frac{x^2}{2} + \frac{x^3}{6}.$$

The forward error in this approximation is then given by

$$\hat{f}(x) - f(x).$$

To determine the backward error, we need to know the input value $\hat{x}$ for f that gives the output value we actually obtained for $\hat{f}$, that is, for which $f(\hat{x}) = \hat{f}(x)$. For the exponential function, we know that this value is given by

$$\hat{x} = \log(\hat{f}(x)).$$

Thus, for the particular input value $x = 1$, we have, to seven decimal places,

$$f(x) = 2.718282, \quad \hat{f}(x) = 2.666667,$$

$$\hat{x} = \log(2.666667) = 0.980829,$$

$$\text{Forward error} = \hat{f}(x) - f(x) = -0.051615,$$

$$\text{Backward error} = \hat{x} - x = -0.019171.$$

The point here is not to compare the numerical values of the forward and backward errors quantitatively, but merely to illustrate the concepts involved and to show that both are legitimate approaches to assessing accuracy. In this case, the forward error indicates that the accuracy is fairly good because the output is close to what we wanted to compute, whereas the backward error indicates that the accuracy is fairly good because the output we obtained is correct for an input that is only slightly perturbed.

1.2.7 Stability and Accuracy

The concept of stability of a computational algorithm is analogous to conditioning of a mathematical problem. Both concepts have to do with sensitivity to perturbations, but the term *stability* is usually used for algorithms and *conditioning* for problems (although stability is sometimes used for problems as well, especially in differential equations). An algorithm is *stable* if the result it produces is relatively insensitive to perturbations resulting from approximations made during the computation. From the viewpoint of backward error analysis, an algorithm is stable if the result it produces is the exact solution to a nearby problem.

Accuracy, on the other hand, refers to the closeness of a computed solution to the true solution of the problem under consideration. Stability of an algorithm does not by itself guarantee that the computed solution is accurate: accuracy depends on the conditioning of the problem as well as the stability of the algorithm. Stability tells us that the solution obtained is exact for a nearby problem, but the solution to that nearby problem is not necessarily close to the solution to the original problem unless the problem is well-conditioned. Thus, inaccuracy can result from applying a stable algorithm to an ill-conditioned problem as well as from applying an unstable algorithm to a well-conditioned problem.

1.3 COMPUTER ARITHMETIC

As noted earlier, one type of approximation inevitably made in scientific computing is in representing real numbers on a computer. In this section we will examine in some detail the finite-precision arithmetic systems that are used for most scientific computations on digital computers.

1.3.1 Floating-Point Numbers

In a digital computer, the real number system of mathematics is represented approximately by a *floating-point* number system. The basic idea resembles *scientific notation,* in which a number of very large or very small magnitude is expressed as a number of moderate size times an appropriate power of ten. For example, 2347 and 0.0007396 are written as 2.347×10^3 and 7.396×10^{-4}, respectively. In this format, the decimal point moves, or *floats,* as the power of 10 changes. Formally, a floating-point number system is characterized by four integers:

β	Base or radix
t	Precision
$[L, U]$	Exponent range

Any number x in the floating-point system is represented as follows:

$$x = \pm\left(d_0 + \frac{d_1}{\beta} + \frac{d_2}{\beta^2} + \cdots + \frac{d_{t-1}}{\beta^{t-1}}\right)\beta^e,$$

where

$$0 \le d_i \le \beta - 1, \quad i = 0, \ldots, t - 1,$$

$$L \le e \le U.$$

The part in parentheses, represented by the string of base-β digits $d_0 d_1 \cdots d_{t-1}$, is called the *mantissa* or *significand*, and e is called the *exponent* or *characteristic* of the floating-point number x. The portion $d_1 d_2 \cdots d_{t-1}$ of the mantissa is called the *fraction*. In a computer, the sign, exponent, and mantissa are stored in separate *fields* of a given floating-point word, each of which has a fixed width. The number zero is represented uniquely by having both its mantissa and its exponent equal to zero.

Most computers today use binary ($\beta = 2$) arithmetic, but other bases have also been used in the past, such as hexadecimal ($\beta = 16$) in IBM mainframes and $\beta = 3$ in an ill-fated Russian computer. Octal ($\beta = 8$) and hexadecimal notations are also commonly used as a convenient shorthand for writing binary numbers in groups of three or four binary digits (*bits*), respectively. For obvious reasons, decimal ($\beta = 10$) arithmetic is popular in hand-held calculators. To facilitate human interaction, a computer usually converts numerical values from decimal notation on input and to decimal notation for output, regardless of the base it uses internally. Parameters for some typical floating-point systems are given in Table 1.1, which illustrates the trade-off between precision and exponent range implied by their respective field widths. For example, working with the same 64-bit word length, the Cray system has a wider exponent range than does IEEE double precision, but at the expense of carrying less precision.

The IEEE standard single-precision (SP) and double-precision (DP) binary floating-point systems are by far the most important today. They have been almost universally adopted for personal computers and workstations, and also for many mainframes and supercomputers as well. The IEEE standard was carefully crafted to eliminate the many anomalies and ambiguities in earlier vendor-specific floating-point implementations and has greatly facilitated the development of portable and reliable numerical software. It also allows for sensible and consistent handling of exceptional situations, such as division by zero.

TABLE 1.1

Parameters for some typical floating-point systems

System	β	t	L	U
IEEE SP	2	24	-126	127
IEEE DP	2	53	$-1{,}022$	1,023
Cray	2	48	$-16{,}383$	16,384
HP calculator	10	12	-499	499
IBM mainframe	16	6	-64	63

1.3.2 Normalization

A floating-point system is said to be *normalized* if the leading digit d_0 is always nonzero unless the number represented is zero. Thus, in a normalized floating-point system, the mantissa m of a given nonzero floating-point number always satisfies

$$1 \leq m < \beta.$$

(An alternative convention is that d_0 is *always* zero, in which case a floating-point number is said to be normalized if $d_1 \neq 0$, and $\beta^{-1} \leq m < 1$ instead.) Floating-point systems are usually normalized because

- The representation of each number is then unique.
- No digits are wasted on leading zeros, thereby maximizing precision.
- In a binary ($\beta = 2$) system, the leading bit is always 1 and thus need not be stored, thereby gaining one extra bit of precision for a given field width.

1.3.3 Properties of Floating-Point Systems

A floating-point number system is finite and discrete. The number of normalized floating-point numbers is

$$2(\beta - 1)\beta^{t-1}(U - L + 1) + 1$$

because there are two choices of sign, $\beta - 1$ choices for the leading digit of the mantissa, β choices for each of the remaining $t - 1$ digits of the mantissa, and $U - L + 1$ possible values for the exponent. The 1 is added because the number could be zero.

There is a smallest positive normalized floating-point number,

$$\text{Underflow level} = \text{UFL} = \beta^L,$$

which has a 1 as the leading digit and 0 for the remaining digits of the mantissa, and the smallest possible value for the exponent. There is a largest floating-point number,

$$\text{Overflow level} = \text{OFL} = \beta^{U+1}(1 - \beta^{-t}),$$

which has $\beta - 1$ as the value for each digit of the mantissa and the largest possible value for the exponent. Any number larger than OFL cannot be represented in the given floating-point system, nor can any positive number smaller than UFL.

Floating-point numbers are not uniformly distributed throughout their range, but are equally spaced only between successive powers of β. Not all real numbers are exactly representable in a floating-point system. Real numbers that are exactly representable in a given floating-point system are sometimes called *machine numbers*.

EXAMPLE 1.5 FLOATING-POINT SYSTEM. An example floating-point system is illustrated in Fig. 1.2, where the tick marks indicate all of the 25 floating-point numbers in a system having $\beta = 2$, $t = 3$, $L = -1$, and $U = 1$. For this system, the largest number is OFL $= (1.11)_2 \times 2^1 = (3.5)_{10}$, and the smallest positive normalized number is UFL $= (1.00)_2 \times 2^{-1} = (0.5)_{10}$. This is a very tiny, toy system for illustrative purposes only, but

FIGURE 1.2
Example of a floating-point number system.

> it is in fact characteristic of floating-point systems in general: at a sufficiently high level of magnification, every normalized floating-point system looks essentially like this one—grainy and unequally spaced.

1.3.4 Rounding

If a given real number x is not exactly representable as a floating-point number, then it must be approximated by some "nearby" floating-point number. We denote the floating-point approximation of a given real number x by $\mathrm{fl}(x)$. The process of choosing a nearby floating-point number $\mathrm{fl}(x)$ to approximate a given real number x is called *rounding*, and the error introduced by such an approximation is called *rounding error*, or *roundoff error*. Two of the most commonly used rounding rules are

- *Chop:* The base-β expansion of x is truncated after the $(t-1)$st digit. Since $\mathrm{fl}(x)$ is the next floating-point number towards zero from x, this rule is also sometimes called *round toward zero.*
- *Round to nearest:* $\mathrm{fl}(x)$ is the nearest floating-point number to x; in case of a tie, we use the floating-point number whose last stored digit is even. Because of the latter property, this rule is also sometimes called *round to even.*

Rounding to nearest is the most accurate, but it is somewhat more expensive to implement correctly. Some systems in the past have used rounding rules that are cheaper to implement, such as chopping, but rounding to nearest is the default rounding rule in IEEE standard systems.

EXAMPLE 1.6 ROUNDING RULES. Rounding the following decimal numbers to two digits using each of the rounding rules gives the following results:

Number	Chop	Round to nearest	Number	Chop	Round to nearest
1.649	1.6	1.6	1.749	1.7	1.7
1.650	1.6	1.6	1.750	1.7	1.8
1.651	1.6	1.7	1.751	1.7	1.8
1.699	1.6	1.7	1.799	1.7	1.8

A potential source of additional error that is often overlooked is in the decimal-to-binary and binary-to-decimal conversions that usually take place upon input and output of floating-point numbers. Such conversions are not covered by the IEEE standard, which governs only internal arithmetic operations. Correctly rounded input and output can be obtained at reasonable cost, but not all computer systems do so. Efficient, portable routines for correctly rounded binary-to-decimal and decimal-to-binary conversions—**dtoa** and **strtod**, respectively—are available from **netlib** (see Section 1.4.1).

1.3.5 Machine Precision

The accuracy of a floating-point system can be characterized by a quantity variously known as the *unit roundoff*, *machine precision*, or *machine epsilon*. Its value, which we denote by ϵ_{mach}, depends on the particular rounding rule used. With rounding by chopping,

$$\epsilon_{mach} = \beta^{1-t},$$

whereas with rounding to nearest,

$$\epsilon_{mach} = \tfrac{1}{2}\beta^{1-t}.$$

The unit roundoff is important because it determines the maximum possible *relative error* in representing a nonzero real number x in a floating-point system:

$$\left| \frac{fl(x) - x}{x} \right| \leq \epsilon_{mach}.$$

An alternative characterization of the unit roundoff that you may sometimes see is that it is the smallest number ϵ such that

$$fl(1 + \epsilon) > 1,$$

but this is not quite equivalent to the previous definition if the round-to-even rule is used. Another definition sometimes used is that ϵ_{mach} is the distance from 1 to the next larger floating-point number, but this may differ from either of the other definitions. Although they can differ in detail, all three definitions of ϵ_{mach} have the same basic intent as measures of the granularity of a floating-point system.

For the toy illustrative system in Example 1.5, $\epsilon_{mach} = 0.25$ with rounding by chopping, and $\epsilon_{mach} = 0.125$ with rounding to nearest. For IEEE binary floating-point systems, $\epsilon_{mach} = 2^{-24} \approx 10^{-7}$ in single precision and $\epsilon_{mach} = 2^{-53} \approx 10^{-16}$ in double precision. We thus say that the IEEE single- and double-precision floating-point systems have about 7 and 16 decimal digits of precision, respectively.

Though both are "small," the unit roundoff should not be confused with the underflow level. The unit roundoff ϵ_{mach} is determined by the number of digits in the mantissa field of a floating-point system, whereas the underflow level UFL is determined by the number of digits in the exponent field. In all practical floating-point systems,

$$0 < UFL < \epsilon_{mach} < OFL.$$

1.3.6 Subnormals and Gradual Underflow

In the toy floating-point system illustrated in Fig. 1.2, there is a noticeable gap around zero. This gap, which is present to some degree in any floating-point system, is due to normalization: the smallest possible mantissa is $1.00\ldots$, and the smallest possible exponent is L, so there are no floating-point numbers between zero and β^L. If we relax our insistence on normalization and allow leading digits to be zero (but only when the exponent is at its minimum value), then the gap around zero can be "filled in" by additional floating-point numbers. For our toy illustrative system, this relaxation gains six additional floating-point numbers, the smallest positive one of which is $(0.01)_2 \times 2^{-1} = (0.125)_{10}$, as shown in Fig. 1.3.

The extra numbers added to the system in this way are referred to as *subnormal* or *denormalized* floating-point numbers. Although they usefully extend the range of magnitudes representable, subnormal numbers have inherently lower precision than normalized numbers because they have fewer significant digits in their fractional parts. In particular, extending the range in this manner does not make the unit roundoff ϵ_{mach} any smaller.

Such an augmented floating-point system is sometimes said to exhibit *gradual underflow*, since it extends the lower range of magnitudes representable rather than underflowing to zero as soon as the minimum exponent value would otherwise be exceeded. The IEEE standard provides for such subnormal numbers and gradual underflow. Gradual underflow is implemented through a special reserved value of the exponent field because the leading binary digit is not stored and hence cannot be used to indicate a denormalized number.

1.3.7 Exceptional Values

The IEEE floating-point standard provides two additional special values that indicate exceptional situations:

- **Inf**, which stands for "infinity," results from dividing a finite number by zero, such as 1/0.
- **NaN**, which stands for "not a number," results from undefined or indeterminate operations such as 0/0, 0 ∗ **Inf**, or **Inf/Inf**.

Inf and **NaN** are implemented in IEEE arithmetic through special reserved values of the exponent field.

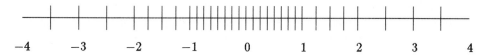

FIGURE 1.3
Example of a floating-point system with subnormals.

Whether **Inf** and **NaN** are supported at the user level in a given computing environment depends on the language, compiler, and run-time system. If available, these quantities can be helpful in designing software that deals gracefully with exceptional situations rather than abruptly aborting the program. In **MATLAB** (see Section 1.4.2), for example, if **Inf** and **NaN** arise, they are propagated sensibly through a computation (e.g., $1 + $ **Inf** $= $ **Inf**). It is still desirable, however, to avoid such exceptional situations entirely, if possible. In addition to alerting the user to arithmetic exceptions, these special values can also be useful as flags that cannot be confused with any legitimate numeric value. For example, **NaN** might be used to indicate a portion of an array that has not yet been defined.

1.3.8 Floating-Point Arithmetic

In adding or subtracting two floating-point numbers, their exponents must match before their mantissas can be added or subtracted. If they do not match initially, then the mantissa of one of the numbers must be shifted until the exponents do match. In performing such a shift, some of the trailing digits of the smaller (in magnitude) number will be shifted off the end of the mantissa field, and thus the correct result of the arithmetic operation cannot be represented exactly in the floating-point system. Indeed, if the difference in magnitude is too great, then the entire mantissa of the smaller number may be shifted completely beyond the field width so that the result is simply the larger of the operands. Another way of saying this is that if the true sum of two t-digit numbers contains more than t digits, then the excess digits will be lost when the result is rounded to t digits, and in the worst case the operand of smaller magnitude may be lost completely.

Multiplication of two floating-point numbers does not require that their exponents match—the exponents are simply summed and the mantissas multiplied. However, the product of two t-digit mantissas will in general contain up to $2t$ digits, and thus once again the correct result cannot be represented exactly in the floating-point system and must be rounded.

EXAMPLE 1.7 FLOATING-POINT ARITHMETIC. Consider a floating-point system with $\beta = 10$ and $t = 6$. If $x = 1.92403 \times 10^2$ and $y = 6.35782 \times 10^{-1}$, then floating-point addition gives the result $x + y = 1.93039 \times 10^2$, assuming rounding to nearest. Note that the last two digits of y have no effect on the result. With an even smaller exponent, y could have had no effect at all on the result. Similarly, floating-point multiplication gives the result $x * y = 1.22326 \times 10^2$, which discards half of the digits of the true product.

Division of two floating-point numbers may also give a result that cannot be represented exactly. For example, 1 and 10 are both exactly representable as binary floating-point numbers, but their quotient, 1/10, has a nonterminating binary expansion and thus is not a binary floating-point number.

In each of the cases just cited, the result of a floating-point arithmetic operation may differ from the result that would be given by the corresponding real arithmetic operation on the same operands because there is insufficient precision to represent the correct real result. The real result may also be unrepresentable because its exponent is beyond the range available in the floating-point system (overflow or underflow). Overflow is usually a more serious problem than underflow in the sense that there is *no* good approximation in a floating-point system to arbitrarily large numbers, whereas zero is often a reasonable approximation for arbitrarily small numbers. For this reason, on many computer systems the occurrence of an overflow aborts the program with a fatal error, but an underflow may be silently set to zero without disrupting execution.

EXAMPLE 1.8 SUMMING A SERIES. As an illustration of these issues, the infinite series

$$\sum_{n=1}^{\infty} \frac{1}{n}$$

has a finite sum in floating-point arithmetic even though the real series is divergent. At first blush, one might think that this result occurs because $1/n$ will eventually underflow, or the partial sum will eventually overflow, as indeed they must. But before either of these occurs, the partial sum ceases to change once $1/n$ becomes negligible relative to the partial sum, i.e., when $1/n < \epsilon_{mach} \sum_{k=1}^{n-1}(1/k)$, and thus the sum is finite (see Computer Problem 1.8).

As we have noted, a real arithmetic operation on two floating-point numbers does not necessarily result in another floating-point number. If a number that is not exactly representable as a floating-point number is entered into the computer or is produced by a subsequent arithmetic operation, then it must be rounded (using one of the rounding rules given earlier) to obtain a floating-point number. Because floating-point numbers are not equally spaced, the absolute error made in such an approximation is not uniform, but the relative error is bounded by the unit roundoff ϵ_{mach}.

Ideally, x **flop** $y = \text{fl}(x$ **op** $y)$ (i.e., floating-point arithmetic operations produce correctly rounded results); and many computers, such as those meeting the IEEE floating-point standard, achieve this ideal as long as x **op** y is within the range of the floating-point system. Nevertheless, some familiar laws of real arithmetic are not necessarily valid in a floating-point system. In particular, floating-point addition and multiplication are commutative but *not* associative. For example, if ϵ is a positive floating-point number slightly smaller than the unit roundoff ϵ_{mach}, then $(1+\epsilon)+\epsilon = 1$, but $1 + (\epsilon + \epsilon) > 1$.

The failure of floating-point arithmetic to satisfy the normal laws of real arithmetic is one reason that forward error analysis can be difficult. One advantage of backward error analysis is that it permits the use of real arithmetic in the analysis.

1.3.9 Cancellation

Rounding is not the only necessary evil in finite-precision arithmetic. Subtraction between two t-digit numbers having the same sign and similar magnitudes yields a result with *fewer* than t significant digits, and hence it is always exactly representable (provided the two numbers involved do not differ in magnitude by more than a factor of two). The reason is that the leading digits of the two numbers cancel (i.e., their difference is zero). For example, again taking $\beta = 10$ and $t = 6$, if $x = 1.92403 \times 10^2$ and $z = 1.92275 \times 10^2$, then we obtain the result $x - z = 1.28000 \times 10^{-1}$, which, with only three significant digits, is exactly representable.

Despite the exactness of the result, however, such cancellation nevertheless often implies a serious loss of information. The problem is that the operands are often uncertain, owing to rounding or other previous errors, in which case the relative uncertainty in the difference may be large. In effect, if two nearly equal numbers are accurate only to within rounding error, then taking their difference leaves only rounding error as a result.

As a simple example, if ϵ is a positive number slightly smaller than the unit roundoff ϵ_{mach}, then $(1 + \epsilon) - (1 - \epsilon) = 1 - 1 = 0$ in floating-point arithmetic, which is correct for the actual operands of the final subtraction, but the true result of the overall computation, 2ϵ, has been completely lost. The subtraction itself is not at fault: it merely signals the loss of information that had already occurred.

Of course, the loss of information is not always complete, but the fact remains that the digits lost to cancellation are the most significant, leading digits, whereas the digits lost in rounding are the least significant, trailing digits. Because of this effect, computing a small quantity as a difference of large quantities is generally a bad idea, for rounding error is likely to dominate the result. For example, summing an alternating series, such as

$$e^x = 1 + x + \frac{x^2}{2!} + \frac{x^3}{3!} + \cdots$$

for $x < 0$, may give disastrous results because of catastrophic cancellation (see Computer Problem 1.9).

EXAMPLE 1.9 CANCELLATION. Cancellation is an issue not only in computer arithmetic, but also in any situation in which limited precision is attainable, such as empirical measurements or laboratory experiments. For example, determining the distance from Manhattan to Staten Island by using their respective distances from Los Angeles will produce a very poor result unless the latter distances are known with extraordinarily high accuracy.

As another example, for many years physicists have been trying to compute the total energy of the helium atom from first principles using Monte Carlo techniques. The accuracy of these computations is determined largely by the number of random trials used. As faster computers become available and computational techniques are refined, the attainable accuracy improves. The total energy is the sum of the kinetic energy and the potential energy, which are computed separately and have opposite signs. Thus, the total energy is computed as a difference and suffers cancellation. Table 1.2 gives a sequence of values obtained over a number of years (these data were kindly provided by Dr. Robert Panoff). During this span the computed values for the kinetic and potential energies changed by only 6 percent or less, yet the resulting estimate for the total energy changed by 144 percent. The one or two significant digits in the earlier computations were completely lost in the subsequent subtraction.

TABLE 1.2
Computed values for the total
energy of the helium atom

Year	Kinetic	Potential	Total
1971	13.0	−14.0	−1.0
1977	12.76	−14.02	−1.26
1980	12.22	−14.35	−2.13
1985	12.28	−14.65	−2.37
1988	12.40	−14.84	−2.44

EXAMPLE 1.10 QUADRATIC FORMULA. Cancellation and other numerical difficulties need not involve a long series of computations. For example, use of the standard formula for the roots of a quadratic equation is fraught with numerical pitfalls. As every schoolchild learns, the two solutions of the quadratic equation

$$ax^2 + bx + c = 0$$

are given by

$$x = \frac{-b \pm \sqrt{b^2 - 4ac}}{2a}.$$

For some values of the coefficients, naive use of this formula in floating-point arithmetic can produce overflow, underflow, or catastrophic cancellation.

For example, if the coefficients are very large or very small, then b^2 or $4ac$ may overflow or underflow. The possibility of overflow can be avoided by rescaling the coefficients, such as dividing all three coefficients by the coefficient of largest magnitude. Such a rescaling does not change the roots of the quadratic equation, but now the largest coefficient is 1 and overflow cannot occur in computing b^2 or $4ac$. Such rescaling does not eliminate the possibility of underflow, but it does prevent *needless* underflow, which could otherwise occur when all three coefficients are very small.

Cancellation between $-b$ and the square root can be avoided by computing one of the roots using the alternative formula

$$x = \frac{2c}{-b \mp \sqrt{b^2 - 4ac}},$$

which has the opposite sign pattern from that of the standard formula. But cancellation inside the square root cannot be easily avoided without using higher precision (if the discriminant is small relative to the coefficients, then the two roots are close to each other, and the problem is inherently ill-conditioned).

As an illustration, we use four-digit decimal arithmetic, with rounding to nearest, to compute the roots of the quadratic equation having coefficients $a = 0.05010$, $b = -98.78$, and $c = 5.015$. For comparison, the correct roots, rounded to 10 significant digits, are

$$1971.605916 \quad \text{and} \quad 0.05077069387.$$

Computing the discriminant in four-digit arithmetic produces

$$b^2 - 4ac = 9757 - 1.005 = 9756,$$

so that

$$\sqrt{b^2 - 4ac} = 98.77.$$

The standard quadratic formula then gives the roots

$$\frac{98.78 \pm 98.77}{0.1002} = 1972 \quad \text{and} \quad 0.0998.$$

The first root is the correctly rounded four-digit result, but the other root is completely wrong, with an error of about 100 percent. The culprit is cancellation, not in the sense that the final subtraction is wrong (indeed it is exactly correct), but in the sense that cancellation of the leading digits has left nothing remaining but previous rounding errors. The alternative quadratic formula gives the roots

$$\frac{10.03}{98.78 \mp 98.77} = 1003 \quad \text{and} \quad 0.05077.$$

Once again we have obtained one fully accurate root and one completely erroneous root, but in each case it is the opposite root from the one obtained previously. Cancellation is again the explanation, but the different sign pattern causes the opposite root to be contaminated. In general, for computing each root we should choose whichever formula avoids this cancellation, depending on the sign of b.

EXAMPLE 1.11 FINITE DIFFERENCE APPROXIMATION. Consider the finite difference approximation to the first derivative

$$f'(x) \approx \frac{f(x + h) - f(x)}{h}.$$

We want h to be small so that the approximation will be accurate, but if h is too small, then $\mathrm{fl}(x+h)$ may not differ from $\mathrm{fl}(x)$. Even if $\mathrm{fl}(x+h) \neq \mathrm{fl}(x)$, we might still have $\mathrm{fl}(f(x+h)) = \mathrm{fl}(f(x))$ if f is slowly varying. In any case, we can expect some cancellation in computing the difference $f(x + h) - f(x)$. Thus, there is a trade-off between truncation error and rounding error in choosing the size of h.

If the relative error in the function values is bounded by ϵ, then the rounding error in the approximate derivative value is bounded by $2\epsilon|f(x)|/h$. The Taylor series expansion

$$f(x + h) = f(x) + f'(x)h + f''(x)h^2/2 + \cdots$$

gives an estimate of $Mh/2$ for the truncation error, where M is a bound for $|f''(x)|$. The total error is therefore bounded by

$$\frac{2\epsilon|f(x)|}{h} + \frac{Mh}{2},$$

which is minimized when

$$h = 2\sqrt{\epsilon|f(x)|/M}.$$

If we assume that the function values are accurate to machine precision and that f and f'' have roughly the same magnitude, then we obtain the rule of thumb that it is usually best to perturb about half the digits of x by taking

$$h \approx \sqrt{\epsilon_{\mathrm{mach}}} \cdot |x|.$$

A typical example is shown in Fig. 1.4, where the error in the finite difference approximation for a particular function is plotted as a function of the stepsize h. This computation was done in IEEE single precision with $x = 1$, and the error indeed reaches a minimum at $h \approx \sqrt{\epsilon_{\mathrm{mach}}}$. The error increases for smaller values of h because of rounding error, and increases for larger values of h because of truncation error.

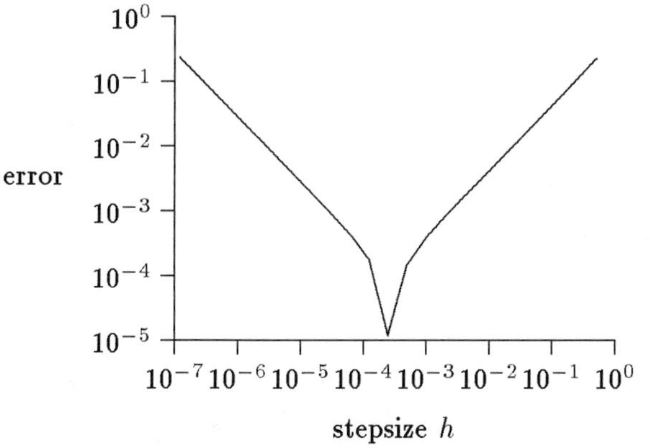

FIGURE 1.4
Error in finite difference approximation
as a function of stepsize.

The rounding error can be reduced by working with higher-precision arithmetic. Truncation error can be reduced by using a more accurate formula, such as the centered difference approximation (see Section 8.7.1)

$$f'(x) \approx \frac{f(x + h) - f(x - h)}{2h}.$$

EXAMPLE 1.12 STANDARD DEVIATION. The *mean* of a finite sequence of real values $x_i, i = 1, \ldots, n$, is defined by

$$\bar{x} = \frac{1}{n} \sum_{i=1}^{n} x_i,$$

and the *standard deviation* is defined by

$$\sigma = \left[\frac{1}{n-1} \sum_{i=1}^{n} (x_i - \bar{x})^2 \right]^{1/2}.$$

Use of these formulas requires two passes through the data: one to compute the mean and another to compute the standard deviation. For better efficiency, it is tempting to use the mathematically equivalent formula

$$\sigma = \left[\frac{1}{n-1} \left(\sum_{i=1}^{n} x_i^2 - n\bar{x}^2 \right) \right]^{1/2}$$

to compute the standard deviation, since both the sum and the sum of squares can be computed in a single pass through the data.

Unfortunately, the single cancellation at the end of the one-pass formula is often much more damaging numerically than all of the cancellations in the two-pass formula combined. The problem is that the two quantities being subtracted in the one-pass formula are apt to be relatively large and nearly equal, and hence the relative error in the difference may be large (indeed, the result can even be negative, causing the square root to fail).

EXAMPLE 1.13 COMPUTING RESIDUALS. Assessing the accuracy of a computation is often difficult if one uses only the same precision as that of the computation itself. Perhaps this observation should not be surprising: if we knew the actual error, we could have used it to obtain a more accurate result in the first place.

As a simple example, suppose we are solving the scalar linear equation $ax = b$ for the unknown x, and we have obtained an approximate solution $\hat{x}$. As one measure of the quality of our answer, we wish to compute the residual $r = b - a\hat{x}$. In floating-point arithmetic,

$$a \times_\text{fl} \hat{x} = a\hat{x}(1 + \delta_1)$$

for some $\delta_1 \leq \epsilon_\text{mach}$. So

$$
\begin{aligned}
b -{}_\text{fl}(a \times_\text{fl} \hat{x}) &= [b - a\hat{x}(1 + \delta_1)](1 + \delta_2) \\
&= [r - \delta_1 a\hat{x}](1 + \delta_2) \\
&= r + \delta_2 r - \delta_1 a\hat{x} - \delta_1 \delta_2 a\hat{x} \\
&\approx r + \delta_2 r - \delta_1 b.
\end{aligned}
$$

But $\delta_1 b$ may be as large as $\epsilon_\text{mach} b$, which may be as large as r. Thus, higher precision may be required to enable a meaningful computation of the residual r.

1.4 MATHEMATICAL SOFTWARE

This book covers a wide range of topics in numerical analysis and scientific computing. We will discuss the essential aspects of each topic but will not have the luxury of examining any topic in great detail. To be able to solve interesting computational problems, we will often rely on mathematical software written by professionals. Leaving the algorithmic details to such software will allow us to focus on proper problem formulation and interpretation of results. We will consider only the most fundamental algorithms for each type of problem, motivated primarily by the insight to be gained into choosing an appropriate method and using it wisely. Our primary goal is to become intelligent users, rather than creators, of mathematical software.

Before citing some specific sources of good mathematical software, let us summarize the desirable characteristics that such software should possess, in no particular order of importance:

- **Reliability:** always works correctly for easy problems
- **Robustness:** usually works for hard problems, but fails gracefully and informatively when it does fail
- **Accuracy:** produces results as accurate as warranted by the problem and input data, preferably with an estimate of the accuracy achieved
- **Efficiency:** requires execution time and storage that are close to the minimum possible for the problem being solved
- **Maintainability:** is easy to understand and modify
- **Portability:** adapts with little or no change to new computing environments
- **Usability:** has a convenient and well-documented user interface
- **Applicability:** solves a broad range of problems

Obviously, these properties often conflict, and it is rare software indeed that satisfies all of them. Nevertheless, this list gives mathematical software users some idea what qualities to look for and developers some worthy goals to strive for.

1.4.1 Mathematical Software Libraries

Several widely available sources of general-purpose mathematical software are listed here. The software listed is written in Fortran unless otherwise noted. At the end of each chapter of this book, specific routines are listed for given types of problems, both from these general libraries and from more specialized packages. For additional information about available mathematical software, see the URL **http://gams.nist.gov** on the Internet's World-Wide Web.

- **FMM**: A collection of software accompanying the book *Computer Methods for Mathematical Computations,* by Forsythe, Malcolm, and Moler [82]; available from **netlib** (see below).
- **HSL** (Harwell Subroutine Library): A collection of software developed at Harwell Laboratory in England. See URL **http://www.rl.ac.uk/departments/ccd/numerical/hsl/hsl.html**.
- **IMSL** (International Mathematical and Statistical Libraries): A commercial product of Visual Numerics Inc., Houston, Texas. A comprehensive library of mathematical software; the full library is available in Fortran, and a subset is available in C. See URL **http://www.vni.com**.
- **KMN**: A collection of software accompanying the book *Numerical Methods and Software,* by Kahaner, Moler, and Nash [142].
- **NAG** (Numerical Algorithms Group): A commercial product of NAG Inc., Downers Grove, Illinois. A comprehensive library of mathematical software; the full library is available in Fortran, and a subset is available in C. See URL **http://www.nag.com**.
- **NAPACK**: A collection of software designed to complement the book *Applied Numerical Linear Algebra,* by Hager [116]. In addition to linear algebra, also contains routines for nonlinear equations, unconstrained optimization, and fast Fourier transforms. Available from **netlib**.
- **netlib**: A collection of free software from diverse sources available over the Internet. See URL **http://www.netlib.org**, or send email containing the request "send index" to **netlib@ornl.gov**, or **ftp** to one of several mirror sites, such as **netlib.bell-labs.com** or **netlib2.cs.utk.edu**.
- **NR** (Numerical Recipes): A collection of software accompanying the book *Numerical Recipes,* by Press, Teukolsky, Vetterling, and Flannery [205]. Available in C and Fortran editions.
- **NUMAL**: A collection of software developed at the Mathematisch Centrum, Amsterdam. Also available in Algol and Fortran, but most readily available in C from the book *A Numerical Library in C for Scientists and Engineers*, by Lau [162].
- **PORT**: A collection of software developed at Bell Laboratories. Some portions are available from **netlib**, but other portions must be obtained commercially and licensed for use. See the **port** directory in **netlib** for further information.
- **SLATEC**: A collection of software compiled by a consortium of U.S. government laboratories. Available from **netlib**.
- **SOL**: A collection of software for optimization and related problems from the Systems Optimization Laboratory at Stanford University. For further information, see URL **http://www-or.stanford.edu**.

- **TOMS**: A collection of software appearing in *ACM Transactions on Mathematical Software* (formerly *Collected Algorithms of the ACM*). Available from **netlib**. The algorithms are identified by number (in order of appearance) as well as by name.

1.4.2 Scientific Computing Environments

The software libraries just listed contain subroutines that are meant to be called by user-written programs, usually in a conventional programming language such as Fortran or C. An increasingly popular alternative for scientific computing is interactive environments that provide powerful, conveniently accessible, built-in mathematical capabilities, often combined with sophisticated graphics and a very high-level programming language designed for rapid prototyping of new algorithms.

One of the most widely used such computing environments is **MATLAB**, which is a proprietary commercial product of The MathWorks, Inc. (see URL **http://www.mathworks.com**). **MATLAB**, which stands for MATrix LABoratory, is an interactive system that integrates extensive mathematical capabilities, especially in linear algebra, with powerful scientific visualization, a high-level programming language, and a variety of optional "toolboxes" that provide specialized capabilities in particular applications, such as signal processing, image processing, control, system identification, optimization, and statistics. There is also a **MATLAB** interface for the **NAG** mathematical software library mentioned in Section 1.4.1. **MATLAB** is available for a wide variety of personal computers, workstations, and supercomputers, and comes in both professional and inexpensive student editions. If **MATLAB** is not available on your computer system, there are similar, though less powerful, packages that are freely available by **ftp**, including **octave (ftp.che.utexas.edu/pub/octave)** and **RLaB (evans.ee.adfa.oz.au/pub/RLaB)**. Other similar commercial products include **GAUSS**, **HiQ**, **IDL**, **Mathcad**, and **PV-WAVE**.

Another family of interactive computing environments is based primarily on *symbolic* (rather than numeric) computation, often called *computer algebra*. These packages, which include **Axiom**, **Derive**, **Macsyma**, **Maple**, **Mathematica**, **Reduce**, and **Scratchpad**, provide many of the same mathematical and graphical capabilities, and in addition provide symbolic differentiation, integration, equation solving, polynomial manipulation, and the like, as well as arbitrary precision arithmetic.

Because **MATLAB** is probably the most widely used of these environments for the types of problems discussed in this book, specific **MATLAB** functions, either from the basic environment or from the supplementary toolboxes, are mentioned in the summaries of available software for each problem category, along with software from the major conventional software libraries. Note that **MATLAB** has recently added symbolic computation to its capabilities via a "symbolic math" toolbox based on **Maple**.

1.4.3 Practical Advice on Software

This section contains some practical advice on obtaining and using the software mentioned throughout the book, especially for the purpose of programming assignments based on the computer problems at the end of each chapter. The computer problems do not depend on any particular software or programming language, and thus many options are available. The best choice in a given case will depend on the user's experience, resources, and objectives.

The software cited comes from a variety of sources, including large commercial libraries such as **IMSL** and **NAG**, public repositories of free software such as **netlib**, and scientific computing environments such as **MATLAB**. Many academic and industrial computing centers and workstation laboratories will have a representative sample of such software already installed and available for use. In any case, ample software is available free via the Internet or at nominal cost from other sources (e.g., accompanying textbooks) for all of the computer problems in this book. Locating, downloading, and installing suitable software is useful real-world experience, and the skills learned in doing so are an important practical adjunct to the other skills taught in this book.

Perhaps the most important choice is that of a programming language. Fortran is the traditional language of scientific computing, and the overwhelming majority of existing software libraries and applications codes are in Fortran, although C is catching up fast with respect to available resources. In working with this book, the Fortran user will benefit from the widest variety of available software and from compatibility with the preponderance of existing applications codes. In addition, since Fortran is a relatively restrictive language and compilers for it have had the benefit of many years of tuning, Fortran produces somewhat more efficient executable code on some computer systems.

C is a more versatile and expressive language than Fortran, and currently C is probably the language most commonly taught in beginning programming courses. C also has the advantage of being freely available (or at nominal cost) on almost any computer system, whereas Fortran may be unavailable or considerably more expensive in some cases. C has long been used as a primary language for systems programming, but more recently it has become increasingly popular for scientific programming as well. If you desire to use C with this book, there should be plenty of software available. For example, both major commercial libraries, **IMSL** and **NAG**, have substantial subsets available in C, and the **NR** and **NUMAL** libraries are also available in C at nominal cost (see Section 1.4.1).

In addition, on many computer systems it is fairly straightforward to call Fortran routines from C programs. The main differences to watch out for are that the routine names may be slightly modified (often with an underscore before and/or after the usual name), all arguments to Fortran subroutines should be passed by address (i.e., as pointers in C), and C and Fortran have opposite array storage conventions (C matrices are stored row-wise, Fortran matrices are stored column-wise). Finally, one can automatically convert Fortran source code directly into C using the **f2c** converter that is available free from Bell Laboratories or **netlib**, so that Fortran routines obtained via the Internet, for example, can easily be used with C programs.

A third choice of programming language that should be seriously considered is an interactive scientific computing environment, such as **MATLAB**. The user of such an environment will enjoy several benefits. User programs will generally be much shorter, because of the elimination of declarations, storage management, and many explicit loops. In addition, these environments often have built-in functions for many of the problems we will encounter, which greatly simplifies the interface with such routines because much of the necessary information (array sizes, etc.) is passed implicitly by the environment. An additional bonus is built-in graphics, which avoids having to do this separately in a postprocessing phase. Even if you intend to use a standard language such as C or Fortran in the long run, you may still find it beneficial to learn a package such as **MATLAB** for its usefulness as a rapid prototyping environment in which new algorithms can be tried out quickly then later recoded in a standard language, if necessary, for greater efficiency or compatibility. If you wish to learn **MATLAB**, in addition to the superb tutorial and reference documentation that comes with it you might also find one of the many books on **MATLAB** useful (see [18, 71, 120, 200, 204, 206, 229]).

Some of the computer problems in the book call for graphical output. Depending on your computing environment, several options are available for producing the required plots. In a Unix environment, simple plots can be made using the **graph** and **plot** commands (see the corresponding **man** pages). In X-Windows, simple plots can be made on the screen with the **xgraph** tool, and then hard copies can be made using the **xwd** and **xpr** utilities, or their equivalents. Somewhat more sophisticated graphs can be made using free packages such as **gnuplot** (available by **ftp** from **dartmouth.edu/pub/gnuplot**) or **plplot** (available by **ftp** from **dino.ph.utexas.edu/plplot**), which are available for Unix and several other operating systems. Much more sophisticated and powerful scientific visualization systems are also available, but their capabilities go well beyond the simple plots needed for the problems in this book. If you use a PC or Mac, dozens of graphics programs are available, far too many to mention individually. Again, note that **MATLAB** and similar environments have built-in graphics, which is a great convenience.

Another important programming consideration is *performance*. The performance of today's microprocessor-based computer systems often depends critically on judicious exploitation of a memory hierarchy (registers, cache, RAM, disk, etc.) both by the user and by the optimizing compiler. Thus, it is important not only to choose the right algorithm but also to implement it carefully to maximize the reuse of data while they are held in the portions of the memory hierarchy with faster access times. Fortunately, the details of such programming are usually hidden from the user inside the library routines recommended in this text. This feature is just one of the many benefits of using existing, professionally written software for scientific computing whenever possible.

If you use a scientific computing environment such as **MATLAB**, you should be aware that there may be significant differences in performance between the built-in operations, which are generally very fast, and those you program explicitly yourself, which tend to be much slower owing to the interpreted mode of operation and to memory management overhead. Thus, one should be very careful in making performance comparisons under these circumstances. For example, one algorithm may be inferior to another in principle, yet perform better because of more effective utilization of fast built-in operations.

For general advice on many practical aspects of using workstations, Unix, X-Windows, graphics, and many other packages of interest in scientific computing, as well as performance considerations in programming, see [67, 85, 158].

1.5 HISTORICAL NOTES AND FURTHER READING

The subject we now call numerical analysis or scientific computing vastly predates the advent of modern computers. Most of the concepts and many of the algorithms that are in use today were first formulated by pre-twentieth century giants—Newton, Gauss, Euler, Jacobi, and many others—whose names recur throughout this book. The main concern then, as it is now, was finding efficient methods for obtaining approximate solutions to mathematical problems that arose in physics, astronomy, surveying, and other disciplines. Indeed, efficient use of computational resources is even more critical when using pencil, paper, and brain power (or perhaps a hand calculator) than when using a modern high-speed computer.

For the most part, modern computers have simply increased the size of problems that are feasible to tackle. They have also necessitated more careful analysis and control of rounding error, for the computation is no longer done by a human who can easily carry additional precision as needed. There is no question, however, that the development of digital computers was the impetus for the flowering of numerical analysis into the fertile and vigorously growing field that has enabled the ubiquitous role computation now plays throughout modern science and engineering. Indeed, computation has come to be regarded as an equal and indispensable partner, along with theory and experiment, in the advance of scientific knowledge and engineering practice [145].

For an account of the early history of numerical analysis, see [100]; for the more recent development of scientific computing, see [188]. The literature of numerical analysis, from textbooks to research monographs and journals, is much too vast to be covered adequately here. This text will try to give appropriate credit for the major ideas presented (at least those not already obvious from the name) and cite (usually secondary) sources for further reading, but these citations and recommendations are by no means complete. There are too many excellent general textbooks on numerical analysis to mention them all, but many of these still make worthwhile reading (even some of the older ones, several of which have recently been reissued in inexpensive reprint editions). Only those most directly relevant to our discussion will be cited.

Most numerical analysis textbooks contain a general discussion of error analysis. The seminal reference on the analysis of rounding errors is [274], which is a treasure trove of valuable insights. Its author, James H. Wilkinson, played a major role in developing and popularizing the notion of backward error analysis and was also responsible for a number of famous "computational counterexamples" that reveal various numerical instabilities in unsuspected problems and algorithms. A more recent work in a similar spirit is [126]. For various approaches to automating error analysis, see [5, 175, 180]. A **MATLAB** toolbox for error analysis is discussed in [36].

Recent general treatments of computer arithmetic include [152, 193]. The book by Sterbenz [237], though somewhat dated, remains the only book-length treatment of floating-point arithmetic. See [150] for a more concise account. The effort to standardize floating-point arithmetic and the high quality of the resulting standard were largely inspired by William Kahan, who is also responsible for many well known computational counterexamples. The IEEE floating-point standard can be found in [131]. A useful tutorial on floating-point arithmetic and the IEEE standard is [97]. Although it is no substitute for careful problem formulation and solution, extended precision arithmetic can occasionally be useful for highly sensitive problems; several software packages providing multiple precision floating-point arithmetic are available, including **MP**(#524), **FM**(#693), and **MPFUN**(#719) from **TOMS**.

For an account of the emergence of mathematical software as a subdiscipline of numerical analysis and computer science, see the survey [41] and the collections [44, 73, 122, 134, 209, 210]. Perhaps the earliest numerical methods textbook to be based on professional quality software (not just code fragments for illustration) was [225], which is similar in tone, style, and content to the very influential book by Forsythe, Malcolm and Moler [82] that popularized this approach. In addition to the books mentioned in Section 1.4.1, the following numerical methods textbooks focus on the specific software libraries or packages listed: **IMSL** [211], **NAG** [128, 151], **MATLAB** [165, 187, 262], and **Mathematica** [231]. Other textbooks that provide additional discussion and examples at an introductory level include [11, 29, 30, 38, 43, 94, 173, 240]. More advanced general textbooks include [47, 59, 103, 118, 132, 149, 195, 222, 242]. The books of Acton [2, 3] entertainingly present practical advice on avoiding pitfalls in numerical computation.

The book of Strang [243] provides excellent background and insights on many aspects of applied mathematics that are relevant to numerical computation in general, and in particular to almost every chapter of this book. For an elementary introduction to scientific programming, see [261]. For advice on designing, implementing, and testing numerical software, as opposed to simply using it, see [174]. Additional computer exercises and projects can be found in [45, 72, 85, 89, 107, 109, 157].

REVIEW QUESTIONS

1.1. True or false: A problem is ill-conditioned if its solution is highly sensitive to small changes in the problem data.

1.2. True or false: Using higher-precision arithmetic will make an ill-conditioned problem better conditioned.

1.3. True or false: The conditioning of a problem depends on the algorithm used to solve it.

1.4. True or false: A good algorithm will produce an accurate solution regardless of the condition of the problem being solved.

1.5. True or false: The choice of algorithm for solving a problem has no effect on the propagated data error.

1.6. True or false: If two real numbers are exactly representable as floating-point numbers, then the result of a real arithmetic operation on them will also be representable as a floating-point number.

1.7. True or false: Floating-point numbers are distributed uniformly throughout their range.

1.8. True or false: Floating-point addition is associative but not commutative.

1.9. True or false: In a floating-point number system, the underflow level is the smallest positive number that perturbs the number 1 when added to it.

1.10. Explain the distinction between truncation (or discretization) and rounding.

1.11. Explain the distinction between absolute error and relative error.

1.12. Explain the distinction between computational error and propagated data error.

1.13. (*a*) What is meant by the *conditioning* of a problem?

(*b*) Is it affected by the algorithm used to solve the problem?

(*c*) Is it affected by the precision of the arithmetic used to solve the problem?

1.14. If a computational problem has a condition number of 1, is this good or bad? Why?

1.15. When is an approximate solution to a given problem considered to be good according to backward error analysis?

1.16. For a given floating-point number system, describe in words the distribution of machine numbers along the real line.

1.17. In floating-point arithmetic, which is generally more harmful, underflow or overflow? Why?

1.18. In floating-point arithmetic, which of the following operations on two positive floating-point operands can produce an overflow?

(*a*) Addition
(*b*) Subtraction
(*c*) Multiplication
(*d*) Division

1.19. In floating-point arithmetic, which of the following operations on two positive floating-point operands can produce an underflow?

(*a*) Addition
(*b*) Subtraction
(*c*) Multiplication
(*d*) Division

1.20. List two reasons why floating-point number systems are usually normalized.

1.21. In a floating-point system, what quantity determines the maximum relative error in representing a given real number by a machine number?

1.22. (*a*) Explain the difference between the rounding rules "round toward zero" and "round to nearest" in a floating-point system.

(*b*) Which of these two rounding rules is more accurate?

(*c*) What quantitative difference does this make in the unit roundoff ϵ_{mach}?

1.23. In a t-digit binary floating-point system with rounding to nearest, what is the value of the unit roundoff ϵ_{mach}?

1.24. In a floating-point system with gradual underflow (subnormal numbers), is the representation of each number still unique? Why?

1.25. In a floating-point system, is the product of two machine numbers usually exactly representable in the floating-point system? Why?

1.26. In a floating-point system, is the quotient of two nonzero machine numbers always exactly representable in the floating-point system? Why?

1.27. (*a*) Give an example to show that floating-point addition is not necessarily associative.

(*b*) Give an example to show that floating-point multiplication is not necessarily associative.

1.28. Give an example of a number whose decimal representation is finite (i.e., it has only a finite number of nonzero digits) but whose binary representation is not.

1.29. Give examples of floating-point arithmetic operations that would produce each of the exceptional values **Inf** and **NaN**.

1.30. Explain why the cancellation that occurs when two numbers of similar magnitude are subtracted is often bad even though the result may be exactly correct for the actual operands involved.

1.31. Assume a decimal (base 10) floating-point system having machine precision $\epsilon_{mach} = 10^{-5}$ and an exponent range of ± 20. What is the result of each of the following floating-point arithmetic operations?

(*a*) $1 + 10^{-7}$
(*b*) $1 + 10^3$
(*c*) $1 + 10^7$
(*d*) $10^{10} + 10^3$
(*e*) $10^{10}/10^{-15}$
(*f*) $10^{-10} \times 10^{-15}$

1.32. In a floating-point number system having an underflow level of UFL $= 10^{-38}$, which of the following computations will incur an underflow?

(*a*) $a = \sqrt{b^2 + c^2}$, with $b = 1, c = 10^{-25}$.
(*b*) $a = \sqrt{b^2 + c^2}$, with $b = c = 10^{-25}$.

(c) $u = (v \times w)/(y \times z)$, with $v = 10^{-15}$, $w = 10^{-30}$, $y = 10^{-20}$, and $z = 10^{-25}$.

In each case where underflow occurs, is it reasonable simply to set to zero the quantity that underflows?

1.33. (a) Explain in words the difference between the unit roundoff, ϵ_{mach}, and the underflow level, UFL, in a floating-point system.

Of these two quantities,

(b) Which one depends only on the number of digits in the mantissa field?

(c) Which one depends only on the number of digits in the exponent field?

(d) Which one does *not* depend on the rounding rule used?

(e) Which one is *not* affected by allowing subnormal numbers?

1.34. Let x_k be a monotonically decreasing, finite sequence of positive numbers (i.e., $x_k > x_{k+1}$ for each k). Assuming it is practical to take the numbers in any order we choose, in what order should the sequence be summed to minimize rounding error?

1.35. Is cancellation an example of rounding error? Why?

1.36. (a) Explain why a divergent infinite series, such as

$$\sum_{n=1}^{\infty} \frac{1}{n},$$

can have a finite sum in floating-point arithmetic.

(b) At what point will the partial sums cease to change?

1.37. In floating-point arithmetic, if you are computing the sum of a convergent infinite series

$$S = \sum_{i=1}^{\infty} x_i$$

of positive terms in the natural order, what stopping criterion would you use to attain the maximum possible accuracy using the smallest number of terms?

1.38. Explain why an alternating infinite series, such as

$$e^x = 1 + x + \frac{x^2}{2!} + \frac{x^3}{3!} + \cdots$$

for $x < 0$, is difficult to evaluate accurately in floating-point arithmetic.

1.39. If f is a real-valued function of a real variable, the truncation error of the finite difference approximation to the derivative

$$f'(x) \approx \frac{f(x + h) - f(x)}{h}$$

goes to zero as $h \to 0$. If we use floating-point arithmetic, list two factors that limit how small a value of h we can use in practice.

1.40. For computing the midpoint m of an interval $[x, y]$, which of the following two formulas is preferable in floating-point arithmetic? Why?

(a) $m = (x + y)/2.0$

(b) $m = x + (y - x)/2.0$

1.41. List at least two ways in which evaluation of the quadratic formula

$$x = \frac{-b \pm \sqrt{b^2 - 4ac}}{2a}$$

may suffer numerical difficulties in floating-point arithmetic.

EXERCISES

1.1. The average normal human body temperature is usually quoted as 98.6 degrees Fahrenheit, which might be presumed to have been determined by computing the average over a large population and then rounding to three significant digits. In fact, however, 98.6 is simply the Fahrenheit equivalent of 37 degrees Celsius, which is accurate to only two significant digits.

(a) What is the maximum relative error in the accepted value, assuming it is accurate to within $\pm 0.05°$ F?

(b) What is the maximum relative error in the accepted value, assuming it is accurate to within $\pm 0.5°$ C?

1.2. What are the absolute and relative errors in approximating π by each of the following quantities?

    (*a*) 3

    (*b*) 3.14

    (*c*) 22/7

1.3. If a is an approximate value for a quantity whose true value is t, and a has relative error r, prove from the definitions of these terms that $a = t(1 + r)$.

1.4. Consider the problem of evaluating the function $\sin(x)$, in particular, the propagated data error, i.e., the error in the function value due to a perturbation h in the argument x.

    (*a*) Estimate the absolute error in evaluating $\sin(x)$.

    (*b*) Estimate the relative error in evaluating $\sin(x)$.

    (*c*) Estimate the condition number for this problem.

    (*d*) For what values of the argument x is this problem highly sensitive?

1.5. Consider the function $f: \mathbb{R}^2 \rightarrow \mathbb{R}$ defined by $f(x, y) = x - y$. Measuring the size of the input (x, y) by $|x|+|y|$, and assuming that $|x|+|y| \approx 1$ and $x-y \approx \epsilon$, show that $\mathrm{cond}(f) \approx 1/\epsilon$. What can you conclude about the sensitivity of subtraction?

1.6. The sine function is given by the infinite series

$$\sin(x) = x - \frac{x^3}{3!} + \frac{x^5}{5!} - \frac{x^7}{7!} + \cdots.$$

    (*a*) What are the forward and backward errors if we approximate the sine function by using only the first term in the series, i.e., $\sin(x) \approx x$, for $x = 0.1, 0.5$, and 1.0?

    (*b*) What are the forward and backward errors if we approximate the sine function by using the first two terms in the series, i.e., $\sin(x) \approx x - x^3/6$, for $x = 0.1$, 0.5, and 1.0?

1.7. A floating-point number system is characterized by four integers: the base β, the precision t, and the lower and upper limits L and U of the exponent range.

    (*a*) If $\beta = 10$, what are the smallest values of t and U, and largest value of L, such that both 2365.27 and 0.0000512 can be represented *exactly* in a *normalized* floating-point system?

    (*b*) How would your answer change if the system is not normalized, i.e., if gradual underflow is allowed?

1.8. In a floating-point system with precision $t = 6$ decimal digits, let $x = 1.23456$ and $y = 1.23579$.

    (*a*) How many significant digits does the difference $y - x$ contain?

    (*b*) If the floating-point system is normalized, what is the minimum exponent range for which x, y, and $y - x$ are all exactly representable?

    (*c*) Is the difference $y - x$ exactly representable, regardless of exponent range, if gradual underflow is allowed? Why?

1.9. (*a*) Using four-digit decimal arithmetic and the formula given in Example 1.1, compute the surface area of the Earth, with $r = 6370$ km.

    (*b*) Using the same formula and precision, compute the difference in surface area if the value for the radius is increased by 1 km.

    (*c*) Since $dA/dr = 8\pi r$, the change in surface area is approximated by $8\pi rh$, where h is the change in radius. Use this formula, still with four-digit arithmetic, to compute the difference in surface area due to an increase of 1 km in radius. How does the value obtained using this approximate formula compare with that obtained from the "exact" formula in part *b*?

    (*d*) Determine which answer is more nearly correct by repeating both computations using higher precision, say, six-digit decimal arithmetic.

    (*e*) Explain the results you obtained in parts *a–d*.

    (*f*) Try this problem on a computer. How small must the change h in radius be for the same phenomenon to occur? Try both single precision and double precision, if available.

1.10. Consider the expression

$$\frac{1}{1 - x} - \frac{1}{1 + x},$$

assuming $x \neq \pm 1$.

    (*a*) For what range of values of x is it difficult to compute this expression accurately in floating-point arithmetic?

    (*b*) Give a rearrangement of the terms such that, for the range of x in part *a*, the computation is more accurate in floating-point arithmetic.

1.11. If $x \approx y$, then we would expect some cancellation in computing $\log(x) - \log(y)$. On the other hand, $\log(x) - \log(y) = \log(x/y)$, and the latter involves no cancellation. Does this mean that computing $\log(x/y)$ is likely to give a better result? (*Hint*: For what value is the log function sensitive?)

1.12. (*a*) Which of the two mathematically equivalent expressions

$$x^2 - y^2 \quad \text{and} \quad (x - y)(x + y)$$

can be evaluated more accurately in floating-point arithmetic? Why?

(*b*) For what values of x and y, relative to each other, is there a substantial difference in the accuracy of the two expressions?

1.13. The Euclidean norm of an n-dimensional vector x is defined by

$$\|x\|_2 = \left(\sum_{i=1}^{n} x_i^2 \right)^{1/2}.$$

How would you avoid overflow and harmful underflow in this computation?

1.14. Give specific examples to show that floating-point addition is not associative in each of the following floating-point systems:

(*a*) The toy floating-point system of Example 1.5

(*b*) IEEE single-precision floating-point arithmetic

1.15. Explain how the various definitions for the unit roundoff ϵ_{mach} given in Section 1.3.5 can differ in practice. (*Hint*: Consider the toy floating-point system of Example 1.5.)

1.16. Let x be a given nonzero floating-point number in a normalized system, and let y be an adjacent floating-point number, also nonzero.

(*a*) What is the minimum possible spacing between x and y?

(*b*) What is the maximum possible spacing between x and y?

1.17. How many normalized machine numbers are there in a single-precision IEEE floating-point system? How many additional machine numbers are gained if subnormals are allowed?

1.18. In a single-precision IEEE floating-point system, what are the values of the largest machine number, OFL, and the smallest positive normalized machine number, UFL? How do your answers change if subnormals are allowed?

1.19. What is the IEEE single-precision binary floating-point representation of the decimal fraction 0.1

(*a*) with chopping?

(*b*) with rounding to nearest?

1.20. (*a*) In a floating-point system, is the unit roundoff ϵ_{mach} necessarily a machine number?

(*b*) Is it possible to have a floating-point system in which $\epsilon_{\text{mach}} < \text{UFL}$? If so, give an example.

1.21. Assume that you are solving the quadratic equation $ax^2 + bx + c = 0$, with $a = 1.22$, $b = 3.34$, and $c = 2.28$, using a normalized floating-point system with $\beta = 10, t = 3$.

(*a*) What is the computed value of the discriminant $b^2 - 4ac$?

(*b*) What is the correct value of the discriminant in real (exact) arithmetic?

(*c*) What is the relative error in the computed value of the discriminant?

1.22. Assume a normalized floating-point system with $\beta = 10, t = 3$, and $L = -98$.

(*a*) What is the value of the underflow level UFL for this system?

(*b*) If $x = 6.87 \times 10^{-97}$ and $y = 6.81 \times 10^{-97}$, what is the result of $x - y$?

(*c*) What would be the result of $x - y$ if the system permitted gradual underflow?

1.23. Consider the following claim: if two floating-point numbers x and y with the same sign differ by a factor of at most the base β (i.e., $1/\beta \le x/y \le \beta$), then their difference, $x - y$, is exactly representable in the floating-point system. Show that this claim is true for $\beta = 2$, but give a counterexample for $\beta > 2$.

1.24. Some microprocessors have an instruction **mpyadd(a,b,c)**, for multiply-add, which takes single-length inputs and adds **c** to the double-length product of **a** and **b** before normalizing and returning a single-length result. How can such an instruction be used to compute double-precision products *without* using any double-length variables (i.e., the double-length product of **a** and **b** will be contained in two single-length variables, say, **s** and **t**)?

1.25. Verify that the alternative quadratic formula given in Example 1.10 indeed gives the correct roots to the quadratic equation (in exact arithmetic).

1.26. Give a detailed explanation of the numerical inferiority of the one-pass formula for computing the standard deviation compared with the two-pass formula given in Example 1.12.

COMPUTER PROBLEMS

1.1. Write a program to compute the absolute and relative errors in Stirling's approximation

$$n! \approx \sqrt{2\pi n}\,(n/e)^n$$

for $n = 1, \ldots, 10$. Does the absolute error grow or shrink as n increases? Does the relative error grow or shrink as n increases?

1.2. Write a program to determine approximate values for the unit roundoff ϵ_{mach} and the underflow level UFL, and test it on a real computer. (*Optional*: Can you also determine the overflow level OFL on your machine? This is trickier because an actual overflow may be fatal.) Print the resulting values in decimal, and also try to determine the number of bits in the mantissa and exponent fields of the floating-point system you use.

1.3. In most floating-point systems, a quick approximation to the unit roundoff can be obtained by evaluating the expression

$$\epsilon_{mach} \approx |3 \ * \ (4/3 \ - \ 1) \ - \ 1|.$$

(a) Explain why this trick works.

(b) Try it on a variety of computers (in both single and double precision) and calculators to confirm that it works.

(c) Would this trick work in a floating-point system with base $\beta = 3$?

1.4. Write a program to compute the mathematical constant e, the base of natural logarithms, from the definition

$$e = \lim_{n \to \infty} (1 + 1/n)^n.$$

Specifically, compute $(1 + 1/n)^n$ for $n = 10^k$, $k = 1, 2, \ldots, 20$. If the programming language you use does not have an operator for exponentiation, you may use the equivalent formula

$$(1 + 1/n)^n = \exp(n \log(1 + 1/n)),$$

where exp and log are built-in functions. Determine the error in your successive approximations by comparing them with the value of exp(1). Does the error always decrease as n increases? Explain your results.

1.5. (a) Consider the function

$$f(x) = (e^x - 1)/x.$$

Use l'Hôpital's rule to show that

$$\lim_{x \to 0} f(x) = 1.$$

(b) Check this result empirically by writing a program to compute $f(x)$ for $x = 10^{-k}$, $k = 1, \ldots, 16$. Do your results agree with theoretical expectations? Explain why.

(c) Perform the experiment in part b again, this time using the mathematically equivalent formulation

$$f(x) = (e^x - 1)/\log(e^x),$$

evaluated as indicated, with no simplification. If this works any better, can you explain why?

1.6. Suppose you need to generate $n + 1$ equally spaced points on the interval $[a, b]$, with spacing $h = (b - a)/n$.

(a) In floating-point arithmetic, which of the following methods,

$$x_0 = a, \quad x_k = x_{k-1} + h, \quad k = 1, \ldots, n$$

or

$$x_k = a + kh, \quad k = 0, \ldots, n,$$

is better, and why?

(b) Write a program implementing both methods and find an example, say, with $a = 0$ and $b = 1$, that illustrates the difference between them.

1.7. (a) Write a program to compute an approximate value for the derivative of a function using the finite-difference formula

$$f'(x) \approx \frac{f(x + h) - f(x)}{h}.$$

Test your program using the function $\sin(x)$ for $x = 1$. Determine the error by comparing with the built-in function $\cos(x)$. Plot the magnitude of the error as a function of h, for $h = \frac{1}{2}, \frac{1}{4}, \frac{1}{8}, \ldots$. You should use a log scale for h and for the magnitude of the error. Is there a minimum value for the magnitude of the error? How does the corresponding value for h compare with the rule of thumb

$$h \approx \sqrt{\epsilon_{mach}} \cdot |x| \; ?$$

(b) Repeat the exercise using the centered difference approximation

$$f'(x) \approx \frac{f(x + h) - f(x - h)}{2h}.$$

1.8. Consider the infinite series

$$\sum_{n=1}^{\infty} \frac{1}{n}.$$

(a) Prove that the series is divergent. (*Hint*: Group the terms in sets containing terms $1/(2^{k-1} + 1)$ down to $1/2^k$, for $k = 1, 2, \ldots$.)

(b) Explain why summing the series in floating-point arithmetic yields a finite sum.

(c) Try to predict when the partial sum will cease to change in both IEEE single-precision and double-precision floating-point arithmetic. Given the execution rate of your computer for floating-point operations, try to predict how long each computation would take to complete.

(d) Write two programs to compute the sum of the series, one in single precision and the other in double precision. Monitor the progress of the summation by printing out the index and partial sum periodically. What stopping criterion should you use? What result is actually produced on your computer? Compare your results with your predictions, including the execution time required. (*Caution*: Your single-precision version should terminate fairly quickly, but your double-precision version may take *much* longer, so it may not be practical to run it to completion, even if your computer budget is generous.)

1.9. (a) Write a program to compute the exponential function e^x using the infinite series

$$e^x = 1 + x + \frac{x^2}{2!} + \frac{x^3}{3!} + \cdots.$$

(b) Summing in the natural order, what stopping criterion should you use?

(c) Test your program for

$$x = \pm 1, \pm 5, \pm 10, \pm 15, \pm 20,$$

and compare your results with the built-in function $\exp(x)$.

(d) Can you use the series in this form to get accurate results for $x < 0$? (*Hint*: $e^{-x} = 1/e^x$.)

(e) Can you rearrange the series or regroup the terms in any way to get more accurate results for $x < 0$?

1.10. Write a program to solve the quadratic equation $ax^2 + bx + c = 0$ using the standard quadratic formula

$$x = \frac{-b \pm \sqrt{b^2 - 4ac}}{2a}$$

or the alternative formula

$$x = \frac{2c}{-b \mp \sqrt{b^2 - 4ac}}.$$

Your program should accept values for the coefficients a, b, and c as input and produce the two roots of the equation as output. Your program should detect when the roots are imaginary, but need not use complex arithmetic explicitly. You should guard against unnecessary overflow, underflow, and cancellation. When should you use each of the two formulas? Try to make your program robust when given unusual input values. Any root that is within the range of the floating-point system should be computed accurately, even if the other is out of range. Test your program using the following values for the coefficients:

a	b	c
6	5	-4
6×10^{30}	5×10^{30}	-4×10^{30}
0	1	1
1	-10^5	1
1	-4	3.999999
10^{-30}	-10^{30}	10^{30}

1.11. A cubic equation

$$ax^3 + bx^2 + cx + d = 0,$$

where the coefficients are real and $a \neq 0$, has at least one real root, which can be computed in closed form as follows. Make the substitution $y = x + b/(3a)$. Then the original equation becomes

$$y^3 + 3py + q = 0,$$

where

$$p = \frac{3ac - b^2}{9a^2}$$

and

$$q = \frac{27a^2d - 9abc + 2b^3}{27a^3}.$$

If we now take

$$\alpha = \frac{-q + \sqrt{4p^3 + q^2}}{2}$$

and

$$\beta = \frac{-q - \sqrt{4p^3 + q^2}}{2},$$

then one real root of the original cubic equation is given by

$$x = \sqrt[3]{\alpha} - \sqrt[3]{\beta}.$$

Write a routine using this method to compute one real root of an arbitrary cubic equation given its (real) coefficients. Try to make your routine as robust as possible, guarding against unnecessary overflow, underflow, and cancellation. What should your routine do if $a = 0$? Test your routine for various values of the coefficients, analogous to those used in the previous exercise.

1.12. (a) Write a program to compute the mean $\bar{x}$ and standard deviation σ of a finite sequence x_i. Your program should accept a vector x of dimension n as input and produce the mean and standard deviation of the sequence as output. For the standard deviation, try both the two-pass formula

$$\sigma = \left[\frac{1}{n-1} \sum_{i=1}^{n} (x_i - \bar{x})^2 \right]^{1/2}$$

and the one-pass formula

$$\sigma = \left[\frac{1}{n-1} \left(\sum_{i=1}^{n} x_i^2 - n\bar{x}^2 \right) \right]^{1/2}$$

and compare the results for an input sequence of your choice.

(b) Can you devise an input data sequence that dramatically illustrates the numerical difference between these two mathematically equivalent formulas? (*Caution*: Beware of taking the square root of a negative number.)

1.13. If an amount a is invested at interest rate r compounded n times per year, then the final value f at the end of one year is given by

$$f = a(1 + r/n)^n.$$

This is the familiar formula for *compound interest*. With simple interest, $n = 1$. Typically, compounding is done quarterly, $n = 4$, or perhaps even daily, $n = 365$. Obviously, the more frequent the compounding, the greater the final amount, because more interest is paid on previous interest. But how much difference does this frequency actually make? Write a program that implements the compound interest formula. Test your program using an initial investment of $a = 100$, an interest rate of 5 percent (i.e., $r = 0.05$), and the following values for n: 1, 4, 12, 365, 10,000, and 20,000. Implement the compound interest formula in two different ways:

(a) If the programming language you use does not have an operator for exponentiation (e.g., C), then you might implement the compound interest formula using a loop that repeatedly multiplies a by $(1 + r/n)$ for a total of n times. Even if your programming language does have an operator for exponentiation (e.g., Fortran), try implementing the compound interest formula using such a loop and print your results for the input values. Does the final amount always grow with the frequency of compounding, as it should? Can you explain this behavior?

(b) With the functions $\exp(x)$ and $\log(x)$, the compound interest formula can also be written

$$f = a\exp(n\log(1 + r/n)).$$

Implement this formula using the corresponding built-in functions and compare your results with those for the first implementation using the loop, for the same input values.

1.14. The polynomial $(x-1)^6$ has the value zero at $x = 1$ and is positive elsewhere. The expanded form of the polynomial, $x^6 - 6x^5 + 15x^4 - 20x^3 + 15x^2 - 6x + 1$, is mathematically equivalent but may not give the same results numerically. Compute and plot the values of this polynomial, using each of the two forms, for 101 equally spaced points in the interval [0.995, 1.005], i.e., with a spacing of 0.0001. Your plot should be scaled so that the values for x and for the polynomial use the full ranges of their respective axes. Can you explain this behavior?

1.15. Write a program that sums n random, single-precision floating-point numbers x_i, uniformly distributed on the interval $[0, 1]$ (see Table 13.1 for an appropriate random number generator). Sum the numbers in each of the following ways (use only single-precision floating-point variables unless specifically indicated otherwise):

(*a*) Sum the numbers in the order in which they were generated, using a double-precision variable in which to accumulate the sum.

(*b*) Sum the numbers in the order in which they were generated, this time using a single-precision accumulator.

(*c*) Use the following algorithm (due to Kahan), again using only single precision, to sum the numbers in the order in which they were generated:

$s = x_1$
$c = 0$
for $i = 2$ **to** n
    $y = x_i - c$
    $t = s + y$
    $c = (t - s) - y$
    $s = t$
end

(*d*) Sum the numbers in order of increasing magnitude (this will require that the numbers be sorted before summing, for which you may use a library sorting routine).

(*e*) Sum the numbers in order of decreasing magnitude (i.e., reverse the order of summation from part *d*).

Run your program for various values of n and compare the results for methods *a* through *e*. You may need to use a fairly large value for n to see a substantial difference. How do the methods rank in terms of accuracy, and why? How do the methods compare in cost? Can you explain why the algorithm in part *c* works?

1.16. Write a program to generate the first n terms in the sequence given by the difference equation

$$x_{k+1} = 2.25x_k - 0.5x_{k-1},$$

with starting values

$$x_1 = \tfrac{1}{3} \quad \text{and} \quad x_2 = \tfrac{1}{12}.$$

Use $n = 225$ if you are working in single precision, $n = 60$ if you are working in double precision. Make a semilog plot of the values you obtain as a function of k. The exact solution of the difference equation is given by

$$x_k = \frac{4^{1-k}}{3},$$

which decreases monotonically as k increases. Does your graph confirm this theoretically expected behavior? Can you explain your results? (*Hint:* Find the general solution to the difference equation.)

1.17. Write a program to generate the first n terms in the sequence given by the difference equation

$$x_{k+1} = 111 - (1130 - 3000/x_{k-1})/x_k,$$

with starting values

$$x_1 = \tfrac{11}{2} \quad \text{and} \quad x_2 = \tfrac{61}{11}.$$

Use $n = 10$ if you are working in single precision, $n = 20$ if you are working in double precision. The exact solution is a monotonically increasing sequence converging to 6. Can you explain your results?

1.18. The Euclidean norm of an n-dimensional vector x is defined by

$$\|x\|_2 = \left(\sum_{i=1}^{n} x_i^2 \right)^{1/2}.$$

Implement a robust routine for computing this quantity for any given input vector x. Your routine should avoid overflow and harmful underflow. Compare both the accuracy and performance of your robust routine with a more straightforward naive implementation. Can you devise a vector that produces significantly different results from the two routines? How much performance does the robust routine sacrifice?

CHAPTER 2

Systems of Linear Equations

2.1 LINEAR SYSTEMS

Systems of linear algebraic equations arise in almost every aspect of applied mathematics and scientific computation. Such systems often occur naturally, but they are also frequently the result of approximating nonlinear equations by linear equations or differential equations by algebraic equations. We will see many examples of such approximations throughout this book. For these reasons, the efficient and accurate solution of linear systems forms the cornerstone of many numerical methods for solving a wide variety of practical computational problems.

In matrix-vector notation, a system of linear algebraic equations has the form

$$Ax = b,$$

where A is an $m \times n$ matrix, b is a given m-vector, and x is the unknown solution n-vector to be determined. Such a system of equations asks the question, "Can the vector b be expressed as a linear combination of the columns of the matrix A?" If so, the coefficients of this linear combination are given by the components of the solution vector x. There may or may not be a solution; and if there is a solution, it may or may not be unique. In this chapter we will consider only *square* systems, which means that $m = n$, i.e., the matrix has the same number of rows and columns. In later chapters we will consider systems where $m \neq n$.

2.1.1 Singularity and Nonsingularity

An $n \times n$ matrix A is said to be *singular* if it has any one of the following equivalent properties:

1. A has no inverse (i.e., there is no matrix M such that $AM = MA = I$, the identity matrix).

2. $\det(A) = 0$.
3. $\text{rank}(A) < n$ (the *rank* of a matrix is the maximum number of linearly independent rows or columns it contains).
4. $Az = 0$ for some vector $z \neq 0$.

Otherwise, the matrix is *nonsingular*. The solvability of a system of linear equations $Ax = b$ is determined by whether the matrix A is singular or nonsingular. If the matrix A is nonsingular, then its inverse, denoted by A^{-1}, exists, and the system $Ax = b$ always has a unique solution $x = A^{-1}b$ regardless of the value for b. If, on the other hand, the matrix A is singular, then the *number* of solutions is determined by the right-hand-side vector b: for a given value of b there may be no solution, but if there is a solution x, so that $Ax = b$, then we also have $A(x + \gamma z) = b$ for any scalar γ, where the vector z is as in the foregoing definition. Thus, if a singular system has a solution, then the solution cannot be unique. To summarize the possibilities, for a given matrix A and right-hand-side vector b, the system may have

One solution:	nonsingular
No solution:	singular
Infinitely many solutions:	singular

In two dimensions, each linear equation determines a straight line in the plane. The solution of the system is the intersection point of the two lines. If the two straight lines are not parallel, then they have a unique intersection point (the nonsingular case). If the two straight lines are parallel, then either they do not intersect at all (there is no solution) or the two lines are the same (any point along the line is a solution). In higher dimensions, each equation determines a hyperplane. In the nonsingular case, the unique solution is the intersection point of all of the hyperplanes.

EXAMPLE 2.1 SINGULARITY AND NONSINGULARITY. The 2×2 system

$$2x_1 + 3x_2 = b_1,$$
$$5x_1 + 4x_2 = b_2,$$

or in matrix-vector notation

$$\begin{bmatrix} 2 & 3 \\ 5 & 4 \end{bmatrix} \begin{bmatrix} x_1 \\ x_2 \end{bmatrix} = \begin{bmatrix} b_1 \\ b_2 \end{bmatrix},$$

is nonsingular regardless of the value of b. If $b = \begin{bmatrix} 8 & 13 \end{bmatrix}^T$, for example, then the unique solution is $x = \begin{bmatrix} 1 & 2 \end{bmatrix}^T$.

The 2×2 system

$$\begin{bmatrix} 2 & 3 \\ 4 & 6 \end{bmatrix} \begin{bmatrix} x_1 \\ x_2 \end{bmatrix} = \begin{bmatrix} b_1 \\ b_2 \end{bmatrix}$$

is singular regardless of the value of b. With $b = \begin{bmatrix} 4 & 7 \end{bmatrix}^T$, there is no solution. With $b = \begin{bmatrix} 4 & 8 \end{bmatrix}^T$, then

$$x = \begin{bmatrix} \gamma \\ (4 - 2\gamma)/3 \end{bmatrix}$$

is a solution for any real number γ.

2.2 SOLVING LINEAR SYSTEMS

To solve a linear system, the general strategy outlined in Section 1.1.1 suggests that we should transform the system into one whose solution is the same as that of the original system but is easier to compute. What type of transformation of a linear system leaves the solution unchanged? The answer is that we can premultiply (i.e., multiply from the left) both sides of the linear system $Ax = b$ by any nonsingular matrix M without affecting the solution. To see why this is so, note that the solution to the linear system $MAx = Mb$ is given by

$$x = (MA)^{-1}Mb = A^{-1}M^{-1}Mb = A^{-1}b.$$

EXAMPLE 2.2 PERMUTATIONS. An important example of such a transformation is the fact that the rows of A and corresponding entries of b can be reordered without changing the solution x. This is intuitively obvious: all of the equations in the system must be satisfied simultaneously in any case, so the order in which they happen to be written down is irrelevant; they may as well have been drawn randomly from a hat. Formally, such a reordering of the rows is accomplished by premultiplying both sides of the equation by a *permutation* matrix P, which is a square matrix having exactly one 1 in each row and column and zeros elsewhere (i.e., an identity matrix with its rows and columns permuted). For example,

$$\begin{bmatrix} 0 & 0 & 1 \\ 1 & 0 & 0 \\ 0 & 1 & 0 \end{bmatrix} \begin{bmatrix} b_1 \\ b_2 \\ b_3 \end{bmatrix} = \begin{bmatrix} b_3 \\ b_1 \\ b_2 \end{bmatrix}.$$

A permutation matrix is always nonsingular; in fact, its inverse is simply its transpose, $P^{-1} = P^T$ (the *transpose* of a matrix M, denoted by M^T, is a matrix whose columns are the rows of M, that is, if $N = M^T$, then $n_{ij} = m_{ji}$). Thus, the reordered system can be written $PAx = Pb$, and the solution x is unchanged.

Postmultiplying (i.e., multiplying from the right) by a permutation matrix reorders the columns of the matrix instead of the rows. Such a transformation *does* change the solution, but only in that the components of the solution are permuted. To see this, observe that the solution to the system $APx = b$ is given by

$$x = (AP)^{-1}b = P^{-1}A^{-1}b = P^T(A^{-1}b).$$

EXAMPLE 2.3 DIAGONAL SCALING. Another simple but important type of transformation is *diagonal scaling*. Recall that a matrix D is *diagonal* if $d_{ij} = 0$ for all $i \neq j$, that is, the only nonzero entries are d_{ii}, $i = 1, \ldots, n$, on the *main diagonal*. Premultiplying both sides of a linear system $Ax = b$ by a nonsingular diagonal matrix D multiplies each row of the matrix and right-hand side by the corresponding diagonal entry of D, and hence is called *row scaling*. In principle, row scaling does not change the solution to the linear system, but in practice it can affect the numerical solution process and the accuracy that can be attained for a given problem, as we will see.

Column scaling—postmultiplying the matrix of a linear system by a nonsingular diagonal matrix D—multiplies each column of the matrix by the corresponding diagonal entry of D. Such a transformation does alter the solution, in effect changing the units in which the components of the solution are measured. The solution to the scaled system $ADx = b$ is given by

$$x = (AD)^{-1}b = D^{-1}A^{-1}b,$$

and hence the solution to the original system is given by Dx.

2.2.1 Triangular Linear Systems

The next question is what type of linear system is easy to solve. Suppose there is an equation in the system $Ax = b$ that involves only one of the unknown solution components (i.e., only one entry in that row of A is nonzero). Then that equation can easily be solved (by division) for that unknown. Now suppose there is another equation in the system that involves only two unknowns, one of which is the one already determined. By substituting the one solution component already determined into this second equation, we can then easily solve for its other unknown. If this pattern continues, with only one new unknown component arising per equation, then all of the solution components can be computed in succession. A matrix with this special property is called *triangular*, for reasons that will soon become apparent. Because triangular linear systems are easily solved by this successive substitution process, they are a suitable target in transforming a general linear system.

Although the general triangular form just described is all that is required to enable the system to be solved by successive substitution, it is convenient to define two specific triangular forms for computational purposes. A matrix is *upper triangular* if all of its entries below the main diagonal are zero (i.e., if $a_{ij} = 0$ for $i > j$). Similarly, a matrix is *lower triangular* if all of its entries above the main diagonal are zero (i.e., if $a_{ij} = 0$ for $i < j$). For an upper triangular system $Ax = b$, the successive substitution process is called *back-substitution* and can be expressed as follows:

$$x_n = b_n/a_{nn},$$

$$x_i = \left(b_i - \sum_{j=i+1}^{n} a_{ij}x_j\right)/a_{ii}, \qquad i = n-1, \ldots, 1.$$

Similarly, for a lower triangular system $Ax = b$, the successive substitution process is called *forward-substitution* and can be expressed as follows:

$$x_1 = b_1/a_{11},$$

$$x_i = \left(b_i - \sum_{j=1}^{i-1} a_{ij}x_j\right)/a_{ii}, \qquad i = 2, \ldots, n.$$

A matrix that is triangular in the more general sense defined earlier can be permuted into upper or lower triangular form by a suitable permutation of its rows or columns.

EXAMPLE 2.4 TRIANGULAR LINEAR SYSTEM. Consider the upper triangular linear system

$$\begin{bmatrix} 2 & 4 & -2 \\ 0 & 1 & 1 \\ 0 & 0 & 4 \end{bmatrix} \begin{bmatrix} x_1 \\ x_2 \\ x_3 \end{bmatrix} = \begin{bmatrix} 2 \\ 4 \\ 8 \end{bmatrix}.$$

The last equation, $4x_3 = 8$, can be solved directly for $x_3 = 2$. This value can then be substituted into the second equation to obtain $x_2 = 2$, and finally both x_3 and x_2 are substituted into the first equation to obtain $x_1 = -1$.

2.2.2 Elementary Elimination Matrices

Our strategy then is to devise a nonsingular linear transformation that transforms a given general linear system into a triangular linear system that we can then solve easily by successive substitution. Thus, we need a transformation that replaces selected nonzero entries of the given matrix with zeros. This can be accomplished by taking appropriate linear combinations of the rows of the matrix, as we will now show.

Consider the 2-vector $a = \begin{bmatrix} a_1 & a_2 \end{bmatrix}^T$. If $a_1 \neq 0$, then

$$\begin{bmatrix} 1 & 0 \\ -a_2/a_1 & 1 \end{bmatrix} \begin{bmatrix} a_1 \\ a_2 \end{bmatrix} = \begin{bmatrix} a_1 \\ 0 \end{bmatrix}.$$

More generally, given an n-vector a, we can annihilate *all* of its entries below the kth position, provided that $a_k \neq 0$, by the following transformation:

$$M_k a = \begin{bmatrix} 1 & \cdots & 0 & 0 & \cdots & 0 \\ \vdots & \ddots & \vdots & \vdots & \ddots & \vdots \\ 0 & \cdots & 1 & 0 & \cdots & 0 \\ 0 & \cdots & -m_{k+1} & 1 & \cdots & 0 \\ \vdots & \ddots & \vdots & \vdots & \ddots & \vdots \\ 0 & \cdots & -m_n & 0 & \cdots & 1 \end{bmatrix} \begin{bmatrix} a_1 \\ \vdots \\ a_k \\ a_{k+1} \\ \vdots \\ a_n \end{bmatrix} = \begin{bmatrix} a_1 \\ \vdots \\ a_k \\ 0 \\ \vdots \\ 0 \end{bmatrix},$$

where $m_i = a_i/a_k$, $i = k + 1, \ldots, n$. The divisor a_k is called the *pivot*. A matrix of this form is sometimes called an *elementary elimination matrix* or *Gauss transformation,* and its effect on a vector is to add a multiple of row k to each subsequent row, with the multipliers m_i chosen so that the result in each case is zero. Note the following about these elementary elimination matrices:

1. M_k is a lower triangular matrix with unit main diagonal, and hence it must be nonsingular.
2. $M_k = I - m e_k^T$, where $m = [0, \ldots, 0, m_{k+1}, \ldots, m_n]^T$ and e_k is the kth column of the identity matrix.
3. $M_k^{-1} = I + m e_k^T$, which means that M_k^{-1}, which we will denote by L_k, is the same as M_k except that the signs of the multipliers are reversed.
4. If M_j, $j > k$, is another elementary elimination matrix, with vector of multipliers t, then

$$M_k M_j = I - m e_k^T - t e_j^T - m e_k^T t e_j^T = I - m e_k^T - t e_j^T,$$

since $e_k^T t = 0$. Thus, their product is essentially their "union." Because they have the same form, a similar result holds for the product of their inverses, $L_k L_j$. Note that the order of multiplication is significant; these results do not hold for the reverse product.

EXAMPLE 2.5 ELEMENTARY ELIMINATION MATRICES. If $a = \begin{bmatrix} 2 & 4 & -2 \end{bmatrix}^T$, then

$$M_1 a = \begin{bmatrix} 1 & 0 & 0 \\ -2 & 1 & 0 \\ 1 & 0 & 1 \end{bmatrix} \begin{bmatrix} 2 \\ 4 \\ -2 \end{bmatrix} = \begin{bmatrix} 2 \\ 0 \\ 0 \end{bmatrix}, \quad \text{and} \quad M_2 a = \begin{bmatrix} 1 & 0 & 0 \\ 0 & 1 & 0 \\ 0 & \frac{1}{2} & 1 \end{bmatrix} \begin{bmatrix} 2 \\ 4 \\ -2 \end{bmatrix} = \begin{bmatrix} 2 \\ 4 \\ 0 \end{bmatrix}.$$

We also note that

$$L_1 = M_1^{-1} = \begin{bmatrix} 1 & 0 & 0 \\ 2 & 1 & 0 \\ -1 & 0 & 1 \end{bmatrix}, \qquad L_2 = M_2^{-1} = \begin{bmatrix} 1 & 0 & 0 \\ 0 & 1 & 0 \\ 0 & -\frac{1}{2} & 1 \end{bmatrix},$$

and

$$M_1 M_2 = \begin{bmatrix} 1 & 0 & 0 \\ -2 & 1 & 0 \\ 1 & \frac{1}{2} & 1 \end{bmatrix}, \qquad L_1 L_2 = \begin{bmatrix} 1 & 0 & 0 \\ 2 & 1 & 0 \\ -1 & -\frac{1}{2} & 1 \end{bmatrix}.$$

2.2.3 Gaussian Elimination and LU Factorization

With elementary elimination matrices, it is a fairly simple matter to reduce a general linear system $Ax = b$ to upper triangular form. We first choose an elementary elimination matrix M_1 according to the recipe given in Section 2.2.2, with the first diagonal entry a_{11} as pivot, so that, when premultiplied by M_1, the first column of A becomes zero below the first row. Of course, all of the remaining columns of A, as well as the right-hand-side vector b, are also multiplied by M_1, so the new system becomes $M_1 A x = M_1 b$, but by our previous discussion the solution is unchanged.

Next we use the second diagonal entry as pivot to determine a second elementary elimination matrix M_2 that annihilates all of the entries of the second column of the new matrix, $M_1 A$, below the second row. Again, M_2 must be applied to the entire matrix and right-hand-side vector, so that we obtain the further modified linear system $M_2 M_1 A x = M_2 M_1 b$. Note that the first column of the matrix $M_1 A$ is not affected by M_2 because all of its entries are zero in the relevant rows. This process is continued for each successive column until all of the subdiagonal entries of the matrix have been annihilated, so that the linear system

$$MA = M_{n-1} \cdots M_1 A x = M_{n-1} \cdots M_1 b = Mb$$

is upper triangular and can be solved by back-substitution to obtain the solution to the original linear system $Ax = b$.

The process we have just described is known as *Gaussian elimination*. It is also known as *LU factorization* or *LU decomposition* because it decomposes the matrix A into a product of a unit lower triangular matrix, L, and an upper triangular matrix, U. To see this, recall that the product $L_k L_j$ is unit lower triangular if $k < j$, so that

$$L = M^{-1} = (M_{n-1} \cdots M_1)^{-1} = M_1^{-1} \cdots M_{n-1}^{-1} = L_1 \cdots L_{n-1}$$

is unit lower triangular. We have already seen that, by design, the matrix $U = MA$ is upper triangular. Therefore, we have expressed A as a product

$$A = LU,$$

where L is unit lower triangular and U is upper triangular. Given such a factorization, the linear system $Ax = b$ can then be written as $LUx = b$ and hence can be solved by first solving the lower triangular system $Ly = b$ by forward-substitution, then the upper triangular system $Ux = y$ by back-substitution. Note that the intermediate solution y is the same as the transformed right-hand-side vector, Mb, in the previous formulation.

Thus, Gaussian elimination and LU factorization are simply two ways of expressing the same solution process.

EXAMPLE 2.6 GAUSSIAN ELIMINATION. We illustrate Gaussian elimination by solving the linear system

$$2x_1 + 4x_2 - 2x_3 = 2,$$
$$4x_1 + 9x_2 - 3x_3 = 8,$$
$$-2x_1 - 3x_2 + 7x_3 = 10,$$

or in matrix notation

$$\begin{bmatrix} 2 & 4 & -2 \\ 4 & 9 & -3 \\ -2 & -3 & 7 \end{bmatrix} \begin{bmatrix} x_1 \\ x_2 \\ x_3 \end{bmatrix} = \begin{bmatrix} 2 \\ 8 \\ 10 \end{bmatrix}.$$

To annihilate the subdiagonal entries of the first column of A, we subtract two times the first row from the second row, and add the first row to the third row:

$$M_1 A = \begin{bmatrix} 1 & 0 & 0 \\ -2 & 1 & 0 \\ 1 & 0 & 1 \end{bmatrix} \begin{bmatrix} 2 & 4 & -2 \\ 4 & 9 & -3 \\ -2 & -3 & 7 \end{bmatrix} = \begin{bmatrix} 2 & 4 & -2 \\ 0 & 1 & 1 \\ 0 & 1 & 5 \end{bmatrix},$$

$$M_1 b = \begin{bmatrix} 1 & 0 & 0 \\ -2 & 1 & 0 \\ 1 & 0 & 1 \end{bmatrix} \begin{bmatrix} 2 \\ 8 \\ 10 \end{bmatrix} = \begin{bmatrix} 2 \\ 4 \\ 12 \end{bmatrix}.$$

Now to annihilate the subdiagonal entry of the second column of $M_1 A$, we subtract the second row from the third row:

$$M_2 M_1 A = \begin{bmatrix} 1 & 0 & 0 \\ 0 & 1 & 0 \\ 0 & -1 & 1 \end{bmatrix} \begin{bmatrix} 2 & 4 & -2 \\ 0 & 1 & 1 \\ 0 & 1 & 5 \end{bmatrix} = \begin{bmatrix} 2 & 4 & -2 \\ 0 & 1 & 1 \\ 0 & 0 & 4 \end{bmatrix},$$

$$M_2 M_1 b = \begin{bmatrix} 1 & 0 & 0 \\ 0 & 1 & 0 \\ 0 & -1 & 1 \end{bmatrix} \begin{bmatrix} 2 \\ 4 \\ 12 \end{bmatrix} = \begin{bmatrix} 2 \\ 4 \\ 8 \end{bmatrix}.$$

We have therefore reduced the original system to the equivalent upper triangular system

$$\begin{bmatrix} 2 & 4 & -2 \\ 0 & 1 & 1 \\ 0 & 0 & 4 \end{bmatrix} \begin{bmatrix} x_1 \\ x_2 \\ x_3 \end{bmatrix} = \begin{bmatrix} 2 \\ 4 \\ 8 \end{bmatrix},$$

which can now be solved by back-substitution (as in Example 2.4) to obtain $x = \begin{bmatrix} -1 & 2 & 2 \end{bmatrix}^T$. To write out the LU factorization explicitly, we have

$$L = L_1 L_2 = \begin{bmatrix} 1 & 0 & 0 \\ 2 & 1 & 0 \\ -1 & 0 & 1 \end{bmatrix} \begin{bmatrix} 1 & 0 & 0 \\ 0 & 1 & 0 \\ 0 & 1 & 1 \end{bmatrix} = \begin{bmatrix} 1 & 0 & 0 \\ 2 & 1 & 0 \\ -1 & 1 & 1 \end{bmatrix},$$

so that

$$A = \begin{bmatrix} 2 & 4 & -2 \\ 4 & 9 & -3 \\ -2 & -3 & 7 \end{bmatrix} = \begin{bmatrix} 1 & 0 & 0 \\ 2 & 1 & 0 \\ -1 & 1 & 1 \end{bmatrix} \begin{bmatrix} 2 & 4 & -2 \\ 0 & 1 & 1 \\ 0 & 0 & 4 \end{bmatrix} = LU.$$

2.2.4 Pivoting

There is one obvious problem with the Gaussian elimination process as we have described it, as well as another, somewhat more subtle, problem. The obvious potential difficulty is that the process breaks down if the leading diagonal entry of the remaining unreduced portion of the matrix is zero at any stage, as computing the multipliers m_i for a given column requires division by the diagonal entry in that column. The solution to this problem is almost equally obvious: if the diagonal entry is zero at stage k, then interchange row k of the system with some subsequent row whose entry in column k is nonzero. As we know from Example 2.2, such an interchange does not alter the solution to the system. With a nonzero diagonal entry as pivot, the process can then proceed as usual.

But what if there is no nonzero entry on or below the diagonal in column k? Then there is nothing to do at this stage, since all the entries to be annihilated are already zero, and we can simply move on to the next column (i.e., $M_k = I$). Note that this step leaves a zero on the diagonal, and hence the resulting upper triangular matrix U is singular, but the LU factorization can still be completed. It does mean, however, that the subsequent back-substitution process will fail, since it requires a division by each diagonal entry of U, but this is not surprising because the original matrix must have been singular anyway. A more insidious problem is that in floating-point arithmetic we may not get an exact zero, but only a very small diagonal entry, which brings us to the more subtle point.

In principle, any nonzero value will do as the pivot for computing the multipliers, but in practice the choice should be made with some care to minimize error. When the remaining portion of the matrix is multiplied by the resulting elementary elimination matrix, we should try to limit the growth of the entries of the transformed matrix in order not to amplify rounding errors. For this reason, it is desirable for the multipliers not to exceed 1 in magnitude. This requirement can be met by choosing the entry of largest magnitude on or below the diagonal as pivot. Such a policy is called *partial pivoting,* and it is essential in practice for a numerically stable implementation of Gaussian elimination for general linear systems.

The row interchanges required by partial pivoting slightly complicate the formal description of LU factorization given earlier. In particular, each elementary elimination matrix M_k is preceded by a permutation matrix P_k that interchanges rows to bring the entry of largest magnitude into the diagonal pivot position. We still have $MA = U$, where U is upper triangular, but now

$$M = M_{n-1}P_{n-1}\cdots M_1 P_1.$$

M^{-1} is still triangular in the general sense defined earlier, but because of the permutations, M^{-1} is not necessarily *lower* triangular, though we still denote it by L. Thus, "LU" factorization no longer literally means "lower times upper" triangular, but it is still equally useful for solving linear systems by successive substitution.

We note that the permutation matrix

$$P = P_{n-1}\cdots P_1$$

permutes the rows of A into the order determined by partial pivoting. An alternative interpretation, therefore, is to think of partial pivoting as a way of determining a row ordering for the system under which no pivoting would be required for numerical stability. Thus, we obtain the factorization

$$PA = LU,$$

where now L really is lower triangular. To solve the linear system $Ax = b$, we first solve the lower triangular system $Ly = Pb$ by forward-substitution, then the upper triangular system $Ux = y$ by back-substitution.

The name "partial" pivoting comes from the fact that only the current column is searched for a suitable pivot. A more exhaustive pivoting strategy is *complete pivoting,* in which the entire remaining unreduced submatrix is searched for the largest entry, which is then permuted into the diagonal pivot position. Note that this requires interchanging columns as well as rows, and hence it leads to a factorization of the form

$$PAQ = LU,$$

where L is unit lower triangular, U is upper triangular, and P and Q are permutation matrices that reorder the rows and columns, respectively, of A. To solve the linear system $Ax = b$, we first solve the lower triangular system $Ly = Pb$ by forward-substitution, then the upper triangular system $Uz = y$ by back-substitution, and finally we permute the solution components to obtain $x = Qz$. Although the numerical stability of complete pivoting is theoretically superior, it requires a much more expensive pivot search than partial pivoting. Because the numerical stability of partial pivoting is more than adequate in practice, it is almost universally used in solving linear systems by Gaussian elimination.

Since pivot selection depends on the magnitudes of individual matrix entries, the particular choice obviously depends on the scaling of the matrix. A diagonal scaling of the matrix (recall Example 2.3) may result in a different sequence of pivots. For example, any nonzero entry in a given column can be made the largest in magnitude simply by giving that row a sufficiently heavy weighting. This does not mean that an arbitrary pivot sequence is acceptable, however: a badly skewed scaling can result in an inherently sensitive system and a correspondingly inaccurate solution. A well-formulated problem should have appropriately commensurate units for measuring the unknown variables (column scaling), and a weighting of the individual equations that properly reflects their relative importance (row scaling). It should also account for the relative accuracy of the input data. Under these circumstances, the pivoting procedure will usually produce a solution that is as accurate as the problem warrants (see Section 2.4).

EXAMPLE 2.7 PIVOTING. Here are some examples to illustrate the necessity of pivoting, both in theory and practice, for a stable implementation of Gaussian elimination. We first observe that the need for pivoting has nothing to do with whether the matrix is singular or nearly singular. For example, the matrix

$$A = \begin{bmatrix} 0 & 1 \\ 1 & 0 \end{bmatrix}$$

is nonsingular yet has no LU factorization unless we interchange rows, whereas the singular matrix

$$A = \begin{bmatrix} 1 & 1 \\ 1 & 1 \end{bmatrix}$$

does have an LU factorization.

In practice, using finite-precision arithmetic, we must avoid not only zero pivots but also *small* pivots in order to prevent unacceptable error growth, as shown in the following example. Let

$$A = \begin{bmatrix} \epsilon & 1 \\ 1 & 1 \end{bmatrix},$$

where ϵ is a positive number smaller than the machine precision ϵ_{mach} in a given floating-point system. If we do not interchange rows, then the pivot is ϵ and the resulting multiplier is $-1/\epsilon$, so that we get the elimination matrix

$$M = \begin{bmatrix} 1 & 0 \\ -1/\epsilon & 1 \end{bmatrix},$$

and hence

$$L = \begin{bmatrix} 1 & 0 \\ 1/\epsilon & 1 \end{bmatrix} \quad \text{and} \quad U = \begin{bmatrix} \epsilon & 1 \\ 0 & 1 - 1/\epsilon \end{bmatrix} = \begin{bmatrix} \epsilon & 1 \\ 0 & -1/\epsilon \end{bmatrix}$$

in floating-point arithmetic. But then

$$LU = \begin{bmatrix} 1 & 0 \\ 1/\epsilon & 1 \end{bmatrix}\begin{bmatrix} \epsilon & 1 \\ 0 & -1/\epsilon \end{bmatrix} = \begin{bmatrix} \epsilon & 1 \\ 1 & 0 \end{bmatrix} \neq A.$$

Using a small pivot, and a correspondingly large multiplier, has caused an unrecoverable loss of information in the transformed matrix. If we interchange rows, on the other hand, then the pivot is 1 and the resulting multiplier is $-\epsilon$, so that we get the elimination matrix

$$M = \begin{bmatrix} 1 & 0 \\ -\epsilon & 1 \end{bmatrix},$$

and hence

$$L = \begin{bmatrix} 1 & 0 \\ \epsilon & 1 \end{bmatrix} \quad \text{and} \quad U = \begin{bmatrix} 1 & 1 \\ 0 & 1 - \epsilon \end{bmatrix} = \begin{bmatrix} 1 & 1 \\ 0 & 1 \end{bmatrix}$$

in floating-point arithmetic. We therefore have

$$LU = \begin{bmatrix} 1 & 0 \\ \epsilon & 1 \end{bmatrix}\begin{bmatrix} 1 & 1 \\ 0 & 1 \end{bmatrix} = \begin{bmatrix} 1 & 1 \\ \epsilon & 1 \end{bmatrix},$$

which is the correct result after permutation.

Although the foregoing example is rather extreme, the principle holds in general that larger pivots produce smaller multipliers and hence smaller errors. In particular, if the largest entry on or below the diagonal in each column is used as pivot (partial pivoting), then the multipliers are bounded in magnitude by 1. In Example 2.6, we did not use row interchanges, and some of the multipliers were greater than 1. For illustration, we now repeat that example, this time using partial pivoting. The system in Example 2.6 is

$$\begin{bmatrix} 2 & 4 & -2 \\ 4 & 9 & -3 \\ -2 & -3 & 7 \end{bmatrix} \begin{bmatrix} x_1 \\ x_2 \\ x_3 \end{bmatrix} = \begin{bmatrix} 2 \\ 8 \\ 10 \end{bmatrix}.$$

The largest entry in the first column is 4, so we interchange the first two rows using the permutation matrix

$$P_1 = \begin{bmatrix} 0 & 1 & 0 \\ 1 & 0 & 0 \\ 0 & 0 & 1 \end{bmatrix},$$

obtaining the permuted system

$$P_1 A = \begin{bmatrix} 4 & 9 & -3 \\ 2 & 4 & -2 \\ -2 & -3 & 7 \end{bmatrix} \begin{bmatrix} x_1 \\ x_2 \\ x_3 \end{bmatrix} = \begin{bmatrix} 8 \\ 2 \\ 10 \end{bmatrix} = P_1 b.$$

To annihilate the subdiagonal entries of the first column, we use the elimination matrix

$$M_1 = \begin{bmatrix} 1 & 0 & 0 \\ -\frac{1}{2} & 1 & 0 \\ \frac{1}{2} & 0 & 1 \end{bmatrix},$$

obtaining the transformed system

$$M_1 P_1 A = \begin{bmatrix} 4 & 9 & -3 \\ 0 & -\frac{1}{2} & -\frac{1}{2} \\ 0 & \frac{3}{2} & \frac{11}{2} \end{bmatrix} = \begin{bmatrix} 8 \\ -2 \\ 14 \end{bmatrix} = M_1 P_1 b.$$

The largest entry in the second column on or below the diagonal is $\frac{3}{2}$, so we interchange the last two rows using the permutation matrix

$$P_2 = \begin{bmatrix} 1 & 0 & 0 \\ 0 & 0 & 1 \\ 0 & 1 & 0 \end{bmatrix},$$

obtaining the permuted system

$$P_2 M_1 P_1 A = \begin{bmatrix} 4 & 9 & -3 \\ 0 & \frac{3}{2} & \frac{11}{2} \\ 0 & -\frac{1}{2} & -\frac{1}{2} \end{bmatrix} \begin{bmatrix} x_1 \\ x_2 \\ x_3 \end{bmatrix} = \begin{bmatrix} 8 \\ 14 \\ -2 \end{bmatrix} = P_2 M_1 P_1 b.$$

To annihilate the subdiagonal entry of the second column, we use the elimination matrix

$$M_2 = \begin{bmatrix} 1 & 0 & 0 \\ 0 & 1 & 0 \\ 0 & \frac{1}{3} & 1 \end{bmatrix},$$

obtaining the transformed system

$$M_2 P_2 M_1 P_1 A = \begin{bmatrix} 4 & 9 & -3 \\ 0 & \frac{3}{2} & \frac{11}{2} \\ 0 & 0 & \frac{4}{3} \end{bmatrix} = \begin{bmatrix} 8 \\ 14 \\ \frac{8}{3} \end{bmatrix} = M_2 P_2 M_1 P_1 b.$$

We have therefore reduced the original system to an equivalent upper triangular system, which can now be solved by back-substitution to obtain the same answer as before.

To write out the LU factorization explicitly, we have

$$L = M^{-1} = (M_2 P_2 M_1 P_1)^{-1} = P_1^T L_1 P_2^T L_2 =$$

$$
\begin{bmatrix} 0 & 1 & 0 \\ 1 & 0 & 0 \\ 0 & 0 & 1 \end{bmatrix}
\begin{bmatrix} 1 & 0 & 0 \\ \frac{1}{2} & 1 & 0 \\ -\frac{1}{2} & 0 & 1 \end{bmatrix}
\begin{bmatrix} 1 & 0 & 0 \\ 0 & 0 & 1 \\ 0 & 1 & 0 \end{bmatrix}
\begin{bmatrix} 1 & 0 & 0 \\ 0 & 1 & 0 \\ 0 & -\frac{1}{3} & 1 \end{bmatrix}
=
\begin{bmatrix} \frac{1}{2} & -\frac{1}{3} & 1 \\ 1 & 0 & 0 \\ -\frac{1}{2} & 1 & 0 \end{bmatrix},
$$

and hence

$$
A = \begin{bmatrix} \frac{1}{2} & -\frac{1}{3} & 1 \\ 1 & 0 & 0 \\ -\frac{1}{2} & 1 & 0 \end{bmatrix}
\begin{bmatrix} 4 & 9 & -3 \\ 0 & \frac{3}{2} & \frac{11}{2} \\ 0 & 0 & \frac{4}{3} \end{bmatrix} = LU.
$$

Note that L is not lower triangular, but it is triangular in the more general sense (it is a permutation of a lower triangular matrix). Alternatively, we can take

$$
P = P_2 P_1 = \begin{bmatrix} 1 & 0 & 0 \\ 0 & 0 & 1 \\ 0 & 1 & 0 \end{bmatrix}
\begin{bmatrix} 0 & 1 & 0 \\ 1 & 0 & 0 \\ 0 & 0 & 1 \end{bmatrix}
= \begin{bmatrix} 0 & 1 & 0 \\ 0 & 0 & 1 \\ 1 & 0 & 0 \end{bmatrix},
$$

and

$$
L = \begin{bmatrix} 1 & 0 & 0 \\ -\frac{1}{2} & 1 & 0 \\ \frac{1}{2} & -\frac{1}{3} & 1 \end{bmatrix},
$$

so that

$$
PA = \begin{bmatrix} 0 & 1 & 0 \\ 0 & 0 & 1 \\ 1 & 0 & 0 \end{bmatrix}
\begin{bmatrix} 2 & 4 & -2 \\ 4 & 9 & -3 \\ -2 & -3 & 7 \end{bmatrix}
= \begin{bmatrix} 1 & 0 & 0 \\ -\frac{1}{2} & 1 & 0 \\ \frac{1}{2} & -\frac{1}{3} & 1 \end{bmatrix}
\begin{bmatrix} 4 & 9 & -3 \\ 0 & \frac{3}{2} & \frac{11}{2} \\ 0 & 0 & \frac{4}{3} \end{bmatrix} = LU,
$$

where L now really is lower triangular but A is permuted.

As we have just seen, pivoting is generally required for Gaussian elimination to be stable. There are some classes of matrices, however, for which Gaussian elimination is stable *without* pivoting. For example, if the matrix A is *diagonally dominant* by *columns*, which means that each diagonal entry is larger in magnitude than the sum of the magnitudes of the other entries in its column,

$$\sum_{i=1, i \neq j}^{n} |a_{ij}| < |a_{jj}|, \qquad j = 1, \ldots, n,$$

then pivoting is not required in computing its LU factorization by Gaussian elimination. If partial pivoting is used on such a matrix, then no row interchanges will actually occur. Another important class for which pivoting is not required is matrices that are symmetric and positive definite, which will be defined in Section 2.5. Avoiding an unnecessary pivot search can save a significant amount of time in computing the factorization.

2.2.5 Implementation of Gaussian Elimination

Gaussian elimination, or LU factorization, has the general form of a triple-nested loop,

> **for** _____
>   **for** _____
>   **for** _____
> $a_{ij} = a_{ij} - (a_{ik}/a_{kk})a_{kj}$
>   **end**
>   **end**
> **end**

where the indices i, j, and k of the **for** loops can be taken in any order, for a total of $3! = 6$ different ways of arranging the loops. Some of the indicated arithmetic operations can be moved outside the innermost loop for greater efficiency, depending on the specific indices involved, and additional reorderings of the operations that do not have strictly nested loops are also possible. These variations of the basic algorithm have different memory access patterns (e.g., accessing memory row-wise or column-wise), and also differ in their ability to take advantage of the architectural features of a given computer (e.g., cache, paging, vectorization, multiple processors). Thus, their performance may vary widely on a given computer or across different computers, and no single arrangement may be uniformly superior.

Numerous implementation details of the algorithm are subject to variation in this way. For example, the partial pivoting procedure we described searches along columns and interchanges rows, but alternatively, one could search along rows and interchange columns. We have also taken L to have unit diagonal, but one could instead arrange for U to have unit diagonal. Some of these variations of Gaussian elimination are of sufficient importance to have been given names, such as the Crout and Doolittle methods.

Although the many possible variations on Gaussian elimination may have a dramatic effect on performance, they all produce essentially the same factorization. Provided the row pivot sequence is the same, if we have two LU factorizations $PA = LU = \hat{L}\hat{U}$, then this expression implies that $\hat{L}^{-1}L = \hat{U}U^{-1} = D$ is both lower and upper triangular, and hence diagonal. If both L and $\hat{L}$ are assumed to be unit lower triangular, then D must in fact be the identity, and hence $L = \hat{L}$ and $U = \hat{U}$, so that the factorization is unique. Even without this assumption, however, we may still conclude that that the LU factorization is unique up to diagonal scaling of the factors. This uniqueness is made explicit in the LDU factorization $PA = LDU$, where L is unit lower triangular, U is unit upper triangular, and D is diagonal.

Storage management is another important implementation issue. The numerous matrices we considered—the elementary elimination matrices M_k, their inverses L_k, and the permutation matrices P_k—merely describe the factorization process formally. They are not formed explicitly in an actual implementation. To conserve storage, the L and U factors overwrite the initial storage for the input matrix A, with the transformed matrix U occupying the upper triangle of A (including the diagonal), and the multipliers that make up the strict lower triangle of L occupying the (now zero) strict lower triangle of A. The unit diagonal of L need not be stored.

To minimize data movement, the row interchanges required by pivoting are not usually carried out explicitly. Instead, the rows remain in their original locations, and an auxiliary integer vector is used to keep track of the new row order. Note that a single such vector suffices, because the net effect of all of the interchanges is still just a permutation of the integers $1, \ldots, n$.

2.2.6 Complexity of Solving Linear Systems

The Gaussian elimination process for computing the LU factorization requires about $n^3/3$ floating-point multiplications and a similar number of additions. Solving the resulting triangular system for a single right-hand-side vector by forward- and back-substitution requires about n^2 multiplications and a similar number of additions. Thus, as the order n of the matrix grows, the LU factorization phase becomes increasingly dominant in the cost of solving linear systems.

We can also solve a linear system by explicitly inverting the matrix so that the solution is given by $x = A^{-1}b$. But computing A^{-1} is tantamount to solving n linear systems: it requires an LU factorization of A followed by n forward- and back-substitutions, one for each column of the identity matrix. The total operation count is about n^3 multiplications and a similar number of additions (taking advantage of the zeros in the right-hand-side vectors for the forward-substitution).

Thus, explicit inversion is three times as expensive as LU factorization. The subsequent matrix-vector multiplication $x = A^{-1}b$ to solve a linear system requires about n^2 multiplications and a similar number of additions, which is similar to the total cost of forward- and back-substitution. Hence, even for multiple right-hand-side vectors, matrix inversion is more costly than LU factorization for solving linear systems. In addition, explicit inversion gives a less accurate answer. As a simple example, if we solve the 1×1 linear system $3x = 18$ by division, we get $x = 18/3 = 6$, but explicit inversion would give $x = 3^{-1} \times 18 = 0.333 \times 18 = 5.99$ using three-digit arithmetic. In this small example, inversion requires an additional arithmetic operation and obtains a less accurate result. The disadvantages of inversion become worse as the size of the system grows.

Explicit matrix inverses often occur as a convenient notation in various formulas, but this practice does not mean that an explicit inverse is required to implement such a formula. One merely need solve a linear system with an appropriate right-hand-side, which might itself be a matrix. Thus, for example, a product of the form $A^{-1}B$ should be computed by LU factorization of A, followed by forward- and back-substitutions using each column of B. It is extremely rare in practice that an explicit matrix inverse is actually needed, so whenever you see a matrix inverse in a formula, you should think "solve a system" rather than "invert a matrix."

Another method for solving linear systems that should be avoided is *Cramer's rule*, in which each component of the solution is computed as a ratio of determinants. Though often taught in elementary linear algebra courses, this method is astronomically expensive for full matrices of nontrivial size. Cramer's rule is useful mostly as a theoretical tool.

2.2.7 Gauss-Jordan Elimination

The motivation for Gaussian elimination is to reduce a general matrix to triangular form, because the resulting linear system is easy to solve. Diagonal linear systems are even easier to solve, however, so diagonal form would appear to be an even more desirable target. *Gauss-Jordan elimination* is a variation of standard Gaussian elimination in which the matrix is reduced to diagonal form rather than merely to triangular form. The same type of row combinations are used to eliminate matrix entries as in standard Gaussian elimination, but they are applied to annihilate entries above as well as below the diagonal. Thus, the elimination matrix used for a given column vector a is of the form

$$
\begin{bmatrix}
1 & \cdots & 0 & -m_1 & 0 & \cdots & 0 \\
\vdots & \ddots & \vdots & \vdots & \vdots & \ddots & \vdots \\
0 & \cdots & 1 & -m_{k-1} & 0 & \cdots & 0 \\
0 & \cdots & 0 & 1 & 0 & \cdots & 0 \\
0 & \cdots & 0 & -m_{k+1} & 1 & \cdots & 0 \\
\vdots & \ddots & \vdots & \vdots & \vdots & \ddots & \vdots \\
0 & \cdots & 0 & -m_n & 0 & \cdots & 1
\end{bmatrix}
\begin{bmatrix}
a_1 \\ \vdots \\ a_{k-1} \\ a_k \\ a_{k+1} \\ \vdots \\ a_n
\end{bmatrix}
=
\begin{bmatrix}
0 \\ \vdots \\ 0 \\ a_k \\ 0 \\ \vdots \\ 0
\end{bmatrix},
$$

where $m_i = a_i/a_k$, $i = 1, \ldots, n$. This process requires about $n^3/2$ multiplications and a similar number of additions, which is 50 percent more expensive than standard Gaussian elimination.

During the elimination phase, the same row operations are also applied to the right-hand-side vector (or vectors) of a system of linear equations. Once the elimination phase has been completed and the matrix is in diagonal form, then the components of the solution to the linear system can be computed simply by dividing each entry of the transformed right-hand-side by the corresponding diagonal entry of the matrix. This computation requires a total of only n divisions, which is significantly cheaper than solving a triangular system, but not enough to make up for the more costly elimination phase. Gauss-Jordan elimination also has the numerical disadvantage that the multipliers can exceed 1 in magnitude even if pivoting is used.

Despite its higher overall cost, Gauss-Jordan elimination may be preferred in some situations because of the extreme simplicity of its final solution phase. For example, it is occasionally advocated for implementation on parallel computers because it has a uniform workload throughout the factorization phase, and then all of the solution components can be computed simultaneously rather than one at a time as in ordinary back-substitution.

Gauss-Jordan elimination is also sometimes used to compute the inverse of a matrix explicitly, if desired. If the right-hand-side matrix is initialized to be the identity matrix and the given matrix A is reduced to the identity matrix by Gauss-Jordan elimination, then the transformed right-hand-side matrix will be the inverse of A. For computing the inverse, Gauss-Jordan elimination has about the same operation count as explicit inversion by Gaussian elimination followed by forward- and back-substitution.

EXAMPLE 2.8 GAUSS-JORDAN ELIMINATION. We illustrate Gauss-Jordan elimination by using it to compute the inverse of the matrix of Example 2.6. For simplicity, we omit pivoting. We begin with the matrix A, augmented by the identity matrix as right-hand side, and repeatedly apply elimination matrices to annihilate off-diagonal entries of A until we reach diagonal form, then scale by the remaining diagonal entries to produce the identity matrix on the left.

$$\begin{bmatrix} 1 & 0 & 0 \\ -2 & 1 & 0 \\ 1 & 0 & 1 \end{bmatrix}\begin{bmatrix} 2 & 4 & -2 \\ 4 & 9 & -3 \\ -2 & -3 & 7 \end{bmatrix}\begin{array}{ccc} 1 & 0 & 0 \\ 0 & 1 & 0 \\ 0 & 0 & 1 \end{array} = \begin{bmatrix} 2 & 4 & -2 \\ 0 & 1 & 1 \\ 0 & 1 & 5 \end{bmatrix}\begin{array}{ccc} 1 & 0 & 0 \\ -2 & 1 & 0 \\ 1 & 0 & 1 \end{array},$$

$$\begin{bmatrix} 1 & -4 & 0 \\ 0 & 1 & 0 \\ 0 & -1 & 1 \end{bmatrix}\begin{bmatrix} 2 & 4 & -2 \\ 0 & 1 & 1 \\ 0 & 1 & 5 \end{bmatrix}\begin{array}{ccc} 1 & 0 & 0 \\ -2 & 1 & 0 \\ 1 & 0 & 1 \end{array} = \begin{bmatrix} 2 & 0 & -6 \\ 0 & 1 & 1 \\ 0 & 0 & 4 \end{bmatrix}\begin{array}{ccc} 9 & -4 & 0 \\ -2 & 1 & 0 \\ 3 & -1 & 1 \end{array},$$

$$\begin{bmatrix} 1 & 0 & \frac{3}{2} \\ 0 & 1 & -\frac{1}{4} \\ 0 & 0 & 1 \end{bmatrix}\begin{bmatrix} 2 & 0 & -6 \\ 0 & 1 & 1 \\ 0 & 0 & 4 \end{bmatrix}\begin{array}{ccc} 9 & -4 & 0 \\ -2 & 1 & 0 \\ 3 & -1 & 1 \end{array} = \begin{bmatrix} 2 & 0 & 0 \\ 0 & 1 & 0 \\ 0 & 0 & 4 \end{bmatrix}\begin{array}{ccc} \frac{27}{2} & -\frac{11}{2} & \frac{3}{2} \\ -\frac{11}{4} & \frac{5}{4} & -\frac{1}{4} \\ 3 & -1 & 1 \end{array},$$

$$\begin{bmatrix} \frac{1}{2} & 0 & 0 \\ 0 & 1 & 0 \\ 0 & 0 & \frac{1}{4} \end{bmatrix}\begin{bmatrix} 2 & 0 & 0 \\ 0 & 1 & 0 \\ 0 & 0 & 4 \end{bmatrix}\begin{array}{ccc} \frac{27}{2} & -\frac{11}{2} & \frac{3}{2} \\ -\frac{11}{4} & \frac{5}{4} & -\frac{1}{4} \\ 3 & -1 & 1 \end{array} = \begin{bmatrix} 1 & 0 & 0 \\ 0 & 1 & 0 \\ 0 & 0 & 1 \end{bmatrix}\begin{array}{ccc} \frac{27}{4} & -\frac{11}{4} & \frac{3}{4} \\ -\frac{11}{4} & \frac{5}{4} & -\frac{1}{4} \\ \frac{3}{4} & -\frac{1}{4} & \frac{1}{4} \end{array},$$

so

$$A^{-1} = \frac{1}{4}\begin{bmatrix} 27 & -11 & 3 \\ -11 & 5 & -1 \\ 3 & -1 & 1 \end{bmatrix}.$$

2.2.8 Solving Modified Problems

In many practical situations linear systems do not occur in isolation but as part of a sequence of related problems that change in some systematic way. For example, one may need to solve a sequence of linear systems $Ax = b$ having the same matrix A but different right-hand sides b. After having solved the initial system by Gaussian elimination, then the L and U factors already computed can be used to solve the additional systems by forward- and back-substitution. The factorization phase need not be repeated in solving subsequent linear systems unless the matrix changes. This procedure represents a substantial savings in work, since additional triangular solutions cost only $\mathcal{O}(n^2)$ work, in contrast to the $\mathcal{O}(n^3)$ cost of a factorization.

In fact, in some important special cases a new factorization can be avoided even when the matrix does change. One such case that arises frequently is the addition of a matrix that is an outer product uv^T of two nonzero vectors u and v. This is called a *rank-one change* because the outer product matrix uv^T has rank one (i.e., only one linearly independent row or column), and any rank-one matrix can be expressed as such an outer product of two vectors. For example, if a single entry of the matrix A changes (say the (j, k) entry changes from a_{jk} to $\tilde{a}_{jk}$), then the new matrix is $A - \alpha e_j e_k^T$, where e_j and e_k are the corresponding columns of the identity matrix and $\alpha = a_{jk} - \tilde{a}_{jk}$.

The *Sherman-Morrison formula* gives the inverse of a matrix resulting from a rank-one change to a matrix whose inverse is already known:

$$(A - uv^T)^{-1} = A^{-1} + A^{-1}u(1 - v^T A^{-1}u)^{-1}v^T A^{-1},$$

where u and v are n-vectors. Evaluation of this formula requires only $\mathcal{O}(n^2)$ work (for matrix-vector multiplications) rather than the $\mathcal{O}(n^3)$ work normally required for inversion.

To solve a linear system $(A - uv^T)x = b$ with the new matrix, we could use the foregoing formula to obtain

$$x = (A - uv^T)^{-1}b = A^{-1}b + A^{-1}u(1 - v^T A^{-1}u)^{-1}v^T A^{-1}b.$$

We would prefer to avoid explicit inversion altogether, however. If we have an LU factorization for A, then the following steps can easily be computed to obtain the solution to the modified system:

1. Solve $Az = u$ for z, so that $z = A^{-1}u$.
2. Solve $Ay = b$ for y, so that $y = A^{-1}b$.
3. Compute $x = y + [(v^T y)/(1 - v^T z)]z$.

Note that the first step is independent of b and hence need not be repeated if there are multiple right-hand-side vectors b. Again, this procedure requires only triangular solutions and inner products, so it requires only $\mathcal{O}(n^2)$ work and no explicit inverses.

The *Woodbury formula,* in which u and v become $n \times k$ matrices U and V, generalizes the Sherman-Morrison formula to a rank-k change in the matrix:

$$(A - UV^T)^{-1} = A^{-1} + A^{-1}U(I - V^T A^{-1}U)^{-1}V^T A^{-1}.$$

Using similar techniques, it is possible to update the factorization rather than the inverse or the solution. Caution must be exercised in using these updating formulas, however, because in general there is no guarantee of numerical stability through successive updates as the matrix changes.

EXAMPLE 2.9 RANK-ONE UPDATING OF SOLUTIONS. To illustrate the use of the Sherman-Morrison formula, we solve the linear system

$$\begin{bmatrix} 2 & 4 & -2 \\ 4 & 9 & -3 \\ -2 & -1 & 7 \end{bmatrix} \begin{bmatrix} x_1 \\ x_2 \\ x_3 \end{bmatrix} = \begin{bmatrix} 2 \\ 8 \\ 10 \end{bmatrix},$$

which is a rank-one modification of the system in Example 2.6 (only the $(3, 2)$ entry has changed). We take A to be the matrix of Example 2.6, so we can use the LU factorization already computed. One way to choose the update vectors is

$$u = \begin{bmatrix} 0 \\ 0 \\ -2 \end{bmatrix} \quad \text{and} \quad v = \begin{bmatrix} 0 \\ 1 \\ 0 \end{bmatrix},$$

so that the matrix of the new system is $A - uv^T$, and the right-hand-side vector b has not changed. We can use the previously computed LU factorization of A to solve $Az = u$ to obtain $z = \begin{bmatrix} -\frac{3}{2} & \frac{1}{2} & -\frac{1}{2} \end{bmatrix}^T$, and we had already solved $Ay = b$ to obtain $y = \begin{bmatrix} -1 & 2 & 2 \end{bmatrix}^T$.

The final step is then to compute the updated solution

$$
x = y + \frac{v^T y}{1 - v^T z} z = \begin{bmatrix} -1 \\ 2 \\ 2 \end{bmatrix} + \frac{2}{1 - \dfrac{1}{2}} \begin{bmatrix} -\frac{3}{2} \\ \frac{1}{2} \\ -\frac{1}{2} \end{bmatrix} = \begin{bmatrix} -7 \\ 4 \\ 0 \end{bmatrix}.
$$

We have thus computed the solution to the new system without refactoring the modified matrix.

2.3 NORMS AND CONDITION NUMBERS

2.3.1 Vector Norms

To measure errors and sensitivity in solving linear systems, we need some notion of the "size" of vectors and matrices. The scalar concept of magnitude, modulus, or absolute value can be generalized to the concept of *norms* for vectors and matrices. Although a more general definition is possible, all of the vector norms we will use are instances of *p*-norms, which for an integer $p > 0$ and a vector x of dimension n are defined by

$$
\|x\|_p = \left(\sum_{i=1}^{n} |x_i|^p \right)^{1/p}.
$$

Important special cases are as follows:

- 1-norm:

$$
\|x\|_1 = \sum_{i=1}^{n} |x_i|,
$$

sometimes called the Manhattan norm because in the plane it corresponds to the distance between two points as measured in "city blocks."

- 2-norm:

$$
\|x\|_2 = \left(\sum_{i=1}^{n} |x_i|^2 \right)^{1/2},
$$

which corresponds to the usual notion of distance in Euclidean space.

- ∞-norm:

$$
\|x\|_\infty = \max_i |x_i|,
$$

which can be viewed as a limiting case as $p \to \infty$.

All of these norms give the same results qualitatively, but in certain circumstances a particular norm may be easiest to work with analytically or computationally. The 1-norm or the ∞-norm is usually used in analyzing the sensitivity of solutions to linear

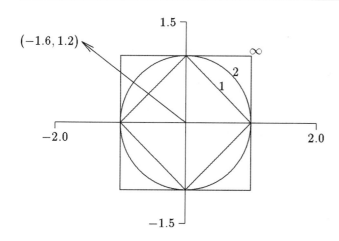

FIGURE 2.1
The unit sphere in various vector norms.

systems. We will also use the 2-norm later on in other contexts. The differences among these norms are illustrated in Fig. 2.1, which shows the *unit sphere*, $\{x: \|x\| = 1\}$, in two dimensions for each norm.

The norm of a vector is simply the factor by which the corresponding unit sphere must be expanded or shrunk to encompass the vector. For example, the norms have the following values for the vector shown in Fig. 2.1:

$$\left\|\begin{bmatrix} -1.6 \\ 1.2 \end{bmatrix}\right\|_1 = 2.8, \qquad \left\|\begin{bmatrix} -1.6 \\ 1.2 \end{bmatrix}\right\|_2 = 2.0, \qquad \left\|\begin{bmatrix} -1.6 \\ 1.2 \end{bmatrix}\right\|_\infty = 1.6.$$

In general, for any vector x in $\mathbb{R}^n$, we have

$$\|x\|_1 \geq \|x\|_2 \geq \|x\|_\infty.$$

On the other hand, we also have

$$\|x\|_1 \leq \sqrt{n}\,\|x\|_2, \qquad \|x\|_2 \leq \sqrt{n}\,\|x\|_\infty, \qquad \text{and} \qquad \|x\|_1 \leq n\,\|x\|_\infty.$$

Thus, for a given n, any two of the norms differ by at most a constant, so they are all equivalent in the sense that if one is small, they must all be proportionally small. Hence, we can choose whichever norm is most convenient in a given context. In the remainder of this book, an appropriate subscript will be used to indicate a specific norm, when necessary, but the subscript will be omitted when it does not matter which particular norm is used.

For any vector norm, the following important properties hold, where x and y are any vectors:

1. $\|x\| > 0$ if $x \neq 0$.
2. $\|\gamma x\| = |\gamma| \cdot \|x\|$ for any scalar γ.
3. $\|x + y\| \leq \|x\| + \|y\|$ (triangle inequality).

In a more general treatment, these three properties can be taken as the *definition* of a vector norm. A useful variation on the triangle inequality is

$$\|x - y\| \geq \|x\| - \|y\|.$$

2.3.2 Matrix Norms

We also need some way to measure the size or magnitude of matrices. Again, a more general definition is possible, but all of the matrix norms we will use are defined in terms of an underlying vector norm. Specifically, given a vector norm, we define the corresponding matrix norm as follows:

$$\|A\| = \max_{x \neq 0} \frac{\|Ax\|}{\|x\|}.$$

Such a matrix norm is said to be *subordinate* to the vector norm. Intuitively, the norm of a matrix measures the maximum stretching the matrix does to any vector, as measured in the given vector norm.

Some matrix norms are much easier to compute than others. For example, the matrix norm corresponding to the vector 1-norm is simply the maximum absolute column sum of the matrix,

$$\|A\|_1 = \max_j \sum_{i=1}^n |a_{ij}|,$$

and the matrix norm corresponding to the vector ∞-norm is simply the maximum absolute row sum of the matrix,

$$\|A\|_\infty = \max_i \sum_{j=1}^n |a_{ij}|.$$

A handy way to remember these is that the matrix norms agree with the corresponding vector norms for an $n \times 1$ matrix. Unfortunately, the matrix norm corresponding to the vector 2-norm is not so simple to compute; it turns out to be equal to the square root of the largest eigenvalue of the matrix $A^T A$, or, as we shall see later, the largest singular value of A (see Section 4.5.2).

The matrix norms we have defined satisfy the following important properties, where A and B are any matrices:

1. $\|A\| > 0$ if $A \neq 0$.
2. $\|\gamma A\| = |\gamma| \cdot \|A\|$ for any scalar γ.
3. $\|A + B\| \leq \|A\| + \|B\|$.
4. $\|AB\| \leq \|A\| \cdot \|B\|$.
5. $\|Ax\| \leq \|A\| \cdot \|x\|$ for any vector x.

In a more general treatment, the first three properties can be taken as the *definition* of a matrix norm. The remaining two properties, known as *submultiplicative* or *consistency* conditions, may or may not hold for these more general matrix norms, but they always hold for the matrix norms subordinate to the vector *p*-norms.

2.3.3 Condition Number of a Matrix

The *condition number* of a square nonsingular matrix A with respect to a given norm is defined as

$$\text{cond}(A) = \|A\| \cdot \|A^{-1}\|.$$

By convention, $\text{cond}(A) = \infty$ if A is singular. Since

$$\|A\| \cdot \|A^{-1}\| = \left(\max_{x \neq 0} \frac{\|Ax\|}{\|x\|}\right) \cdot \left(\min_{x \neq 0} \frac{\|Ax\|}{\|x\|}\right)^{-1},$$

the condition number of a matrix measures the ratio of the maximum stretching that the matrix does to any nonzero vector to the maximum shrinking. We will see in Section 2.4.2 that this concept is consistent with the general notion of condition number defined in Section 1.2.5: the condition number of the matrix bounds the ratio of the relative change in the solution of a linear system to a given relative change in the input data.

The condition number is a measure of how close a matrix is to being singular: a matrix with a large condition number (which we will quantify in Section 2.4.2) is nearly singular, whereas a matrix with a condition number close to 1 is far from being singular. Note that the determinant of a matrix is *not* a good indicator of near singularity: although a matrix A is singular if $\det(A) = 0$, the magnitude of a nonzero determinant, large or small, gives no information on how close to singular the matrix may be. For example, $\det(\alpha I_n) = \alpha^n$, which can be arbitrarily small for $|\alpha| < 1$, yet the matrix is perfectly well-conditioned for any nonzero α, with a condition number of 1.

Some important properties of the condition number are

1. For any matrix A, $\text{cond}(A) \geq 1$.
2. For the identity matrix, $\text{cond}(I) = 1$.
3. For any permutation matrix P, $\text{cond}(P) = 1$.
4. For any matrix A and nonzero scalar γ, $\text{cond}(\gamma A) = \text{cond}(A)$.
5. For any diagonal matrix $D = \text{diag}(d_i)$, $\text{cond}(D) = (\max|d_i|)/(\min|d_i|)$.

As we will see shortly, the usefulness of the condition number is in assessing the accuracy of solutions to linear systems. Since the definition of the condition number involves the inverse of the matrix, computing its value is obviously a nontrivial task. In fact, to compute the condition number literally would require substantially more work than solving the linear system whose accuracy is to be assessed using the condition number. In practice, therefore, the condition number is merely estimated, to perhaps within an order of magnitude, as a relatively inexpensive byproduct of the solution process.

The matrix norm $\|A\|$ is easily computed as the maximum absolute column sum (or row sum, depending on the norm used). It is estimating $\|A^{-1}\|$ at low cost that presents a challenge. From the properties of norms, we know that if z is the solution to $Az = y$, then

$$\frac{\|z\|}{\|y\|} \leq \|A^{-1}\|,$$

and the bound is achieved for some optimally chosen vector y. We thus wish to pick a vector y so that the ratio $\|z\|/\|y\|$ is as large as possible and therefore is a reasonable estimate for $\|A^{-1}\|$. Finding the optimal y would be prohibitively expensive, but a useful approximation can be obtained much more cheaply. One heuristic is to choose y as the solution to the system $A^T y = c$, where c is a vector whose components are ± 1, with the signs chosen successively to make the resulting y as large as possible.

The motivation for this approach may not be obvious now, but it is essentially equivalent to one step of inverse iteration for computing the singular vector corresponding to the smallest singular value of A (see Chapter 4). An alternative approach to condition estimation is to treat it as a convex optimization problem that can be solved very efficiently in practice using a heuristic algorithm. Most good modern software packages for solving linear systems provide an efficient and reliable condition estimator, based on a sophisticated implementation of one of the methods outlined here.

2.4 ACCURACY OF SOLUTIONS

2.4.1 Residual of a Solution

Intuitively, the most obvious way to check the validity of a solution is to substitute it into the equation to see how closely the two sides match. The *residual vector* of an approximate solution $\hat{x}$ to the $n \times n$ linear system $Ax = b$ is defined as

$$r = b - A\hat{x}.$$

In theory, if A is nonsingular, then the error $\|\hat{x} - x\| = 0$ if and only if $\|r\| = 0$. In practice, however, these quantities are not necessarily small simultaneously. If the computed solution $\hat{x}$ exactly satisfies

$$(A + E)\hat{x} = b,$$

then
$$\|r\| = \|b - A\hat{x}\| = \|E\hat{x}\| \leq \|E\| \cdot \|\hat{x}\|,$$

so that we have the inequality

$$\frac{\|r\|}{\|A\| \cdot \|\hat{x}\|} \leq \frac{\|E\|}{\|A\|}$$

relating the *relative residual* to the relative change in the matrix. Thus, a large relative residual implies a large backward error in the matrix, which means that the algorithm used to compute the solution is unstable.

But how large is $\|E\|$ likely to be in practice? Wilkinson [273] showed that for LU factorization by Gaussian elimination, a bound of the form

$$\frac{\|E\|}{\|A\|} \leq \rho\, n\, \epsilon_{\text{mach}}$$

holds, where ρ, called the *growth factor*, is the ratio of the largest entry of U to the largest entry of A. Without pivoting, ρ can be arbitrarily large, and hence Gaussian elimination without pivoting is unstable, as we have already seen. With partial pivoting, the growth factor can still be as large as 2^{n-1} (since in the worst case the size of the entries can double at each stage of elimination), but such behavior is extremely rare. In practice, there is little or no growth in the size of the entries, so that

$$\frac{\|E\|}{\|A\|} \approx n\, \epsilon_{\text{mach}}.$$

This relation means that solving a linear system by Gaussian elimination with partial pivoting followed by back-substitution almost always yields a very small relative residual, regardless of how ill-conditioned the system may be. Thus, a small relative residual is not necessarily a good indicator that a computed solution is close to the "true" solution unless the system is well-conditioned.

Complete pivoting yields an even smaller growth factor, in both theory and practice, but the additional margin of stability it provides is usually not worth the extra expense.

EXAMPLE 2.10 SMALL RESIDUAL. Using three-digit decimal arithmetic to solve the system

$$\begin{bmatrix} 0.641 & 0.242 \\ 0.321 & 0.121 \end{bmatrix} \begin{bmatrix} x_1 \\ x_2 \end{bmatrix} = \begin{bmatrix} 0.883 \\ 0.442 \end{bmatrix},$$

Gaussian elimination with partial pivoting yields the triangular system

$$\begin{bmatrix} 0.641 & 0.242 \\ 0 & 0.000242 \end{bmatrix} \begin{bmatrix} x_1 \\ x_2 \end{bmatrix} = \begin{bmatrix} 0.883 \\ -0.000383 \end{bmatrix},$$

and back-substitution then gives the computed solution

$$x = \begin{bmatrix} 0.782 \\ 1.58 \end{bmatrix}.$$

The exact residual for this solution is

$$r = b - Ax = \begin{bmatrix} -0.000622 \\ -0.000202 \end{bmatrix},$$

which is as small as we can expect using only three-digit arithmetic. Yet the exact solution for this system is easily seen to be

$$x = \begin{bmatrix} 1.00 \\ 1.00 \end{bmatrix},$$

so that the error is almost as large as the solution. The cause of this phenomenon is that the matrix is very nearly singular (its condition number is more than 4000). The division that determines x_2 is between two quantities that are both on the order of rounding error, and hence the result is essentially arbitrary. Yet, by design, when this arbitrary value for x_2 is then substituted into the first equation, a value for x_1 is computed so that the first equation is satisfied. Thus, we get a small residual, but a poor solution.

2.4.2 Estimating Accuracy

In addition to being a reliable indicator of near singularity, the condition number also provides a quantitative estimate for the error in the computed solution to a linear system, as we will now see. Let x be the solution to the nonsingular linear system $Ax = b$, and let $\hat{x}$ be the solution to the system $A\hat{x} = b + \Delta b$ with a perturbed right-hand side. If we define $\Delta x = \hat{x} - x$, then we have

$$b + \Delta b = A\hat{x} = A(x + \Delta x) = Ax + A\Delta x.$$

Since $Ax = b$, we must have $A\Delta x = \Delta b$, and hence $\Delta x = A^{-1}\Delta b$. Now

$$b = Ax \;\Rightarrow\; \|b\| \le \|A\| \cdot \|x\|,$$

and
$$\Delta x = A^{-1}\Delta b \;\Rightarrow\; \|\Delta x\| \le \|A^{-1}\| \cdot \|\Delta b\|,$$

which, upon using the definition $\text{cond}(A) = \|A\| \cdot \|A^{-1}\|$, yields the estimate

$$\frac{\|\Delta x\|}{\|x\|} \le \text{cond}(A)\frac{\|\Delta b\|}{\|b\|}.$$

Thus, the condition number of the matrix determines the possible relative change in the solution due to a given relative change in the right-hand-side vector, regardless of the algorithm used to compute the solution (compare with the general notion of condition number defined in Section 1.2.5). A similar result holds for relative changes in the entries of the matrix A. If $Ax = b$ and

$$(A + E)\hat{x} = b,$$

then
$$x - \hat{x} = A^{-1}(b - A\hat{x}) = A^{-1}E\hat{x},$$

so that
$$\|\Delta x\| \le \|A^{-1}\| \cdot \|E\| \cdot \|\hat{x}\|,$$

which yields the estimate

$$\frac{\|\Delta x\|}{\|\hat{x}\|} \le \text{cond}(A)\frac{\|E\|}{\|A\|}.$$

As an alternative to the algebraic derivations just given, calculus can be used to estimate the sensitivity of linear systems. Introducing the real-valued parameter t, we define $A(t) = A + tE$ and $b(t) = b + t\Delta b$, and consider the solution $x(t)$ to the linear system $A(t)x(t) = b(t)$. Differentiating this equation with respect to t, we obtain

$$A'(t)x(t) + A(t)x'(t) = b'(t),$$

so that we have

$$x'(t) = -A^{-1}(t)A'(t)x(t) + A^{-1}(t)b'(t),$$

and hence, evaluating at $t = 0$ and taking norms,

$$\frac{\|x'\|}{\|x\|} \le \|A^{-1}\| \cdot \|A'\| + \|A^{-1}\| \cdot \frac{\|b'\|}{\|x\|} \le \text{cond}(A)\left(\frac{\|A'\|}{\|A\|} + \frac{\|b'\|}{\|b\|}\right).$$

Thus, we again see that the relative change in the solution is bounded by the condition number times the relative change in the problem data.

A geometric interpretation in two dimensions of these sensitivity results is that if the two straight lines defined by the two equations are nearly parallel, then their point of intersection is not sharply defined if the lines are a bit fuzzy because of rounding errors or other sources of error. If, on the other hand, the lines are far from parallel, say nearly perpendicular, then their intersection is relatively sharply defined. These two cases are illustrated in Fig. 2.2, where the dashed lines indicate the region of uncertainty for each solid line, so that the intersection point in each case could be anywhere within

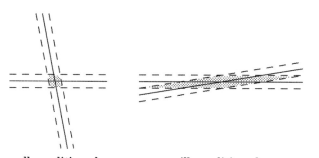

FIGURE 2.2
Well-conditioned and ill-conditioned linear systems.

well-conditioned   ill-conditioned

the shaded parallelogram. Thus, a large condition number is associated with a large uncertainty in the solution.

To summarize, if the input data are accurate to machine precision, then a reasonable estimate for the relative error in the computed solution to a linear system is given by

$$\frac{\|\hat{x} - x\|}{\|x\|} \approx \text{cond}(A)\,\epsilon_{\text{mach}}.$$

One simple way of interpreting these results is that the computed solution loses about $\log_{10}(\text{cond}(A))$ decimal digits of accuracy relative to the accuracy of the input. In Example 2.10, for instance, with a condition number greater than 10^3, we lost all of the three-digit precision available and obtained an arbitrary solution.

Before leaving the subject of assessing accuracy in terms of condition numbers, note these two caveats:

- The foregoing analysis estimates the relative error in the *largest* components of the solution vector. The *relative* error in the smaller components can be much larger, because a vector norm is dominated by the largest components of a vector. Componentwise error bounds can be obtained but are somewhat more complicated to compute, and we will not pursue this topic. Componentwise bounds are of particular interest when the system is poorly scaled.
- The condition number of a matrix is affected by the scaling of the matrix (recall Example 2.3). A large condition number can result simply from poor scaling, as well as from near singularity. Rescaling the matrix can help the former, but not the latter (see Section 2.4.3).

2.4.3 Improving Accuracy

Although the accuracy that can be expected in the solution of a linear system may seem set in concrete, accuracy can be enhanced in some cases by rescaling the system or by iteratively improving the initial computed solution. These measures are not always practicable, but they may be worth trying.

Recall from Example 2.3 that diagonal scaling of a linear system leaves the solution either unchanged (row scaling) or changed in such a way that the solution is easily recoverable (column scaling). In practice, however, scaling affects the conditioning of the system and the selection of pivots in Gaussian elimination, both of which in turn affect the accuracy of the computed solution. Thus, row scaling and column scaling of a linear system can potentially improve (or degrade) numerical stability and accuracy.

Accuracy is usually enhanced if all the entries of the matrix have about the same order of magnitude or, better still, if the uncertainties in the matrix entries are all of about the same size. Sometimes it is obvious by inspection how to scale the matrix to accomplish such balance by the choice of measurement units for the respective variables and by weighting each equation according to its relative importance and accuracy. No general automatic technique has ever been developed, however, that produces optimal scaling in an efficient and foolproof manner. Moreover, the scaling process itself can introduce rounding errors unless care is taken (for example, by using only powers of the arithmetic base as scaling factors).

EXAMPLE 2.11 SCALING. As a simple example, the linear system

$$\begin{bmatrix} 1 & 0 \\ 0 & \epsilon \end{bmatrix} \begin{bmatrix} x_1 \\ x_2 \end{bmatrix} = \begin{bmatrix} 1 \\ \epsilon \end{bmatrix}$$

has condition number $1/\epsilon$ and hence is very ill-conditioned if ϵ is very small. This ill-conditioning means that small perturbations in the input data can cause relatively large changes in the solution. For example, perturbing the right-hand side by the vector $\begin{bmatrix} 0 & -\epsilon \end{bmatrix}^T$ changes the solution from $\begin{bmatrix} 1 & 1 \end{bmatrix}^T$ to $\begin{bmatrix} 1 & 0 \end{bmatrix}^T$. If the second row is first multiplied by $1/\epsilon$, however, then the system becomes perfectly well-conditioned, and the same perturbation now produces a commensurately small change in the solution. Thus, the apparent ill-conditioning was due purely to poor scaling. Unfortunately, how to correct poor scaling for general matrices is much less obvious.

Iterative refinement is another means of potentially improving the accuracy of a computed solution. Given an approximate solution x_1 to the linear system $Ax = b$, compute the residual

$$r_1 = b - Ax_1.$$

Now solve the linear system

$$Az_1 = r_1$$

and take

$$x_2 = x_1 + z_1$$

as a new and "better" approximate solution, since

$$Ax_2 = A(x_1 + z_1) = Ax_1 + Az_1 = (b - r_1) + r_1 = b.$$

This process can be repeated to refine the solution successively until convergence, potentially producing a solution that is accurate to full machine precision.

Unfortunately, iterative refinement requires double the storage, since both the original matrix and its LU factorization are required (to compute the residual and to solve the subsequent systems, respectively). Moreover, for iterative refinement to produce meaningful improvement in the solution, the residual must usually be computed with higher precision than that used in computing the initial solution (recall Example 1.13).

For these reasons, iterative improvement is often impractical to use routinely, but it can still be useful in some circumstances. For example, iterative refinement can recover full accuracy for systems that are badly scaled, and can sometimes stabilize solution methods that are otherwise potentially unstable. Ironically, if the initial solution is relatively poor, then the residual may be large enough to be computed without requiring extra precision. We will return to iterative refinement later in Example 11.6.

2.5 SPECIAL TYPES OF LINEAR SYSTEMS

Thus far we have assumed that the linear system has a general matrix and is *dense*, meaning that essentially all of the matrix entries are nonzero. If the matrix has some special properties, then work and storage can often be saved in solving the linear system. Some examples of special properties that can be exploited include the following:

- *Symmetric:* $A = A^T$, i.e., $a_{ij} = a_{ji}$ for all i, j.
- *Positive definite:* $x^T A x > 0$ for all $x \neq 0$.
- *Band:* $a_{ij} = 0$ for all $|i - j| > \beta$, where β is the *bandwidth* of A. An important special case is a *tridiagonal matrix*, for which $\beta = 1$.
- *Sparse*: most entries of A are zero.

Techniques for handling symmetric and band systems are relatively straightforward variations on Gaussian elimination for dense systems. Sparse linear systems with more general nonzero patterns, on the other hand, require more sophisticated algorithms and data structures in order to avoid storing or operating on the zeros in the matrix (see Section 11.4.1).

The properties just defined for real matrices have analogues for complex matrices, but in the complex case the ordinary matrix transpose is replaced by the conjugate transpose, denoted by a superscript H. If $\gamma = \alpha + i\beta$ is a complex number, where α and β are real numbers and $i = \sqrt{-1}$, then its *complex conjugate* is defined by $\bar{\gamma} = \alpha - i\beta$. The *conjugate transpose* of a matrix A is then given by $\{A^H\}_{ij} = \bar{a}_{ji}$. Of course, for a real matrix A, $A^H = A^T$. A complex matrix is *Hermitian* if $A = A^H$, and positive definite if $x^H A x > 0$ for all complex vectors $x \neq 0$.

2.5.1 Symmetric Positive Definite Systems

If the matrix A is symmetric and positive definite, then an LU factorization can be arranged so that $U = L^T$, that is, $A = LL^T$, where L is lower triangular and has positive diagonal entries (but not, in general, a unit diagonal). This is known as the *Cholesky factorization* of A, and an algorithm for computing it can be derived simply by equating the corresponding entries of A and LL^T and then generating the entries of L in the correct order. In the 2×2 case, for example, we have

$$\begin{bmatrix} a_{11} & a_{21} \\ a_{21} & a_{22} \end{bmatrix} = \begin{bmatrix} l_{11} & 0 \\ l_{21} & l_{22} \end{bmatrix} \begin{bmatrix} l_{11} & l_{21} \\ 0 & l_{22} \end{bmatrix},$$

which implies that

$$l_{11} = \sqrt{a_{11}}, \qquad l_{21} = a_{21}/l_{11}, \qquad l_{22} = \sqrt{a_{22} - l_{21}^2}.$$

One way to write the resulting general algorithm, in which the Cholesky factor L overwrites the original matrix A, is as follows:

> **for** $j = 1$ **to** n { for each column j }
>   **for** $k = 1$ **to** $j - 1$ { loop over all prior columns k }
>   **for** $i = j$ **to** n { subtract a multiple of
> $a_{ij} = a_{ij} - a_{ik} \cdot a_{jk}$ column k from column j }
>   **end**
>   **end**
> $a_{jj} = \sqrt{a_{jj}}$
>   **for** $k = j + 1$ **to** n { scale column j by square
> $a_{kj} = a_{kj}/a_{jj}$ root of diagonal entry }
>   **end**
> **end**

A number of facts about the Cholesky factorization algorithm make it very attractive and popular for symmetric positive definite matrices:

- The n square roots required are all of positive numbers, so the algorithm is well-defined.
- No pivoting is required for numerical stability.
- Only the lower triangle of A is accessed, and hence the upper triangular portion need not be stored.
- Only about $n^3/6$ multiplications and a similar number of additions are required.

Thus, Cholesky factorization requires only about half as much work and half as much storage as are required for LU factorization of a general matrix by Gaussian elimination. Unfortunately, taking advantage of this gain in storage usually requires that one triangle of the symmetric matrix be packed into a one-dimensional array, which is less convenient than the usual two-dimensional storage for a matrix. For this reason, linear algebra software packages commonly offer both packed storage and standard two-dimensional array storage versions for symmetric matrices so that the user can choose between convenience and storage conservation.

In some circumstances it may be advantageous to express the Cholesky factorization in the form $A = LDL^T$, where L is unit lower triangular and D is diagonal with positive diagonal entries. Such a factorization can be computed by a simple variant of the standard Cholesky algorithm, and it has the advantage of not requiring any square roots. The diagonal entries of D in the LDL^T factorization are simply the squares of the diagonal entries of L in the LL^T factorization.

EXAMPLE 2.12 CHOLESKY FACTORIZATION. To illustrate the algorithm, we compute the Cholesky factorization of the symmetric positive definite matrix

$$A = \begin{bmatrix} 5.0 & 0 & 2.5 \\ 0 & 2.5 & 0 \\ 2.5 & 0 & 2.125 \end{bmatrix}.$$

The successive transformations of the lower triangle of the matrix will be shown, as the algorithm touches only this portion of the matrix. The first column has no prior columns, so it is merely scaled by the square root of the diagonal entry, $\sqrt{5}$, to give

$$
\begin{bmatrix}
2.236 & & \\
0 & 2.5 & \\
1.118 & 0 & 2.125
\end{bmatrix}.
$$

The second column now requires updating by subtracting a multiple of the first column. But in this case the multiplier in the second row of the first column is zero, so that the second column is unaffected by the first column. Thus, the second column is simply scaled by the square root of its diagonal entry, $\sqrt{2.5}$, to give

$$
\begin{bmatrix}
2.236 & & \\
0 & 1.581 & \\
1.118 & 0 & 2.125
\end{bmatrix}.
$$

Finally, the third column must be updated by subtracting multiples of the previous two columns. The multipliers for the first two columns, found in the third row, are 1.118 and zero, respectively. Updating the third column accordingly gives

$$
\begin{bmatrix}
2.236 & & \\
0 & 1.581 & \\
1.118 & 0 & 0.875
\end{bmatrix}.
$$

Taking the square root of the third diagonal entry then yields the final result

$$
L = \begin{bmatrix}
2.236 & & \\
0 & 1.581 & \\
1.118 & 0 & 0.935
\end{bmatrix}.
$$

2.5.2 Symmetric Indefinite Systems

If the matrix A is symmetric but indefinite (i.e., $x^T A x$ can take on both positive and negative values), then Cholesky factorization is not applicable, and some form of pivoting is generally required for numerical stability. Obviously, any pivoting must be symmetric—of the form PAP^T, where P is a permutation matrix—if the symmetry of the matrix is to be preserved.

We would like to obtain a factorization of the form $PAP^T = LDL^T$, where L is unit lower triangular and D is diagonal. Unfortunately, such a factorization, with diagonal D, may not exist, and in any case it generally cannot be computed stably using only symmetric pivoting. The best we can do is to take D to be either tridiagonal or block diagonal with 1×1 and 2×2 diagonal blocks. (A block matrix is a matrix whose entries are partitioned into submatrices, or "blocks," of compatible dimensions. In a block diagonal matrix, all of these submatrices are zero except those on the main block diagonal.)

Efficient algorithms have been developed by Aasen for the tridiagonal factorization, and by Bunch and Parlett (with subsequent improvements in the pivoting procedure by Bunch and Kaufman) for the block diagonal factorization (see [104]). In either case, the pivoting procedure yields a stable factorization that requires only about $n^3/6$ multiplications and a similar number of additions. Also, in either case, the subsequent solution phase requires only $\mathcal{O}(n^2)$ work. Thus, the cost of solving symmetric indefinite systems is similar to that for positive definite systems using Cholesky factorization, and only about half the cost for nonsymmetric systems using Gaussian elimination.

2.5.3 Band Systems

Gaussian elimination for band matrices differs little from the general case—the only algorithmic changes are in the ranges of the loops. Of course, one should also use a data structure for a band matrix that avoids storing zero entries. A common choice when the band is dense is to store the matrix in a two-dimensional array by diagonals. If pivoting is required for numerical stability, then the algorithm becomes slightly more complicated in that the bandwidth can grow (but no more than double). Thus, a general-purpose band solver for arbitrary bandwidth is very similar to a code for Gaussian elimination for general matrices.

For a fixed small bandwidth, however, a band solver can be extremely simple, especially if pivoting is not required for stability. Consider, for example, the tridiagonal matrix

$$
A = \begin{bmatrix}
b_1 & c_1 & 0 & \cdots & & 0 \\
a_2 & b_2 & c_2 & \ddots & & \vdots \\
0 & \ddots & \ddots & \ddots & & 0 \\
\vdots & \ddots & a_{n-1} & b_{n-1} & c_{n-1} \\
0 & \cdots & 0 & a_n & b_n
\end{bmatrix}.
$$

If pivoting is not required for stability, which is often the case for tridiagonal systems arising in practice (e.g., if the matrix is diagonally dominant or positive definite), then Gaussian elimination reduces to the following simple algorithm:

$$
\begin{aligned}
&d_1 = b_1 \\
&\textbf{for } i = 2 \textbf{ to } n \\
&\qquad m_i = a_i/d_{i-1} \\
&\qquad d_i = b_i - m_i c_{i-1} \\
&\textbf{end}
\end{aligned}
$$

and the resulting LU factorization of A is given by

$$
L = \begin{bmatrix}
1 & 0 & \cdots & & \cdots & 0 \\
m_2 & 1 & \ddots & & \ddots & \vdots \\
0 & \ddots & \ddots & & \ddots & \vdots \\
\vdots & \ddots & m_{n-1} & 1 & 0 \\
0 & \cdots & 0 & m_n & 1
\end{bmatrix}, \quad
U = \begin{bmatrix}
d_1 & c_1 & 0 & \cdots & & 0 \\
0 & d_2 & c_2 & \ddots & & \vdots \\
\vdots & \ddots & \ddots & \ddots & & 0 \\
\vdots & & \ddots & \ddots & d_{n-1} & c_{n-1} \\
0 & \cdots & & \cdots & 0 & d_n
\end{bmatrix}.
$$

In general, a band system of bandwidth β requires only $\mathcal{O}(\beta n)$ storage, and the factorization requires only $\mathcal{O}(\beta^2 n)$ work, both of which represent substantial savings over full systems if $\beta \ll n$.

2.6 ITERATIVE METHODS FOR LINEAR SYSTEMS

Gaussian elimination is an example of a direct method for solving linear systems, i.e., one that produces the exact solution (assuming exact arithmetic) to a linear system in a finite number of steps. Iterative methods for solving linear systems begin with an initial estimate for the solution and successively improve it until the solution is as accurate as desired. In theory, an infinite number of iterations might be required to converge to the exact solution, but in practice the iterations terminate after the residual $\|b - Ax\|$, or some other measure of error, is as small as desired. For some types of problems, iterative methods may have significant advantages over direct methods. Iterative methods for solving linear systems will be postponed until Chapter 11, where we consider the numerical solution of partial differential equations, which leads to sparse linear systems that are often best solved by iterative methods.

2.7 SOFTWARE FOR LINEAR SYSTEMS

Almost any software library for scientific computing contains routines for solving linear systems of various types. Table 2.1 is a list of appropriate routines for solving real, general, dense linear systems, and also for estimating the condition number, in some widely available software collections. Some packages use different prefixes or suffixes in the routine names to indicate the data type, typically **s** for single-precision real, **d**

TABLE 2.1
Software for solving general linear systems

Source	Factor	Solve	Condition estimator
FMM	decomp	solve	
HSL	ma21	ma21	
IMSL	lftrg	lfsrg	lfcrg
KMN	sgefs	sgefs	sgefs
LAPACK	sgetrf	sgetrs	sgecon
LINPACK	sgefa	sgesl	sgeco
MATLAB	lu	\	rcond
NAG	f07adf	f07aef	f07agf
NAPACK	fact	solve	con
NR	ludcmp	lubksb	
NUMAL	dec	sol	
SLATEC	sgefa	sgesl	sgeco

TABLE 2.2
Software for solving special linear systems

Source	Symmetric positive definite	Symmetric indefinite	General band
HSL	ma22	ma29	ma35
IMSL	lftds/lfsds	lftsf/lfssf	lftrb/lfsrb
LAPACK	spotrf/spotrs	ssytrf/ssytrs	sgbtrf/sgbtrs
LINPACK	spofa/sposl	ssifa/ssisl	sgbfa/sgbsl
NAG	f07fdf/f07fef	f07mdf/f07mef	f07bdf/f07bef
NAPACK	sfact/ssolve	ifact/isolve	bfact/bsolve
NR	choldc/cholsl		bandec/banbks
NUMAL	chldec2/chlsol2	decsym2/solsym2	decbnd/solbnd
SLATEC	spofa/sposl	ssifa/ssisl	sgbfa/sgbsl

for double-precision real, **c** for single-precision complex, and **z** for double-precision complex; only the single-precision real versions are listed here. In most such subroutine libraries, more specialized routines are available for particular types of linear systems, such as positive definite, symmetric, banded, or combinations of these. Some of these routines are listed in Table 2.2; other routines that are more storage efficient or cater to other special tasks may also be available.

Conventional software for solving linear systems $Ax = b$ is sometimes implemented as a single routine, or it may be split into two routines: one for computing a factorization and another for solving the resulting triangular system. In either case, repeating the factorization should not be necessary if additional solutions are needed with the same matrix but different right-hand sides. The input typically required includes a two-dimensional array containing the matrix A, a one-dimensional array containing the right-hand-side vector b (or a two-dimensional array for multiple right-hand-side vectors), the integer order of the system n, the leading dimension of the array containing A (so that the subroutine can interpret subscripts properly in the array), and possibly some work space and a flag indicating the particular task to be performed. On return, the solution x usually overwrites the storage for b, and the matrix factorization overwrites the storage for A. Additional output may include a status flag to indicate any errors or warnings and an estimate of the condition number of the matrix (or sometimes the reciprocal of the condition number). Because of the additional cost of condition estimation, this feature is usually optional.

Solving linear systems using an interactive environment such as **MATLAB** is simpler than when using conventional software because the package keeps track internally of details such as the dimensions of vectors and matrices, and many matrix operations are built into the syntax and semantics of the language. For example, the solution to the linear system $Ax = b$ is given in **MATLAB** by the "left division" operator, denoted by backslash, so that **x = A \ b**. Internally, the solution is computed by LU factorization and forward- and back-substitution, but the user need not be aware of this. The LU factorization can be computed explicitly, if desired, by the **MATLAB** **lu** function, **[L, U] = lu(A)**.

2.7.1 LINPACK and LAPACK

LINPACK is a standard software package for solving a wide variety of systems of linear equations, both general dense systems and those having various special properties, such as symmetric or banded. Solving linear systems is of such fundamental importance in scientific computing that **LINPACK** has become a standard benchmark for comparing the performance of computers. The **LINPACK** manual [63] is a useful source of practical advice on solving systems of linear equations.

A more recent package called **LAPACK** updates the entire **LINPACK** collection for higher performance on modern computer architectures, including some parallel computers. In many cases, the newer algorithms in **LAPACK** also achieve greater accuracy, robustness, and functionality than their predecessors in **LINPACK**. **LAPACK** includes both simple and expert drivers for all of the major computational problems in linear algebra, as well as the many underlying computational and auxiliary routines required for various factorizations, triangular solutions, norm estimation, scaling, and iterative refinement. Both **LINPACK** and **LAPACK** are available from **netlib**, and the linear system solvers in many other libraries and packages are based directly on them.

2.7.2 Basic Linear Algebra Subprograms

The high-level routines in **LINPACK** and **LAPACK** are based on lower-level Basic Linear Algebra Subprograms (**BLAS**). The **BLAS** were originally designed to encapsulate basic operations on vectors so that they could be optimized for a given computer architecture while the high-level routines that call them remain portable. New computer architectures have prompted the development of higher-level **BLAS** that encapsulate matrix-vector and matrix-matrix operations for better utilization of hierarchical memory such as cache, vector registers, and virtual memory with paging. A few of the most important **BLAS** routines of each level are listed in Table 2.3.

TABLE 2.3
Examples of basic linear algebra subprograms (BLAS)

Level	TOMS #	Work	Examples	Function
1	539	$\mathcal{O}(n)$	**saxpy**	Scalar times vector plus vector
			sdot	Inner product of two vectors
			snrm2	Euclidean norm of a vector
2	656	$\mathcal{O}(n^2)$	**sgemv**	Matrix-vector multiplication
			strsv	Triangular solution
			sger	Rank-one update
3	679	$\mathcal{O}(n^3)$	**sgemm**	Matrix-matrix multiplication
			strsm	Multiple triangular solutions
			ssyrk	Rank-k update

The key to good performance is *data reuse,* that is, performing as many arithmetic operations as possible involving a given data item while it is held in the portion of the memory hierarchy with the most rapid access. The level-3 **BLAS** have greater opportunity for data reuse because they perform $\mathcal{O}(n^3)$ operations on $\mathcal{O}(n^2)$ data items, whereas in the lower-level **BLAS** the number of operations is proportional to the number of data items. Generic versions of the **BLAS** are available from **netlib**, and many computer vendors provide custom versions that are optimized for highest performance on their particular systems.

2.8 HISTORICAL NOTES AND FURTHER READING

Elimination methods for solving systems of linear equations date from the nineteenth century and earlier. Their careful error analysis, however, began only with the computer era. Indeed, a grave concern of the early pioneers of digital computation, such as von Neumann and Turing, was whether accumulated rounding error in solving large linear systems by Gaussian elimination would render the results useless, and initially there was considerable pessimism on this score. Computational experience soon showed that the method was surprisingly stable and accurate in practice, however, and analyses eventually followed to explain this good fortune (see especially the work of Wilkinson [273, 274, 275]).

As it turns out, Gaussian elimination with partial pivoting has a worse than optimal operation count [248], is unstable in the worst case [273], and in a theoretical sense cannot be implemented efficiently in parallel [264]. Yet it is consistently effective in practice, even on parallel computers, and is one of the principal workhorses of scientific computing. Most numerical algorithms obey Murphy's law—"if anything can go wrong, it will"—but Gaussian elimination seems to be a happy exception. For further discussion of some of the "mysteries" of this remarkable algorithm, see [257].

For background on linear algebra, the reader may wish to consult the excellent textbooks by Strang [244, 246]. Additional examples, exercises, and practical applications of computational linear algebra can be found in [127, 171]. The definitive reference on matrix computations is [104]. More tutorial treatments include [49, 96, 116, 138, 239, 258, 268]. An influential early work on solving linear systems, and one of the first to include high-quality software, is [83]. A useful tutorial handbook on matrix computations, both in Fortran and **MATLAB**, is [42].

For a comprehensive treatment of error analysis and perturbation theory for linear systems and many other problems in linear algebra, see [126, 241]. An overview of condition number estimation is given in [124]. A detailed survey of componentwise (as opposed to normwise) perturbation theory in linear algebra is given in [125]. **LINPACK** and **LAPACK** are documented in [63] and [8], respectively. For the **BLAS** (Basic Linear Algebra Subprograms) see [61, 62, 164]. One of the earliest papers to examine the effect of the computing environment on the performance of Gaussian elimination and other matrix computations was [177]. For a sample of the now large literature on this topic, see [55, 64, 65, 194].

REVIEW QUESTIONS

2.1. True or false: If a matrix A is nonsingular, then the number of solutions to the linear system $Ax = b$ depends on the particular choice of right-hand-side vector b.

2.2. True or false: If a matrix has a very small determinant, then the matrix is nearly singular.

2.3. True or false: If a triangular matrix has a zero entry on its main diagonal, then the matrix is necessarily singular.

2.4. True or false: If a matrix has a zero entry on its main diagonal, then the matrix is necessarily singular.

2.5. True or false: An underdetermined system of linear equations $Ax = b$, where A is an $m \times n$ matrix with $m < n$, always has a solution.

2.6. True or false: The product of two upper triangular matrices is upper triangular.

2.7. True or false: The product of two symmetric matrices is symmetric.

2.8. True or false: The inverse of a nonsingular upper triangular matrix is upper triangular.

2.9. True or false: If the rows of an $n \times n$ matrix A are linearly dependent, then the columns of the matrix are also linearly dependent.

2.10. True or false: A system of linear equations $Ax = b$ has a solution if and only if the $m \times n$ matrix A and the augmented $m \times (n + 1)$ matrix $[A \ \ b]$ have the same rank.

2.11. True or false: If A is any $n \times n$ matrix and P is any $n \times n$ permutation matrix, then $PA = AP$.

2.12. True or false: Provided row interchanges are allowed, the LU factorization always exists, even for a singular matrix A.

2.13. True or false: If a linear system is well-conditioned, then pivoting is unnecessary in Gaussian elimination.

2.14. True or false: If a matrix is singular then it cannot have an LU factorization.

2.15. True or false: If a nonsingular symmetric matrix is not positive definite, then it cannot have a Cholesky factorization.

2.16. True or false: A symmetric positive definite matrix is always well-conditioned.

2.17. True or false: Gaussian elimination without pivoting fails only when the matrix is ill-conditioned or singular.

2.18. True or false: Once the LU factorization of a matrix A has been computed to solve a linear system $Ax = b$, then subsequent linear systems with the same matrix but different right-hand-side vectors can be solved without refactoring the matrix.

2.19. True or false: In explicitly inverting a matrix by LU factorization and triangular solution, the majority of the work is due to the factorization.

2.20. True or false: If x is any n-vector, then $\|x\|_1 \geq \|x\|_\infty$.

2.21. True or false: The norm of a singular matrix is zero.

2.22. True or false: If $\|A\| = 0$, then $A = 0$.

2.23. True or false: $\|A\|_1 = \|A^T\|_\infty$.

2.24. True or false: If A is any $n \times n$ nonsingular matrix, then $\text{cond}(A) = \text{cond}(A^{-1})$.

2.25. True or false: In solving a nonsingular system of linear equations, Gaussian elimination with partial pivoting usually yields a small residual even if the matrix is ill-conditioned.

2.26. True or false: Since the multipliers in Gaussian elimination with partial pivoting are bounded by 1 in magnitude, the elements of the successive reduced matrices cannot grow in magnitude.

2.27. Can a system of linear equations $Ax = b$ have exactly two distinct solutions?

2.28. Can the number of solutions to a linear system $Ax = b$ ever be determined solely from the matrix A without knowing the right-hand-side vector b?

2.29. In solving a square system of linear equations $Ax = b$, which would be a more serious difficulty: that the rows of A are linearly dependent, or that the columns of A are linearly dependent? Explain.

2.30. (*a*) State one defining property of a *singular* matrix A.

(*b*) Suppose that the linear system $Ax = b$ has two distinct solutions x and y. Use the property you gave in part *a* to prove that A must be singular.

2.31. Given a nonsingular system of linear equations $Ax = b$, what effect on the solution vector x results from each of the following actions?

(*a*) Permuting the rows of $\begin{bmatrix} A & b \end{bmatrix}$

(*b*) Permuting the columns of A

(*c*) Multiplying both sides of the equation from the left by a nonsingular matrix M

2.32. Suppose that both sides of a system of linear equations $Ax = b$ are multiplied by a nonzero scalar α.

(*a*) Does this change the true solution x?

(*b*) Does this change the residual vector $r = b - Ax$ for a given x?

(*c*) What conclusion can be drawn about assessing the quality of a computed solution?

2.33. Suppose that both sides of a system of linear equations $Ax = b$ are premultiplied by a nonsingular diagonal matrix.

(*a*) Does this change the true solution x?

(*b*) Can this affect the conditioning of the system?

(*c*) Can this affect the choice of pivots in Gaussian elimination?

2.34. With a singular matrix and the use of exact arithmetic, at what point will the solution process break down in solving a linear system by Gaussian elimination

(*a*) With partial pivoting?

(*b*) Without pivoting?

2.35. (*a*) What is the difference between partial pivoting and complete pivoting in Gaussian elimination?

(*b*) State one advantage of each type of pivoting relative to the other.

2.36. Consider the following matrix A, whose LU factorization we wish to compute using Gaussian elimination:

$$A = \begin{bmatrix} 4 & -8 & 1 \\ 6 & 5 & 7 \\ 0 & -10 & -3 \end{bmatrix}.$$

What will the initial pivot element be if

(*a*) No pivoting is used?

(*b*) Partial pivoting is used?

(*c*) Complete pivoting is used?

2.37. Give two reasons why pivoting is essential for a numerically stable implementation of Gaussian elimination.

2.38. If A is an ill-conditioned matrix, and its LU factorization is computed by Gaussian elimination with partial pivoting, would you expect the ill-conditioning to be reflected in L, in U, or both? Why?

2.39. (*a*) What is the inverse of the following matrix?

$$\begin{bmatrix} 1 & 0 & 0 & 0 \\ 0 & 1 & 0 & 0 \\ 0 & m_1 & 1 & 0 \\ 0 & m_2 & 0 & 1 \end{bmatrix}$$

(*b*) How might such a matrix arise in computational practice?

2.40. (*a*) Can every nonsingular $n \times n$ matrix A be written as a product, $A = LU$, where L is a lower triangular matrix and U is an upper triangular matrix?

(*b*) If so, what is an algorithm for accomplishing this? If not, give a counterexample to illustrate.

2.41. Given an $n \times n$ nonsingular matrix A and a second $n \times n$ matrix B, what is the best way to compute the $n \times n$ matrix $A^{-1}B$?

2.42. If A and B are $n \times n$ matrices, with A nonsingular, and c is an n-vector, how would you efficiently compute the product $A^{-1}Bc$?

2.43. If A is an $n \times n$ matrix and x is an n-vector, which of the following computations requires less work? Explain.

(a) $y = (x x^T) A$
(b) $y = x (x^T A)$

2.44. How does the computational work in solving an $n \times n$ triangular system of linear equations compare with that for solving a general $n \times n$ system of linear equations?

2.45. Assume that you have already computed the LU factorization, $A = LU$, of the nonsingular matrix A. How would you use it to solve the linear system $A^T x = b$?

2.46. If L is a nonsingular lower triangular matrix, P is a permutation matrix, and b is a given vector, how would you solve each of the following linear systems?

(a) $LPx = b$
(b) $PLx = b$

2.47. In the plane $\mathbb{R}^2$, is it possible to have a vector $x \neq 0$ such that $\|x\|_1 = \|x\|_\infty$? If so, give an example.

2.48. In the plane $\mathbb{R}^2$, is it possible to have two vectors x and y such that $\|x\|_1 > \|y\|_1$, but $\|x\|_\infty < \|y\|_\infty$? If so, give an example.

2.49. In general, which matrix norm is easier to compute, $\|A\|_1$ or $\|A\|_2$?

2.50. (a) Is the magnitude of the determinant of a matrix a good indicator of whether the matrix is nearly singular?

(b) If so, why? If not, what is a better indicator of near singularity?

2.51. (a) How is the condition number of a matrix A defined for a given matrix norm?

(b) How is the condition number used in estimating the accuracy of a computed solution to a linear system $Ax = b$?

2.52. Why is computing the condition number of a general matrix a nontrivial problem?

2.53. Give an example of a 3×3 matrix A, other than the identity matrix, such that cond(A) = 1.

2.54. Suppose that the $n \times n$ matrix A is perfectly well-conditioned, i.e., cond(A) = 1. Which of the following matrices would then necessarily share this same property?

(a) cA, where c is any nonzero scalar
(b) DA, where D is any nonsingular diagonal matrix
(c) PA, where P is any permutation matrix
(d) BA, where B is any nonsingular matrix
(e) A^{-1}, the inverse of A
(f) A^T, the transpose of A

2.55. Let $A = \text{diag}(\frac{1}{2})$ be an $n \times n$ diagonal matrix with all its diagonal entries equal to $\frac{1}{2}$.

(a) What is the value of det(A)?
(b) What is the value of cond(A)?
(c) What conclusion can you draw from these results?

2.56. Suppose that the $n \times n$ matrix A is exactly singular, but that its floating-point representation, fl(A), is nonsingular. In this case, what would you expect the order of magnitude of the condition number cond(fl(A)) to be?

2.57. Classify each of the following matrices as well-conditioned or ill-conditioned:

(a) $\begin{bmatrix} 10^{10} & 0 \\ 0 & 10^{-10} \end{bmatrix}$

(b) $\begin{bmatrix} 10^{10} & 0 \\ 0 & 10^{10} \end{bmatrix}$

(c) $\begin{bmatrix} 10^{-10} & 0 \\ 0 & 10^{-10} \end{bmatrix}$

(d) $\begin{bmatrix} 1 & 2 \\ 2 & 4 \end{bmatrix}$

2.58. Which of the following are good indicators that a matrix is nearly singular?

(a) Its determinant is small.
(b) Its norm is small.
(c) Its norm is large.
(d) Its condition number is large.

2.59. In a floating-point system having 10 decimal digits of precision, if Gaussian elimination with partial pivoting is used to solve a linear system whose matrix has a condition number of 10^3, and whose input data are accurate to full machine precision, about how many digits of accuracy would you expect in the solution?

2.60. Assume that you are solving a system of linear equations $Ax = b$ on a computer whose floating-point number system has 12 decimal digits of precision, and that the problem data are correct to full machine precision. About how large can the condition number of the matrix A be before the computed solution x will contain no significant digits?

2.61. Under what circumstances does a small residual vector $r = b - Ax$ imply that x is an accurate solution to the linear system $Ax = b$?

2.62. Let A be an arbitrary square matrix and c an arbitrary scalar. Which of the following statements must necessarily hold?
    (a) $\|cA\| = |c| \cdot \|A\|$.
    (b) $\text{cond}(cA) = |c| \cdot \text{cond}(A)$.

2.63. (a) What is the main difference between Gaussian elimination and Gauss-Jordan elimination?
    (b) State one advantage of each type of elimination relative to the other.

2.64. Rank the following methods according to the amount of work required for solving a general system of linear equations of order n:
    (a) Gauss-Jordan elimination
    (b) Gaussian elimination with partial pivoting
    (c) Cramer's rule
    (d) Explicit matrix inversion followed by matrix-vector multiplication

2.65. (a) How much storage is required to store an $n \times n$ matrix of rank one efficiently?
    (b) How many arithmetic operations are required to multiply an n-vector by an $n \times n$ matrix of rank one efficiently?

2.66. In a comparison of ordinary Gaussian elimination with Gauss-Jordan elimination for solving a linear system $Ax = b$,
    (a) Which has a more expensive factorization?
    (b) Which has a more expensive back-substitution?
    (c) Which has a higher cost overall?

2.67. For each of the following elimination algorithms for solving linear systems, is there any pivoting strategy that can guarantee that all of the multipliers will be at most 1 in absolute value?
    (a) Gaussian elimination
    (b) Gauss-Jordan elimination

2.68. What two properties of a matrix A together imply that A has a Cholesky factorization?

2.69. List three advantages of Cholesky factorization compared with LU factorization.

2.70. How many square roots are required to compute the Cholesky factorization of an $n \times n$ symmetric positive definite matrix?

2.71. Let $A = \{a_{ij}\}$ be an $n \times n$ symmetric positive definite matrix.
    (a) What is the $(1, 1)$ entry of its Cholesky factor L?
    (b) What is the $(n, 1)$ entry of its Cholesky factor L?

2.72. What is the Cholesky factorization of the following matrix?

$$\begin{bmatrix} 4 & 2 \\ 2 & 2 \end{bmatrix}$$

2.73. (a) Is it possible, in general, to solve a symmetric indefinite linear system at a cost similar to that for using Cholesky factorization to solve a symmetric positive definite linear system?
    (b) If so, what is an algorithm for accomplishing this? If not, why?

2.74. Give two reasons why iterative improvement for solutions of linear systems is often impractical to implement.

2.75. Suppose you have already solved the $n \times n$ linear system $Ax = b$ by LU factorization and back-substitution. What is the further cost (order of magnitude will suffice) of solving a new system
    (a) With the same matrix A but a different right-hand-side vector?
    (b) With the matrix changed by adding a matrix of rank one?
    (c) With the matrix A changed completely?

EXERCISES

2.1. In Section 2.1.1, four defining properties are given for a singular matrix. Show that these four properties are indeed equivalent.

2.2. Suppose that each of the row sums of an $n \times n$ matrix A is equal to zero. Show that A must be singular.

2.3. Suppose that A is a singular $n \times n$ matrix. Prove that if the linear system $Ax = b$ has at least one solution x, then it has infinitely many solutions.

2.4. (a) Show that the following matrix is singular.

$$A = \begin{bmatrix} 1 & 1 & 0 \\ 1 & 2 & 1 \\ 1 & 3 & 2 \end{bmatrix}$$

(b) If $b = \begin{bmatrix} 2 & 4 & 6 \end{bmatrix}^T$, how many solutions are there to the system $Ax = b$?

2.5. What is the inverse of the following matrix?

$$A = \begin{bmatrix} 1 & 0 & 0 \\ 1 & -1 & 0 \\ 1 & -2 & 1 \end{bmatrix}$$

2.6. Let A be an $n \times n$ matrix such that $A^2 = 0$, the zero matrix. Show that A must be singular.

2.7. Let

$$A = \begin{bmatrix} 1 & 1 + \epsilon \\ 1 - \epsilon & 1 \end{bmatrix}.$$

(a) What is the determinant of A?

(b) In floating-point arithmetic, for what range of values of ϵ will the computed value of the determinant be zero?

(c) What is the LU factorization of A?

(d) In floating-point arithmetic, for what range of values of ϵ will the computed value of U be singular?

2.8. Let A and B be any two $n \times n$ matrices.

(a) Prove that $(AB)^T = B^T A^T$.

(b) If A and B are both nonsingular, prove that $(AB)^{-1} = B^{-1}A^{-1}$.

2.9. Let A be any nonsingular matrix. Prove that $(A^{-1})^T = (A^T)^{-1}$. For this reason, the notation A^{-T} can be used unambiguously to denote this matrix.

2.10. Let P be any permutation matrix.

(a) Prove that $P^{-1} = P^T$.

(b) Prove that P can be expressed as a product of pairwise interchanges.

2.11. Write out a detailed algorithm for solving a lower triangular linear system $Lx = b$ by forward-substitution.

2.12. Verify that the dominant term in the operation count (number of multiplications or number of additions) for solving a lower triangular system of order n by forward substitution is $n^2/2$.

2.13. How would you solve a partitioned linear system of the form

$$\begin{bmatrix} L_1 & 0 \\ B & L_2 \end{bmatrix} \begin{bmatrix} x \\ y \end{bmatrix} = \begin{bmatrix} b \\ c \end{bmatrix},$$

where L_1 and L_2 are nonsingular lower triangular matrices, and the solution and right-hand-side vectors are partitioned accordingly? Show the specific steps you would perform in terms of the given submatrices and vectors.

2.14. Prove each of the four properties of elementary elimination matrices enumerated in Section 2.2.2.

2.15. (a) Prove that the product of two lower triangular matrices is lower triangular.

(b) Prove that the inverse of a nonsingular lower triangular matrix is lower triangular.

2.16. (a) What is the LU factorization of the following matrix?

$$\begin{bmatrix} 1 & a \\ c & b \end{bmatrix}$$

(b) Under what condition is this matrix singular?

2.17. Write out the LU factorization of the following matrix (show both the L and U matrices explicitly):

$$\begin{bmatrix} 1 & -1 & 0 \\ -1 & 2 & -1 \\ 0 & -1 & 1 \end{bmatrix}.$$

2.18. Prove that the matrix

$$A = \begin{bmatrix} 0 & 1 \\ 1 & 0 \end{bmatrix}$$

has no LU factorization; i.e., no lower triangular matrix L and upper triangular matrix U exist such that $A = LU$.

2.19. Let A be an $n \times n$ nonsingular matrix. Consider the following algorithm:

1. Scan columns 1 through n of A in succession, and permute rows, if necessary, so that the diagonal entry is the largest entry in magnitude on or below the diagonal in each column. The result is PA for some permutation matrix P.
2. Now carry out Gaussian elimination *without* pivoting to compute the LU factorization of PA.

(*a*) Is this algorithm numerically stable?

(*b*) If so, explain why. If not, give a counterexample to illustrate.

2.20. Prove that if Gaussian elimination with partial pivoting is applied to a matrix A that is diagonally dominant by columns, then no row interchanges will occur.

2.21. If A, B, and C are $n \times n$ matrices, with B and C nonsingular, and b is an n-vector, how would you implement the formula

$$x = B^{-1}(2A + I)(C^{-1} + A)b$$

without computing any matrix inverses?

2.22. Verify that the dominant term in the operation count (number of multiplications or number of additions) for LU factorization of a matrix of order n by Gaussian elimination is $n^3/3$.

2.23. Verify that the dominant term in the operation count (number of multiplications or number of additions) for computing the inverse of a matrix of order n by Gaussian elimination is n^3.

2.24. Verify that the dominant term in the operation count (number of multiplications or number of additions) for Gauss-Jordan elimination for a matrix of order n is $n^3/2$.

2.25. (*a*) If u and v are nonzero n-vectors, prove that the $n \times n$ outer product matrix uv^T has rank one.

(*b*) If A is an $n \times n$ matrix such that rank(A) = 1, prove that there exist nonzero n-vectors u and v such that $A = uv^T$.

2.26. An $n \times n$ matrix A is said to be *elementary* if it differs from the identity matrix by a matrix of rank one, i.e., if $A = I - uv^T$ for some n-vectors u and v.

(*a*) If A is elementary, what condition on u and v ensures that A is nonsingular?

(*b*) If A is elementary and nonsingular, prove that A^{-1} is also elementary by showing that $A^{-1} = I - \sigma uv^T$ for some scalar σ. What is the specific value for σ, in terms of u and v?

(*c*) Is an elementary elimination matrix, as defined in Section 2.2.2, elementary? If so, what are u, v, and σ in this case?

2.27. Prove that the Sherman-Morrison formula

$$(A - uv^T)^{-1} = A^{-1} + A^{-1}u(1 - v^T A^{-1}u)^{-1}v^T A^{-1}$$

given in Section 2.2.8 is correct. (*Hint*: Multiply both sides by $A - uv^T$.)

2.28. Prove that the Woodbury formula

$$(A - UV^T)^{-1} = A^{-1} + A^{-1}U(1 - V^T A^{-1}U)^{-1}V^T A^{-1}$$

given in Section 2.2.8 is correct. (*Hint*: Multiply both sides by $A - UV^T$.)

2.29. Prove that the vector p-norms satisfy the properties given in Section 2.3.1 for $p = 1, 2$, and ∞.

2.30. Prove that the matrix p-norms satisfy the properties given in Section 2.3.2 for $p = 1$ and ∞.

2.31. Let A be a symmetric positive definite matrix. Show that the function

$$\|x\|_A = (x^T Ax)^{1/2}$$

satisfies the three properties of a vector norm given in Section 2.3.1. This vector norm is said to be *induced* by the matrix A.

2.32. Show that the following functions satisfy the first three properties of a matrix norm given in Section 2.3.2

and hence are matrix norms in the more general sense mentioned there.

(a)
$$\|A\|_{max} = \max_{i,j} |a_{ij}|$$

Note that this is simply the ∞-norm of A considered as a vector in $\mathbb{R}^{n^2}$.

(b)
$$\|A\|_F = \left(\sum_{i,j} |a_{ij}|^2\right)^{1/2}$$

Note that this is simply the 2-norm of A considered as a vector in $\mathbb{R}^{n^2}$. It is called the *Frobenius* norm.

2.33. Prove or give a counterexample: If A is a nonsingular matrix, then $\|A^{-1}\| = \|A\|^{-1}$.

2.34. Suppose that A is a positive definite matrix.
(a) Show that A must be nonsingular.
(b) Show that A^{-1} must be positive definite.

2.35. Suppose that the matrix A has a factorization of the form $A = BB^T$, with B nonsingular. Show that A must be symmetric and positive definite.

2.36. Derive an algorithm for computing the Cholesky factorization LL^T of an $n \times n$ symmetric positive definite matrix A by equating the corresponding entries of A and LL^T.

2.37. Suppose that the symmetric matrix
$$B = \begin{bmatrix} \alpha & a^T \\ a & A \end{bmatrix}$$
of order $n + 1$ is positive definite.
(a) Show that the scalar α must be positive and the $n \times n$ matrix A must be positive definite.
(b) What is the Cholesky factorization of B in terms of α, a, and A?

2.38. Suppose that the symmetric matrix
$$B = \begin{bmatrix} A & a \\ a^T & \alpha \end{bmatrix}$$
of order $n + 1$ is positive definite.
(a) Show that the scalar α must be positive and the $n \times n$ matrix A must be positive definite.

(b) What is the Cholesky factorization of B in terms of the constituent submatrices?

2.39. Verify that the dominant term in the operation count (number of multiplications or number of additions) for Cholesky factorization of a symmetric positive definite matrix of order n is $n^3/6$.

2.40. Let A be a band matrix with bandwidth β, and suppose that the LU factorization $PA = LU$ is computed using Gaussian elimination with partial pivoting. Show that the bandwidth of the upper triangular factor U is at most 2β.

2.41. Let A be a nonsingular tridiagonal matrix.
(a) Show that in general A^{-1} is dense.
(b) Compare the work and storage required in this case to solve the linear system $Ax = b$ by Gaussian elimination and back-substitution with those required to solve the system by explicit matrix inversion.

This example illustrates yet another reason why explicit matrix inversion is usually a bad idea.

2.42. (a) Devise an algorithm for computing the inverse of a nonsingular $n \times n$ triangular matrix *in place,* i.e., with no additional array storage.
(b) Is it possible to compute the inverse of a general nonsingular $n \times n$ matrix in place? If so, sketch an algorithm for doing so, and if not, explain why. For purposes of this exercise, you may assume that pivoting is not required.

2.43. Suppose you need to solve the linear system $Cz = d$, where C is a complex $n \times n$ matrix and d and z are complex n-vectors, but your linear equation solver handles only real systems. Let $C = A + iB$ and $d = b + ic$, where A, B, b, and c are real and $i = \sqrt{-1}$. Show that the solution $z = x + iy$ is given by the $2n \times 2n$ real linear system
$$\begin{bmatrix} A & -B \\ B & A \end{bmatrix}\begin{bmatrix} x \\ y \end{bmatrix} = \begin{bmatrix} b \\ c \end{bmatrix}.$$

Is this a good way to solve this problem? Why?

COMPUTER PROBLEMS

2.1. (*a*) Show that the matrix

$$A = \begin{bmatrix} 0.1 & 0.2 & 0.3 \\ 0.4 & 0.5 & 0.6 \\ 0.7 & 0.8 & 0.9 \end{bmatrix}$$

is singular. Describe the set of solutions to the system $Ax = b$ if

$$b = \begin{bmatrix} 0.1 \\ 0.3 \\ 0.5 \end{bmatrix}.$$

(*b*) If we were to use Gaussian elimination with partial pivoting to solve this system using exact arithmetic, at what point would the process fail?

(*c*) Since some of the entries of A are not exactly representable in a binary floating-point system, the matrix is no longer exactly singular when entered into a computer; thus, solving the system by Gaussian elimination will not necessarily fail. Solve this system on a computer using a library routine for Gaussian elimination. Compare the computed solution with your description of the solution set in part *a*. If your software includes a condition estimator, what is the estimated value for cond(A)? How many digits of accuracy in the solution would this lead you to expect?

2.2. (*a*) Use a library routine for Gaussian elimination to solve the system $Ax = b$, where

$$A = \begin{bmatrix} 2 & 4 & -2 \\ 4 & 9 & -3 \\ -2 & -1 & 7 \end{bmatrix}, \qquad b = \begin{bmatrix} 2 \\ 8 \\ 10 \end{bmatrix}.$$

(*b*) Use the LU factorization of A already computed to solve the system $Ay = c$, where

$$c = \begin{bmatrix} 4 \\ 8 \\ -6 \end{bmatrix},$$

without refactoring the matrix.

(*c*) If the matrix A changes so that $a_{1,2} = 2$, use the Sherman-Morrison updating technique to compute the new solution x without refactoring the matrix, using the original right-hand-side vector b.

2.3. The following diagram depicts a plane truss having 13 members (the numbered lines) connected by 10 joints (the numbered circles). The indicated loads, in tons, are applied at joints 2, 5, and 6, and we wish to

determine the resulting force on each member of the truss.

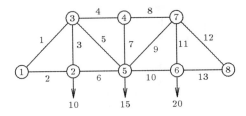

For the truss to be in static equilibrium, there must be no net force, horizontally or vertically, at any joint. Thus, we can determine the member forces by equating the horizontal forces to the left and right at each joint, and similarly equating the vertical forces upward and downward at each joint. For the eight joints, this would give 16 equations, which is more than the 13 unknown forces to be determined. For the truss to be statically determinate, that is, for there to be a unique solution, we assume that joint 1 is rigidly fixed both horizontally and vertically, and that joint 8 is fixed vertically. Resolving the member forces into horizontal and vertical components and defining $\alpha = \sqrt{2}/2$, we obtain the following system of equations for the member forces f_i:

$$\text{Joint 2}: \begin{cases} f_2 = f_6 \\ f_3 = 10 \end{cases}$$

$$\text{Joint 3}: \begin{cases} \alpha f_1 = f_4 + \alpha f_5 \\ \alpha f_1 + f_3 + \alpha f_5 = 0 \end{cases}$$

$$\text{Joint 4}: \begin{cases} f_4 = f_8 \\ f_7 = 0 \end{cases}$$

$$\text{Joint 5}: \begin{cases} \alpha f_5 + f_6 = \alpha f_9 + f_{10} \\ \alpha f_5 + f_7 + \alpha f_9 = 15 \end{cases}$$

$$\text{Joint 6}: \begin{cases} f_{10} = f_{13} \\ f_{11} = 20 \end{cases}$$

$$\text{Joint 7}: \begin{cases} f_8 + \alpha f_9 = \alpha f_{12} \\ \alpha f_9 + f_{11} + \alpha f_{12} = 0 \end{cases}$$

$$\text{Joint 8}: \{ f_{13} + \alpha f_{12} = 0$$

Use a library routine to solve this system of linear equations for the vector f of member forces. Note that the matrix of this system is quite sparse, so you may wish to experiment with a band solver or more general sparse solver, although this particular problem instance is too small for these to offer significant advantage over a general solver.

2.4. Write a routine for estimating the condition number of a matrix A. You may use either the 1-norm or the ∞-norm (or try both and compare the results). You will need to compute $\|A\|$, which is easy, and estimate $\|A^{-1}\|$, which is more challenging. As discussed in Section 2.3.3, one way to estimate $\|A^{-1}\|$ is to pick a vector y such that the ratio $\|z\|/\|y\|$ is large, where z is the solution to $Az = y$. Try two different approaches to picking y:

(a) Choose y as the solution to the system $A^T y = c$, where c is a vector each of whose components is ± 1, with the sign for each component chosen by the following heuristic. Using the factorization $A = LU$, the system $A^T y = c$ is solved in two stages, successively solving the triangular systems $U^T v = c$ and $L^T y = v$. At each step of the first triangular solution, choose the corresponding component of c to be 1 or -1, depending on which will make the resulting component of v larger in magnitude. (You will need to write a custom triangular solution routine to implement this.) Then solve the second triangular system in the usual way for y. The idea here is that any ill-conditioning in A will be reflected in U, resulting in a relatively large v. The relatively well-conditioned unit triangular matrix L will then preserve this relationship, resulting in a relatively large y.

(b) Choose some small number, say, five, different vectors y randomly and use the one producing the largest ratio $\|z\|/\|y\|$. (For this you can use an ordinary triangular solution routine.)

You may use a library routine to obtain the necessary LU factorization of A. Test your program on the following matrices:

$$A = \begin{bmatrix} 0.641 & 0.242 \\ 0.321 & 0.121 \end{bmatrix},$$

$$B = \begin{bmatrix} 10 & -7 & 0 \\ -3 & 2 & 6 \\ 5 & -1 & 5 \end{bmatrix}.$$

How do the results using these two methods compare? To check the quality of your estimates, compute A^{-1} explicitly to determine its true norm (this computation can also make use of the LU factorization already computed). If you have access to linear equations software that already includes a condition estimator, how do your results compare with its?

2.5. (a) Use a single-precision routine for Gaussian elimination to solve the system $Ax = b$, where

$$A = \begin{bmatrix} 21.0 & 67.0 & 88.0 & 73.0 \\ 76.0 & 63.0 & 7.0 & 20.0 \\ 0.0 & 85.0 & 56.0 & 54.0 \\ 19.3 & 43.0 & 30.2 & 29.4 \end{bmatrix},$$

$$b = \begin{bmatrix} 141.0 \\ 109.0 \\ 218.0 \\ 93.7 \end{bmatrix}.$$

(b) Compute the residual $r = b - Ax$ using double-precision arithmetic, if available (but storing the final result in a single-precision vector r). Note that the solution routine may destroy the array containing A, so you may need to save a separate copy for computing the residual. (If only one precision is available in the computing environment you use, then do all of this problem in that precision.)

(c) Solve the linear system $Az = r$ to obtain the "improved" solution $x + z$. Note that A need not be refactored.

(d) Repeat steps b and c until no further improvement is observed.

2.6. An $n \times n$ *Hilbert* matrix H has entries $h_{ij} = 1/(i + j - 1)$, so it has the form

$$\begin{bmatrix} 1 & \frac{1}{2} & \frac{1}{3} & \cdots \\ \frac{1}{2} & \frac{1}{3} & \frac{1}{4} & \cdots \\ \frac{1}{3} & \frac{1}{4} & \frac{1}{5} & \cdots \\ \vdots & \vdots & \vdots & \ddots \end{bmatrix}.$$

For $n = 2, 3, \ldots$, generate the Hilbert matrix of order n, and also generate the n-vector $b = Hx$, where x is the n-vector with all of its components equal to 1. Use a library routine for Gaussian elimination (or Cholesky factorization, since the Hilbert matrix is symmetric and positive definite) to solve the resulting linear system $Hx = b$, obtaining an approximate solution $\hat{x}$. Compute the ∞-norm of the residual $r = b - H\hat{x}$ and of the error $\Delta x = \hat{x} - x$, where x is the vector of all ones. How large can you take n before the error is 100 percent (i.e., there are no significant digits in the solution)? Also use a condition estimator to obtain $\text{cond}(H)$ for each value of n. Try to characterize the condition number as a function of n. As n varies, how does the number of correct digits in the components of the computed solution relate to the condition number of the matrix?

2.7. (*a*) What happens when Gaussian elimination with partial pivoting is used on a matrix of the following form?

$$\begin{bmatrix} 1 & 0 & 0 & 0 & 1 \\ -1 & 1 & 0 & 0 & 1 \\ -1 & -1 & 1 & 0 & 1 \\ -1 & -1 & -1 & 1 & 1 \\ -1 & -1 & -1 & -1 & 1 \end{bmatrix}$$

Do the entries of the transformed matrix grow? What happens if complete pivoting is used instead? (Note that part *a* does not require a computer.)

(*b*) Use a library routine for Gaussian elimination with partial pivoting to solve various sizes of linear systems of this form, using right-hand-side vectors chosen so that the solution is known. How do the error, residual, and condition number behave as the systems become larger? This artificially contrived system illustrates the worst-case growth factor cited in Section 2.4.1 and is not indicative of the usual behavior of Gaussian elimination with partial pivoting.

2.8. Multiplying both sides of a linear system $Ax = b$ by a nonsingular diagonal matrix D to obtain a new system $DAx = Db$ simply rescales the rows of the system and in theory does not change the solution. Such scaling does affect the condition number of the matrix and the choice of pivots in Gaussian elimination, however, so it may affect the accuracy of the solution in finite-precision arithmetic. Note that scaling can introduce some rounding error in the matrix unless the entries of D are powers of the base of the floating-point arithmetic system being used (why?).

Using a linear system with randomly chosen matrix A, and right-hand-side vector b chosen so that the solution is known, experiment with various scaling matrices D to see what effect they have on the condition number of the matrix DA and the solution given by a library routine for solving the linear system $DAx = Db$. Be sure to try some fairly skewed scalings, where the magnitudes of the diagonal entries of D vary widely (the purpose is to simulate a system with badly chosen units). Compare both the relative residuals and the error given by the various scalings. Can you find a scaling that gives very poor accuracy? Is the residual still small in this case?

2.9. (*a*) Use Gaussian elimination *without* pivoting to solve the linear system

$$\begin{bmatrix} \epsilon & 1 \\ 1 & 1 \end{bmatrix}\begin{bmatrix} x_1 \\ x_2 \end{bmatrix} = \begin{bmatrix} 1 + \epsilon \\ 2 \end{bmatrix}$$

for $\epsilon = 10^{-2k}$, $k = 1, \ldots, 10$. The exact solution is $x = \begin{bmatrix} 1 & 1 \end{bmatrix}^T$, independent of the value of ϵ. How does the accuracy of the computed solution behave as the value of ϵ decreases?

(*b*) Repeat part *a*, still using Gaussian elimination without pivoting, but this time use one iteration of iterative refinement to improve the solution, computing the residual in the same precision as the rest of the computations. Now how does the accuracy of the computed solution behave as the value of ϵ decreases?

2.10. Consider the linear system

$$\begin{bmatrix} 1 & 1 + \epsilon \\ 1 - \epsilon & 1 \end{bmatrix}\begin{bmatrix} x_1 \\ x_2 \end{bmatrix} = \begin{bmatrix} 1 + (1 + \epsilon)\epsilon \\ 1 \end{bmatrix},$$

where ϵ is a small parameter to be specified. The exact solution is obviously

$$x = \begin{bmatrix} 1 \\ \epsilon \end{bmatrix}$$

for any value of ϵ.

Use a library routine based on Gaussian elimination to solve this system. Experiment with various values for ϵ, especially values near $\sqrt{\epsilon_{\text{mach}}}$ for your computer. For each value of ϵ you try, compute an estimate of the condition number of the matrix and the relative error in each component of the solution. How accurately is each component determined? How does the accuracy attained for each component compare with expectations based on the condition number of the matrix and the error bounds given in Section 2.4.2? What conclusions can you draw from this experiment?

2.11. (*a*) Write programs implementing Gaussian elimination with no pivoting, partial pivoting, and complete pivoting.

(*b*) Generate several linear systems with random matrices (i.e., use a random number generator to obtain the matrix entries) and right-hand sides chosen so that the solutions are known, and compare the accuracy, residuals, and performance of the three implementations.

(*c*) Can you devise a (nonrandom) matrix for which complete pivoting is significantly more accurate than partial pivoting?

2.12. Write a routine for solving tridiagonal systems of linear equations using the algorithm given in Section 2.5.3 and test it on some sample systems. How does your routine change if you include partial pivoting? How does your routine change if the system is positive definite and you compute the Cholesky factorization instead of the LU factorization?

2.13. The determinant of a triangular matrix is equal to the product of its diagonal entries. Use this fact to develop a routine for computing the determinant of an arbitrary $n \times n$ matrix A by using its LU factorization. You may use a library routine for Gaussian elimination with partial pivoting to obtain the LU factorization, or you may design your own routine. How can you determine the proper sign for the determinant? To avoid risk of overflow or underflow, you may wish to consider computing the logarithm of the determinant instead of the actual value of the determinant.

2.14. Write programs implementing matrix multiplication $C = AB$, where A is $m \times n$ and B is $n \times k$, in two different ways:

(*a*) Compute the mk inner products of rows of A with columns of B.

(*b*) Form each column of C as a linear combination of columns of A.

In **BLAS** terminology (see Section 2.7.2), the first implementation uses **sdot**, whereas the second uses **saxpy**. Compare the performance of these two implementations on your computer. You may need to try fairly large matrices before the differences in performance become significant. Find out as much as you can about your computer system (e.g., cache size and cache management policy), and use this information to explain the results you observe.

2.15. Implement Gaussian elimination using each of the six different orderings of the triple-nested loop and compare their performance on your computer. For purposes of this exercise, you may ignore pivoting for numerical stability, but be sure to use test matrices that do not require pivoting. You may need to try a fairly large system before the differences in performance become significant. Find out as much as you can about your computer system (e.g., cache size and cache management policy), and use this information to explain the results you observe.

2.16. Both forward- and back-substitution for solving triangular linear systems involve nested loops whose two indices can be taken in either order. Implement both forward- and back-substitution using each of the two index orderings (a total of four algorithms), and compare their performance for triangular test matrices of various sizes. You may need to try a fairly large system before the differences in performance become significant. Is the best choice of index orderings the same for both algorithms? Find out as much as you can about your computer system (e.g., cache size and cache management policy), and use this information to explain the results you observe.

2.17. Consider a horizontal cantilevered beam that is clamped at one end but free along the remainder of its length. A discrete model of the forces on the beam yields a system of linear equations $Ax = b$, where the $n \times n$ matrix A has the banded form

$$
\begin{bmatrix}
9 & -4 & 1 & 0 & \cdots & \cdots & 0 \\
-4 & 6 & -4 & 1 & \ddots & & \vdots \\
1 & -4 & 6 & -4 & 1 & \ddots & \vdots \\
0 & \ddots & \ddots & \ddots & \ddots & \ddots & 0 \\
\vdots & \ddots & 1 & -4 & 6 & -4 & 1 \\
\vdots & & \ddots & 1 & -4 & 5 & -2 \\
0 & \cdots & \cdots & 0 & 1 & -2 & 1
\end{bmatrix}.
$$

the n-vector b is the known load on the bar (including its own weight), and the n-vector x represents the resulting deflection of the bar that is to be determined. We will take the bar to be uniformly loaded, with $b_i = 1$ for each component of the load vector.

(*a*) Letting $n = 100$, solve this linear system using both a standard library routine for dense linear systems and a library routine designed for band (or more general sparse) systems. How do the two routines compare in the time required to compute the solution? How well do the answers obtained agree with each other?

(*b*) Verify that the matrix A has the UL factorization $A = RR^T$, where R is an upper triangular matrix of the form

$$
\begin{bmatrix}
2 & -2 & 1 & 0 & \cdots & & 0 \\
0 & 1 & -2 & 1 & \ddots & & \vdots \\
\vdots & \ddots & \ddots & \ddots & \ddots & & 0 \\
\vdots & & \ddots & 1 & -2 & 1 & \\
\vdots & & & \ddots & 1 & -2 & \\
0 & \cdots & \cdots & \cdots & & 0 & 1
\end{bmatrix}.
$$

Letting $n = 1000$, solve the linear system using this factorization (two triangular solutions will be required). Also solve the system in its original form using a band solver as in part *a*. How well do the answers obtained agree with each other? Which approach seems more ac-

curate? What is the condition number of A, and what accuracy does it suggest that you should expect? Try iterative refinement to see if the accuracy or residual improves for the less accurate method.

CHAPTER 3

Linear Least Squares

What meaning should we attribute to a system of linear equations $Ax = b$ if the matrix A is not square? Since a nonsquare matrix cannot have an inverse, the system of equations must have either no solution or a nonunique solution. Nevertheless, it is often useful to define a unique vector x that satisfies the linear system in an approximate sense. In this chapter we will see how such problems arise and consider methods for solving them.

Let A be an $m \times n$ matrix. We will be concerned primarily with the most commonly occurring case, $m > n$, which is called *overdetermined* because there are more equations than unknowns. Such a system usually has no exact solution in the usual sense. Later on we will also briefly consider the *underdetermined* case, $m < n$, with fewer equations than unknowns.

3.1 DATA FITTING

Perhaps the most common source of overdetermined linear systems is *data fitting*, especially when the data have some random error associated with them, as do most empirical laboratory measurements or other observations of nature. Given m data points (t_i, y_i), we wish to find the n-vector x of parameters that gives the "best fit" to the model function $f(t, x)$, where $f: \mathbb{R}^{n+1} \to \mathbb{R}$. By best fit we mean

$$\min_x \sum_{i=1}^{m} (y_i - f(t_i, x))^2,$$

which is called a *least squares* solution because the sum of squares of differences between model and data is minimized. Such a problem is usually known as *regression analysis* in statistics. Note that the quantity being minimized is just the square of the Euclidean 2-norm. Other norms, such as the 1-norm or ∞-norm, can be used instead, but they are less convenient computationally and give different results with different statistical properties.

A least squares problem is *linear* if the function f is linear in the components of the parameter vector x, which means that f is a linear combination

$$f(t, x) = x_1\phi_1(t) + x_2\phi_2(t) + \cdots + x_n\phi_n(t)$$

of functions ϕ_j that depend only on t.

EXAMPLE 3.1 DATA FITTING. Polynomial fitting, with

$$f(t, x) = x_1 + x_2 t + x_3 t^2 + \cdots + x_n t^{n-1},$$

is a linear least squares problem because a polynomial is linear in its coefficients, although nonlinear in the independent variable t. An example of a nonlinear least squares data-fitting problem is a sum of exponentials

$$f(t, x) = x_1 e^{x_2 t} + \cdots + x_{n-1} e^{x_n t}.$$

We will consider nonlinear least squares problems in Section 6.4, but in this chapter we will confine our attention to linear least squares problems. We will be concerned only with numerical algorithms for solving least squares problems. For the many important statistical considerations in formulating least squares problems and in interpreting the results, consult any book on regression analysis or multivariate statistics.

3.2 LINEAR LEAST SQUARES

A linear least squares data-fitting problem can be written in matrix notation as

$$Ax \approx b,$$

where $a_{ij} = \phi_j(t_i)$ and $b_i = y_i$. For example, in fitting a quadratic polynomial, which has three parameters, to the five data points $(t_1, y_1), \ldots, (t_5, y_5)$, the matrix A is 5×3, and the problem has the form

$$Ax = \begin{bmatrix} 1 & t_1 & t_1^2 \\ 1 & t_2 & t_2^2 \\ 1 & t_3 & t_3^2 \\ 1 & t_4 & t_4^2 \\ 1 & t_5 & t_5^2 \end{bmatrix} \begin{bmatrix} x_1 \\ x_2 \\ x_3 \end{bmatrix} \approx \begin{bmatrix} y_1 \\ y_2 \\ y_3 \\ y_4 \\ y_5 \end{bmatrix} = b.$$

A matrix A of this particular form, whose columns (or rows) are successive powers of some independent variable, is called a *Vandermonde matrix*.

In least squares problems we write $Ax \approx b$ rather than $Ax = b$ because the "equation" is not usually satisfiable exactly. The approximate nature of least squares solutions should not disturb us, however, because the goal is to smooth out random errors in the data and capture the underlying trend. The method of least squares was developed by Gauss for solving problems in astronomy, particularly determining the orbits of celestial bodies such as planets and comets. The elliptical orbit of such a body is determined by five parameters, so in principle only five observations of its position should be necessary to determine the complete orbit. Owing to measurement errors, however, an orbit based on only five observations would be highly unreliable. Instead, many more observations are taken and a least squares fit performed in order to smooth out the errors and obtain more accurate values for the orbital parameters.

As we will see, an $m \times n$ linear least squares problem $Ax \approx b$ has a unique solution provided that rank$(A) = n$ (i.e., the columns of A are linearly independent). If rank$(A) < n$, then A is said to be *rank-deficient*, and the corresponding linear least squares problem does not have a unique solution. We will consider the implications of rank deficiency later, but for now we will assume that A has full rank.

EXAMPLE 3.2 LINEAR LEAST SQUARES DATA FITTING. We illustrate linear least squares by fitting a quadratic polynomial to the following five data points:

t	−1.0	−0.5	0.0	0.5	1.0
y	1.0	0.5	0.0	0.5	2.0

The overdetermined 5×3 linear system is therefore

$$Ax = \begin{bmatrix} 1 & -1.0 & 1.0 \\ 1 & -0.5 & 0.25 \\ 1 & 0.0 & 0.0 \\ 1 & 0.5 & 0.25 \\ 1 & 1.0 & 1.0 \end{bmatrix} \begin{bmatrix} x_1 \\ x_2 \\ x_3 \end{bmatrix} \approx \begin{bmatrix} 1.0 \\ 0.5 \\ 0.0 \\ 0.5 \\ 2.0 \end{bmatrix} = b.$$

The solution to this system, which we will see later how to compute, turns out to be $x = \begin{bmatrix} 0.086 & 0.40 & 1.4 \end{bmatrix}^T$, which means that the approximating polynomial is

$$p(t) = 0.086 + 0.4t + 1.4t^2.$$

The resulting curve and the original data points are shown in Fig. 3.1. The least squares solution minimizes the sum of squares of vertical distances between the data points and the curve over all possible quadratic polynomials.

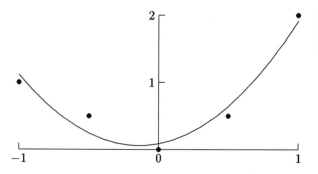

FIGURE 3.1
Least squares fit of a quadratic polynomial to the given data.

3.3 NORMAL EQUATIONS METHOD

The classical method for solving least squares problems, due to Gauss, can be derived in a variety of ways. We first show how it can be derived using calculus. In matrix notation, the least squares criterion for data fitting can be expressed as minimizing the squared Euclidean norm

$$\|r\|_2^2 = r^T r$$

of the residual vector

$$r = b - Ax.$$

To minimize

$$\|r\|_2^2 = r^T r = (b - Ax)^T (b - Ax) = b^T b - 2x^T A^T b + x^T A^T Ax,$$

we take the derivative with respect to x and set it to zero:

$$2A^T Ax - 2A^T b = 0,$$

which reduces to an $n \times n$ square linear system

$$A^T Ax = A^T b,$$

commonly known as the system of *normal equations*. The name comes from the fact that the (i, j) entry of the matrix $A^T A$ is the inner product of the ith and jth columns of A; for this reason $A^T A$ is also sometimes called the *cross-product matrix* of A. Provided rank$(A) = n$ (i.e., the columns of A are linearly independent), the matrix $A^T A$ is nonsingular, so that the system of normal equations has a unique solution, which is also the unique solution to the original least squares problem.

3.3.1 Orthogonality

A more geometric derivation of the normal equations is based on the concept of orthogonality. Two vectors y and z are said to be *orthogonal* to each other, which is a synonym for *perpendicular* or *normal*, if their inner product is zero, $y^T z = 0$.

Since the matrix A has n columns, the space spanned by the columns of A (i.e., the set of all vectors of the form Ax), known as the *column space* or *range space* of A, is of dimension n at most. In the usual case for least squares, $m > n$, this fact implies that the m-vector b generally does not lie in the column space of A, and hence there is no exact solution to the equation $Ax = b$. Rather than an exact solution, however, in least squares problems we seek the vector in the column space of A that is closest to b (in the Euclidean norm), which is given by the orthogonal projection of b onto the column space of A. For this vector, the residual $r = b - Ax$ is orthogonal to the column space of A. Thus, we have

$$0 = A^T r = A^T (b - Ax),$$

or

$$A^T Ax = A^T b,$$

which is again the system of normal equations. The geometric relationships we have just described are shown in Fig. 3.2. This interpretation also suggests when the least

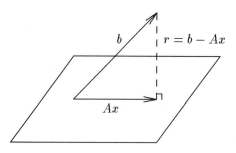

FIGURE 3.2
Geometric depiction of a linear least squares problem.

squares solution will be unique, for the orthogonal projection of b onto the column space of A will have a unique representation of the form Ax if and only if the columns of A are linearly independent.

3.3.2 Normal Equations Method

If A has full column rank, then the matrix $A^T A$ is nonsingular. Therefore, the $n \times n$ system of normal equations

$$A^T A x = A^T b$$

can be used to obtain the solution x to the linear least squares problem $Ax \approx b$. In fact, in this case $A^T A$ is symmetric and positive definite, so we can compute its Cholesky factorization,

$$A^T A = LL^T,$$

where L is lower triangular. The solution x to the least squares problem can then be computed by solving the triangular systems $Ly = A^T b$ and $L^T x = y$.

The normal equations method is an example of the general strategy noted earlier, where a difficult problem is converted to successively easier ones having the same solution. In this case, the sequence of problem transformations is

$$\text{Rectangular} \quad \longrightarrow \quad \text{square} \quad \longrightarrow \quad \text{triangular.}$$

Unfortunately, this method also illustrates another important fact, namely, that a problem transformation that is legitimate theoretically is not always advisable numerically, as we will see shortly.

EXAMPLE 3.3 NORMAL EQUATIONS METHOD. We illustrate the normal equations method by using it to solve the quadratic polynomial data-fitting problem given in Example 3.2:

$$A^T A = \begin{bmatrix} 1 & 1 & 1 & 1 & 1 \\ -1.0 & -0.5 & 0.0 & 0.5 & 1.0 \\ 1.0 & 0.25 & 0.0 & 0.25 & 1.0 \end{bmatrix} \begin{bmatrix} 1 & -1.0 & 1.0 \\ 1 & -0.5 & 0.25 \\ 1 & 0.0 & 0.0 \\ 1 & 0.5 & 0.25 \\ 1 & 1.0 & 1.0 \end{bmatrix} = \begin{bmatrix} 5.0 & 0.0 & 2.5 \\ 0.0 & 2.5 & 0.0 \\ 2.5 & 0.0 & 2.125 \end{bmatrix},$$

$$A^T b = \begin{bmatrix} 1 & 1 & 1 & 1 & 1 \\ -1.0 & -0.5 & 0.0 & 0.5 & 1.0 \\ 1.0 & 0.25 & 0.0 & 0.25 & 1.0 \end{bmatrix} \begin{bmatrix} 1.0 \\ 0.5 \\ 0.0 \\ 0.5 \\ 2.0 \end{bmatrix} = \begin{bmatrix} 4.0 \\ 1.0 \\ 3.25 \end{bmatrix}.$$

We previously computed the Cholesky factorization of this symmetric positive definite matrix in Example 2.12:

$$\begin{bmatrix} 5.0 & 0.0 & 2.5 \\ 0.0 & 2.5 & 0.0 \\ 2.5 & 0.0 & 2.125 \end{bmatrix} = \begin{bmatrix} 2.236 & 0 & 0 \\ 0 & 1.581 & 0 \\ 1.118 & 0 & 0.935 \end{bmatrix} \begin{bmatrix} 2.236 & 0 & 1.118 \\ 0 & 1.581 & 0 \\ 0 & 0 & 0.935 \end{bmatrix} = LL^T.$$

Solving the lower triangular system $Ly = A^T b$ by forward substitution, we obtain

$$y = \begin{bmatrix} 1.789 \\ 0.632 \\ 1.336 \end{bmatrix}.$$

Finally, solving the upper triangular system $L^T x = y$ by back-substitution, we obtain

$$x = \begin{bmatrix} 0.086 \\ 0.400 \\ 1.429 \end{bmatrix}.$$

In theory the system of normal equations gives the exact solution to a linear least squares problem, but in practice this system can provide disappointingly inaccurate results. Some of the potential difficulties are these:

1. Information can be lost in forming the normal equations matrix and right-hand-side vector. For example, take

$$A = \begin{bmatrix} 1 & 1 \\ \epsilon & 0 \\ 0 & \epsilon \end{bmatrix},$$

where ϵ is a positive number smaller than the square root of machine precision, $\sqrt{\epsilon_{mach}}$, in a given floating-point system. Then

$$A^T A = \begin{bmatrix} 1 + \epsilon^2 & 1 \\ 1 & 1 + \epsilon^2 \end{bmatrix},$$

so that in floating-point arithmetic

$$fl(A^T A) = \begin{bmatrix} 1 & 1 \\ 1 & 1 \end{bmatrix},$$

which is exactly singular.

2. The sensitivity of the solution is worsened, in that the condition of the normal equations matrix is worse than that of the original matrix A. Specifically, the condition number of the matrix is squared:

$$\text{cond}(A^T A) = [\text{cond}(A)]^2.$$

(We will see in Section 4.5.2 how to assign a condition number to a rectangular matrix. For now, think of it as a measure of the distance to the closest rank-deficient matrix.)

These shortcomings do not make the normal equations method useless, but they are cause for concern and provide motivation for seeking more numerically robust methods for linear least squares problems.

3.3.3 Augmented System Method

The *augmented system method* is a variant of the normal equations method that can be useful in some situations. Together, the definition of the residual vector r and the requirement that the residual be orthogonal to the columns of A give the system of two equations

$$r + Ax = b,$$

$$A^T r = 0,$$

which can be written in matrix form as the $(m + n) \times (m + n)$ augmented system

$$\begin{bmatrix} I & A \\ A^T & 0 \end{bmatrix} \begin{bmatrix} r \\ x \end{bmatrix} = \begin{bmatrix} b \\ 0 \end{bmatrix},$$

whose solution yields both the desired vector x and the residual vector r.

At first glance, this method does not look promising: The augmented system is symmetric but not positive definite, it is larger than the original system, and it requires that we store two copies of A. Moreover, if we simply pivot along the diagonal (equivalent to block elimination in the block 2×2 system), we reproduce the normal equations, whose potential numerical shortcomings we have already observed. The one advantage we have gained is that other pivoting strategies are now available, which can be beneficial for numerical or other reasons.

The selection of pivots in computing a symmetric indefinite (see Section 2.5.2) or LU factorization of the augmented system matrix will obviously depend on the relative magnitudes of the entries in the upper and lower block rows. Since the relative scales of r and x are arbitrary, we introduce a scaling parameter α for the residual, giving the new system

$$\begin{bmatrix} \alpha I & A \\ A^T & 0 \end{bmatrix} \begin{bmatrix} r/\alpha \\ x \end{bmatrix} = \begin{bmatrix} b \\ 0 \end{bmatrix}.$$

The parameter α controls the relative weights of the entries in the two subsystems in choosing pivots from either. A reasonable rule of thumb is to take

$$\alpha = \max_{i,j} |a_{ij}|/1000,$$

but some experimentation may be required to determine the best value.

A straightforward implementation of this method can be prohibitive in cost [proportional to $(m+n)^3$], so the special structure of the augmented matrix must be carefully exploited. For example, the augmented system method is used effectively in **MATLAB** for large sparse linear least squares problems.

3.4 ORTHOGONALIZATION METHODS

Owing to the potential numerical difficulties with the normal equations system, we need an alternative method that does not require formation of the normal equations matrix and right-hand-side vector. Thus, we seek a more numerically robust transformation that produces a new problem whose solution is the same as that of the original least squares problem but is more easily computed. We will see that, as with square linear systems, triangular form is a suitable target in simplifying least squares problems. To preserve the solution, however, we will need a new type of transformation to achieve triangular form.

3.4.1 Triangular Least Squares Problems

As we did with square linear systems, let us consider a least squares problem having an upper triangular matrix. In the overdetermined case, where $m > n$, such a problem has the form

$$\begin{bmatrix} R \\ 0 \end{bmatrix} x \approx \begin{bmatrix} b_1 \\ b_2 \end{bmatrix},$$

where R is an $n \times n$ upper triangular matrix and where we have partitioned the right-hand-side vector b similarly. Then we have

$$\|r\|_2^2 = \|b - Ax\|_2^2 = \|b_1 - Rx\|_2^2 + \|b_2\|_2^2.$$

We have no control over the second term, $\|b_2\|_2^2$, in the foregoing sum, but the first term can be forced to be zero by choosing x to satisfy the triangular system

$$Rx = b_1,$$

which can be solved by back-substitution. We have therefore found the least squares solution x and can also conclude that the minimum sum of squares is

$$\|r\|_2^2 = \|b_2\|_2^2.$$

3.4.2 Orthogonal Transformations

Reducing a matrix to triangular form via Gaussian elimination is not appropriate for solving least squares problems, for such a transformation does not preserve the Euclidean norm and hence does not preserve the solution to the problem. We now define a type of linear transformation that does preserve the Euclidean norm.

A matrix Q is said to be *orthogonal* if its columns are orthonormal, i.e., if $Q^T Q = I$, the identity matrix. Orthogonal transformations preserve the Euclidean norm, since

$$\|Qx\|_2^2 = (Qx)^T Qx = x^T Q^T Qx = x^T x = \|x\|_2^2.$$

Orthogonal matrices can transform vectors in various ways, such as rotation or reflection; but they do not change the Euclidean length of a vector. Hence, they preserve the solution to a linear least squares problem.

Orthogonal matrices are of great importance in many areas of numerical computation because their norm-preserving property means that they do not amplify error. Thus, for example, orthogonal transformations can be used to solve square linear systems *without* the need for pivoting for numerical stability. Unfortunately, orthogonalization methods are significantly more expensive computationally than methods based on Gaussian elimination, so their superior numerical properties come at a price that may or may not be worthwhile, depending on context.

3.4.3 QR Factorization

Given an $m \times n$ matrix A, with $m \geq n$, we seek an $m \times m$ orthogonal matrix Q such that

$$A = Q \begin{bmatrix} R \\ 0 \end{bmatrix},$$

where R is $n \times n$ and upper triangular. Such a *QR factorization* transforms the linear least squares problem $Ax \approx b$ into a triangular least squares problem having the same solution because

$$\|b - Ax\|_2 = \left\| b - Q \begin{bmatrix} R \\ 0 \end{bmatrix} x \right\|_2 = \left\| Q^T b - \begin{bmatrix} R \\ 0 \end{bmatrix} x \right\|_2.$$

As with Gaussian elimination, we wish to introduce zeros successively into the matrix A, eventually reaching upper triangular form, but doing so using orthogonal transformations. A number of methods are possible, including

- Householder transformations (elementary reflectors)
- Givens transformations (plane rotations)
- Gram-Schmidt orthogonalization

We will focus mainly on the use of Householder transformations, the most popular and generally the most effective approach in this context; but we will sketch the other two methods as well.

QR factorization has many other uses besides solving least squares problems. For example, if we partition Q into Q_1, containing the first n columns, and Q_2, containing the remaining $m - n$ columns, then we have

$$A = Q \begin{bmatrix} R \\ 0 \end{bmatrix} = [Q_1 \quad Q_2] \begin{bmatrix} R \\ 0 \end{bmatrix} = Q_1 R.$$

Thus, if A has full column rank, so that R is nonsingular, then the columns of Q_1 form an orthonormal basis for the range space of A; and the columns of Q_2 form an orthonormal basis for its orthogonal complement, which is the same as the *null space* of A^T (i.e., the set of all vectors x such that $A^T x = 0$). Such orthonormal bases are useful in eigenvalue computations, optimization, and many other problems, as we will see.

3.4.4 Householder Transformations

A Householder transformation H is a matrix of the form

$$H = I - 2\frac{vv^T}{v^T v},$$

where v is a nonzero vector. From the definition, we see that $H = H^T = H^{-1}$, so that H is both orthogonal and symmetric. Given a vector a, we wish to choose the vector v so that

$$Ha = \begin{bmatrix} \alpha \\ 0 \\ \vdots \\ 0 \end{bmatrix} = \alpha \begin{bmatrix} 1 \\ 0 \\ \vdots \\ 0 \end{bmatrix} = \alpha e_1.$$

Using the formula for H, we have

$$\alpha e_1 = Ha = (I - 2\frac{vv^T}{v^T v})a = a - v\frac{2v^T a}{v^T v},$$

and hence

$$v = (a - \alpha e_1)\frac{v^T v}{2v^T a}.$$

But the scalar factor is irrelevant in determining v, since it divides out in the formula for H anyway, so we can take

$$v = a - \alpha e_1.$$

To preserve the norm, we must have $\alpha = \pm\|a\|_2$, and the sign should be chosen to avoid cancellation. Another potential numerical difficulty is that the computation of $\|a\|_2$ could incur unnecessary overflow or underflow if the components of a are very large or very small. Dividing a at the outset by its component of largest magnitude prevents this problem. Again, such a scale factor does not change the resulting transformation H.

EXAMPLE 3.4 HOUSEHOLDER TRANSFORMATION. To illustrate the construction just described, we determine a Householder transformation that annihilates all but the first component of the vector

$$a = \begin{bmatrix} 2 \\ 1 \\ 2 \end{bmatrix}.$$

Following the foregoing recipe, we choose the vector

$$v = a - \alpha e_1 = \begin{bmatrix} 2 \\ 1 \\ 2 \end{bmatrix} - \alpha \begin{bmatrix} 1 \\ 0 \\ 0 \end{bmatrix} = \begin{bmatrix} 2 \\ 1 \\ 2 \end{bmatrix} - \begin{bmatrix} \alpha \\ 0 \\ 0 \end{bmatrix},$$

where $\alpha = \pm \|a\|_2 = \pm 3$. Since a_1 is positive, we can avoid cancellation by choosing the negative sign for α. We therefore have

$$v = \begin{bmatrix} 2 \\ 1 \\ 2 \end{bmatrix} - \begin{bmatrix} -3 \\ 0 \\ 0 \end{bmatrix} = \begin{bmatrix} 5 \\ 1 \\ 2 \end{bmatrix}.$$

To confirm that the Householder transformation performs as expected, we compute

$$Ha = a - 2\frac{v^T a}{v^T v}v = \begin{bmatrix} 2 \\ 1 \\ 2 \end{bmatrix} - 2\frac{15}{30}\begin{bmatrix} 5 \\ 1 \\ 2 \end{bmatrix} = \begin{bmatrix} -3 \\ 0 \\ 0 \end{bmatrix},$$

which shows that the zero pattern of the result is correct and that the norm is preserved. Note that there is no need to form the matrix H explicitly, as the vector v is all we need to apply H to any vector.

Using Householder transformations, we can successively introduce zeros column by column below the diagonal of a matrix A to reduce it to upper triangular form. Each Householder transformation must be applied to the remaining unreduced portion of the matrix, but it will not affect any columns already reduced (and hence the zeros are preserved). In applying a Householder transformation H to an arbitrary vector x, we note that

$$Hx = \left(I - 2\frac{vv^T}{v^T v}\right)x = x - \left(2\frac{v^T x}{v^T v}\right)v,$$

which is substantially cheaper to compute than a general matrix-vector multiplication and requires only that we know the vector v.

The process just described produces a factorization of the form

$$H_n \cdots H_1 A = \begin{bmatrix} R \\ 0 \end{bmatrix},$$

where R is upper triangular. The product of the successive Householder transformations $H_n \cdots H_1$ is itself an orthogonal matrix. Thus, if we take

$$Q^T = H_n \cdots H_1, \quad \text{or equivalently,} \quad Q = H_1^T \cdots H_n^T,$$

then

$$A = Q\begin{bmatrix} R \\ 0 \end{bmatrix}.$$

Hence, we have indeed computed the QR factorization of the matrix A, which we can now use to solve the linear least squares problem. To preserve the solution, however, we must also transform the right-hand-side vector b by the same sequence of Householder transformations. We thus solve the equivalent triangular least squares problem

$$\begin{bmatrix} R \\ 0 \end{bmatrix} x \approx Q^T b.$$

For purposes of solving the linear least squares problem, the product Q of the Householder transformations need not be explicitly formed. In most software for this problem, R is stored in the upper triangle of the original array containing A, while the vectors v required for forming the individual Householder transformations are stored in the (now zero) lower triangular portion of A. (Technically, one additional vector of storage is required, since the main diagonals of both Q and R must be stored.) As we have already seen, Householder transformations are most easily applied in this form anyway (as opposed to explicit matrix-vector multiplication), so the vectors v are all that is needed to solve the original least squares problem as well as any subsequent problems having the same matrix but different right-hand-side vectors. If Q is needed explicitly for some other reason, however, then it can be computed by multiplying each Householder transformation in sequence times a matrix that is initially the identity, but this computation will require additional storage.

EXAMPLE 3.5 HOUSEHOLDER QR FACTORIZATION. We illustrate Householder QR factorization by using it to solve the quadratic polynomial data-fitting problem in Example 3.2, with

$$A = \begin{bmatrix} 1 & -1.0 & 1.0 \\ 1 & -0.5 & 0.25 \\ 1 & 0.0 & 0.0 \\ 1 & 0.5 & 0.25 \\ 1 & 1.0 & 1.0 \end{bmatrix}, \qquad b = \begin{bmatrix} 1.0 \\ 0.5 \\ 0.0 \\ 0.5 \\ 2.0 \end{bmatrix}.$$

The Householder vector v_1 for annihilating the subdiagonal entries of the first column of A is

$$v_1 = \begin{bmatrix} 1 \\ 1 \\ 1 \\ 1 \\ 1 \end{bmatrix} - \begin{bmatrix} -2.236 \\ 0 \\ 0 \\ 0 \\ 0 \end{bmatrix} = \begin{bmatrix} 3.236 \\ 1 \\ 1 \\ 1 \\ 1 \end{bmatrix}.$$

Applying the resulting Householder transformation H_1 yields the transformed matrix and right-hand side

$$H_1 A = \begin{bmatrix} -2.236 & 0 & -1.118 \\ 0 & -0.191 & -0.405 \\ 0 & 0.309 & -0.655 \\ 0 & 0.809 & -0.405 \\ 0 & 1.309 & 0.345 \end{bmatrix}, \qquad H_1 b = \begin{bmatrix} -1.789 \\ -0.362 \\ -0.862 \\ -0.362 \\ 1.138 \end{bmatrix}.$$

The Householder vector v_2 for annihilating the subdiagonal entries of the second column of $H_1 A$ is

$$v_2 = \begin{bmatrix} 0 \\ -0.191 \\ 0.309 \\ 0.809 \\ 1.309 \end{bmatrix} - \begin{bmatrix} 0 \\ 1.581 \\ 0 \\ 0 \\ 0 \end{bmatrix} = \begin{bmatrix} 0 \\ -1.772 \\ 0.309 \\ 0.809 \\ 1.309 \end{bmatrix}.$$

Applying the resulting Householder transformation H_2 yields

$$H_2 H_1 A = \begin{bmatrix} -2.236 & 0 & -1.118 \\ 0 & 1.581 & 0 \\ 0 & 0 & -0.725 \\ 0 & 0 & -0.589 \\ 0 & 0 & 0.047 \end{bmatrix}, \qquad H_2 H_1 b = \begin{bmatrix} -1.789 \\ 0.632 \\ -1.035 \\ -0.816 \\ 0.404 \end{bmatrix}.$$

The Householder vector v_3 for annihilating the subdiagonal entries of the third column of $H_2 H_1 A$ is

$$v_3 = \begin{bmatrix} 0 \\ 0 \\ -0.725 \\ -0.589 \\ 0.047 \end{bmatrix} - \begin{bmatrix} 0 \\ 0 \\ 0.935 \\ 0 \\ 0 \end{bmatrix} = \begin{bmatrix} 0 \\ 0 \\ -1.660 \\ -0.589 \\ 0.047 \end{bmatrix}.$$

Applying the resulting Householder transformation H_3 yields

$$H_3 H_2 H_1 A = \begin{bmatrix} -2.236 & 0 & -1.118 \\ 0 & 1.581 & 0 \\ 0 & 0 & 0.935 \\ 0 & 0 & 0 \\ 0 & 0 & 0 \end{bmatrix}, \qquad H_3 H_2 H_1 b = \begin{bmatrix} -1.789 \\ 0.632 \\ 1.336 \\ 0.026 \\ 0.337 \end{bmatrix}.$$

We can now solve the upper triangular system $Rx = y$, where y consists of the first three components of the transformed right-hand side, by back-substitution to obtain

$$x = \begin{bmatrix} 0.086 \\ 0.400 \\ 1.429 \end{bmatrix}.$$

3.4.5 Givens Rotations

Householder transformations introduce many zeros in a column at once. Although generally good for efficiency, this approach can be a bit heavy-handed when greater selectivity is needed in introducing zeros. For this reason, some algorithms use Givens rotations instead, which introduce zeros one at a time.

We seek an orthogonal matrix that annihilates a single given component of a vector. One such orthogonal matrix is a *plane rotation*, often called a Givens rotation in the context of QR factorization. Given a 2-vector $a = \begin{bmatrix} a_1 & a_2 \end{bmatrix}^T$, we want to choose scalars c and s, which can be interpreted as the cosine and sine of the angle of rotation, such that

$$\begin{bmatrix} c & s \\ -s & c \end{bmatrix} \begin{bmatrix} a_1 \\ a_2 \end{bmatrix} = \begin{bmatrix} \alpha \\ 0 \end{bmatrix},$$

with $c^2 + s^2 = 1$, or, equivalently, $\alpha = \sqrt{a_1^2 + a_2^2}$. In effect, we will rotate a so that it is aligned with the first coordinate axis. Then its second component will become zero. The previous equation can be rewritten as

$$\begin{bmatrix} a_1 & a_2 \\ a_2 & -a_1 \end{bmatrix} \begin{bmatrix} c \\ s \end{bmatrix} = \begin{bmatrix} \alpha \\ 0 \end{bmatrix}.$$

We can now perform Gaussian elimination on this system to obtain the triangular system

$$\begin{bmatrix} a_1 & a_2 \\ 0 & -a_1 - a_2^2/a_1 \end{bmatrix} \begin{bmatrix} c \\ s \end{bmatrix} = \begin{bmatrix} \alpha \\ -\alpha a_2/a_1 \end{bmatrix}.$$

Back-substitution then gives

$$s = \frac{\alpha a_2}{a_1^2 + a_2^2}, \qquad c = \frac{\alpha a_1}{a_1^2 + a_2^2}.$$

Finally, the requirement that $c^2 + s^2 = 1$, or $\alpha = \sqrt{a_1^2 + a_2^2}$, implies that

$$c = \frac{a_1}{\sqrt{a_1^2 + a_2^2}}, \qquad s = \frac{a_2}{\sqrt{a_1^2 + a_2^2}}.$$

As with Householder transformations, unnecessary overflow or underflow can be avoided by appropriate scaling. If $|a_1| > |a_2|$, then we can work with the tangent of the angle of rotation, $t = s/c = a_2/a_1$, so that the cosine and sine are given by

$$c = 1/\sqrt{1 + t^2}, \qquad s = c \cdot t.$$

If $|a_2| > |a_1|$, on the other hand, then we can use the analogous formulas involving the cotangent $\tau = c/s = a_1/a_2$, obtaining

$$s = 1/\sqrt{1 + \tau^2}, \qquad c = s \cdot \tau.$$

In either case, we can avoid squaring any magnitude larger than 1. Note that the angle of rotation need not be determined explicitly, as only its cosine and sine are actually needed.

EXAMPLE 3.6 GIVENS ROTATION. To illustrate the construction just described, we determine a Givens rotation that annihilates the second component of the vector

$$a = \begin{bmatrix} 4 \\ 3 \end{bmatrix}.$$

For this problem, we can safely compute the cosine and sine directly, obtaining

$$c = \frac{a_1}{\sqrt{a_1^2 + a_2^2}} = \frac{4}{5} = 0.8 \quad \text{and} \quad s = \frac{a_2}{\sqrt{a_1^2 + a_2^2}} = \frac{3}{5} = 0.6,$$

or, equivalently, we can use the tangent $t = a_2/a_1 = 3/4 = 0.75$ to obtain

$$c = \frac{1}{\sqrt{1 + (0.75)^2}} = \frac{1}{1.25} = 0.8 \quad \text{and} \quad s = c \cdot t = (0.8)(0.75) = 0.6.$$

Thus, the rotation is given by

$$G = \begin{bmatrix} c & s \\ -s & c \end{bmatrix} = \begin{bmatrix} 0.8 & 0.6 \\ -0.6 & 0.8 \end{bmatrix}.$$

To confirm that the rotation performs as expected, we compute

$$Ga = \begin{bmatrix} 0.8 & 0.6 \\ -0.6 & 0.8 \end{bmatrix} \begin{bmatrix} 4 \\ 3 \end{bmatrix} = \begin{bmatrix} 5 \\ 0 \end{bmatrix},$$

which shows that the zero pattern of the result is correct and that the norm is preserved. Note that the value of the angle rotation, which in this case is about 36.87 degrees, does not enter directly into the computation and need not be determined explicitly.

We have seen how to design a plane rotation to annihilate a given component of a vector in two dimensions. To annihilate a selected component of a vector in n dimensions, we can apply the same technique by rotating the target component, say j, with another component, say i. The two selected components of the vector are used as before to determine the appropriate 2×2 rotation matrix, which is then embedded as a 2×2 submatrix in rows and columns i and j of the n-dimensional identity matrix, as illustrated here for the case $n = 5$, $i = 2$, $j = 4$:

$$\begin{bmatrix} 1 & 0 & 0 & 0 & 0 \\ 0 & c & 0 & s & 0 \\ 0 & 0 & 1 & 0 & 0 \\ 0 & -s & 0 & c & 0 \\ 0 & 0 & 0 & 0 & 1 \end{bmatrix} \begin{bmatrix} a_1 \\ a_2 \\ a_3 \\ a_4 \\ a_5 \end{bmatrix} = \begin{bmatrix} a_1 \\ \alpha \\ a_3 \\ 0 \\ a_5 \end{bmatrix}.$$

Using a sequence of such Givens rotations, we can selectively and systematically annihilate entries of a matrix A to reduce the matrix to upper triangular form. The only restriction on the order in which we annihilate entries is that we should avoid reintroducing nonzero values into matrix entries that have previously been annihilated, but this can be accomplished by a number of different orderings. Once again, the product of all of the rotations is itself an orthogonal matrix that gives us the desired QR factorization.

A straightforward implementation of the Givens method for solving general linear least squares problems requires about 50 percent more work than the Householder method. It also requires more storage, since each rotation requires two numbers, c and s, to define it (and hence the zeroed entry a_{ij} does not suffice for storage). These work and storage disadvantages can be overcome to make the Givens method competitive with the Householder method, but at the cost of a more complicated implementation. Therefore, the Givens method is generally reserved for situations in which its greater selectivity is of paramount importance, such as when the matrix is sparse or when some particular pattern of existing zeros must be maintained.

As with Householder transformations, the matrix Q need not be formed explicitly because multiplication by the successive rotations produces the same effect as multiplication by Q. If Q is needed explicitly for some other reason, however, then it can be computed by multiplying each rotation in sequence times a matrix that is initially the identity.

EXAMPLE 3.7 GIVENS QR FACTORIZATION. We illustrate Givens QR factorization by using it to solve the quadratic polynomial data-fitting problem in Example 3.2, with

$$
A = \begin{bmatrix} 1 & -1.0 & 1.0 \\ 1 & -0.5 & 0.25 \\ 1 & 0.0 & 0.0 \\ 1 & 0.5 & 0.25 \\ 1 & 1.0 & 1.0 \end{bmatrix}, \qquad b = \begin{bmatrix} 1.0 \\ 0.5 \\ 0.0 \\ 0.5 \\ 2.0 \end{bmatrix}.
$$

We can annihilate the $(5,1)$ entry of A using a Givens rotation based on the fourth and fifth entries of the first column. The appropriate rotation is given by $c = 0.707$, $s = 0.707$. Applying this rotation G_1 to A and b yields

$$
G_1 A = \begin{bmatrix} 1 & 0 & 0 & 0 & 0 \\ 0 & 1 & 0 & 0 & 0 \\ 0 & 0 & 1 & 0 & 0 \\ 0 & 0 & 0 & 0.707 & 0.707 \\ 0 & 0 & 0 & -0.707 & 0.707 \end{bmatrix} \begin{bmatrix} 1 & -1.0 & 1.0 \\ 1 & -0.5 & 0.25 \\ 1 & 0.0 & 0.0 \\ 1 & 0.5 & 0.25 \\ 1 & 1.0 & 1.0 \end{bmatrix} = \begin{bmatrix} 1 & -1.0 & 1.0 \\ 1 & -0.5 & 0.25 \\ 1 & 0.0 & 0.0 \\ 1.414 & 1.061 & 0.884 \\ 0 & 0.354 & 0.530 \end{bmatrix}
$$

and

$$
G_1 b = \begin{bmatrix} 1 & 0 & 0 & 0 & 0 \\ 0 & 1 & 0 & 0 & 0 \\ 0 & 0 & 1 & 0 & 0 \\ 0 & 0 & 0 & 0.707 & 0.707 \\ 0 & 0 & 0 & -0.707 & 0.707 \end{bmatrix} \begin{bmatrix} 1.0 \\ 0.5 \\ 0.0 \\ 0.5 \\ 2.0 \end{bmatrix} = \begin{bmatrix} 1.0 \\ 0.5 \\ 0.0 \\ 1.768 \\ 1.061 \end{bmatrix}.
$$

We next annihilate the $(4,1)$ entry using a Givens rotation based on the third and fourth entries of the first column. The appropriate rotation is given by $c = 0.577$, $s = 0.816$. Applying this rotation G_2 yields

$$
G_2 G_1 A = \begin{bmatrix} 1 & 0 & 0 & 0 & 0 \\ 0 & 1 & 0 & 0 & 0 \\ 0 & 0 & 0.577 & 0.816 & 0 \\ 0 & 0 & -0.816 & 0.577 & 0 \\ 0 & 0 & 0 & 0 & 1 \end{bmatrix} \begin{bmatrix} 1 & -1.0 & 1.0 \\ 1 & -0.5 & 0.25 \\ 1 & 0.0 & 0.0 \\ 1.414 & 1.061 & 0.884 \\ 0 & 0.354 & 0.530 \end{bmatrix} = \begin{bmatrix} 1 & -1.0 & 1.0 \\ 1 & -0.5 & 0.25 \\ 1.732 & 0.866 & 0.722 \\ 0 & 0.612 & 0.510 \\ 0 & 0.354 & 0.530 \end{bmatrix}
$$

and

$$
G_2 G_1 b = \begin{bmatrix} 1 & 0 & 0 & 0 & 0 \\ 0 & 1 & 0 & 0 & 0 \\ 0 & 0 & 0.577 & 0.816 & 0 \\ 0 & 0 & -0.816 & 0.577 & 0 \\ 0 & 0 & 0 & 0 & 1 \end{bmatrix} \begin{bmatrix} 1.0 \\ 0.5 \\ 0.0 \\ 1.768 \\ 1.061 \end{bmatrix} = \begin{bmatrix} 1.0 \\ 0.5 \\ 1.443 \\ 1.020 \\ 1.061 \end{bmatrix}.
$$

We continue up the first column in this manner until all of its subdiagonal entries have been annihilated. We then proceed similarly to the second and third columns, eventually producing the upper triangular matrix and transformed right-hand side

$$Q^T A = \begin{bmatrix} 2.236 & 0 & 1.118 \\ 0 & 1.581 & 0 \\ 0 & 0 & 0.935 \\ 0 & 0 & 0 \\ 0 & 0 & 0 \end{bmatrix}, \quad Q^T b = \begin{bmatrix} 1.789 \\ 0.632 \\ 1.336 \\ 0.338 \\ 0 \end{bmatrix},$$

where Q^T is the product of all of the Givens rotations used. We can now solve the upper triangular system by back-substitution to obtain

$$x = \begin{bmatrix} 0.086 \\ 0.400 \\ 1.429 \end{bmatrix}.$$

3.4.6 Gram-Schmidt Orthogonalization

Another method for computing the QR factorization is the Gram-Schmidt orthogonalization process, which you may have seen in a calculus or linear algebra course. Given two vectors a_1 and a_2, we can determine two orthonormal vectors q_1 and q_2 that span the same subspace by orthogonalizing one of the given vectors against the other, as shown in Fig. 3.3.

This process can be extended to an arbitrary number of vectors a_k (up to the dimension of the space) by orthogonalizing each successive vector against all of the previous ones, giving the classical Gram-Schmidt orthogonalization procedure:

> **for** $k = 1$ **to** n
> $\quad q_k = a_k$
> $\quad$ **for** $j = 1$ **to** $k - 1$
> $\quad\quad r_{jk} = q_j^T a_k$
> $\quad\quad q_k = q_k - r_{jk} q_j$
> $\quad$ **end**
> $\quad r_{kk} = \|q_k\|_2$
> $\quad q_k = q_k / r_{kk}$
> **end**

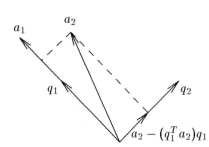

FIGURE 3.3
One step of Gram-Schmidt orthogonalization.

If we take the a_k to be the columns of the matrix A, then the resulting q_k are the columns of Q and the r_{ij} are the entries of the upper triangular matrix R in the QR factorization of A.

Unfortunately, the classical Gram-Schmidt procedure requires separate storage for A, Q, and R because the original a_k are needed in the inner loop, and hence the q_k cannot overwrite the columns of A. This shortcoming can be alleviated, however, if we orthogonalize each chosen vector in turn against all of the subsequent vectors, in effect generating the upper triangular matrix R by rows rather than by columns. This rearrangement of the computation is known as *modified* Gram-Schmidt orthogonalization:

> **for** $k = 1$ **to** n
> $\quad r_{kk} = \|a_k\|_2$
> $\quad q_k = a_k/r_{kk}$
> $\quad$ **for** $j = k + 1$ **to** n
> $\quad\quad r_{kj} = q_k^T a_j$
> $\quad\quad a_j = a_j - r_{kj} q_k$
> $\quad$ **end**
> **end**

We have continued to write the a_k and q_k separately for clarity, but now they can in fact share the same storage. (A programmer would have formulated the algorithm this way in the first place.) Unfortunately, separate storage for Q and R is still required, a disadvantage compared with the Householder method, for which Q and R can share the space formerly occupied by A. On the other hand, Gram-Schmidt provides an explicit representation for Q, which, if desired, would require additional storage with the Householder method.

In addition to requiring less storage than the classical procedure, an added bonus of modified Gram-Schmidt is that it is also numerically superior to classical Gram-Schmidt: the two procedures are mathematically equivalent, but in finite-precision arithmetic the classical procedure tends to lose orthogonality among the computed q_k. The modified procedure also permits the use of column pivoting to deal with possible rank deficiency (see Section 3.4.8). Although the modified Gram-Schmidt procedure has advantages in some circumstances, for solving least squares problems it is somewhat inferior to the Householder method in storage, work, and accuracy.

EXAMPLE 3.8 GRAM-SCHMIDT QR FACTORIZATION. We illustrate modified Gram-Schmidt orthogonalization by again solving the quadratic polynomial data-fitting problem in Example 3.2, with

$$A = \begin{bmatrix} 1 & -1.0 & 1.0 \\ 1 & -0.5 & 0.25 \\ 1 & 0.0 & 0.0 \\ 1 & 0.5 & 0.25 \\ 1 & 1.0 & 1.0 \end{bmatrix}, \qquad b = \begin{bmatrix} 1.0 \\ 0.5 \\ 0.0 \\ 0.5 \\ 2.0 \end{bmatrix}.$$

Normalizing the first column of A, we compute

$$r_{1,1} = \|a_1\|_2 = 2.236, \qquad q_1 = a_1/r_{1,1} = \begin{bmatrix} 0.447 \\ 0.447 \\ 0.447 \\ 0.447 \\ 0.447 \end{bmatrix}.$$

Orthogonalizing the first column against the subsequent columns, we get

$$r_{1,2} = q_1^T a_2 = 0, \qquad r_{1,3} = q_1^T a_3 = 1.118,$$

so that the matrix is transformed to become

$$\begin{bmatrix} 0.477 & -1.0 & 0.50 \\ 0.447 & -0.5 & -0.25 \\ 0.447 & 0.0 & -0.50 \\ 0.447 & 0.5 & -0.25 \\ 0.447 & 1.0 & 0.50 \end{bmatrix}.$$

Normalizing the second column, we compute

$$r_{2,2} = \|a_2\|_2 = 1.581, \qquad q_2 = a_2/r_{2,2} = \begin{bmatrix} -0.632 \\ -0.316 \\ 0 \\ 0.316 \\ 0.632 \end{bmatrix}.$$

Orthogonalizing the second column against the third column, we get

$$r_{2,3} = q_2^T a_3 = 0,$$

so that the third column is unaffected. Finally, we normalize the third column

$$r_{3,3} = \|a_3\|_2 = 0.935, \qquad q_3 = a_3/r_{3,3} = \begin{bmatrix} 0.535 \\ -0.267 \\ -0.535 \\ -0.267 \\ 0.535 \end{bmatrix}.$$

We have thus obtained the QR factorization

$$A = \begin{bmatrix} 0.447 & -0.632 & 0.535 \\ 0.447 & -0.316 & -0.267 \\ 0.447 & 0 & -0.535 \\ 0.447 & 0.316 & -0.267 \\ 0.447 & 0.632 & 0.535 \end{bmatrix} \begin{bmatrix} 2.236 & 0 & 1.118 \\ 0 & 1.581 & 0 \\ 0 & 0 & 0.935 \end{bmatrix} = QR.$$

The transformed right-hand side is obtained from

$$Q^T b = \begin{bmatrix} 0.447 & 0.447 & 0.447 & 0.447 & 0.447 \\ -0.632 & -0.316 & 0 & 0.316 & 0.632 \\ 0.535 & -0.267 & -0.535 & -0.267 & 0.535 \end{bmatrix} \begin{bmatrix} 1.0 \\ 0.5 \\ 0.0 \\ 0.5 \\ 2.0 \end{bmatrix} = \begin{bmatrix} 1.789 \\ 0.632 \\ 1.336 \end{bmatrix}.$$

We can now solve the upper triangular system $Rx = Q^T b$ by back-substitution to obtain

$$x = \begin{bmatrix} 0.086 \\ 0.400 \\ 1.429 \end{bmatrix}.$$

3.4.7 Rank Deficiency

So far we have assumed that A is of full rank, $\text{rank}(A) = n$. If this is not the case, i.e., if A has linearly dependent columns, then the QR factorization still exists, but the upper triangular factor R is singular (as is $A^T A$). Thus, many vectors x give the same minimum residual norm, and the least squares solution is not unique. This situation usually arises from a poorly designed experiment, insufficient data, or an inadequate or redundant model. Thus, the problem should probably be reformulated or rethought.

If one insists on forging ahead as is, however, then a common practice is to select the minimum residual solution x having the smallest norm. This may be computed by QR factorization with column pivoting, which we consider next, or by the singular value decomposition (SVD), which we will study in Section 4.5. Note that such a procedure for dealing with rank deficiency also enables us to handle underdetermined problems, where $m < n$, since the columns of A are necessarily linearly dependent in that case.

In practice, the rank of a matrix is often not clear-cut. Thus, a relative tolerance is used to detect near rank deficiency of least squares problems, just as in detecting near singularity of square linear systems. If a least squares problem is nearly rank-deficient, then the solution will be sensitive to perturbations in the input data. We will be able to examine these issues more precisely when we introduce the singular value decomposition of a matrix in Section 4.5. Within the context of QR factorization, the most robust method for detecting and dealing with possible rank deficiency is *column pivoting,* which we consider next.

EXAMPLE 3.9 NEAR RANK DEFICIENCY. Consider the 3×2 matrix

$$A = \begin{bmatrix} 0.641 & 0.242 \\ 0.321 & 0.121 \\ 0.962 & 0.363 \end{bmatrix}.$$

If we compute the QR factorization of A, we find that

$$R = \begin{bmatrix} 1.1997 & 0.4527 \\ 0 & 0.0002 \end{bmatrix}.$$

Thus, R is extremely close to being singular (indeed, it is exactly singular to the three-digit accuracy with which the problem was stated), and if we use R to solve a least squares problem, the result will be correspondingly sensitive to perturbations in the right-hand side. For practical purposes, the rank of A is only one rather than two, since its columns are nearly linearly dependent.

3.4.8 Column Pivoting

The columns of a matrix A can be viewed as an unordered set of vectors from which we wish to select a maximal linearly independent subset. Rather than processing the columns in the natural order in computing the QR factorization, we instead select for reduction at each stage the column of the remaining unreduced submatrix having maximum Euclidean norm. This column is interchanged (explicitly or implicitly) with the next column in the natural order and then is zeroed below the diagonal in the usual manner. The transformation required to do this must then be applied to the remaining unreduced columns, and the process is repeated. The process just described is called *column pivoting*.

If rank$(A) = k < n$, then after k steps of this procedure, the norms of the remaining unreduced columns will be zero (or "negligible" in finite-precision arithmetic) below row k. Thus, we have produced an orthogonal factorization of the form

$$Q^T A P = \begin{bmatrix} R & S \\ 0 & 0 \end{bmatrix},$$

where R is $k \times k$, upper triangular, and nonsingular, and P is a permutation matrix that performs the column interchanges. At this point, a *basic solution* (i.e., a solution with only k nonzero components) to the least squares problem $Ax \approx b$ can be computed by solving the triangular system $Ry = c$, where c is a vector composed of the first k components of $Q^T b$, and then taking

$$x = P \begin{bmatrix} y \\ 0 \end{bmatrix}.$$

In the context of data fitting, this procedure amounts to ignoring components of the model that are redundant or not well-determined. If a *minimum-norm solution* is desired, however, it can be computed at the expense of some additional processing (from the right) to annihilate S as well.

In practice, the rank of A is usually unknown, so the column pivoting process is used to discover the rank by monitoring the norms of the remaining unreduced columns and terminating the factorization when the maximum value falls below some relative tolerance.

3.5 COMPARISON OF METHODS

We have now seen a number of methods for solving least squares problems. The choice among them depends on the particular problem being solved and involves trade-offs among efficiency, accuracy, and robustness.

The normal equations method is easy to implement: it simply requires matrix multiplication and Cholesky factorization. Moreover, reducing the problem to an $n \times n$ system is very attractive when $m \gg n$. By taking advantage of its symmetry, the formation of the normal equations matrix $A^T A$ requires about $n^2 m / 2$ multiplications and a similar number of additions. Solving the resulting linear system by Cholesky factorization requires about $n^3/6$ multiplications and a similar number of additions. Unfortunately, the normal equations method produces a solution whose relative error is proportional to $[\text{cond}(A)]^2$, and the required Cholesky factorization can be expected to break down if $\text{cond}(A) \approx 1/\sqrt{\epsilon_{\text{mach}}}$ or worse.

For solving dense linear least squares problems, the Householder method is generally the most efficient and accurate of the orthogonalization methods. It requires about $n^2 m - n^3/3$ multiplications and a similar number of additions. It can be shown that the Householder method produces a solution whose relative error is proportional to $\text{cond}(A) + \|r\|_2[\text{cond}(A)]^2$, which is the best that can be expected since this is the inherent sensitivity of the solution to the least squares problem itself. Moreover, the Householder method can be expected to break down (in the back-substitution phase) only if $\text{cond}(A) \approx 1/\epsilon_{\text{mach}}$ or worse.

For nearly square problems, $m \approx n$, the normal equations and Householder methods require about the same amount of work. But for highly overdetermined problems, $m \gg n$, the Householder method requires about twice as much work as the normal equations method. On the other hand, the Householder method is more accurate and more broadly applicable than the normal equations method. These advantages may not be worth the additional cost, however, when the problem is sufficiently well-conditioned that the normal equations method provides adequate accuracy. For rank-deficient or nearly rank-deficient problems, of course, the Householder method with column pivoting can produce a useful solution when the normal equations method would fail outright.

3.6 SOFTWARE FOR LINEAR LEAST SQUARES

Table 3.1 is a list of appropriate routines for solving linear least squares problems, both those having full rank and those that are rank-deficient. Most of the routines listed are based on QR factorization. Many packages also include software for the singular value decomposition (SVD), which can be used to solve least squares problems, although at greater computational expense. The SVD provides a particularly robust method for determining numerical rank and dealing with possible rank deficiency, as we will see in Section 4.5.

Conventional software for solving linear least squares problems $Ax \approx b$ is sometimes implemented as a single routine, or it may be split into two routines: one for computing a factorization and another for solving the resulting triangular system. The input typically required includes a two-dimensional array containing A, a one-dimensional array containing the right-hand-side vector b (or a two-dimensional array for multiple right-hand-side vectors), the number of rows m and number of columns n in the matrix, the leading dimension of the array containing A (so that the subroutine can interpret subscripts properly in the array), and possibly some work space and a flag indicating the particular task to be performed. The user may also need to supply the relevant tolerance if column pivoting or other means of rank determination is performed. On return, the solution x usually overwrites the storage for b, and the matrix factorization overwrites the storage for A.

TABLE 3.1
Software for linear least squares problems

Source	Factor	Solve	Rank-deficient
FMM	svd		svd
IMSL	lqrrr	lqrsl	lsqrr
KMN	sqrls	sqrls	ssvdc
LAPACK	sgeqrf	sormqr/strtrs	sgeqpf/stzrqf
Lawson/Hanson [163]	hft	hs1	hfti
LINPACK	sqrdc	sqrsl	sqrst
MATLAB	qr	\	svd
NAG	f01axf	f04anf	f04jgf
NAPACK	qr	over	sing/rsolve
NR	qrdcmp^a	qrsolv	svdcmp/svbksb
NUMAL	lsqortdec	lsqsol	solovr
SLATEC	sqrdc	sqrsl	llsia/sglss/minfit
SOL [279]	hredl	qrvslv	mnlnls

^{a}As published, qrdcmp and qrsolv handle only square matrices, but they are easily modified to handle rectangular matrices.

In **MATLAB**, the backslash operator used for solving square linear systems is extended to include rectangular systems as well. Thus, the least squares solution to the overdetermined system $Ax \approx b$ is given by **x = A \ b**. Internally, the solution is computed by QR factorization, but the user need not be aware of this. The QR factorization can be computed explicitly, if desired, by the **MATLAB qr** function, **[Q, R] = qr(A)**.

In addition to mathematical software libraries such as those listed in the table, many statistical packages have extensive software for solving least squares problems in various contexts, and they often include many diagnostic features for assessing the quality of the results. Well-known packages in this category include **BMDP**, **Minitab**, **Omnitab**, **S**, **SAS**, and **SPSS**. There is also a statistics toolbox available for **MATLAB**. Additional software is available for data fitting using criteria other than least squares, particularly for the 1-norm and the ∞-norm, which are preferable in some contexts.

3.7 HISTORICAL NOTES AND FURTHER READING

The normal equations method for least squares problems, due to Gauss, dates from around 1800, and Gram-Schmidt orthogonalization from around 1900. The orthogonalization methods of Householder and Givens date from the late 1950s, and the numerically stable modified form of Gram-Schmidt orthogonalization dates from the 1960s. The use of orthogonalization, particularly the Householder method, for solving least squares problems was popularized by Golub [101]. A tutorial introduction to Householder transformations (treating only square systems) can be found in [28]. Comprehensive references on least squares computations include [19, 76, 163]. The books on matrix computations cited in Chapter 2 also discuss linear least squares problems in some detail. For a statistical perspective on least squares computations, see [148, 254].

We have discussed only the simplest type of least squares problems, in which the model function is linear, only the values y_i of the dependent variable are subject to random error (i.e., the values t_i of the independent variable t are taken as exact), and all of the data points are weighted equally. We will discuss nonlinear least squares problems in Section 6.4. Incorporating varying weights for the data points or more general cross-correlations among the variables is relatively straightforward within the framework we have discussed. Allowing varying weights for the data points, for example, simply involves multiplying both sides of the least squares system by a diagonal matrix. When all of the variables are subject to random error, so that the entries of the matrix A as well as those of the right-hand-side vector b are uncertain, then minimizing the vertical distances between the data points and the fitted curve may no longer be appropriate. Minimizing the orthogonal distances between the data points and the curve is a reasonable alternative. It yields a more complicated computational problem, but one that is still tractable using the singular value decomposition (see Section 4.5.2). For a thorough discussion of this approach, called *total least squares*, see [259].

REVIEW QUESTIONS

3.1. True or false: If you are given four or more data points, then fitting a straight line to the data is a linear least squares problem, whereas fitting a quadratic polynomial to the data is a nonlinear least squares problem.

3.2. True or false: At the solution to a linear least squares problem $Ax \approx b$, the residual vector $r = b - Ax$ is orthogonal to the column space of A.

3.3. True or false: An overdetermined linear least squares problem $Ax \approx b$ always has a unique solution x that minimizes the Euclidean norm of the residual vector $r = b - Ax$.

3.4. True or false: In solving a linear least squares problem $Ax \approx b$, if the vector b lies in the column space of the matrix A, then the residual is 0.

3.5. True or false: In solving a linear least squares problem $Ax \approx b$, if the residual is 0, then the solution x must be unique.

3.6. True or false: The product of a Householder transformation and a Givens rotation is always an orthogonal matrix.

3.7. True or false: If the $n \times n$ matrix Q is a Householder transformation, and x is an arbitrary n-vector,

then the last k components of the vector Qx are zero for some $k < n$.

3.8. True or false: Methods based on orthogonal factorization are generally more expensive computationally than methods based on the normal equations for solving linear least squares problems.

3.9. (*a*) In a data-fitting problem in which m data points (t_i, y_i) are fit by a model function $f(t, x)$, where t is the independent variable and x is an n-vector of parameters to be determined, what does it mean for the function f to be *linear* in the components of x?

(*b*) Give an example of a model function $f(t, x)$ that is linear in this sense.

(*c*) Give an example of a model function $f(t, x)$ that is nonlinear.

3.10. In a linear least squares problem $Ax \approx b$, where A is an $m \times n$ matrix, if $\text{rank}(A) < n$, then which of the following situations are possible?

(*a*) There is no solution.

(*b*) There is a unique solution.

(*c*) There is a solution, but it is not unique.

3.11. In solving an overdetermined least squares problem $Ax \approx b$, which would be a more serious difficulty: that the rows of A are linearly dependent, or that the columns of A are linearly dependent? Explain.

3.12. In an overdetermined linear least squares problem with model function $f(t, x) = x_1\phi_1(t) + x_2\phi_2(t) + x_3\phi_3(t)$, what will be the rank of the resulting least squares matrix A if we take $\phi_1(t) = 1$, $\phi_2(t) = t$, and $\phi_3(t) = 1 - t$?

3.13. What is the system of normal equations for the linear least squares problem $Ax \approx b$?

3.14. List two ways in which use of the normal equations for solving linear least squares problems may suffer loss of numerical accuracy.

3.15. Let A be an $m \times n$ matrix. Under what conditions on the matrix A will the matrix $A^T A$ be
  (a) Symmetric?
  (b) Nonsingular?
  (c) Positive definite?

3.16. Which of the following properties of an $m \times n$ matrix A, with $m > n$, indicate that the minimum residual solution of the least squares problem $Ax \approx b$ is **not** unique?
  (a) The columns of A are linearly dependent.
  (b) The rows of A are linearly dependent.
  (c) The matrix $A^T A$ is singular.

3.17. (a) Can Gaussian elimination with pivoting be used to compute an LU factorization of a rectangular $m \times n$ matrix A, where L is an $m \times k$ matrix whose entries above its main diagonal are all zero, U is a $k \times n$ matrix whose entries below its main diagonal are all zero, and $k = \min\{m, n\}$?
  (b) If this were possible, would it provide a way to solve an overdetermined least squares problem $Ax \approx b$, where $m > n$? Why?

3.18. (a) What is meant by two vectors x and y being *orthogonal* to each other?
  (b) Prove that if two nonzero vectors are orthogonal to each other, then they must also be linearly independent.
  (c) Give an example of two nonzero vectors in the plane that are orthogonal to each other.
  (d) Give an example of two nonzero vectors in the plane that are not orthogonal to each other.
  (e) List two ways in which orthogonality is important in the context of linear least squares problems.

3.19. In Euclidean n-space, is orthogonality a transitive relation? That is, if x is orthogonal to y, and y is orthogonal to z, is x necessarily orthogonal to z?

3.20. (a) Why are orthogonal transformations, such as Householder or Givens, often used to solve least squares problems?
  (b) Why are such methods not often used to solve square linear systems?
  (c) Do orthogonal transformations have any advantage over Gaussian elimination for solving square linear systems? If so, state one.

3.21. Which of the following matrices are orthogonal?
  (a) $\begin{bmatrix} 0 & 1 \\ 1 & 0 \end{bmatrix}$

  (b) $\begin{bmatrix} 1 & 0 \\ 0 & -1 \end{bmatrix}$

  (c) $\begin{bmatrix} 2 & 0 \\ 0 & \frac{1}{2} \end{bmatrix}$

  (d) $\begin{bmatrix} \sqrt{2}/2 & \sqrt{2}/2 \\ -\sqrt{2}/2 & \sqrt{2}/2 \end{bmatrix}$

3.22. Which of the following properties does an $n \times n$ orthogonal matrix necessarily have?
  (a) It is nonsingular.
  (b) It preserves the Euclidean vector norm when multiplied times a vector.
  (c) Its transpose is its inverse.
  (d) Its columns are orthonormal.
  (e) It is symmetric.
  (f) It is diagonal.
  (g) Its Euclidean matrix norm is 1.
  (h) Its condition number in the Euclidean norm is 1.

3.23. Which of the following types of matrices are necessarily orthogonal?
  (a) Permutation
  (b) Symmetric positive definite
  (c) Householder transformation
  (d) Givens rotation
  (e) Nonsingular
  (f) Diagonal

3.24. Show that multiplication by an orthogonal matrix Q preserves the Euclidean norm of a vector x.

3.25. What condition must a nonzero n-vector w satisfy to ensure that the matrix $H = I - 2ww^T$ is orthogonal?

3.26. If Q is a 2×2 orthogonal matrix such that

$$Q\begin{bmatrix}1\\1\end{bmatrix} = \begin{bmatrix}\alpha\\0\end{bmatrix},$$

what must the value of α be?

3.27. How many scalar multiplications are required to multiply an arbitrary n-vector by an $n \times n$ Householder transformation matrix $H = I - 2ww^T$, where w is an n-vector with $\|w\|_2 = 1$?

3.28. Given a vector a, in designing a Householder transformation H such that $Ha = \alpha e_1$, we know that $\alpha = \pm\|a\|_2$. On what basis should the sign be chosen?

3.29. List one advantage and one disadvantage of Givens rotations for QR factorization compared with Householder transformations.

3.30. When used to annihilate the second component of a 2-vector, does a Householder transformation always give the same result as a Givens rotation?

3.31. In addition to the input array containing the matrix A, which can be overwritten, how much additional auxiliary array storage is required to compute and store the following?

(*a*) The LU factorization of A by Gaussian elimination with partial pivoting, where A is $n \times n$

(*b*) The QR factorization of A by Householder transformations, where A is $m \times n$

3.32. In solving a linear least squares problem $Ax \approx b$, where A is an $m \times n$ matrix with $m \geq n$ and rank(A) <

n, at what point will the least squares solution process break down (assuming exact arithmetic)?

(*a*) Using Cholesky factorization to solve the normal equations

(*b*) Using QR factorization by Householder transformations

3.33. Compared to the classical Gram-Schmidt procedure, which of the following are advantages of modified Gram-Schmidt orthogonalization?

(*a*) Requires less storage

(*b*) Requires less work

(*c*) Is more stable numerically

3.34. For computing the QR factorization of an $m \times n$ matrix, with $m \geq n$, how large must n be before there is a difference between the classical and modified Gram-Schmidt procedures?

3.35. Explain why the Householder method requires less storage than the modified Gram-Schmidt method for computing the QR factorization of a matrix A.

3.36. Explain how QR factorization with column pivoting can be used to determine the rank of a matrix.

3.37. Explain why column pivoting can be used with the modified Gram-Schmidt orthogonalization procedure but not with the classical Gram-Schmidt procedure.

3.38. In terms of the condition number of the matrix A, compare the range of applicability of the normal equations method and the Householder QR method for solving the linear least squares problem $Ax \approx b$ [i.e., for what values of cond(A) can each method be expected to break down?].

EXERCISES

3.1. If a vertical beam has a downward force applied at its lower end, the amount by which it stretches will be proportional to the magnitude of the force. Thus, the total length y of the beam is given by the equation

$$y = x_1 + x_2 t,$$

where x_1 is its original length, t is the force applied, and x_2 is the proportionality constant. Suppose that the following measurements are taken:

t	10	15	20
y	11.60	11.85	12.25

(a) Set up the overdetermined 3×2 system of linear equations corresponding to the data collected.

(b) Is this system consistent? If not, compute each possible pair of values for (x_1, x_2) obtained by selecting any two of the equations from the system. Is there any reason to prefer any one of these results?

(c) Set up the system of normal equations and solve it to obtain the least squares solution to the overdetermined system. Compare your result with those obtained in part b.

3.2. Suppose you are fitting a straight line to the three data points $(0, 1)$, $(1, 2)$, $(3, 3)$.

(a) Set up the overdetermined linear system for the least squares problem.

(b) Set up the corresponding normal equations.

(c) Compute the least squares solution by Cholesky factorization.

3.3. Set up the linear least squares system $Ax \approx b$ for fitting the model function $f(t, x) = x_1 t + x_2 e^t$ to the three data points $(1, 2)$, $(2, 3)$, $(3, 5)$.

3.4. In fitting a straight line $y = x_0 + x_1 t$ to the three data points $(t_i, y_i) = (0, 0)$, $(1, 0)$, $(1, 1)$, is the least squares solution unique? Why?

3.5. Let x be the solution to the linear least squares problem $Ax \approx b$, where

$$A = \begin{bmatrix} 1 & 0 \\ 1 & 1 \\ 1 & 2 \\ 1 & 3 \end{bmatrix}.$$

Let $r = b - Ax$ be the corresponding residual vector. Which of the following three vectors is a possible value for r? Why?

(a) $\begin{bmatrix} 1 \\ 1 \\ 1 \\ 1 \end{bmatrix}$ (b) $\begin{bmatrix} -1 \\ -1 \\ 1 \\ 1 \end{bmatrix}$ (c) $\begin{bmatrix} -1 \\ 1 \\ 1 \\ -1 \end{bmatrix}$

3.6. (a) What is the Euclidean norm of the minimum residual vector for the following linear least squares problem?

$$\begin{bmatrix} 1 & 1 \\ 0 & 1 \\ 0 & 0 \end{bmatrix} \begin{bmatrix} x_1 \\ x_2 \end{bmatrix} \approx \begin{bmatrix} 2 \\ 1 \\ 1 \end{bmatrix}$$

(b) What is the solution vector x for this problem?

3.7. Let A be an $m \times n$ matrix and b an m-vector.

(a) Prove that a solution to the least squares problem $Ax \approx b$ always exists.

(b) Prove that such a solution is unique if and only if rank$(A) = n$.

3.8. Suppose that A is an $m \times n$ matrix of rank n. Prove that the matrix $A^T A$ is positive definite.

3.9. Prove that the augmented system matrix in Section 3.3.3 *cannot* be positive definite.

3.10. Let A be an $n \times n$ matrix, and assume that A is both orthogonal and triangular.

(a) Prove that A must be diagonal.

(b) What are the diagonal entries of A?

3.11. Suppose that the partitioned matrix

$$\begin{bmatrix} A & B \\ 0 & C \end{bmatrix}$$

is orthogonal, where the submatrices A and C are square. Prove that A and C must be orthogonal, and $B = 0$.

3.12. (a) Let A be an $n \times n$ matrix. Show that any two of the following conditions imply the other:

$$A^T = A$$
$$A^T A = I$$
$$A^2 = I$$

(b) Give a specific example, other than the identity matrix or a permutation of it, of a 3×3 matrix that has all three of these properties.

(c) Name a nontrivial class of matrices that have all three of these properties.

3.13. Show that if the vector $v \neq 0$, then the matrix

$$H = I - 2\frac{vv^T}{v^T v}$$

is orthogonal and symmetric.

3.14. Let a be any nonzero vector. If $v = a - \alpha e_1$, where $\alpha = \pm \|a\|_2$, and

$$H = I - 2\frac{vv^T}{v^T v},$$

show that $Ha = \alpha e_1$.

3.15. Consider the vector a as an $n \times 1$ matrix.

(a) Write out its QR factorization, showing the matrices Q and R explicitly.

(b) What is the solution to the linear least squares problem $ax \approx b$, where b is a given n-vector?

3.16. Determine the Householder transformation that annihilates all but the first entry of the vector $\begin{bmatrix} 1 & 1 & 1 & 1 \end{bmatrix}^T$. Specifically, if

$$\left(I - 2\frac{vv^T}{v^T v}\right)\begin{bmatrix} 1 \\ 1 \\ 1 \\ 1 \end{bmatrix} = \begin{bmatrix} \alpha \\ 0 \\ 0 \\ 0 \end{bmatrix},$$

what are the values of the scalar α and the vector v?

3.17. Suppose that you are computing the QR factorization of the matrix

$$\begin{bmatrix} 1 & 1 & 1 \\ 1 & 2 & 4 \\ 1 & 3 & 9 \\ 1 & 4 & 16 \end{bmatrix}$$

by Householder transformations.

(a) How many Householder transformations are required?

(b) What does the first column of A become as a result of applying the first Householder transformation?

(c) What does the first column then become as a result of applying the second Householder transformation?

(d) How many Givens rotations would be required to compute the QR factorization of the same matrix?

3.18. Consider the vector

$$a = \begin{bmatrix} 2 \\ 3 \\ 4 \end{bmatrix}.$$

(a) Specify an elementary elimination matrix that annihilates the third component of a.

(b) Specify a Householder transformation that annihilates the third component of a.

(c) Specify a Givens rotation that annihilates the third component of a.

(d) When annihilating a given nonzero component of any vector, is it ever possible for the corresponding elementary elimination matrix and Householder transformation to be the same? Why?

(e) When annihilating a given nonzero component of any vector, is it ever possible for the corresponding Householder transformation and Givens rotation to be the same? Why?

3.19. Suppose you want to annihilate the second component of a vector

$$a = \begin{bmatrix} a_1 \\ a_2 \end{bmatrix}$$

using a Givens rotation, but a_1 is already zero.

(a) Is it still possible to annihilate a_2 with a Givens rotation? If so, specify an appropriate Givens rotation; if not, explain why.

(b) Under these circumstances, can a_2 be annihilated with an elementary elimination matrix? If so, how? If not, why?

3.20. A Givens rotation is defined by two parameters, c and s, and therefore would appear to require two storage locations in a computer implementation. The two parameters depend on a single angle of rotation, however, so in principle it should be possible to record the rotation by storing only one number. Devise an algorithm for storing and recovering Givens rotations using only one storage location per rotation.

3.21. Let A be an $m \times n$ matrix of rank n. Let

$$A = Q\begin{bmatrix} R \\ 0 \end{bmatrix}$$

be the QR factorization of A, with Q orthogonal and R an $n \times n$ upper triangular matrix. Let $A^T A = LL^T$ be the Cholesky factorization of $A^T A$.

(a) Show that $R^T R = LL^T$.

(b) Can one conclude that $R = L^T$? Why?

3.22. In Section 3.3 we observed that the normal equations matrix $A^T A$ is exactly singular in floating-point arithmetic if

$$A = \begin{bmatrix} 1 & 1 \\ \epsilon & 0 \\ 0 & \epsilon \end{bmatrix},$$

where ϵ is a positive number smaller than the square root of machine precision ϵ_{mach} in a given floating-point system. Show that if $A = QR$ is the QR factorization for this matrix A, then R is *not* singular, even in floating-point arithmetic.

3.23. Verify that the dominant terms in the operation count (number of multiplications or number of additions) for solving an $m \times n$ linear least squares problem by the normal equations and Cholesky factorization are $n^2m/2 + n^3/6$.

3.24. Verify that the dominant terms in the operation count (number of multiplications or number of additions) for QR factorization of an $m \times n$ matrix by Householder transformations are $n^2m - n^3/3$.

3.25. An $n \times n$ matrix P is a *projector* if it is both idempotent ($P^2 = P$) and symmetric ($P = P^T$). Such a matrix projects any given n-vector onto a subspace (namely, the column space of P) but leaves unchanged any vector that is already in that subspace.

(*a*) Suppose that Q is an $n \times k$ matrix whose columns form an orthonormal basis for a subspace S of $\mathbb{R}^n$. Show that QQ^T is a projector onto S.

(*b*) If A is a matrix with linearly independent columns, show that $A(A^T A)^{-1} A^T$ is a projector onto the column space of A. How does this result relate to the linear least squares problem?

(*c*) If P is a projector onto a subspace S, show that $I - P$ is a projector onto the orthogonal complement of S.

(*d*) Let v be any nonzero n-vector. What is the projector onto the subspace spanned by v?

(*e*) In the Gram-Schmidt procedure of Section 3.4.6, if we define the projectors $P_k = q_k q_k^T$, $k = 1, \ldots, n$, show that the classical Gram-Schmidt procedure is equivalent to

$$q_k = (I - (P_1 + \cdots + P_{k-1}))a_k,$$

whereas the modified Gram-Schmidt procedure is equivalent to

$$q_k = (I - P_{k-1})\cdots(I - P_1)a_k.$$

(*f*) An alternative way to stabilize the classical procedure is to apply it more than once (i.e., iterative

refinement), which is equivalent to taking

$$q_k = (I - (P_1 + \cdots + P_{k-1}))^m a_k,$$

where $m = 2$ is typically sufficient. Show that all three of these variations are mathematically equivalent (though they may differ markedly in finite-precision arithmetic).

3.26 Let v be a nonzero n-vector. The hyperplane normal to v is the $(n - 1)$-dimensional subspace of all vectors y such that $v^T y = 0$. A *reflector* is a linear transformation R such that $Rx = -x$ if x is a scalar multiple of v, and $Rx = x$ if $v^T x = 0$. Thus, the hyperplane acts as a mirror: for any vector, its component within the hyperplane is invariant, whereas its component orthogonal to the hyperplane is reversed.

(*a*) Show that $R = 2P - I$, where P is the projector onto the hyperplane normal to v. Draw a picture to illustrate this result geometrically.

(*b*) Show that R is symmetric and orthogonal.

(*c*) Show that the Householder transformation

$$H = I - 2\frac{vv^T}{v^T v},$$

is a reflector.

(*d*) Show that for any two vectors s and t such that $s \neq t$ and $\|s\|_2 = \|t\|_2$, there is a reflector R such that $Rs = t$.

(*e*) Show that any orthogonal matrix Q is a product of reflectors.

(*f*) Illustrate the previous result by expressing the plane rotation

$$\begin{bmatrix} c & s \\ -s & c \end{bmatrix},$$

where $c^2 + s^2 = 1$, as a product of two reflectors. For some specific angle of rotation, draw a picture to show the mirrors.

COMPUTER PROBLEMS

3.1. For $n = 0, 1, \ldots, 5$, fit a polynomial of degree n by least squares to the following data:

t	0.0	1.0	2.0	3.0	4.0	5.0
y	1.0	2.7	5.8	6.6	7.5	9.9

Make a plot of the original data points along with each resulting polynomial curve (you may make separate graphs for each curve or a single graph containing all of the curves). Which polynomial would you say captures the general trend of the data better? Obviously, this is a subjective question, and its answer depends on both the nature of the given data (e.g., the uncertainty of the data values) and the purpose of the fit. Explain your assumptions in answering.

3.2. A common problem in surveying is to determine the altitudes of a series of points with respect to some reference point. Since the measurements are subject to error, more observations are taken than are strictly necessary to determine the altitudes, and the resulting overdetermined system is solved in the least squares sense to smooth out errors. Suppose that there are four points whose altitudes x_1, x_2, x_3, x_4 are to be determined. In addition to direct measurements of each x_i with respect to the reference point, measurements are also taken of each point with respect to all of the others. The resulting set of measurements is as follows:

$$x_1 = 2.95, \qquad x_2 = 1.74,$$
$$x_3 = -1.45, \qquad x_4 = 1.32,$$
$$x_1 - x_2 = 1.23, \qquad x_1 - x_3 = 4.45,$$
$$x_1 - x_4 = 1.61, \qquad x_2 - x_3 = 3.21,$$
$$x_2 - x_4 = 0.45, \qquad x_3 - x_4 = -2.75.$$

Set up the corresponding least squares system $Ax \approx b$ and use a library routine, or one of your own design, to solve it for the best values of the altitudes. How do the computed values compare with the direct measurements of the same quantities?

3.3. (*a*) For a series of matrices A of order n, record the execution times for a library routine to compute the LU factorization of A. Using a linear least squares routine, or one of your own design, fit a cubic polynomial to the execution times as a function of n. To obtain reliable results, use a fairly wide range of values for n, say, in increments of 100 from 100 up to several hundred, depending on the speed and available memory of the computer you use. You may obtain more accurate timings by averaging several runs for a given matrix size. The resulting cubic polynomial could be used to predict the execution time for other values of n not tried, such as very large values for n. What is the predicted execution time for a matrix of order 10,000?

(*b*) Try to determine the basic execution rate (in floating-point operations per second, or *flops*) for your computer by timing a known computation, such as matrix multiplication. You can then use this information to determine the complexity of LU factorization, based on

the polynomial fit to the execution times. After converting to floating-point operations, how does the dominant term compare with the theoretically expected value of $\frac{4}{3} n^3$ (counting both additions and multiplications)? Try to explain any discrepancy. If you use a system that provides operation counts automatically, such as **MATLAB** or some supercomputers, try this same experiment fitting the operation counts directly.

3.4. (*a*) Solve the following least squares problem using any method you like:

$$\begin{bmatrix} 0.16 & 0.10 \\ 0.17 & 0.11 \\ 2.02 & 1.29 \end{bmatrix} \begin{bmatrix} x_1 \\ x_2 \end{bmatrix} \approx \begin{bmatrix} 0.26 \\ 0.28 \\ 3.31 \end{bmatrix}.$$

(*b*) Now solve the same least squares problem again, but this time use the slightly perturbed right-hand side

$$b = \begin{bmatrix} 0.27 \\ 0.25 \\ 3.33 \end{bmatrix}.$$

(*c*) Compare your results from parts *a* and *b*. Can you explain this difference?

3.5. A planet follows an elliptical orbit, which can be represented in a Cartesian (x, y) coordinate system by the equation

$$ay^2 + bxy + cx + dy + e = x^2.$$

(*a*) Use a library routine, or one of your own design, for linear least squares to determine the orbital parameters a, b, c, d, e, given the following observations of the planet's position:

x	1.02	0.95	0.87	0.77	0.67
y	0.39	0.32	0.27	0.22	0.18

x	0.56	0.44	0.30	0.16	0.01
y	0.15	0.13	0.12	0.13	0.15

In addition to printing the values for the orbital parameters, plot the resulting orbit and the given data points in the (x, y) plane.

(*b*) This least squares problem is nearly rank-deficient. To see what effect this has on the solution, perturb the input data slightly by adding to each coordinate of each data point a random number uniformly distributed on the interval $[-0.005, 0.005]$ (see Section 13.5) and solve the least squares problem with the perturbed data. Compare the new values for the parameters with those previously computed. What effect does this difference have on the plot of the orbit? Can you explain this behavior?

(c) Solve the same least squares problem again, for both the original and the perturbed data, this time using a library routine (or one of your own design) specifically designed to deal with rank deficiency (by using column pivoting, for example). Such a routine usually includes as an input parameter a tolerance to be used in determining the numerical rank of the matrix. Experiment with various values for the tolerance, say, 10^{-k}, $k = 1, \ldots, 5$. What is the resulting rank of the matrix for each value of the tolerance? Compare the behavior of the two solutions (for the original and the perturbed data) with each other as the tolerance and the resulting rank change. How well do the resulting orbits fit the data points as the tolerance and rank vary? Which solution would you regard as better: one that fits the data more closely, or one that is less sensitive to small perturbations in the data? Why?

3.6. To demonstrate the numerical difference betwen the normal equations method and QR factorization for linear least squares, we need a problem that is ill-conditioned and also has a small residual. We can generate such a problem as follows. We will fit a polynomial of degree $n - 1$,

$$p_{n-1}(t) = x_1 + x_2 t + x_3 t^2 + \cdots + x_n t^{n-1}$$

to m data points (t_i, y_i), with $m > n$. We choose $t_i = (i - 1)/(m - 1)$, $i = 1, \ldots, m$, so that the data points are equally spaced on the interval $[0, 1]$. We will generate the corresponding values y_i by first choosing values for the x_j, say, $x_j = 1$, $j = 1, \ldots, n$, and evaluating the resulting polynomial to obtain $y_i = p_{n-1}(t_i)$, $i = 1, \ldots, m$. We could now see whether we can recover the x_j that we used to generate the y_i, but to make it more interesting, we first randomly perturb the y_i values to simulate the data error typical of least squares problems. Specifically, we take $y_i = y_i + (2u_i - 1) * \epsilon$, $i = 1, \ldots, m$, where each u_i is a random number uniformly distributed on the interval $[0, 1)$ (see Section 13.5) and ϵ is a small positive number that determines the maximum perturbation. If you are using the equivalent of IEEE double precision, reasonable parameters for this problem are $m = 21$, $n = 12$, and $\epsilon = 10^{-10}$.

Having generated the data set (t_i, y_i) as just outlined, we will now compare the two methods for computing the least squares solution to this polynomial data-fitting problem. First, form the system of normal equations for this problem and solve it using a library routine for Cholesky factorization. Next, solve the least squares system using a library routine for QR factorization. Compare the two resulting solution vectors x. For which method is the solution more sensitive to the perturbation we introduced into the data? Which method comes closer to recovering the x that we used to generate the data? Does the difference in solutions affect our ability to fit the data points (t_i, y_i) closely by the polynomial? Why?

3.7. Use the augmented system method of Section 3.3.3 to solve the least squares problem derived in the previous exercise. The augmented system is symmetric but not positive definite, so Cholesky factorization is not applicable, but you can use a symmetric indefinite or LU factorization. Experiment with various values for the scaling parameter α. How do the accuracy and execution time of this method compare with those of the normal equations and QR factorization methods?

3.8. The *covariance matrix* for the $m \times n$ least squares problem $Ax \approx b$ is given by $\sigma^2(A^T A)^{-1}$, where $\sigma^2 = \|b - Ax\|_2^2/(m - n)$ at the least squares solution x. The entries of this matrix contain important information about the goodness of the fit and any cross-correlations among the fitted parameters. The covariance matrix is an exception to the general rule that inverses of matrices should never be computed explicitly. If an orthogonalization method is used to solve the least squares problem, then the normal equations matrix $A^T A$ is never formed, so we need an alternative method for computing the covariance matrix.

(a) Show that $(A^T A)^{-1} = (R^T R)^{-1}$, where R is the upper triangular factor obtained by QR factorization of A.

(b) Based on this fact, implement a routine for computing the covariance matrix using only the already computed R. (For purposes of this exercise, you may ignore the scalar factor σ^2.) Test your routine on a few example matrices to confirm that it gives the same result as computing $(A^T A)^{-1}$.

3.9. Most library routines for computing the QR factorization of an $m \times n$ matrix A return the matrix R in the upper triangle of the storage for A and the Householder vectors in the lower triangle of A, with an extra vector to accommodate the overlap on the diagonal. Write a routine that takes this output array and auxiliary vector and forms the orthogonal matrix Q explicitly by multiplying the corresponding sequence of Householder transformations times an $m \times m$ matrix that is initialized to the identity. Of course, the latter will require a separate array. Test your program on several randomly chosen matrices and confirm that your computed Q is indeed orthogonal and that the product

$$Q \begin{bmatrix} R \\ 0 \end{bmatrix}$$

recovers A.

3.10. (*a*) Implement both the classical and modified Gram-Schmidt procedures and use each to generate an orthogonal matrix Q whose columns form an orthogonal basis for the column space of the Hilbert matrix H, with entries $h_{ij} = 1/(i + j - 1)$, for $n = 2, \ldots, 12$ (see Computer Problem 2.6). As a measure of the quality of the results (specifically, the potential loss of orthogonality), plot the quantity $-\log_{10}(\|I - Q^T Q\|)$, which can be interpreted as "digits of accuracy," for each method as a function of n. In addition, try applying the classical procedure twice (i.e., apply your classical Gram-Schmidt routine to its own output Q to obtain a new Q), and again plot the resulting departure from orthogonality. How do the three methods compare in speed, storage, and accuracy?

(*b*) Repeat the previous experiment, but this time use the Householder method, that is, use the explicitly computed orthogonal matrix Q resulting from Householder QR factorization of the Hilbert matrix. Note that if the routine you use for Householder QR factorization does not form Q explicitly, then you can obtain Q by multiplying the sequence of Householder transformations times a matrix that is initialized to the identity (see previous exercise). Again, plot the departure from orthogonality for this method and compare it with that of the previous methods.

(*c*) Yet another way to compute an orthogonal basis is to use the normal equations. If we form the normal equations matrix and compute its Cholesky factorization $A^T A = L L^T$, then we have

$$I = L^{-1}(A^T A)L^{-T}$$
$$= (AL^{-T})^T(AL^{-T}),$$

which means that $Q = AL^{-T}$ is orthogonal, and its column space is obviously the same as that of A. Repeat the previous experiment using Hilbert matrices again, this time using the Q obtained in this way from the normal equations (the required triangular solution may be a little tricky, depending on the software you use). Again, plot the resulting departure from orthogonality and compare it with that of the previous methods.

(*d*) Can you explain the relative quality of the results you obtained for the various methods used in these experiments?

3.11. What is the exact solution to the linear least squares problem

$$\begin{bmatrix} 1 & 1 & 1 \\ \epsilon & 0 & 0 \\ 0 & \epsilon & 0 \\ 0 & 0 & \epsilon \end{bmatrix} \approx \begin{bmatrix} 1 \\ 0 \\ 0 \\ 0 \end{bmatrix}$$

as a function of ϵ?

Solve this least squares problem using each of the following methods. For each method, experiment with the value of the parameter ϵ to see how small you can take it and still obtain an accurate solution. Pay particular attention to values around $\epsilon \approx \sqrt{\epsilon_{\text{mach}}}$ and $\epsilon \approx \epsilon_{\text{mach}}$.

   (*a*) Normal equations method
   (*b*) Augmented system method
   (*c*) Householder QR method
   (*d*) Givens QR method
   (*e*) Classical Gram-Schmidt orthogonalization
   (*f*) Modified Gram-Schmidt orthogonalization
   (*g*) Classical Gram-Schmidt orthogonalization with iterative refinement (i.e., CGS applied twice)

CHAPTER 4

Eigenvalues and Singular Values

4.1 EIGENVALUES AND EIGENVECTORS

The standard *algebraic eigenvalue problem* is as follows: Given an $n \times n$ matrix A, find a scalar λ and a nonzero vector x such that

$$Ax = \lambda x.$$

Such a scalar λ is called an *eigenvalue,* and x is a corresponding *eigenvector.* In addition to the "right" eigenvector defined above, we could also define a "left" eigenvector y such that $y^T A = \lambda y^T$, but since a left eigenvector of A is a right eigenvector of A^T, we will consider only right eigenvectors. The set of all the eigenvalues of a matrix A, denoted by $\lambda(A)$, is called the *spectrum* of A. The maximum modulus of the eigenvalues, $\max\{|\lambda| : \lambda \in \lambda(A)\}$, is called the *spectral radius* of A, denoted by $\rho(A)$.

An eigenvector of a matrix determines a direction in which the effect of the matrix is particularly simple: The matrix expands or shrinks any vector lying in that direction by a scalar multiple, and the expansion or contraction factor is given by the corresponding eigenvalue λ. Thus, eigenvalues and eigenvectors provide a means of understanding the complicated behavior of a general linear transformation by decomposing it into simpler actions.

Eigenvalue problems occur in many areas of science and engineering. For example, the natural modes and frequencies of vibration of a structure are determined by the eigenvectors and eigenvalues of an appropriate matrix. The stability of the structure is determined by the locations of the eigenvalues, and thus their computation is of critical interest. We will also see later in this book that eigenvalues can be very useful in analyzing numerical methods, such as the convergence analysis of iterative methods for solving systems of algebraic equations, and the stability analysis of methods for solving systems of differential equations.

Although most of our examples will involve only real matrices, both the theory and computational procedures we will discuss in this chapter are generally applicable to complex matrices. Notationally, the only difference in dealing with complex matrices is that the conjugate transpose, denoted by A^H, is used instead of the usual matrix transpose, A^T (recall the definitions of transpose and conjugate transpose from Section 2.5).

EXAMPLE 4.1 EIGENVALUES AND EIGENVECTORS

1. $A = \begin{bmatrix} 1 & 0 \\ 0 & 2 \end{bmatrix}$: $\lambda = 1,\ x = \begin{bmatrix} 1 \\ 0 \end{bmatrix}$ and $\lambda = 2,\ x = \begin{bmatrix} 0 \\ 1 \end{bmatrix}$.

2. $A = \begin{bmatrix} 1 & 1 \\ 0 & 2 \end{bmatrix}$: $\lambda = 1,\ x = \begin{bmatrix} 1 \\ 0 \end{bmatrix}$ and $\lambda = 2,\ x = \begin{bmatrix} 1 \\ 1 \end{bmatrix}$.

3. $A = \begin{bmatrix} 3 & -1 \\ -1 & 3 \end{bmatrix}$: $\lambda = 2,\ x = \begin{bmatrix} 1 \\ 1 \end{bmatrix}$ and $\lambda = 4,\ x = \begin{bmatrix} 1 \\ -1 \end{bmatrix}$.

4. $A = \begin{bmatrix} 1.5 & 0.5 \\ 0.5 & 1.5 \end{bmatrix}$: $\lambda = 2,\ x = \begin{bmatrix} 1 \\ 1 \end{bmatrix}$ and $\lambda = 1,\ x = \begin{bmatrix} -1 \\ 1 \end{bmatrix}$.

5. $A = \begin{bmatrix} 0 & 1 \\ -1 & 0 \end{bmatrix}$: $\lambda = i,\ x = \begin{bmatrix} 1 \\ i \end{bmatrix}$ and $\lambda = -i,\ x = \begin{bmatrix} i \\ 1 \end{bmatrix}$, where $i = \sqrt{-1}$.

Note that for Examples 1 and 2 the eigenvalues are the diagonal entries of A, and for Example 1 the eigenvectors are the columns of the identity matrix. The matrices in Examples 3 and 4 are symmetric, and the eigenvalues are real. Example 5 shows, however, that a nonsymmetric real matrix need not have real eigenvalues.

4.1.1 Nonuniqueness

Neither eigenvalues nor eigenvectors are necessarily unique, in the following senses:

- The eigenvalues of a matrix are not necessarily all distinct. That is, more than one direction may have the same expansion or contraction factor. In this case, we say that the matrix has a *multiple eigenvalue*. For example, 1 is an eigenvalue of multiplicity n for the $n \times n$ identity matrix.
- Eigenvectors can obviously be scaled arbitrarily: if $Ax = \lambda x$, then $A(\gamma x) = \lambda(\gamma x)$ for any scalar γ, so that γx is also an eigenvector corresponding to λ. For example,

$$\text{If}\quad A = \begin{bmatrix} 1 & 1 \\ 0 & 2 \end{bmatrix}, \qquad \text{then} \qquad \gamma x = \gamma \begin{bmatrix} 1 \\ 1 \end{bmatrix} = \begin{bmatrix} \gamma \\ \gamma \end{bmatrix}$$

is an eigenvector corresponding to the eigenvalue $\lambda = 2$ for any nonzero scalar γ. Consequently, eigenvectors are usually *normalized* by requiring some norm of the vector to be 1.

4.1.2 Characteristic Polynomial

The equation $Ax = \lambda x$ is equivalent to

$$(A - \lambda I)x = 0.$$

This homogeneous equation has a nonzero solution x if and only if its matrix is singular. Thus, the eigenvalues of A are the values λ such that

$$\det(A - \lambda I) = 0.$$

Now $\det(A - \lambda I)$ is a polynomial of degree n in λ, called the *characteristic polynomial* of A, and its roots are the eigenvalues of A.

EXAMPLE 4.2 CHARACTERISTIC POLYNOMIAL. As an example, consider the characteristic polynomial of one of the matrices in Example 4.1:

$$\det\left(\begin{bmatrix} 3 & -1 \\ -1 & 3 \end{bmatrix} - \lambda \begin{bmatrix} 1 & 0 \\ 0 & 1 \end{bmatrix}\right) = \det\left(\begin{bmatrix} 3 - \lambda & -1 \\ -1 & 3 - \lambda \end{bmatrix}\right)$$

$$= (3 - \lambda)(3 - \lambda) - (-1)(-1) = \lambda^2 - 6\lambda + 8 = 0,$$

so that the eigenvalues are given by

$$\lambda = \frac{6 \pm \sqrt{36 - 32}}{2} = \frac{6 \pm 2}{2} = 2 \quad \text{and} \quad 4.$$

Because the eigenvalues of a matrix are the roots of its characteristic polynomial, we can conclude from the Fundamental Theorem of Algebra that an $n \times n$ matrix A always has n eigenvalues, but they need be neither distinct nor real. The *algebraic multiplicity* of an eigenvalue is its multiplicity as a root of the characteristic polynomial. An eigenvalue of algebraic multiplicity 1 is said to be *simple*. The *geometric multiplicity* of an eigenvalue is the number of linearly independent eigenvectors corresponding to that eigenvalue. The geometric multiplicity of an eigenvalue cannot exceed the algebraic multiplicity, but it can be less than the algebraic multiplicity. An eigenvalue with the latter property is said to be *defective*. Similarly, an $n \times n$ matrix that has fewer than n linearly independent eigenvectors is said to be defective.

Although the eigenvalues are not necessarily real, complex eigenvalues of a real matrix must occur in complex conjugate pairs (i.e., if $\alpha + i\beta$ is an eigenvalue of a real matrix, then so is $\alpha - i\beta$, where $i = \sqrt{-1}$).

4.1.3 Properties of Eigenvalue Problems

Some properties of an eigenvalue problem that affect the choice of algorithm and software to solve it are as follows:

- Are all of the eigenvalues needed, or only a few?
- Are only the eigenvalues needed, or are the corresponding eigenvectors also needed?
- Is the matrix real, or complex?
- Is the matrix relatively small and dense, or large and sparse?
- Does the matrix have any special properties, such as symmetry, or is it a general matrix?

TABLE 4.1
Some properties of matrices
relevant to eigenvalue problems

Property	Definition
Symmetric	$A = A^T$
Hermitian	$A = A^H$
Orthogonal	$A^T A = A A^T = I$
Unitary	$A^H A = A A^H = I$
Normal	$A^H A = A A^H$

Some properties that a square matrix may have that are relevant to eigenvalue problems are defined in Table 4.1 (see also Section 2.5).

EXAMPLE 4.3 MATRIX PROPERTIES. The following examples illustrate some of the matrix properties relevant to eigenvalue problems:

$$\text{Transpose:} \quad \begin{bmatrix} 1 & 2 \\ 3 & 4 \end{bmatrix}^T = \begin{bmatrix} 1 & 3 \\ 2 & 4 \end{bmatrix},$$

$$\text{Conjugate transpose:} \quad \begin{bmatrix} 1+i & 1+2i \\ 2-i & 2-2i \end{bmatrix}^H = \begin{bmatrix} 1-i & 2+i \\ 1-2i & 2+2i \end{bmatrix},$$

$$\text{Symmetric:} \quad \begin{bmatrix} 1 & 2 \\ 2 & 3 \end{bmatrix}, \quad \text{nonsymmetric:} \quad \begin{bmatrix} 1 & 3 \\ 2 & 4 \end{bmatrix},$$

$$\text{Hermitian:} \quad \begin{bmatrix} 1 & 1+i \\ 1-i & 2 \end{bmatrix}, \quad \text{nonHermitian:} \quad \begin{bmatrix} 1 & 1+i \\ 1+i & 2 \end{bmatrix},$$

$$\text{Orthogonal:} \quad \begin{bmatrix} 0 & 1 \\ 1 & 0 \end{bmatrix}, \quad \begin{bmatrix} -1 & 0 \\ 0 & -1 \end{bmatrix}, \quad \text{nonorthogonal:} \quad \begin{bmatrix} 1 & 1 \\ 1 & 2 \end{bmatrix},$$

$$\text{Orthogonal:} \quad \begin{bmatrix} \sqrt{2}/2 & \sqrt{2}/2 \\ -\sqrt{2}/2 & \sqrt{2}/2 \end{bmatrix}, \quad \text{unitary:} \quad \begin{bmatrix} i\sqrt{2}/2 & \sqrt{2}/2 \\ -\sqrt{2}/2 & -i\sqrt{2}/2 \end{bmatrix},$$

$$\text{Normal:} \quad \begin{bmatrix} 1 & 2 & 0 \\ 0 & 1 & 2 \\ 2 & 0 & 1 \end{bmatrix}, \quad \text{nonnormal:} \quad \begin{bmatrix} 1 & 1 \\ 0 & 1 \end{bmatrix}.$$

4.1.4 Similarity Transformations

In keeping with our general strategy, many numerical methods for computing eigenvalues and eigenvectors are based on reducing the original matrix to a simpler form, whose eigenvalues and eigenvectors are then easily determined. Thus, we need to identify what types of transformations preserve eigenvalues, and for what types of matrices the eigenvalues are easily determined.

A matrix B is *similar* to a matrix A if there is a nonsingular matrix T such that

$$B = T^{-1}AT.$$

Then

$$By = \lambda y \quad \Rightarrow \quad T^{-1}ATy = \lambda y \quad \Rightarrow \quad A(Ty) = \lambda(Ty),$$

so that A and B have the same eigenvalues, and if y is an eigenvector of B, then $x = Ty$ is an eigenvector of A. Thus, similarity transformations preserve eigenvalues, and, although they do not preserve eigenvectors, the eigenvectors are still easily recovered. Note that the converse is not true: two matrices that are similar must have the same eigenvalues, but two matrices that have the same eigenvalues are not necessarily similar.

EXAMPLE 4.4 SIMILARITY TRANSFORMATION. From the eigenvalues and eigenvectors for one of the matrices in Example 4.1, we see that

$$AT = \begin{bmatrix} 3 & -1 \\ -1 & 3 \end{bmatrix}\begin{bmatrix} 1 & 1 \\ 1 & -1 \end{bmatrix} = \begin{bmatrix} 1 & 1 \\ 1 & -1 \end{bmatrix}\begin{bmatrix} 2 & 0 \\ 0 & 4 \end{bmatrix} = T\Lambda,$$

and hence $\quad T^{-1}AT = \begin{bmatrix} 0.5 & 0.5 \\ 0.5 & -0.5 \end{bmatrix}\begin{bmatrix} 3 & -1 \\ -1 & 3 \end{bmatrix}\begin{bmatrix} 1 & 1 \\ 1 & -1 \end{bmatrix} = \begin{bmatrix} 2 & 0 \\ 0 & 4 \end{bmatrix} = \Lambda,$

so that the original matrix is similar to the diagonal matrix, and in this case the eigenvectors form the columns of the transformation matrix T.

The eigenvalues of a diagonal matrix are its diagonal entries, and the eigenvectors are the corresponding columns of the identity matrix. Thus, diagonal form is a desirable target in simplifying eigenvalue problems for general matrices by similarity transformations. Unfortunately, some matrices cannot be transformed into diagonal form by a similarity transformation. The best that can be done, in general, is *Jordan form,* in which the matrix is reduced nearly to diagonal form but may yet have a few nonzero entries on the first superdiagonal, corresponding to one or more multiple eigenvalues.

Fortunately, every matrix can be transformed into triangular form—called *Schur form* in this context—by a similarity transformation, and the eigenvalues of a triangular matrix are also the diagonal entries, for $A - \lambda I$ must have a zero on its diagonal if A is triangular and λ is any diagonal entry of A. The eigenvectors of a triangular matrix are not quite so obvious but are still straightforward to compute. If

$$A - \lambda I = \begin{bmatrix} U_{11} & u & U_{13} \\ 0 & 0 & v^T \\ 0 & 0 & U_{33} \end{bmatrix}$$

is triangular, then the system $U_{11}y = u$ can be solved for y, so that

$$x = \begin{bmatrix} y \\ -1 \\ 0 \end{bmatrix}$$

TABLE 4.2
Forms attainable by similarity transformations for various types of matrices

A	T	B
Distinct eigenvalues	Nonsingular	Diagonal
Real symmetric	Orthogonal	Real diagonal
Complex Hermitian	Unitary	Real diagonal
Normal	Unitary	Diagonal
Arbitrary	Unitary	Upper triangular (Schur form)
Arbitrary	Nonsingular	Almost diagonal (Jordan form)

is an eigenvector. (We have assumed that U_{11} is nonsingular, which means that we are working with the *first* occurrence of λ on the diagonal.)

The simplest form attainable by a similarity transformation, as well as the type of similarity transformation, depends on the properties of the given matrix. We obviously prefer the simpler diagonal form when possible, and we also prefer orthogonal (or unitary) similarity transformations when possible, for both theoretical and numerical reasons. Unfortunately, not all matrices are unitarily diagonalizable, and some matrices are not diagonalizable at all. Table 4.2 indicates what form is attainable for a given type of matrix and a given type of similarity transformation. Given a matrix A with one of the properties indicated, there exist matrices B and T having the indicated properties such that $B = T^{-1}AT$. In the first four cases, the columns of T are the eigenvectors. In all cases, the diagonal entries of B are the eigenvalues.

4.1.5 Conditioning of Eigenvalue Problems

The condition of an eigenvalue problem is the sensitivity of the eigenvalues and eigenvectors to small changes in the matrix. The condition of a matrix eigenvalue problem is *not* the same as the condition of the matrix for solving linear equations. Different eigenvalues or eigenvectors of a given matrix are not necessarily equally sensitive to perturbations in the matrix.

The condition of a simple eigenvalue λ of a matrix A is given by $1/|y^H x|$, where x and y are corresponding right and left eigenvectors normalized so that $x^H x = y^H y = 1$. In other words, the sensitivity of a simple eigenvalue is proportional to the reciprocal of the cosine of the angle between the corresponding left and right eigenvectors. Thus, a perturbation of order ϵ in A may perturb the eigenvalue λ by as much as $\epsilon/|y^H x|$. The sensitivity of an eigenvector depends on both the sensitivity of the corresponding eigenvalue and the distance of that eigenvalue from other eigenvalues.

For a symmetric or Hermitian matrix, the right and left eigenvectors are the same, so we have $y^H x = x^H x = 1$, and hence the eigenvalues are inherently well-conditioned. More generally, the eigenvalues are well-conditioned for normal matrices, but for nonnormal matrices the eigenvalues need not be well-conditioned. In particular, multiple or close eigenvalues can be poorly conditioned and therefore difficult to compute accurately, especially if the matrix is defective. Balancing—scaling by a diagonal similarity transformation—can improve the condition of an eigenvalue problem, and many software packages for eigenvalue problems offer such an option.

4.2 METHODS FOR COMPUTING ALL EIGENVALUES

4.2.1 Characteristic Polynomial

Perhaps the most obvious method for computing the eigenvalues of a matrix A is by means of its characteristic polynomial,

$$\det(A - \lambda I) = 0.$$

This is not recommended as a general numerical procedure, however, because the coefficients of the characteristic polynomial are not well-determined numerically, and its roots can be very sensitive to perturbations in the coefficients. Moreover, solving for the roots of a polynomial of high degree requires a great deal of work. In other words, the characteristic polynomial gives an equivalent problem in theory, but in practice the solution is not preserved numerically; and in any case, computing the roots of the polynomial is no simpler than the original eigenvalue problem. Indeed, one of the better ways of computing the roots of a polynomial $p(\lambda) = a_0 + a_1\lambda + \cdots + a_{n-1}\lambda^{n-1} + \lambda^n$ is to compute the eigenvalues of the *companion matrix*

$$\begin{bmatrix} 0 & 1 & 0 & \cdots & 0 \\ 0 & 0 & 1 & \cdots & 0 \\ \vdots & \vdots & \vdots & \ddots & \vdots \\ 0 & 0 & 0 & \cdots & 1 \\ -a_0 & -a_1 & -a_2 & \cdots & -a_{n-1} \end{bmatrix}$$

using the methods discussed in this chapter.

Although it is not useful numerically, the characteristic polynomial does permit us to make an important theoretical observation about computing eigenvalues. Abel proved that the roots of a polynomial of degree greater than four cannot always be expressed by a closed-form formula in the coefficients using ordinary arithmetic operations and root extractions. Thus, in general, computing the eigenvalues of matrices of order greater than four requires a (theoretically infinite) iterative process.

EXAMPLE 4.5 CHARACTERISTIC POLYNOMIAL. To illustrate some of the numerical difficulties associated with the characteristic polynomial, consider the matrix

$$A = \begin{bmatrix} 1 & \epsilon \\ \epsilon & 1 \end{bmatrix},$$

where ϵ is a positive number slightly smaller than the square root of machine precision in a given floating-point system. The exact eigenvalues of A are $1 + \epsilon$ and $1 - \epsilon$. Computing the characteristic polynomial of A in floating-point arithmetic, we get

$$\det(A - \lambda I) = \lambda^2 - 2\lambda + (1 - \epsilon^2) = \lambda^2 - 2\lambda + 1,$$

which has 1 as a double root. Thus, we cannot resolve the two eigenvalues by this method even though they are quite distinct in the working precision. We would need up to twice the precision in the coefficients of the characteristic polynomial to compute the eigenvalues to the same precision as that of the input matrix.

4.2.2 Jacobi Method for Symmetric Matrices

One of the oldest methods for computing eigenvalues of symmetric matrices is due to Jacobi. Starting with a symmetric matrix $A_0 = A$, each iteration has the form

$$A_{k+1} = J_k^T A_k J_k,$$

where J_k is a plane rotation chosen to annihilate a symmetric pair of entries in the matrix A_k (so that the symmetry of the original matrix is preserved). Recall from Section 3.4.5 that a plane rotation is an orthogonal matrix that differs from the identity matrix in only four entries, and this 2×2 submatrix has the form

$$\begin{bmatrix} c & s \\ -s & c \end{bmatrix},$$

with c and s the cosine and sine of the angle of rotation, respectively, so that $c^2 + s^2 = 1$. The choice of c and s is slightly more complicated in this context than in the Givens method for QR factorization because we are annihilating a symmetric pair of matrix entries by a similarity transformation, as opposed to annihilating a single entry by a one-sided transformation.

As before, it suffices to consider only the 2×2 case,

$$
J^T A J = \begin{bmatrix} c & -s \\ s & c \end{bmatrix} \begin{bmatrix} a & b \\ b & d \end{bmatrix} \begin{bmatrix} c & s \\ -s & c \end{bmatrix}
$$

$$
= \begin{bmatrix} c^2 a - 2csb + s^2 d & c^2 b + cs(a-d) - s^2 b \\ c^2 b + cs(a-d) - s^2 b & c^2 d + 2csb + s^2 a \end{bmatrix},
$$

where $b \neq 0$ (else there is nothing to do). The transformed matrix will be diagonal if

$$c^2 b + cs(a - d) - s^2 b = 0.$$

Dividing both sides of this equation by $c^2 b$, we obtain

$$1 + \frac{s}{c} \frac{(a-d)}{b} - \frac{s^2}{c^2} = 0.$$

Making the substitution $t = s/c$, we obtain a quadratic equation

$$1 + t \frac{(a-d)}{b} - t^2 = 0$$

for t, the tangent of the angle of rotation, from which we can recover $c = 1/\sqrt{1 + t^2}$ and $s = c \cdot t$. It is advantageous numerically to use the root of smaller magnitude of the equation for t.

EXAMPLE 4.6 PLANE ROTATION. To illustrate the use of a plane rotation to annihilate a symmetric pair of off-diagonal entries, we consider the 2×2 matrix

$$A = \begin{bmatrix} 1 & 2 \\ 2 & 1 \end{bmatrix}.$$

The quadratic equation for the tangent reduces to $t^2 = 1$ in this case, so we have $t = \pm 1$. Since the two roots are of the same magnitude, we arbitrarily choose $t = -1$, which yields $c = 1/\sqrt{2}$ and $s = -1/\sqrt{2}$. Using the resulting plane rotation J, we then have

$$J^T A J = \begin{bmatrix} 1/\sqrt{2} & 1/\sqrt{2} \\ -1/\sqrt{2} & 1/\sqrt{2} \end{bmatrix} \begin{bmatrix} 1 & 2 \\ 2 & 1 \end{bmatrix} \begin{bmatrix} 1/\sqrt{2} & -1/\sqrt{2} \\ 1/\sqrt{2} & 1/\sqrt{2} \end{bmatrix} = \begin{bmatrix} 3 & 0 \\ 0 & -1 \end{bmatrix}.$$

In the Jacobi method, plane rotations determined in this manner are repeatedly applied from both sides in systematic sweeps through the matrix until the off-diagonal mass of the matrix is reduced to within some tolerance of zero. The resulting approximately diagonal matrix is orthogonally similar to the original matrix; hence, we have the approximate eigenvalues on the diagonal, and the product of all of the plane rotations gives the eigenvectors.

Although the Jacobi method is reliable, simple to program, and capable of very high accuracy, it converges rather slowly. It is also difficult to generalize beyond symmetric (or Hermitian) matrices. Except for very small problems, the Jacobi method usually requires 5 to 10 times more work than more modern methods. Recently, however, the Jacobi method has regained popularity because it is relatively easy to implement on parallel computers.

The main source of inefficiency in the Jacobi method is that entries that have been annihilated by a previous iteration can subsequently become nonzero again, thereby requiring repeated annihilation. The main computational advantage of more modern methods is that they are carefully designed to preserve zero entries once they have been introduced into the matrix.

EXAMPLE 4.7 JACOBI METHOD. Let

$$A_0 = \begin{bmatrix} 1 & 0 & 2 \\ 0 & 2 & 1 \\ 2 & 1 & 1 \end{bmatrix}.$$

We will repeatedly sweep through the matrix by rows and columns, annihilating successive matrix entries. We first annihilate the symmetrically placed entries $(1, 3)$ and $(3, 1)$ using the plane rotation

$$J_0 = \begin{bmatrix} 0.707 & 0 & -0.707 \\ 0 & 1 & 0 \\ 0.707 & 0 & 0.707 \end{bmatrix} \quad \text{to obtain} \quad A_1 = J_0^T A_0 J_0 = \begin{bmatrix} 3 & 0.707 & 0 \\ 0.707 & 2 & 0.707 \\ 0 & 0.707 & -1 \end{bmatrix}.$$

We next annihilate the symmetrically placed entries $(1, 2)$ and $(2, 1)$ using the plane rotation

$$J_1 = \begin{bmatrix} 0.888 & -0.460 & 0 \\ 0.460 & 0.888 & 0 \\ 0 & 0 & 1 \end{bmatrix} \quad \text{to obtain} \quad A_2 = J_1^T A_1 J_1 = \begin{bmatrix} 3.366 & 0 & 0.325 \\ 0 & 1.634 & 0.628 \\ 0.325 & 0.628 & -1 \end{bmatrix}.$$

We next annihilate the symmetrically placed entries $(2, 3)$ and $(3, 2)$ using the plane rotation

$$J_2 = \begin{bmatrix} 1 & 0 & 0 \\ 0 & 0.975 & -0.221 \\ 0 & 0.221 & 0.975 \end{bmatrix} \quad \text{to obtain} \quad A_3 = J_2^T A_2 J_2 = \begin{bmatrix} 3.366 & 0.072 & 0.317 \\ 0.072 & 1.776 & 0 \\ 0.317 & 0 & -1.142 \end{bmatrix}.$$

Beginning a new sweep, we again annihilate the symmetrically placed entries (1, 3) and (3, 1) using the plane rotation

$$
J_3 = \begin{bmatrix} 0.998 & 0 & -0.070 \\ 0 & 1 & 0 \\ 0.070 & 0 & 0.998 \end{bmatrix} \quad \text{to obtain} \quad A_4 = J_3^T A_3 J_3 = \begin{bmatrix} 3.388 & 0.072 & 0 \\ 0.072 & 1.776 & 0.005 \\ 0 & 0.005 & -1.164 \end{bmatrix}.
$$

This process continues until the off-diagonal entries are reduced to as small a magnitude as desired. The result is an approximately diagonal matrix that is orthogonally similar to the original matrix, with the orthogonal similarity transformation given by the product of the plane rotations.

4.2.3 QR Iteration

QR iteration for computing eigenvalues and eigenvectors makes repeated use of the QR factorization to produce a unitary similarity transformation of the matrix to diagonal or triangular form. We initially take $A_0 = A$, then at iteration k we compute the QR factorization

$$
A_k = Q_k R_k,
$$

and then form the reverse product

$$
A_{k+1} = R_k Q_k.
$$

Since

$$
R_k Q_k = Q_k^H A_k Q_k,
$$

we see that the successive matrices A_k are unitarily similar to each other. Moreover, it can be shown that if the moduli of the eigenvalues are all distinct, then the A_k converge to triangular form for a general initial matrix, or diagonal form for a symmetric initial matrix. This condition is not a serious restriction in practice because eigenvalues are deflated out as they are determined, which in this context simply means that we deal with successively smaller submatrices as each eigenvalue is determined. For example, after the last row of the matrix has converged to within some tolerance of zero (except, of course, for the diagonal entry, which is then an approximate eigenvalue), it need be processed no further and attention can be restricted to the leading submatrix of dimension $n - 1$. Such reductions continue successively until all the eigenvalues have been found.

EXAMPLE 4.8 QR ITERATION. Let

$$
A_0 = \begin{bmatrix} 7 & 2 \\ 2 & 4 \end{bmatrix}.
$$

We first compute the QR factorization $A_0 = Q_0 R_0$, obtaining

$$
Q_0 = \begin{bmatrix} 0.962 & -0.275 \\ 0.275 & 0.962 \end{bmatrix} \quad \text{and} \quad R_0 = \begin{bmatrix} 7.28 & 3.02 \\ 0 & 3.30 \end{bmatrix}.
$$

We next form the reverse product

$$A_1 = R_0 Q_0 = \begin{bmatrix} 7.83 & 0.906 \\ 0.906 & 3.17 \end{bmatrix}.$$

We see that the off-diagonal entries are now smaller, so that the matrix is closer to being diagonal, and the diagonal entries are now closer to the eigenvalues, which are 8 and 3 for this problem. Repetition of this process would continue until the matrix is within tolerance of being diagonal, and the diagonal entries would then closely approximate the eigenvalues. The product of the orthogonal matrices Q_k would yield the corresponding eigenvectors.

The convergence rate of QR iteration can be accelerated by incorporating *shifts* of the following form:

$$A_k - \sigma_k I = Q_k R_k,$$
$$A_{k+1} = R_k Q_k + \sigma_k I,$$

where σ_k is a rough approximation to an eigenvalue. This is called a shift because the entire spectrum of the matrix is displaced temporarily by the amount σ_k and then subsequently restored. One choice for the shift is simply the lower right corner entry of the matrix. A better shift can be determined by computing the eigenvalues of the 2×2 submatrix in the lower right corner of the matrix. In either case, such a shift will become increasingly better (i.e., closer to an eigenvalue) as the matrix converges to diagonal or triangular form.

EXAMPLE 4.9 QR ITERATION WITH SHIFTS. To illustrate the QR algorithm with shifts, we repeat the previous example using a shift of $\sigma_0 = 4$, which is the lower right corner entry of the matrix. Thus, we first compute the QR factorization $A_0 - \sigma_0 I = Q_0 R_0$ so that we have

$$Q_0 = \begin{bmatrix} 0.832 & 0.555 \\ 0.555 & -0.832 \end{bmatrix} \quad \text{and} \quad R_0 = \begin{bmatrix} 3.61 & 1.66 \\ 0 & 1.11 \end{bmatrix}.$$

We next form the reverse product and add back the shift to obtain

$$A_1 = R_0 Q_0 + \sigma_0 I = \begin{bmatrix} 7.92 & 0.615 \\ 0.615 & 3.08 \end{bmatrix}.$$

Compared with the unshifted algorithm, the off-diagonal entries are smaller after one iteration, and the diagonal entries are closer approximations to the eigenvalues. For the next iteration, we would use the new value of the lower right corner entry as the shift.

4.2.4 Preliminary Reduction

In the simple form just given, each iteration of the QR method requires $\mathcal{O}(n^3)$ work. The work per iteration can be reduced if the matrix is initially transformed into a simpler form. In particular, it is advantageous if the matrix is as close as possible to triangular (or diagonal for a symmetric matrix) before the QR iterations begin. A *Hessenberg matrix* is triangular except for one additional nonzero diagonal immediately adjacent to the main diagonal. Note that a symmetric Hessenberg matrix is tridiagonal. Any matrix can be reduced to Hessenberg form in a finite number of steps by an orthogonal similarity transformation, for example, by using Householder transformations. Moreover, upper Hessenberg or tridiagonal form can then be preserved during the subsequent QR iterations. The advantages of this initial reduction to upper Hessenberg or tridiagonal form are

- The work per QR iteration is reduced to at most $\mathcal{O}(n^2)$.
- The convergence rate of the QR iterations is enhanced.
- If there are any multiple eigenvalues, then the problem can be broken into two or more smaller subproblems because there will be at least one zero entry on the first subdiagonal of the upper Hessenberg matrix.

Thus, the QR method is usually implemented as a two-stage process:

$$\text{Symmetric} \longrightarrow \text{tridiagonal} \longrightarrow \text{diagonal}$$

or

$$\text{General} \longrightarrow \text{Hessenberg} \longrightarrow \text{triangular}$$

The preliminary reduction requires a definite number of steps, whereas the subsequent iterative stage continues until convergence. In practice, however, only a modest number of iterations are usually required, so the $\mathcal{O}(n^3)$ cost of the preliminary reduction is a significant fraction of the total. The total cost is strongly affected by whether the eigenvectors are needed because their inclusion determines whether the orthogonal transformations must be accumulated. For the symmetric case, the overall cost is roughly $\frac{4}{3}n^3$ arithmetic operations (counting both additions and multiplications) if only the eigenvalues are needed, and about $9n^3$ operations if the eigenvectors are also desired. For the general case, the overall cost is roughly $10n^3$ operations if only the eigenvalues are needed, and about $25n^3$ operations if the eigenvectors are also desired.

4.3 METHODS FOR COMPUTING SELECTED EIGENVALUES

4.3.1 Power Method

The QR and Jacobi methods are designed to compute all of the eigenvalues of a matrix and consequently require a great deal of work. In practice, one may need only one or a few eigenvalues and corresponding eigenvectors. The simplest method for computing a single eigenvalue and eigenvector of a matrix is the *power method,* which in effect takes successively higher powers of the matrix times an initial starting vector. Assume that the matrix has a unique eigenvalue λ_1 of maximum modulus, with corresponding eigenvector u_1. Then, starting from a given nonzero vector x_0, the iteration scheme

$$x_k = Ax_{k-1}$$

converges to a multiple of u_1, the eigenvector corresponding to the dominant eigenvalue λ_1.

To see why, we first express the starting vector x_0 as a linear combination, $x_0 = \sum_{i=1}^{n} \alpha_i u_i$, where the u_i are eigenvectors of A. We then have

$$x_k = A x_{k-1} = A^2 x_{k-2} = \cdots = A^k x_0$$

$$= A^k \sum_{i=1}^{n} \alpha_i u_i = \sum_{i=1}^{n} \alpha_i A^k u_i = \sum_{i=1}^{n} \lambda_i^k \alpha_i u_i$$

$$= \lambda_1^k (\alpha_1 u_1 + \sum_{i=2}^{n} (\lambda_i / \lambda_1)^k \alpha_i u_i).$$

Since $|\lambda_i / \lambda_1| < 1$ for $i > 1$, successively higher powers go to zero, leaving only the component corresponding to u_1.

EXAMPLE 4.10 POWER METHOD. In the sequence of vectors produced by the power method, the ratio of the values of a given component of x_k from one iteration to the next converges to the dominant eigenvalue λ_1. For example, if

$$A = \begin{bmatrix} 1.5 & 0.5 \\ 0.5 & 1.5 \end{bmatrix} \quad \text{and} \quad x_0 = \begin{bmatrix} 0 \\ 1 \end{bmatrix},$$

then we obtain the following sequence.

k	x_k^T		Ratio
0	0.0	1.0	
1	0.5	1.5	1.500
2	1.5	2.5	1.667
3	3.5	4.5	1.800
4	7.5	8.5	1.889
5	15.5	16.5	1.941
6	31.5	32.5	1.970
7	63.5	64.5	1.985
8	127.5	128.5	1.992

The sequence of vectors x_k is converging to a multiple of the eigenvector $\begin{bmatrix} 1 & 1 \end{bmatrix}^T$, and the ratio of successive iterates for each component is converging to the corresponding eigenvalue, 2, which we saw in Example 4.1 is indeed the largest eigenvalue of this matrix.

In practice the power method usually works, but it can fail for any of a number of reasons:

- The starting vector may have *no* component in the dominant eigenvector u_1 (i.e., $\alpha_1 = 0$). This possibility is not a problem in practice, because rounding error usually introduces such a component in any case.
- For a real matrix and starting vector, the iteration can never converge to a complex vector.
- There may be more than one eigenvalue having the same (maximum) modulus, in which case the iteration may converge to a vector that is a linear combination of the corresponding eigenvectors.

4.3.2 Normalization

Geometric growth of the components at each iteration risks eventual overflow (or underflow if the dominant eigenvalue is less than 1 in magnitude), so normalizing the approximate eigenvector at each iteration is preferable, say, by requiring its largest component to have modulus 1. This step gives the iteration scheme

$$y_k = Ax_{k-1},$$
$$x_k = y_k / \|y_k\|_\infty.$$

With this normalization, $\|y_k\|_\infty \to |\lambda_1|$, and $x_k \to u_1 / \|u_1\|_\infty$.

EXAMPLE 4.11 POWER METHOD WITH NORMALIZATION. Repeating the previous example with this normalized scheme, we get the following sequence:

k	x_k^T		$\|y_k\|_\infty$
0	0.000	1.0	
1	0.333	1.0	1.500
2	0.600	1.0	1.667
3	0.778	1.0	1.800
4	0.882	1.0	1.889
5	0.939	1.0	1.941
6	0.969	1.0	1.970
7	0.984	1.0	1.985
8	0.992	1.0	1.992

The eigenvalue estimates have not changed, but now the approximate eigenvector is normalized at each iteration, thereby avoiding geometric growth or shrinkage of its components.

4.3.3 Geometric Interpretation

The behavior of the power method is depicted geometrically in Fig. 4.1. The eigenvectors of the example matrix are shown by dashed arrows. The initial vector

$$x_0 = \begin{bmatrix} 0 \\ 1 \end{bmatrix} = 1 \begin{bmatrix} 1 \\ 1 \end{bmatrix} + 1 \begin{bmatrix} -1 \\ 1 \end{bmatrix}$$

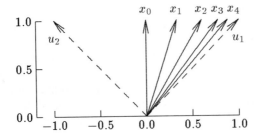

FIGURE 4.1
Geometric interpretation of the power method.

contains equal components in the two eigenvectors. Repeated multiplication by the matrix A, however, causes the component in the first eigenvector (corresponding to the larger eigenvalue, 2) to dominate, and hence the sequence of vectors converges to that eigenvector.

4.3.4 Shifts

The convergence rate of the power method depends on the ratio $|\lambda_2/\lambda_1|$, where λ_2 is the eigenvalue having second-largest modulus: the smaller this ratio, the faster the convergence. It may be possible to choose a shift, $A - \sigma I$, such that

$$\left|\frac{\lambda_2 - \sigma}{\lambda_1 - \sigma}\right| < \left|\frac{\lambda_2}{\lambda_1}\right|,$$

and thus convergence is accelerated. Of course, the shift must then be added to the result to obtain the eigenvalue of the original matrix. In our earlier example, for instance, if we pick a shift of $\sigma = 1$ (which is equal to the other eigenvalue), then the ratio becomes zero and the method converges in a single iteration. In general, we would not be able to make such a fortuitous choice, but such shifts can still be extremely useful in some contexts, as we will see later.

4.3.5 Deflation

Suppose that an eigenvalue λ_1 and corresponding eigenvector x_1 for a matrix A have been computed. We now consider how to compute additional eigenvalues $\lambda_2, \ldots, \lambda_n$ of A, if needed, by a process called *deflation*, which effectively removes the known eigenvalue.

Let H be any nonsingular matrix such that $Hx_1 = \alpha e_1$, a scalar multiple of the first column of the identity matrix (for example, an appropriate Householder transformation is a good choice for H). Then the similarity transformation determined by H transforms A into the form

$$HAH^{-1} = \begin{bmatrix} \lambda_1 & b^T \\ 0 & B \end{bmatrix},$$

where B is a matrix of order $n - 1$ having eigenvalues $\lambda_2, \ldots, \lambda_n$. Thus, we can work with B to compute the next eigenvalue λ_2. Moreover, if y_2 is an eigenvector of B corresponding to λ_2, then

$$x_2 = H^{-1} \begin{bmatrix} \alpha \\ y_2 \end{bmatrix}, \quad \text{where} \quad \alpha = \frac{b^T y_2}{\lambda_2 - \lambda_1},$$

is an eigenvector corresponding to λ_2 for the original matrix A, provided $\lambda_1 \neq \lambda_2$. This process can be repeated to find additional eigenvalues and eigenvectors, as needed.

An alternative approach to deflation is to let v_1 be any vector such that $v_1^T x_1 = \lambda_1$. Then the matrix $A - x_1 v_1^T$ has eigenvalues $0, \lambda_2, \ldots, \lambda_n$. Possible choices for v_1 include

- $v_1 = \lambda_1 x_1$, if A is symmetric and x_1 is normalized so that $\|x_1\|_2 = 1$
- $v_1 = \lambda_1 y_1$, where y_1 is the corresponding left eigenvector (i.e., $A^T y_1 = \lambda_1 y_1$) normalized so that $y_1^T x_1 = 1$
- $v_1 = A^T e_k$, if x_1 is normalized so that $\|x_1\|_\infty = 1$ and the kth component of x_1 is 1

4.3.6 Inverse Iteration

For some applications, the smallest eigenvalue of a matrix is required rather than the largest. We can make use of the fact that the eigenvalues of A^{-1} are the reciprocals of those of A, and hence the smallest eigenvalue of A is the reciprocal of the largest eigenvalue of A^{-1}. We therefore use the *inverse iteration* scheme

$$Ay_k = x_{k-1},$$

$$x_k = y_k / \|y_k\|_\infty,$$

which is equivalent to the power method applied to A^{-1}. Of course, the inverse of A is not computed explicitly. Instead the system of linear equations is solved at each iteration, perhaps by LU factorization, which need be done only once. Inverse iteration converges to the eigenvector corresponding to the smallest eigenvalue of A. The eigenvalue obtained is the dominant eigenvalue of A^{-1}, and hence its reciprocal is the smallest eigenvalue of A in modulus.

As before, a shifting strategy (working with $A - \sigma I$ for some scalar σ) can greatly improve convergence. For this reason, inverse iteration is particularly useful for computing the eigenvector corresponding to an approximate eigenvalue that has already been computed by some other means because it converges very rapidly when applied to the matrix $A - \lambda I$, where λ is an approximate eigenvalue. Inverse iteration is also useful for computing the eigenvalue of a matrix closest to a given value β, for if β is used as shift, then the desired eigenvalue corresponds to the smallest eigenvalue of the shifted matrix.

EXAMPLE 4.12 INVERSE ITERATION. As an illustration of inverse iteration, we apply it to our previous example to compute the smallest eigenvalue, obtaining the sequence

k	x_k^T		$\|y_k\|_\infty$
0	0.000	1.0	
1	-0.333	1.0	0.750
2	-0.600	1.0	0.833
3	-0.778	1.0	0.900
4	-0.882	1.0	0.944
5	-0.939	1.0	0.971
6	-0.969	1.0	0.985

which is converging to the eigenvector $\begin{bmatrix} -1 & 1 \end{bmatrix}^T$ corresponding to the dominant eigenvalue of A^{-1}, which is the same as the eigenvector corresponding to the smallest eigenvalue of A. The approximate eigenvalue is converging to 1, which is its own reciprocal in this case.

4.3.7 Rayleigh Quotient

If one is given an approximate eigenvector x for a real matrix A, determining the best estimate for the corresponding eigenvalue λ can be considered as an $n \times 1$ linear least squares approximation problem

$$x\lambda \approx Ax.$$

From the normal equation $x^T x\lambda = x^T Ax$, we see that the least squares solution is given by

$$\lambda = \frac{x^T Ax}{x^T x}.$$

The latter quantity, known as the *Rayleigh quotient*, has many useful properties. For example, it can be used to accelerate the convergence of an iterative method such as the power method, since at iteration k the Rayleigh quotient $x_k^T Ax_k / x_k^T x_k$ gives a better approximation to an eigenvalue than that provided by the basic method alone.

EXAMPLE 4.13 RAYLEIGH QUOTIENT. For Example 4.11 using the power method, the value of the Rayleigh quotient at each iteration is shown next.

k	x_k^T		$\|y_k\|_\infty$	$x_k^T Ax_k / x_k^T x_k$
0	0.000	1.0		1.500
1	0.333	1.0	1.500	1.800
2	0.600	1.0	1.667	1.941
3	0.778	1.0	1.800	1.985
4	0.882	1.0	1.889	1.996
5	0.939	1.0	1.941	1.999
6	0.969	1.0	1.970	2.000

Thus, the Rayleigh quotient converges to the dominant eigenvalue, 2, faster than the successive approximations produced by the power method alone.

4.3.8 Rayleigh Quotient Iteration

Given an approximate eigenvector, the Rayleigh quotient yields a very good estimate for the corresponding eigenvalue. Conversely, inverse iteration converges very rapidly to an eigenvector if an approximate eigenvalue is used as shift, with a single iteration often sufficing. It is natural, therefore, to combine these two ideas in the *Rayleigh quotient iteration*

$$\sigma_k = x_k^T Ax_k / x_k^T x_k,$$
$$(A - \sigma_k I)y_{k+1} = x_k,$$
$$x_{k+1} = y_{k+1} / \|y_{k+1}\|_\infty,$$

starting from a given nonzero vector x_0. This iteration scheme is especially effective for symmetric matrices and usually converges very rapidly.

On the other hand, using a different shift at each iteration means that the matrix must be refactored each time to solve the linear system, so that the cost per iteration is relatively high unless the matrix has some special form that makes the factorization easy. In general, the power method, inverse iteration, and Rayleigh quotient iteration show the expected trade-off, with faster convergence coming at the expense of more work per iteration.

Rayleigh quotient iteration also works for complex matrices, for which the transpose is replaced by conjugate transpose, and the Rayleigh quotient becomes $x^H A x / x^H x$.

EXAMPLE 4.14 RAYLEIGH QUOTIENT ITERATION. Using the same matrix as our previous examples and a randomly chosen starting vector x_0, Rayleigh quotient iteration converges to the accuracy shown in only two iterations:

k	x_k^T		σ_k
0	0.807	0.397	1.896
1	0.924	1.000	1.998
2	1.000	1.000	2.000

4.3.9 Lanczos Method for Symmetric Matrices

The power method produces a sequence of vectors, each of which is a successively better approximation to an eigenvector. At any point in the process, however, the approximation is based on a single vector, which spans a one-dimensional subspace. A better approximation should result if we compute the best approximation to an eigenvector over an entire subspace of higher dimension. The *Rayleigh-Ritz procedure* is a method for doing just that.

Let A be an $n \times n$ symmetric matrix, and let S be an $n \times m$ matrix, $n \geq m$, whose columns span a subspace of dimension m. Orthogonalize the columns of S (see Section 3.4), if necessary, to obtain an $n \times m$ matrix Q with orthonormal columns spanning the same subspace. Form the $m \times m$ symmetric matrix $B = Q^T A Q$. Denote the eigenvalues and corresponding eigenvectors of B by γ_i and y_i, respectively, and let $z_i = Qy_i$, $i = 1, \ldots, m$. Then it can be shown that the γ_i and z_i, which are called *Ritz values* and *Ritz vectors*, respectively, are the best possible approximations to eigenvalue-eigenvector pairs of A over the subspace spanned by S. One must still compute the eigenvalues of B, but if $m \ll n$, this problem should be much easier.

So how can we obtain a suitable subspace? The answer is that we can use the *Krylov subspace* spanned by the vectors

$$x, Ax, A^2 x, \ldots, A^{m-1} x,$$

where x is any nonzero starting vector. Note that this is just the sequence of vectors generated by the power method, which means that we will obtain the best eigenvalue-eigenvector approximation over the entire subspace spanned by all of the iterates, rather than using only the last vector in the sequence. Orthogonalization of an arbitrary set of vectors would be very expensive, but for the Krylov sequence, it can be shown that the successive orthogonal vectors satisfy a three-term recurrence, so that each new vector need be orthogonalized only against the previous two, rather than all of the previous vectors (which means that they need not be saved). Thus, in this case the $m \times m$ matrix $Q^T A Q$ is tridiagonal, and we denote it by T_m. As m increases, the eigenvalues of T_m become increasingly better approximations to the extreme (largest and smallest) eigenvalues of A.

The ideas we have just outlined—using the Rayleigh-Ritz approximation over the Krylov subspace and taking advantage of the resulting three-term recurrence—form the basis for the *Lanczos method* for computing eigenvalues and eigenvectors of symmetric matrices. Beginning with an arbitrary nonzero starting vector r_0, and taking $\beta_0 = \|r_0\|_2$ and $q_0 = 0$, the following steps are repeated for $k = 1, \ldots, m$:

1. $q_k = r_{k-1}/\beta_{k-1}$.
2. $u_k = A q_k$.
3. $r_k = u_k - \beta_{k-1} q_{k-1}$.
4. $\alpha_k = q_k^T r_k$.
5. $r_k = r_k - \alpha_k q_k$.
6. $\beta_k = \|r_k\|_2$.

The α_k, $k = 1, \ldots, m$, and β_k, $k = 1, \ldots, m - 1$, are the diagonal and subdiagonal entries, respectively, of the symmetric tridiagonal matrix T_m. If at any point $\beta_k = 0$, then the algorithm appears to break down, but in that case an invariant subspace has already been identified (i.e., the Ritz values and vectors are already exact at that point). Note that the algorithm as just stated does not produce the eigenvalues and eigenvectors directly but rather the tridiagonal matrix T_m, whose eigenvalues and eigenvectors must then be computed by some other method to obtain the Ritz values and vectors.

In principle, if the foregoing algorithm were run until $m = n$, then the resulting tridiagonal matrix would be orthogonally similar to A. In practice, unfortunately, rounding error causes a loss of orthogonality that invalidates this expectation. This problem can be overcome by reorthogonalizing the vectors as needed, but the expense of doing so can be substantial. Alternatively, one can ignore the problem, in which case the algorithm still produces good eigenvalue approximations, but multiple copies of some eigenvalues may be generated, which can be a nuisance to say the least. In any case, there are better ways to tridiagonalize a matrix (e.g., Householder's method) than running the Lanczos algorithm for n steps. The great virtue of the Lanczos method is its ability to produce good approximations to the extreme eigenvalues with $m \ll n$, often on the order of $\sqrt{n}$. Moreover, the algorithm requires only one matrix-vector multiplication by A per step and very little auxiliary storage, so it is ideally suited to large sparse matrices, unlike methods that alter the entries of A.

EXAMPLE 4.15 LANCZOS METHOD. The behavior of the Lanczos method is illustrated in Fig. 4.2, where the algorithm is applied to a matrix of order 29 whose eigenvalues are $1, \ldots, 29$. The iteration count is plotted on the vertical axis and the corresponding Ritz values

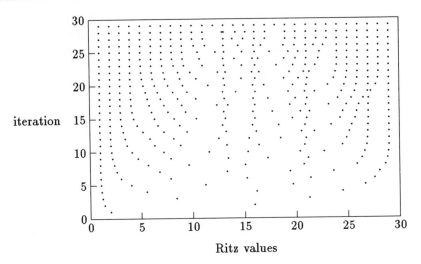

FIGURE 4.2
Convergence of Ritz values to eigenvalues in the Lanczos method.

are on the horizontal axis. At each iteration k, the points $(\gamma_i, k), i = 1, \ldots, k$, are plotted. We see that the extreme eigenvalues are closely approximated by Ritz values after only a few iterations, but the interior eigenvalues take much longer to appear. For this small matrix with well-separated eigenvalues, the Ritz values are identical to the eigenvalues after 29 iterations, as theory predicts, but for more realistic problems this cannot be relied upon owing to rounding error. Moreover, running the algorithm for a full n iterations may not be feasible if n is very large. The main point, however, is the relatively rapid convergence to the extreme eigenvalues, which is typical of the Lanczos method in general.

The Lanczos method most quickly produces approximate eigenvalues near the ends of the spectrum. If eigenvalues are needed in the middle of the spectrum, say, near the value σ, then the algorithm can be applied to the matrix $(A - \sigma I)^{-1}$, assuming that it is practical to solve systems of the form $(A - \sigma I)x = y$. Such a "shift-and-invert" strategy enables much more rapid convergence to interior eigenvalues, since they correspond to extreme eigenvalues of the new matrix.

A generalization of the Lanczos method to nonsymmetric matrices, known as the *Arnoldi method*, reduces the input matrix to Hessenberg form rather than tridiagonal form. Several software packages that implement the Lanczos and Arnoldi methods are available.

4.3.10 Spectrum-Slicing Methods for Symmetric Matrices

Another family of methods is based on *counting* eigenvalues. For real symmetric matrices, there are various methods for determining the number of eigenvalues that are less than a given real number σ. By systematically choosing various values for σ (slicing the spectrum at σ) and monitoring the resulting count, any eigenvalue can be isolated as accurately as desired. We sketch such methods briefly here.

Let A be a real symmetric matrix. The *inertia* of A is a triple of integers consisting of the numbers of positive, negative, and zero eigenvalues. A *congruence transformation* has the form SAS^T, where S is any nonsingular matrix. Unless $S^T = S^{-1}$ (i.e., S is orthogonal), a congruence is not a similarity transformation and hence does not preserve the eigenvalues of A. However, by Sylvester's Law of Inertia, a congruence transformation does preserve the inertia of A, i.e., the numbers of positive, negative, and zero eigenvalues are invariant under congruences.

If we can find a congruence transformation that makes the inertia easy to determine, then we can apply it to the matrix $A - \sigma I$ to determine the numbers of eigenvalues to the right or left of σ. An obvious candidate is the LDL^T factorization discussed in Section 2.5.2, where D is a matrix whose inertia is easily determined. By computing the LDL^T factorization, and hence the inertia, of $A - \sigma I$ for any desired value of σ, individual eigenvalues can be isolated as accurately as desired using an interval bisection technique (see Section 5.2.1).

Another spectrum-slicing method for computing individual eigenvalues is based on the *Sturm sequence* property of symmetric matrices. Let A be a symmetric matrix and let $p_k(\sigma)$ denote the determinant of the leading principal submatrix of order k of $A - \sigma I$. Then the zeros of $p_k(\sigma)$ strictly separate (i.e., are interleaved with) those of $p_{k-1}(\sigma)$. Furthermore, the number of agreements in sign of successive members of the sequence $p_k(\sigma)$, for $k = 1, \ldots, n$, is equal to the number of eigenvalues of A that are strictly greater than σ. This property allows the computation of the number of eigenvalues lying in a given interval. The determinants $p_k(\sigma)$ are especially easy to compute if A is tridiagonal, so A is usually transformed to this form before applying the Sturm sequence technique.

4.4 GENERALIZED EIGENVALUE PROBLEMS

Many eigenvalue problems occurring in practice have the form of a *generalized eigenvalue problem*

$$Ax = \lambda Bx,$$

where A and B are given $n \times n$ matrices. In structural vibration problems, for example, A represents the *stiffness matrix* and B the *mass matrix*, and the eigenvalues and eigenvectors determine the natural frequencies and modes of vibration of the structure (see Computer Problem 4.12 for an example). A detailed study of the theory and algorithms for this and other generalized eigenvalue problems is beyond the scope of this book, but the basic methods available for their solution are briefly outlined next.

If either of the matrices A or B is nonsingular, then the generalized eigenvalue problem can be converted to a standard eigenvalue problem, either

$$(B^{-1}A)x = \lambda x \quad \text{or} \quad (A^{-1}B)x = (1/\lambda)x.$$

Such a transformation is not generally recommended, however, since it may cause

- Loss of accuracy due to rounding error in forming the product matrix, especially when A or B is ill-conditioned
- Loss of symmetry when A and B are symmetric

If A and B are symmetric, and one of them is positive definite, then symmetry can still be retained by using the Cholesky factorization. For example, if $B = LL^T$, then the generalized eigenvalue problem can be rewritten as the standard symmetric eigenvalue problem

$$(L^{-1}AL^{-T})y = \lambda y,$$

and x can be recovered from the triangular linear system $L^T x = y$. Transformation to a standard eigenvalue problem may still incur unnecessary rounding error, however, and it offers no help if both A and B are singular.

   A numerically superior approach, which is applicable even when the matrices are singular or indefinite, is the QZ algorithm. Note that if A and B are both triangular, then the eigenvalues are given by $\lambda_i = a_{ii}/b_{ii}$ for $b_{ii} \neq 0$. This circumstance is the motivation for the QZ algorithm, which reduces A and B simultaneously to upper triangular form by orthogonal transformations. First, B is reduced to upper triangular form by an orthogonal transformation Q_0 applied on the left, and the same orthogonal transformation is also applied to A. Then a sequence of orthogonal transformations Q_k is applied to both matrices from the left to reduce A to upper Hessenberg form, and these alternate with orthogonal transformations Z_k applied on the right to restore B to upper triangular form. Finally, in a process analogous to QR iteration for the standard eigenvalue problem, additional orthogonal transformations are applied, alternating on the left and right, so that A converges to upper triangular form while maintaining the upper triangular form of B. The product of all the transformations on the left is denoted by Q, and the product of those on the right is denoted by Z, giving the algorithm its name. The eigenvalues can now be determined from the mutually triangular form, and the eigenvectors can be recovered via Q and Z.

4.5 SINGULAR VALUES

4.5.1 Singular Value Decomposition

The *singular value decomposition* (SVD) is an eigenvalue-like decomposition for rectangular matrices. Let A be an $m \times n$ real matrix. Then the singular value decomposition has the form

$$A = U\Sigma V^T,$$

where U is an $m \times m$ orthogonal matrix, V is an $n \times n$ orthogonal matrix, and Σ is an $m \times n$ diagonal matrix, with

$$\sigma_{ij} = \begin{cases} 0 & \text{for } i \neq j \\ \sigma_i \geq 0 & \text{for } i = j \end{cases}.$$

The diagonal entries σ_i are called the *singular values* of A and are usually ordered so that $\sigma_i \geq \sigma_{i+1}$, for $i = 1, \ldots, n - 1$. The columns u_i of U and v_i of V are the corresponding *singular vectors*.

EXAMPLE 4.16 SINGULAR VALUE DECOMPOSITION. The singular value decomposition of

$$A = \begin{bmatrix} 1 & 2 & 3 \\ 4 & 5 & 6 \\ 7 & 8 & 9 \\ 10 & 11 & 12 \end{bmatrix}$$

is given by $U\Sigma V^T =$

$$\begin{bmatrix} 0.141 & 0.825 & -0.420 & -0.351 \\ 0.344 & 0.426 & 0.298 & 0.782 \\ 0.547 & 0.028 & 0.664 & -0.509 \\ 0.750 & -0.371 & -0.542 & 0.079 \end{bmatrix} \begin{bmatrix} 25.5 & 0 & 0 \\ 0 & 1.29 & 0 \\ 0 & 0 & 0 \\ 0 & 0 & 0 \end{bmatrix} \begin{bmatrix} 0.504 & 0.574 & 0.644 \\ -0.761 & -0.057 & 0.646 \\ 0.408 & -0.816 & 0.408 \end{bmatrix}.$$

Thus, we have $\sigma_1 = 25.5$, $\sigma_2 = 1.29$, and $\sigma_3 = 0$. A singular value of zero indicates that the matrix is rank-deficient; in general, the rank of a matrix is equal to the number of nonzero singular values, which in this example is two.

The singular values of A are the nonnegative square roots of the eigenvalues of $A^T A$, and the columns of U and V are orthonormal eigenvectors of AA^T and $A^T A$, respectively. Algorithms for computing the SVD work directly with A, however, without forming AA^T or $A^T A$, thereby avoiding any loss of information associated with forming these matrix products explicitly.

The SVD is usually computed by a variant of QR iteration. First, A is reduced to bidiagonal form by orthogonal transformations, then the remaining off-diagonal entries are annihilated iteratively. The SVD can also be computed by a variant of the Jacobi method, which can be useful on parallel computers or if the matrix has some special structure. The total number of arithmetic operations required to compute the SVD of an $m \times n$ dense matrix is proportional to $mn^2 + n^3$, with the proportionality constants ranging from 2 to 10 or more, depending on the particular algorithm used and the combination of singular values and right or left singular vectors desired. If the matrix is large and sparse, then bidiagonalization is most effectively performed by a variant of the Lanczos algorithm, which is especially suitable if only a few of the extreme singular values and corresponding singular vectors are needed.

4.5.2 Applications of SVD

The singular value decomposition $A = U\Sigma V^T$ has many important applications, among which are the following:

- Euclidean norm of a matrix. The matrix norm subordinate to the Euclidean vector norm is given by the largest singular value of the matrix,

$$\|A\|_2 = \max_{x \neq 0} \frac{\|Ax\|_2}{\|x\|_2} = \sigma_{\max}.$$

- Condition number of a matrix. The condition number of a matrix A with respect to the Euclidean norm is given by the ratio

$$\text{cond}(A) = \sigma_{\max}/\sigma_{\min}.$$

This result agrees with the definition of cond(A) for a square matrix given in Section 2.3.3 when using the Euclidean norm, and it also enables us to assign a condition number to a rectangular matrix. Just as the condition number of a square matrix measures closeness to singularity, the condition number of a rectangular matrix measures closeness to rank deficiency.

- Rank of a matrix. In theory, the rank of a matrix is equal to the number of nonzero singular values it has. In practice, however, the rank may not be well-determined in that some singular values may be very small but nonzero. For many purposes it may be better to regard any singular values falling below some threshold as negligible in determining the "numerical rank" of the matrix. One way to interpret this is that the given matrix is very near to (i.e., within the given threshold of) a matrix of the rank so determined.

- Solving linear systems or linear least squares problems. The minimum Euclidean norm solution to $Ax \approx b$ is given by

$$x = \sum_{\sigma_i \neq 0} \frac{u_i^T b}{\sigma_i} v_i.$$

The SVD is especially useful for ill-conditioned or rank-deficient problems, since "small" singular values can be dropped from the summation, thereby stabilizing the solution (making it much less sensitive to perturbations in the data).

- Pseudoinverse of a matrix. Define the pseudoinverse of a scalar σ to be $1/\sigma$ if $\sigma \neq 0$, and zero otherwise. Define the pseudoinverse of a (possibly rectangular) diagonal matrix by transposing the matrix and taking the scalar pseudoinverse of each entry. Then the *pseudoinverse* of a general real $m \times n$ matrix A, denoted by A^+, is given by

$$A^+ = V\Sigma^+ U^T.$$

Note that the pseudoinverse always exists regardless of whether the matrix is square or of full rank. If A is square and nonsingular, then the pseudoinverse is the same as the usual matrix inverse, A^{-1}. In any case, the least squares solution to $Ax \approx b$ of minimum Euclidean norm is given by $A^+ b$.

- Orthonormal bases for range and null spaces. The columns of V corresponding to zero singular values form an orthonormal basis for the null space of A. The remaining columns of V form an orthonormal basis for the orthogonal complement of the null space. Similarly, the columns of U corresponding to nonzero singular values form an orthonormal basis for the range space of A, and the remaining columns of U form an orthonormal basis for the orthogonal complement of the range space.

- Approximating a matrix by one of lower rank. Another way to write the SVD is

$$A = U\Sigma V^T = \sigma_1 E_1 + \sigma_2 E_2 + \cdots + \sigma_n E_n,$$

where $E_i = u_i v_i^T$. Each E_i is of rank 1 and can be stored using only $m + n$ storage locations. Moreover, the product $E_i x$ can be formed using only $m + n$ multiplications. Thus, a useful condensed approximation to A can be obtained by omitting from the foregoing summation those terms corresponding to the smaller singular values, since they have relatively little effect on the sum. It can be shown that this approximation using the k largest singular values is the closest matrix of rank k to A in the Frobenius norm. (The *Frobenius norm* of an $m \times n$ matrix is the Euclidean norm of the matrix considered as a vector in R^{mn}.) Such an approximation is useful in image processing, data compression, cryptography, and numerous other applications.

- Total least squares. In an ordinary linear least squares problem $Ax \approx b$, we implicitly assume that the entries of A are known exactly, whereas the entries of b are subject to error. In curve-fitting or regression problems where all of the variables are subject to measurement error or other uncertainty, it may make more sense to minimize the orthogonal distances between the data points and the curve rather than the vertical distances as in ordinary least squares. Such a total least squares solution can be computed using the singular value decomposition $\begin{bmatrix} A & b \end{bmatrix} = U\Sigma V^T$. Provided that σ_{n+1} is simple and $v_{n+1,n+1} \neq 0$, the total least squares solution is then given by

$$x = -\frac{1}{v_{n+1,n+1}} \begin{bmatrix} v_{1,n+1} \\ \vdots \\ v_{n,n+1} \end{bmatrix}.$$

More general problems, for example with multiple right-hand sides and with some of the variables known exactly, can be handled by a similar approach but are rather more complicated (see [259] for details).

4.6 SOFTWARE FOR EIGENVALUES AND SINGULAR VALUES

Table 4.3 is a list of some of the software available for eigenvalue and singular value problems. The routines listed are in most cases high-level drivers whose underlying routines can also be called directly if greater user control is required. Only the most comprehensive and commonly occurring cases are listed, and only for real matrices. There are many additional routines available in these packages, including routines for complex matrices and for various special situations, such as when only the eigenvalues and not the eigenvectors are needed, or when only a few eigenvalues are needed, or when the matrix has some special property, such as being banded. Routines are also available for both symmetric and nonsymmetric generalized eigenvalue problems. **EISPACK** and its successor **LAPACK** are the standards in software for dense eigenvalue problems, and the eigenvalue routines in most other libraries are based on them.

Conventional software for computing eigenvalues is fairly complicated, especially if eigenvectors are also computed. The standard approach, QR iteration, is typically broken into separate routines for the preliminary reduction to tridiagonal or Hessenberg

TABLE 4.3

Software for standard dense eigenvalue and singular value problems

Source	Eigenvalues/eigenvectors		Singular value decomposition
	General	Symmetric	
EISPACK	rg	rs	svd
FMM			svd
HSL	eb06	ea06	eb10
IMSL	evcrg	evcsf	lsvrr
LAPACK	sgeev	ssyev	sgesvd
Lawson/Hanson [163]			svdrs
LINPACK			ssvdc
MATLAB	eig	eig	svd
NAG	f02agf	f02abf	f02wef
NAPACK	diag	sdiag	sing
NR	elmhes/hqr	tred2/tqli	svdcmp
NUMAL	comeig1	qrisym	qrisngvaldec
SLATEC	rg	rs	ssvdc

form, and then QR iteration for computing the eigenvalues. The orthogonal or unitary similarity transformations may or may not be accumulated, depending on whether eigenvectors are also desired. Because of the complexity of the underlying routines, higher-level drivers are often provided for applications that do not require fine control. Typically, the input required is a two-dimensional array containing the matrix, together with information about the size of the matrix and the array containing it. The eigenvalues are returned in one or two one-dimensional arrays, depending on whether they are real or complex; and normalized eigenvectors, if requested, are similarly returned in one or two two-dimensional arrays. Similar remarks apply to software for computing the singular value decomposition except that arrays must be provided for both left and right singular vectors, if requested, and the decomposition is always real if the input matrix is real.

As usual, life is simpler using an interactive environment such as **MATLAB**, in which functions for eigenvalue and singular value computations are built in. A diagonal matrix D of eigenvalues and full matrix V of eigenvectors of a (real or complex) matrix A are given by the **MATLAB** function **[V, D] = eig(A)**. Internally, the eigenvalues and eigenvectors are computed by Hessenberg reduction and then QR iteration to obtain the Schur form of the matrix, but the user need not be aware of this. If the Hessenberg or Schur forms are desired explicitly, they can be computed by the **MATLAB** functions **hess** and **schur**. The **MATLAB** function for computing the singular value decomposition has the form **[U, S, V] = svd(A)**.

For software implementing the Lanczos algorithm for large sparse symmetric eigenvalue problems, see **laso** from **netlib**, **ea15** from the Harwell library, **lancz** from **napack**, or the software published in [46]. In addition, the Arnoldi method for large sparse nonsymmetric eigenvalue problems is implemented in **arpack**, and the Lanczos method for computing singular values and vectors of large sparse matrices is implemented in **svdpack**, both of which are available from **netlib**. For solving total least squares problems, **dtls** is available from **netlib**.

4.7 HISTORICAL NOTES AND FURTHER READING

The Jacobi method for computing eigenvalues dates from the mid-nineteenth century. The power method is sufficiently obvious to have been rediscovered repeatedly, but as a practical method its use dates from early in this century. Inverse iteration was proposed by Wielandt in 1944. The Lanczos method was first published in 1950, and Arnoldi's generalization of it to nonsymmetric matrices followed in 1951. QR iteration was discovered independently and simultaneously by Francis and Kublanovskaya in 1961, based on the earlier LR method of Rutishauser (1958), which uses less stable elementary eliminations instead of orthogonal transformations. The first practical algorithm for computing the singular value decomposition was proposed by Golub and Kahan in 1965, and the basic algorithm that is still in use today was published by Businger and Golub in 1969. The direct precursors of most modern software for eigenvalue and related problems were collected in [276], published in 1971.

The definitive reference on eigenvalue computations is [275]. Other excellent references on this topic include [37, 108, 199]. Most of the books on matrix computations cited in Chapter 2 also discuss eigenvalue and singular value computations in some detail, especially [104]. **EISPACK** is documented in [90, 233], and its successor **LAPACK** is documented in [8]. For a detailed discussion of methods for large eigenvalue problems, see [46, 217]. For a graphic example of the use of the SVD in image processing, see [9], and for its use in cryptography, see [178].

REVIEW QUESTIONS

4.1. True or false: The eigenvalues of a matrix are not necessarily all distinct.

4.2. True or false: All the eigenvalues of a real matrix are necessarily real.

4.3. True or false: An eigenvector corresponding to a given eigenvalue of a matrix is unique.

4.4. True or false: Every $n \times n$ matrix A has n linearly independent eigenvectors.

4.5. True or false: If an $n \times n$ matrix is singular, then it does not have a full set of n linearly independent eigenvectors.

4.6. True or false: A square matrix A is singular if and only if 0 is one of its eigenvalues.

4.7. True or false: If $\lambda = 0$ for every eigenvalue λ of a matrix A, then $A = 0$.

4.8. True or false: The diagonal elements of a complex Hermitian matrix must be real.

4.9. True or false: The eigenvalues of a complex Hermitian matrix must be real.

4.10. True or false: If two matrices have the same eigenvalues, then the two matrices are similar.

4.11. True or false: If two matrices are similar, then they have the same eigenvectors.

4.12. True or false: Given any arbitrary square matrix, there is some diagonal matrix that is similar to it.

4.13. True or false: Given any arbitrary square matrix, there is some triangular matrix that is unitarily similar to it.

4.14. True or false: The condition number of a matrix that determines the sensitivity of the solution to a system of linear equations also determines the sensitivity of the eigenvalues and eigenvectors to perturbations in the matrix.

4.15. True or false: A matrix that is both symmetric and Hessenberg must be tridiagonal.

4.16. True or false: If an $n \times n$ matrix A has distinct eigenvalues, then QR iteration applied to A necessarily converges to a diagonal matrix.

4.17. True or false: For a square matrix, the eigenvalues and the singular values are the same thing.

4.18. For a given matrix A,
  (*a*) Can the same eigenvalue correspond to two different eigenvectors?
  (*b*) Can the same eigenvector correspond to two different eigenvalues?

4.19. What are the eigenvalues and eigenvectors of a diagonal matrix?

4.20. Which of the following conditions necessarily imply that an $n \times n$ real matrix A is diagonalizable (i.e., is similar to a diagonal matrix)?
  (*a*) A has n distinct eigenvalues.
  (*b*) A has only real eigenvalues.
  (*c*) A is nonsingular.
  (*d*) A is equal to its transpose.
  (*e*) A commutes with its transpose.

4.21. Which of the following classes of matrices necessarily have all real eigenvalues?
  (*a*) Real symmetric
  (*b*) Real triangular
  (*c*) Arbitrary real
  (*d*) Complex symmetric
  (*e*) Complex Hermitian
  (*f*) Complex triangular with real diagonal
  (*g*) Arbitrary complex

4.22. Let A and B be similar matrices, i.e., $B = T^{-1}AT$ for some nonsingular matrix T. If y is an eigenvector of B, then exhibit an eigenvector of A.

4.23. The eigenvalues of a matrix are the roots of its characteristic polynomial. Does this fact provide a generally effective numerical method for computing the eigenvalues? Why?

4.24. Before applying QR iteration to find the eigenvalues of a matrix, the matrix is usually first transformed to a simpler form. For each type of matrix listed below, what intermediate form is appropriate?
  (*a*) A general real matrix
  (*b*) A real symmetric matrix

4.25. A general matrix can be reduced to triangular form by a single QR factorization, and the eigenvalues of a triangular matrix are its diagonal entries. Does this procedure suffice to compute the eigenvalues of the original matrix? Why?

4.26. Gauss-Jordan elimination reduces a matrix to diagonal form. Does this make the eigenvalues of the matrix obvious? Why?

4.27. (*a*) Why is the Jacobi method for computing all the eigenvalues of a real symmetric matrix relatively slowly convergent?
  (*b*) Name a method that is faster, and explain briefly why it is faster.

4.28. For which of the following classes of matrices of order n can the eigenvalues be computed in a finite number of steps for arbitrary n?
  (*a*) Diagonal
  (*b*) Tridiagonal
  (*c*) Triangular
  (*d*) Hessenberg
  (*e*) General real matrix with distinct eigenvalues
  (*f*) General real matrix with eigenvalues that are not necessarily distinct

4.29. In using QR iteration for computing the eigenvalues of a matrix, why is the matrix usually first reduced to some simpler form, such as Hessenberg or tridiagonal?

4.30. Applied to a given matrix A, QR iteration for computing eigenvalues converges to either diagonal or triangular form. What property of A determines which of these two forms is obtained?

4.31. As a preliminary step before computing its eigenvalues, a matrix A is often first reduced to Hessenberg form by a unitary similarity transformation. Why stop there? If such a preliminary reduction to Hessenberg form is good, wouldn't triangular form be even better? What is wrong with this argument?

4.32. Order the following algorithms 1 through 4, from least work required to most work required, for a general square matrix A:

  (*a*) LU factorization by Gaussian elimination with partial pivoting

  (*b*) Computing all of the eigenvalues and eigenvectors

  (*c*) Solving a triangular system by back-substitution

  (*d*) Computing the inverse of the matrix

4.33. The power method converges to which eigenvector of a matrix?

4.34. (*a*) If a matrix A has a simple dominant eigenvalue λ_1, what quantity determines the convergence rate of the power method for computing λ_1?

  (*b*) How can the convergence rate of the power method be improved?

4.35. Given an approximate eigenvector x for a matrix A, what is the best estimate (in the least squares sense) for the corresponding eigenvalue?

4.36. List three conditions under which the power method for computing an eigenvalue may fail.

4.37. Inverse iteration converges to which eigenvector of a matrix?

4.38. In the power method or inverse iteration for computing eigenvalues and eigenvectors, why are the vector iterates normalized at each iteration?

4.39. What is the main reason that shifts are used in iterative methods for computing eigenvalues, such as the power, inverse iteration, and QR iteration methods?

4.40. Given a general square matrix A, what method would you use to find the following?

  (*a*) The smallest eigenvalue of A

  (*b*) The largest eigenvalue of A

  (*c*) The eigenvalue of A closest to some specified scalar β

  (*d*) All of the eigenvalues of A

4.41. (*a*) Given an approximate eigenvalue λ for a matrix, how can one obtain a good approximate eigenvector?

  (*b*) Given an approximate eigenvector x for a matrix, how can one obtain a good approximate eigenvalue?

4.42. What is a Krylov sequence, and for what purpose is it useful?

4.43. Why is the Lanczos method faster than the power method for computing a few eigenvalues of a real symmetric matrix?

4.44. What features make the Lanczos method suitable for large sparse symmetric eigenvalue problems?

4.45. What is meant by the *inertia* of a real symmetric matrix?

4.46. (*a*) What is meant by a *congruence* transformation of a real symmetric matrix?

  (*b*) What properties of the matrix, if any, are preserved by such a transformation?

4.47. Explain briefly how spectrum-slicing methods work for computing individual eigenvalues of a real symmetric matrix.

4.48. (*a*) List two reasons why converting a generalized eigenvalue problem $Ax = \lambda Bx$ to the standard eigenvalue problem $(B^{-1}A)x = \lambda x$ might not be a good idea.

  (*b*) What is a better approach?

4.49. List at least two applications for the singular value decomposition (SVD) of a matrix.

4.50. How are the singular values of an $m \times n$ matrix A related to the eigenvalues of the $n \times n$ matrix $A^T A$?

4.51. Let A be an $m \times n$ matrix.

  (*a*) What is the maximum number of nonzero singular values that A can have?

  (*b*) If rank(A) $= k$, how many nonzero singular values does A have?

4.52. Let a be a nonzero column vector. Considered as an $n \times 1$ matrix, a has only one positive singular value. What is its value?

4.53. Is forming $A^T A$ and computing its eigenvalues a good way to compute the singular values of a matrix A? Why?

4.54. What is the condition number of a matrix with respect to the Euclidean vector norm, expressed in terms of the singular values of the matrix?

4.55. List two reliable methods for determining the rank of a rectangular matrix numerically.

4.56. If A is a $2n \times n$ matrix, rank the following methods according to the amount of work required to solve the linear least squares problem $Ax \approx b$.

    (*a*) QR factorization by Householder transformations

    (*b*) Normal equations

    (*c*) Singular value decomposition

EXERCISES

4.1. (*a*) Prove that 5 is an eigenvalue of the matrix

$$A = \begin{bmatrix} 6 & 3 & 3 & 1 \\ 0 & 7 & 4 & 5 \\ 0 & 0 & 5 & 4 \\ 0 & 0 & 0 & 8 \end{bmatrix}.$$

    (*b*) Exhibit an eigenvector of A corresponding to the eigenvalue 5.

4.2. What are the eigenvalues and corresponding eigenvectors of the following matrix?

$$\begin{bmatrix} 1 & 2 & -4 \\ 0 & 2 & 1 \\ 0 & 0 & 3 \end{bmatrix}$$

4.3. Let

$$A = \begin{bmatrix} 1 & 4 \\ 1 & 1 \end{bmatrix}.$$

Your answers to the following questions should be numeric and specific to this particular matrix, not just the general definitions.

    (*a*) What is the characteristic polynomial of A?

    (*b*) What are the roots of the characteristic polynomial of A?

    (*c*) What are the eigenvalues of A?

    (*d*) What are the corresponding eigenvectors of A?

    (*e*) Perform one iteration of the power method on A, using $x_0 = \begin{bmatrix} 1 & 1 \end{bmatrix}^T$ as starting vector.

    (*f*) To what eigenvector of A will the power method ultimately converge?

    (*g*) What eigenvalue estimate is given by the Rayleigh quotient, using the vector $x = \begin{bmatrix} 1 & 1 \end{bmatrix}^T$?

    (*h*) To what eigenvector of A would inverse iteration ultimately converge?

    (*i*) What eigenvalue of A would be obtained if inverse iteration were used with shift $\sigma = 2$?

    (*j*) If QR iteration were applied to A, to what form would it converge: diagonal or triangular? Why?

4.4. Give an example of a 2×2 matrix A and a nonzero starting vector x_0 such that the power method fails to converge to the eigenvector corresponding to the dominant eigenvalue of A.

4.5. Suppose that all of the row sums of an $n \times n$ matrix A have the same value, say, α.

    (*a*) Show that α is an eigenvalue of A.

    (*b*) What is the corresponding eigenvector?

4.6. Show that an $n \times n$ matrix A is singular if and only if zero is one of its eigenvalues.

4.7. Let A be an $n \times n$ matrix.

    (*a*) Show that A and A^T have the same eigenvalues.

    (*b*) Do A and A^T also have the same eigenvectors? Prove or give a counterexample.

4.8. Prove that an $n \times n$ matrix A is diagonalizable by a similarity transformation if and only if it has a complete set of n linearly independent eigenvectors.

4.9. (*a*) Prove that all the eigenvalues of a real symmetric matrix A are real (*Hint*: Consider $x^T A x$).

    (*b*) Prove that all the eigenvalues of a complex Hermitian matrix A are real (*Hint*: Consider $x^H A x$).

4.10. Prove that the eigenvalues of a positive definite matrix A are all positive.

4.11. Prove that for any matrix norm subordinate to a vector norm, $\rho(A) \leq \|A\|$.

4.12. Is there any real value for the parameter α such that the matrix

$$\begin{bmatrix} 1 & 0 & \alpha \\ 4 & 2 & 0 \\ 6 & 5 & 3 \end{bmatrix}$$

(a) Has all real eigenvalues?

(b) Has all complex eigenvalues with nonzero imaginary parts?

In each case, either give such a value for α or give a reason why none exists.

4.13. Give an example of a symmetric complex matrix (not Hermitian) that has complex eigenvalues (i.e., with nonzero imaginary parts).

4.14. If A and B are $n \times n$ matrices and A is nonsingular, show that the matrices AB and BA are similar.

4.15. Assume that A is a nonsingular $n \times n$ matrix.

(a) What is the relationship between the eigenvalues of A and those of A^{-1}? Prove your answer.

(b) What is the relationship between the eigenvectors of A and those of A^{-1}? Prove your answer.

4.16. If λ is an eigenvalue of an $n \times n$ matrix A, show that λ^2 is an eigenvalue of A^2.

4.17. Prove that if $A^k = 0$ for some positive integer k (such a matrix is said to be *nilpotent*), then all of the eigenvalues of A are zero.

4.18. What are the eigenvalues of an *idempotent* matrix (i.e., $A^2 = A$)?

4.19. (a) Let A be an $n \times n$ matrix, and suppose that A is symmetric. If λ and γ are eigenvalues of A, with $\lambda \neq \gamma$, show that $y^T x = 0$ (i.e., eigenvectors corresponding to distinct eigenvalues of a symmetric matrix are orthogonal).

(b) More generally, suppose now that A is not necessarily symmetric. If $Ax = \lambda x$ and $A^T y = \gamma y$, with $\lambda \neq \gamma$, show that $y^T x = 0$ (i.e., right and left eigenvectors corresponding to distinct eigenvalues are orthogonal).

4.20. Let A be an $n \times n$ matrix such that $\rho(A) < 1$.

(a) Show that the matrix $I - A$ is nonsingular.

(b) Show that

$$(I - A)^{-1} = \sum_{k=0}^{\infty} A^k.$$

4.21. If A is an $n \times n$ matrix of rank one, then A must have the form $A = uv^T$ for some nonzero vectors u and v.

(a) Show that the scalar $u^T v$ is an eigenvalue of A.

(b) What are the other eigenvalues of A?

(c) If the power method is applied to A, how many iterations are required for it to converge exactly to the eigenvector corresponding to the dominant eigenvalue?

4.22. Let $\lambda_1 \leq \lambda_2 \leq \cdots \leq \lambda_n$ be the (real) eigenvalues of an $n \times n$ real symmetric matrix A.

(a) To which of the eigenvalues of A is it possible for the power method to converge by using an appropriately chosen shift σ?

(b) In each such case, what value for the shift gives the most rapid convergence?

(c) Answer the same two questions for the inverse iteration method.

4.23. Let the $n \times n$ complex Hermitian matrix C be written as $C = A + iB$ (i.e., the matrices A and B are its real and imaginary parts, respectively). Define the $2n \times 2n$ real matrix $\bar{C}$ by

$$\bar{C} = \begin{bmatrix} A & -B \\ B & A \end{bmatrix}.$$

Let λ be an eigenvalue of C with corresponding eigenvector $x + iy$.

(a) Show that $\bar{C}$ is symmetric.

(b) Show that λ is an eigenvalue of $\bar{C}$, with both

$$\begin{bmatrix} x \\ y \end{bmatrix} \quad \text{and} \quad \begin{bmatrix} -y \\ x \end{bmatrix}$$

as corresponding eigenvectors.

(c) The previous results show that a routine for real symmetric eigenvalue problems can be used to solve complex Hermitian eigenvalue problems. Is this a good approach? Why?

4.24. (a) What are the eigenvalues of the following complex symmetric matrix?

$$\begin{bmatrix} 2i & 1 \\ 1 & 0 \end{bmatrix}$$

(b) How many linearly independent eigenvectors does it have?

(c) Contrast this situation with that for a real symmetric or complex Hermitian matrix.

4.25. (a) If λ is an eigenvalue of an orthogonal matrix Q, show that $|\lambda| = 1$.

(b) What are the singular values of an orthogonal matrix?

4.26. (a) What are the eigenvalues of the Householder transformation

$$H = I - 2\frac{vv^T}{v^Tv},$$

where v is any nonzero vector?

(b) What are the eigenvalues of the plane rotation

$$G = \begin{bmatrix} c & s \\ -s & c \end{bmatrix},$$

where $c^2 + s^2 = 1$?

4.27. Let A be an upper Hessenberg matrix having no zero entries on its subdiagonal. Show that A must have distinct eigenvalues.

4.28. Let A be a *singular* upper Hessenberg matrix having no zero entries on its subdiagonal. Show that the QR method applied to A produces an exact eigenvalue after only one iteration. This result suggests that the convergence of the QR method will be very rapid if we use a shift that is approximately equal to an eigenvalue.

4.29. Verify that the successive orthogonal vectors produced by the Lanczos algorithm (Section 4.3.9) satisfy a three-term recurrence. For example, Aq_3 is already orthogonal to q_1 and hence need be orthogonalized only against q_2 and q_3.

4.30. (a) Consider the column vector a as an $n \times 1$ matrix. Write out its singular value decomposition, showing the matrices U, Σ, and V explicitly.

(b) Consider the row vector a^T as a $1 \times n$ matrix. Write out its singular value decomposition, showing the matrices U, Σ, and V explicitly.

4.31. If A is an $m \times n$ matrix and b is an m-vector, prove that the solution x of minimum Euclidean norm to the least squares problem $Ax \approx b$ is given by

$$x = \sum_{\sigma_i \neq 0} \frac{u_i^T b}{\sigma_i} v_i,$$

where the σ_i, u_i, and v_i are the singular values and corresponding singular vectors of A.

4.32. Let A be an $m \times n$ real matrix. Consider the symmetric eigenvalue problem

$$\begin{bmatrix} 0 & A \\ A^T & 0 \end{bmatrix}\begin{bmatrix} u \\ v \end{bmatrix} = \lambda \begin{bmatrix} u \\ v \end{bmatrix}.$$

(a) Show that if λ, u, and v satisfy this relationship, with u and v suitably normalized, then $|\lambda|$ is a singular value of A with corresponding left and right singular vectors u and v, respectively.

(b) Is solving this eigenvalue problem a good way to compute the SVD of the matrix A? Why?

4.33. Prove that the pseudoinverse A^+ of an $m \times n$ matrix A, as defined using the SVD in Section 4.5.2, satisfies the following four properties, known as the *Moore-Penrose conditions.*

(a) $AA^+A = A$.

(b) $A^+AA^+ = A^+$.

(c) $(AA^+)^T = AA^+$.

(d) $(A^+A)^T = A^+A$.

4.34. (a) If an $n \times n$ matrix A is nonsingular, prove that $A^+ = A^{-1}$.

(b) If an $m \times n$ matrix A has rank n, prove that $A^+ = (A^TA)^{-1}A^T$.

(c) If an $m \times n$ matrix A has rank m, prove that $A^+ = A^T(AA^T)^{-1}$.

4.35. (a) What is the pseudoinverse of the following matrix?

$$\begin{bmatrix} 1 & 0 \\ 0 & 0 \end{bmatrix}$$

(b) If $\epsilon > 0$, what is the pseudoinverse of the following matrix?

$$\begin{bmatrix} 1 & 0 \\ 0 & \epsilon \end{bmatrix}$$

(c) What do these results imply about the conditioning of the problem of computing the pseudoinverse of a given matrix?

COMPUTER PROBLEMS

4.1. (*a*) Implement the power method to find the dominant eigenvalue and a corresponding eigenvector of the matrix

$$A = \begin{bmatrix} 2 & 3 & 2 \\ 10 & 3 & 4 \\ 3 & 6 & 1 \end{bmatrix}.$$

As starting vector, take $x_0 = \begin{bmatrix} 0 & 0 & 1 \end{bmatrix}^T$.

(*b*) Using any of the methods for deflation given in Section 4.3.5, deflate out the eigenvalue found in part *a* and apply the power method again to find the second largest eigenvalue of the same matrix.

(*c*) Use a general real eigensystem library routine to compute all of the eigenvalues and eigenvectors of the matrix, and compare the results with those obtained in parts *a* and *b*.

4.2. (*a*) Implement inverse iteration with a shift to compute the eigenvalue nearest to 2, and the corresponding eigenvector, of the matrix

$$A = \begin{bmatrix} 6 & 2 & 1 \\ 2 & 3 & 1 \\ 1 & 1 & 1 \end{bmatrix}.$$

You may use an arbitrary starting vector.

(*b*) Use a real symmetric eigensystem library routine to compute all of the eigenvalues and eigenvectors of the matrix, and compare the results with those obtained in part *a*.

4.3. Write a program implementing Rayleigh quotient iteration for computing an eigenvalue and corresponding eigenvector of a matrix. Test your program on the matrix in the previous exercise, using a random starting vector.

4.4. (*a*) Use a library routine to compute the eigenvalues of the matrix

$$A = \begin{bmatrix} -149 & -50 & -154 \\ 537 & 180 & 546 \\ -27 & -9 & -25 \end{bmatrix}.$$

(*b*) Compute the eigenvalues of the same matrix again, except with the a_{22} entry changed to 180.01.

(*c*) Compute the eigenvalues of the same matrix again, except with the a_{22} entry changed to 179.99.

(*d*) What conclusion can you draw about the conditioning of the eigenvalues of A?

4.5. Implement the following simple version of QR iteration with shifts for computing the eigenvalues of a general real matrix A. Repeat until convergence:

1. $\sigma = a_{n,n}$ (i.e., use corner entry as shift).
2. Compute QR factorization $A - \sigma I = QR$.
3. $A = RQ + \sigma I$.

(These steps will be easy if you use a package such as **MATLAB** but more involved if you use a library routine for the QR factorization or write your own.)

What convergence test should you use? Test your program on the matrices in the first two computer exercises above.

4.6. Write a program implementing the Lanczos method as given in Section 4.3.9. Test your program using a random symmetric matrix A of order n having eigenvalues $1, 2, \ldots, n$. To generate such a matrix, first generate an $n \times n$ matrix B with random entries uniformly distributed on the interval $[0, 1)$ (see Section 13.5), and then compute the QR factorization $B = QR$. Now take $A = QDQ^T$, where $D = \text{diag}(1, \ldots, n)$. The Lanczos algorithm generates only the tridiagonal matrix T_k at iteration k, so you will need to compute its eigenvalues (i.e., the Ritz values γ_i, $i = 1, \ldots, k$) at each iteration, say, by using a library routine based on QR iteration. For the purpose of this exercise, run the Lanczos algorithm for a full n iterations.

To see graphically how the Ritz values behave as iterations proceed, construct a plot with the iteration number on the vertical axis and the Ritz values at each iteration on the horizontal axis. Plot each pair (γ_i, k), $i = 1, \ldots, k$, as a discrete point at each iteration k (see Fig. 4.2). As iterations proceed and the number of Ritz values grows correspondingly, you should see vertical "trails" of Ritz values converging on the true eigenvalues. Try several values for n, say, $n = 10, 20, \ldots, 50$, making a separate plot for each.

4.7. Compute all the roots of the polynomial

$$p(x) = 24 - 40x + 35x^2 - 13x^3 + x^4$$

by forming the companion matrix (see Section 4.2.1) and then calling an eigenvalue routine to compute its eigenvalues. Note that the companion matrix is already in lower Hessenberg form (there is also an equivalent upper Hessenberg form), which you may be able to take advantage of, depending on the specific software you use. Compare the speed and accuracy of the companion matrix method with those of a library routine designed specifically for computing roots of polynomials (see Table 5.2). You may need to experiment with polynomials of larger degree to see a significant difference.

4.8. Compute the eigenvalues of the Hilbert matrix of order n (see Computer Problem 2.6) for several values of n, say, up to $n = 20$. Can you characterize the range of magnitudes of the eigenvalues as a function of n?

4.9. A singular matrix must have a zero eigenvalue, but must a nearly singular matrix have a "small" eigenvalue? Consider a matrix of the form

$$\begin{bmatrix} 1 & -1 & -1 & -1 & -1 \\ 0 & 1 & -1 & -1 & -1 \\ 0 & 0 & 1 & -1 & -1 \\ 0 & 0 & 0 & 1 & -1 \\ 0 & 0 & 0 & 0 & 1 \end{bmatrix},$$

whose eigenvalues are obviously all ones. Use a library routine to compute the singular values of such a matrix for various orders. How does the ratio $\sigma_{max}/\sigma_{min}$ behave as the order of the matrix grows? What conclusions can you draw?

4.10. A symmetric tridiagonal matrix with a multiple eigenvalue must have a zero on its subdiagonal, but do a close pair of eigenvalues imply that some subdiagonal element must be small? Consider the symmetric tridiagonal matrix of order $n = 2k + 1$ having $k, k - 1, \ldots, 1, 0, 1, \ldots, k$ as its diagonal entries and all ones as its subdiagonal and superdiagonal entries. Compute the eigenvalues of this matrix for various values of n. Does it have any multiple or nearly multiple eigenvalues? What conclusions can you draw?

4.11. A *Markov chain* is a system that has n possible states and passes through a series of transitions from one state to another. The probability of a transition from state j to state i is given by a_{ij}, where $0 \le a_{ij} \le 1$ and $\sum_{i=1}^{n} a_{ij} = 1$. Let A denote the matrix of transition probabilities, and let $x_i^{(k)}$ denote the probability that the system is in state i after transition k. If the initial probability distribution vector is $x^{(0)}$, then the probability distribution vector after k steps is given by

$$x^{(k)} = Ax^{(k-1)} = A^k x^{(0)}.$$

The long-term behavior of the system is therefore determined by the value of $\lim_{k \to \infty} A^k$.

Consider a system with three states and transition matrix

$$A = \begin{bmatrix} 0.8 & 0.2 & 0.1 \\ 0.1 & 0.7 & 0.3 \\ 0.1 & 0.1 & 0.6 \end{bmatrix},$$

and suppose that the system is initially in state 1.

(*a*) What is the probability distribution vector after three steps?

(*b*) What is the long-term value of the probability distribution vector?

(*c*) Does the long-term value of the probability distribution vector depend on the particular starting value $x^{(0)}$?

(*d*) What is the value of $\lim_{k \to \infty} A^k$, and what is the rank of this matrix?

(*e*) Explain your previous results in terms of the eigenvalues and eigenvectors of A.

(*f*) Must 1 *always* be an eigenvalue of the transition matrix of a Markov chain? Why?

(*g*) A probability distribution vector x is said to be *stationary* if $Ax = x$. How can you determine such a stationary value x using the eigenvalues and eigenvectors of A?

(*h*) How can you determine a stationary value x *without* knowledge of the eigenvalues and eigenvectors of A?

(*i*) In this particular example, is it possible for a previous distribution vector to recur, other than a stationary distribution? For Markov chains in general, is such nontrivial cyclic behavior possible? If not, why? If so, give an example. (*Hint:* Think about the location of the eigenvalues of A in the complex plane.)

(*j*) Can there be more than one stationary distribution vector for a given Markov chain? If not, why? If so, give an example.

(*k*) Of what numerical method does this problem remind you?

4.12. Consider the spring-mass system

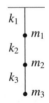

with three masses m_1, m_2, and m_3 at vertical locations y_1, y_2, and y_3 connected by three springs having spring constants k_1, k_2, and k_3. According to Newton's Second Law, the motion of the system is governed by the system of ordinary differential equations

$$My'' + Ky = 0,$$

where

$$M = \begin{bmatrix} m_1 & 0 & 0 \\ 0 & m_2 & 0 \\ 0 & 0 & m_3 \end{bmatrix}$$

is the *mass matrix* and

$$K = \begin{bmatrix} k_1 + k_2 & -k_2 & 0 \\ -k_2 & k_2 + k_3 & -k_3 \\ 0 & -k_3 & k_3 \end{bmatrix}$$

is the *stiffness matrix*. Such a system exhibits simple harmonic motion with natural frequency ω, i.e., the solution components are given by

$$y_k(t) = x_k e^{i\omega t},$$

where x_k is the amplitude, $k = 1, 2, 3$, and $i = \sqrt{-1}$. To determine the frequency ω and mode of vibration (i.e., the amplitudes x_k), we note that for each solution component,

$$y_k''(t) = -\omega^2 x_k e^{i\omega t}.$$

Substituting this relationship into the differential equation, we obtain the algebraic equation

$$Kx = \lambda M x,$$

where $\lambda = \omega^2$. Thus, the natural frequencies and modes of vibration can be determined by solving a generalized eigenvalue problem (see Section 4.4).

For purposes of this problem, assume the values $k_1 = k_2 = k_3 = 1$, $m_1 = 2$, $m_2 = 3$, and $m_4 = 4$, in arbitrary units.

(a) For this particular problem, the mass matrix M is diagonal, so there is no harm in converting the generalized eigenvalue problem to a standard eigenvalue problem. Taking this approach, determine all three natural frequencies and modes of vibration for the system, using any combination you choose of the power and inverse iteration methods (you may use shifts, deflation, or both).

(b) If you have access to a library routine for solving generalized eigenvalue problems, use it to solve this problem directly in its original form, and compare the results with those obtained in part a.

4.13. (a) The *matrix exponential* function of an $n \times n$ matrix A is defined by the infinite series

$$\exp(A) = I + A + \frac{A^2}{2!} + \frac{A^3}{3!} + \cdots.$$

Write a program to evaluate $\exp(A)$ using the foregoing series definition.

(b) An alternative way to compute the matrix exponential uses the eigenvalue-eigenvector decomposition

$$A = U \operatorname{diag}(\lambda_1, \ldots, \lambda_n) U^{-1},$$

where $\lambda_1, \ldots, \lambda_n$ are the eigenvalues of A and U is a matrix whose columns are corresponding eigenvectors. Then the matrix exponential is given by

$$\exp(A) = U \operatorname{diag}(e^{\lambda_1}, \ldots, e^{\lambda_n}) U^{-1}.$$

Write a second program to evaluate $\exp(A)$ using this method.

Test both methods using each of the following test matrices:

$$A = \begin{bmatrix} 2 & -1 \\ -1 & 2 \end{bmatrix},$$

$$B = \begin{bmatrix} 113 & -114 \\ 152 & -153 \end{bmatrix}.$$

Compare your results with those for a library routine for computing the matrix exponential, if you have access to one. Which of your two routines is more accurate and robust? Try to explain why. See [179] for several additional methods for computing the matrix exponential.

4.14. Write a routine for solving an arbitrary, possibly rank-deficient, linear least squares problem $Ax \approx b$ using the singular value decomposition. You may call a library routine to compute the SVD, then use its output to compute the least squares solution (see Section 4.5.2). The input to your routine should include the matrix A, right-hand-side vector b, and a tolerance for determining the numerical rank of A. Test your routine on some of the linear least squares problems in Chapter 3.

4.15. (a) Write a routine that uses a one-sided plane rotation to symmetrize an arbitrary 2×2 matrix. That is, given a 2×2 matrix A, choose c and s so that

$$\begin{bmatrix} c & s \\ -s & c \end{bmatrix} \begin{bmatrix} a_{11} & a_{12} \\ a_{21} & a_{22} \end{bmatrix} = \begin{bmatrix} b_{11} & b_{12} \\ b_{12} & b_{22} \end{bmatrix}$$

is symmetric.

(b) Write a routine that uses a two-sided plane rotation to annihilate the off-diagonal entries of an arbitrary 2×2 symmetric matrix. That is, given a symmetric 2×2 matrix B, choose c and s so that

$$\begin{bmatrix} c & -s \\ s & c \end{bmatrix} \begin{bmatrix} b_{11} & b_{12} \\ b_{12} & b_{22} \end{bmatrix} \begin{bmatrix} c & s \\ -s & c \end{bmatrix} = \begin{bmatrix} d_{11} & 0 \\ 0 & d_{22} \end{bmatrix}$$

is diagonal.

(c) Combine the two routines developed in parts a and b to obtain a routine for computing the singular value decomposition $A = U\Sigma V^T$ of an arbitrary 2×2 matrix A. Note that U will be a product to two plane rotations, whereas V will be a single plane rotation. Test your routine on a few randomly chosen 2×2 matrices and compare the results with those for a library SVD routine.

By systematically solving successive 2×2 subproblems, the module you have just developed can be used to compute the SVD of an arbitrary $m \times n$ matrix in a manner analogous to the Jacobi method for the symmetric eigenvalue problem.

4.16. We will revisit Computer Problem 3.5 concerning the elliptical orbit of a planet, represented in a Cartesian (x, y) coordinate system by the equation

$$ay^2 + bxy + cx + dy + e = x^2.$$

The orbital parameters a, b, c, d, e can be determined by a linear least squares fit to the following observations of the planet's position:

x	1.02	0.95	0.87	0.77	0.67
y	0.39	0.32	0.27	0.22	0.18
x	0.56	0.44	0.30	0.16	0.01
y	0.15	0.13	0.12	0.13	0.15

(a) Use a library routine to compute the singular value decomposition of the 10×5 least squares matrix.

(b) Use the singular value decomposition to compute the solution to the least squares problem. With the singular values in order of decreasing magnitude, compute the solutions using the first k singular values, $k = 1, \ldots, 5$. For each of the five solutions obtained, print the values for the orbital parameters and also plot the resulting orbits along with the given data points in the (x, y) plane.

(c) Perturb the input data slightly by adding to each coordinate of each data point a random number uniformly distributed on the interval $[-0.005, 0.005]$. Compute the singular value decomposition of the new

least squares matrix, and solve the least squares problem with the perturbed data as in part b. Compare the new values for the parameters with those previously computed for each value of k. What effect does this difference have on the plot of the orbits? Can you explain this behavior? Which solution would you regard as better: one that fits the data more closely, or one that is less sensitive to small perturbations in the data? Why?

4.17. Write a routine for computing the pseudoinverse of an arbitrary $m \times n$ matrix. You may call a library routine to compute the singular value decomposition, then use its output to compute the pseudoinverse (see Section 4.5.2). Consider the use of a tolerance for declaring relatively small singular values to be zero. Test your routine on both singular and nonsingular matrices. In the latter case, of course, your results should agree with those of standard matrix inversion. What happens when the matrix is nonsingular, but severely ill-conditioned (e.g., a Hilbert matrix)?

4.18. Consider the problem of fitting the model function

$$f(t, x) = xt$$

(i.e., a straight line through the origin, with slope x to be determined) to the following data points:

t	-2	-1	3
y	-1	3	-2

(a) Perform a standard linear least squares fit of such a line to y as a function of t, minimizing the vertical distances between the data points and the line (this procedure is appropriate if y is subject to error and t is known exactly).

(b) Perform a standard linear least squares fit of such a line to t as a function of y, minimizing the horizontal distances between the data points and the line (this procedure is appropriate if t is subject to error and y is known exactly).

(c) Perform a total least squares fit of the line to the data, minimizing the orthogonal distances between the data points and the line (this procedure is appropriate if both variables are subject to error). Such a fit can be done using the singular value decomposition (see Section 4.5.2).

(d) What is the resulting slope x of the line in each case? Plot the data points and all three lines on a single graph.

CHAPTER 5

Nonlinear Equations

5.1 NONLINEAR EQUATIONS

We will now consider methods for solving *nonlinear equations*. Given a nonlinear function f, we seek a value x for which

$$f(x) = 0.$$

Such a solution value for x is called a *root* of the equation, and a *zero* of the function f. Though technically they have distinct meanings, these two terms are informally used more or less interchangeably, with the obvious meaning. Thus, this problem is often referred to as *root finding* or *zero finding*.

In discussing numerical methods for solving nonlinear equations, we will distinguish two cases:

$$f: \mathbb{R} \rightarrow \mathbb{R} \quad \text{(scalar)},$$

and

$$f: \mathbb{R}^n \rightarrow \mathbb{R}^n \quad \text{(vector)}.$$

The latter is referred to as a *system* of nonlinear equations.

EXAMPLE 5.1 NONLINEAR EQUATIONS. An example of a nonlinear equation in one dimension is

$$x^2 - 4\sin(x) = 0,$$

for which one approximate solution is $x = 1.9$. An example of a system of nonlinear equations in two dimensions is

$$x_1^2 - x_2 + 0.25 = 0,$$
$$-x_1 + x_2^2 + 0.25 = 0,$$

for which the solution vector is $x = \begin{bmatrix} 0.5 & 0.5 \end{bmatrix}^T$.

5.1.1 Solutions of Nonlinear Equations

A system of linear equations always has a unique solution unless the matrix of the system is singular. The existence and uniqueness of solutions for nonlinear equations are often much more complicated and difficult to determine, and a much wider variety of behavior is possible. Curved lines can intersect, or fail to intersect, in many more ways than straight lines can. For example, unlike straight lines, two curved lines can be tangent without being coincident. Whereas for systems of linear equations the number of solutions must be either zero, one, or infinitely many, nonlinear equations can have any number of solutions.

EXAMPLE 5.2 SOLUTIONS OF NONLINEAR EQUATIONS. For example:

- $e^x + 1 = 0$ has no solution.
- $e^{-x} - x = 0$ has one solution.
- $x^2 - 4\sin(x) = 0$ has two solutions.
- $x^3 + 6x^2 + 11x - 6 = 0$ has three solutions.
- $\sin(x) = 0$ has infinitely many solutions.

In addition, a nonlinear equation may have a *multiple root*, where both the function *and* its derivative are zero, i.e., $f(x) = 0$ and $f'(x) = 0$. In one dimension, this property means that the curve has a horizontal tangent on the x axis. If $f(x) = 0$ and $f'(x) \neq 0$, then x is said to be a *simple root*.

EXAMPLE 5.3 MULTIPLE ROOT. Examples of equations having a multiple root include

$$x^2 - 2x + 1 = 0 \quad \text{and} \quad x^3 - 3x^2 + 3x - 1 = 0,$$

which are illustrated in Fig. 5.1.

What do we mean by an approximate solution $\hat{x}$ to a nonlinear system,

$$\|f(\hat{x})\| \approx 0 \quad \text{or} \quad \|\hat{x} - x^*\| \approx 0,$$

where x^* is the "true" solution to $f(x) = 0$? The first corresponds to having a small residual, whereas the second measures closeness to the (usually unknown) true solution. As with linear systems, these two criteria for a solution are not necessarily "small"

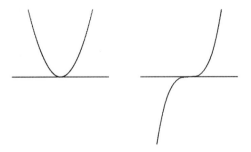

FIGURE 5.1
Nonlinear equations having a multiple root.

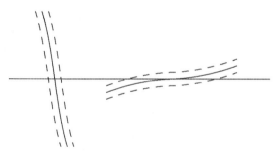

FIGURE 5.2
Conditioning of roots of nonlinear equations.

well-conditioned   ill-conditioned

simultaneously. This feature is illustrated in Fig. 5.2, where the two functions have about the same uncertainty in their values (e.g., due to rounding error or measurement error) but very different uncertainties in the locations of their roots (compare with Fig. 2.2). Thus, we see that the same concept of sensitivity or conditioning applies to nonlinear equations: it is the relative change in the solution due to a given relative change in the input data. For example, a multiple root tends to be ill-conditioned, since by definition the curve has a horizontal tangent at such a root, and is therefore locally approximately parallel to the x axis.

The conditioning of the root-finding problem for a given function is the opposite of that for *evaluating* the function: if the function value is insensitive to the value of the argument, then the root will be sensitive, whereas if the function value is sensitive to the argument, then the root will be insensitive. This property makes sense, because the two problems are inverses of each other: if $y = f(x)$, then finding x given y has the opposite conditioning from finding y given x.

5.1.2 Convergence Rates of Iterative Methods

Unlike linear equations, most nonlinear equations cannot be solved in a finite number of steps. Thus, we must usually resort to an iterative method that produces increasingly accurate approximations to the solution, and we terminate the iteration when the result is sufficiently accurate. The total cost of solving the problem depends on both the cost per iteration and the number of iterations required for convergence, and there is often a trade-off between these two factors.

To compare the effectiveness of iterative methods, we need to characterize their convergence rates. We denote the error at iteration k by e_k, and it is usually given by $e_k = x_k - x^*$, where x_k is the approximate solution at iteration k, and x^* is the true solution. Some methods for one-dimensional problems do not actually produce a specific approximate solution x_k, however, but merely produce an interval known to contain the solution, with the length of the interval decreasing as iterations proceed. For such methods, we take e_k to be the length of this interval at iteration k. In either case, a method is said to converge with rate r if

$$\lim_{k \to \infty} \frac{\|e_{k+1}\|}{\|e_k\|^r} = C$$

for some finite nonzero constant C. Some particular cases of interest are these:

- If $r = 1$ and $C < 1$, the convergence rate is *linear*.
- If $r > 1$, the convergence rate is *superlinear*.
- If $r = 2$, the convergence rate is *quadratic*.

One way to interpret the distinction between linear and superlinear convergence is that, asymptotically, a linearly convergent sequence gains a constant number of digits of accuracy per iteration, whereas a superlinearly convergent sequence gains an increasing number of digits of accuracy with each iteration. Specifically, a linearly convergent sequence gains $-\log_\beta(C)$ base-β digits per iteration, but a superlinearly convergent sequence has r times as many digits of accuracy after each iteration as it had the previous iteration. In particular, a quadratically convergent method doubles the number of digits of accuracy with each iteration.

5.2 NONLINEAR EQUATIONS IN ONE DIMENSION

We first consider methods for nonlinear equations in one dimension. Given a function $f\colon \mathbb{R} \to \mathbb{R}$, we seek a point x such that $f(x) = 0$.

5.2.1 Bisection Method

In finite-precision arithmetic, there may not be a floating-point number x such that $f(x)$ is exactly zero. One alternative is to look for a very short interval $[a, b]$ in which f has a change of sign, since the corresponding continuous function must be zero somewhere within such an interval. An interval for which the sign of f differs at its endpoints is called a *bracket*. The *bisection method* begins with an initial bracket and successively reduces its length until the solution has been isolated as accurately as desired. At each iteration, the function is evaluated at the midpoint of the current interval, and half of the interval can then be discarded, depending on the sign of the function at the midpoint. More formally, the algorithm is as follows, where $\text{sign}(x) = 1$ if $x \geq 0$ and $\text{sign}(x) = -1$ if $x < 0$:

Initial input: a function f, an interval $[a, b]$ such that $\text{sign}(f(a)) \neq \text{sign}(f(b))$, and an error tolerance *tol*.

while $((b - a) > tol)$ **do**
    $m = a + (b - a)/2$
    if $\text{sign}(f(a)) = \text{sign}(f(m))$ **then**
        $a = m$
    else
        $b = m$
    end
end

EXAMPLE 5.4 BISECTION METHOD. We illustrate the bisection method by finding a root of the equation

$$f(x) = x^2 - 4\sin(x) = 0.$$

For the initial bracketing interval $[a, b]$, we take $a = 1$ and $b = 3$. All that really matters is that the function values differ in sign at the two points. We evaluate the function at the midpoint $m = a + (b - a)/2 = 2$ and find that $f(m)$ has the opposite sign from $f(a)$, so we retain the first half of the initial interval by setting $b = m$. We then repeat the process until the bracketing interval isolates the root of the equation as accurately as desired. The sequence of iterations is shown here.

a	$f(a)$	b	$f(b)$
1.000000	−2.365884	3.000000	8.435520
1.000000	−2.365884	2.000000	0.362810
1.500000	−1.739980	2.000000	0.362810
1.750000	−0.873444	2.000000	0.362810
1.875000	−0.300718	2.000000	0.362810
1.875000	−0.300718	1.937500	0.019849
1.906250	−0.143255	1.937500	0.019849
1.921875	−0.652406	1.937500	0.019849
1.929688	−0.021454	1.937500	0.019849
1.933594	−0.000846	1.937500	0.019849
1.933594	−0.000846	1.935547	0.009491
1.933594	−0.000846	1.934570	0.004320
1.933594	−0.000846	1.934082	0.001736
1.933594	−0.000846	1.933838	0.000445
1.933716	−0.000201	1.933838	0.000445
1.933716	−0.000201	1.933777	0.000122
1.933746	−0.000039	1.933777	0.000122
1.933746	−0.000039	1.933762	0.000041
1.933746	−0.000039	1.933754	0.000001
1.933750	−0.000019	1.933754	0.000001
1.933752	−0.000009	1.933754	0.000001
1.933753	−0.000004	1.933754	0.000001

The bisection method makes no use of the magnitudes of the function values, only their signs. As a result, bisection is certain to converge but does so rather slowly. Specifically, at each successive iteration the length of the interval containing the solution, and hence a bound on the possible error, is reduced by half. This means that the bisection method is linearly convergent, with $r = 1$ and $C = 0.5$. Another way of stating this is that we gain one bit of accuracy in the approximate solution for each iteration of bisection. Given a starting interval $[a, b]$, the length of the interval after k iterations is $(b - a)/2^k$, so that achieving an error tolerance of tol requires

$$\left\lceil \log_2\left(\frac{b - a}{tol}\right) \right\rceil$$

iterations, regardless of the particular function f involved.

5.2.2 Fixed-Point Iteration

Given a function $g\colon \mathbb{R} \to \mathbb{R}$, a value x such that

$$x = g(x)$$

is called a *fixed point* of the function g, since x is unchanged when g is applied to it. Fixed-point problems often arise directly in practice, but they are also important because a nonlinear equation can often be recast as a fixed-point problem for a related nonlinear function. Indeed, many iterative algorithms for solving nonlinear systems are based on iteration schemes of the form

$$x_{k+1} = g(x_k),$$

where g is a suitably chosen function whose fixed points are solutions for $f(x) = 0$. Such a scheme is called *fixed-point iteration* or sometimes *functional iteration*, since the function g is applied repeatedly to an initial starting value x_0.

For a given equation $f(x) = 0$, there may be many equivalent fixed-point problems $x = g(x)$ with different choices for the function g. But not all fixed-point formulations are equally useful in deriving an iteration scheme for solving a given nonlinear equation. The resulting iteration schemes may differ not only in their convergence rates but also in whether they converge at all.

EXAMPLE 5.5 FIXED-POINT PROBLEMS. For the nonlinear equation

$$f(x) = x^2 - x - 2 = 0,$$

any of the choices

$$g(x) = x^2 - 2,$$
$$g(x) = \sqrt{x + 2},$$
$$g(x) = 1 + 2/x,$$
$$g(x) = \frac{x^2 + 2}{2x - 1}$$

is a function whose fixed points are solutions to the equation $f(x) = 0$. Each of these functions is plotted in Fig. 5.3, where we see that the intersection of the curve $y = g(x)$ with the line $y = x$ is what we seek. By design, each of the functions passes through the point $(2, 2)$, and indeed $f(2) = 0$.

The corresponding iteration schemes are depicted graphically in Fig. 5.4. A vertical arrow corresponds to evaluation of the function at a point, and a horizontal arrow pointing to the line $y = x$ indicates that the result of the previous function evaluation is used as the argument for the next. For the first of these functions, even with a starting point very near the solution, the iteration scheme diverges. For the other three functions, the iteration scheme converges to the fixed point even if it is started relatively far from the solution, although the apparent rates of convergence vary somewhat.

As one can see from Fig. 5.4, the behavior of fixed-point iteration schemes can vary widely, from divergence, to slow convergence, to rapid convergence. What makes

FIGURE 5.3
A fixed point of some nonlinear functions.

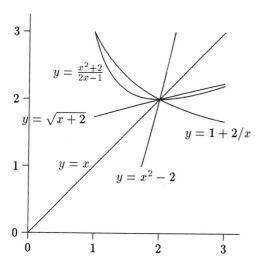

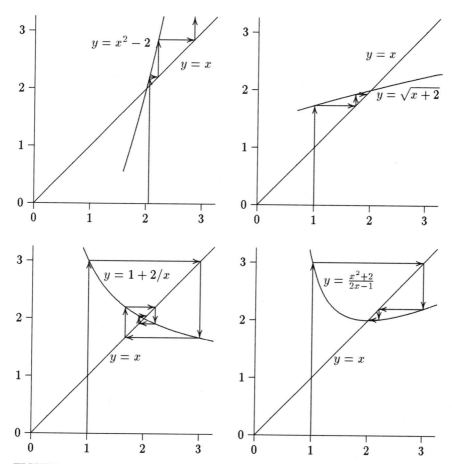

FIGURE 5.4
Fixed-point iterations for some nonlinear functions.

the difference? The simplest (though not the most general) way to characterize the behavior of an iterative scheme $x_{k+1} = g(x_k)$ for the fixed-point problem $x = g(x)$ is to consider the derivative of g at the solution x^*, assuming that g is smooth. In particular, if $x^* = g(x^*)$ and

$$|g'(x^*)| < 1,$$

then the iterative scheme is *locally convergent*, i.e., there is an interval containing x^* such that the corresponding iterative scheme is convergent if started within that interval. If, on the other hand, $|g'(x^*)| > 1$, then the corresponding iterative scheme diverges.

The proof of this result is simple and instructive, so we sketch it here. If x^* is a fixed point, then for the error at the kth iteration we have

$$e_{k+1} = x_{k+1} - x^* = g(x_k) - g(x^*).$$

By the Mean Value Theorem, there is a point θ_k between x_k and x^* such that

$$g(x_k) - g(x^*) = g'(\theta_k)(x_k - x^*),$$

so that

$$e_{k+1} = g'(\theta_k)e_k.$$

We do not know the value of θ_k, but if $|g'(x^*)| < 1$, then by starting the iterations close enough to x^*, we can be assured that there is a constant C such that $|g'(\theta_k)| \le C < 1$, for $k = 0, 1, \ldots$. Thus, we have

$$|e_{k+1}| \le C|e_k| \le \cdots \le C^k|e_0|,$$

and since $C^k \to 0$, then $|e_k| \to 0$ and the sequence converges.

As we can see from the proof, the asymptotic convergence rate of a fixed-point iteration scheme is usually linear, with constant $C = |g'(x^*)|$. The smaller the constant, the faster the convergence, so ideally we would like to have $g'(x^*) = 0$, in which case a similar proof shows that the convergence rate is at least quadratic. We will next see a systematic way of choosing g so that this occurs.

5.2.3 Newton's Method

The bisection technique makes no use of the function values other than their signs, which results in sure but slow convergence. More rapidly convergent methods can be derived by using the function values to obtain a more accurate approximation to the solution at each iteration. In particular, the truncated Taylor series

$$f(x + h) \approx f(x) + f'(x)h$$

is a linear function of h that approximates f near a given x. We can therefore replace the nonlinear function f with this linear function, whose zero is easily determined to be $h = -f(x)/f'(x)$, assuming that $f'(x) \ne 0$. Of course, the zeros of the two functions are not identical in general, so we repeat the process. This motivates the following iteration scheme, known as *Newton's method*:

$$x_{k+1} = x_k - f(x_k)/f'(x_k).$$

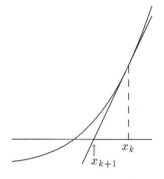

FIGURE 5.5
Newton's method for solving a nonlinear equation.

Newton's method can be interpreted as approximating the function f near x_k by the tangent line at $f(x_k)$. We can then take the next approximate solution to be the zero of this linear function, and repeat the process. Newton's method is illustrated in Fig. 5.5.

EXAMPLE 5.6 NEWTON'S METHOD. We illustrate Newton's method by again finding a root of the equation

$$f(x) = x^2 - 4\sin(x) = 0.$$

The derivative of this function is given by

$$f'(x) = 2x - 4\cos(x),$$

so that the iteration scheme is given by

$$x_{k+1} = x_k - \frac{x_k^2 - 4\sin(x_k)}{2x_k - 4\cos(x_k)}.$$

Taking $x_0 = 3$ as starting value, we get the sequence of iterations shown next, where $h = -f(x)/f'(x)$ denotes the change in x at each iteration. The iteration is terminated when $|h|$ is as small as desired relative to $|x|$.

x	$f(x)$	$f'(x)$	h
3.000000	8.435520	9.959970	−0.846942
2.153058	1.294772	6.505771	−0.199019
1.954039	0.108438	5.403795	−0.020067
1.933972	0.001152	5.288919	−0.000218
1.933754	0.000000	5.287670	0.000000

We can view Newton's method as a systematic way of transforming a nonlinear equation $f(x) = 0$ into a fixed-point problem $x = g(x)$, where

$$g(x) = x - f(x)/f'(x).$$

To study the convergence of this scheme, we therefore determine the derivative

$$g'(x) = f(x)f''(x)/(f'(x))^2.$$

If x^* is a simple root (i.e., $f(x^*) = 0$ and $f'(x^*) \neq 0$), then $g'(x^*) = 0$. Thus, the asymptotic convergence rate of Newton's method for a simple root is quadratic, i.e., $r = 2$. We have already seen an illustration of this: the fourth fixed-point iteration scheme in Example 5.5 is Newton's method for solving that example equation (note that the fourth iteration function in Fig. 5.4 has a horizontal tangent at the fixed point).

The quadratic convergence rate of Newton's method for a simple root means that asymptotically the error is squared at each iteration. Another way of stating this is that the number of digits of accuracy in the approximate solution is doubled at each iteration of Newton's method. For a multiple root, on the other hand, Newton's method is only linearly convergent [with constant $C = 1 - (1/m)$, where m is the multiplicity]. It is important to remember, however, that these convergence results are only local, and Newton's method may not converge at all unless started close enough to the solution. For example, a relatively small value for $f'(x_k)$ (i.e., a nearly horizontal tangent) tends to cause the next iterate to lie far away from the current approximation.

EXAMPLE 5.7 NEWTON'S METHOD FOR A MULTIPLE ROOT. Both types of behavior are shown in the following examples, where the first shows quadratic convergence to a simple root and the second shows linear convergence to a multiple root. The multiplicity for the second problem is 2, so $C = 0.5$.

$f(x) = x^2 - 1$		$f(x) = x^2 - 2x + 1$
k	x_k	x_k
0	2.0	2.0
1	1.25	1.5
2	1.025	1.25
3	1.0003	1.125
4	1.00000005	1.0625
5	1.0	1.03125

5.2.4 Secant Method

One drawback of Newton's method is that both the function and its derivative must be evaluated at each iteration. The derivative may be inconvenient or expensive to evaluate, so we might consider approximating it by a finite difference quotient over some small stepsize h, as in Example 1.11; but this would require a second evaluation of the function at each iteration purely for the purpose of obtaining derivative information. A better idea is to base the finite difference approximation on successive iterates, where the function must be evaluated anyway. This approach gives the *secant method:*

$$x_{k+1} = x_k - f(x_k)\frac{x_k - x_{k-1}}{f(x_k) - f(x_{k-1})}.$$

The secant method can be interpreted as approximating the function f by the secant line through the previous two iterates, and taking the zero of the resulting linear function to be the next approximate solution, as illustrated in Fig. 5.6.

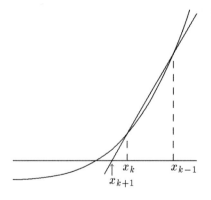

FIGURE 5.6
Secant method for solving a nonlinear equation.

EXAMPLE 5.8 SECANT METHOD. We illustrate the secant method by again finding a root of the equation

$$f(x) = x^2 - 4\sin(x) = 0.$$

We take $x_0 = 1$ and $x_1 = 3$ as our two starting guesses for the solution. We evaluate the function at each of these two points and generate a new approximate solution by fitting a straight line to the two function values according to the secant formula. We then repeat the process using this new value and the more recent of our two previous values. Note that only one new function evaluation is needed per iteration. The sequence of iterations is shown next, where h denotes the change in x at each iteration.

x	$f(x)$	h
1.000000	−2.365884	
3.000000	8.435520	−1.561930
1.438070	−1.896774	0.286735
1.724805	−0.977706	0.305029
2.029833	0.534305	−0.107789
1.922044	−0.061523	0.011130
1.933174	−0.003064	0.000583
1.933757	0.000019	−0.000004
1.933754	0.000000	0.000000

Because each new approximate solution produced by the secant method depends on two previous iterates, its convergence behavior is somewhat more complicated to analyze, so we omit most of the details. It can be shown that the errors satisfy

$$\lim_{k \to \infty} \frac{|e_{k+1}|}{|e_k| \cdot |e_{k-1}|} = c$$

for some finite nonzero constant c, which implies that the sequence is locally convergent and suggests that the rate is superlinear. For each k we define

$$s_k = |e_{k+1}| / |e_k|^r,$$

where r is the convergence rate to be determined. Thus, we have

$$|e_{k+1}| = s_k|e_k|^r = s_k(s_{k-1}|e_{k-1}|^r)^r = s_k s_{k-1}^r |e_{k-1}|^{r^2},$$

so that

$$\frac{|e_{k+1}|}{|e_k| \cdot |e_{k-1}|} = \frac{s_k s_{k-1}^r |e_{k-1}|^{r^2}}{s_{k-1}|e_{k-1}|^r |e_{k-1}|} = s_k s_{k-1}^{r-1} |e_{k-1}|^{r^2-r-1}.$$

But $|e_k| \to 0$, whereas the foregoing ratio on the left tends to a nonzero constant; so we must have $r^2 - r - 1 = 0$, which implies that the convergence rate is given by the positive solution to this quadratic equation, $r = (1 + \sqrt{5})/2 \approx 1.618$. Thus, the secant method is normally superlinearly convergent, but, like Newton's method, it must be started close enough to the solution in order to converge.

Compared with Newton's method, the secant method has the advantage of requiring only one new function evaluation per iteration, but it has the disadvantages of requiring two starting guesses and converging somewhat more slowly, though still superlinearly. The lower cost per iteration of the secant method often more than offsets the larger number of iterations required for convergence, however, so that the total cost of finding a root is often less for the secant method than for Newton's method.

5.2.5 Inverse Interpolation

At each iteration of the secant method, a straight line is fit to two values of the function whose zero is sought. A higher convergence rate (but not exceeding $r = 2$) can be obtained by fitting a higher-degree polynomial to the appropriate number of function values. For example, one could fit a quadratic polynomial to three successive iterates and use one of its roots as the next approximate solution. There are several difficulties with this idea, however: the polynomial may not have real roots, and even if it does they may not be easy to compute, and it may not be easy to choose which root to use as the next iterate. (On the other hand, if one seeks a *complex root*, then a polynomial having complex roots is desirable; in *Muller's method*, for example, a quadratic polynomial is used in approximating complex roots.)

An answer to these difficulties is provided by *inverse interpolation*, in which one fits the values x_k as a function of the values $y_k = f(x_k)$, say, by a polynomial $p(y)$, so that the next approximate solution is simply $p(0)$. This idea is illustrated in Fig. 5.7, where a parabola fitting y as a function of x has no real root (i.e., it fails to cross the x axis), but a parabola fitting x as a function of y is merely evaluated at zero to obtain the next iterate.

Using inverse quadratic interpolation, at each iteration we have three approximate solution values, which we denote by a, b, and c, with corresponding function values f_a, f_b, and f_c, respectively. The next approximate solution is found by fitting a quadratic polynomial to a, b, and c as a function of f_a, f_b, and f_c, and then evaluating the polynomial at 0. This task is accomplished by the following formulas, whose derivation will become clearer after we study Lagrange interpolation in Section 7.2.2:

$$u = f_b/f_c, \qquad v = f_b/f_a, \qquad w = f_a/f_c,$$
$$p = v(w(u - w)(c - b) - (1 - u)(b - a)), \qquad q = (w - 1)(u - 1)(v - 1).$$

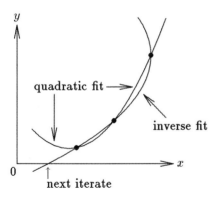

FIGURE 5.7
Inverse interpolation for finding a root.

The new approximate solution is given by $b + p/q$. The process is then repeated with b replaced by the new approximation, a replaced by the old b, and c replaced by the old a. Note that only one new function evaluation is needed per iteration. The convergence rate of inverse quadratic interpolation for root finding is $r \approx 1.839$, which is the same as for regular quadratic interpolation (Muller's method). Again this result is local, and the iterations must be started close enough to the solution to obtain convergence.

EXAMPLE 5.9 INVERSE QUADRATIC INTERPOLATION. We illustrate inverse quadratic interpolation by again finding a root of the equation

$$f(x) = x^2 - 4\sin(x) = 0.$$

Taking $a = 1$, $b = 2$, and $c = 3$ as starting values, the sequence of iterations is shown next, where $h = p/q$ denotes the change in x at each iteration.

x	$f(x)$	h
1.000000	−2.365884	
2.000000	0.362810	
3.000000	8.435520	
1.885318	−0.244343	−0.113682
1.939558	0.030786	0.053240
1.933742	−0.000060	−0.005815
1.933754	0.000000	0.000011

5.2.6 Linear Fractional Interpolation

The zero-finding methods we have considered thus far may have difficulty if the function whose zero is sought has a horizontal or vertical asymptote. A horizontal asymptote may yield a tangent or secant line that is almost horizontal, causing the next approximate solution to be far afield, and a vertical asymptote may be skipped over, placing the approximation on the wrong branch of the function. Linear fractional interpolation, which uses a rational fraction of the form

$$\phi(x) = \frac{x - u}{vx - w},$$

is a useful alternative in such cases. This function has a zero at $x = u$, a vertical asymptote at $x = w/v$, and a horizontal asymptote at $y = 1/v$.

In seeking a zero of a nonlinear function $f(x)$, suppose that we have three approximate solution values, which we denote by a, b, and c, with corresponding function values f_a, f_b, and f_c, respectively. Fitting the linear fraction ϕ to the three data points yields a 3×3 system of linear equations

$$\begin{bmatrix} 1 & -af_a & f_a \\ 1 & -bf_b & f_b \\ 1 & -cf_c & f_c \end{bmatrix} \begin{bmatrix} u \\ v \\ w \end{bmatrix} = \begin{bmatrix} a \\ b \\ c \end{bmatrix},$$

whose solution determines the coefficients u, v, and w. We now replace a and b with b and c, respectively, and take the next approximate solution to be the zero of the linear fraction, $c = u$. Since v and w play no direct role, the solution to the foregoing system is most conveniently implemented as a single formula for the change h in c, which is given by

$$h = \frac{(a - c)(b - c)(f_a - f_b)f_c}{(a - c)(f_c - f_b)f_a - (b - c)(f_c - f_a)f_b}.$$

Linear fractional interpolation is also effective as a general-purpose one-dimensional zero finder, as the following example illustrates. Its asymptotic convergence rate is the same as that given by quadratic interpolation (inverse or regular), $r \approx 1.839$. Once again this result is local, and the iterations must be started close enough to the solution to obtain convergence.

EXAMPLE 5.10 LINEAR FRACTIONAL INTERPOLATION. We illustrate linear fractional interpolation by again finding a root of the equation

$$f(x) = x^2 - 4\sin(x) = 0.$$

Taking $a = 1$, $b = 2$, and $c = 3$ as starting values, the sequence of iterations is shown next.

x	$f(x)$	h
1.000000	−2.365884	
2.000000	0.362810	
3.000000	8.435520	
1.906953	−0.139647	−1.093047
1.933351	−0.002131	0.026398
1.933756	0.000013	−0.000406
1.933754	0.000000	−0.000003

5.2.7 Safeguarded Methods

Rapidly convergent methods for solving nonlinear equations, such as Newton's method, the secant method, and other types of methods based on interpolation, are unsafe in that they may not converge unless they are started close enough to the solution. Safe methods, such as bisection, on the other hand, are slow and therefore costly. Which should one choose?

A solution to this dilemma is provided by hybrid methods that combine features of both types of methods. For example, one could use a rapidly convergent method but maintain a bracket around the solution. If the next approximate solution given by the rapid algorithm falls outside the bracketing interval, one would fall back on a safe method, such as bisection, for one iteration. Then one can try the rapid method again on a smaller interval with a greater chance of success. Ultimately, the fast convergence rate should prevail. This approach seldom does worse than the slow method and usually does much better.

A popular implementation of such a hybrid approach was originally developed by Dekker and van Wijngaarden and later improved by Brent. This method, which is found in a number of subroutine libraries, combines the safety of bisection with the faster convergence of inverse quadratic interpolation. By avoiding Newton's method, derivatives of the function are not required. A careful implementation must address a number of potential pitfalls in floating-point arithmetic, such as underflow, overflow, or an unrealistically tight user-supplied error tolerance.

5.2.8 Zeros of Polynomials

Thus far we have discussed methods for finding a single zero of an arbitrary function in one dimension. For the special case of a polynomial $p(x)$ of degree n, one often may need to find all n of its zeros, which may be complex even if the coefficients are real. Several approaches are available:

- Use one of the methods we have discussed, such as Newton's method or Muller's method, to find a single root x_1 (keeping in mind that the root may be complex), then consider the deflated polynomial $p(x)/(x - x_1)$ of degree one less. Repeat until all roots have been found. It is a good idea to go back and refine each root using the original polynomial $p(x)$ to avoid contamination due to rounding error in the deflated polynomials.
- Form the companion matrix of the given polynomial and use an eigenvalue routine to compute all of its eigenvalues (see Section 4.2.1). This method is reliable but relatively inefficient in both work and storage.
- Use a method designed specifically for finding all the roots of a polynomial. Some of these methods are based on classical techniques for isolating the roots of a polynomial in a region of the complex plane, typically a union of discs, and then refining it in a manner similar in spirit to bisection until the roots have been localized as accurately as desired. Like bisection, such methods are guaranteed to work but are only linearly convergent. More rapidly convergent methods are available, however, such as that

of Jenkins and Traub [136, 137], which is probably the most effective method available for finding all of the roots of a polynomial.

The first two of these approaches are relatively simple to implement since they make use of other software for the primary subtasks. The third approach is rather complicated, but fortunately good software implementations are available.

5.3 SYSTEMS OF NONLINEAR EQUATIONS

We now consider nonlinear equations in more than one dimension. The multidimensional case is much more difficult than the scalar case for a variety of reasons:

- A much wider range of behavior is possible, so that a theoretical analysis of the existence and number of solutions is much more complex.
- It is not possible, in general, to guarantee convergence to the correct solution or to bracket the solution to produce an absolutely safe method.
- Computational overhead increases rapidly with the dimension of the problem.

EXAMPLE 5.11 SYSTEMS OF NONLINEAR EQUATIONS. Consider the system of two nonlinear equations in two unknowns

$$x_1^2 - x_2 + \gamma = 0,$$
$$-x_1 + x_2^2 + \gamma = 0,$$

where x_1 and x_2 are the unknowns and γ is a given parameter. Each of the two equations defines a parabola, and any point where the two parabolas intersect is a solution to the system. Depending on the particular value for γ, this system can have either zero, one, two, or four solutions, as illustrated in Fig. 5.8.

5.3.1 Fixed-Point Iteration

Just as for one dimension, a system of nonlinear equations can be converted into a fixed-point problem, so we now briefly consider the multidimensional case. If $g: \mathbb{R}^n \to \mathbb{R}^n$, then a fixed-point problem for g is to find an n-vector x such that

$$x = g(x).$$

The corresponding fixed-point iteration is simply

$$x_{k+1} = g(x_k),$$

given some starting vector x_0. (In discussing iterative methods for multidimensional problems, subscripts may indicate either a vector in a sequence or a particular component of a given vector; the distinction should be clear from the context.)

In one dimension, we saw that the convergence (and convergence rate) of fixed-point iteration is determined by $|g'(x^*)|$, where x^* is the solution. In higher dimensions

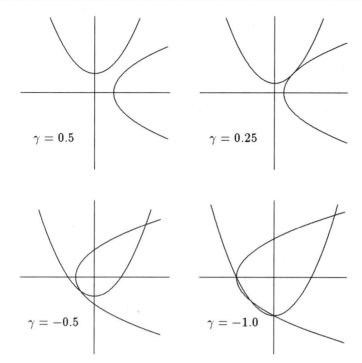

FIGURE 5.8
Some systems of nonlinear equations.

the analogous condition is

$$\rho(G(x^*)) < 1,$$

where $G(x)$ denotes the *Jacobian matrix* of g evaluated at x,

$$\{G(x)\}_{ij} = \frac{\partial g_i(x)}{\partial x_j},$$

and ρ denotes the *spectral radius*, which is defined to be the maximum modulus of the eigenvalues of the matrix (see Section 4.1). If the foregoing condition is satisfied, then the fixed-point iteration converges if started close enough to the solution. (Note that testing this condition does not necessarily require computing the eigenvalues, since $\rho(A) \le \|A\|$ for any matrix norm subordinate to a vector norm; see Exercise 4.11.) As with scalar systems, the smaller the spectral radius the faster the convergence rate. In particular, if $G(x^*) = 0$, the zero matrix, then the convergence rate is at least quadratic. We will next see that Newton's method is a systematic way of selecting g so that this happens.

5.3.2 Newton's Method

Many one-dimensional methods do not generalize directly to n dimensions. The most popular and powerful method that does generalize is Newton's method, which in n

dimensions has the form

$$x_{k+1} = x_k - J_f(x_k)^{-1} f(x_k),$$

where $J_f(x)$ is the Jacobian matrix of f,

$$\{J_f(x)\}_{ij} = \frac{\partial f_i(x)}{\partial x_j}.$$

In practice, we do not explicitly invert $J_f(x_k)$ but instead solve the linear system

$$J_f(x_k)s_k = -f(x_k),$$

then take as the next iterate

$$x_{k+1} = x_k + s_k.$$

In this sense, Newton's method replaces a system of nonlinear equations with a system of linear equations, but since the solutions of the two systems are not identical in general, the process must be repeated until the approximate solution is as accurate as desired.

EXAMPLE 5.12 NEWTON'S METHOD. We illustrate Newton's method by solving the nonlinear system

$$f(x) = \begin{bmatrix} x_1 + 2x_2 - 2 \\ x_1^2 + 4x_2^2 - 4 \end{bmatrix} = 0,$$

for which the Jacobian matrix is given by

$$J_f(x) = \begin{bmatrix} 1 & 2 \\ 2x_1 & 8x_2 \end{bmatrix}.$$

If we take $x_0 = \begin{bmatrix} 1 & 2 \end{bmatrix}^T$, then

$$f(x_0) = \begin{bmatrix} 3 \\ 13 \end{bmatrix} \quad \text{and} \quad J_f(x_0) = \begin{bmatrix} 1 & 2 \\ 2 & 16 \end{bmatrix}.$$

Solving the system

$$\begin{bmatrix} 1 & 2 \\ 2 & 16 \end{bmatrix} s_0 = \begin{bmatrix} -3 \\ -13 \end{bmatrix}$$

gives $s_0 = \begin{bmatrix} -1.83 & -0.58 \end{bmatrix}^T$, and hence

$$x_1 = x_0 + s_0 = \begin{bmatrix} -0.83 \\ 1.42 \end{bmatrix}, \quad f(x_1) = \begin{bmatrix} 0 \\ 4.72 \end{bmatrix}, \quad J_f(x_1) = \begin{bmatrix} 1 & 2 \\ -1.67 & 11.3 \end{bmatrix}.$$

Solving the system

$$\begin{bmatrix} 1 & 2 \\ -1.67 & 11.3 \end{bmatrix} s_1 = \begin{bmatrix} 0 \\ -4.72 \end{bmatrix}$$

gives $s_1 = \begin{bmatrix} 0.64 & -0.32 \end{bmatrix}^T$, and hence

$$x_2 = x_1 + s_1 = \begin{bmatrix} -0.19 \\ 1.10 \end{bmatrix}, \quad f(x_2) = \begin{bmatrix} 0 \\ 0.83 \end{bmatrix}, \quad J_f(x_2) = \begin{bmatrix} 1 & 2 \\ -0.38 & 8.76 \end{bmatrix}.$$

Iterations continue until convergence to the solution $x^* = \begin{bmatrix} 0 & 1 \end{bmatrix}^T$.

We can determine the convergence rate of Newton's method in n dimensions by differentiating the corresponding fixed-point operator (assuming it is smooth) and evaluating the resulting Jacobian matrix at the solution x^*:

$$g(x) = x - J_f(x)^{-1} f(x),$$

$$G(x^*) = I - (J_f(x^*)^{-1} J_f(x^*) + \sum_{i=1}^{n} f_i(x^*) H_i(x^*)) = 0,$$

where $H_i(x)$ denotes a component matrix of the derivative of $J_f(x)^{-1}$ (which is a tensor). Thus, the convergence rate of Newton's method for solving a nonlinear system is normally quadratic, provided that the Jacobian matrix $J_f(x^*)$ is nonsingular, but the algorithm may have to be started close to the solution in order to converge.

The arithmetic overhead per iteration for Newton's method in n dimensions can be substantial:

- Computing the Jacobian matrix, either in closed form or by finite differences, requires the equivalent of n^2 scalar function evaluations for a dense problem (i.e., if every component function of f depends on every variable). Computation of the Jacobian may be much cheaper if it is sparse or has some special structure. Another alternative that may be cheaper for computing derivatives is automatic differentiation (see Section 8.7.2).
- Solving the linear system by Gaussian elimination costs $\mathcal{O}(n^3)$ arithmetic operations, again assuming the Jacobian matrix is dense.

5.3.3 Secant Updating Methods

The high cost per iteration of Newton's method and its finite difference variants has led to the development of methods, analogous to the one-dimensional secant method, that gradually build up an approximation to the Jacobian based on successive iterates and function values without explicitly evaluating derivatives. Moreover, these methods save on computational overhead by updating a factorization of the approximate Jacobian matrix at each iteration (using techniques similar to the Sherman-Morrison formula) rather than refactoring it each time. Because of these two features, such methods are usually called *secant updating methods*.

These savings in computational overhead are not without their own cost, however, in that secant updating methods generally have superlinear but not quadratic convergence rates. Nevertheless, there is often a net reduction in the overall cost of finding a solution, especially when the problem function and its derivatives are expensive to evaluate.

5.3.4 Broyden's Method

One of the simplest and most effective secant updating methods for solving nonlinear systems is *Broyden's method*, which begins with an approximate Jacobian matrix and updates it (or a factorization of it) at each iteration. The initial Jacobian approximation

B_0 can be taken as the correct Jacobian (or a finite difference approximation to it) at the starting point x_0, or, to avoid computing derivatives altogether, B_0 can simply be initialized to be the identity matrix. The steps of the algorithm at iteration k are as follows:

1. Solve $B_k s_k = -f(x_k)$ for s_k.
2. $x_{k+1} = x_k + s_k$.
3. $y_k = f(x_{k+1}) - f(x_k)$.
4. $B_{k+1} = B_k + ((y_k - B_k s_k)s_k^T)/(s_k^T s_k)$.

The motivation for the formula for B_{k+1} is that it gives the least change to B_k subject to satisfying the *secant equation*

$$B_{k+1}(x_{k+1} - x_k) = f(x_{k+1}) - f(x_k).$$

In this way, the sequence of matrices B_k gains and maintains information about the behavior of the function f along the various directions generated by the algorithm, without the need for the function to be sampled purely for the purpose of obtaining derivative information.

Updating B_k as just indicated would still leave one needing to solve a linear system at each iteration at a cost of $\mathcal{O}(n^3)$ arithmetic. Therefore, in practice a factorization of B_k is updated instead of B_k directly, so that the total cost per iteration is only $\mathcal{O}(n^2)$.

EXAMPLE 5.13 BROYDEN'S METHOD. We illustrate Broyden's method by again solving the nonlinear system of Example 5.12,

$$f(x) = \begin{bmatrix} x_1 + 2x_2 - 2 \\ x_1^2 + 4x_2^2 - 4 \end{bmatrix} = 0.$$

Again we let $x_0 = \begin{bmatrix} 1 & 2 \end{bmatrix}^T$, so $f(x_0) = \begin{bmatrix} 3 & 13 \end{bmatrix}^T$, and we let

$$B_0 = J_f(x_0) = \begin{bmatrix} 1 & 2 \\ 2 & 16 \end{bmatrix}.$$

Solving the system

$$\begin{bmatrix} 1 & 2 \\ 2 & 16 \end{bmatrix} s_0 = \begin{bmatrix} -3 \\ -13 \end{bmatrix}$$

gives $s_0 = \begin{bmatrix} -1.83 & -0.58 \end{bmatrix}^T$, and hence

$$x_1 = x_0 + s_0 = \begin{bmatrix} -0.83 \\ 1.42 \end{bmatrix}, \qquad f(x_1) = \begin{bmatrix} 0 \\ 4.72 \end{bmatrix}, \qquad y_0 = \begin{bmatrix} -3 \\ -8.28 \end{bmatrix}.$$

From the updating formula, we therefore have

$$B_1 = \begin{bmatrix} 1 & 2 \\ 2 & 16 \end{bmatrix} + \begin{bmatrix} 0 & 0 \\ -2.34 & -0.74 \end{bmatrix} = \begin{bmatrix} 1 & 2 \\ -0.34 & 15.3 \end{bmatrix}.$$

Solving the system

$$\begin{bmatrix} 1 & 2 \\ -0.34 & 15.3 \end{bmatrix} s_1 = \begin{bmatrix} 0 \\ -4.72 \end{bmatrix}$$

gives $s_1 = \begin{bmatrix} 0.59 & -0.30 \end{bmatrix}^T$, and hence

$$x_2 = x_1 + s_1 = \begin{bmatrix} -0.24 \\ 1.120 \end{bmatrix}, \qquad f(x_2) = \begin{bmatrix} 0 \\ 1.08 \end{bmatrix}, \qquad y_1 = \begin{bmatrix} 0 \\ -3.64 \end{bmatrix}.$$

From the updating formula, we therefore have

$$B_2 = \begin{bmatrix} 1 & 2 \\ -0.34 & 15.3 \end{bmatrix} + \begin{bmatrix} 0 & 0 \\ 1.46 & -0.73 \end{bmatrix} = \begin{bmatrix} 1 & 2 \\ 1.12 & 14.5 \end{bmatrix}.$$

Iterations continue until convergence to the solution $x^* = \begin{bmatrix} 0 & 1 \end{bmatrix}^T$.

5.3.5 Robust Newton-Like Methods

Newton's method and its variants may fail to converge when started far from a solution. Unfortunately, in n dimensions there is no analogue of bisection in one dimension that can provide a fail-safe hybrid method. Nevertheless, safeguards can be taken that may substantially widen the region of convergence for Newton-like methods.

The simplest of these precautions is the *damped Newton method*, in which the Newton (or Newton-like) step s_k is computed as usual at each iteration, but then the new iterate is taken to be

$$x_{k+1} = x_k + \alpha_k s_k,$$

where α_k is a scalar parameter to be chosen. The motivation is that far from a solution the full Newton step is likely to be unreliable—often much too large—and so α_k can be adjusted to ensure that x_{k+1} is a better approximation to the solution than x_k. One way to enforce this condition is to monitor $\|f(x_k)\|_2$ and make sure that it decreases sufficiently with each iteration. One might even minimize $\|f(x_k + \alpha_k s_k)\|_2$ with respect to α_k at each iteration (see the discussion of line searches in Chapter 6). Whatever the strategy for choosing α_k, when the iterates become close enough to a solution, the value $\alpha_k = 1$ should suffice, and indeed the α_k must approach 1 in order to maintain the usual convergence rate. Although this damping technique can improve the robustness of Newton-like methods, it is not foolproof. For example, there may be no value for α_k that produces sufficient decrease, or the iterations may converge to a local minimum of $\|f(x)\|_2$ such that the function value is not 0.

A somewhat more complicated but often more effective approach to making Newton-like methods more robust is to maintain an estimate of the radius of a *trust region* within which the Taylor series approximation, upon which Newton's method is based, is sufficiently accurate for the resulting computed step to be reliable. By adjusting the size of the trust region as necessary to constrain the stepsize, these methods can usually make progress toward a solution even when started far away, yet still converge rapidly once near a solution, since the trust radius should then be large enough to permit full Newton steps to be taken. Again, however, the point to which such a method converges may be a local minimum of $\|f(x)\|_2$ without being a solution of the equation $f(x) = 0$. Unlike damped Newton methods, trust region methods may modify the direction as well as the length of the Newton step when necessary, and hence they are generally more robust. See Section 6.3.3 for further discussion and a graphical illustration (Fig. 6.6).

5.4 SOFTWARE FOR NONLINEAR EQUATIONS

Table 5.1 is a list of some of the software available for solving general nonlinear equations. In the multidimensional case, we distinguish between routines that do or do not require the user to supply derivatives for the functions, although in some cases the routines mentioned offer both options.

Software for solving a nonlinear equation $f(x) = 0$ typically requires the user to supply the name of a routine that computes the value of the function f for any given value of x. The user must also supply absolute or relative error tolerances that are used in the stopping criterion for the iterative solution process. Additional input for one-dimensional problems usually includes the endpoints of an interval in which the function has a change of sign. Additional input for multidimensional problems includes the number of functions and variables in the system and a starting guess for the solution, and may also include the name of a routine for computing the Jacobian of the function and the name of an array to be used as workspace for storing the Jacobian or an approximation to it. In addition to the solution x, the output typically includes a status flag indicating any warnings or errors.

For both single equations and systems, it is highly advisable to make a preliminary plot, or at least a rough sketch, of the function(s) involved to determine a good starting guess or bracketing interval. Some trial and error may be required to determine an initial guess for which a zero finder converges, or finds the desired root in cases with more than one solution.

Some additional packages available for solving systems of nonlinear equations are based on methods not covered in this book. One such approach is *homotopy methods* or *continuation methods*. Such methods parameterize the problem space and then track a curve between a trivial problem instance and the actual problem to be solved. See Computer Problem 9.6 for an example of this approach, which can be especially

TABLE 5.1
Software for nonlinear equations

Source	One-dimensional, No derivatives	Multidimensional No derivatives	Derivatives
Brent [23]	zero		
FMM	zeroin		
HSL	nb01/nb02	ns11	
IMSL	zbren	neqbf	neqnj
Dennis/Schnabel [57]		nedriver	nedriver
KMN	fzero	snsqe	snsqe
MATLAB	fzero	fsolve	
MINPACK [182]		hybrd1	hybrj1
NAG	c05adf	c05nbf	c05pbf
NAPACK	root	quasi	
NR	zbrent	broydn	newt
NUMAL	zeroin	quanewbnd	
SLATEC	fzero	snsq/sos	
TOMS	zero1(#631)	brentm(#554)	

TABLE 5.2
Software for finding all the zeros of a polynomial

Source	Real	Complex
HSL	pa17	pa16
IMSL	zporc/zplrc	zpocc
MATLAB	roots	roots
NAG	c02agf	c02aff
NAPACK		czero
NR	zrhqr	zroots
SLATEC	rpzero/rpqr79	cpzero/cpqr79
TOMS	rpoly(#493)	cpoly(#419)

useful for very difficult nonlinear problems for which a good starting guess for the solution is unavailable. Software implementing such methods includes **fixpt(#555)**, **dafne(#617)**, and **hompack(#652)**, all available from **TOMS**. Yet another approach is generalized bisection, which is implemented in the routines **chabis(#666)** and **intbis(#681)** available from **TOMS**.

Table 5.2 is a list of specialized software for finding all the zeros of a polynomial with real or complex coefficients.

5.5 HISTORICAL NOTES AND FURTHER READING

Most of the methods we discussed for solving nonlinear equations in one dimension—including bisection, Newton, and secant—are quite venerable. Hybrid, safeguarded methods for one-dimensional problems, as popularized by Brent [23], are a relatively recent development. For systems of nonlinear equations, Newton's method has served to motivate most other methods, and it is the standard by which they are measured. Indeed, "Newton's method" has become as much a paradigm as a specific algorithm, synonymous with local linear approximations to nonlinear problems of many different types. Secant updating methods were first developed for optimization problems around 1959, but analogous methods were soon developed for solving systems of nonlinear equations; Broyden's method was published in 1965.

The basic methods for solving nonlinear equations in one variable are discussed in almost every general textbook on numerical methods. More detailed treatment of the classical methods can be found in [129, 197, 256]. For zero finding using linear fractional interpolation, see [135]; more general rational functions for this purpose are discussed in [161]. Definitive references on solving systems of nonlinear equations are [57, 196]. For a survey of recent developments, see [147]. An incisive overview of the theory and convergence analysis of secant updating methods appears in [56]. Homotopy, or continuation, methods are the subject of [6]. The **MINPACK** software for nonlinear equations is documented in [182].

REVIEW QUESTIONS

5.1. True or false: If an iterative method for solving a nonlinear equation gains more than one bit of accuracy per iteration, then it is said to have a superlinear convergence rate.

5.2. True or false: For a given fixed level of accuracy, a superlinearly convergent iterative method always requires fewer iterations than a linearly convergent method to find a solution to that level of accuracy.

5.3. True or false: A small residual $\|f(x)\|$ guarantees an accurate solution of a system of nonlinear equations $f(x) = 0$.

5.4. True or false: Newton's method is an example of a fixed-point iteration scheme.

5.5. Suppose you are using an iterative method to solve a nonlinear equation $f(x) = 0$ for a root that is ill-conditioned, and you need to choose a convergence test. Would it be better to terminate the iteration when you find an iterate x_k for which $\|f(x_k)\|$ is small, or when $\|x_k - x_{k-1}\|$ is small? Why?

5.6. (*a*) What is the definition of the convergence rate r of an iterative method?
(*b*) Is it possible to have a cubically convergent method ($r = 3$) for finding a zero of a function?
(*c*) If not, why, and if so, how might such a scheme be derived?

5.7. If the errors at successive iterations of an iterative method are as follows, how would you characterize the convergence rate?
(*a*) $10^{-2}, 10^{-4}, 10^{-8}, 10^{-16}, \ldots$
(*b*) $10^{-2}, 10^{-4}, 10^{-6}, 10^{-8}, \ldots$

5.8. What condition ensures that the bisection method will find a zero of a continuous nonlinear function f in the interval $[a, b]$?

5.9. (*a*) If the bisection method for finding a zero of a function $f: \mathbb{R} \to \mathbb{R}$ starts with an initial bracket of length 1, what is the length of the interval containing the root after six iterations?
(*b*) Do you need to know the particular function f to answer the question in part *a*?

(*c*) If we assume that it is started with a bracket for the solution in which there is a sign change, is the convergence rate of the bisection method dependent on whether the solution sought is a simple root or a multiple root? Why?

5.10. Suppose you are using the bisection method to find a zero of a nonlinear function, starting with an initial bracketing interval $[a, b]$. Give a general expression for the number of iterations that will be required to achieve an error tolerance of *tol* for the length of the final bracketing interval.

5.11. What is meant by a *quadratic* convergence rate for an iterative method?

5.12. If an iterative method squares the error every *two* iterations, what is its convergence rate r?

5.13. (*a*) What does it mean for a root of an equation to be a *multiple* root?
(*b*) What is the effect of a multiple root on the convergence rate of the bisection method?
(*c*) What is the effect of a multiple root on the convergence rate of Newton's method?

5.14. Which of the following behaviors are possible in using Newton's method for solving a nonlinear equation?
(*a*) It may converge linearly.
(*b*) It may converge quadratically.
(*c*) It may not converge at all.

5.15. What is the convergence rate for Newton's method for finding the root $x = 2$ of each of the following equations?
(*a*) $f(x) = (x - 1)(x - 2)^2 = 0$
(*b*) $f(x) = (x - 1)^2(x - 2) = 0$

5.16. (*a*) What is meant by a *fixed point* of a function $g(x)$?
(*b*) Given a nonlinear equation $f(x) = 0$, how can you determine an equivalent fixed-point problem, that is, a function $g(x)$ such that a fixed point x of g is a solution to the nonlinear equation $f(x) = 0$?
(*c*) Specifically, what function $g(x)$ results from this approach?

5.17. In using the secant method for solving a one-dimensional nonlinear equation,

(*a*) How many starting guesses for the solution are required?

(*b*) How many new function evaluations are required per iteration?

5.18. Let g: $\mathbb{R} \to \mathbb{R}$ be a smooth function having a fixed point x^*.

(*a*) What condition determines whether the iteration scheme $x_{k+1} = g(x_k)$ is locally convergent to x^*?

(*b*) What is the convergence rate?

(*c*) What additional condition implies that the convergence rate is quadratic?

(*d*) Is Newton's method for finding a zero of a smooth function f: $\mathbb{R} \to \mathbb{R}$ an example of such a fixed-point iteration scheme? If so, what is the function g in this case? If not, then explain why not.

5.19. In bracketing a zero of a nonlinear function, one needs to determine if two function values, say $f(a)$ and $f(b)$, differ in sign. Is the following a good way to test for this condition: if $(f(a) * f(b) < 0)$…? Why?

5.20. Let g: $\mathbb{R} \to \mathbb{R}$ be a smooth function, and let x^* be a point such that $g(x^*) = x^*$.

(*a*) State a general condition under which the iteration scheme $x_{k+1} = g(x_k)$ converges quadratically to x^*, assuming that the starting guess x_0 is close enough to x^*.

(*b*) Use this condition to prove that Newton's method is locally quadratically convergent to a simple zero x^* of a smooth function f: $\mathbb{R} \to \mathbb{R}$.

5.21. List one advantage and one disadvantage of the secant method compared with the bisection method for finding a simple zero of a single nonlinear equation.

5.22. List one advantage and one disadvantage of the secant method compared with Newton's method for solving a nonlinear equation in one dimension.

5.23. The secant method for solving a one-dimensional nonlinear equation uses linear interpolation of the given function at two points. Interpolation at more points by a higher-degree polynomial would increase the convergence rate of the iteration.

(*a*) Give three reasons why such an approach might not work well.

(*b*) What alternative approach using higher-degree interpolation in this context avoids these difficulties?

5.24. For solving a one-dimensional nonlinear equation, how many function or derivative evaluations are required per iteration of each of the following methods?

(*a*) Newton's method

(*b*) Secant method

5.25. Rank the following methods 1 through 3, from slowest convergence rate to fastest convergence rate, for finding a simple root of a nonlinear equation in one dimension:

(*a*) Bisection method

(*b*) Newton's method

(*c*) Secant method

5.26. In solving a nonlinear equation in one dimension, how many bits of accuracy are gained per iteration of

(*a*) Bisection method?

(*b*) Newton's method?

5.27. In solving a nonlinear equation $f(x) = 0$, if you assume that the cost of evaluating the derivative $f'(x)$ is about the same as the cost of evaluating $f(x)$, how does the cost of Newton's method compare with the cost of the secant method per iteration?

5.28. Suppose that you are using fixed-point iteration based on the fixed-point problem $x = g(x)$ to find a solution x^* to a nonlinear equation $f(x) = 0$. Which would be more favorable for the convergence rate: a horizontal tangent of g at x^* or a horizontal tangent of f at x^*? Why?

5.29. Suggest a procedure for safeguarding the secant method for solving a one-dimensional nonlinear equation so that it will still converge even if started far from a root.

5.30. For what type of function is linear fractional interpolation a particularly good choice of zero finder?

5.31. Each of the following methods for computing a root of a nonlinear equation has the same asymptotic convergence rate. For each method, specify a situation in which that method is particularly appropriate.

(*a*) Regular quadratic interpolation

(*b*) Inverse quadratic interpolation

(*c*) Linear fractional interpolation

5.32. State at least one method for finding all the zeros of a polynomial, and discuss its advantages and disadvantages.

5.33. Does the bisection method generalize to finding zeros of multidimensional functions? Why?

5.34. For solving an n-dimensional nonlinear equation, how many scalar function evaluations are required per iteration of Newton's method?

5.35. Relative to Newton's method, which of the following factors motivate secant updating methods for solving systems of nonlinear equations?
    (*a*) Lower cost per iteration
    (*b*) Faster convergence rate
    (*c*) Greater robustness far from solution
    (*d*) Avoidance of computing derivatives

5.36. Give two reasons why secant updating methods for solving systems of nonlinear equations are often more efficient than Newton's method despite converging more slowly.

EXERCISES

5.1. Consider the nonlinear equation

$$f(x) = x^2 - 2 = 0.$$

    (*a*) With $x_0 = 1$ as a starting point, what is the value of x_1 if you use Newton's method for solving this problem?
    (*b*) With $x_0 = 1$ and $x_1 = 2$ as starting points, what is the value of x_2 if you use the secant method for the same problem?

5.2. Write out Newton's iteration for solving each of the following nonlinear equations:
    (*a*) $x^3 - 2x - 5 = 0$.
    (*b*) $e^{-x} = x$.
    (*c*) $x \sin(x) = 1$.

5.3. Newton's method is sometimes used to implement the built-in square root function on a computer, with the initial guess supplied by a lookup table.
    (*a*) What is the Newton iteration for computing the square root of a positive number y (i.e., for solving the equation $f(x) = x^2 - y = 0$, given y)?
    (*b*) If we assume that the starting guess has an accuracy of 4 bits, how many iterations would be necessary to attain 24-bit accuracy? 53-bit accuracy?

5.4. On a computer with no functional unit for floating-point division, one might instead use multiplication by the reciprocal of the divisor. Apply Newton's method to produce an iterative scheme for approximating the reciprocal of a number $y > 0$ (i.e., to solve the equation $f(x) = (1/x) - y = 0$, given y). Considering the intended application, your formula should not contain any divisions!

5.5. (*a*) Show that the iterative method

$$x_{k+1} = \frac{x_{k-1} f(x_k) - x_k f(x_{k-1})}{f(x_k) - f(x_{k-1})}$$

is mathematically equivalent to the secant method for solving a scalar nonlinear equation $f(x) = 0$.
    (*b*) Why is the formula given in part *a* inferior in practice to the usual formula for the secant method?

5.6. Suppose we wish to develop an iterative method to compute the square root of a given positive number y, i.e., to solve the nonlinear equation $f(x) = x^2 - y = 0$ given the value of y. Each of the functions g_1 and g_2 listed next gives a fixed-point problem that is equivalent to the equation $f(x) = 0$. For each of these functions, determine whether the corresponding fixed-point iteration scheme $x_{k+1} = g_i(x_k)$ is locally convergent to $\sqrt{y}$ if $y = 3$. Explain your reasoning in each case.
    (*a*) $g_1(x) = y + x - x^2$.
    (*b*) $g_2(x) = 1 + x - x^2/y$.
    (*c*) What is the fixed-point iteration *function* given by Newton's method for this particular problem?

5.7. The gamma function has the following known values: $\Gamma(0.5) = \sqrt{\pi}$, $\Gamma(1) = 1$, $\Gamma(0.75) = \sqrt{\pi}/2$. From these three values, determine the approximate value x for which $\Gamma(x) = 1.5$, using one step of each of the following methods.
    (*a*) Quadratic interpolation
    (*b*) Inverse quadratic interpolation
    (*c*) Linear fractional interpolation

5.8. Express the Newton iteration for solving each of the following systems of nonlinear equations.

(a)
$$x_1^2 + x_2^2 = 1,$$
$$x_1^2 - x_2 = 0.$$

(b)
$$x_1^2 + x_1 x_2^3 = 9,$$
$$3x_1^2 x_2 - x_2^3 = 4.$$

(c)
$$x_1 + x_2 - 2x_1 x_2 = 0,$$
$$x_1^2 + x_2^2 - 2x_1 + 2x_2 = -1.$$

(d)
$$x_1^3 - x_2^2 = 0,$$
$$x_1 + x_1^2 x_2 = 2.$$

(e)
$$2\sin(x_1) + \cos(x_2) - 5x_1 = 0,$$
$$4\cos(x_1) + 2\sin(x_2) - 5x_2 = 0.$$

5.9. Carry out one iteration of Newton's method applied to the system of nonlinear equations
$$x_1^2 - x_2^2 = 0,$$
$$2x_1 x_2 = 1,$$
with starting value $x_0 = \begin{bmatrix} 0 & 1 \end{bmatrix}^T$.

5.10. Suppose you are using the secant method to find a root x^* of a nonlinear equation $f(x) = 0$. Show that if at any iteration it happens to be the case that either $x_k = x^*$ or $x_{k-1} = x^*$ (but not both), then it will also be true that $x_{k+1} = x^*$.

5.11. Newton's method for solving a scalar nonlinear equation $f(x) = 0$ requires computation of the derivative of f at each iteration. Suppose that we instead replace the true derivative with a constant value d, that is, we use the iteration scheme
$$x_{k+1} = x_k - f(x_k)/d.$$

(a) Under what condition on the value of d will this scheme be locally convergent?

(b) What will be the convergence rate, in general?

(c) Is there any value for d that would still yield quadratic convergence?

5.12. Consider the system of equations
$$x_1 - 1 = 0,$$
$$x_1 x_2 - 1 = 0.$$

For what starting point or points, if any, will Newton's method for solving this system fail? Why?

5.13. Supply the details of a proof that if x^* is a fixed point of the smooth function $g \colon \mathbb{R} \to \mathbb{R}$, and $g'(x^*) = 0$, then the convergence rate of the fixed-point iteration scheme $x_{k+1} = g(x_k)$ is at least quadratic if started close enough to x^*.

5.14. Verify the formula given in Section 5.2.6 for the change h in c when using linear fractional interpolation to find a zero of a nonlinear function.

COMPUTER PROBLEMS

5.1. For the equation
$$f(x) = x^2 - x - 2 = 0,$$
each of the following functions yields an equivalent fixed-point problem:
$$g_1(x) = x^2 - 2,$$
$$g_2(x) = \sqrt{x + 2},$$
$$g_3(x) = 1 + 2/x,$$
$$g_4(x) = (x^2 + 2)/(2x - 1).$$

(a) Analyze the convergence properties of each of the corresponding fixed-point iteration schemes for the root $x = 2$ by considering $|g_i'(2)|$.

(b) Confirm your analysis by implementing each of the schemes and verifying its convergence (or lack thereof) and approximate convergence rate.

5.2. Implement the bisection, Newton, and secant methods for solving nonlinear equations in one dimension, and test your implementations by finding at least one root for each of the following equations. What termination criterion should you use? What convergence rate is achieved in each case? Compare your results (solutions and convergence rates) with those for a library routine for solving nonlinear equations.

(a) $x^3 - 2x - 5 = 0$.

(b) $e^{-x} = x$.

(c) $x \sin(x) = 1$.

(d) $x^3 - 3x^2 + 3x - 1 = 0$.

5.3. Repeat the previous exercise, this time implementing the inverse quadratic interpolation and linear fractional interpolation methods, and answer the same questions as before.

5.4. Consider the function

$$f(x) = (((x - 0.5) + x) - 0.5) + x,$$

evaluated as indicated (i.e., without any simplification). On your computer, is there any floating-point value x such that $f(x)$ is *exactly* zero? If you use a zero-finding routine on this function, what result is returned, and what is the value of f for this argument? Experiment with the error tolerance to determine its effect on the results obtained.

5.5. Compute the first several iterations of Newton's method for solving each of the following equations, starting with the given initial guess.

    (*a*) $x^2 - 1 = 0$, $x_0 = 10^6$.
    (*b*) $(x - 1)^4 = 0$, $x_0 = 10$.

    For each equation, answer the following questions: What is the apparent convergence rate of the sequence initially? What should the asymptotic convergence rate of Newton's method be for this equation? How many iterations are required before the asymptotic range is reached? Give an analytical explanation of the behavior you observe empirically.

5.6. Consider the problem of finding the smallest positive root of the nonlinear equation

$$\cos(x) + 1/(1 + e^{-2x}) = 0.$$

Investigate, both theoretically and empirically, the following iterative schemes for solving this problem using the starting point $x_0 = 3$. For each scheme, you should show that it is indeed an equivalent fixed-point problem, determine analytically whether it is locally convergent and its expected convergence rate, and then implement the method to confirm your results.

    (*a*) $x_{k+1} = \arccos(-1/(1 + e^{-2x_k}))$.
    (*b*) $x_{k+1} = 0.5 \log(-1/(1 + 1/\cos(x_k)))$.
    (*c*) Newton's method.

5.7. In celestial mechanics, *Kepler's equation*

$$M = E - e \sin(E)$$

relates the mean anomaly M to the eccentric anomaly E of an elliptical orbit of eccentricity e, where $0 < e < 1$.

    (*a*) Prove that fixed-point iteration using the iteration function

$$g(E) = M + e \sin(E)$$

is locally convergent.

    (*b*) Use the fixed-point iteration scheme in part *a* to solve Kepler's equation for the eccentric anomaly E corresponding to a mean anomaly of $M = 1$ (radians) and an eccentricity of $e = 0.5$.

    (*c*) Use Newton's method to solve the same problem.

    (*d*) Use a library zero finder to solve the same problem.

5.8. In neutron transport theory, the critical length of a fuel rod is determined by the roots of the equation

$$\cot(x) = (x^2 - 1)/(2x).$$

Use a zero finder to determine the smallest positive root of this equation.

5.9. The natural frequencies of vibration of a uniform beam of unit length, clamped on one end and free on the other, satisfy the equation

$$\tan(x) \tanh(x) = -1.$$

Use a zero finder to determine the smallest positive root of this equation.

5.10. The vertical distance y that a parachutist falls before opening the parachute is given by the equation

$$y = \log(\cosh(t \sqrt{gk}))/k,$$

where t is the elapsed time in seconds, $g = 9.8065$ m/s^2 is the acceleration due to gravity, and $k = 0.00341$ m^{-1} is a constant related to air resistance. Use a zero finder to determine the elapsed time required to fall a distance of 1 km.

5.11. If an amount a is borrowed at interest rate r for n years, then the total amount to be repaid is given by

$$a(1 + r)^n.$$

Yearly payments of p each would reduce this amount by

$$\sum_{0}^{n-1} p(1 + r)^i = p \frac{(1 + r)^n - 1}{r}.$$

The loan will be repaid when these two quantities are equal.

(a) For a loan of $a = \$100,000$ and yearly payments of $p = \$10,000$, how long will it take to pay off the loan if the interest rate is 6 percent, i.e., $r = 0.06$?

(b) For a loan of $a = \$100,000$ and yearly payments of $p = \$10,000$, what interest rate r would be required for the loan to be paid off in $n = 20$ years?

(c) For a loan of $a = \$100,000$, how large must the yearly payments p be for the loan to be paid off in $n = 20$ years at 6 percent interest?

You may use any method you like to solve the given equation in each case. For the purpose of this problem, we will treat n as a continuous variable (i.e., it can have fractional values).

5.12. (a) Write a program using Newton's method to compute the nth root of a given number y, that is, to solve the nonlinear equation $f(x) = x^n - y = 0$ for x, given y and n. Since we want to be able to compute any nth root, your routine should work for complex as well as real roots. Test your program by computing the complex cube root of 3 lying in the upper left quadrant of the complex plane, using $x_0 = -1 + i$ as starting guess.

(b) Repeat part a, but this time use Muller's method (i.e., successive quadratic polynomial interpolation). For this method, you will need two additional starting guesses.

5.13. Write a program to solve the system of nonlinear equations

$$16x^4 + 16y^4 + z^4 = 16,$$
$$x^2 + y^2 + z^2 = 3,$$
$$x^3 - y = 0$$

using Newton's method. You may solve the resulting linear system at each iteration either by a library routine or by a linear system solver of your own design. As starting guess, you may take each variable to be 1. In addition, try nonlinear solvers from a subroutine library, based on both Newton and secant updating methods, and compare the solutions obtained and the convergence rates with those for your program.

5.14. The derivation of a two-point Gaussian quadrature rule (which we will consider in Section 8.3) on the interval $[-1, 1]$ using the method of undetermined coefficients leads to the following system of nonlinear equations for the nodes x_1, x_2 and weights w_1, w_2:

$$w_1 + w_2 = 2,$$
$$w_1 x_1 + w_2 x_2 = 0,$$
$$w_1 x_1^2 + w_2 x_2^2 = \tfrac{2}{3},$$
$$w_1 x_1^3 + w_2 x_2^3 = 0.$$

Solve this system for x_1, x_2, w_1, and w_2 using a library routine or one of your own design. How many different solutions can you find?

5.15. Use a library routine, or one of your own design, to solve the following system of nonlinear equations:

$$\sin(x) + y^2 + \log(z) = 3,$$
$$3x + 2^y - z^3 = 0,$$
$$x^2 + y^2 + z^3 = 6.$$

Try to find as many different solutions as you can. You should find at least four.

5.16. Each of the following systems of nonlinear equations may present some difficulty in computing a solution. Use a library routine, or one of your own design, to solve each of the systems from the given starting point. In some cases, the nonlinear solver may fail to converge or may converge to a point other than a solution. When this happens, try to explain the reason for the observed behavior. Also note the convergence rate attained, and if it is slower than expected, try to explain why.

(a) $x_1 + x_2(x_2(5 - x_2) - 2) = 13,$
$$x_1 + x_2(x_2(1 + x_2) - 14) = 29,$$
starting from $x_1 = 15$, $x_2 = -2$.

(b) $x_1^2 + x_2^2 + x_3^2 = 5,$
$$x_1 + x_2 = 1,$$
$$x_1 + x_3 = 3,$$
starting from $x_1 = (1 + \sqrt{3})/2$, $x_2 = (1 - \sqrt{3})/2$, $x_3 = \sqrt{3}$.

(c) $x_1 + 10x_2 = 0,$
$$\sqrt{5}(x_3 - x_4) = 0,$$
$$(x_2 - x_3)^2 = 0,$$
$$\sqrt{10}(x_1 - x_4)^2 = 0,$$
starting from $x_1 = 1$, $x_2 = 2$, $x_3 = 1$, $x_4 = 1$.

(d) $x_1 = 0,$
$$10x_1/(x_1 + 0.1) + 2x_2^2 = 0,$$
starting from $x_1 = 1.8$, $x_2 = 0$.

(e)
$$10^4 x_1 x_2 = 1,$$
$$e^{-x_1} + e^{-x_2} = 1.0001,$$

starting from $x_1 = 0$, $x_2 = 1$.

5.17. Newton's method can be used to compute the inverse of a nonsingular $n \times n$ matrix A. If we define the function $F: \mathbb{R}^{n \times n} \to \mathbb{R}^{n \times n}$ by

$$F(X) = I - AX,$$

where X is an $n \times n$ matrix, then $F(X) = 0$ precisely when $X = A^{-1}$. Since $F'(X) = -A$, Newton's method for solving this equation has the form

$$X_{k+1} = X_k - [F'(X_k)]^{-1} F(X_k)$$
$$= X_k + A^{-1}(I - AX_k).$$

But A^{-1} is what we are trying to compute, so instead we use the current approximation to A^{-1}, namely X_k. Thus, the iteration scheme takes the form

$$X_{k+1} = X_k + X_k(I - AX_k).$$

(*a*) If we define the residual matrix

$$R_k = I - AX_k$$

and the error matrix

$$E_k = A^{-1} - X_k,$$

show that

$$R_{k+1} = R_k^2 \quad \text{and} \quad E_{k+1} = E_k A E_k,$$

from which we can conclude that the convergence rate is quadratic, despite using only an approximate derivative.

(*b*) Write a program to compute the inverse of a given input matrix A using this iteration scheme. A reasonable starting guess is to take

$$X_0 = \frac{A^T}{\|A\|_1 \cdot \|A\|_\infty}.$$

Test your program on a few randomly chosen matrices and compare its accuracy and efficiency with conventional methods for computing the inverse, such as LU factorization or Gauss-Jordan elimination.

5.18. Newton's method can be used to compute an eigenvalue λ and corresponding eigenvector x of an $n \times n$ matrix A. If we define the function $f: \mathbb{R}^{n+1} \to \mathbb{R}^{n+1}$ by

$$f(x, \lambda) = \begin{bmatrix} Ax - \lambda x \\ x^T x - 1 \end{bmatrix},$$

then $f(x, \lambda) = 0$ precisely when λ is an eigenvalue and x is a corresponding normalized eigenvector. Since

$$J_f(x, \lambda) = \begin{bmatrix} A - \lambda I & -x \\ 2x^T & 0 \end{bmatrix},$$

Newton's method for solving this equation has the form

$$\begin{bmatrix} x_{k+1} \\ \lambda_{k+1} \end{bmatrix} = \begin{bmatrix} x_k \\ \lambda_k \end{bmatrix} + \begin{bmatrix} s_k \\ \delta_k \end{bmatrix},$$

where $\begin{bmatrix} s_k & \delta_k \end{bmatrix}^T$ is the solution to the linear system

$$\begin{bmatrix} A - \lambda_k I & -x_k \\ 2x_k^T & 0 \end{bmatrix} \begin{bmatrix} s_k \\ \delta_k \end{bmatrix} = - \begin{bmatrix} Ax_k - \lambda_k x_k \\ x_k^T x_k - 1 \end{bmatrix}.$$

Write a program to compute an eigenvalue-eigenvector pair of a given input matrix A using this iteration scheme. A reasonable starting guess is to take x_0 to be an arbitrary normalized nonzero vector (i.e., $x_0^T x_0 = 1$) and take $\lambda_0 = x_0^T A x_0$ (why?). Test your program on a few randomly chosen matrices and compare its accuracy and efficiency with those of conventional methods for computing a single eigenvalue-eigenvector pair, such as the power method. Note, however, that Newton's method does not necessarily converge to the dominant eigenvalue.

CHAPTER 6

Optimization

6.1 OPTIMIZATION PROBLEMS

We now turn to the problem of determining extreme values, or optimum values (maxima or minima), that a given function has on a given domain. More formally, given a function $f: \mathbb{R}^n \to \mathbb{R}$, and a set $S \subseteq \mathbb{R}^n$, we seek $x \in S$ such that f attains a minimum on S at x, i.e., $f(x) \leq f(y)$ for all $y \in S$. Such a point x is called a *minimizer*, or simply a *minimum*, of f. Since a maximum of f is a minimum of $-f$, it suffices to consider only minimization.

The *objective function*, f, may be linear or nonlinear, and it is usually assumed to be differentiable. The constraint set S is usually defined by a system of equations or inequalities, or both, that may be linear or nonlinear. A point $x \in S$ that satisfies the constraints is called a *feasible point*. If $S = \mathbb{R}^n$, then the problem is *unconstrained*.

General *continuous* optimization problems have the form

$$\min_x f(x) \qquad \text{subject to} \qquad g(x) = 0 \qquad \text{and} \qquad h(x) \leq 0,$$

where $f: \mathbb{R}^n \to \mathbb{R}$, $g: \mathbb{R}^n \to \mathbb{R}^m$, and $h: \mathbb{R}^n \to \mathbb{R}^k$. Optimization problems are classified by the properties of the functions involved. For example, if f, g, and h are all linear, then we have a *linear programming* problem.[1] If any of the functions involved are nonlinear, then we have a *nonlinear programming* problem. Important subclasses of the latter include problems with a nonlinear objective function and linear constraints, or a nonlinear objective function and no constraints. We will focus mainly on optimization problems in one dimension and unconstrained problems in n dimensions.

We will not address *discrete* optimization problems—such as *integer programming*, in which the variables can take on only integer values—because such problems

---

[1]The use of the term *programming* in optimization has nothing to do with computer programming, but instead refers to planning activities in the sense of operations research or management science.

usually require combinatorial rather than numerical techniques. In addition to traditional combinatorial techniques, such as branch-and-bound, there has been a great deal of research in recent years on new approaches to discrete optimization, such as simulated annealing and genetic algorithms, but these topics are beyond the scope of this book.

EXAMPLE 6.1 OPTIMIZATION PROBLEMS. Optimization problems arise in many areas of science, engineering, economics, and business. One might want to minimize the weight of a structure subject to a constraint on its strength, or maximize its strength subject to a constraint on its weight (note the duality here, which is common in optimization). One might want to minimize the cost of a diet subject to nutritional constraints, and so on.

A concrete example is to minimize the surface area of a cylinder subject to a constraint on its volume:

$$\min_{x_1, x_2} f(x_1, x_2) = 2\pi x_1(x_1 + x_2) \qquad \text{subject to} \qquad g(x_1, x_2) = \pi x_1^2 x_2 = V,$$

where x_1 and x_2 are the radius and height of the cylinder, respectively, and V is the required volume. The solution to this problem minimizes the amount of material required to make an appropriate container for the given quantity of liquid. (A sphere with the given volume would require even less surface area but would not make a practical container.)

6.1.1 Local versus Global Optimization

A function f has a *global minimum* at a feasible point x^* if $f(x^*) \le f(x)$ for all feasible points x. We say that f has a *local minimum* at a feasible point x^* if $f(x^*) \le f(x)$ for all feasible points x in a neighborhood of x^*. These concepts are illustrated for a one-dimensional unconstrained problem in Fig. 6.1.

Finding the global minimum of a function, or even verifying that a point is the global minimum after it has been found, is a very difficult problem unless the function has special properties. Most optimization methods are designed to find a local minimum, which may or may not be the global minimum. In general, there is no foolproof way to guarantee that a specific local minimum, or in particular the global minimum, will be found. Usually the best one can do is to start the iterative solution process with an initial guess as close as possible to the desired minimum point.

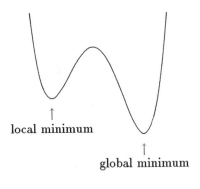

FIGURE 6.1
Local and global minima.

For many purposes, a local minimum of a function may suffice. If the global minimum is desired, however, one way to try to find it is to use several different, widely separated starting points. If they all produce the same result, then there is a good chance that the global minimum has been found. If they produce different results, then taking the lowest of the local minima is the best one can do; but there may still be other unexplored regions with even lower values.

Global optimization for general problems is an active area of research, but with few ironclad results. For special categories of problems, however, global optimization is much more tractable. For example, global solutions to linear programming problems, or more generally *convex* programming problems, are routinely obtained by very efficient methods.

6.1.2 Relationship to Nonlinear Equations

Optimization is related to finding zeros of functions because extrema of smooth functions correspond to zeros of their derivatives. For example, if x^* minimizes an unconstrained function $f : \mathbb{R}^n \to \mathbb{R}$, then the partial derivative of f with respect to each variable x_i is zero, which means that x^* is a solution to the system of equations $\nabla f(x) = 0$. [Recall that the *gradient* of f evaluated at x, denoted by $\nabla f(x)$, is a vector-valued function whose ith component function is the partial derivative of f with respect to x_i, $\partial f(x)/\partial x_i$.]

The converse is not true, however: a solution to the system of nonlinear equations $\nabla f(x) = 0$, which is known as a *stationary point* or *critical point*, may be a minimum, a maximum, or neither (i.e., a saddle point) of f. Nevertheless, many methods for optimization are based on seeking a critical point of a gradient function, which is a system of (generally nonlinear) equations. Any candidate solution found by such a method should be checked for optimality.

A critical point x of an unconstrained objective function f can be checked for optimality by considering the *Hessian matrix* $H_f(x)$ of second partial derivatives of f,

$$\{H_f(x)\}_{ij} = \frac{\partial^2 f(x)}{\partial x_i \partial x_j},$$

evaluated at x. If f has continuous second partial derivatives, the Hessian matrix $H_f(x)$ is symmetric. At a critical point x, where $\nabla f(x) = 0$,

- If $H_f(x)$ is positive definite, then x is a minimum of f.
- If $H_f(x)$ is negative definite, then x is a maximum of f.
- If $H_f(x)$ is indefinite, then x is a saddle point of f.

There are a number of ways to test a symmetric matrix for positive definiteness. One of the simplest and cheapest is to try to compute its Cholesky factorization: the Cholesky algorithm will succeed if and only if the matrix is positive definite (of course, this suggestion assumes that one has a Cholesky routine that fails gracefully when given a nonpositive definite matrix as input). Another good method is to compute the inertia of the matrix (see Section 4.3.10) using a symmetric factorization of the form LDL^T, as in Section 2.5.2. A much more expensive approach is to compute the eigenvalues of the matrix and check whether they are all positive.

6.1.3 Accuracy of Solutions

Consider the Taylor series expansion

$$f(x + h) = f(x) + f'(x)h + \frac{f''(x)}{2}h^2 + \mathcal{O}(h^3),$$

where $f : \mathbb{R} \to \mathbb{R}$. If $f(x^*) = 0$ and $f'(x^*) \neq 0$, as is usually the case in solving a nonlinear equation, then the foregoing expansion indicates that for small values of h, $f(x^* + h) \approx ch$, where $c = f'(x^*)$. This expression implies that small changes in x^* cause proportionally small changes in $f(x^*)$, and hence the solution can be computed about as accurately as the function values can be evaluated, which is often at the level of machine precision.

In a minimization problem, however, we usually have $f'(x^*) = 0$ and $f''(x^*) \neq 0$, so that for small values of h, $f(x^* + h) \approx f(x^*) + ch^2$, where $c = f''(x^*)/2$. This expression implies that a small change of order h in x^* causes a change of order h^2 in $f(x^*)$, and hence one cannot expect the accuracy of the solution to be less than the square root of the error in the function values. Geometrically, a minimum is analogous to a multiple root of a nonlinear equation: in either case a horizontal tangent implies that the function is locally approximately parallel to the x axis, and hence the solution is relatively poorly conditioned. Although simple zeros of a function can often be found to an accuracy of nearly full machine precision, minimizers of a function can be found to an accuracy of only about half precision (i.e., $\sqrt{\epsilon_{\text{mach}}}$). This fact should be kept in mind when selecting an error tolerance for an optimization problem: an unrealistically tight tolerance may drive up the cost of computing a solution without producing a concomitant gain in accuracy.

6.2 ONE-DIMENSIONAL OPTIMIZATION

We begin our study of methods for optimization with problems in one dimension. The one-dimensional case is simpler than multidimensional optimization yet illustrates many of the ideas and issues that arise in higher dimensions.

First, we need a way of bracketing a minimum in an interval, analogous to the way we used a sign change for bracketing solutions to nonlinear equations in one dimension. A real-valued function f is *unimodal* on an interval if there is a unique value x^* in the interval such that $f(x^*)$ is the minimum of f on the interval, and f is strictly decreasing for $x \leq x^*$ and strictly increasing for $x^* \leq x$. The significance of this property is that it enables us to refine an interval containing a solution by computing sample values of the function within the interval and discarding portions of the interval according to the function values obtained, analogous to bisection for solving nonlinear equations.

6.2.1 Golden Section Search

Suppose f is a real-valued function that is unimodal on the interval $[a, b]$. Let x_1 and x_2 be two points within the interval, with $x_1 < x_2$. Comparing the function values $f(x_1)$

and $f(x_2)$ and using the unimodality property will enable us to discard a subinterval, either $(x_2, b]$ or $[a, x_1)$, and know that the minimum of the function lies within the remaining subinterval. In particular, if $f(x_1) < f(x_2)$, then the minimum cannot lie in the interval $(x_2, b]$; and if $f(x_1) > f(x_2)$, then the minimum cannot lie in the interval $[a, x_1)$. Thus, we are left with a shorter interval, either $[a, x_2]$ or $[x_1, b]$, within which we have already computed one function value, either $f(x_1)$ or $f(x_2)$, respectively. Hence, we will need to compute only one new function evaluation to repeat this process.

To make consistent progress in reducing the length of the interval containing the minimum, we would like for each new pair of points to have the same relationship with respect to the new interval that the previous pair had with respect to the previous interval. Such an arrangement will enable us to reduce the length of the interval by a fixed fraction at each iteration, much as we reduced the length by half at each iteration of the bisection method for computing zeros of functions.

To accomplish this objective, we choose the relative positions of the two points as τ and $1 - \tau$, where $\tau^2 = 1 - \tau$, so that $\tau = (\sqrt{5} - 1)/2 \approx 0.618$ and $1 - \tau \approx 0.382$. With this choice, no matter which subinterval is retained, its length will be τ relative to the previous interval, and the interior point retained will be at position either τ or $1 - \tau$ relative to the new interval. Thus, we need to compute only one new function value, at the complementary point, to continue the iteration. This choice of sample points is called *golden section search*. The complete algorithm is as follows:

Initial input: a function f, an interval $[a, b]$ on which f is unimodal, and an error tolerance *tol*.

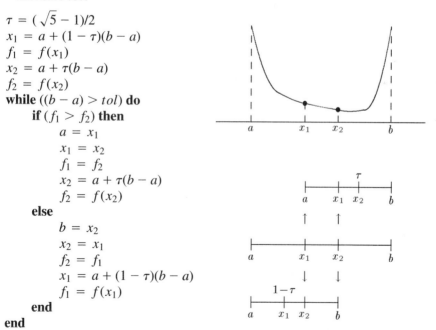

$\tau = (\sqrt{5} - 1)/2$
$x_1 = a + (1 - \tau)(b - a)$
$f_1 = f(x_1)$
$x_2 = a + \tau(b - a)$
$f_2 = f(x_2)$
while $((b - a) > tol)$ **do**
    if $(f_1 > f_2)$ **then**
        $a = x_1$
        $x_1 = x_2$
        $f_1 = f_2$
        $x_2 = a + \tau(b - a)$
        $f_2 = f(x_2)$
    else
        $b = x_2$
        $x_2 = x_1$
        $f_2 = f_1$
        $x_1 = a + (1 - \tau)(b - a)$
        $f_1 = f(x_1)$
    end
end

Golden section search is safe but slowly convergent. Specifically, it is linearly convergent, with $r = 1$ and $C \approx 0.618$.

EXAMPLE 6.2 GOLDEN SECTION SEARCH. We illustrate golden section search by using it to minimize the function

$$f(x) = 0.5 - xe^{-x^2}.$$

Starting with the initial interval $[0, 2]$, we evaluate the function at points $x_1 = 0.764$ and $x_2 = 1.236$, obtaining $f_1 = 0.074$ and $f_2 = 0.232$. Since $f_1 < f_2$, we know that the minimum must lie in the interval $[a, x_2]$, and thus we may replace b by x_2 and repeat the process. The first iteration is depicted in Fig. 6.2, and the full sequence of iterations is given next.

x_1	f_1	x_2	f_2
0.764	0.074	1.236	0.232
0.472	0.122	0.764	0.074
0.764	0.074	0.944	0.113
0.652	0.074	0.764	0.074
0.584	0.085	0.652	0.074
0.652	0.074	0.695	0.071
0.695	0.071	0.721	0.071
0.679	0.072	0.695	0.071
0.695	0.071	0.705	0.071

Although unimodality plays a role in optimization similar to that played by a sign change in root finding, there are important practical differences. A sign change brackets a root of an equation regardless of how large the bracketing interval may be. The same is true of unimodality, but in practice most functions cannot be expected to be unimodal unless the interval is reasonably close to a minimum. Thus, rather more trial and error may be required to find a suitable starting interval for optimization than that typically required for root finding. In practice one might simply look for three points such that the value of the objective function is lower at the inner point than at the two outer points. Although golden section search always converges, it is not guaranteed to find the global minimum, or even a local minimum, unless the objective function is unimodal on the starting interval.

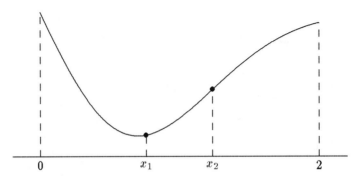

FIGURE 6.2
First iteration of golden section search for example problem.

6.2.2 Successive Parabolic Interpolation

Like bisection for solving nonlinear equations, golden section search makes no use of the numerical function values other than to compare them, so one might conjecture that making greater use of the function values would lead to faster methods. Indeed, as in solving nonlinear equations, faster convergence can be attained by replacing the objective function locally by a simple function that matches its values at some sample points.

An example of this approach is *successive parabolic interpolation*. Initially, the function is evaluated at three points and a quadratic polynomial is fit to the three resulting values. The minimum of the parabola, if it has one, is taken to be a new estimate for the minimum of the function. This new point then replaces the oldest of the three previous points and the process is repeated until convergence. This process is illustrated in Fig. 6.3. Successive parabolic interpolation is riskier than golden section search, since it does not necessarily maintain a bracketing interval in which the solution is known to lie, but asymptotically it converges superlinearly with convergence rate $r \approx 1.324$.

EXAMPLE 6.3 SUCCESSIVE PARABOLIC INTERPOLATION. We illustrate successive parabolic interpolation by using it to minimize the function of Example 6.2,

$$f(x) = 0.5 - xe^{-x^2}.$$

We evaluate the function at three points, say, $x_0 = 0$, $x_1 = 0.6$, and $x_2 = 1.2$, obtaining $f(x_0) = 0.5$, $f(x_1) = 0.081$, $f(x_2) = 0.216$. We fit a parabola to these three points and take its minimizer, $x_3 = 0.754$, to be the next approximation to the solution. We then discard x_0 and repeat the process with the three remaining points. The first iteration is depicted in Fig. 6.4, and the full sequence of iterations is given next.

x_k	$f(x_k)$
0.000	0.500
0.600	0.081
1.200	0.216
0.754	0.073
0.721	0.071
0.692	0.071
0.707	0.071

6.2.3 Newton's Method

A local quadratic approximation to the objective function is useful because the minimum of a quadratic is easy to compute. Another way to obtain a local quadratic approximation is to use a truncated Taylor series expansion,

$$f(x + h) \approx f(x) + f'(x)h + \frac{f''(x)}{2}h^2.$$

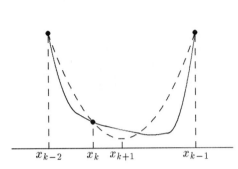

FIGURE 6.3
Successive parabolic iteration for minimizing a function.

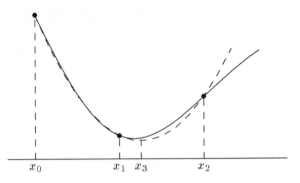

FIGURE 6.4
First iteration of successive parabolic iteration for example problem.

By differentiation, we find that the minimum of this quadratic function of h is given by $h = -f'(x)/f''(x)$. This result suggests the iteration scheme

$$x_{k+1} = x_k - f'(x_k)/f''(x_k),$$

which is simply Newton's method for solving the nonlinear equation $f'(x) = 0$. As usual, Newton's method for finding a minimum normally has a quadratic convergence rate. Unless it is started near the desired solution, however, Newton's method may fail to converge, or it may converge to a maximum or to an inflection point of the function.

EXAMPLE 6.4 NEWTON'S METHOD. We illustrate Newton's method by using it to minimize the function of Example 6.2,

$$f(x) = 0.5 - xe^{-x^2}.$$

The first and second derivatives of f are given by

$$f'(x) = (2x^2 - 1)e^{-x^2}$$

and $$f''(x) = 2x(3 - 2x^2)e^{-x^2},$$

so the Newton iteration for finding a zero of f' is given by

$$x_{k+1} = x_k - (2x_k^2 - 1)/(2x_k(3 - 2x_k^2)).$$

Using a starting guess of $x_0 = 1$, we get the sequence of iterates shown next.

x_k	$f(x_k)$
1.000	0.132
0.500	0.111
0.700	0.071
0.707	0.071

6.2.4 Safeguarded Methods

As with solving nonlinear equations in one dimension, slow-but-sure and fast-but-risky optimization methods can be combined to provide both safety and efficiency. A bracketing interval, in which the solution is known to lie, is maintained so that if the fast method generates an iterate that would lie outside the interval, then the safe method can be used to reduce the length of the bracketing interval before trying the fast method again, with a better chance of producing a reliable result. Most library routines for one-dimensional optimization are based on such a hybrid approach. One popular combination, which requires no derivatives of the objective function, is golden section search and successive parabolic interpolation.

6.3 MULTIDIMENSIONAL UNCONSTRAINED OPTIMIZATION

We turn now to multidimensional unconstrained optimization, which has a number of features in common with both one-dimensional optimization and with solving systems of nonlinear equations in n dimensions.

6.3.1 Direct Search Methods

Recall that golden section search for one-dimensional optimization makes no use of the objective function values other than to compare them. Direct search methods for multidimensional optimization share this property, although they do not retain the convergence guarantee of golden section search. Perhaps the best known of these is the method of Nelder and Mead. For minimizing a function f of n variables, the method begins with a set of $n + 1$ starting points, forming a *simplex* in $\mathbb{R}^n$, at which f is evaluated. A move is then made to a new point along a straight line from the worst current point through the centroid of all of the points. The new point then replaces the worst point, and the process is repeated. The algorithm involves several parameters that determine how far to move along the line and how much to expand or contract the simplex, depending on whether the search is successful or not. Such direct search methods can be attractive for a nonsmooth objective function, for which few other methods are applicable, and they are sometimes fairly effective when n is small, but they tend to be quite expensive when n is larger than two or three.

6.3.2 Steepest Descent Method

As expected, greater use of the objective function and its derivatives leads to faster methods. Let $f : \mathbb{R}^n \to \mathbb{R}$ be a real-valued function of n real variables. Recall that the gradient of f evaluated at x, denoted by $\nabla f(x)$, is a vector-valued function whose ith component function is the partial derivative of f with respect to x_i, $\partial f(x)/\partial x_i$. From calculus, we know that at a given point x where the gradient vector is nonzero, the negative gradient, $-\nabla f(x)$, points downhill toward lower values of the function f. In fact, $-\nabla f(x)$ is locally the direction of *steepest descent* for the function f in the sense that the value of the function decreases more rapidly along the direction of the negative gradient than along any other direction.

This fact leads to one of the oldest methods for multidimensional optimization, the *steepest descent method*. Starting from some initial guess x_0, each successive approximate solution is given by

$$x_{k+1} = x_k - \alpha_k \nabla f(x_k),$$

where α_k is a *line search* parameter that determines how far to go in the given direction.

Given a direction of descent, such as the negative gradient, determination of an appropriate value for the line search parameter α_k at each iteration is a one-dimensional minimization problem

$$\min_{\alpha} f(x_k - \alpha \nabla f(x_k))$$

that can be solved by the methods discussed in Section 6.2.

The steepest descent method is very reliable in that it can always make progress provided the gradient is nonzero. But as the following example demonstrates, the method is rather myopic in its view of the behavior of the function, and the resulting iterates can zigzag back and forth, making very slow progress toward a solution. In general, the convergence rate of steepest descent is only linear, with a constant factor that can be arbitrarily close to 1.

EXAMPLE 6.5 STEEPEST DESCENT. We illustrate the steepest descent method by using it to minimize the function

$$f(x) = 0.5x_1^2 + 2.5x_2^2,$$

whose gradient is given by

$$\nabla f(x) = \begin{bmatrix} x_1 \\ 5x_2 \end{bmatrix}.$$

If we take $x_0 = [5 \quad 1]^T$ as starting point, the gradient is $\nabla f(x_0) = [5 \quad 5]^T$. We next perform a line search along the negative gradient direction, i.e.,

$$\min_{\alpha} f(x_0 - \alpha \nabla f(x_0)).$$

One-dimensional minimization of f as a function of α along the line gives $\alpha_0 = \frac{1}{3}$, so that the next approximation is $x_1 = [3.333 \quad -0.667]^T$. We then evaluate the gradient at this new point to determine the next search direction and repeat the process. The resulting sequence of iterations is shown numerically in the following table and graphically in Fig. 6.5, where the ellipses represent level curves, or contours, on which the function f has a constant value. The gradient direction at any given point is always normal to the level curve passing through that point. Note that the minimum along a given search direction occurs when the gradient at the new point is orthogonal to the search direction. The sequence of iterates given by steepest descent is converging slowly toward the solution, which for this problem is at the origin, where the minimum function value is zero.

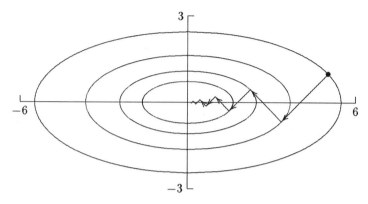

FIGURE 6.5
Convergence of steepest descent.

x_k		$f(x_k)$	$\nabla f(x_k)$	
5.000	1.000	15.000	5.000	5.000
3.333	−0.667	6.667	3.333	−3.333
2.222	0.444	2.963	2.222	2.222
1.481	−0.296	1.317	1.481	−1.481
0.988	0.198	0.585	0.988	0.988
0.658	−0.132	0.260	0.658	−0.658
0.439	0.088	0.116	0.439	0.439
0.293	−0.059	0.051	0.293	−0.293
0.195	0.039	0.023	0.195	0.195
0.130	−0.026	0.010	0.130	−0.130

6.3.3 Newton's Method

A broader view of the function can be obtained by a local quadratic approximation, which as we have seen is equivalent to Newton's method. In the case of multidimensional optimization, we seek a zero of the gradient. Thus, the iteration scheme for Newton's method has the form

$$x_{k+1} = x_k - H_f^{-1}(x_k)\nabla f(x_k),$$

where $H_f(x)$ is the *Hessian matrix* of second partial derivatives of f,

$$\{H_f(x)\}_{ij} = \frac{\partial^2 f(x)}{\partial x_i \partial x_j},$$

evaluated at x_k. As usual, we do not explicitly invert the Hessian matrix but instead use it to solve a linear system

$$H_f(x_k)s_k = -\nabla f(x_k)$$

for s_k, then take as next iterate

$$x_{k+1} = x_k + s_k.$$

The convergence rate of Newton's method for minimization is normally quadratic. As usual, however, Newton's method is unreliable unless started close enough to the solution.

EXAMPLE 6.6 NEWTON'S METHOD. We illustrate Newton's method by again minimizing the function of Example 6.5,

$$f(x) = 0.5x_1^2 + 2.5x_2^2,$$

whose gradient and Hessian are given by

$$\nabla f(x) = \begin{bmatrix} x_1 \\ 5x_2 \end{bmatrix} \quad \text{and} \quad H_f(x) = \begin{bmatrix} 1 & 0 \\ 0 & 5 \end{bmatrix}.$$

If we take $x_0 = \begin{bmatrix} 5 & 1 \end{bmatrix}^T$ as starting point, the gradient is $\nabla f(x_0) = \begin{bmatrix} 5 & 5 \end{bmatrix}^T$. The linear system to be solved for the Newton step is therefore

$$\begin{bmatrix} 1 & 0 \\ 0 & 5 \end{bmatrix} s_0 = \begin{bmatrix} -5 \\ -5 \end{bmatrix},$$

and hence the next approximate solution is

$$x_1 = x_0 + s_0 = \begin{bmatrix} 5 \\ 1 \end{bmatrix} + \begin{bmatrix} -5 \\ -1 \end{bmatrix} = \begin{bmatrix} 0 \\ 0 \end{bmatrix},$$

which is the exact solution for this problem. That Newton's method has converged in a single iteration in this case should not be surprising, since the function being minimized is a quadratic. Of course, the quadratic model used by Newton's method is not exact in general, but nevertheless it enables Newton's method to take a more global view of the problem, yielding much more rapid convergence than the steepest descent method.

Intuitively, unconstrained minimization is like finding the bottom of a bowl by rolling a marble down the side. If the bowl is oblong, then the marble will rock back and forth along the valley before eventually settling at the bottom, analogous to the zigzagging path taken by the steepest descent method. With Newton's method, the metric of the space is redefined so that the bowl becomes circular, and hence the marble rolls directly to the bottom.

Unlike the steepest descent method, Newton's method does not require a line search parameter because the quadratic model determines an appropriate length as well as direction for the step to the next approximate solution. When started far from a solution, however, it may still be advisable to perform a line search along the direction of the Newton step s_k in order to make the method more robust (this procedure is sometimes called the *damped Newton method*). Once the iterations are near the solution, then the value $\alpha_k = 1$ for the line search parameter should suffice for subsequent iterations.

An alternative to a line search is a *trust region method*, in which an estimate is maintained of the radius of a region in which the quadratic model is sufficiently accurate for the computed Newton step to be reliable (see Section 5.3.5), and thus the next

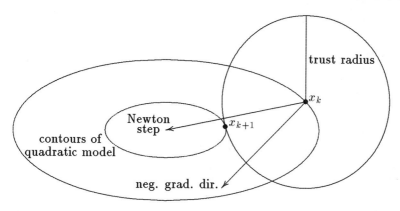

FIGURE 6.6
Modification of Newton step by trust region method.

approximate solution is constrained to lie within the trust region. If the current trust radius is binding, minimizing the quadratic model function subject to this constraint may modify the direction as well as the length of the Newton step, as illustrated in Fig. 6.6. The accuracy of the quadratic model at a given step is assessed by comparing the actual decrease in the objective function value with that predicted by the quadratic model, and the trust radius is then increased or decreased accordingly. Once near a solution, the trust radius should be large enough to permit full Newton steps, yielding rapid local convergence.

If the objective function f has continuous second partial derivatives, then the Hessian matrix H_f is symmetric; and near a minimum it is positive definite. Thus, the linear system for the step to the next iterate can be solved by Cholesky factorization, requiring only about half of the work required by LU factorization. Far from a minimum, however, $H_f(x_k)$ may not be positive definite and thus may require a symmetric indefinite factorization. The resulting Newton step s_k may not even be a *descent direction* for the function, i.e., we may not have

$$\nabla f(x_k)^T s_k < 0.$$

In this case, an alternative descent direction can be computed, such as the negative gradient or a *direction of negative curvature* (i.e., a vector s_k such that $s_k^T H_f(x_k)s_k < 0$, which can be obtained readily from a symmetric indefinite factorization of $H_f(x_k)$), and a line search performed. Such alternative measures should become unnecessary once the approximate solution is sufficiently close to the true solution, so that the ultimate quadratic convergence rate of Newton's method can still be attained.

6.3.4 Quasi-Newton Methods

Newton's method usually converges very rapidly once it nears a solution, but it requires a substantial amount of work per iteration, specifically $\mathcal{O}(n^3)$ arithmetic and $\mathcal{O}(n^2)$ scalar function evaluations per iteration for a dense problem. This drawback has motivated the development of quasi-Newton methods that converge somewhat less rapidly but require much less work per iteration (and are often more robust as well).

Many variants of Newton's method have been developed to improve its reliability and reduce its overhead. These *quasi-Newton methods* have the form

$$x_{k+1} = x_k - \alpha_k B_k^{-1} \nabla f(x_k),$$

where α_k is a line search parameter and B_k is some approximation to the Hessian matrix obtained in any of a number of ways, including secant updating, finite differences, periodic reevaluation, or neglecting some terms in the true Hessian of the objective function.

Many quasi-Newton methods are more robust than the pure Newton method, are superlinearly convergent, and have considerably lower overhead per iteration. For example, *secant updating* methods for this problem require no second derivative evaluations, require only one gradient evaluation per iteration, and solve the necessary linear system at each iteration by updating methods that require only $\mathcal{O}(n^2)$ work rather than the $\mathcal{O}(n^3)$ work that would be required by a matrix factorization at each step. This substantial savings in work per iteration more than offsets their somewhat slower convergence rate (generally superlinear but not quadratic), so that they usually take less total time to find a solution.

6.3.5 Secant Updating Methods

As with secant updating methods for solving nonlinear equations, the motivation for secant updating methods for minimization is to reduce the work per iteration of Newton's method and possibly improve its robustness. One could simply use Broyden's method to seek a zero of the gradient, but this approach would not preserve the symmetry of the Hessian matrix. Several secant updating formulas for unconstrained minimization have been developed that not only preserve symmetry in the approximate Hessian matrix but also preserve positive definiteness. Symmetry reduces the amount of work required by about half, and positive definiteness guarantees that the quasi-Newton step will be a descent direction.

One of the most effective of these secant updating methods for minimization is called BFGS, after the initials of its four coinventors. Starting with an initial guess x_0 and a symmetric positive definite approximate Hessian matrix B_0, the following steps are repeated until convergence.

1. Solve $B_k s_k = -\nabla f(x_k)$ for s_k.
2. $x_{k+1} = x_k + s_k$.
3. $y_k = \nabla f(x_{k+1}) - \nabla f(x_k)$.
4. $B_{k+1} = B_k + (y_k y_k^T)/(y_k^T s_k) - (B_k s_k s_k^T B_k)/(s_k^T B_k s_k)$.

In practice, a factorization of B_k is updated rather than B_k itself, so that the linear system for the quasi-Newton step s_k can be solved at a cost of $\mathcal{O}(n^2)$ rather than $\mathcal{O}(n^3)$ work. Note that unlike Newton's method for minimization, no second derivatives are required. These methods are often started with $B_0 = I$, which means that the initial step is along the negative gradient (i.e., the direction of steepest descent); and then second derivative information is gradually built up in the approximate Hessian matrix through successive iterations.

Like most secant updating methods, BFGS normally has a superlinear convergence rate, even though the approximate Hessian does not necessarily converge to the true Hessian. A line search can also be used to enhance the effectiveness of the method. Indeed, for a quadratic objective function, if an exact line search is performed at each iteration, then the BFGS method terminates at the exact solution in at most n iterations, where n is the dimension of the problem.

EXAMPLE 6.7 BFGS METHOD. We illustrate the BFGS method by again minimizing the function of Example 6.5,

$$f(x) = 0.5x_1^2 + 2.5x_2^2,$$

whose gradient is given by

$$\nabla f(x) = \begin{bmatrix} x_1 \\ 5x_2 \end{bmatrix}.$$

Starting with $x_0 = \begin{bmatrix} 5 & 1 \end{bmatrix}^T$ and $B_0 = I$, the initial step is simply the negative gradient, so

$$x_1 = x_0 + s_0 = \begin{bmatrix} 5 \\ 1 \end{bmatrix} + \begin{bmatrix} -5 \\ -5 \end{bmatrix} = \begin{bmatrix} 0 \\ -4 \end{bmatrix}.$$

Updating the approximate Hessian according to the BFGS formula, we get

$$B_1 = \begin{bmatrix} 0.667 & 0.333 \\ 0.333 & 0.667 \end{bmatrix}.$$

A new step is now computed and the process continued. The sequence of iterations is shown in the following table:

x_k		$f(x_k)$	$\nabla f(x_k)$	
5.000	1.000	15.000	5.000	5.000
0.000	−4.000	40.000	0.000	−20.000
−2.222	0.444	2.963	−2.222	2.222
0.816	0.082	0.350	0.816	0.408
−0.009	−0.015	0.001	−0.009	−0.077
−0.001	0.001	0.000	−0.001	0.005

The increase in function value on the first iteration could have been avoided by using a line search.

6.3.6 Conjugate Gradient Method

The conjugate gradient method is another alternative to Newton's method that does not require explicit second derivatives. Indeed, unlike secant updating methods, the conjugate gradient method does not even store an approximation to the Hessian matrix, which makes it especially suitable for very large problems.

As we saw in Section 6.3.2, the steepest descent method tends to search in the same directions repeatedly, leading to very slow convergence. As its name suggests, the conjugate gradient method also uses gradients, but it avoids repeated searches by modifying the gradient at each step to remove components in previous directions. The resulting sequence of conjugate (i.e., orthogonal in some inner product) search directions implicitly accumulates information about the Hessian matrix as iterations proceed. Theoretically, the method is exact after at most n iterations for a quadratic objective function in n dimensions, but it is usually quite effective for more general unconstrained minimization problems as well. The motivation for this algorithm is discussed in Section 11.5.5.

To minimize f starting from an initial guess x_0, we initialize $g_0 = \nabla f(x_0)$ and $s_0 = -g_0$; then the following steps are repeated until convergence.

1. $x_{k+1} = x_k + \alpha_k s_k$, where α_k is determined by a line search.
2. $g_{k+1} = \nabla f(x_{k+1})$.
3. $\beta_{k+1} = (g_{k+1}^T g_{k+1})/(g_k^T g_k)$.
4. $s_{k+1} = -g_{k+1} + \beta_{k+1} s_k$.

The formula for β_{k+1} given above is due to Fletcher and Reeves. An alternative formula, due to Polak and Ribiere, is

$$\beta_{k+1} = ((g_{k+1} - g_k)^T g_{k+1})/(g_k^T g_k).$$

It is common to restart the algorithm after every n iterations, reinitializing to use the negative gradient at the current point.

EXAMPLE 6.8 CONJUGATE GRADIENT METHOD. We illustrate the conjugate gradient method by using it to minimize the function

$$f(x) = 0.5x_1^2 + 2.5x_2^2,$$

whose gradient is given by

$$\nabla f(x) = \begin{bmatrix} x_1 \\ 5x_2 \end{bmatrix}.$$

Starting with $x_0 = [5 \quad 1]^T$, the initial search direction is the negative gradient,

$$s_0 = -g_0 = -\nabla f(x_0) = \begin{bmatrix} -5 \\ -5 \end{bmatrix}.$$

The exact minimum along this line is given by $\alpha_0 = \frac{1}{3}$, so that the next approximation is $x_1 = [3.333 \quad -0.667]^T$, at which point we compute the new gradient,

$$g_1 = \nabla f(x_1) = \begin{bmatrix} 3.333 \\ -3.333 \end{bmatrix}.$$

So far there is no difference from the steepest descent method. At this point, however, rather than search along the new negative gradient, we compute instead the quantity

$$\beta_0 = (g_1^T g_1)/(g_0^T g_0) = 0.444,$$

which gives as the next search direction

$$s_1 = -g_1 + \beta_0 s_0 = \begin{bmatrix} -3.333 \\ 3.333 \end{bmatrix} + 0.444 \begin{bmatrix} -5 \\ -5 \end{bmatrix} = \begin{bmatrix} -5.556 \\ 1.111 \end{bmatrix}.$$

The minimum along this direction is given by $\alpha_1 = 0.6$, which gives the exact solution at the origin. Thus, as expected for a quadratic function, the conjugate gradient method converges in $n = 2$ steps in this case.

6.3.7 Truncated Newton Methods

Despite its rapid asymptotic convergence, Newton's method can be unattractive because of its high cost per iteration, especially for very large problems, for which storage requirements are also an important consideration. Another way of potentially reducing the work per iteration is to solve the linear system for the Newton step,

$$B_k s_k = -\nabla f(x_k),$$

where B_k is the true or approximate Hessian matrix, by an iterative method (see Section 11.5) rather than by a direct method based on factorization of B_k. One advantage is that only a few iterations of the iterative method may be sufficient to produce a step s_k that is almost as good as the true Newton step. Indeed, far from the minimum the true Newton step may offer no special advantage, yet can be very costly to compute exactly. Such an approach is called an *inexact* or *truncated* Newton method, since the linear system for the Newton step is solved inexactly by terminating the linear iterative solver before convergence.

A good choice for the linear iterative solver is the conjugate gradient method (see Section 11.5.5). The conjugate gradient method begins with the negative gradient vector and eventually converges to the true Newton step, so truncating the iterations produces a step that is intermediate between these two vectors and is always a descent direction provided B_k is positive definite. Moreover, since the conjugate gradient method requires only matrix-vector products, the Hessian matrix need not be formed explicitly, which can mean a substantial savings in storage. To supply the product $B_k v$, for example, the finite difference approximation

$$B_k v \approx \frac{\nabla f(x_k + hv) - \nabla f(x_k)}{h}$$

can be computed instead, without ever forming B_k.

In implementing a truncated Newton method, the termination criterion for the inner iteration must be chosen carefully to preserve the superlinear convergence rate of the outer iteration. In addition, special measures may be required if the matrix B_k is not positive definite. Nevertheless, truncated Newton methods are usually very effective in practice and are among the best methods available for large sparse problems.

6.4 NONLINEAR LEAST SQUARES

Least squares data fitting can be viewed as an optimization problem. Given m data points (t_i, y_i), we wish to find the n-vector x of parameters that gives the best fit in the least squares sense to the model function $f(t, x)$. If we define the components of the residual function $r(x)$,

$$r_i(x) = y_i - f(t_i, x), \qquad i = 1, \dots, m,$$

then we wish to minimize the function $g(x) = \frac{1}{2}r^T(x)r(x)$. The gradient vector and Hessian matrix of g are given by

$$\nabla g(x) = J^T(x)r(x)$$

and

$$H_g(x) = J^T(x)J(x) + \sum_{i=1}^{m} r_i(x)H_i(x),$$

where $J(x)$ is the Jacobian matrix of the vector function $r(x)$, and $H_i(x)$ denotes the Hessian matrix of the component function $r_i(x)$. Thus, if x_k is an approximate solution, the Newton step s_k is given by the linear system

$$[J^T(x_k)J(x_k) + \sum_{i=1}^{m} r_i(x_k)H_i(x_k)]s_k = -J^T(x_k)r(x_k).$$

6.4.1 Gauss-Newton Method

The m Hessian matrices H_i are usually inconvenient and expensive to compute. Moreover, in H_g each of these matrices is multiplied by the residual component function r_i, which should be small at a solution if the fit of the model function to the data is reasonably good. These features motivate the *Gauss-Newton method* for nonlinear least squares, in which the second-order term is dropped and the linear system

$$J^T(x_k)J(x_k)s_k = -J^T(x_k)r(x_k)$$

is solved for the approximate Newton step s_k at each iteration. But we recognize this system as the normal equations (see Section 3.3) for the linear least squares problem

$$J(x_k)s_k \approx -r(x_k),$$

which can be solved more reliably by orthogonal factorization (see Section 3.4). The next approximate solution is then given by

$$x_{k+1} = x_k + s_k,$$

and the process is repeated until convergence. In effect, the Gauss-Newton method replaces a nonlinear least squares problem with a sequence of linear least squares problems whose solutions converge to the solution of the original nonlinear problem.

EXAMPLE 6.9 GAUSS-NEWTON METHOD. We illustrate the Gauss-Newton method for nonlinear least squares by fitting the nonlinear model function

$$f(t, x) = x_1 e^{x_2 t}$$

to the data

t	0.0	1.0	2.0	3.0
y	2.0	0.7	0.3	0.1

For this model function, the entries of the Jacobian matrix of the residual function r are given by

$$\{J(x)\}_{i,1} = \frac{\partial r_i(x)}{\partial x_1} = -e^{x_2 t_i}, \quad \{J(x)\}_{i,2} = \frac{\partial r_i(x)}{\partial x_2} = -x_1 t_i e^{x_2 t_i}.$$

If we take $x_0 = \begin{bmatrix} 1 & 0 \end{bmatrix}^T$ as starting point, then the linear least squares problem to be solved for the Gauss-Newton correction step s_0 is

$$\begin{bmatrix} -1 & 0 \\ -1 & -1 \\ -1 & -2 \\ -1 & -3 \end{bmatrix} s_0 \approx \begin{bmatrix} -1 \\ 0.3 \\ 0.7 \\ 0.9 \end{bmatrix}.$$

The least squares solution to this system is $s_0 = [0.69 \quad -0.61]^T$. We take $x_1 = x_0 + s_0$ as the next approximate solution and repeat the process until convergence. The sequence of iterations is shown next.

x_k		$\|r(x_k)\|_2^2$
1.000	0.000	2.390
1.690	−0.610	0.212
1.975	−0.930	0.007
1.994	−1.004	0.002
1.995	−1.009	0.002
1.995	−1.010	0.002

Like all methods based on Newton's method, the Gauss-Newton method for solving nonlinear least squares problems may fail to converge if it is started too far from the solution. A line search can be used to improve its robustness, but additional modifications may be necessary to ensure that the computed step is a descent direction when far from the solution.

In addition, if the residual function at the solution is too large, then the second-order term omitted from the Hessian matrix may not be negligible, which means that the Gauss-Newton approximation is not sufficiently accurate, so that the method converges very slowly at best and may not converge at all. In such "large-residual" cases, it may be best to use a general nonlinear minimization method that takes into account the true full Hessian matrix.

6.4.2 Levenberg-Marquardt Method

The *Levenberg-Marquardt method* is another useful alternative when the Gauss-Newton approximation is inadequate or yields a rank-deficient linear least squares subproblem. In this method, the linear system at each iteration is of the form

$$(J^T(x_k)J(x_k) + \mu_k I)s_k = -J^T(x_k)r(x_k),$$

where μ_k is a scalar parameter chosen by some strategy. The corresponding linear least squares problem to be solved is

$$\begin{bmatrix} J(x_k) \\ \sqrt{\mu_k}I \end{bmatrix} s_k \approx \begin{bmatrix} -r(x_k) \\ 0 \end{bmatrix}.$$

This method can be variously interpreted as replacing the term omitted from the true Hessian by a scalar multiple of the identity, or as shifting the spectrum of the approximate Hessian to make it positive definite (or equivalently, as boosting the rank of the corresponding least squares problem), or as using a weighted combination of the Gauss-Newton step and the steepest descent direction. With a suitable strategy for choosing the parameter μ_k, the Levenberg-Marquardt method can be very robust in practice, and it forms the basis for several effective software packages for solving nonlinear least squares problems.

6.5 CONSTRAINED OPTIMIZATION

A thorough study of constrained optimization is beyond the scope of this book, but the basic ideas of some of the concepts and algorithms involved are briefly sketched here. Consider the minimization of a nonlinear function subject to nonlinear equality constraints,

$$\min_x f(x) \quad \text{subject to} \quad g(x) = 0,$$

where $f \colon \mathbb{R}^n \to \mathbb{R}$ and $g \colon \mathbb{R}^n \to \mathbb{R}^m$, with $m \le n$. From multivariate calculus, we know that a necessary condition for a feasible point x to be a solution to this problem is that the negative gradient of f lies in the space spanned by the constraint normals, i.e., that

$$-\nabla f(x) = J_g^T(x)\lambda,$$

where J_g is the Jacobian matrix of g and λ is an m-vector of *Lagrange multipliers*. This condition says that we cannot reduce the objective function without violating the constraints, and it motivates the definition of the *Lagrangian function*, $\mathcal{L} \colon \mathbb{R}^{n+m} \to \mathbb{R}$, given by

$$\mathcal{L}(x, \lambda) = f(x) + \lambda^T g(x),$$

whose gradient and Hessian are given by

$$\nabla \mathcal{L}(x, \lambda) = \begin{bmatrix} \nabla_x \mathcal{L}(x, \lambda) \\ \nabla_\lambda \mathcal{L}(x, \lambda) \end{bmatrix} = \begin{bmatrix} \nabla f(x) + J_g^T(x)\lambda \\ g(x) \end{bmatrix}$$

and

$$H_{\mathcal{L}}(x, \lambda) = \begin{bmatrix} B(x, \lambda) & J_g^T(x) \\ J_g(x) & 0 \end{bmatrix},$$

where $B(x, \lambda) = \nabla_{xx} \mathcal{L}(x, \lambda) = H_f(x) + \sum_{i=1}^m \lambda_i H_{g_i}(x)$. Together, the necessary condition and the requirement of feasibility say that we are looking for a critical point of the Lagrangian function, which is expressed by the system of nonlinear equations

$$\begin{bmatrix} \nabla f(x) + J_g^T(x)\lambda \\ g(x) \end{bmatrix} = 0.$$

It is important to note that the block 2×2 matrix $H_{\mathcal{L}}$ is symmetric but cannot be positive definite, even if the matrix B is positive definite (in general, B is not positive definite, but an extra "penalty" term is sometimes added to the Lagrangian to make it so). Thus, a critical point of $\mathcal{L}$ is necessarily a saddle point rather than a minimum or maximum.

If the Hessian of the Lagrangian is never positive definite, even at a constrained minimum, then how can we check a critical point of the Lagrangian for optimality? It turns out that a sufficient condition for a constrained minimum is that the matrix $B(x, \lambda)$ at the critical point be positive definite on the *tangent space* to the constraint surface, which is simply the null space of J_g (i.e., the set of all vectors orthogonal to the rows of J_g). If Z is a matrix whose columns form a basis for this subspace, then we check whether the symmetric matrix $Z^T B Z$ is positive definite. This condition says that we need positive definiteness only with respect to locally feasible directions (i.e., parallel to the constraint surface), for movement orthogonal to the constraint surface would violate the constraints. A suitable matrix Z can be obtained from an orthogonal factorization of J_g^T (see Section 3.4.3).

Applying Newton's method to the foregoing nonlinear system, we obtain a system of linear equations

$$\begin{bmatrix} B(x, \lambda) & J_g^T(x) \\ J_g(x) & 0 \end{bmatrix} \begin{bmatrix} s \\ \delta \end{bmatrix} = - \begin{bmatrix} \nabla f(x) + J_g^T(x)\lambda \\ g(x) \end{bmatrix}$$

for the Newton step (s, δ) in (x, λ) at each iteration. Many of the algorithms for solving constrained optimization problems amount to different ways of solving this block 2×2 linear system or some variant of it. Methods for constrained optimization fall roughly into three categories:

- Range space methods, which are based on block elimination in the block 2×2 linear system, yielding an approach akin to the normal equations for linear least squares
- Null space methods, which are based on orthogonal factorization of the matrix of constraint normals, $J_g^T(x)$
- Methods that solve the entire block 2×2 system directly, with an appropriate pivoting strategy that takes advantage of its symmetry and sparsity

The methods just outlined for equality constraints can be extended to handle inequality constraints by using an *active set strategy* in which the inequality constraints are provisionally divided into those that are satisfied already (and can therefore be temporarily disregarded) and those that are violated (and are therefore temporarily treated as equality constraints). This division of the constraints is revised as iterations proceed until eventually the correct constraints that are binding at the solution are identified.

EXAMPLE 6.10 CONSTRAINED OPTIMIZATION. As a simple illustration of constrained optimization, we minimize the same quadratic function as in our previous examples,

$$f(x) = 0.5x_1^2 + 2.5x_2^2,$$

but this time subject to the constraint

$$g(x) = x_1 - x_2 - 1 = 0.$$

The Lagrangian function is given by

$$\mathcal{L}(x, \lambda) = f(x) + \lambda^T g(x) = 0.5x_1^2 + 2.5x_2^2 + \lambda(x_1 - x_2 - 1),$$

where the Lagrange multiplier λ is a scalar in this instance because there is only one constraint. Since

$$\nabla f(x) = \begin{bmatrix} x_1 \\ 5x_2 \end{bmatrix} \quad \text{and} \quad J_g(x) = [1 \quad -1],$$

we have

$$\nabla_x \mathcal{L}(x, \lambda) = \nabla f(x) + J_g^T(x)\lambda = \begin{bmatrix} x_1 \\ 5x_2 \end{bmatrix} + \lambda \begin{bmatrix} 1 \\ -1 \end{bmatrix}.$$

Therefore, the system of equations to be solved for a critical point of the Lagrangian is

$$x_1 + \lambda = 0,$$

$$5x_2 - \lambda = 0,$$

$$x_1 - x_2 = 1,$$

which in this case is a linear system whose matrix formulation is

$$\begin{bmatrix} 1 & 0 & 1 \\ 0 & 5 & -1 \\ 1 & -1 & 0 \end{bmatrix} \begin{bmatrix} x_1 \\ x_2 \\ \lambda \end{bmatrix} = \begin{bmatrix} 0 \\ 0 \\ 1 \end{bmatrix}.$$

Solving this system, we obtain the solution

$$x_1 = 0.833, \qquad x_2 = -0.167, \qquad \lambda = -0.833.$$

The solution is illustrated in Fig. 6.7. The necessary condition for optimality requires that the negative gradient of the objective function line up with the gradient of the constraint, and that the point lie on the line $x_1 - x_2 = 1$. The only point satisfying both requirements is the solution we computed, indicated by a bullet in the diagram.

6.5.1 Linear Programming

One of the most important and commonly occurring constrained optimization problems is *linear programming*. A standard form for such problems is

$$\min_x f(x) = c^T x \quad \text{subject to} \quad Ax = b \quad \text{and} \quad x \geq 0,$$

where c is an n-vector, A is an $m \times n$ matrix, $m < n$, and b is an m-vector.

The feasible region for such a problem is a convex polyhedron in n-dimensional space, and the minimum must occur at one of its vertices. The standard method for solving linear programming problems, called the *simplex method*, systematically examines a sequence of vertices to find the one yielding the minimum.

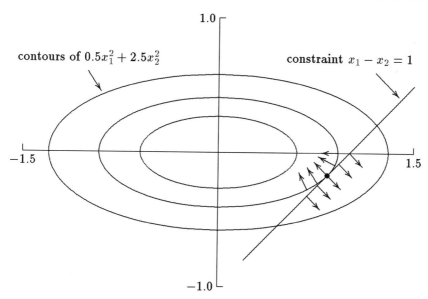

FIGURE 6.7
Solution to constrained optimization problem.

A detailed description of the simplex method is beyond the scope of this book; but the main procedures, sketched here, make use of a number of tools we have already seen. Phase 1 of the simplex method is to find a vertex of the feasible region. A vertex of the feasible region is a point where all of the constraints are satisfied, and $n - m$ of the inequality constraints are binding (i.e., $x_i = 0$). If we choose any subset of $n - m$ variables, called *basic variables*, and set them to zero, then we can use the equality constraints to solve for the m remaining *nonbasic variables*. If the resulting values for the nonbasic variables are nonnegative, then we have found a feasible vertex. Otherwise, we must choose a different set of basic variables and try again. There are systematic procedures, which involve adding new artificial variables and constraints, to ensure that a feasible vertex is found rapidly and efficiently.

Phase 2 of the simplex method moves systematically from vertex to vertex until the minimum point is found. Starting from the feasible vertex found in Phase 1, a neighboring vertex that has a smaller value for the objective function is selected. The specific new vertex chosen is obtained by exchanging one of the current basic variables for the nonbasic variable that produces the greatest reduction in the value of the objective function, subject to remaining feasible. This process is then repeated until no vertex has a lower function value than the current point, which must therefore be optimal.

The linear system solutions required at each step of the simplex method use matrix factorization and updating techniques similar to those in Chapter 2. In particular, much of the efficiency of the method depends on updating the factorization at each step as variables are added or deleted one at a time.

In this brief sketch of the simplex method, we have glossed over many details, such as the various degeneracies that can arise, the detection of infeasible or unbounded problems, the updating of the factorization, and the optimality test. Suffice it to say that all of these can be addressed effectively, so that the method is very reliable and efficient in practice, able to solve problems having thousands of variables and constraints.

The efficiency of the simplex method in practice is somewhat surprising, since the number of vertices that must potentially be examined is

$$\binom{n}{m} = \frac{n!}{m!\,(n-m)!},$$

which is enormous for problems of realistic size. Yet in practice, the number of iterations required is usually only a small multiple of the number of constraints m, essentially independent of the number of variables n (the value of n affects the cost per iteration, but not the number of iterations).

Although the simplex method is extremely effective in practice, in theory it can require in the worst case a solution time that is exponential in the size of the problem, and there are contrived examples for which such behavior actually occurs. In recent years, new methods for linear programming have been developed, such as those of Khachiyan and of Karmarkar, whose worst-case solution time is polynomial in the size of the problem. These methods move through the interior of the feasible region, not restricting themselves to investigating only its vertices. Although interior point methods are having significant practical impact, the simplex method is still the predominant method in standard packages for linear programming, and its effectiveness in practice is excellent.

EXAMPLE 6.11 LINEAR PROGRAMMING. To illustrate linear programming we consider a graphical solution of the problem

$$\min_{x} f(x) = c^T x = -8x_1 - 11x_2$$

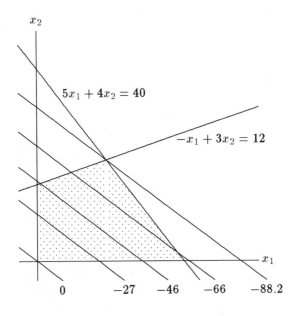

$5x_1 + 4x_2 = 40$

$-x_1 + 3x_2 = 12$

0 -27 -46 -66 -88.2

FIGURE 6.8
Linear programming problem from Example 6.11.

subject to the linear inequality constraints

$$5x_1 + 4x_2 \leq 40, \quad -x_1 + 3x_2 \leq 12, \quad x_1 \geq 0, \quad x_2 \geq 0.$$

The feasible region, which is bounded by the coordinate axes and the other two straight lines, is shaded in Fig. 6.8. Contour lines of the objective function are drawn, with corresponding values of the objective function shown along the bottom of the graph. The minimum value necessarily occurs at one of the vertices of the feasible region, in this case the point $x_1 = 3.79$, $x_2 = 5.26$, where the objective function has the value -88.2.

6.6 SOFTWARE FOR OPTIMIZATION

Table 6.1 is a list of some of the software available for solving one-dimensional and unconstrained optimization problems. In the multidimensional case, we distinguish between routines that do or do not require the user to supply derivatives for the functions, although in some cases the routines mentioned offer both options.

Software for minimizing a function $f(x)$ typically requires the user to supply the name of a routine that computes the value of the function f for any given value of x. The user must also supply absolute or relative error tolerances that are used in the stopping criterion for the iterative solution process. Additional input for one-dimensional problems usually includes the endpoints of an interval in which the function is unimodal. (If the function is not unimodal, then the routine often will still find a local minimum, but it may not be the global minimum on the interval.) Additional input for multidimensional problems includes the dimension of the problem and a starting guess for

TABLE 6.1
Software for one-dimensional and unconstrained optimization

Source	One-dimensional No derivatives	Multidimensional	
		No derivatives	Derivatives
Brent [23]	localmin	praxis	
FMM	fmin		
HSL	vd01/vd04	va04/va08/va09	va06/va10/va13
IMSL	uvmif	uminf	umiah
KMN	fmin	uncmin	
MATLAB	fmin	fmins	
NAG	e04abf	e04jaf	e04laf
NAPAK			cg
NR	brent	powell	dfpmin
NUMAL	minin	praxis	flemin/rnk1min
PORT		mnf	mng
Schnabel et al. [220]		uncmin	uncmin
TOMS			mini (#500)
TOMS		smsno (#611)	sumsl (#611)
TOMS		bbvscg (#630)	bbvscg (#630)
TOMS			tnpack (#702)
TOMS		tensor (#739)	tensor (#739)

TABLE 6.2
Software for nonlinear least squares and constrained optimization

Source	Nonlinear least squares	Linear programming	Nonlinear programming
HSL	ns13/va07/vb01/vb03	la01	vf01/vf04/vf13
IMSL	unlsf	dlprs	nconf/ncong
MATLAB	leastsq	lp	constr
MINPACK	lmdif1		
NAG	e04fdf	e04mbf	e04vdf
NETLIB	varpro/dqed		
NR	mrqmin	simplx	
NUMAL	gssnewton/marquardt		
PORT	n2f/n2g/nsf/nsg		
SLATEC	snls1	splp	
SOL		minos	npsol
TOMS	nl2sol(#573)		

the solution, and may also include the name of a routine for computing the gradient (and possibly the Hessian) of the function and the name of an array to be used as workspace for storing the Hessian or an approximation to it. In addition to the solution x, the output typically includes a status flag indicating any warnings or errors. A preliminary plot of the functions involved can help greatly in determining a suitable starting guess.

Table 6.2 is a list of some of the software available for solving nonlinear least squares problems, linear programming problems, and general nonlinear constrained optimization problems. Good software is also available from a number of sources for solving many other types of optimization problems, including quadratic programming, linear or simple bounds constraints, network flow problems, etc. There is an optimization toolbox for **MATLAB** in which some of the software listed in the tables can be found, along with numerous additional routines for various other optimization problems. For the nonlinear analogue of total least squares, called *orthogonal distance regression*, odrpack(#676) is available from **TOMS**. A comprehensive survey of optimization software can be found in [184].

6.7 HISTORICAL NOTES AND FURTHER READING

As with nonlinear equations in one dimension, the one-dimensional optimization methods based on Newton's method or interpolation are classical. A theory of optimal one-dimensional search methods using only function value comparisons was initiated in the 1950s by Kiefer, who showed that Fibonacci search, in which successive evaluation points are determined by ratios of Fibonacci numbers, is optimal in the sense that it produces the minimum interval of uncertainty for a given number of function evaluations. What we usually want, however, is to fix the error tolerance rather than the number of function evaluations, so golden section search, which can be viewed as a limiting case of Fibonacci search, turned out to be more practical. See [272] for a detailed discussion of these methods. As with nonlinear equations, hybrid safeguarded methods for one-dimensional optimization were popularized by Brent [23].

For multidimensional optimization, most of the basic direct search methods were proposed in the 1960s. The method of Nelder and Mead is based on an earlier method of Spendley, Hext, and Himsworth. Another popular direct search method is that of Hooke and Jeeves. For a survey of these methods, see [252].

Steepest descent method and Newton's method for multidimensional optimization were analyzed as practical algorithms by Cauchy. Secant updating methods were originated by Davidon (who used the term *variable metric* method) in 1959. In 1963, Fletcher and Powell published an improved implementation, which came to be known as the DFP method. Continuing this trend of initialisms, the BFGS method was developed independently by Broyden, Fletcher, Goldfarb, and Shanno in 1970. Many other secant updates have been proposed, but these two have been the most successful, with BFGS having a slight edge. The conjugate gradient method was originally developed by Hestenes and Stiefel in the early 1950s to solve symmetric linear systems by minimizing a quadratic function. It was later adapted to minimize general nonlinear functions by Fletcher and Reeves in 1964.

The Levenberg-Marquardt method for nonlinear least squares was originally developed by Levenberg in 1944 and improved by Marquardt in 1963. A definitive modern implementation of this method, due to Moré [181], can be found in **MINPACK** [182].

The simplex method for linear programming, which is still the workhorse for such problems, was originated by Dantzig in the late 1940s. The first polynomial-time algorithm for linear programming, the ellipsoid algorithm published by Khachiyan in 1979, was based on earlier work in the 1970s by Shor and by Judin and Nemirovskii (Khachiyan's main contribution was to show that the algorithm indeed has polynomial complexity). A much more practical polynomial-time algorithm is the interior point method of Karmarkar, published in 1984, which is related to earlier barrier methods popularized by Fiacco and McCormick [78].

Good general references on optimization, with an emphasis on numerical algorithms, are [40, 80, 95, 167, 189]. Algorithms for unconstrained optimization are covered in [57] and the more recent surveys [98, 192]. The theory and convergence analysis of Newton's method and quasi-Newton methods are summarized in [183] and [56], respectively. For a detailed discussion of nonlinear least squares, see [14]. The classic account of the simplex method for linear programming is [48]. More recent treatments of the simplex method can be found in [96, 167, 189]. For an overview of linear programming that includes polynomial-time algorithms, see [99]. For a review of interior point methods in constrained optimization, see [278].

REVIEW QUESTIONS

6.1. True or false: Points that minimize a nonlinear function are inherently less accurately determined than points for which a nonlinear function has a zero value.

6.2. True or false: If a function is unimodal on a closed interval, then it has exactly one minimum on the interval.

6.3. True or false: In minimizing a unimodal function of one variable by golden section search, the point discarded at each iteration is always the point having the largest function value.

6.4. True or false: For minimizing a real-valued function of several variables, the steepest descent method is usually more rapidly convergent than Newton's method.

6.5. True or false: The solution to a linear programming problem must occur at one of the vertices of the feasible region.

6.6. True or false: The approximate solution produced at each step of the simplex method for linear programming is a feasible point.

6.7. Suppose that the real-valued function f is unimodal on the interval $[a, b]$. Let x_1 and x_2 be two points in the interval, with $a < x_1 < x_2 < b$. If $f(x_1) = 1.232$ and $f(x_2) = 3.576$, then which of the following statements is valid?

(*i*) The minimum of f must lie in the subinterval $[x_1, b]$.

(*ii*) The minimum of f must lie in the subinterval $[a, x_2]$.

(*iii*) You can't tell which of these two subintervals the minimum must lie in without knowing the values of $f(a)$ and $f(b)$.

6.8. (*a*) In minimizing a unimodal function of one variable on the interval $[0, 1]$ by golden section search, at what two points in the interval is the function initially evaluated?

(*b*) Why are those particular points chosen?

6.9. If the real-valued function f is monotonic on the interval $[a, b]$, will golden section search to find a minimum of f still converge? If not, why, and if so, to what point?

6.10. Suppose that the real-valued function f is unimodal on the interval $[a, b]$, and x_1 and x_2 are points in the interval such that $x_1 < x_2$ and $f(x_1) < f(x_2)$.

(*a*) What is the shortest interval in which you know that the minimum of f must lie?

(*b*) How would your answer change if we happened to have $f(x_1) = f(x_2)$?

6.11. List one advantage and one disadvantage of golden section search compared with successive parabolic interpolation for minimizing a function of one variable.

6.12. (*a*) Why is linear interpolation of a function $f : \mathbb{R} \to \mathbb{R}$ not useful for finding a minimum of f?

(*b*) In using quadratic interpolation for one-dimensional problems, why would one use inverse quadratic interpolation for finding a zero but regular quadratic interpolation for finding a minimum?

6.13. For minimizing a function $f : \mathbb{R} \to \mathbb{R}$, successive parabolic interpolation and Newton's method both fit a quadratic polynomial to the function f and then take its minimum as the next approximate solution.

(*a*) How do these two methods differ in choosing the quadratic polynomials they use?

(*b*) What difference does this make in their respective convergence rates?

6.14. Explain why Newton's method minimizes a quadratic function in one iteration but does not solve a quadratic equation in one iteration.

6.15. Suppose you want to minimize a function of one variable, $f : \mathbb{R} \to \mathbb{R}$. For each convergence rate given, name a method that normally has that convergence rate for this problem:

(*a*) Linear but not superlinear

(*b*) Superlinear but not quadratic

(*c*) Quadratic

6.16. Suppose you want to minimize a function of several variables, $f : \mathbb{R}^n \to \mathbb{R}$. For each convergence rate given, name a method that normally has that convergence rate for this problem:

(*a*) Linear but not superlinear

(*b*) Superlinear but not quadratic

(*c*) Quadratic

6.17. Which of the following iterative methods have a superlinear convergence rate under normal circumstances?

(*a*) Successive parabolic interpolation for minimizing a function

(*b*) Golden section search for minimizing a function

(*c*) Interval bisection for finding a zero of a function

(d) Secant updating methods for minimizing a function of n variables

(e) Steepest descent method for minimizing a function of n variables

6.18. (a) For minimizing a real-valued function f of n variables, what is the initial search direction in the conjugate gradient method?

(b) Under what condition will the BFGS method for minimization use this same initial search direction?

6.19. For minimizing a quadratic function of n variables, what is the maximum number of iterations required to converge to the exact solution (assuming exact arithmetic) from an arbitrary starting point for each of the following algorithms?

(a) Conjugate gradient method

(b) Newton's method

(c) BFGS secant updating method with exact line search

6.20. (a) What is meant by a *critical point* (or *stationary point*) of a smooth nonlinear function $f : \mathbb{R}^n \to \mathbb{R}$?

(b) Is a critical point always a minimum or maximum of the function?

(c) How can you test a given critical point to determine which type it is?

6.21. Let $f : \mathbb{R}^2 \to \mathbb{R}$ be a real-valued function of two variables. What is the geometrical interpretation of the vector

$$\nabla f(x) = \begin{bmatrix} \partial f(x)/\partial x_1 \\ \partial f(x)/\partial x_2 \end{bmatrix}?$$

Specifically, explain the meaning of the direction and magnitude of $\nabla f(x)$.

6.22. (a) If $f : \mathbb{R}^n \to \mathbb{R}$, what do we call the Jacobian matrix of the gradient $\nabla f(x)$?

(b) What special property does this matrix have, assuming f is twice continuously differentiable?

(c) What additional special property does this matrix have near a local minimum of f?

6.23. The steepest descent method for minimizing a function of several variables is usually slow but reliable. However, it can sometimes fail, and it can also sometimes converge rapidly. Under what conditions would each of these two types of behavior occur?

6.24. Consider Newton's method for minimizing a function of n variables:

(a) When might the use of a line search parameter be beneficial?

(b) When might the use of a line search parameter *not* be beneficial?

6.25. Many iterative methods for solving multidimensional nonlinear problems replace the given nonlinear problem by a sequence of linear problems, each of which can be solved by some matrix factorization. For each method listed, what is the most appropriate matrix factorization for solving the linear subproblems? (Assume that we start close enough to a solution to avoid any potential difficulties.)

(a) Newton's method for solving a system of nonlinear equations

(b) Newton's method for minimizing a function of several variables

(c) Gauss-Newton method for solving a nonlinear least squares problem

6.26. Let $f : \mathbb{R}^n \to \mathbb{R}^n$ be a nonlinear function. Since $\| f(x) \| = 0$ if and only if $f(x) = 0$, does this relation mean that searching for a minimum of $\| f(x) \|$ is equivalent to solving the nonlinear system $f(x) = 0$? Why?

6.27. (a) Why is a line search parameter *always* used in the steepest descent method for minimizing a general function of several variables?

(b) Why might one use a line search parameter in Newton's method for minimizing a function of several variables?

(c) Asymptotically, as the solution is approached, what should be the value of this line search parameter for Newton's method?

6.28. What is a good way to test a symmetric matrix to determine whether it is positive definite?

6.29. Suppose we want to minimize a function $f : \mathbb{R}^n \to \mathbb{R}$ using a secant updating method. Why would one *not* just apply Broyden's method for finding a zero of the gradient of f?

6.30. To what method does the first iteration of the BFGS method for minimization reduce if the initial approximate Hessian is

(a) The identity matrix?

(b) The exact Hessian at the starting point?

6.31. In secant updating methods for solving systems of nonlinear equations or minimizing a function of several variables, why is it preferable to update a factorization of the approximate Jacobian or Hessian matrix rather than update the matrix itself?

6.32. For solving a very large unconstrained optimization problem whose objective function has a sparse Hessian matrix, which type of method would be better, a secant updating method such as BFGS or the conjugate gradient method? Why?

6.33. How does the conjugate gradient method for minimizing an unconstrained nonlinear function differ from a truncated Newton method for the same problem, assuming the conjugate gradient method is used in the latter as the iterative solver for the Newton linear system?

6.34. For what type of nonlinear least squares problem, if any, would you expect the Gauss-Newton method to converge quadratically?

6.35. For what type of nonlinear least squares problem may the Gauss-Newton method converge very slowly or not at all? Why?

6.36. For what two general classes of least squares problems is the Gauss-Newton approximation to the Hessian exact at the solution?

6.37. The Levenberg-Marquardt method adds an extra term to the Gauss-Newton approximation to the Hessian. Give a geometric or algebraic interpretation of this additional term.

6.38. What are Lagrange multipliers, and what is their relevance to constrained optimization problems?

6.39. Consider the optimization problem min $f(x)$ subject to $g(x) = 0$, where $f : \mathbb{R}^n \to \mathbb{R}$ and $g : \mathbb{R}^n \to \mathbb{R}^m$.
  (a) What is the Lagrangian function for this problem?
  (b) What is a necessary condition for optimality for this problem?

6.40. Explain the difference between range space methods and null space methods for solving constrained optimization problems.

6.41. What is meant by an *active set strategy* for inequality-constrained optimization problems?

6.42. (a) Is it possible, in general, to solve linear programming problems by an algorithm whose computational complexity is polynomial in the size of the problem data?
  (b) Does the simplex method have this property?

EXERCISES

6.1. Consider the function $f : \mathbb{R}^2 \to \mathbb{R}$ defined by
$$f(x) = \tfrac{1}{2}(x_1^2 - x_2)^2 + \tfrac{1}{2}(1 - x_1)^2.$$
  (a) At what point does f attain a minimum?
  (b) Perform one iteration of Newton's method for minimizing f using as starting point $x_0 = [2 \quad 2]^T$.
  (c) In what sense is this a good step?
  (d) In what sense is this a bad step?

6.2. Let $f : \mathbb{R}^n \to \mathbb{R}$ be given by
$$f(x) = \tfrac{1}{2}x^T A x - x^T b + c,$$
where A is an $n \times n$ symmetric positive definite matrix, b is an n-vector, and c is a scalar.

  (a) Show that Newton's method for minimizing this function converges in one iteration from any starting point x_0.
  (b) If the steepest descent method is used on this problem, what happens if the starting value x_0 is an eigenvector of A?

6.3. Prove that the block 2×2 Hessian matrix of the Lagrangian function for constrained optimization (see Section 6.5) cannot be positive definite.

6.4. Consider the linear programming problem
$$\min_x f(x) = -3x_1 - 2x_2$$

subject to the inequality constraints

$$5x_1 + x_2 \leq 6, \qquad 3x_1 + 4x_2 \leq 6,$$
$$4x_1 + 3x_2 \leq 6, \qquad x_1 \geq 0, \qquad x_2 \geq 0.$$

(a) How many vertices does the feasible region have?

(b) Since the solution must occur at a vertex, solve the problem by evaluating the objective function at each vertex and choosing the one that gives the lowest value.

(c) Obtain a graphical solution to the problem by drawing the feasible region and contours of the objective function, as in Fig. 6.8.

6.5. How can the linear programming problem given in Example 6.11 be stated in the standard form given at the beginning of Section 6.5.1? (*Hint*: Additional variables may be needed.)

COMPUTER PROBLEMS

6.1. (a) The function

$$f(x) = x^2 - 2x + 2$$

has a minimum at $x^* = 1$. On your computer, for what range of values of x near x^* is $f(x) = f(x^*)$? Can you explain this phenomenon? What are the implications regarding the accuracy with which a minimum can be computed?

(b) Repeat the preceding exercise, this time using the function

$$f(x) = 0.5 - xe^{-x^2},$$

which has a minimum at $x^* = \sqrt{2}/2$.

6.2. Consider the function f defined by

$$f(x) = \begin{cases} 1/2 & \text{if } x = 0 \\ (1 - \cos(x))/x^2 & \text{if } x \neq 0 \end{cases}.$$

(a) Use l'Hôpital's rule to show that f is continuous at $x = 0$.

(b) Use differentiation to show that f has a local maximum at $x = 0$.

(c) Use a library routine, or one of your own design, to find a maximum of f on the interval $[-2\pi, 2\pi]$, on which $-f$ is unimodal. Experiment with the error tolerance to determine how accurately the routine can approximate the known solution at $x = 0$.

(d) If you have difficulty in obtaining a highly accurate result, try to explain why. (*Hint*: Make a plot of f in the vicinity of $x = 0$, say on the interval $[-0.001, 0.001]$ with a spacing of 0.00001 between points.)

(e) Can you devise an alternative formulation of f such that the maximum can be determined more accurately? (*Hint*: Consider a double angle formula.)

6.3. Use a library routine, or one of your own design, to find a minimum of each of the following functions on the interval $[0, 3]$. Draw a plot of each function to confirm that it is unimodal.

(a) $f(x) = x^4 - 14x^3 + 60x^2 - 70x$.
(b) $f(x) = 0.5x^2 - \sin(x)$.
(c) $f(x) = x^2 + 4\cos(x)$.
(d) $f(x) = \Gamma(x)$. (The gamma function, defined by

$$\Gamma(x) = \int_0^\infty t^{x-1}e^{-t}\,dt, \quad x > 0,$$

is a built-in function on many computer systems.)

6.4. Try using a library routine for one-dimensional optimization on a function that is *not* unimodal and see what happens. Does it find the global minimum on the given interval, merely a local minimum, or neither? Experiment with various functions and different intervals to determine the range of behavior that is possible.

6.5. If a water hose with initial water velocity v is aimed at angle α with respect to the ground to hit a target of height h, then the horizontal distance x from nozzle to target satisfies the quadratic equation

$$(g/(2v^2 \cos^2 \alpha))x^2 - (\tan \alpha)x + h = 0,$$

where $g = 9.8065$ m/s^2 is the acceleration due to gravity. How do you interpret the two roots of this quadratic equation? Assuming that $v = 20$ m/s and $h = 13.5$ m, use a one-dimensional optimization routine to find the maximum distance x at which the target can still be hit, and the angle α for which the maximum occurs.

6.6. Write a general-purpose line search routine. Your routine should take as input a vector defining the starting point, a second vector defining the search direction, the name of a routine defining the objective function, and a convergence tolerance. For the resulting one-dimensional optimization problem, you may call a library routine or one of your own design. In any case, you will need to determine a bracket for the minimum along the search direction using some heuristic procedure. Test your routine for a variety of objective functions and search directions. This routine will be useful in some of the other computer exercises in this section.

6.7. Consider the function $f: \mathbb{R}^2 \to \mathbb{R}$ defined by

$$f(x) = 2x_1^3 - 3x_1^2 - 6x_1 x_2 (x_1 - x_2 - 1).$$

(a) Determine all of the critical (stationary) points of f analytically (i.e., without using a computer).

(b) Classify each critical point found in part a as a minimum, a maximum, or a saddle point, again working analytically.

(c) Verify your analysis graphically by creating a contour plot or three-dimensional surface plot of f over the region $-2 \leq x_i \leq 2$, $i = 1, 2$.

(d) Use a library routine for minimization to find the minima of both f and $-f$. Experiment with various starting points to see how well the routine gets around other types of critical points to find minima and maxima. You may find it instructive to plot the sequence of iterates generated by the routine.

6.8. Consider the function $f: \mathbb{R}^2 \to \mathbb{R}$ defined by

$$f(x) = 2x_1^2 - 1.05x_1^4 + x_1^6/6 + x_1 x_2 + x_2^2.$$

Using any method or routine you like, how many stationary points can you find for this function? Classify each stationary point you find as a local minimum, a local maximum, or a saddle point. What is the global minimum of this function?

6.9. Write a program to find a minimum of Rosenbrock's function,

$$f(x_1, x_2) = 100(x_2 - x_1^2)^2 + (1 - x_1)^2$$

using each of the following methods:

(a) Steepest descent

(b) Newton

(c) Damped Newton (Newton's method with a line search)

You should try each of the methods from each of the three starting points $x_0 = [-1 \quad 1]^T$, $[0 \quad 1]^T$, and $[2 \quad 1]^T$. For any line searches and linear system solutions required, you may use either library routines or routines of your own design. Plot the path taken in the plane by the approximate solutions for each method from each starting point.

6.10. Let A be an $n \times n$ real symmetric matrix with eigenvalues $\lambda_1 \leq \cdots \leq \lambda_n$. It can be shown that the stationary points of the Rayleigh quotient (see Section 4.3.7) are eigenvectors of A, and in particular

$$\lambda_1 = \min_x \frac{x^T A x}{x^T x}$$

and

$$\lambda_n = \max_x \frac{x^T A x}{x^T x},$$

with the minimum and maximum occurring at the corresponding eigenvectors. Thus, we can in principle compute the extreme eigenvalues and corresponding eigenvectors of A using any suitable method for optimization.

(a) Use an unconstrained optimization routine to compute the extreme eigenvalues and corresponding eigenvectors of the matrix

$$A = \begin{bmatrix} 6 & 2 & 1 \\ 2 & 3 & 1 \\ 1 & 1 & 1 \end{bmatrix}.$$

Is the solution unique in each case? Why?

(b) The foregoing characterization of λ_1 and λ_n remains valid if we restrict the vector x to be normalized by taking $x^T x = 1$. Repeat part a, but use a constrained optimization routine to impose this normalization constraint. What is the significance of the Lagrange multiplier in this context?

6.11. Write a routine implementing the BFGS method of Section 6.3.5 for unconstrained minimization. For the purpose of this exercise, you may refactor the resulting matrix B at each iteration, whereas in a real implementation you would update either B^{-1} or a factorization of B to reduce the amount of work per iteration. You may use an initial value of $B_0 = I$, but you might also wish to include an option to compute a finite difference approximation to the Hessian of the objective function to use as the initial B_0. You may wish to include a line search to enhance the robustness of your routine. Test your routine on some of the other computer problems in this chapter, and compare its robustness and convergence rate with those of Newton's method and the method of steepest descent.

6.12. Write a routine implementing the conjugate gradient method of Section 6.3.6 for unconstrained minimization. You will need a line search routine to determine the parameter α_k at each iteration. Try both the Fletcher-Reeves and Polak-Ribiere formulas for computing β_{k+1} to see how much difference this makes. Test your routine on both quadratic and nonquadratic objective functions. For a reasonable error tolerance, does your routine terminate in at most n steps for a quadratic function of n variables?

6.13. Using a library routine or one of your own design, find least squares solutions to the following overdetermined systems of nonlinear equations:

(a)
$$x_1^2 + x_2^2 = 2,$$
$$(x_1 - 2)^2 + x_2^2 = 2,$$
$$(x_1 - 1)^2 + x_2^2 = 9.$$

(b)
$$x_1^2 + x_2^2 + x_1 x_2 = 0,$$
$$\sin^2(x_1) = 0,$$
$$\cos^2(x_2) = 0.$$

6.14. The concentration of a drug in the bloodstream is expected to diminish exponentially with time. We will fit the model function

$$f(t, x) = x_1 e^{x_2 t}$$

to the following data:

t	0.5	1.0	1.5	2.0
y	7.80	4.00	2.50	1.75

t	2.5	3.0	3.5	4.0
y	1.48	1.25	1.20	1.15

(a) Perform the exponential fit using nonlinear least squares. You may use a library routine or one of your own design, perhaps using the Gauss-Newton method.

(b) Taking the logarithm of the model function gives $\log(x_1) + x_2 t$, which is now linear in x_2. Thus, an exponential fit can also be done using linear least squares, assuming that we also take logarithms of the data points y_i. Use a linear least squares routine, or one

of your own design, to compute x_1 and x_2 in this manner. Do the values obtained agree with those determined in part a? Why?

6.15. A bacterial population P grows according to the geometric progression

$$P_k = r P_{k-1},$$

where r is the growth rate. The following population counts (in billions) are observed:

k	1	2	3	4
P_k	.19	.36	.69	1.3

k	5	6	7	8
P_k	2.5	4.7	8.5	14

(a) Perform a nonlinear least squares fit of the growth function to these data to estimate the initial population P_0 and the growth rate r.

(b) By using logarithms, a fit to these data can also be done by linear least squares (see previous exercise). Perform such a linear least squares fit to obtain estimates for P_0 and r, and compare your results with those for the nonlinear fit.

6.16. The *Michaelis-Menten equation* describes the chemical kinetics of enzyme reactions. According to this equation, if v_0 is the initial velocity, V is the maximum velocity, K_m is the Michaelis constant, and S is the substrate concentration, then

$$v_0 = \frac{V}{1 + K_m/S}.$$

In a typical experiment, v_0 is measured as S is varied, and then V and K_m are to be determined from the resulting data.

(a) Given the measured data,

S	2.5	5.0	10.0
v_0	0.024	0.036	0.053

S	15.0	20.0
v_0	0.060	0.064

determine V and K_m by performing a nonlinear least squares fit of v_0 as a function of S. You may use a library routine or one of your own design, perhaps using the Gauss-Newton method.

(b) To avoid a nonlinear fit, a number of researchers have rearranged the Michaelis-Menten equation so that a linear least squares fit will suffice. For example, Lineweaver and Burk used the rearrangement

$$\frac{1}{v_o} = \frac{1}{V} + \frac{K_m}{V} \cdot \frac{1}{S}$$

and performed a linear fit of $1/v_o$ as a function of $1/S$ to determine $1/V$ and K_m/V, from which the values of V and K_m can then be derived. Similarly, Dixon used the rearrangement

$$\frac{S}{v_0} = \frac{K_m}{V} + \frac{1}{V} \cdot S$$

and performed a linear fit of S/v_0 as a function of S to determine K_m/V and $1/V$, from which the values of V and K_m can then be derived. Finally, Eadie and Hofstee used the rearrangement

$$v_0 = V - K_m \cdot \frac{v_0}{S}$$

and performed a linear fit of v_0 as a function of v_0/S to determine V and K_m.

Verify the algebraic validity of each of these rearrangements. Perform the indicated linear least squares fit in each case, using the same data as in part a, and determine the resulting values for V and K_m. Compare the results with those obtained in part a. Why do they differ? For which of these linear fits are the resulting parameter values closest to those determined by the true nonlinear fit for these data?

6.17. We wish to fit the model function

$$f(t, x) = x_1 + x_2 t + x_3 t^2 + x_4 e^{x_5 t}$$

to the following data:

t	0.00	0.25	0.50
y	20.00	51.58	68.73

t	0.75	1.00	1.25
y	75.46	74.36	67.09

t	1.50	1.75	2.00
y	54.73	37.98	17.28

We must determine the values for the five parameters x_i that best fit the data in the least squares sense. The model function is linear in the first four parameters, but it is a nonlinear function of the fifth parameter, x_5. We will solve this problem in five different ways:

(a) Use a general multidimensional unconstrained minimization routine with $g(x) = \frac{1}{2}r^T(x)r(x)$ as objective function, where r is the residual function defined by $r_i(x) = y_i - f(t_i, x)$. This method will determine all five parameters (i.e., the five components of x) simultaneously.

(b) Use a multidimensional nonlinear equation solver to solve the system of nonlinear equations $\nabla g(x) = 0$.

(c) Given a value for x_5, the best values for the remaining four parameters can be determined by linear least squares. Thus, we can view the problem as a one-dimensional nonlinear minimization problem with an objective function whose input is x_5 and whose output is the residual sum of squares of the resulting linear least squares problem. Use a one-dimensional minimization routine to solve the problem in this manner. (*Hint*: Your routine for computing the objective function will in turn call a linear least squares routine.)

(d) Solve the problem in the same manner as c, except use a one-dimensional nonlinear equation solver to find a zero of the derivative of the objective function in part c.

(e) Use the Gauss-Newton method for nonlinear least squares to solve the problem. You will need to call a linear least squares routine to solve the linear least squares subproblem at each iteration.

In each of the five methods, you may compute any derivatives required either analytically or by finite differences. You may need to do some experimentation to find a suitable starting value for which each method converges. Of course, after you have solved the problem once, you will know the correct answer, but try to use "fair" starting guesses for the remaining methods. You may need to use global variables in **MATLAB** or C, or common blocks in Fortran, to pass information to subroutines in some cases.

6.18. Use a library routine for linear programming to solve the following problem:

$$\max_{x} f(x) = 2x_1 + 4x_2 + x_3 + x_4$$

subject to the constraints

$$x_1 + 3x_2 + x_4 \le 4$$
$$2x_1 + x_2 \le 3$$
$$x_2 + 4x_3 + x_4 \le 3$$

and

$$x_i \ge 0, \qquad i = 1, 2, 3, 4.$$

6.19. Use the method of Lagrange multipliers to solve each of the following constrained optimization problems. To solve the resulting system of nonlinear equations, you may use a library routine or one of your own design. Once you find a critical point of the Lagrangian function, remember to check it for optimality, either by sampling the objective at nearby feasible points, or using the second-order optimality condition. You may also wish to compare your results with those of a library routine designed for constrained optimization.

(*a*) Quadratic objective function and linear constraints:

$$\min_x f(x) = (4x_1 - x_2)^2 + (x_2 + x_3 - 2)^2$$
$$+ (x_4 - 1)^2 + (x_5 - 1)^2$$

subject to

$$x_1 + 3x_2 = 0,$$
$$x_3 + x_4 - 2x_5 = 0,$$
$$x_2 - x_5 = 0.$$

(*b*) Quadratic objective function and nonlinear constraints:

$$\min_x f(x) = 4x_1^2 + 2x_2^2 + 2x_3^2$$
$$- 33x_1 + 16x_2 - 24x_3$$

subject to

$$3x_1 - 2x_2^2 = 7,$$
$$4x_1 - x_3^2 = 11.$$

(*c*) Nonquadratic objective function and nonlinear constraints:

$$\min_x f(x) = (x_1 - 1)^2 + (x_1 - x_2)^2$$
$$+ (x_2 - x_3)^2 + (x_3 - x_4)^4 + (x_4 - x_5)^4$$

subject to

$$x_1 + x_2^2 + x_3^3 = 3\sqrt{2} + 2,$$
$$x_2 - x_3^2 + x_4 = 2\sqrt{2} - 2,$$
$$x_1 x_5 = 2.$$

6.20. Use the method of Lagrange multipliers to find the radius and height of a cylinder having minimum surface area subject to the constraint that its volume is one liter (1000 cc). See Example 6.1. How does the resulting shape compare with that of one-liter cans or bottles you see in a grocery store? How does the resulting surface area compare with that of a sphere having the same volume?

CHAPTER 7

Interpolation

7.1 INTERPOLATION

Interpolation simply means fitting some function to given data so that the function has the same values as the given data. We have already seen several instances of interpolation in various numerical methods, such as linear interpolation in the secant method for nonlinear equations and successive parabolic interpolation for minimization. We will now make a more general and systematic study of interpolation.

In general, the simplest interpolation problem in one dimension is of the following form: for given data

$$(t_i, y_i), \qquad i = 1, \ldots, n,$$

with $t_1 < t_2 < \cdots < t_n$, we seek a function f such that

$$f(t_i) = y_i, \qquad i = 1, \ldots, n.$$

We call f an *interpolating function*, or simply an *interpolant*, for the given data. It is often desirable for $f(t)$ to have "reasonable" values for t between the data points, but such a requirement may be difficult to quantify. In more complicated interpolation problems, additional data might be prescribed, such as the slope of the interpolant at given points, or additional constraints might be imposed on the interpolant, such as monotonicity, convexity, or the degree of smoothness required. One could also consider higher-dimensional interpolation in which f is a function of more than one variable, but we will not do so in this book.

7.1.1 Purposes for Interpolation

Interpolation problems arise from many different sources and may have many different purposes. Some of these include:

- Plotting a smooth curve through discrete data points
- Quick and easy evaluation of a mathematical function
- Replacing a "difficult" function by an "easy" one
- "Reading between the lines" of a table
- Differentiating or integrating tabular data

7.1.2 Interpolation versus Approximation

By definition, an interpolating function fits the given data points exactly. Interpolation is usually not appropriate if the data points are subject to experimental errors or other sources of significant error. It is usually preferable to smooth out such noisy data by a technique such as least squares approximation (see Chapter 3).

Another context in which approximation is generally more appropriate than interpolation is in the design of library routines for computing special functions, such as those usually supplied by the Fortran and C math libraries. In this case, it is important that the approximating function be close to the exact underlying mathematical function for arguments throughout some domain, but it is not essential that the function values match exactly at any particular points. An appropriate type of approximation in this case is to minimize the maximum deviation between the given function and the approximating function over some interval. This approach is variously known as uniform, Chebyshev, or minimax approximation. A general study of approximation theory and algorithms is beyond the scope of this book, however, and we will confine our attention to interpolation.

7.1.3 Choice of Interpolating Function

It is important to realize that there is some arbitrariness in most interpolation problems. There are arbitrarily many functions that interpolate a given set of data points. Simply requiring that some mathematical function fit the data points exactly leaves open such questions as:

- What form should the function have? There may be relevant mathematical or physical considerations that suggest a particular form of interpolant.
- How should the function behave between data points?
- Should the function inherit properties of the data, such as monotonicity, convexity, or periodicity?
- If the function and data are plotted, should the results be visually pleasing?
- Are we interested primarily in the values of the parameters that define the interpolating function, or simply in evaluating the function at various points for plotting or other purposes?

The choice of interpolating function depends on the answers to these questions as well as the data to be fit.

The selection of a function for interpolation is usually based on:

- How easy the function is to work with (determining its parameters from the data, evaluating the function at a given point, differentiating or integrating the function, etc.)
- How well the properties of the function match the properties of the data to be fit (smoothness, monotonicity, convexity, periodicity, etc.)

Some families of functions commonly used for interpolation include:

- Polynomials
- Piecewise polynomials
- Trigonometric functions
- Exponentials
- Rational functions

In this chapter we will focus on interpolation by polynomials and piecewise polynomials. We will consider trigonometric interpolation in Chapter 12. We have already seen an example of interpolation by a rational function, namely, linear fractional interpolation, in Section 5.2.6. The use of more general rational functions of arbitrary degree, known as *Padé approximation*, is an important topic, but it is beyond the scope of this book.

7.1.4 Basis Functions

The family of functions chosen for interpolating a given set of data points is spanned by a set of *basis functions* $\phi_1(t), \ldots, \phi_n(t)$. The interpolating function f is chosen as a linear combination of these basis functions,

$$f(t) = \sum_{j=1}^{n} x_j \phi_j(t),$$

where the parameters x_j are to be determined. Requiring that f interpolate the data (t_i, y_i) means that

$$f(t_i) = \sum_{j=1}^{n} x_j \phi_j(t_i) = y_i, \qquad i = 1, \ldots, n,$$

which is a system of linear equations

$$Ax = y$$

for the parameters x_j, where the entries of the matrix A are given by $a_{ij} = \phi_j(t_i)$.

We have chosen the number of basis functions to be the same as the number of data points so that we obtain a square linear system, and hence the data points can be fit exactly. In other contexts, these two values would not necessarily be the same. In least squares approximation, for example, the number of basis functions, and thus the number of parameters to be determined, is usually smaller than the number of data points (i.e., the system is overdetermined in that there are more equations than unknowns). Therefore, the data usually cannot be fit exactly.

For a given family of functions, there may be many different choices of basis functions. The particular choice of basis functions affects the conditioning of the linear system $Ax = y$, the work required to solve it, and the ease with which the resulting interpolating function can be evaluated or otherwise manipulated.

7.2 POLYNOMIAL INTERPOLATION

The simplest and commonest type of interpolation uses polynomials. There is a unique polynomial of degree at most $n - 1$ passing through n data points (t_i, y_i), $i = 1, \ldots, n$, where the t_i are distinct. There are many ways to represent or compute this polynomial, but all must give the same mathematical function. (Simple proof: if there were two, then their difference would be a polynomial of degree at most $n - 1$ having n zeros, which must be the zero polynomial.)

For example, with the *monomial basis*,

$$\phi_j(t) = t^{j-1}, \qquad j = 1, \ldots, n,$$

the interpolating polynomial has the form

$$p_{n-1}(t) = x_1 + x_2 t + \cdots + x_n t^{n-1},$$

and its coefficients are determined by the $n \times n$ linear system

$$\begin{bmatrix} 1 & t_1 & \cdots & t_1^{n-1} \\ 1 & t_2 & \cdots & t_2^{n-1} \\ \vdots & \vdots & \ddots & \vdots \\ 1 & t_n & \cdots & t_n^{n-1} \end{bmatrix} \begin{bmatrix} x_1 \\ x_2 \\ \vdots \\ x_n \end{bmatrix} = \begin{bmatrix} y_1 \\ y_2 \\ \vdots \\ y_n \end{bmatrix}.$$

As we saw in Section 3.2, a matrix of this form is called a Vandermonde matrix.

EXAMPLE 7.1 MONOMIAL BASIS. To illustrate polynomial interpolation using the monomial basis, we will find a polynomial of degree two interpolating the three data points $(-2, -27)$, $(0, -1)$, $(1, 0)$. In general, there is a unique polynomial

$$p_2(t) = x_1 + x_2 t + x_3 t^2$$

of degree two interpolating three points (t_1, y_1), (t_2, y_2), (t_3, y_3). With the monomial basis, the coefficients of the polynomial are given by the system of linear equations

$$\begin{bmatrix} 1 & t_1 & t_1^2 \\ 1 & t_2 & t_2^2 \\ 1 & t_3 & t_3^2 \end{bmatrix} \begin{bmatrix} x_1 \\ x_2 \\ x_3 \end{bmatrix} = \begin{bmatrix} y_1 \\ y_2 \\ y_3 \end{bmatrix}.$$

For this particular set of data, this system becomes

$$\begin{bmatrix} 1 & -2 & 4 \\ 1 & 0 & 0 \\ 1 & 1 & 1 \end{bmatrix} \begin{bmatrix} x_1 \\ x_2 \\ x_3 \end{bmatrix} = \begin{bmatrix} -27 \\ -1 \\ 0 \end{bmatrix}.$$

Solving this system by Gaussian elimination yields the solution $x = [-1 \quad 5 \quad -4]^T$, so that the interpolating polynomial is

$$p_2(t) = -1 + 5t - 4t^2.$$

Note that polynomial interpolation and polynomial evaluation are inverses of each other in the following sense: if A is a Vandermonde matrix as just defined, then computing the matrix-vector product Ax evaluates at n points the polynomial whose coefficients are given by the components of x, whereas computing the product $A^{-1}y$ (i.e., solving the linear system $Ax = y$) determines the coefficients of the polynomial whose values at n points are given by the components of y.

Solving the system $Ax = y$ using a standard linear equation solver to determine the coefficients of the interpolating polynomial requires $\mathcal{O}(n^3)$ work. [Solvers for Vandermonde systems with $\mathcal{O}(n^2)$ complexity are possible, but they are based on other polynomial representations that we will see shortly.] Moreover, when using the monomial basis, the resulting Vandermonde matrix A is often ill-conditioned, especially for high-degree polynomials. The reason for this is illustrated in Fig. 7.1, in which the first several monomials are plotted on the interval $[0, 1]$. These functions are progressively less distinguishable as the degree increases, which makes the columns of the Vandermonde matrix nearly linearly dependent. For most choices of data points t_i, the condition number of the Vandermonde matrix grows at least exponentially with the number of data points n.

Note that this ill-conditioning does not prevent fitting the data points well, since the residual for the solution to the linear system will be small in any case, but it does mean that the values of the coefficients may be poorly determined. Both the conditioning of the linear system and the amount of computational work required to solve it can be improved by using a different basis. A change of basis still gives the same interpolating polynomial for a given data set (recall that the interpolating polynomial is unique). What does change is the *representation* of that polynomial in a different basis.

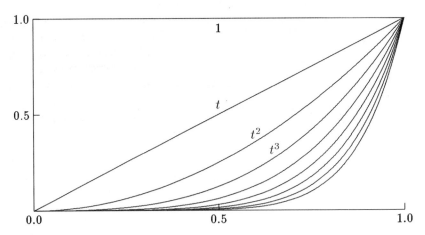

FIGURE 7.1
Monomial basis functions.

The conditioning of the monomial basis can be improved somewhat by shifting and scaling the independent variable t so that

$$\phi_j(t) = \left(\frac{t-c}{d}\right)^{j-1},$$

where, for example, $c = (t_1 + t_n)/2$ and $d = (t_n - t_1)/2$ are the midpoint and half the range of the data, respectively. Thus, the new independent variable lies in the interval $[-1, 1]$. Such a transformation also helps avoid overflow or harmful underflow in computing the entries of the basis matrix or evaluating the resulting polynomial. Even with optimal shifting and scaling, however, the monomial basis is usually still poorly conditioned, and we must seek superior alternatives.

7.2.1 Evaluating Polynomials

In addition to the cost of determining the interpolating function, the cost of evaluating it at a given point is an important factor in choosing an interpolation method. When represented in the monomial basis, a polynomial

$$p_{n-1}(t) = x_1 + x_2 t + \cdots + x_n t^{n-1}$$

can be evaluated very efficiently using *Horner's method*, also known as *nested evaluation* or *synthetic division*:

$$p_{n-1}(t) = x_1 + t(x_2 + t(x_3 + t(\cdots(x_{n-1} + x_n t)\cdots))),$$

which requires only n additions and n multiplications. For example,

$$1 - 4t + 5t^2 - 2t^3 + 3t^4 = 1 + t(-4 + t(5 + t(-2 + 3t))).$$

The same principle applies in forming a Vandermonde matrix:

$$a_{i,j} = \phi_j(t_i) = t_i^{j-1} = t_i \phi_{j-1}(t_i) = t_i a_{i,j-1} \qquad \text{for} \qquad j = 2, \ldots, n,$$

which is superior to using explicit exponentiation.

Other manipulations of the interpolating polynomial, such as differentiation or integration, are also relatively easy with the monomial basis representation.

7.2.2 Lagrange Interpolation

For a given set of data points (t_i, y_i), $i = 1, \ldots, n$, the *Lagrange basis* functions are given by

$$l_j(t) = \frac{\prod_{k=1,\, k\neq j}^{n} (t - t_k)}{\prod_{k=1,\, k\neq j}^{n} (t_j - t_k)}.$$

For the Lagrange basis, we have

$$l_j(t_i) = \begin{cases} 1 & \text{if } i = j \\ 0 & \text{if } i \neq j \end{cases},$$

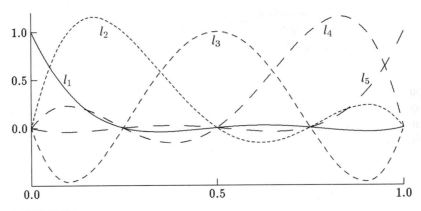

FIGURE 7.2
Lagrange basis functions.

which means that the matrix of the linear system $Ax = y$ is the identity. Thus, in the Lagrange basis the polynomial interpolating the data points (t_i, y_i) is given by

$$p_{n-1}(t) = y_1 l_1(t) + y_2 l_2(t) + \cdots + y_n l_n(t).$$

Figure 7.2 shows the Lagrange basis functions for five equally spaced points on the interval $[0, 1]$. Compare this graph with the corresponding graph for the monomial basis functions in Fig. 7.1.

Lagrange interpolation makes it easy to determine the interpolating polynomial for a given set of data points, but the Lagrangian form of the polynomial is more expensive to evaluate for a given argument compared with the monomial basis representation. The Lagrangian form is also more difficult to differentiate, integrate, etc.

EXAMPLE 7.2 LAGRANGE INTERPOLATION. We illustrate Lagrange interpolation by using it to find the interpolating polynomial for the three data points $(-2, -27)$, $(0, -1)$, $(1, 0)$ of Example 7.1. The Lagrange form for the polynomial of degree two interpolating three points (t_1, y_1), (t_2, y_2), (t_3, y_3) is

$$p_2(t) = y_1 \frac{(t - t_2)(t - t_3)}{(t_1 - t_2)(t_1 - t_3)} + y_2 \frac{(t - t_1)(t - t_3)}{(t_2 - t_1)(t_2 - t_3)} + y_3 \frac{(t - t_1)(t - t_2)}{(t_3 - t_1)(t_3 - t_2)}.$$

For this particular set of data, this formula becomes

$$p_2(t) = -27 \frac{(t - 0)(t - 1)}{(-2 - 0)(-2 - 1)} + (-1) \frac{(t - (-2))(t - 1)}{(0 - (-2))(0 - 1)} + 0 \frac{(t - (-2))(t - 0)}{(1 - (-2))(1 - 0)}$$

$$= -27 \frac{t(t - 1)}{6} + \frac{(t + 2)(t - 1)}{2}.$$

Depending on the use to be made of it, the polynomial can be evaluated in this form for any t, or it can be simplified to produce the same result as we saw previously for the same data using the monomial basis (as expected, since the interpolating polynomial is unique).

7.2.3 Newton Interpolation

We have thus far seen two methods for polynomial interpolation, one for which the basis matrix A is full (Vandermonde) and the other for which it is diagonal (Lagrange). As a result, these two methods have very different trade-offs between the cost of computing the interpolant and the cost of evaluating it for a given argument. We will now consider Newton interpolation, for which the basis matrix is between these two extremes.

For a given set of data points (t_i, y_i), $i = 1, \ldots, n$, the Newton interpolating polynomial has the form

$$p_{n-1}(t) = x_1 + x_2(t - t_1) + x_3(t - t_1)(t - t_2) + \cdots + x_n(t - t_1)(t - t_2)\cdots(t - t_{n-1}).$$

Thus, the basis functions for Newton interpolation are given by

$$\phi_j(t) = \prod_{k=1}^{j-1}(t - t_k), \qquad j = 1, \ldots, n,$$

where we take the value of the product to be 1 when the limits make it vacuous. For $i < j$, we then have $\phi_j(t_i) = 0$, so that the basis matrix A, with $a_{ij} = \phi_j(t_i)$, is lower triangular. Hence, the solution x to the system $Ax = y$, which determines the coefficients of the basis functions in the interpolant, can be computed by forward-substitution in $\mathcal{O}(n^2)$ arithmetic operations. In practice, the triangular matrix need not be formed explicitly, since its entries can be computed as needed during the forward-substitution process.

Figure 7.3 shows the Newton basis functions for five equally spaced points on the interval $[0, 2]$. Compare this graph with the corresponding graphs for the monomial and Lagrange basis functions given earlier.

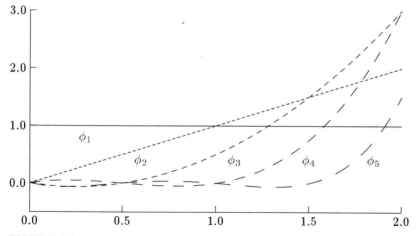

FIGURE 7.3
Newton basis functions.

EXAMPLE 7.3 NEWTON INTERPOLATION. We illustrate Newton interpolation by using it to find the interpolating polynomial for the three data points $(-2, -27)$, $(0, -1)$, $(1, 0)$ of Example 7.1. With the Newton basis, we have the triangular linear system

$$
\begin{bmatrix}
1 & 0 & 0 \\
1 & t_2 - t_1 & 0 \\
1 & t_3 - t_1 & (t_3 - t_1)(t_3 - t_2)
\end{bmatrix}
\begin{bmatrix}
x_1 \\
x_2 \\
x_3
\end{bmatrix}
=
\begin{bmatrix}
y_1 \\
y_2 \\
y_3
\end{bmatrix}.
$$

For this particular set of data, this system becomes

$$
\begin{bmatrix}
1 & 0 & 0 \\
1 & 2 & 0 \\
1 & 3 & 3
\end{bmatrix}
\begin{bmatrix}
x_1 \\
x_2 \\
x_3
\end{bmatrix}
=
\begin{bmatrix}
-27 \\
-1 \\
0
\end{bmatrix},
$$

whose solution, obtained by forward-substitution, is $x = [-27 \quad 13 \quad -4]^T$. Thus, the interpolating polynomial is

$$
p(t) = -27 + 13(t + 2) - 4(t + 2)t,
$$

which reduces to the same polynomial we obtained earlier by the other two methods.

Once the coefficients x_j have been determined, the resulting Newton polynomial interpolant can be evaluated efficiently for any argument using Horner's nested evaluation scheme:

$$
p_{n-1}(t) = x_1 + (t - t_1)(x_2 + (t - t_2)(x_3 + (t - t_3)(\cdots(x_{n-1} + x_n(t - t_{n-1}))\cdots))).
$$

Thus, Newton interpolation has a better balance between the cost of computing the interpolant and the cost of evaluating it for a given argument than the other two methods.

The Newton basis functions can be derived by considering the problem of building a polynomial interpolant incrementally as successive new data points are added. If $p_j(t)$ is a polynomial of degree $j - 1$ interpolating j given points, then for any constant x_{j+1}

$$
p_{j+1}(t) = p_j(t) + x_{j+1}\phi_{j+1}(t)
$$

is a polynomial of degree j that also interpolates the same j points. The free parameter x_{j+1} can then be chosen so that $p_{j+1}(t)$ interpolates the $(j + 1)$st point, y_{j+1}. Specifically,

$$
x_{j+1} = \frac{y_{j+1} - p_j(t_{j+1})}{\phi_{j+1}(t_{j+1})}.
$$

In this manner, Newton interpolation begins with the constant polynomial $p_1(t) = y_1$ interpolating the first data point and builds successively from there to incorporate the remaining data points into the interpolant.

EXAMPLE 7.4 INCREMENTAL NEWTON INTERPOLATION. We illustrate by building the Newton interpolant for the previous example incrementally as new data points are added. We begin with the first data point, $(t_1, y_1) = (-2, -27)$, which is interpolated by the constant polynomial

$$
p_1(t) = y_1 = -27.
$$

Adding the second data point, $(t_2, y_2) = (0, -1)$, we modify the previous polynomial so that it interpolates the new data point as well:

$$p_2(t) = p_1(t) + x_2\phi_2(t) = p_1(t) + \frac{y_2 - p_1(t_2)}{\phi_2(t_2)}\phi_2(t)$$

$$= p_1(t) + \frac{y_2 - y_1}{t_2 - t_1}(t - t_1) = -27 + 13(t + 2).$$

Finally, we add the third data point, $(t_3, y_3) = (1, 0)$, modifying the previous polynomial so that it interpolates the new data point as well:

$$p_3(t) = p_2(t) + x_3\phi_3(t) = p_2(t) + \frac{y_3 - p_2(t_3)}{\phi_3(t_3)}\phi_3(t)$$

$$= p_2(t) + \frac{y_3 - p_2(t_3)}{(t_3 - t_1)(t_3 - t_2)}(t - t_1)(t - t_2)$$

$$= -27 + 13(t + 2) - 4(t + 2)t.$$

Given a set of data points (t_i, y_i), $i = 1, \dots, n$, an alternative method for computing the coefficients x_k of the Newton polynomial interpolant is via quantities known as *divided differences*, which are usually denoted by $f[\ ]$ and are defined recursively by the formula

$$f[t_1, t_2, \dots, t_k] = \frac{f[t_2, t_3, \dots, t_k] - f[t_1, t_2, \dots, t_{k-1}]}{t_k - t_1},$$

where the recursion begins with $f[t_k] = y_k$, $k = 1, \dots, n$. It turns out that the coefficient of the jth basis function in the Newton interpolant is given by $x_j = f[t_1, t_2, \dots, t_j]$. Like forward-substitution, use of this recursion also requires $\mathcal{O}(n^2)$ arithmetic operations to compute the coefficients of the Newton interpolant, but it is less prone to overflow or underflow than is direct formation of the entries of the triangular Newton basis matrix.

EXAMPLE 7.5 DIVIDED DIFFERENCES. We illustrate divided differences by using this approach to derive the Newton interpolant for the same data points as in the previous examples.

$$f[t_1] = y_1 = -27, \qquad f[t_2] = y_2 = -1, \qquad f[t_3] = y_3 = 0,$$

$$f[t_1, t_2] = \frac{f[t_2] - f[t_1]}{t_2 - t_1} = \frac{-1 - (-27)}{0 - (-2)} = 13,$$

$$f[t_2, t_3] = \frac{f[t_3] - f[t_2]}{t_3 - t_2} = \frac{0 - (-1)}{1 - 0} = 1,$$

$$f[t_1, t_2, t_3] = \frac{f[t_2, t_3] - f[t_1, t_2]}{t_3 - t_1} = \frac{1 - 13}{1 - (-2)} = -4.$$

Thus, the Newton polynomial is given by

$$p(t) = f[t_1]\phi_1(t) + f[t_1, t_2]\phi_2(t) + f[t_1, t_2, t_3]\phi_3(t)$$

$$= f[t_1] + f[t_1, t_2](t - t_1) + f[t_1, t_2, t_3](t - t_1)(t - t_2)$$

$$= -27 + 13(t + 2) - 4(t + 2)t.$$

Note that the validity of Newton interpolation does not depend on any particular ordering of the points $t_1, \ldots, t_n$: in principle any ordering gives the same polynomial. However, the conditioning of the triangular basis matrix A does depend on the ordering of the points. Thus, the sensitivity of the coefficients to perturbations in the data depends on the particular ordering chosen, and the "left-to-right" ordering is not necessarily the best. For example, it is often better to take the points in order of their distances from their mean or their distances from a specific point at which the resulting interpolant will be evaluated.

7.2.4 Orthogonal Polynomials

Orthogonal polynomials are yet another useful type of basis function for polynomials. An inner product can be defined on the space of polynomials on an interval $[a, b]$ by taking

$$(p, q) = \int_a^b p(t)q(t)w(t)\, dt,$$

where $w(t)$ is a nonnegative *weight function*. Two polynomials p and q are said to be *orthogonal* if $(p, q) = 0$. A set of polynomials $\{p_i\}$ is said to be *orthonormal* if

$$(p_i, p_j) = \begin{cases} 1 & \text{for } i = j \\ 0 & \text{for } i \neq j \end{cases}.$$

Given a set of polynomials, the Gram-Schmidt orthogonalization process (see Section 3.4.6) can be used to generate an orthonormal set spanning the same space. For example, with the inner product given by the weight function $w(t) \equiv 1$ on the interval $[-1, 1]$, if we apply the Gram-Schmidt process to the set of monomials, $1, t, t^2, t^3, \ldots$, and scale the results so that $p_k(1) = 1$ for each k, we obtain the *Legendre polynomials*

$$1, \quad t, \quad (3t^2 - 1)/2, \quad (5t^3 - 3t)/2, \quad (35t^4 - 30t^2 + 3)/8, \quad (63t^5 - 70t^3 + 15t)/8, \quad \ldots,$$

the first n of which form an orthogonal basis for the set of polynomials of degree at most $n - 1$. The first few Legendre polynomials are plotted in Fig. 7.4. Other choices of interval and weight function similarly yield other well-known sets of orthogonal polynomials, some of which are listed in Table 7.1.

Orthogonal polynomials have many useful properties and are the subject of an elegant theory. One of their most important properties is that they satisfy a three-term recurrence of the form

$$p_{k+1}(t) = (\alpha_k t + \beta_k)p_k(t) - \gamma_k p_{k-1}(t),$$

which makes them very efficient to generate and evaluate. For example, the Legendre polynomials satisfy the recurrence

$$(k + 1)p_{k+1}(t) = (2k + 1)tp_k(t) - kp_{k-1}(t).$$

Orthogonality makes such polynomials very convenient for least squares approximation of a given function by a polynomial of any desired degree, since the matrix of the resulting system of normal equations is diagonal. Orthogonal polynomials are also useful in generating Gaussian quadrature rules, a topic considered in Section 8.3.

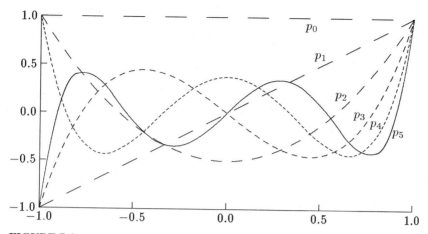

FIGURE 7.4
The first six Legendre polynomials.

TABLE 7.1
Some commonly occurring sets of orthogonal polynomials

Name	Interval	Weight function	
Legendre	$[-1, 1]$	1	
Chebyshev, first kind	$[-1, 1]$	$(1 - t^2)^{-1/2}$	
Chebyshev, second kind	$[-1, 1]$	$(1 - t^2)^{1/2}$	
Jacobi	$[-1, 1]$	$(1 - t)^\alpha (1 + t)^\beta,$	$\alpha, \beta > -1$
Laguerre	$[0, \infty]$	e^{-t}	
Hermite	$[-\infty, \infty]$	e^{-t^2}	

7.2.5 Interpolating a Function

Thus far we have thought only in terms of interpolating a discrete set of data points, so little could be said about the behavior of the interpolant between the data points. If the data points represent a discrete sample of an underlying continuous function, however, then we may wish to know how closely the interpolant approximates the given function between the sample points.

For polynomial interpolation, an answer to this question is given by the following relationship, where f is a sufficiently smooth function, p_{n-1} is the unique polynomial of degree at most $n - 1$ that interpolates f at n points $t_1, \ldots, t_n$, and θ is some (unknown) point in the interval $[t_1, t_n]$:

$$f(t) - p_{n-1}(t) = \frac{f^{(n)}(\theta)}{n!}(t - t_1)(t - t_2) \cdots (t - t_n).$$

Since the point θ is unknown, this result is not particularly useful unless we have a bound on the appropriate derivative of f, but it still provides some insight into the factors affecting the accuracy of polynomial interpolation.

Another useful form of polynomial interpolation for an underlying smooth function f is the polynomial given by the truncated Taylor series

$$p_n(t) = f(a) + f'(a)(t - a) + \frac{f''(a)}{2}(t - a)^2 + \cdots + \frac{f^{(n)}(a)}{n!}(t - a)^n.$$

This *Taylor polynomial* interpolates f in the sense that the values of p_n and its first n derivatives match those of f and its first n derivatives evaluated at $t = a$, so that $p_n(t)$ is a good approximation to $f(t)$ for t near a. We have seen the usefulness of this type of polynomial interpolant in Newton's method for root finding (where we used a linear polynomial) and for minimization (where we used a quadratic polynomial).

7.2.6 High-Degree Polynomial Interpolation

High-degree interpolating polynomials are expensive to determine and evaluate. Moreover, in some bases the coefficients of the polynomial may be poorly determined as a result of ill-conditioning of the linear system to be solved. In addition to these undesirable computational properties, the use of high-degree polynomials for interpolation has some undesirable theoretical consequences as well. Simply put, a high-degree polynomial necessarily has lots of "wiggles," which may bear no relation to the data to be fit. Although the polynomial goes through the required data points, it may oscillate wildly between data points and thus be useless for many of the purposes for which interpolation is done in the first place.

One manifestation of this difficulty is the potential lack of uniform convergence of the interpolating polynomial to an underlying continuous function as the number of equally spaced points (and hence the polynomial degree) increases. This phenomenon is illustrated by Runge's function, shown graphically in Fig. 7.5, where we see that the interpolating polynomials of increasing degree converge nicely to the function in the middle of the interval, but diverge near the endpoints.

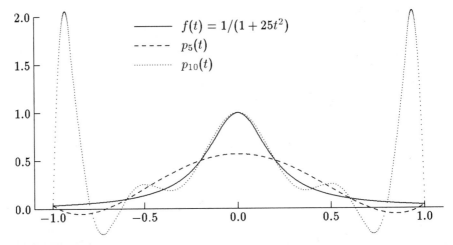

FIGURE 7.5
Interpolation of Runge's function at equally spaced points.

7.2.7 Placement of Interpolation Points

As we have just seen, equally spaced interpolation points may give unsatisfactory results, especially near the ends of the interval. If, instead of being equally spaced, the points are bunched near the ends of the interval, more satisfactory results are likely to be obtained with polynomial interpolation. One way to accomplish this is to use the *Chebyshev points*

$$t_k = -\cos\left(\frac{(2k-1)\pi}{2n}\right), \qquad k = 1, \ldots, n,$$

on the interval $[-1, 1]$, or a suitable transformation of these points to an arbitrary interval. The Chebyshev points are the abscissas of n points in the plane that are equally spaced around the unit circle but have abscissas appropriately bunched near the ends of the interval $[-1, 1]$, as illustrated in Fig. 7.6. The name comes from the fact that the points t_k are the zeros of the nth Chebyshev polynomial of the first kind.

Use of the Chebyshev points for polynomial interpolation distributes the error more evenly and yields convergence throughout the interval for any sufficiently smooth underlying function, as illustrated for Runge's function in Fig. 7.7. Of course, one may have no choice in placing the interpolation points, either because of existing measured

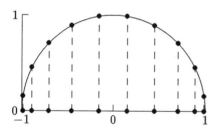

FIGURE 7.6
Chebyshev points for interpolation.

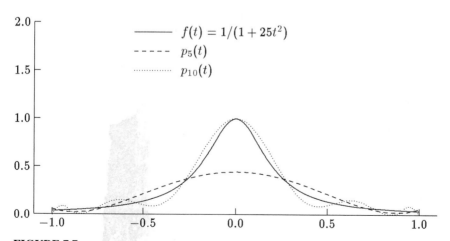

FIGURE 7.7
Interpolation of Runge's function at the Chebyshev points.

data or because a particular distribution (such as equally spaced) is required for other reasons.

7.3 PIECEWISE POLYNOMIAL INTERPOLATION

An appropriate choice of basis functions and interpolation points can mitigate some of the difficulties associated with interpolation by a polynomial of high degree. Nevertheless, fitting a single polynomial to a large number of data points is still likely to yield unsatisfactory oscillating behavior in the interpolant. Piecewise polynomial interpolation provides an alternative to the practical and theoretical difficulties incurred by high-degree polynomial interpolation. The main advantage of piecewise polynomial interpolation is that a large number of data points can be fit with low-degree polynomials.

In piecewise polynomial interpolation of a given set of data points (t_i, y_i), a *different* polynomial is used in each subinterval $[t_i, t_{i+1}]$. For this reason, the abscissas t_i at which the interpolant changes from one polynomial to another are called *knots*, *breakpoints*, or *control points*. The simplest example is piecewise linear interpolation, in which successive data points are connected by straight lines.

Although piecewise polynomial interpolation eliminates the problems of excessive oscillation and nonconvergence, it appears to sacrifice smoothness of the interpolating function. There are many degrees of freedom in choosing a piecewise polynomial interpolant, however, which can be exploited to obtain a smooth interpolating function despite its piecewise nature.

7.3.1 Hermite Cubic Interpolation

In *Hermite*, or *osculatory*, interpolation, the derivatives as well as the values of the interpolating function are specified at the data points. Specifying derivative values simply adds more equations to the linear system that determines the parameters of the interpolating function. To have a well-defined solution, the number of equations and the number of parameters to be determined must be equal.

To provide adequate flexibility while maintaining simplicity and computational efficiency, piecewise cubic polynomials are the most common choice of function for Hermite interpolation. A *Hermite cubic* interpolant is a piecewise cubic polynomial interpolant with a continuous first derivative. A piecewise cubic polynomial with n knots has $4(n - 1)$ parameters to be determined, since there are $n - 1$ different cubics and each has four parameters. Interpolating the given data gives $2(n - 1)$ equations, because each of the $n - 1$ cubics must match the two data points at either end of its subinterval. Requiring the derivative to be continuous gives $n - 2$ additional equations, for at each of the $n - 2$ interior data points the derivatives of the cubics on either side must match. We therefore have a total of $3n - 4$ equations, which still leaves n free parameters. Thus, a Hermite cubic interpolant is not unique, and the remaining free parameters can be chosen so that the result is visually pleasing or satisfies additional constraints, such as monotonicity or convexity.

7.3.2 Cubic Spline Interpolation

In general, a *spline* is a piecewise polynomial of degree k that is continuously differentiable $k - 1$ times. For example, a linear spline is a piecewise linear polynomial that has degree one and is continuous but not differentiable (it could be described as a "broken line"). A *cubic spline* is a piecewise cubic polynomial that is twice continuously differentiable. As with a Hermite cubic, interpolating the given data and requiring continuity of the first derivative imposes $3n - 4$ constraints on the cubic spline. Requiring a continuous second derivative imposes $n - 2$ additional constraints, leaving two remaining free parameters.

The final two parameters can be fixed in a number of ways, such as:

- Specifying the first derivative at the endpoints t_1 and t_n, based either on desired boundary conditions or on estimates of the derivative from the data
- Forcing the second derivative to be zero at the endpoints, which gives the so-called *natural* spline
- Enforcing a "not-a-knot" condition, which effectively forces two consecutive cubic pieces to be the same, at t_2 and at t_{n-1}
- Forcing the first derivatives as well as the second derivatives to match at the endpoints t_1 and t_n (if the spline is to be periodic)

EXAMPLE 7.6 CUBIC SPLINE INTERPOLATION. To illustrate spline interpolation, we will determine the natural cubic spline interpolating three data points (t_i, y_i), $i = 1, 2, 3$. The required interpolant is a piecewise cubic function defined by separate cubic polynomials in each of the two intervals $[t_1, t_2]$ and $[t_2, t_3]$. Denote these two polynomials by

$$p_1(t) = \alpha_1 + \alpha_2 t + \alpha_3 t^2 + \alpha_4 t^3, \qquad p_2(t) = \beta_1 + \beta_2 t + \beta_3 t^2 + \beta_4 t^3.$$

Eight parameters are to be determined, and we will therefore need eight equations. Requiring the first cubic to interpolate the data at the endpoints of the first interval gives the two equations

$$\alpha_1 + \alpha_2 t_1 + \alpha_3 t_1^2 + \alpha_4 t_1^3 = y_1, \qquad \alpha_1 + \alpha_2 t_2 + \alpha_3 t_2^2 + \alpha_4 t_2^3 = y_2.$$

Requiring the second cubic to interpolate the data at the endpoints of the second interval gives the two equations

$$\beta_1 + \beta_2 t_2 + \beta_3 t_2^2 + \beta_4 t_2^3 = y_2, \qquad \beta_1 + \beta_2 t_3 + \beta_3 t_3^2 + \beta_4 t_3^3 = y_3.$$

Requiring the first derivative of the interpolating function to be continuous at t_2 gives the equation

$$\alpha_2 + 2\alpha_3 t_2 + 3\alpha_4 t_2^2 = \beta_2 + 2\beta_3 t_2 + 3\beta_4 t_2^2.$$

Requiring the second derivative of the interpolating function to be continuous at t_2 gives the equation

$$2\alpha_3 + 6\alpha_4 t_2 = 2\beta_3 + 6\beta_4 t_2.$$

Finally, by definition a natural spline has second derivative equal to zero at the endpoints, which gives the two equations

$$2\alpha_3 + 6\alpha_4 t_1 = 0, \qquad 2\beta_3 + 6\beta_4 t_3 = 0.$$

When particular data values are substituted for the t_i and y_i, this system of eight linear equations can be solved for the eight unknown parameters α_i and β_i.

7.3.3 Hermite Cubic versus Cubic Spline Interpolation

The choice between Hermite cubic and spline interpolation depends on the data to be fit and on the purpose for doing interpolation. If smoothness is of paramount importance, then spline interpolation may be most appropriate. On the other hand, a Hermite cubic interpolant may have a more pleasing visual appearance, and it allows the flexibility to preserve monotonicity if the original data are monotonic. These issues are illustrated in Figs. 7.8 and 7.9, where a monotone Hermite cubic and a cubic spline interpolate the same monotonic data points (indicated by the bullets in the figures). We see that the additional degree of smoothness required of the cubic spline causes it to overshoot, and the resulting interpolant is not monotonic. The cubic Hermite, on the other hand, is clearly less smooth, but visually it seems to reflect the behavior of the data better. In

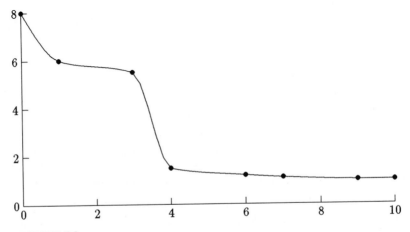

FIGURE 7.8
Monotone cubic Hermite interpolation of monotonic data.

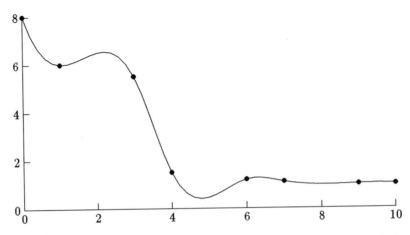

FIGURE 7.9
Cubic spline interpolation of monotonic data.

any case, it is advisable to plot the interpolant and the original data to help assess how well the interpolating function captures the behavior of the data.

7.3.4 B-splines

One might wonder if an arbitrary spline can be represented as a linear combination of basis functions, which we have already seen can be done in various ways for polynomials. An elegant answer to this question is provided by *B-splines*, which get their name from the fact that they form a *basis* for the family of spline functions of a given degree.

B-splines can be defined in a number of different ways, including recursion, convolution, and divided differences. Here we will define them recursively. Although in practice we use only the finite set of knots $t_1, \ldots, t_n$, for notational convenience we will assume an infinite set of knots

$$\cdots < t_{-2} < t_{-1} < t_0 < t_1 < t_2 < \cdots$$

The additional knots can be taken as arbitrarily defined points outside the interval $[t_1, t_n]$. Again for notational convenience, we will also make use of the linear functions

$$v_i^k(t) = \frac{t - t_i}{t_{i+k} - t_i}.$$

To start the recursion, we define B-splines of degree 0 by

$$B_i^0(t) = \begin{cases} 1 & \text{if } t_i \le t < t_{i+1} \\ 0 & \text{otherwise} \end{cases},$$

and then for $k > 0$ we define B-splines of degree k by

$$B_i^k(t) = v_i^k(t) B_i^{k-1}(t) + (1 - v_{i+1}^k(t)) B_{i+1}^{k-1}(t).$$

Since B_i^0 is piecewise constant and v_i^k is linear, we see from the definition that B_i^1 is piecewise linear. Similarly, B_i^2 is in turn piecewise quadratic, and in general, B_i^k is a piecewise polynomial of degree k. The first few B-splines are pictured in Fig. 7.10. Another motivation for their name is their bell shape. For $k = 1$, they are often called "hat" functions.

We note the following important properties of the B-spline functions B_i^k:

1. For $t < t_i$ or $t > t_{i+k+1}$, $B_i^k(t) = 0$.
2. For $t_i < t < t_{i+k+1}$, $B_i^k(t) > 0$.
3. For all t, $\sum_{i=-\infty}^{\infty} B_i^k(t) = 1$.
4. For $k \ge 1$, B_i^k is $k - 1$ times continuously differentiable.
5. The set of functions $\{B_{1-k}^k, \ldots, B_{n-1}^k\}$ is linearly independent on the interval $[t_1, t_n]$.
6. The set of functions $\{B_{1-k}^k, \ldots, B_{n-1}^k\}$ spans the set of all splines of degree k having knots t_i.

Properties 1 and 2 together say that the B-spline functions have local support. Property 3 indicates how the functions are normalized, and property 4 says that they are indeed

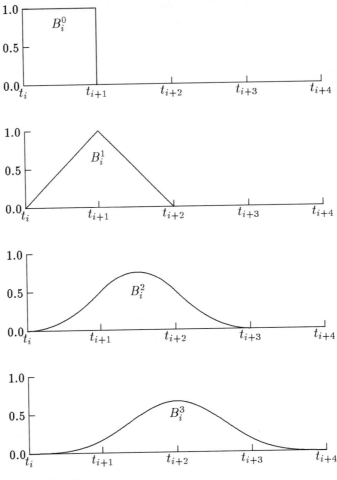

FIGURE 7.10
The first four B-splines.

splines. Properties 5 and 6 together say that for a given k, these functions form a basis for the set of all splines of degree k having the same set of knots. Thus, if we use the B-spline basis, the linear system to be solved for the spline coefficients will be nonsingular and banded. The locality of the B-spline representation also means that if the data value at a given knot changes, then the coefficients of only a few basis functions are affected, which is in marked contrast to the standard polynomial representation, for which changing a single data point changes all of the coefficients of the spline inter-polant.

The use of the B-spline basis yields efficient and stable methods for determining and evaluating spline interpolants, and many library routines for spline interpolation are based on this approach. B-splines are also useful in many other contexts, such as the numerical solution of differential equations, as we will see later.

7.4 SOFTWARE FOR INTERPOLATION

Table 7.2 is a list of some of the software available for polynomial interpolation and for cubic spline interpolation in one dimension. Some of the spline packages offer the option of Hermite cubic interpolation as well. A spline toolbox is also available for **MATLAB**. Tension splines—a particularly flexible approach to spline curve fitting that conveniently allows smoothing and shape preservation, if desired—are implemented in **tspack(#716)** from **TOMS**. We note that software is also available from many of these same sources for interpolation in two or more dimensions, both for regularly placed and for irregularly scattered data. For generating orthogonal polynomials of various types, the software package **orthpol(#726)** is available from **TOMS**.

Software for interpolation often consists of two routines: one for computing an interpolant and another for evaluating it at any given point or set of points. The input to the first routine includes the number of data points and two one-dimensional arrays containing the values of the independent variable and corresponding function values to be fit, and the output includes one or more arrays containing the coefficients of the interpolant. The input to the second routine includes one or more values at which the interpolant is to be evaluated, together with the arrays containing the coefficients previously determined, and the output is the corresponding value(s) of the interpolant (and possibly its derivative) at the desired point(s).

7.4.1 Software for Special Functions

A number of functions that have proved useful in mathematics have become known as *special functions*. Examples include elementary functions such as exponential, logarithmic, and trigonometric functions, as well as functions that commonly occur in mathematical physics (among other areas), such as the gamma and beta functions, Bessel functions, hypergeometric functions, elliptic integrals, and many others. The specialized techniques used in approximating these functions are beyond the scope of this

TABLE 7.2
Software for polynomial and piecewise cubic interpolation

Source	Polynomial interpolation	Compute spline	Evaluate spline
FITPACK [60]		curfit	curev/splev
FMM		spline	seval
HSL	tb02	tb04	tg01
IMSL		csint/csdec/csher	csval
KMN		pchez	pchev
MATLAB	polyfit	spline	ppval
NAG	e01aef	e01baf/e01bef	e02bbf/e01bff
NR	polint	spline	splint
NUMAL	newton		
PPACK [53]		cubspl	ppvalu
SLATEC	polint	bint4/bintk	bvalu/bspev
Späth [236]	newdia/newsol	cubir5/cub2r7	cubval

book, but good software is available for evaluating almost any standard function of interest. The most frequently occurring functions are typically supplied as built-in functions in most programming languages used for scientific computing. Software for many additional functions can be found in most of the general-purpose libraries mentioned in Section 1.4.1. In addition, **netlib** contains several collections of special function routines, including **amos**, **elefunt**, **fdlibm**, **fn**, **specfun**, and **vfnlib**, and routines for numerous individual functions can be found in **TOMS**. Of particular note is the portable elementary function library **fdlibm**, available from **netlib**, which is better than the default libraries supplied by many system vendors. An extensive survey of available software for special functions can be found in [166].

7.5 HISTORICAL NOTES AND FURTHER READING

As the names associated with it—Newton, Lagrange, Hermite, and many others—suggest, polynomial interpolation has long been an important part of applied mathematics. An excellent reference on polynomial interpolation, approximation, orthogonal polynomials, and related topics is [51]. Spline functions were first formulated by Schoenberg in 1946. The theory of splines is presented in detail in [4, 221]. More computationally oriented references on splines are [53, 60, 236], all of which include software. The use of splines in computer graphics and geometric modeling is detailed in [16]. For monotone piecewise cubic interpolation, see [88]. In addition to their use for interpolation, splines can also be used for more general approximation. For example, least squares fitting by cubic splines is a good method for smoothing noisy data; see [207, 208].

REVIEW QUESTIONS

7.1. True or false: There are arbitrarily many different mathematical functions that interpolate a given set of data points.

7.2. True or false: If an interpolating function accurately reproduces the given data values, then this fact implies that the coefficients in the linear combination of basis functions are well-determined.

7.3. True or false: The representation of the polynomial interpolating a given set of data points is unique.

7.4. True or false: When interpolating a continuous function by a polynomial at equally spaced points on a given interval, the polynomial interpolant always converges to the function as the number of interpolation points increases.

7.5. What is the basic distinction between interpolation and approximation of a function?

7.6. State at least two different applications for interpolation.

7.7. Give two examples of numerical methods (for problems other than interpolation itself) that are based on polynomial interpolation.

7.8. Is it ever possible for two distinct polynomials to interpolate the same n data points? If so, under what conditions, and if not, why?

7.9. State at least two important criteria for choosing a particular set of basis functions for use in interpolation.

7.10. Determining the parameters of an interpolant can be interpreted as solving a linear system $Ax = y$, where the matrix A depends on the basis functions used and the vector y contains the function values to be fit. Describe in words the pattern of nonzero entries in the matrix A for polynomial interpolation using each of the following bases:

(a) Monomial basis

(b) Lagrange basis

(c) Newton basis

7.11. (a) Is interpolation an appropriate procedure for fitting a function to noisy data?

(b) If so, why, and if not, what is a good alternative?

7.12. (a) For a given set of data points (t_i, y_i), $i = 1, \ldots, n$, rank the following three methods for polynomial interpolation according to the cost of determining the interpolant (i.e., determining the coefficients of the basis functions), from 1 for the cheapest to 3 for the most expensive:

Monomial basis
Lagrange basis
Newton basis

(b) Which of the three methods has the best-conditioned basis matrix A, where $a_{ij} = \phi_j(t_i)$?

(c) For which of the three methods is evaluating the resulting interpolant at a given point the most expensive?

7.13. (a) What is a Vandermonde matrix?

(b) In what context does such a matrix arise?

(c) Why is such a matrix often ill-conditioned when its order is relatively large?

7.14. Given a set of n data points, (t_i, y_i), $i = 1, \ldots, n$, determining the coefficients x_i of the interpolating polynomial requires the solution of an $n \times n$ system of linear equations $Ax = y$.

(a) If we use the monomial basis $1, t, t^2, \ldots$, give an expression for the entries a_{ij} of the matrix A that is efficient to evaluate.

(b) Does the condition of A tend to get better, or worse, or stay about the same as n grows?

(c) How does this change affect the accuracy with which the interpolating polynomial approximates the given data points?

7.15. For Lagrange polynomial interpolation of n data points (t_i, y_i), $i = 1, \ldots, n$,

(a) What is the degree of each polynomial function $l_j(t)$ in the Lagrange basis?

(b) What function results if we sum the n functions in the Lagrange basis [i.e., if we take $g(t) = \sum_{j=1}^{n} l_j(t)$, what function $g(t)$ results]?

7.16. List one advantage and one disadvantage of Lagrange interpolation compared with using the monomial basis for polynomial interpolation.

7.17. What is the computational cost (number of additions and multiplications) of evaluating a polynomial of degree n using Horner's method?

7.18. Why is interpolation by a polynomial of high degree often unsatisfactory?

7.19. How should the interpolation points be placed in an interval in order to guarantee convergence of the polynomial interpolant to sufficiently smooth functions on the interval as the number of points increases?

7.20. What does it mean for two polynomials p and q to be *orthogonal* to each other on an interval $[a, b]$?

7.21. (a) What is meant by a *Taylor* polynomial?

(b) In what sense does it interpolate a given function?

7.22. In fitting a large number of data points, what is the main advantage of piecewise polynomial interpolation over interpolation by a single polynomial?

7.23. (a) How does Hermite interpolation differ from ordinary interpolation?

(b) How does a cubic spline interpolant differ from a Hermite cubic interpolant?

7.24. In choosing between Hermite cubic and cubic spline interpolation, which should one choose

(a) If maximum smoothness of the interpolant is desired?

(b) If the data are monotonic and this property is to be preserved?

7.25. (a) How many times is a Hermite cubic interpolant continuously differentiable?

(b) How many times is a cubic spline interpolant continuously differentiable?

7.26. The continuity and smoothness requirements on a cubic spline interpolant still leave two free parameters. Give at least two examples of additional constraints that might be imposed to determine the cubic spline interpolant to a set of data points.

7.27. (a) How many parameters are required to define a piecewise cubic polynomial with n knots?

(b) Obviously, a similar number of equations is required to determine those parameters. Assuming the interpolating function is to be a natural cubic spline, explain how the requirements on the function account for the necessary number of equations in the linear system to be solved for the parameters.

7.28. Which of the following interpolants to n data points are unique?

(a) Polynomial of degree at most $n - 1$

(b) Hermite cubic

(c) Cubic spline

7.29. For which of the following types of interpolation is it possible, in general, to preserve monotonicity in a set of n data points (i.e., the interpolant is increasing or decreasing if the data points are increasing or decreasing)?

(a) Polynomial of degree at most $n - 1$

(b) Hermite cubic

(c) Cubic spline

7.30. Why is it advantageous if the basis functions used for interpolation are localized (i.e., each basis function involves only a few data points)?

EXERCISES

7.1. Given the three data points $(-1, 1)$, $(0, 0)$, $(1, 1)$, determine the interpolating polynomial of degree two:

(a) Using the monomial basis

(b) Using the Lagrange basis

(c) Using the Newton basis

Show that the three representations give the same polynomial.

7.2. Express the following polynomial in the correct form for evaluation by Horner's method: $p(t) = 5t^3 - 3t^2 + 7t - 2$.

7.3. Write a formal algorithm for evaluating a polynomial at a given argument using Horner's nested evaluation scheme

(a) For a polynomial expressed in terms of the monomial basis

(b) For a polynomial expressed in Newton form

7.4. How many multiplications are required to evaluate a polynomial $p(t)$ of degree $n - 1$ at a given point t

(a) Represented in the monomial basis?

(b) Represented in the Lagrange basis?

(c) Represented in the Newton basis?

7.5. In general, is it possible to interpolate n data points by a piecewise *quadratic* polynomial, with knots at the given data points, such that the interpolant is

(a) Once continuously differentiable?

(b) Twice continuously differentiable?

In each case, if the answer is "yes," explain why, and if the answer is "no," give the maximum value for n for which it *is* possible.

7.6. Assuming that $t_1, \ldots, t_n$ are distinct, prove that the Vandermonde matrix A given by $a_{ij} = t_i^{j-1}$ is nonsingular.

7.7. Compare the cost of forming a Vandermonde matrix inductively, as in Section 7.2.1, with the cost using explicit exponentiation.

7.8. Use Lagrange interpolation to derive the formulas given in Section 5.2.5 for inverse quadratic interpolation.

7.9. Prove that the formula using divided differences given in Section 7.2.3,

$$x_j = f[t_1, t_2, \ldots, t_j],$$

indeed gives the coefficient of the jth basis function in the Newton polynomial interpolant.

7.10. (*a*) Verify directly that the first six Legendre polynomials given in Section 7.2.4 are indeed mutually orthogonal.

(*b*) Verify directly that they satisfy the three-term recurrence given in Section 7.2.4.

(*c*) Express each of the first six monomials, 1, *t*, ..., t^5, as a linear combination of the first six Legendre polynomials, $p_0, \ldots, p_5$.

7.11. Verify the properties of B-splines enumerated in Section 7.3.4.

COMPUTER PROBLEMS

7.1. (*a*) Write a routine that uses Horner's rule to evaluate a polynomial $p(t)$ given its degree n, an array x containing its coefficients, and the value t of the independent variable at which it is to be evaluated.

(*b*) Add options to your routine to evaluate the derivative $p'(t)$ or the integral $\int_a^b p(t)\,dt$, given a and b.

7.2. (*a*) Write a routine for computing the Newton polynomial interpolant for a given set of data points, and a second routine for evaluating the Newton interpolant at a given argument value using Horner's rule.

(*b*) Write a routine for computing the new Newton polynomial interpolant when a new data point is added.

(*c*) If your programming language supports recursion, write a recursive routine that implements part *a* by calling your routine for part *b* recursively. Compare its performance with that of your original implementation.

7.3. (*a*) Write the system of equations derived in Example 7.6 in matrix form.

(*b*) Use a library routine, or one of your own design, to solve the resulting 8×8 linear system using the data given in Example 7.1.

(*c*) Plot the resulting natural cubic spline, along with the given data points. Also plot the first and second derivatives of the cubic spline and confirm that all of the required conditions are met.

7.4. An experiment has produced the following data:

t	0.0	0.5	1.0	6.0	7.0	9.0
y	0.0	1.6	2.0	2.0	1.5	0.0

We wish to interpolate the data with a smooth curve in the hope of obtaining reasonable values of y for values of t between the points at which measurements were taken.

(*a*) Using any method you like, determine the polynomial of degree 5 that interpolates the given data, and make a smooth plot of it over the range $0 \le t \le 9$.

(*b*) Similarly, determine a cubic spline that interpolates the given data, and make a smooth plot of it over the same range.

(*c*) Which interpolant seems to give more reasonable values between the given data points? Can you explain why each curve behaves the way it does?

(*d*) Might piecewise linear interpolation be a better choice for these particular data? Why?

7.5. Interpolating the data points

t	0	1	4	9	16
y	0	1	2	3	4

t	25	36	49	64
y	5	6	7	8

should give an approximation to the square root function.

(*a*) Compute the polynomial of degree eight that interpolates these 9 data points. Plot the resulting polynomial as well as the corresponding values given by the built-in **sqrt** function over the domain [0, 64].

(*b*) Use a cubic spline routine to interpolate the same data and again plot the resulting curve along with the built-in **sqrt** function.

(*c*) Which of the two interpolants is more accurate over most of the domain?

(*d*) Which of the two interpolants is more accurate between 0 and 1?

7.6. The gamma function is defined by

$$\Gamma(x) = \int_0^\infty t^{x-1} e^{-t}\,dt, \qquad x > 0.$$

For an integer argument n, the gamma function has the value

$$\Gamma(n) = (n-1)!,$$

so interpolating the data points

t	1	2	3	4	5
y	1	1	2	6	24

should yield an approximation to the gamma function over the given range.

(a) Compute the polynomial of degree 4 that interpolates these five data points. Plot the resulting polynomial as well as the corresponding values given by the built-in **gamma** function over the domain [1, 5].

(b) Use a cubic spline routine to interpolate the same data and again plot the resulting curve along with the built-in **gamma** function.

(c) Which of the two interpolants is more accurate over most of the domain?

(d) Which of the two interpolants is more accurate between 1 and 2?

7.7. Consider the following population data for the United States:

Year	Population
1900	76,212,168
1910	92,228,496
1920	106,021,537
1930	123,202,624
1940	132,164,569
1950	151,325,798
1960	179,323,175
1970	203,302,031
1980	226,542,199

There is a unique polynomial of degree 8 that interpolates these nine data points, but of course that polynomial can be represented in many different ways. Consider the following possible sets of basis functions $\phi_j(t)$, $j = 1, \ldots, 9$:

1. $\phi_j(t) = t^{j-1}$
2. $\phi_j(t) = (t - 1900)^{j-1}$
3. $\phi_j(t) = (t - 1940)^{j-1}$
4. $\phi_j(t) = ((t - 1940)/40)^{j-1}$

(a) For each of these four sets of basis functions, generate the corresponding Vandermonde matrix and compute its condition number using a library routine for condition estimation. How do the condition numbers compare? Explain your results.

(b) Using the best-conditioned basis found in part a, compute the polynomial interpolant to the population data. Plot the resulting polynomial, using Horner's nested evaluation scheme to evaluate the polynomial at one-year intervals to obtain a smooth curve. Also plot the original data points on the same graph.

(c) Use a cubic spline routine to interpolate the population data, and again plot the resulting curve on the same graph.

(d) Use both the polynomial and the spline to extrapolate the population to 1990 and compare the values obtained. How close are these to the true value of 248, 709, 873 according to the 1990 census?

(e) Determine the Lagrange interpolant to the same nine data points and evaluate it at the same yearly intervals as in parts b and c. Compare the total execution time with those for Horner's nested evaluation scheme and for evaluating the cubic spline.

(f) Determine the Newton form of the polynomial interpolating the same nine data points. Now determine the Newton polynomial of one degree higher that also interpolates the additional data point for 1990 given in part d, without starting over from scratch (i.e., use the Newton polynomial of degree eight already computed to determine the new Newton polynomial). Plot both of the resulting polynomials (of degree eight and nine) over the interval from 1900 to 1990.

(g) Round the population data for each year to the nearest million and compute the corresponding polynomial interpolant of degree eight using the same basis as in part b. Compare the resulting coefficients with those determined in part b. Explain your results.

CHAPTER 8

Numerical Integration and Differentiation

8.1 NUMERICAL QUADRATURE

The numerical approximation of definite integrals is known as *numerical quadrature*. This name derives from ancient methods for computing areas of curved figures, the most famous example of which is the problem of "squaring the circle" (finding a square having the same area as a given circle). In our case we wish to compute the area under a curve defined over an interval on the real line. Thus, the quantity we wish to compute is of the form

$$I(f) = \int_a^b f(x)\, dx.$$

We will generally take the interval of integration to be finite, and we will assume for the most part that the integrand f is continuous and smooth. We will consider only briefly how to deal with an infinite interval of integration or an integrand function that may have discontinuities or singularities.

Note that we seek a single number as an answer, not a function or a symbolic formula. This feature distinguishes numerical quadrature from the solution of differential equations or the evaluation of indefinite integrals, as in elementary calculus and in many packages for symbolic computation.

An integral is, in effect, an infinite summation. It should come as no surprise that we will approximate this infinite sum by a finite sum. Such a finite sum, in which the integrand function is sampled at a finite number of points in the interval of integration, is called a *quadrature rule*. Our main object of study will be how to choose the sample points and how to weight their contributions to the quadrature formula so that we obtain a desired level of accuracy at a reasonable computational cost. For numerical quadrature, computational work is usually measured by the number of evaluations of the integrand function that are required.

8.1.1 Quadrature Rules

An n-point quadrature formula has the form

$$I(f) = \int_a^b f(x)\, dx = \sum_{i=1}^n w_i f(x_i) + R_n.$$

The points x_i at which the function f is evaluated are called the *nodes* or *abscissas*, the multipliers w_i are called the *weights*, and R_n is the *remainder* or *error*. To estimate the value of the integral, we simply compute the sum

$$I(f) \approx \sum_{i=1}^n w_i f(x_i),$$

which is known as a *quadrature rule*.

The exact error term R_n usually involves information, such as higher derivatives of f, that is inconvenient or even impossible to obtain, so we usually content ourselves with merely estimating the possible error in using a given rule. The error term can be estimated by means of a Taylor series expansion of the integrand function, as we will see in subsequent examples.

Quadrature rules are based on polynomial interpolation. In effect, the integrand function f is sampled at some number of points, the polynomial that interpolates the function at those points is determined, and the integral of the interpolant is then taken as an approximation to the integral of the original function. In practice, however, the interpolating polynomial is not determined explicitly each time a particular integral is to be evaluated. Instead, polynomial interpolation is used to determine the weights corresponding to the chosen nodes in a quadrature rule, which can be stored and then used in approximating any integral over the interval. For example, if Lagrange interpolation is used, then the weights are given by the integrals of the corresponding Lagrange basis functions for the given set of points,

$$w_i = \int_a^b l_i(x)\, dx, \quad i = 1, \ldots, n,$$

and these are independent of any particular integrand.

8.2 NEWTON-COTES QUADRATURE

8.2.1 Newton-Cotes Quadrature Rules

In general, for any value of n, polynomial interpolation of degree $n - 1$ can be used to generate an n-point quadrature rule. If the nodes x_i are equally spaced in the interval $[a, b]$, the resulting interpolatory quadrature rule is known as a *Newton-Cotes quadrature rule*. A Newton-Cotes rule is said to be *closed* if its nodes include the endpoints a and b; otherwise the rule is said to be *open*.

As simple examples, interpolation at one, two, and three equally spaced points gives the first three Newton-Cotes quadrature rules:

- Interpolating the function value at the midpoint of the interval by a constant (i.e., a polynomial of degree zero) gives a one-point quadrature rule known as the *midpoint rule* or *rectangle rule*:

$$I(f) \approx M(f) = (b - a)f\left(\frac{a + b}{2}\right).$$

- Interpolating the function values at the two endpoints of the interval by a straight line (i.e., a polynomial of degree one) gives a two-point quadrature rule known as the *trapezoid rule*:

$$I(f) \approx T(f) = \frac{b - a}{2}(f(a) + f(b)).$$

- Interpolating the function values at three points (the two endpoints and the midpoint) by a quadratic polynomial gives a three-point quadrature rule known as *Simpson's rule*:

$$I(f) \approx S(f) = \frac{b - a}{6}\left[f(a) + 4f\left(\frac{a + b}{2}\right) + f(b)\right].$$

EXAMPLE 8.1 NEWTON-COTES QUADRATURE. As an example, we approximate the integral

$$I(f) = \int_0^1 e^{-x^2}\, dx$$

using each of the first three Newton-Cotes quadrature rules:

$$M(f) = (1 - 0)\exp(-0.25) \approx 0.778801,$$
$$T(f) = \tfrac{1}{2}[\exp(0) + \exp(-1)] \approx 0.683940,$$
$$S(f) = \tfrac{1}{6}[\exp(0) + 4\exp(-0.25) + \exp(-1)] \approx 0.747180.$$

The integrand and the interpolating polynomial for each rule are shown in Fig. 8.1. The correctly rounded result for this problem is 0.746824. It is somewhat surprising to see that the magnitude of the error from the trapezoid rule (0.062884) is about twice that from the midpoint rule (0.031977), and that Simpson's rule, with an error of only 0.000356, seems remarkably accurate considering the size of the interval over which it is applied. We will soon see explanations for these phenomena.

8.2.2 Method of Undetermined Coefficients

As we have seen, a quadrature rule can be derived directly by interpolating the integrand function by a polynomial at a set of points and then integrating the interpolant. An alternative derivation that yields some additional insight is the *method of undetermined*

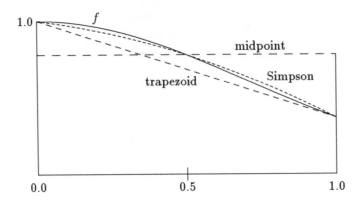

FIGURE 8.1
Integration of $f(x) = e^{-x^2}$ by Newton-Cotes quadrature rules.

coefficients. In deriving a quadrature rule of Newton-Cotes type on an interval $[a, b]$, we take the nodes $x_1, \ldots, x_n$ as given and consider the weights $w_1, \ldots, w_n$ as coefficients to be determined. If we force the quadrature rule to integrate each of the polynomial basis functions exactly, then, by linearity, it will integrate any polynomial of degree $n - 1$ exactly. In this manner we obtain a system of n linear equations in n unknowns that determines the appropriate set of weights for the quadrature rule.

EXAMPLE 8.2 METHOD OF UNDETERMINED COEFFICIENTS. We illustrate the method of undetermined coefficients by deriving a three-point rule

$$I(f) \approx w_1 f(x_1) + w_2 f(x_2) + w_3 f(x_3)$$

on the interval $[a, b]$ using the monomial basis. The three equally spaced points are $x_1 = a$, $x_2 = (a + b)/2$, and $x_3 = b$, and the three monomial basis functions are 1, x, and x^2. The resulting system of equations is

$$w_1 \cdot 1 + w_2 \cdot 1 + w_3 \cdot 1 = \int_a^b 1 \, dx = x|_a^b = b - a,$$

$$w_1 \cdot a + w_2 \cdot (a + b)/2 + w_3 \cdot b = \int_a^b x \, dx = (x^2/2)|_a^b = (b^2 - a^2)/2,$$

$$w_1 \cdot a^2 + w_2 \cdot ((a + b)/2)^2 + w_3 \cdot b^2 = \int_a^b x^2 \, dx = (x^3/3)|_a^b = (b^3 - a^3)/3.$$

Written in matrix form, we recognize this system of equations

$$\begin{bmatrix} 1 & 1 & 1 \\ a & (a + b)/2 & b \\ a^2 & ((a + b)/2)^2 & b^2 \end{bmatrix} \begin{bmatrix} w_1 \\ w_2 \\ w_3 \end{bmatrix} = \begin{bmatrix} b - a \\ (b^2 - a^2)/2 \\ (b^3 - a^3)/3 \end{bmatrix}$$

as a Vandermonde system (recall Section 3.2). Solving it by Gaussian elimination, we obtain the weights

$$w_1 = (b - a)/6, \qquad w_2 = 2(b - a)/3, \qquad w_3 = (b - a)/6,$$

which we recognize as Simpson's rule.

8.2.3 Error Estimation

The error in the midpoint quadrature rule can be estimated by means of a Taylor series expansion about the midpoint $m = (a + b)/2$ of the interval $[a, b]$:

$$f(x) = f(m) + f'(m)(x - m) + \frac{f''(m)}{2}(x - m)^2$$
$$+ \frac{f'''(m)}{6}(x - m)^3 + \frac{f^{iv}(m)}{24}(x - m)^4 + \cdots.$$

When we integrate this expression from a to b, the odd-order terms drop out, yielding

$$I(f) = f(m)(b - a) + \frac{f''(m)}{24}(b - a)^3 + \frac{f^{iv}(m)}{1920}(b - a)^5 + \cdots$$
$$= M(f) + E + F + \cdots,$$

where we have used E and F to represent the first two terms in the error expansion for the midpoint rule.

To derive a comparable error expansion for the trapezoid quadrature rule, we substitute $x = a$ and $x = b$ into the Taylor series, add the two resulting series together, observe once again that the odd-order terms drop out, solve for $f(m)$, and substitute into the midpoint formula to obtain

$$I(f) = T(f) - 2E - 4F - \cdots.$$

Note that

$$T(f) - M(f) = 3E + 5F + \cdots,$$

and hence the difference between the two quadrature rules provides an estimate for the dominant term in their error expansions,

$$E \approx \frac{T - M}{3},$$

provided that the length of the interval, $h = b - a$, is sufficiently small that $h^5 \ll h^3$, and the integrand f is such that f^{iv} is reasonably well-behaved. Under these assumptions, we may draw several conclusions from the previous derivations:

- Halving the length h of the interval decreases the error in either rule by a factor of about $\frac{1}{8}$.
- The midpoint rule is about twice as accurate as the trapezoid rule, despite being based on polynomial interpolation of degree one less.
- The difference between the midpoint rule and the trapezoid rule can be used to estimate the error in either of them.

An appropriately weighted combination of the midpoint and trapezoid rules eliminates the E (i.e., h^3) term from the error expansion:

$$I(f) = \tfrac{2}{3}M(f) + \tfrac{1}{3}T(f) - \tfrac{2}{3}F + \cdots$$
$$= S(f) - \tfrac{2}{3}F + \cdots,$$

which provides an alternative derivation for Simpson's rule as well as an expression for its error term.

EXAMPLE 8.3 ERROR ESTIMATION. We illustrate error estimation by computing the approximate value for the integral $\int_0^1 x^2 \, dx$. Using the midpoint rule, we obtain

$$M(f) = (1 - 0)\left(\tfrac{1}{2}\right)^2 = \tfrac{1}{4},$$

and using the trapezoid rule, we obtain

$$T(f) = \frac{1 - 0}{2}(0^2 + 1^2) = \tfrac{1}{2}.$$

Thus, we have the estimate

$$E \approx \frac{T - M}{3} = \frac{1/4}{3} = \tfrac{1}{12}.$$

We conclude that the error in M is about $\tfrac{1}{12}$ and the error in T is about $-\tfrac{1}{6}$.

In addition, we can now compute the approximate value for the integral given by Simpson's rule,

$$S(f) = \tfrac{2}{3}M + \tfrac{1}{3}T = \tfrac{2}{3} \cdot \tfrac{1}{4} + \tfrac{1}{3} \cdot \tfrac{1}{2} = \tfrac{1}{3},$$

which is the exact value for this integral (as is to be expected since, by design, Simpson's rule is exact for quadratic polynomials). Thus, the error estimates for M and T are in fact exactly correct for this simple problem (though this would not be true in general).

8.2.4 Polynomial Degree

The accuracy of a quadrature rule is conveniently characterized by the notion of *polynomial degree*. A quadrature rule is said to be of polynomial degree d if it is exact (i.e., its remainder is zero) for every polynomial of degree d but is not exact for some polynomial of degree $d + 1$. Since an n-point Newton-Cotes rule is based on an interpolating polynomial of degree $n - 1$, we would expect such a rule to have polynomial degree at least $n - 1$, and we enforced this requirement by construction in the method of undetermined coefficients.

Thus, we would expect the midpoint rule to have polynomial degree zero, the trapezoid rule degree one, Simpson's rule degree two, and so on. We saw from a Taylor series expansion, however, that the error for the midpoint rule depends on the second and higher derivatives of the integrand, which vanish for linear as well as constant polynomials. This implies that the midpoint rule in fact integrates linear polynomials exactly, and hence its polynomial degree is one rather than zero. Similarly, the error for Simpson's rule depends on the fourth and higher derivatives, which vanish for cubics as well as quadratic polynomials, so that Simpson's rule is of polynomial degree three rather than two.

In general, an odd-order Newton-Cotes rule gains an extra degree beyond that of the polynomial interpolant on which it is based. This phenomenon is due to cancellation of positive and negative errors, as illustrated for the midpoint and Simpson rules in Fig. 8.2, which, on the left, shows a linear polynomial and the constant function interpolating it at the midpoint and, on the right, a cubic and the quadratic interpolating

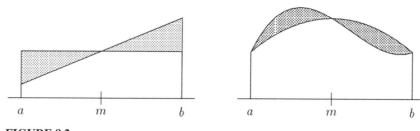

FIGURE 8.2
Cancellation of errors in the midpoint (left) and Simpson (right) rules.

it at the midpoint and endpoints. Integration of the linear polynomial by the midpoint rule yields two congruent triangles of equal area. The inclusion of one of the triangles compensates exactly for the omission of the other. A similar phenomenon occurs for the cubic polynomial, where the two shaded regions also have equal areas, so that the addition of one compensates for the subtraction of the other. Such cancellation does not occur, however, for even-order Newton-Cotes rules. Thus, in general, an n-point Newton-Cotes rule is of polynomial degree $n - 1$ if n is even, but of polynomial degree n if n is odd.

8.3 GAUSSIAN QUADRATURE

8.3.1 Gaussian Quadrature Rules

Newton-Cotes quadrature rules are simple and often effective, but they have a number of drawbacks:

- The use of a large number of equally spaced nodes in a high-order Newton-Cotes rule may incur the erratic behavior and unsatisfactory results often associated with high-degree polynomial interpolation. For example, some of the weights for a high-order rule may be negative, potentially leading to catastrophic cancellation in the summation.
- Closed Newton-Cotes rules require evaluation of the integrand function at the endpoints of the interval, where singularities often lie.
- In general, Newton-Cotes rules are not of the highest polynomial degree possible for the number of nodes used.

These drawbacks are largely overcome by Gaussian quadrature rules. Gaussian rules are based on polynomial interpolation, but the nodes are not equally spaced within the interval. Instead, the locations of the nodes are chosen to maximize the polynomial degree of the resulting rule. In particular, the nodes tend to be bunched near the endpoints but do not include the endpoints themselves. These two properties avoid both singularities at the endpoints and unwanted oscillation in the polynomial interpolant, keeping the weights positive and of reasonable magnitude.

An example of a Gaussian quadrature rule is the two-point rule on the interval $[a, b]$,

$$I(f) \approx G_2(f) = \frac{b-a}{2}\left[f\left(\frac{a+b}{2} - \frac{b-a}{2\sqrt{3}}\right) + f\left(\frac{a+b}{2} + \frac{b-a}{2\sqrt{3}}\right)\right],$$

which has polynomial degree three. In general, for each n there is a unique n-point Gaussian rule, and it is of polynomial degree $2n - 1$. The nodes and weights for many Gaussian quadrature rules are tabulated in [1, 251, 282].

Gaussian quadrature rules are significantly more difficult to derive than Newton-Cotes rules. In particular, the system of equations that determines the nodes and weights is nonlinear, and the resulting values are usually irrational numbers even if the endpoints a and b are rational, as the foregoing two-point rule illustrates. The latter feature makes Gaussian rules relatively inconvenient for hand computation, compared with using the weights for simple Newton-Cotes rules. When using a computer, however, the nodes and weights are usually tabulated in advance and stored in a subroutine that is called when needed, so the user need not know their actual values.

EXAMPLE 8.4 GAUSSIAN QUADRATURE RULE. To illustrate the derivation of a Gaussian quadrature rule, we consider the case of a two-point rule on the interval $[-1, 1]$. We seek a quadrature rule of the form

$$\int_{-1}^{1} f(x)\,dx \approx w_1 f(x_1) + w_2 f(x_2),$$

where the nodes x_i and weights w_i are to be chosen to maximize the polynomial degree of the resulting quadrature rule.

We again use the method of undetermined coefficients, but now the nodes as well as the weights are unknown parameters to be determined. Four parameters are to be determined, so we would expect to be able to integrate cubic polynomials exactly because a cubic depends on four parameters (its coefficients). Thus, we force the quadrature rule to be exact for each member of a basis for the set of polynomials of degree three or less, and hence, by linearity, exact for all cubic polynomials. Requiring the rule to integrate the first four monomials exactly gives the system of four equations

$$w_1 + w_2 = \int_{-1}^{1} 1\,dx = x\big|_{-1}^{1} = 1 + 1 = 2,$$

$$w_1 x_1 + w_2 x_2 = \int_{-1}^{1} x\,dx = \frac{x^2}{2}\bigg|_{-1}^{1} = \tfrac{1}{2} - \tfrac{1}{2} = 0,$$

$$w_1 x_1^2 + w_2 x_2^2 = \int_{-1}^{1} x^2\,dx = \frac{x^3}{3}\bigg|_{-1}^{1} = \tfrac{1}{3} + \tfrac{1}{3} = \tfrac{2}{3},$$

$$w_1 x_1^3 + w_2 x_2^3 = \int_{-1}^{1} x^3\,dx = \frac{x^4}{4}\bigg|_{-1}^{1} = \tfrac{1}{4} - \tfrac{1}{4} = 0$$

in the four unknowns. One solution for this nonlinear system is given by

$$x_1 = -1/\sqrt{3}, \qquad x_2 = 1/\sqrt{3}, \qquad w_1 = 1, \qquad w_2 = 1,$$

and the other solution is obtained by reversing the signs of x_1 and x_2 (see Computer Problem 5.14). Thus, the Gaussian quadrature rule has the form

$$\int_{-1}^{1} f(x)\,dx \approx f(-1/\sqrt{3}) + f(1/\sqrt{3})$$

and has polynomial degree three.

Alternatively, the nodes of a Gaussian quadrature rule can be obtained by using orthogonal polynomials. If p is a polynomial of degree n such that

$$\int_{a}^{b} p(x)x^k\,dx = 0, \qquad k = 0, \ldots, n-1,$$

and hence p is orthogonal on $[a, b]$ to all polynomials of degree less than n, then it is fairly easy to show (see Exercise 8.6) that

1. The n zeros of p are real, simple, and lie in the open interval (a, b).
2. The n-point interpolatory quadrature rule on $[a, b]$ whose nodes are the zeros of p has polynomial degree $2n - 1$; i.e., it is the unique n-point Gaussian rule.

The nth Legendre polynomial (see Section 7.2.4) provides a suitable polynomial p. For this reason, the resulting rule is often called a Gauss-Legendre quadrature rule. Of course, the zeros of the Legendre polynomial must still be computed, and then the corresponding weights for the quadrature rule can be determined in the usual way. This method also extends naturally to various other weight functions and intervals corresponding to other families of orthogonal polynomials. Of particular interest for semi-infinite or infinite intervals are Gauss-Laguerre and Gauss-Hermite quadrature rules. The nodes and weights for a Gaussian quadrature rule can also be computed by means of an eigenvalue problem associated with the corresponding orthogonal polynomials and weight function [105].

8.3.2 Change of Interval

Gaussian rules are somewhat more difficult to apply than Newton-Cotes rules because the weights and nodes are usually derived for some specific interval, such as $[0, 1]$ or $[-1, 1]$, and thus the given interval of integration $[a, b]$ must be transformed into a standard interval for which the nodes and weights have been tabulated. If we wish to use a quadrature rule that is tabulated on the interval $[\alpha, \beta]$,

$$\int_{\alpha}^{\beta} f(x)\,dx \approx \sum_{i=1}^{n} w_i f(x_i),$$

to approximate an integral on the interval $[a, b]$,

$$I(g) = \int_a^b g(t)\, dt,$$

then we must use a change of variable from x in $[\alpha, \beta]$ to t in $[a, b]$. Many such transformations are possible, but a simple linear transformation

$$t = \frac{(b - a)x + a\beta - b\alpha}{\beta - \alpha}$$

has the advantage of preserving the polynomial degree of the rule. The integral is then given by

$$I(g) = \frac{b - a}{\beta - \alpha} \int_\alpha^\beta g\left(\frac{(b - a)x + a\beta - b\alpha}{\beta - \alpha}\right) dx$$

$$\approx \frac{b - a}{\beta - \alpha} \sum_{i=1}^n w_i g\left(\frac{(b - a)x_i + a\beta - b\alpha}{\beta - \alpha}\right).$$

EXAMPLE 8.5 CHANGE OF INTERVAL. To illustrate a change of interval, we use a two-point Gaussian quadrature rule derived for the interval $[-1, 1]$ in Example 8.4 to approximate the integral

$$I(g) = \int_0^1 e^{-t^2}\, dt$$

from Example 8.1. Using the linear transformation of variables just given, we get

$$t = \frac{x + 1}{2},$$

so that the integral is approximated by

$$I(g) \approx \frac{1}{2}\left(\exp\left(-\frac{(-1/\sqrt{3}) + 1}{2}\right)^2 + \exp\left(-\frac{(1/\sqrt{3}) + 1}{2}\right)^2\right) \approx 0.746595,$$

which is slightly more accurate than the result given by Simpson's rule for this integral (see Example 8.1) despite using only two points instead of three.

8.3.3 Gauss-Kronrod Quadrature Rules

As we have seen, one convenient way to obtain an error estimate is by using two different quadrature rules. Since Newton-Cotes quadrature rules use equally spaced nodes, rules of different orders often have nodes in common. For example, the three nodes used in Simpson's rule are the same as those used in the midpoint and trapezoid rules.

We can take advantage of this fact to minimize the number of times that the integrand function must be evaluated in using multiple rules of different orders to estimate the error.

We have seen that Gaussian quadrature rules are more accurate than Newton-Cotes rules for the same number of nodes, but unfortunately, Gaussian rules of different orders do not have any nodes in common (except that Gaussian rules of odd order always have the midpoint as one node). Thus, if we seek to estimate the error by using Gaussian rules of different orders, we must evaluate the integrand function at the full set of nodes of both rules.

Avoiding this additional work is the motivation for Gauss-Kronrod quadrature rules. Such rules come in pairs: an n-point Gaussian rule G_n and a $(2n + 1)$-point Kronrod rule K_{2n+1} whose nodes are optimally chosen subject to the constraint that all of the nodes of G_n are reused in K_{2n+1}. The $(2n + 1)$-point Kronrod rule is of polynomial degree $3n + 1$, whereas a true $(2n + 1)$-point Gaussian rule would be of polynomial degree $4n + 1$.

In using such a Gauss-Kronrod pair, the value of K_{2n+1} is taken as the approximation to the integral, and a realistic but conservative estimate for the error, based partly on theory and partly on experience, is given by

$$(200|G_n - K_{2n+1}|)^{1.5}.$$

Because they efficiently provide both high accuracy and a reliable error estimate, Gauss-Kronrod rules are among the most effective methods for numerical quadrature, and they form the basis for many of the quadrature routines available in major software libraries. The pair of rules (G_7, K_{15}), in particular, has become a commonly used standard.

8.4 COMPOSITE AND ADAPTIVE QUADRATURE

8.4.1 Composite Quadrature Rules

It is not feasible to use arbitrarily high-order quadrature rules in an attempt to attain arbitrarily high accuracy in evaluating an integral over a given interval. A much better alternative is to subdivide the original interval into subintervals, often called *panels* in this context, then apply a lower-order quadrature rule in each panel. Summing all of these partial results then yields an approximation to the overall integral.

This approach is equivalent to using piecewise interpolation to derive a *composite,* or *compound,* quadrature rule over the given interval. For example, if the interval $[a, b]$ is partitioned into n panels, $[x_{i-1}, x_i]$, $i = 1, \ldots, n$, with $a = x_0 < x_1 < x_2 < \cdots < x_{n-1} < x_n = b$, then the composite midpoint rule is given by

$$I(f) \approx M(f) = \sum_{i=1}^{n} (x_i - x_{i-1}) f\left(\frac{x_{i-1} + x_i}{2}\right),$$

and the composite trapezoid rule by

$$I(f) \approx T(f) = \sum_{i=1}^{n} (x_i - x_{i-1}) \frac{f(x_{i-1}) + f(x_i)}{2}.$$

Composite quadrature rules offer a particularly simple means of estimating error by using two rules of different order. For example, we observed in Section 8.2.3 that halving the interval length reduces the error in the midpoint or trapezoid rules by a factor of about $\frac{1}{8}$. For a given interval $[a, b]$, however, halving the width of each panel doubles the number of panels, so the overall reduction in the error is by a factor of about $\frac{1}{4}$.

If h denotes the panel width, and hence the number of panels is $n = 1/h$, then the dominant term in the remainder for the composite midpoint or trapezoid rules is $\mathcal{O}(nh^3) = \mathcal{O}(h^2)$, so the accuracy of these rules is said to be of second order. Similarly, the composite Simpson's rule is of fourth-order accuracy, meaning that the dominant term in its remainder is $\mathcal{O}(h^4)$, and hence halving the panel width reduces the error by a factor of about $\frac{1}{16}$.

8.4.2 Automatic and Adaptive Quadrature

A composite quadrature rule with an error estimate can be used to produce an *automatic* quadrature procedure: simply continue to subdivide all of the panels, say, by half, until the overall error estimate falls below the required tolerance. This approach usually works, but it may require substantially more work than methods tailored for the particular problem. A more intelligent approach is *adaptive* quadrature, in which the domain of integration is selectively refined to reflect the behavior of the particular integrand function.

For example, one might apply a quadrature rule over the entire original interval. If the error tolerance is not met, subdivide the interval into two halves and apply the quadrature rule in each. From this point on, if the sum of the error estimates for the individual panels still exceeds the required tolerance, then the panel with the largest error is further halved, and so on until the error tolerance is eventually met, if possible. In this way the integrand function tends to be sampled most densely in regions where it is most active, as shown by example in Fig. 8.3. Such an adaptive strategy forms the basis for most library subroutines for one-dimensional integration.

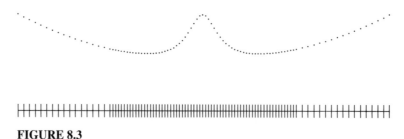

FIGURE 8.3
Typical placement of evaluation points by an adaptive quadrature routine.

It may not be possible, however, to meet a given error tolerance in computing a given integral. The accuracy attainable is limited both by the precision of the arithmetic used and by the accuracy with which the integrand function can be evaluated. If the integrand is noisy, or if the error tolerance is unrealistically tight relative to the machine precision, then an adaptive quadrature routine may be unable to meet the error tolerance and will likely expend a large number of function evaluations only to return a warning message that its subdivision limit was exceeded. Such a result should not be regarded as a fault of the adaptive routine but as a reflection of the difficulty of the problem or unrealistic expectations on the part of the user, or both.

Although adaptive quadrature procedures tend to be very effective in practice, they can be fooled: both the approximate integral and the error estimate can be completely wrong. The reason is that the integrand function is sampled at only a finite number of points, so it is possible that significant features of the integrand may be missed. For example, it may happen that the interval of integration is very wide, but all of the "interesting" behavior of the integrand is confined to a very narrow range. In this case, sampling by the automatic routine may completely miss the interesting part of the integrand's behavior, and the resulting value for the integral may be completely wrong. This situation may seem unlikely, but it can happen, for example, if we are trying to evaluate an integral over an infinite interval and have truncated it unwisely (see Section 8.5.2).

Another potential difficulty with adaptive quadrature routines is that they may be very inefficient in handling discontinuities (finite jumps in the integrand) and integrable singularities (points where the integrand becomes infinite but the integral still exists). For example, an adaptive routine may expend a great many function evaluations in refining the region around a discontinuity of the integrand because it assumes that the integrand is smooth (but very steep). A good way to prevent this behavior is to call the quadrature routine separately to compute the integral on either side of the discontinuity, thereby obviating the need for the routine to resolve the discontinuity. A good strategy for dealing with a singularity is to obtain an analytic formula for the integral in a neighborhood around the singularity and use the adaptive routine to compute the integral elsewhere.

8.5 OTHER INTEGRATION PROBLEMS

8.5.1 Integrating Tabular Data

Thus far we have assumed that the integrand function can be evaluated at any desired point within the interval of integration. This assumption may not be valid if the integrand is defined only by a table of its values at selected points. A reasonable approach to integrating such tabular data is by piecewise interpolation. For example, integrating the piecewise linear interpolant to tabular data gives a composite trapezoid rule.

An excellent method for integrating tabular data is provided by Hermite cubic or cubic spline interpolation. In effect, the overall integral is computed by integrating each of the cubic pieces that make up the interpolant. This facility is provided by some of the spline interpolation packages mentioned in Section 7.4.

8.5.2 Infinite Intervals

Although some quadrature routines are capable of handling integrals over infinite or semi-infinite intervals, one may also be able to deal adequately with such problems using standard quadrature routines for finite intervals. A number of approaches are possible:

- Replace the infinite limits of integration by finite values. Such finite limits should be chosen carefully so that any omitted tail is negligible or its contribution is estimated, if possible. But the remaining finite interval should not be so wide that an automatic quadrature routine will be fooled into sampling badly.
- Transform the variable of integration so that the new interval is finite. Typical transformations include $x = -\log t$ or $x = t/(1 - t)$. Care must be taken not to introduce singularities or other difficulties by such a transformation.
- Apply a quadrature rule, such as Gauss-Laguerre or Gauss-Hermite, designed for an infinite interval.

8.5.3 Double Integrals

Thus far we have considered only one-dimensional integrals, where we wish to determine the area under a curve over an interval. In evaluating a two-dimensional integral, we wish to compute the volume under a surface over a region in the plane. For a rectangular region, a double integral has the form

$$\int_a^b \int_c^d f(x, y)\, dx\, dy.$$

For a more general two-dimensional domain Ω, the integral takes the form

$$\iint_\Omega f(x, y)\, dA.$$

By analogy with numerical quadrature for one-dimensional integrals, the numerical approximation of two-dimensional integrals is sometimes called *numerical cubature*.

To evaluate a double integral, a number of approaches are available, including the following:

- Use an automatic one-dimensional quadrature routine for each dimension, one for the outer integral and the other for the inner integral. Each time the outer routine calls its integrand function, the latter will call the inner quadrature routine. This approach requires some care in setting the error tolerances for the respective quadrature routines.
- Use a product quadrature rule, which results from applying a one-dimensional rule to successive dimensions. This approach is limited to standard domains, such as rectangles.
- Use a nonproduct quadrature rule. In recent years, such rules, including error estimates, have become available. The most important case for automatic adaptive use is for triangles, since many two-dimensional regions can be efficiently triangulated to any desired degree of refinement.

8.5.4 Multiple Integrals

To evaluate a multiple integral in dimensions higher than two, the only generally viable approach is the Monte Carlo method. The function is sampled at n points distributed randomly in the domain of integration, and then the mean of these function values is multiplied by the area (or volume, etc.) of the domain to obtain an estimate for the integral. The error in this estimate goes to zero as $n^{-1/2}$, which means, for example, that to gain an extra decimal place of accuracy the number of sample points must be increased by a factor of 100. For this reason, it is not unusual for Monte Carlo calculations of integrals to require millions of evaluations of the integrand.

The Monte Carlo method is not competitive for integrals in one or two dimensions, but the beauty of the method is that its convergence rate is independent of the number of dimensions. Thus, for example, 1 million points in six dimensions amounts to only 10 points per dimension, which is vastly better than any type of conventional quadrature rule would require for the same level of accuracy. The efficiency of Monte Carlo integration can be enhanced by various methods for biasing the sampling, either to achieve more uniform coverage of the sampled volume (e.g., by avoiding undesirable random clumping of the sample points; see Section 13.4) or to concentrate sampling in regions where the integrand is largest in magnitude (importance sampling) or in variability (stratified sampling), in a spirit similar to adaptive quadrature. See Chapter 13 for further information on the use of random sampling for numerical integration as well as other types of problems.

8.6 INTEGRAL EQUATIONS

An integral equation is an equation in which the unknown to be determined is a *function* inside an integral sign. An integral equation can be thought of as a continuous analogue, or limiting case, of a system of algebraic equations. For example, the analogue of a linear system $Ax = y$ is a Fredholm integral equation of the first kind, which has the form

$$\int_a^b K(s, t)u(t)\, dt = f(s),$$

where the functions K, called the *kernel*, and f are known, and the function u is to be determined. Integral equations arise naturally in many fields of science and engineering, particularly observational sciences (e.g., astronomy, seismology, spectrometry), where the kernel K represents the response function of an instrument (determined by calibration with known signals), f represents measured data, and u represents the underlying signal that is sought. In effect, we are trying to *resolve* the measured data f as a (continuous) linear combination of standard signals. Integral equations can also result from Green's function methods [214] or boundary element methods [154] for solving differential equations (topics beyond the scope of this book).

Establishing the existence and uniqueness of solutions to integral equations is much more problematic than with algebraic equations. Moreover, when a solution does exist, it may be extremely sensitive to perturbations in the input data f, which are often subject to random experimental or measurement errors. The reason for this sensitivity is that integration is a smoothing process, so its inverse (i.e., determining the integrand from the integral) is just the opposite. Integrating an arbitrary function u against a smooth kernel K dampens any high-frequency oscillation, so solving for u tends to *introduce* high-frequency oscillation in the result. For example, Riemann showed that for any integrable kernel K,

$$\lim_{n \to \infty} \int_a^b K(s, t) \sin(nt)\, dt = 0,$$

which implies that an arbitrarily high-frequency component of u has an arbitrarily small effect on f. Thus, integral equations of the first kind with smooth kernels are always ill-conditioned.

A standard technique for solving integral equations numerically is to use a quadrature formula to replace the integral by an approximating finite sum. Denote the nodes and weights of the quadrature rule by t_j and w_j, $j = 1, \ldots, n$. We also choose n points s_i for the variable s, often the same as the t_j, but not necessarily so. Then the approximation to the integral equation becomes

$$\sum_{j=1}^n K(s_i, t_j) w_j u(t_j) = f(s_i), \qquad i = 1, \ldots, n.$$

This system of linear algebraic equations $Ax = y$, where $a_{ij} = K(s_i, t_j) w_j$, $y_i = f(s_i)$, and $x_j = u(t_j)$, can then be solved for x to obtain a discrete sample of approximate values of the function u.

EXAMPLE 8.6 INTEGRAL EQUATION. Consider the integral equation

$$\int_{-1}^1 (1 + \alpha st) u(t)\, dt = 1$$

[i.e., $K(s, t) = 1 + \alpha st$ and $f(s) = 1$], where α is a known positive constant whose value is unspecified for now. Using the composite midpoint quadrature rule with two panels, taking $t_1 = -\frac{1}{2}$, $t_2 = \frac{1}{2}$, and $w_1 = w_2 = 1$, and also taking $s_1 = -\frac{1}{2}$ and $s_2 = \frac{1}{2}$, we obtain the linear system

$$\begin{bmatrix} 1 + \alpha/4 & 1 - \alpha/4 \\ 1 - \alpha/4 & 1 + \alpha/4 \end{bmatrix} \begin{bmatrix} x_1 \\ x_2 \end{bmatrix} = \begin{bmatrix} 1 \\ 1 \end{bmatrix}.$$

It is easily verified that the solution to this linear system is $x = \begin{bmatrix} \frac{1}{2} & \frac{1}{2} \end{bmatrix}^T$, independent of the value of α.

Now suppose that the measured values of $y_1 = f(s_1)$ and $y_2 = f(s_2)$ are in error by ϵ_1 and ϵ_2, respectively. Then by linearity, the change in the solution x is given by the same linear system, but with a right-hand side of $\begin{bmatrix} \epsilon_1 & \epsilon_2 \end{bmatrix}^T$. The resulting change in x is therefore given by

$$\begin{bmatrix} \Delta x_1 \\ \Delta x_2 \end{bmatrix} = \begin{bmatrix} (\epsilon_1 - \epsilon_2)/\alpha + (\epsilon_1 + \epsilon_2)/4 \\ (\epsilon_2 - \epsilon_1)/\alpha + (\epsilon_1 + \epsilon_2)/4 \end{bmatrix}.$$

Thus, if α is sufficiently small, the relative error in the computed value for x can be arbitrarily large. A very small value for α in this particular kernel corresponds to a very insensitive instrument with a very flat response. This is reflected in the conditioning of the matrix A, whose columns become more nearly linearly dependent as α decreases in magnitude. This simple example is typical of integral equations with smooth kernels.

Note that the sensitivity in the previous example is inherent in the problem and is not due to the method of solving it. In general, such an integral operator with a smooth kernel has zero as an eigenvalue (i.e., there are nonzero functions that it annihilates), and hence using a more accurate quadrature rule makes the conditioning of the linear system worse and the resulting solution more erratic. Because of this behavior, additional information may be required to obtain a physically meaningful solution. Such techniques include:

- *Truncated singular value decomposition.* The solution to the system $Ax = y$ is computed using the SVD of A; but the small singular values of A, which reflect the ill-conditioning, are omitted from the solution (see Section 4.5.2).
- *Regularization.* A damped solution is obtained by solving the minimization problem

$$\min_{x}(\| y - Ax \|_2^2 + \mu \| x \|_2^2),$$

where the parameter μ determines the relative weight given to the norm of the residual and the norm of the solution. This minimization problem is equivalent to the linear least squares problem

$$\begin{bmatrix} A \\ \sqrt{\mu}I \end{bmatrix} x \approx \begin{bmatrix} y \\ 0 \end{bmatrix},$$

which can be solved by the methods discussed in Chapter 3. More generally, other norms, usually based on first or second differences between its components, can also be used to weight the smoothness of the solution.
- *Constrained optimization.* Some norm of the residual $\| y - Ax \|$ is minimized subject to constraints on x that disallow nonphysical solutions. In many applications, for example, the components of the solution x are required to be nonnegative. The resulting constrained optimization problem can then be solved by one of the methods discussed in Section 6.5.

A variety of such methods are implemented in the **MATLAB** toolbox documented in [121].

We have considered only Fredholm integral equations of the first kind. Many other types arise in practice, including integral equations of the second kind (eigenvalue problems), Volterra integral equations (in which the upper limit of integration is s instead of b), singular integral equations (in which one or both of the limits of integration are infinite), and nonlinear integral equations. All types of integral equations can be discretized by means of numerical quadrature, yielding a system of algebraic equations. Alternatively, the unknown function u can be expressed as a linear combination $u(t) = \sum_{j=1}^{n} c_j \phi_j(t)$ of suitably chosen basis functions ϕ_j, which leads to a system of algebraic equations for the coefficients c_j. This type of approach will be examined in more detail in Section 10.5, when we consider finite element methods for boundary value problems in differential equations.

8.7 NUMERICAL DIFFERENTIATION

We now turn briefly to numerical differentiation. It is important to realize that differentiation is an inherently sensitive problem, as small perturbations in the data can cause large changes in the result. Integration, on the other hand, is a smoothing process and is inherently stable in this respect. The contrast between differentiation and integration should not be surprising, since they are inverse processes to each other. The difference between them is illustrated in Fig. 8.4, which shows two functions that have very similar definite integrals but very different derivatives.

When approximating the derivative of a function whose values are known only at a discrete set of points, a good approach is to fit some smooth function to the given discrete data and then differentiate the approximating function to approximate the derivatives of the original function. If the given data are sufficiently smooth, then interpolation may be appropriate; but if the given data are noisy, then a smoothing approximating function, such as a least squares spline, is more appropriate.

8.7.1 Finite Difference Approximations

Although finite difference formulas are generally inappropriate for discrete or noisy data, they are very useful for approximating derivatives of a smooth function that is known analytically or can be evaluated accurately for any given argument. We now develop some finite difference formulas that will be useful in our study of the numerical solution of differential equations.

Given a smooth function $f : \mathbb{R} \to \mathbb{R}$, we wish to approximate its first and second derivatives at a point x. Consider the Taylor series expansions

$$f(x + h) = f(x) + f'(x)h + \frac{f''(x)}{2}h^2 + \frac{f'''(x)}{6}h^3 + \cdots$$

and

$$f(x - h) = f(x) - f'(x)h + \frac{f''(x)}{2}h^2 - \frac{f'''(x)}{6}h^3 + \cdots.$$

Solving for $f'(x)$ in the first series, we obtain the forward difference formula

$$f'(x) = \frac{f(x + h) - f(x)}{h} - \frac{f''(x)}{2}h + \cdots$$

$$\approx \frac{f(x + h) - f(x)}{h},$$

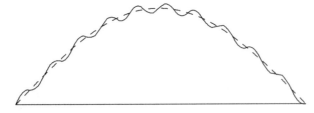

FIGURE 8.4
Two functions whose integrals are similar but whose derivatives are not.

which gives an approximation that is first-order accurate since the dominant term in the remainder of the series is $\mathcal{O}(h)$. Similarly, from the second series we derive the backward difference formula

$$f'(x) = \frac{f(x) - f(x - h)}{h} + \frac{f''(x)}{2}h + \cdots$$

$$\approx \frac{f(x) - f(x - h)}{h},$$

which is also first-order accurate. Subtracting the second series from the first gives the centered difference formula

$$f'(x) = \frac{f(x + h) - f(x - h)}{2h} - \frac{f'''(x)}{6}h^2 + \cdots$$

$$\approx \frac{f(x + h) - f(x - h)}{2h},$$

which is second-order accurate. Finally, adding the two series together gives a centered difference formula for the second derivative

$$f''(x) = \frac{f(x + h) - 2f(x) + f(x - h)}{h^2} - \frac{f^{iv}(x)}{12}h^2 + \cdots$$

$$\approx \frac{f(x + h) - 2f(x) + f(x - h)}{h^2},$$

which is also second-order accurate. By using function values at additional points, $x \pm 2h$, $x \pm 3h$, ..., we can derive similar finite difference approximations with still higher accuracy or for higher-order derivatives.

Note that higher-accuracy difference formulas require more function values. Whether these translate into higher overall cost depends on the particular situation, since a more accurate formula may permit the use of a larger stepsize and correspondingly fewer steps. In choosing a value for h, rounding error must also be considered in addition to the truncation error given by the series expansion (see Example 1.11).

8.7.2 Automatic Differentiation

A number of alternatives are available for computing derivatives of a function, including finite difference approximations and closed-form evaluation using formulas determined either by hand or by a computer algebra package. Each of these methods has significant drawbacks, however: manual differentiation is tedious and error-prone; symbolic derivatives tend to be unwieldy for complicated functions; and finite difference approximations require the sometimes delicate choice of a stepsize, and their accuracy is limited by discretization error.

Another alternative, at least for any function expressed by a computer program, is *automatic differentiation*, often abbreviated as AD. The basic idea of AD is simple: a computer program consists of basic arithmetic operations and elementary functions, each of whose derivatives is easily computed. Thus, the function computed by the program is, in effect, a composite of many simple functions whose derivatives can be propagated through the program by repeated use of the chain rule, effectively computing the derivative of the function step by step along with the function itself. The result is the true derivative of the original function, subject only to rounding error but suffering no discretization error.

Though AD is conceptually simple, its practical implementation is more complicated, requiring careful analysis of the input program and clever strategies for reducing the potentially explosive complexity of the resulting derivative code. Fortunately, most of these practical impediments have been successfully overcome, and a number of effective software packages are now available for automatic differentiation. Some of these packages accept a Fortran or C input code and then output a second code for computing the desired derivatives, whereas other packages use operator overloading to perform derivative computations automatically in addition to the function evaluation. When applicable, AD can be much easier, more efficient, and more accurate than other methods for computing derivatives. AD can also be useful for determining the sensitivity of the output of a program to perturbations in its input parameters. Such information might otherwise be obtainable only through many repeated runs of the program, which could be prohibitively expensive for large, complex programs.

8.8 RICHARDSON EXTRAPOLATION

In many problems, such as numerical integration or differentiation, we compute an approximate value for some quantity based on some stepsize. Ideally, we would like to obtain the limiting value as the stepsize approaches zero, but we cannot take the stepsize to be arbitrarily small because of excessive cost or rounding error. Based on values for nonzero stepsizes, however, we may be able to estimate what the value would be for a stepsize of zero.

Let $F(h)$ denote the value obtained with stepsize h. If we compute the value of F for some nonzero stepsizes, and if we know the theoretical behavior of $F(h)$ as $h \to 0$, then we can extrapolate from the known values to obtain an approximate value for $F(0)$. This extrapolated value should have a higher-order accuracy than the values on which it is based. We emphasize, however, that the extrapolated value, though an improvement, is still only an approximation, not the exact solution, and its accuracy is still limited by the stepsize and arithmetic precision used.

To be more specific, suppose that

$$F(h) = a_0 + a_1 h^p + \mathcal{O}(h^r)$$

as $h \to 0$ for some p and r, with $r > p$. We assume that we know the values of p and r, but not a_0 or a_1. Indeed, $F(0) = a_0$ is the quantity we seek. Suppose that we have computed F for two stepsizes, say, h and qh for some $q > 1$. Then we have

$$F(h) = a_0 + a_1 h^p + \mathcal{O}(h^r)$$

and
$$F(qh) = a_0 + a_1 (qh)^p + \mathcal{O}(h^r).$$

This system of two linear equations in the two unknowns a_0 and a_1 is easily solved to obtain

$$a_0 = F(h) + \frac{F(h) - F(qh)}{q^p - 1} + \mathcal{O}(h^r).$$

Thus, the accuracy of the improved value, a_0, is $\mathcal{O}(h^r)$ rather than only $\mathcal{O}(h^p)$.

If $F(h)$ is known for several values of h, then the extrapolation process can be repeated to produce still more accurate approximations, up to the limitations imposed by finite-precision arithmetic. For example, if we have computed F for the values h, $2h$, and $4h$, then the extrapolated value based on h and $2h$ can be combined with the extrapolated value based on $2h$ and $4h$ in a further extrapolation to produce a still more accurate estimate for $F(0)$.

EXAMPLE 8.7 RICHARDSON EXTRAPOLATION. To illustrate Richardson extrapolation, we use it to improve the accuracy of a finite difference approximation to the derivative of the function $\sin(x)$ at the point $x = 1$. Using the first-order accurate, forward difference formula derived in Section 8.7.1, we have for this problem

$$F(h) = a_0 + a_1 h + \mathcal{O}(h^2)$$

which means that $p = 1$ and $r = 2$ in this case. Using stepsizes of $h = 0.25$ and $2h = 0.5$ (i.e., $q = 2$), we get

$$F(h) = \frac{\sin(1.25) - \sin(1)}{0.25} = 0.430055,$$

and

$$F(2h) = \frac{\sin(1.5) - \sin(1)}{0.5} = 0.312048.$$

The extrapolated value is then given by

$$F(0) = a_0 = F(h) + \frac{F(h) - F(2h)}{2 - 1} = 2F(h) - F(2h) = 0.548061.$$

For comparison, the correctly rounded result is given by $\cos(1) = 0.540302$. In this example the extrapolation is linear, as can be seen on the left in Fig. 8.5, because the lowest-order term in h is linear.

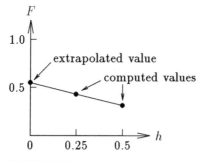
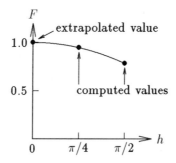

FIGURE 8.5
Richardson extrapolation in Examples 8.7 (left) and 8.8 (right).

EXAMPLE 8.8 ROMBERG INTEGRATION. As another example of Richardson extrapolation, we evaluate the integral

$$\int_0^{\pi/2} \sin(x)\, dx.$$

If we use the composite trapezoid rule, we recall from Section 8.4.1 that

$$F(h) = a_0 + a_1 h^2 + \mathcal{O}(h^4),$$

which means that $p = 2$ and $r = 4$ in this case. With $h = \pi/4$, we obtain the value $F(h) = 0.948059$. With $h = \pi/2$ (i.e., $q = 2$), we obtain the value $F(h) = 0.785398$. The extrapolated value is then given by

$$F(0) = a_0 = F(\pi/4) + \frac{F(\pi/4) - F(\pi/2)}{2^2 - 1}$$

$$= 0.948059 + \frac{0.948059 - 0.785398}{4 - 1} = 1.00228,$$

which is substantially more accurate than either value previously computed (the exact answer is 1). In this example the extrapolation is quadratic, as can be seen on the right in Fig. 8.5, because the lowest-order term in h is quadratic.

Evaluation of the trapezoid rule for additional values of h would permit further extrapolations to attain even higher accuracy, up to the limit imposed by the arithmetic precision. Continued use of Richardson extrapolation in this manner, using the trapezoid quadrature rule with various stepsizes, is called *Romberg integration*. It is capable of producing very high accuracy for well-behaved problems.

8.9 SOFTWARE FOR NUMERICAL INTEGRATION AND DIFFERENTIATION

Table 8.1 is a list of some of the software available for numerical quadrature. Most of the one-dimensional quadrature routines listed are adaptive routines based on Gauss-Kronrod quadrature rules. We note that software for solving initial value problems for ordinary differential equations, which will be covered in Chapter 9, can also be used for computing definite integrals (see Computer Problem 9.5). Several routines are available for generating the nodes and weights for various Gaussian and other quadrature rules, including **gaussq** from **netlib**; and **iqpack**(#**655**), **extend**(#**672**), and **gauss** (the latter is part of the **orthpol**(#**726**) package), all from **TOMS**.

Software for numerical integration typically requires the user to supply the name of a routine that computes the value of the integrand function for any argument. The user must also supply the endpoints of the interval of integration, as well as absolute or relative error tolerances. In addition to the approximate value of the integral, the output usually includes an estimate of the error, a status flag indicating any warnings or error conditions, and possibly a count of the number of function evaluations that were required.

TABLE 8.1
Software for numerical integration and differentiation

Source	One dimension	Two dimensions	n dimensions	Differentiation
FMM	quanc8			
HSL	qa02/qa04/qa05		qb01/qm01	td01
IMSL	qdag/qdags	twodq	qand	deriv
MATLAB	quad/quad8			diff
KMN	q1da			
NAG	d01ajf	d01daf	d01fcf	d04aaf
NUMAL	quadrat	tricub		
NR		vegas/miser	dfridr	
QUADPACK	qag/qags			
SLATEC	qag/qnc/qng/gaus8			
TOMS	squank(#379)/quad(#468)	dcutri(#706)	dcuhre(#698)	

Although adaptive quadrature routines can often be used as black boxes, they can be ineffective for integrals having discontinuities, singularities, or other such difficulties. In such cases, it may be advantageous to transform the problem to enable the automatic routine to arrive at an accurate result more efficiently. For practical advice on handling such problematic integrals, see [2, 3].

In the last column of Table 8.1 are listed some routines for numerical differentiation. In addition, a number of packages are available that implement automatic differentiation (see Section 8.7.2), including **ADIC**, **ADIFOR**, **ADOL-C**, **ADOL-F**, **AMC**, **GRESS**, **Odyssée**, and **PADRE2**. See URL **http://www.mcs.anl.gov/adifor/** for further information.

8.10 HISTORICAL NOTES AND FURTHER READING

As mentioned earlier, quadrature is an ancient technique. Most of the methods we discussed date from the nineteenth century or earlier, as the names associated with them suggest—Simpson, Newton, Cotes, Gauss, and others. Kronrod published the quadrature rules that bear his name in 1964. One of the earliest adaptive quadrature routines was published by McKeeman in 1962. Many others have followed, most notably **squank**, **cadre**, **qnc7**, and **quanc8**, culminating with the **quadpack** package, which represents the current state of the art (see also **TOMS** #**691**).

Comprehensive general references on numerical integration are [52, 70, 74, 153]. The computation of multiple integrals is discussed in [113, 169, 232, 250]. The **quadpack** package is documented in [203]. Cautionary advice on using automatic quadrature routines can be found in [168, 170]. For a comprehensive survey of extrapolation techniques, see [141]. For more details on the numerical solution of integral equations, see [54, 277].

REVIEW QUESTIONS

8.1. True or false: Since the midpoint quadrature rule is based on interpolation by a constant, whereas the trapezoid rule is based on linear interpolation, the trapezoid rule is generally more accurate than the midpoint rule.

8.2. True or false: The polynomial degree of a quadrature rule is the degree of the interpolating polynomial on which the rule is based.

8.3. True or false: An n-point Newton-Cotes quadrature rule is always of polynomial degree $n - 1$.

8.4. True or false: Gaussian quadrature rules of different orders never have any points in common.

8.5. How can you estimate the error in a quadrature formula without computing the derivatives of the integrand function that would be required by a Taylor series approximation?

8.6. (a) If a quadrature rule for an interval $[a, b]$ is based on polynomial interpolation at n equally spaced points in the interval, what is the highest degree such that the rule integrates all polynomials of that degree exactly?

(b) How would your answer change if the points were optimally placed to integrate the highest possible degree polynomials exactly?

8.7. Would you expect an n-point Newton-Cotes quadrature rule to work well for integrating Runge's function, $\int_{-1}^{1}(1 + 25x^2)^{-1}\,dx$, if n is very large? Why?

8.8. (a) What is the polynomial degree of Simpson's rule for numerical quadrature?

(b) What is the polynomial degree of an n-point Gaussian quadrature rule?

8.9. Newton-Cotes and Gaussian quadrature rules are both based on polynomial interpolation.

(a) What specific property characterizes a Newton-Cotes quadrature rule for a given number of nodes?

(b) What specific property characterizes a Gaussian quadrature rule for a given number of nodes?

8.10. (a) Explain how the midpoint rule, which is based on interpolation by a polynomial of degree zero, can nevertheless integrate polynomials of degree one exactly.

(b) Is the midpoint rule a Gaussian quadrature rule? Explain your answer.

8.11. Suppose that the quadrature rule

$$\int_a^b f(x)\,dx \approx \sum_{i=1}^n w_i f(x_i)$$

is exact for all constant functions. What does this imply about the weights w_i or the nodes x_i?

8.12. If the integrand has an integrable singularity at one endpoint of the interval of integration, which type of quadrature rule would be better to use, a closed Newton-Cotes rule or a Gaussian rule? Why?

8.13. What is the polynomial degree of each of the following types of numerical quadrature rules?

(a) An n-point Newton-Cotes rule, where n is odd

(b) An n-point Newton-Cotes rule, where n is even

(c) An n-point Gaussian rule

(d) What accounts for the difference between the answers to parts a and b?

(e) What accounts for the difference between the answers to parts b and c?

8.14. For each of the following properties, state which type of quadrature, Newton-Cotes or Gaussian, more accurately fits the description:

(a) Easier to compute nodes and weights

(b) Easier to apply for a general interval $[a, b]$

(c) More accurate for the same number of nodes

(d) Has maximal polynomial degree for the number of nodes

(e) Nodes easy to reuse as order of rule changes

8.15. What is the relationship between Gaussian quadrature and orthogonal polynomials?

8.16. (a) What is the advantage of using a Gauss-Kronrod pair of quadrature rules, such as G_7 and K_{15}, compared with using two Gaussian rules, such as G_7 and G_{15}, to obtain an approximate integral with error estimate?

(*b*) How many evaluations of the integrand function are required to evaluate *both* of the rules G_7 and K_{15} in a given panel?

8.17. Rank the following types of quadrature rules in order of their polynomial degree for the same number of nodes (1 for highest polynomial degree, etc.):
  (*a*) Newton-Cotes
  (*b*) Gaussian
  (*c*) Kronrod

8.18. (*a*) What is a composite quadrature rule?
  (*b*) Why is a composite quadrature rule preferable to an ordinary quadrature rule for achieving high accuracy in numerically computing a definite integral on a given interval?
  (*c*) In using the composite trapezoid quadrature rule to approximate a definite integral on an interval [*a*, *b*], by what factor is the overall error reduced if the mesh size (i.e. panel width) *h* is halved?

8.19. (*a*) Describe in general terms how adaptive quadrature works.
  (*b*) How can the necessary error estimate be obtained?
  (*c*) Under what circumstances might such a procedure produce a result that is seriously in error?
  (*d*) Under what circumstances might such a procedure be very inefficient?

8.20. What is the most efficient way to use an adaptive quadrature routine for computing a definite integral whose integrand has a known discontinuity within the interval of integration?

8.21. What is a good way to integrate tabular data (i.e., an integrand whose value is known only at a discrete set of points)?

8.22. (*a*) How might one use a standard quadrature routine, designed for integrating over a finite interval, to integrate a function over an infinite interval?
  (*b*) What precautions would need to be taken to ensure a good result?

8.23. How might one use a standard one-dimensional quadrature routine to compute the value of a double integral over a rectangular region?

8.24. Why is Monte Carlo *not* a practical method for computing one-dimensional integrals?

8.25. Relative to other methods for numerical quadrature, why is the Monte Carlo method more effective in higher dimensions than in low dimensions?

8.26. Explain why integral equations of the first kind with smooth kernels are always ill-conditioned.

8.27. Explain how a quadrature rule can be used to solve an integral equation numerically. What type of computational problem results?

8.28. In solving an integral equation of the first kind by numerical quadrature, does the solution always improve if the order of the quadrature rule is increased or the mesh size is decreased? Why?

8.29. List three approaches for obtaining a meaningful solution to an ill-conditioned linear system approximating an integral equation of the first kind.

8.30. Consider the problem of approximating the derivative of a function that is measured or sampled at only a finite number of points.
  (*a*) One way to obtain an approximate derivative is to interpolate the discrete data points and then differentiate the interpolant. Is this a good method for approximating the derivative? Why?
  (*b*) Similarly, one can approximate the integral of a function given by such discrete data by integrating the interpolant. Is this a good method for computing the integral? Why?

8.31. Comparing integration and differentiation, which problem is inherently better conditioned? Why?

8.32. (*a*) Suggest a good method for numerically approximating the derivative of a function whose value is given only at a discrete set of data points.
  (*b*) For this problem, what would be the effect of noisy data, and how would you cope with it in your numerical method?

8.33. (*a*) Explain the basic idea of Richardson extrapolation.
  (*b*) Does it give a more accurate answer than the values on which it is based?

8.34. What is meant by Romberg integration?

EXERCISES

8.1. (*a*) Compute the approximate value of the integral $\int_0^1 x^3 \, dx$, first by the midpoint rule and then by the trapezoid rule.

(*b*) Use the difference between these two results to estimate the error in each of them.

(*c*) Combine the two results to obtain the Simpson's rule approximation to the integral.

(*d*) Would you expect the latter to be exact for this problem? Why?

8.2. (*a*) Using the composite midpoint quadrature rule, compute the approximate value for the integral $\int_0^1 x^3 \, dx$, using a mesh size (panel width) of $h = 0.5$ and also using a mesh size of $h = 1$.

(*b*) Based on the two approximate values computed in part *a*, use Richardson extrapolation to compute a more accurate approximation to the integral.

(*c*) Would you expect the extrapolated result computed in part *b* to be exact in this case? Why?

8.3. If $Q(f) = \sum_{i=1}^n w_i f(x_i)$ is an interpolatory quadrature rule (i.e., based on polynomial interpolation) on the interval $[0, 1]$, then is it true that $\sum_{i=1}^n w_i = 1$? Prove your answer.

8.4. Fill in the details of the derivation of the error estimates for the midpoint and trapezoid quadrature rules given in Section 8.2.3. In particular, show that the odd-order terms drop out in both cases, as claimed.

8.5. Suppose that Lagrange interpolation at a given set of nodes $x_1, \ldots, x_n$ is used to derive a quadrature rule. Prove that the corresponding weights are given by the integrals of the Lagrange basis functions, $w_i = \int_a^b l_i(x) \, dx$, $i = 1, \ldots, n$.

8.6. Let p be a real polynomial of degree n such that

$$\int_a^b p(x) x^k \, dx = 0, \quad k = 0, \ldots, n - 1.$$

(*a*) Show that the n zeros of p are real, simple, and lie in the open interval (a, b). (*Hint*: Consider the polynomial $q_k(x) = (x - x_1)(x - x_2) \cdots (x - x_k)$, where x_i, $i = 1, \ldots k$, are the roots of p in $[a, b]$.)

(*b*) Show that the n-point interpolatory quadrature rule on $[a, b]$ whose nodes are the zeros of p has polynomial degree $2n - 1$. (*Hint*: Consider the quotient and

remainder polynomials when a given polynomial is divided by p.)

8.7. Newton-Cotes quadrature rules are derived by fixing the nodes and then determining the corresponding weights by the method of undetermined coefficients so that the polynomial degree is maximized for the given nodes. The opposite approach could also be taken, with the weights fixed and the nodes to be determined. In a *Chebyshev quadrature rule*, for example, all of the weights are taken to have the same constant value, w, thereby eliminating n multiplications in evaluating the resulting quadrature formula, since the single weight can be factored out of the summation.

(*a*) Use the method of undetermined coefficients to derive a three-point Chebyshev quadrature rule on the interval $[-1, 1]$.

(*b*) What is the polynomial degree of the resulting rule?

8.8. In approximating the first derivative of a function $f : \mathbb{R} \to \mathbb{R}$, the forward difference formula

$$f'(x) \approx \frac{f(x + h) - f(x)}{h}$$

and the backward difference formula

$$f'(x) \approx \frac{f(x) - f(x - h)}{h}$$

are both first-order accurate, meaning that their dominant error terms are $\mathcal{O}(h)$. Show how these two formulas can be combined to produce a difference approximation for the first derivative of f that is second-order accurate, i.e., whose dominant error term is $\mathcal{O}(h^2)$.

8.9. Given a sufficiently smooth function $f : \mathbb{R} \to \mathbb{R}$, use Taylor series to derive a second-order accurate, one-sided difference approximation to $f'(x)$ in terms of the values of $f(x)$, $f(x + h)$, and $f(x + 2h)$.

8.10. Consider the following two methods for approximating the second derivative of a function f at a point x:

1. Evaluate the finite difference quotient

$$\frac{f(x + h) - 2f(x) + f(x - h)}{h^2}.$$

2. Interpolate f at the points $x - h$, x, and $x + h$ by a quadratic polynomial $p(x)$ and then evaluate $p''(x)$.

Do these two methods produce the same result? Why?

8.11. Suppose that the first-order accurate, forward difference approximation to the derivative of a function at a given point produces the value -0.8333 for $h = 0.2$ and the value -0.9091 for $h = 0.1$. Use Richardson extrapolation to obtain a better approximate value for the derivative.

8.12. Archimedes approximated the value of π by computing the perimeter of a regular polygon inscribing or circumscribing a circle of diameter 1. The perimeter of an inscribed polygon with n sides is given by

$$p_n = n \sin(\pi/n),$$

and that of a circumscribed polygon by

$$q_n = n \tan(\pi/n),$$

and these values provide lower and upper bounds, respectively, on the value of π.

    (*a*) Using the Taylor series expansions for the sine and tangent functions, show that p_n and q_n can be expressed in the form

$$p_n = a_0 + a_1 h^2 + a_2 h^4 + \cdots$$

and

$$q_n = b_0 + b_1 h^2 + b_2 h^4 + \cdots,$$

where $h = 1/n$. What are the true values of a_0 and b_0?

    (*b*) Given the values $p_6 = 3.0000$ and $p_{12} = 3.1058$, use Richardson extrapolation to produce a better estimate for π. Similarly, given the values $q_6 = 3.4641$ and $q_{12} = 3.2154$, use Richardson extrapolation to produce a better estimate for π.

COMPUTER PROBLEMS

8.1. Since

$$\int_0^1 \frac{4}{1 + x^2}\, dx = \pi,$$

one can compute an approximate value for π using numerical integration of the given function.

    (*a*) Use the midpoint, trapezoid, and Simpson composite quadrature rules to compute the approximate value for π in this manner for various stepsizes h. Try to characterize the error as a function of h for each rule, and also compare the accuracy of the rules with each other (based on the known value of π). Is there any point beyond which decreasing h yields no further improvement? Why?

    (*b*) Implement Romberg integration and repeat part *a* using it.

    (*c*) Compute π again by the same method, this time using a library routine for adaptive quadrature and various error tolerances. How reliable is the error estimate it produces? Compare the work required (integrand evaluations and elapsed time) with that for parts *a* and *b*.

    (*d*) Compute π again by the same method, this time using Monte Carlo integration with various numbers n of sample points. Try to characterize the error as a function of n, and also compare the work required with that for the previous methods. For a suitable random number generator, see Section 13.5.

8.2. The integral in the previous problem is rather easy. Repeat the problem, this time computing the more difficult integral

$$\int_0^1 \sqrt{x} \, \log(x)\, dx = -\tfrac{4}{9}.$$

8.3. Evaluate each of the following integrals:

    (*a*)

$$\int_{-1}^1 \cos(x)\, dx$$

    (*b*)

$$\int_{-1}^1 \frac{1}{1 + 100x^2}\, dx$$

    (*c*)

$$\int_{-1}^1 \sqrt{|x|}\, dx$$

Try several composite quadrature rules for various fixed mesh sizes and compare their efficiency and accuracy. Also, try one or more automatic adaptive quadrature routines using various error tolerances, and again compare efficiency for a given accuracy.

8.4. Use numerical integration to verify or refute each of the following conjectures.

    (*a*)

$$\int_0^1 \sqrt{x^3}\, dx = 0.4$$

(b)
$$\int_0^1 \frac{1}{1+10x^2}\, dx = 0.4$$

(c)
$$\int_0^1 \frac{e^{-9x^2} + e^{-1024(x-1/4)^2}}{\sqrt{\pi}}\, dx = 0.2$$

(d)
$$\int_0^{10} \frac{50}{\pi(2500x^2+1)}\, dx = 0.5$$

(e)
$$\int_{-9}^{100} \frac{1}{\sqrt{|x|}}\, dx = 26$$

(f)
$$\int_0^{10} 25e^{-25x}\, dx = 1$$

(g)
$$\int_0^1 \log(x)\, dx = -1$$

8.5. Each of the following integrands is defined piecewise over the indicated interval. Use an adaptive quadrature routine to evaluate each integral over the given interval. For the same overall accuracy requirement, compare the cost of evaluating the integral using a single subroutine call over the whole interval with the cost when the routine is called separately in each appropriate subinterval. Experiment with both loose and strict error tolerances.

(a) $f(x) = \begin{cases} 0 & 0 \le x < 0.3 \\ 1 & 0.3 \le x \le 1 \end{cases}$

(b) $f(x) = \begin{cases} 1/(x+2) & 0 \le x < e-2 \\ 0 & e-2 \le x \le 1 \end{cases}$

(c) $f(x) = \begin{cases} e^x & -1 \le x < 0 \\ e^{1-x} & 0 \le x \le 2 \end{cases}$

(d) $f(x) = \begin{cases} e^{10x} & -1 \le x < 0.5 \\ e^{10(1-x)} & 0.5 \le x \le 1.5 \end{cases}$

8.6. Evaluate the following quantities using each of the given methods:

(a) Use an adaptive quadrature routine to evaluate each of the integrals

$$I_k = e^{-1} \int_0^1 x^k e^x\, dx$$

for $k = 0, 1, \ldots, 20$.

(b) Verify that the integrals just defined satisfy the recurrence

$$I_k = 1 - kI_{k-1},$$

and use it to generate the same quantities, starting with $I_0 = 1 - e^{-1}$.

(c) Generate the same quantities using the backward recurrence

$$I_{k-1} = (1 - I_k)/k,$$

beginning with $I_n = 0$ for some chosen value $n > 20$. Experiment with different values of n to see the effect on the accuracy of the values generated.

(d) Compare the three methods with respect to accuracy, stability, and execution time. Can you explain these results?

8.7. The intensity of diffracted light near a straight edge is determined by the values of the *Fresnel integrals*

$$C(x) = \int_0^x \cos\left(\frac{\pi t^2}{2}\right) dt$$

and

$$S(x) = \int_0^x \sin\left(\frac{\pi t^2}{2}\right) dt.$$

Use an adaptive quadrature routine to evaluate these integrals for enough values of x to draw a smooth plot of $C(x)$ and $S(x)$ over the range $0 \le x \le 5$. You may wish to check your results by obtaining a routine for computing Fresnel integrals from a special function library (see Section 7.4.1).

8.8. The period of a simple pendulum is determined by the complete elliptic integral of the first kind

$$K(x) = \int_0^{\pi/2} \frac{d\theta}{\sqrt{1 - x^2 \sin^2\theta}}.$$

Use an adaptive quadrature routine to evaluate this integral for enough values of x to draw a smooth plot of $K(x)$ over the range $0 \le x \le 1$. You may wish to check your results by obtaining a routine for computing elliptic integrals from a special function library (see Section 7.4.1).

8.9. The gamma function is defined by

$$\Gamma(x) = \int_0^\infty t^{x-1} e^{-t}\, dt, \quad x > 0.$$

Write a program to compute the value of this function from the definition using each of the following approaches:

(a) Truncate the infinite interval of integration and use a composite quadrature rule, such as trapezoid or Simpson. You will need to do some experimentation or analysis to determine where to truncate the interval, based on the usual trade-off between efficiency and accuracy.

(b) Truncate the interval and use a standard adaptive quadrature routine. Again, explore the trade-off between accuracy and efficiency.

(c) Gauss-Laguerre quadrature is designed for the interval $[0, \infty]$ and the weight function e^{-t}, so it is ideal for approximating this integral. Look up the nodes and weights for Gauss-Laguerre quadrature rules of various orders (see [1, 251, 282], for example) and compute the resulting estimates for the integral.

(d) If available, use an adaptive quadrature routine designed for an infinite interval of integration.

For each method, compute the approximate value of the integral for several values of x in the range 1 to 10. Compare your results with the values given by the built-in **gamma** function or with the known values for integer arguments,

$$\Gamma(n) = (n - 1)! \,.$$

How do the various methods compare in efficiency for a given level of accuracy?

8.10. Planck's theory of blackbody radiation leads to the integral

$$\int_0^\infty \frac{x^3}{e^x - 1} \, dx.$$

Evaluate this integral using each of the methods in the previous exercise, and compare their efficiency and accuracy.

8.11. In two dimensions, suppose that there is a uniform charge distribution in the region $-1 \le x \le 1$, $-1 \le y \le 1$. Then, with suitably chosen units, the electrostatic potential at a point $(\hat{x}, \hat{y})$ outside the region is given by the double integral

$$\Phi(\hat{x}, \hat{y}) = \int_{-1}^1 \int_{-1}^1 \frac{dx \, dy}{\sqrt{(\hat{x} - x)^2 + (\hat{y} - y)^2}}.$$

Evaluate this integral for enough points $(\hat{x}, \hat{y})$ to plot the $\Phi(\hat{x}, \hat{y})$ surface over the region $2 \le \hat{x} \le 10$, $2 \le \hat{y} \le 10$.

8.12. Using any method you choose, evaluate the double integral

$$\iint e^{-xy} \, dx \, dy$$

over each of the following regions:

(a) The unit square, i.e., $0 \le x \le 1, 0 \le y \le 1$
(b) The quarter of the unit disc lying in the first quadrant, i.e., $x^2 + y^2 \le 1, x \ge 0, y \ge 0$

8.13. (a) Write an automatic quadrature routine using the composite Simpson rule. Successively refine a uniform mesh until a given error tolerance is met. Estimate the error at each stage by comparing the values obtained for consecutive mesh sizes. What kind of data structure is needed for reusing previously computed function values?

(b) Write an adaptive quadrature routine using the composite Simpson rule. Successively refine only those subintervals that have not yet met an error tolerance. What kind of data structure is needed for keeping track of which subintervals have converged?

After debugging, test your routines using some of the integrals in the previous problems and compare the results with those previously obtained. How does the efficiency of your adaptive routine compare with that of your nonadaptive routine?

8.14. Select an automatic adaptive quadrature routine and try to devise an integrand function for which it gives an answer that is completely wrong. (*Hint:* This problem may require at least one round of trial and error.) Can you devise a *smooth* function for which the adaptive routine is seriously in error?

8.15. (a) Solve the integral equation

$$\int_0^1 (s^2 + t^2)^{1/2} u(t) \, dt = \frac{(s^2 + 1)^{3/2} - s^3}{3}$$

on the interval $[0, 1]$ by discretizing the integral using the composite Simpson quadrature rule with n equally spaced points t_j, and also using the same n points for the s_i. Solve the resulting linear system $Ax = y$ using a library routine for Gaussian elimination with partial pivoting. Experiment with various values for n in the range from 3 to 15, comparing your results with the known unique solution, $u(t) = t$. Which value of n gives the best results? Can you explain why?

(b) For each value of n in part a, compute the condition number of the matrix A. How does it behave as a function of n?

(c) Repeat part a, this time solving the linear system using the singular value decomposition, but omit any "small" singular values. Try various thresholds for truncating the singular values, and again compare your results with the known true solution.

(d) Repeat part a, this time using the method of regularization. Experiment with various values for the regularization parameter μ to determine which value yields the best results for a given value of n. For each value of μ, plot a point on a two-dimensional graph whose axes are the norm of the solution and the norm of the residual. What is the shape of the curve traced out as μ varies? Does this shape suggest an optimal value for μ?

(e) Repeat part a, this time using an optimization routine to minimize $\|y - Ax\|_2^2$ subject to the constraint that the components of the solution must be nonnegative. Again, compare your results with the known true solution.

(f) Repeat part e, this time imposing the additional constraint that the solution be monotonically increasing, i.e., $x_1 \geq 0$ and $x_i - x_{i-1} \geq 0, i = 2, \ldots, n$. How much difference does this make in approximating the true solution?

8.16. In this exercise we will experiment with numerical differentiation using data from Computer Problem 3.1:

t	0.0	1.0	2.0	3.0	4.0	5.0
y	1.0	2.7	5.8	6.6	7.5	9.9

For each of the following methods for estimating the derivative, compute the derivative of the original data and also experiment with randomly perturbing the y values to determine the sensitivity of the resulting derivative estimates. For each method, comment on both the reasonableness of the derivative estimates and their sensitivity to perturbations. Note that the data are monotonically increasing, so one might expect the derivative always to be positive.

(a) For $n = 0, 1, \ldots, 5$, fit a polynomial of degree n by least squares to the data, then differentiate the resulting polynomial and evaluate the derivative at each of the given t values.

(b) Interpolate the data with a cubic spline, differentiate the resulting piecewise cubic polynomial, and evaluate the derivative at each of the given t values (some spline routines provide the derivative automatically, but it can be done manually if necessary).

(c) Repeat part b, this time using a smoothing spline routine. Experiment with various levels of smoothing, using whatever mechanism for controlling the degree of smoothing that the routine provides.

(d) Interpolate the data with a monotonic Hermite cubic, differentiate the resulting piecewise cubic polynomial, and evaluate the derivative at each of the given t values.

CHAPTER 9

Initial Value Problems for Ordinary Differential Equations

9.1 ORDINARY DIFFERENTIAL EQUATIONS

We now turn to the study of differential equations, that is, equations involving derivatives of the unknown solution. We have previously considered only *algebraic* equations, for which the unknown solution is a discrete *vector* in a finite-dimensional space. For a *differential* equation, on the other hand, the unknown solution is a continuous *function* in an infinite-dimensional space. Our approach to solving differential equations numerically will be based on finite-dimensional approximations, a process called *discretization*. We will replace differential equations with algebraic equations whose solutions approximate those of the given differential equations.

First, we establish some notation and definitions. A system of ordinary differential equations (ODEs) has the general form

$$y' = f(t, y),$$

where t is a real variable, $y: \mathbb{R} \to \mathbb{R}^n$ is a vector-valued function of t, $f: \mathbb{R}^{n+1} \to \mathbb{R}^n$, and $y' = dy/dt$ denotes the derivative with respect to t, i.e.,

$$\begin{bmatrix} y'_1 \\ y'_2 \\ \vdots \\ y'_n \end{bmatrix} = \begin{bmatrix} dy_1/dt \\ dy_2/dt \\ \vdots \\ dy_n/dt \end{bmatrix}.$$

Thus, we have a *system* of *coupled* differential equations in which we are given the function f and we wish to determine the unknown function y. An important special case, which we will often consider for simplicity, is $n = 1$, i.e., a single scalar ODE.

9.1.1 Initial Value Problems

An ordinary differential equation $y' = f(t, y)$ by itself does not determine a unique solution function because the equation merely specifies the slope $y'(t)$ of the solution function at each point but not its actual value $y(t)$ at any point. Thus, in general, there is an infinite family of functions that satisfy the differential equation, provided f is sufficiently smooth.

To single out a particular solution, we must specify the value, usually denoted by y_0, of the solution function at some point, usually denoted by t_0. Thus, part of the given problem data is the requirement that

$$y(t_0) = y_0.$$

This additional requirement determines a unique solution to the ODE, provided that f is continuously differentiable. Because the independent variable t usually represents time, we think of t_0 as the initial time and y_0 as the initial value. Hence, this is termed an *initial value problem*. The ODE governs the dynamic evolution of the system in time from its initial state y_0 at time t_0 onward, and we seek a function $y(t)$ that describes the state of the system as a function of time.

EXAMPLE 9.1 INITIAL VALUE PROBLEM. Consider the ordinary differential equation $y' = y$. This is an ODE of the form $y' = f(t, y)$, where in this example $f(t, y) = y$. The family of solutions for this equation is given by $y(t) = ce^t$, where c is any real constant. If we impose an *initial condition*, such as requiring that $y(t_0) = y_0$, then this will single out the unique particular solution that satisfies the initial condition. For this example, if $t_0 = 0$, then we get $c = y_0$, which means that the solution is $y(t) = y_0 e^t$. Some members of the family of solutions for this equation are sketched in Fig. 9.1, including the particular solution that satisfies the given initial condition.

9.1.2 Higher-Order ODEs

If the first derivative is the highest-order derivative of the solution function appearing in the equation, an ODE is said to be of *first order.* Equations with higher-order derivatives

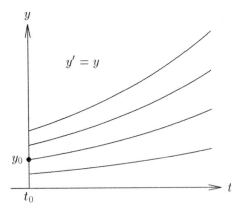

FIGURE 9.1
The family of solution curves for the ODE $y' = y$.

occur frequently in practice but can be transformed into an equivalent first-order system as follows. Given an nth order equation

$$u^{(n)} = f(t, u, u', \ldots, u^{(n-1)}),$$

define the n new unknowns $y_1(t) = u$, $y_2(t) = u'$, ..., $y_n(t) = u^{(n-1)}$, so that the original equation becomes the first-order system of n equations

$$\begin{bmatrix} y_1' \\ y_2' \\ \vdots \\ y_{n-1}' \\ y_n' \end{bmatrix} = \begin{bmatrix} y_2 \\ y_3 \\ \vdots \\ y_n \\ f(t, y_1, y_2, \ldots, y_n) \end{bmatrix}.$$

Thus, in general, a scalar ODE of order n is equivalent to a system of n first-order ODEs. If a system of ODEs contains equations having higher-order derivatives, then each such equation can be transformed into an equivalent first-order system in this same manner. For example, a system of two second-order equations would yield an equivalent system of four first-order equations. For this reason, most ODE software is designed to solve only first-order equations, and we will also restrict our attention to first-order equations in discussing numerical solution methods.

EXAMPLE 9.2 NEWTON'S SECOND LAW. To illustrate the transformation of a higher-order ODE into an equivalent system of first-order ODEs, consider Newton's Second Law of Motion, $F = ma$, in one dimension. This is a second-order ODE, since the acceleration a is the second derivative of the position coordinate, which we denote by x. Thus, the ODE has the form

$$x'' = F/m,$$

where F and m represent force and mass, respectively. To transform this second-order, scalar ODE into a system of two first-order ODEs, we define two new functions $y_1 = x$ and $y_2 = x'$. This step gives us the system of two first-order equations

$$\begin{bmatrix} y_1' \\ y_2' \end{bmatrix} = \begin{bmatrix} y_2 \\ F/m \end{bmatrix}.$$

We can now use a method for first-order equations to solve this system. When we do so, the first component of the solution y_1 will be the same as the solution x to the original second-order equation. In addition, we will also get the second component y_2, which is the same as the velocity x'. In three dimensions, Newton's Law would comprise three second-order equations, one for each spatial coordinate, and would yield an equivalent system of six first-order equations.

9.1.3 Stable and Unstable ODEs

Roughly speaking, if the members of the solution family for an ODE move away from each other with time, then the equation is said to be *unstable*; but if the members of the solution family move closer to each other with time, then the equation is said to be *stable*. If the solution curves are neither converging nor diverging (i.e., they remain nearby but do not actually come together), then the equation is said to be *neutrally stable*. This definition of stability for ODEs is consistent with the general concept of stability discussed in Section 1.2.7 in that it reflects the sensitivity of a solution of the ODE to perturbations. A small perturbation to a solution of a stable equation will be damped out with time because the solution curves are converging, whereas for an unstable equation the perturbation will grow with time because the solution curves are diverging.

The stability of a cone provides a helpful geometric analogy. If a cone resting on its circular base is slightly perturbed, it will return to its original position; the position is stable. If a cone is balanced on its point, any slight perturbation will cause it to fall; the position is unstable. If a cone is resting on its slanted side, then a slight perturbation will move the cone to a new position nearby; the position is neutrally stable.

Note that the concept of stability of an ODE depends on the entire family of solutions, not just on some particular solution. Moreover, both stable and unstable behavior can occur in different portions of the domain of interest for the same equation.

This qualitative concept of stability for an ODE $y' = f(t, y)$ can be made more precise quantitatively by considering the Jacobian matrix J with entries

$$\{J\}_{ij} = \partial f_i/\partial y_j.$$

If any of the eigenvalues of this matrix have positive real parts, then the equation is unstable. If all of the eigenvalues have negative real parts, then the equation is stable. If one or more eigenvalues have zero real parts, and all of the remainder have negative real parts, then the equation is neutrally stable. Since the entries of J are functions of t and y, its eigenvalues may vary with time, and hence the stability of the equation may vary from region to region.

EXAMPLE 9.3 STABLE ODE. In Example 9.1, we considered the ODE $y' = y$ and sketched its family of solution curves $y(t) = ce^t$ in Fig. 9.1. From the exponential growth of the solutions, we know that the solution curves for this equation move away from each other as time increases, as we see in Fig. 9.1. We can therefore conclude that the equation is unstable. More rigorously, we note that the Jacobian of f (i.e., $\partial f/\partial y$) is positive (in fact, it is the constant 1), so the equation is unstable.

EXAMPLE 9.4 UNSTABLE ODE. Let us now consider a different equation, namely, $y' = -y$. The family of solutions for this equation is given by $y(t) = ce^{-t}$, where c is any real constant. For this equation we see that the Jacobian of f is negative ($\partial f/\partial y = -1$), so the equation is stable. We also can see this from the exponential decay of the solutions, as shown in Fig. 9.2, in which some members of the solution family for this equation are drawn.

EXAMPLE 9.5 NEUTRALLY STABLE ODE. Finally, consider the ODE $y' = a$, for a given constant a. The family of solutions is given by $y(t) = at + c$, where c is any real constant. Thus, the solution curves, as illustrated for $a = \frac{1}{2}$ in Fig. 9.3, are parallel straight lines that are neither converging nor diverging, and hence the equation is neutrally stable. Note that $\partial f/\partial y = 0$ for this equation, consistent with its neutral stability. Note also that the issue that determines stability is not whether the solution curves are increasing or decreasing (either case can apply for this equation, depending on whether a is positive or negative) but rather the relationship of the solution curves to each other.

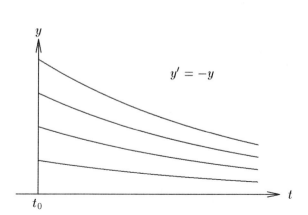

FIGURE 9.2
The family of solution curves for the ODE $y' = -y$.

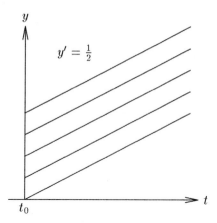

FIGURE 9.3
The family of solution curves for the ODE $y' = \frac{1}{2}$.

EXAMPLE 9.6 LINEAR SYSTEM OF ODEs. A linear, homogeneous system of ODEs with constant coefficients has the form

$$y' = Ay,$$

where A is an $n \times n$ matrix. Suppose we have the initial condition $y(0) = y_0$. Let the eigenvalues of A be denoted by λ_i, and the corresponding eigenvectors by u_i, $i = 1, \ldots, n$. For simplicity, assume that the eigenvectors are linearly independent, so that we can express y_0 as a linear combination

$$y_0 = \sum_{i=1}^{n} \alpha_i u_i.$$

Then it is easily confirmed that

$$y(t) = \sum_{i=1}^{n} \alpha_i u_i e^{\lambda_i t}$$

is a solution to the ODE that satisfies the initial condition. We see that eigenvalues of A with positive real parts yield exponentially growing solution components, eigenvalues with negative real parts yield exponentially decaying solution components, and pure imaginary eigenvalues with zero real parts yield oscillatory solution components. These are consistent with our definitions of instability, stability, and neutral stability, respectively, as $J = A$ for this problem.

9.2 NUMERICAL SOLUTION OF ODEs

An analytical solution of an ODE is a closed-form formula for computing the value of the solution function at any point t. In contrast, a numerical solution of an ODE is a table of approximate values of the solution function at a discrete set of points. Such a numerical solution is obtained by simulating the behavior of the system governed by the differential equation. Approximate solution values are generated step by step in discrete increments moving across the interval in which the solution is sought. For this reason, numerical methods for solving ODEs are sometimes called *discrete variable methods*.

In stepping from one discrete point to the next, we will in general incur some error, which means that our new approximate solution value will lie on a *different* member of the family of solution curves for the ODE from the one on which we started. The stability or instability of the equation determines in part whether such errors are magnified or diminished with time.

9.2.1 Euler's Method

A numerical solution of an ODE is generated by simulating the behavior of the system governed by the ODE. Starting at t_0 with the given initial value, we wish to track the trajectory dictated by the ODE. Evaluating $f(t_0, y_0)$ tells us the slope of the trajectory at that point. We use this information to predict the value y_1 of the solution at some future time $t_1 = t_0 + h$ for some suitably chosen increment h.

The simplest example of this approach is *Euler's method*. Consider the Taylor series

$$y(t + h) = y(t) + y'(t)h + \frac{y''(t)}{2}h^2 + \cdots$$

$$= y(t) + f(t, y(t))h + \frac{y''(t)}{2}h^2 + \cdots.$$

Euler's method is derived by dropping terms of second and higher order to obtain the approximate solution value

$$y_{k+1} = y_k + f(t_k, y_k)h_k,$$

which allows us to step from time t_k to time $t_{k+1} = t_k + h_k$. Equivalently, if we replace the derivative in the differential equation $y' = f(t, y)$ with a finite difference quotient, we obtain an approximating algebraic equation

$$\frac{y_{k+1} - y_k}{h_k} = f(t_k, y_k),$$

which gives Euler's method when solved for y_{k+1}. Thus, Euler's method advances the solution by extrapolating along a straight line whose slope is given by $f(t_k, y_k)$. Euler's method is called a *single-step* method because it depends on information at only one point in time to advance to the next point.

EXAMPLE 9.7 EULER'S METHOD. We previously considered the equation $y' = y$, which is easily solved analytically, but for illustration let us apply Euler's method to solve it numerically. For some stepsize h, we advance the solution from time $t_0 = 0$ to time $t_1 = t_0 + h$:

$$y_1 = y_0 + y_0'h = y_0 + y_0h = y_0(1 + h).$$

Note that the value for the solution we obtain at t_1 is not exact (i.e., $y_1 \neq y(t_1)$). For example, if $t_0 = 0$, $y_0 = 1$, and $h = 0.5$, then we get $y_1 = 1.5$, whereas the exact solution for this initial value is $y(0.5) = \exp(0.5) \approx 1.649$.

From the Taylor series used to derive Euler's method, we know that the error is proportional to h^2, so we can reduce the error for this step by a factor of $\frac{1}{4}$ by reducing the stepsize by a factor of $\frac{1}{2}$, provided rounding error is negligible. For any nonzero error, however, the value y_1 lies on a different member of the family of solution curves from the one on which we started.

To continue the numerical solution process, we take another step from t_1 to $t_2 = t_1 + h = 1.0$, obtaining $y_2 = y_1 + y_1 h = 1.5 + (1.5)(0.5) = 2.25$. Note that y_2 differs not only from the true solution of the original problem at $t = 1$, namely, $y(1) = \exp(1) \approx 2.718$ but it also differs from the solution curve passing through the previous point (t_1, y_1), which has the approximate value 2.473 at $t = 1$. Thus, we have moved to still another member of the family of solution curves for this ODE. We can continue to take additional steps, generating a table of discrete values of the approximate solution over whatever interval we desire. As we do so, we will hop from one member of the solution family to another at each step.

For this unstable equation, the errors we make in the numerical method are amplified with time as a result of the divergence of the solution curves, as shown in Fig. 9.4. For a

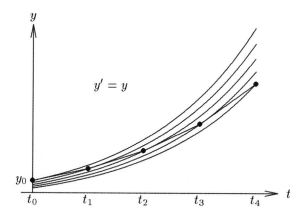

FIGURE 9.4
Euler's method for the ODE $y' = y$.

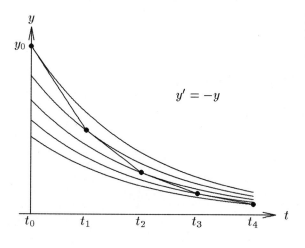

FIGURE 9.5
Euler's method for the ODE $y' = -y$.

stable equation such as $y' = -y$, on the other hand, the errors in the numerical solution may diminish with time, as shown in Fig. 9.5.

9.3 ACCURACY AND STABILITY

9.3.1 Order of Accuracy

Like other methods that replace derivatives with finite differences, a numerical procedure for solving an ODE suffers from two distinct sources of error:

- *Rounding error*, which is due to the finite precision of floating-point arithmetic
- *Truncation error* (or discretization error), which is due to the method used, and which would remain even if all arithmetic could be performed exactly

Although they arise from different sources, these two types of errors are not independent of each other. For example, the truncation error can usually be reduced by using a smaller stepsize h, but doing so may incur greater rounding error (see Example 1.11). In most practical situations, however, truncation error is the dominant factor in determining the accuracy of numerical solutions of ODEs, and we shall henceforth ignore rounding error.

The truncation error at step k of a numerical solution of an ODE can be further broken down into:

- *Local truncation error*, denoted by L_k, which is the error made in one step of the numerical method. More precisely,

$$L_k = y_k - u_{k-1}(t_k),$$

where y_k is the computed solution at t_k, and u_{k-1} is the member of the family of true solutions to the ODE that passes through the previous point (t_{k-1}, y_{k-1}).
- *Global truncation error*, denoted by E_k, which is the difference between the computed solution and the true solution determined by the initial data at t_0. More precisely,

$$E_k = y_k - u_0(t_k) = y_k - y(t_k).$$

The global error is not necessarily the same as the sum of the local errors. The global error will generally be greater than the sum of the local errors if the equation is unstable but may be less than that sum if the equation is stable, as shown in Figs. 9.6 and 9.7, where the local errors are indicated by small vertical bars between solution curves and the global error is indicated by a bar at the end. Having a small global error is obviously what we want, but we can control only the local error directly.

The accuracy of a numerical method is said to be of order p if

$$L_k = O(h_k^{p+1}).$$

The motivation for this definition, with the order one less than the exponent of the stepsize in the local error, is that if the local error is of order $p + 1$, then the *sum* of the

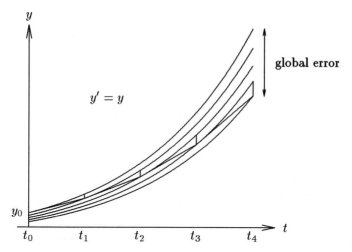

FIGURE 9.6
Local and global errors in Euler's method for the ODE $y' = y$.

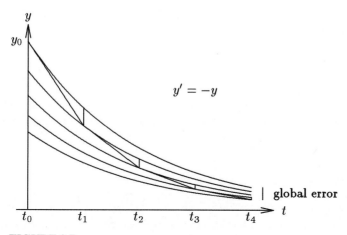

FIGURE 9.7
Local and global errors in Euler's method for the ODE $y' = -y$.

local errors from t_0 to t_k will be

$$\frac{t_k - t_0}{h} O(h^{p+1}) = O(h^p),$$

where h is the average stepsize, and this gives a rough approximation of the global error E_k.

EXAMPLE 9.8 ACCURACY OF EULER'S METHOD. Consider the Taylor series
$$y(t + h) = y(t) + y'(t)h + O(h^2) = y(t) + f(t, y(t))h + O(h^2).$$

If we take $t = t_k$ and $h = h_k$, we get

$$y(t_{k+1}) = y(t_k) + f(t_k, y(t_k))h_k + O(h_k^2).$$

If we now subtract this from Euler's method we get

$$y_{k+1} - y(t_{k+1}) = [y_k - y(t_k)] + [f(t_k, y_k) - f(t_k, y(t_k))]h_k - O(h_k^2).$$

The difference on the left side preceding is the global error E_{k+1}. If there were no prior errors, then we would have $y_k = y(t_k)$, and the first two differences on the right side would be zero, leaving only the $O(h_k^2)$ term, which is the local truncation error. This result means that Euler's method is first-order accurate.

9.3.2 Stability of a Numerical Method

The concept of stability for numerical solutions of ODEs is analogous to, but distinct from, the concept of stability of the ODE itself. Recall that an ODE is stable if its solution curves do not diverge from each other with time. Similarly, a numerical method is said to be *stable* if small perturbations do not cause the resulting numerical solutions to diverge from each other without bound (recall the general notion of stability in Section 1.2.7). Such divergence of numerical solutions could be due to instability of the ODE being solved, but it can also be due to the numerical method itself, even when solving a stable ODE.

EXAMPLE 9.9 STABILITY OF EULER'S METHOD. From the derivation in Example 9.8 we see that the global error is the sum of the local error and what might be termed the *propagated error*. To characterize the latter, note that by the Mean Value Theorem we can write

$$f(t_k, y_k) - f(t_k, y(t_k)) = J(\xi)(y_k - y(t_k))$$

for some (unknown) value ξ, so that we can express the global error at step $k + 1$ as

$$E_{k+1} = (1 + h_k J)E_k + L_{k+1}.$$

Thus, the global error is multiplied at each step by the factor $(1 + h_k J)$, which is called the *amplification factor* or *growth factor*. If $|1 + hJ| < 1$, then the errors do not grow, and the method is stable. This condition is equivalent to requiring hJ to lie in the interval $(-2, 0)$. If this is not the case, then the errors grow and the method is unstable. Note that such instability could be due to instability of the ODE (i.e., $J > 0$), but it can also occur for a stable equation ($J < 0$) if $h > -2/J$. We will see a dramatic example of such numerical instability for a stable equation in Example 9.11.

For a system of equations, the amplification factor for Euler's method is the matrix $(I + hJ)$, and the condition for stability of the method is $\rho(I + hJ) < 1$, which is satisfied if the eigenvalues of hJ lie inside a circle in the complex plane of radius 1 and centered at -1 [notice that this includes the interval $(-2, 0)$ of the single-equation case].

In general, the amplification factor depends on the particular ODE being solved (which determines the Jacobian J), the particular numerical method used (which determines the form of the amplification factor), and the stepsize h.

An alternative approach to assessing the accuracy and stability of a numerical method is to apply the method to the linear ODE $y' = \lambda y$ with initial condition $y(0) = y_0$, whose exact solution is given by $y(t) = y_0 e^{\lambda t}$. This will enable us to determine the accuracy of the method by comparing the computed and exact solutions and to determine stability by characterizing the growth factor of the numerical solution.

For example, applying Euler's method to this equation using a fixed stepsize h, we have

$$y_{k+1} = y_k + \lambda y_k h = (1 + \lambda h) y_k,$$

which means that

$$y_k = (1 + \lambda h)^k y_0.$$

Provided $\lambda < 0$, the exact solution decays to zero as t increases, as will the computed solution if $|1 + \lambda h| < 1$. This result agrees with our earlier stability analysis because $J = \lambda$ for this ODE. We also note that the growth factor $1 + \lambda h$ agrees with the series expansion

$$e^{\lambda h} = 1 + \lambda h + \frac{(\lambda h)^2}{2} + \frac{(\lambda h)^3}{6} + \cdots$$

through terms of first order in h, and hence Euler's method is first-order accurate. Especially for more complicated numerical methods, a linear ODE is easier to work with than a general ODE, and it produces essentially the same stability result if we equate λ with the Jacobian J at a given point. An important caveat, however, is that λ is constant, whereas the Jacobian J varies for a nonlinear equation, and hence the stability can potentially change.

9.3.3 Stepsize Control

In choosing a stepsize h for advancing the numerical solution of an ODE we would like to take as large a step as possible to minimize computational cost, but we must also take into account both stability and accuracy. Obviously, to yield a meaningful solution, the stepsize must obey any stability restrictions imposed by the method being used. In addition, a local error estimate is needed to ensure that the desired accuracy is attained. With Euler's method, for example, we know that the local error is approximately $(y''/2)h^2$, and hence we should choose the stepsize so that

$$h \leq (2 \, tol / |y''|)^{1/2}$$

where tol is the specified local error tolerance. Of course, we do not know the value of y'', but we can estimate it by a difference quotient of the form

$$y'' \approx \frac{y'_k - y'_{k-1}}{t_k - t_{k-1}}.$$

Other methods of obtaining local error estimates are based on the difference between results obtained using methods of different orders or different stepsizes.

9.4 IMPLICIT METHODS

Euler's method is an *explicit* method in that it uses only information at time t_k to advance the solution to time t_{k+1}. This may appear to be a virtue, but we saw that Euler's method has a rather limited stability interval of $(-2, 0)$. A larger stability region can be obtained by using information at time t_{k+1}, which makes the method *implicit*. The simplest example is the *backward Euler method*,

$$y_{k+1} = y_k + f(t_{k+1}, y_{k+1})h_k.$$

This method is implicit because we must evaluate f with the argument y_{k+1} before we know its value. This statement simply means that a value for y_{k+1} that satisfies the preceding equation must be determined, and if f is a nonlinear function of y, as is often the case, then an iterative solution method, such as fixed-point iteration or Newton's method, must be used. A good starting guess for the iteration can be obtained from an explicit integration method, such as Euler's method, or from the solution at the previous time step.

EXAMPLE 9.10 BACKWARD EULER METHOD. Consider the nonlinear ODE

$$y' = -y^3$$

with initial condition $y(0) = 1$. Using the backward Euler method with a stepsize of $h = 0.5$, we obtain the equation

$$y_1 = y_0 + f(t_1, y_1)h = 1 - 0.5y_1^3$$

for the solution value at the next step. This nonlinear equation for y_1 is already set up to solve by fixed-point iteration, repeatedly substituting successive values for y_1 on the right-hand side, or we could use any other method from Chapter 5, such as Newton's method. In any case, we need a starting guess for y_1, for which we could simply use the previous solution value, $y_0 = 1$, or we could use an explicit method to produce a starting guess for the implicit method. Using Euler's method, for example, we would obtain $y_1 = y_0 - 0.5y_0^3 = 0.5$ as a starting guess for the iterative solution of the implicit equation. The iterations eventually converge to the final value $y_1 \approx 0.7709$.

Given the extra trouble and computation in using an implicit method, one might wonder why we would bother. The answer is that implicit methods generally have a significantly larger stability region than comparable explicit methods. To determine the stability of the backward Euler method, we apply it to the linear ODE $y' = \lambda y$, obtaining

$$y_{k+1} = y_k + \lambda y_{k+1}h,$$

or

$$(1 - \lambda h)y_{k+1} = y_k,$$

so that

$$y_k = \left(\frac{1}{1 - \lambda h}\right)^k y_0.$$

Thus, to mimic the exponential decay of the exact solution when $\lambda < 0$, we must have $|1/(1 - \lambda h)| < 1$. Moreover, the growth factor

$$\frac{1}{1-\lambda h} = 1 + \lambda h + (\lambda h)^2 + \cdots$$

agrees with the expansion for $e^{\lambda h}$ through terms of order h, so the backward Euler method is first-order accurate.

More generally, the amplification factor for the backward Euler method for a scalar equation is $1/(1 - hJ)$, which is less than 1 in magnitude for any positive h provided that $J < 0$. Thus, the stability interval for the backward Euler method is $(-\infty, 0)$, or the entire left half of the complex plane in the case of a system of equations, and hence for a stable equation the method is stable for any positive stepsize. Such a method is said to be *unconditionally stable* (other terms sometimes used for this concept are *absolutely stable*, *A-stable,* or *A_0-stable*). The great virtue of an unconditionally stable method is that the desired local accuracy places the only constraint on our choice of stepsize. Thus, we may be able to take much larger steps than for an explicit method of comparable order and attain much higher overall efficiency despite requiring more computation per step.

Although the backward Euler method is unconditionally stable, its first-order accuracy severely limits its usefulness. We can obtain a method of higher-order accuracy by combining the Euler and backward Euler methods. In particular, averaging these two methods yields the implicit *trapezoid rule*

$$y_{k+1} = y_k + \frac{f(t_k, y_k) + f(t_{k+1}, y_{k+1})}{2} h_k.$$

To determine the stability and accuracy of this method, we apply it to the linear ODE $y' = \lambda y$, obtaining

$$y_{k+1} = y_k + \frac{\lambda y_k + \lambda y_{k+1}}{2} h,$$

which implies that

$$y_k = \left(\frac{1 + \lambda h/2}{1 - \lambda h/2}\right)^k y_0.$$

Thus, the method is stable if $|(1 + \lambda h/2)/(1 - \lambda h/2)| < 1$, which is true for any positive value of h provided $\lambda < 0$. In addition, the growth factor

$$\frac{1 + \lambda h/2}{1 - \lambda h/2} = \left(1 + \frac{\lambda h}{2}\right)\left(1 + \frac{\lambda h}{2} + \left(\frac{\lambda h}{2}\right)^2 + \left(\frac{\lambda h}{2}\right)^3 + \cdots\right)$$

$$= 1 + \lambda h + \frac{(\lambda h)^2}{2} + \frac{(\lambda h)^3}{4} + \cdots$$

agrees with the expansion of $e^{\lambda h}$ through terms of order h^2, and hence the trapezoid method is second-order accurate.

More generally, the trapezoid rule has amplification factor $(1 + hJ/2)/(1 - hJ/2)$, which is less than 1 in magnitude for any positive stepsize provided that $J < 0$. The resulting stability regions are the interval $(-\infty, 0)$ for a scalar equation and the entire left half of the complex plane for a system of equations. Thus, the trapezoid rule is unconditionally stable as well as second-order accurate. It turns out that this is the highest-order accuracy possible for an unconditionally stable method.

We have now seen two examples of implicit methods that are unconditionally stable, but not all implicit methods have this property. Implicit methods generally have larger stability regions than explicit methods, but the allowable stepsize is not always unlimited. Implicitness is not sufficient to guarantee stability, and stability is not sufficient to guarantee accuracy.

9.5 STIFF DIFFERENTIAL EQUATIONS

The solution curves for a stable equation converge with time. This convergence has the favorable property of damping errors in a numerical solution, but if it is too rapid, as illustrated in Fig. 9.8, then difficulties of a different type may arise. Such an equation is said to be *stiff*.

Formally, a stable system of ODEs is stiff if the eigenvalues of its Jacobian matrix J have greatly differing magnitudes. There may be an eigenvalue with a large negative real part (corresponding to a strongly damped component of the solution) or a large imaginary part (corresponding to a rapidly oscillating component of the solution). Such a differential equation corresponds to a physical process whose components have disparate time scales or a process whose time scale is small compared to the interval over which it is being studied.

Some numerical methods are very inefficient for stiff equations because the rapidly varying component of the solution forces very small stepsizes to be used to maintain stability. Since the stability restriction depends on the rapidly varying component of the solution, whereas the accuracy restriction depends on the slowly varying component, the stepsize may be much more severely restricted by stability than by the required accuracy. For example, Euler's method with a fixed stepsize is unstable for solving a stiff equation, whereas the implicit backward Euler method is stable for stiff problems. Stiff ODEs need not be difficult to solve numerically, provided a suitable method is chosen.

EXAMPLE 9.11 STIFF ODE. To illustrate the numerical solution of a stiff ODE, consider the equation

$$y' = -100y + 100t + 101$$

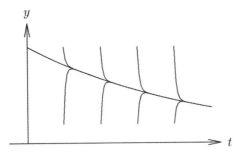

FIGURE 9.8
The family of solution curves for a typical stiff ODE.

with initial condition $y(0) = 1$. The general solution of this ODE is $y(t) = 1 + t + ce^{-100t}$, and the particular solution satisfying the initial condition is $y(t) = 1 + t$ (i.e., $c = 0$). Since the solution is linear, Euler's method is theoretically exact for this problem. However, to illustrate the effect of truncation or rounding errors, let us perturb the initial value slightly. With a stepsize $h = 0.1$, the first few steps for the given initial values are:

t	0.0	0.1	0.2	0.3	0.4
Exact solution	1.00	1.10	1.20	1.30	1.40
Euler solution	0.99	1.19	0.39	8.59	−64.2
Euler solution	1.01	1.01	2.01	−5.99	67.0

The computed solution is incredibly sensitive to the initial value, as each tiny perturbation results in a wildly different solution. An explanation for this behavior is shown in Fig. 9.9. Any point deviating from the desired particular solution, even by only a small amount, lies on a different solution curve, for which $c \neq 0$, and therefore the rapid transient of the general solution is present. Euler's method bases its projection on the derivative at the current point, and the resulting large value causes the numerical solution to diverge radically from the desired solution. This behavior should not surprise us. The Jacobian for this equation is $J = -100$, so the stability condition for Euler's method requires a stepsize $h < 0.02$, which we are violating.

By contrast, the backward Euler method has no trouble solving this problem. In fact, the backward Euler solution is extremely *insensitive* to the initial value, as shown in the following table, and illustrated in Fig. 9.10. Even with a very large perturbation in the initial value, by using the derivative at the next point rather than the current point, the transient is quickly damped out and the backward Euler solution converges to the desired solution curve after only a few steps. This behavior is consistent with the unconditional stability of the backward Euler method for a stable equation.

t	0.0	0.1	0.2	0.3	0.4
Exact solution	1.00	1.10	1.20	1.30	1.40
BE solution	0.00	1.01	1.19	1.30	1.40
BE solution	2.00	1.19	1.21	1.30	1.40

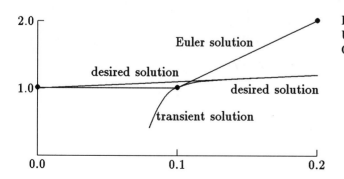

FIGURE 9.9
Unstable solution of stiff ODE using Euler method.

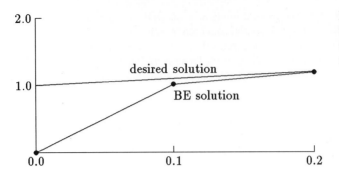

FIGURE 9.10
Stable solution of stiff ODE using backward Euler method.

9.6 SURVEY OF NUMERICAL METHODS FOR ODES

Having covered the basic concepts of solving ordinary differential equations numerically, we now briefly survey each of the major categories of methods for such problems.

9.6.1 Taylor Series Methods

We have already seen that Euler's method can be derived from a Taylor series expansion. By retaining more terms in the Taylor series, we can generate higher-order single-step methods. For example, retaining one additional term in the Taylor series

$$y(t + h) = y(t) + y'(t)h + \frac{y''(t)}{2}h^2 + \frac{y'''(t)}{6}h^3 + \cdots$$

gives the second-order method

$$y_{k+1} = y_k + y'_k h_k + \frac{y''_k}{2}h_k^2.$$

Note, however, that this approach requires the computation of higher derivatives of y. These can be obtained by differentiating $y' = f(t, y)$ using the chain rule, e.g.,

$$y'' = f_t(t, y) + f(t, y)f_y(t, y),$$

where the subscripts indicate partial derivatives with respect to the given variable. As the order increases, such expressions for the derivatives rapidly become too complicated to be practical to compute, so Taylor series methods of higher order have not often been used in practice. Recently, however, the availability of symbolic manipulation and automatic differentiation systems has made these methods more feasible.

EXAMPLE 9.12 TAYLOR SERIES METHOD. To illustrate the second-order Taylor series method, we use it to solve the ODE

$$y' = f(t, y) = -2ty^2,$$

with initial value $y(0) = 1$. We differentiate f to obtain for this problem

$$y'' = f_t(t, y) + f(t, y)f_y(t, y) = -2y^2 + (-2ty^2)(-4t) = 2y^2(4t^2 - 1).$$

Taking a step from $t_0 = 0$ to $t_1 = 0.25$ using stepsize $h = 0.25$, we obtain

$$y_1 = y_0 + y_0'h + \frac{y_0''}{2}h^2 = 1 + 0 - 0.0625 = 0.9375.$$

Continuing with another step from $t_1 = 0.25$ to $t_2 = 0.5$ we obtain

$$y_2 = y_1 + y_1'h + \frac{y_1''}{2}h^2 = 0.9375 - 0.1099 - 0.0412 = 0.7864.$$

For comparison, the exact solution for this problem is $y(t) = 1/(1 + t^2)$, and hence the true solution at the integration points is $y(0.25) = 0.9412$ and $y(0.5) = 0.8$.

9.6.2 Runge-Kutta Methods

Runge-Kutta methods are single-step methods that are similar in motivation to Taylor series methods but do not require the computation of higher derivatives. Instead, Runge-Kutta methods simulate the effect of higher derivatives by evaluating f several times between t_k and t_{k+1}.

EXAMPLE 9.13 DERIVATION OF A RUNGE-KUTTA METHOD. The basic idea of Runge-Kutta methods is best illustrated by example, the simplest of which is *Heun's method*. Recall from Section 9.6.1 that the second derivative of y is given by

$$y'' = f_t + ff_y,$$

where each function is evaluated at (t, y). We can approximate the term on the right by expanding f in a Taylor series in two variables

$$f(t + h, y + hf) = f + hf_t + hff_y + O(h^2),$$

from which we obtain

$$f_t + ff_y = \frac{f(t + h, y + hf) - f(t, y)}{h} + O(h^2).$$

With this approximation to the second derivative, the second-order Taylor series method given in Section 9.6.1 becomes

$$y_{k+1} = y_k + f(t_k, y_k)h_k + \frac{f(t_k + h_k, y_k + h_k f(t_k, y_k)) - f(t_k, y_k)}{2h_k}h_k^2$$

$$= y_k + \frac{f(t_k, y_k) + f(t_k + h_k, y_k + h_k f(t_k, y_k))}{2}h_k,$$

which can be implemented in the form

$$y_{k+1} = y_k + \tfrac{1}{2}(k_1 + k_2),$$

where

$$k_1 = f(t_k, y_k)h_k,$$

$$k_2 = f(t_k + h_k, y_k + k_1)h_k.$$

Heun's method, which is of second-order accuracy, is analogous to the implicit trapezoid rule but remains explicit by using the Euler prediction $y_k + k_1$ instead of y_{k+1} in evaluating f at t_{k+1}.

EXAMPLE 9.14 HEUN'S METHOD. To illustrate the use of Heun's method, we use it to solve the ODE

$$y' = -2ty^2,$$

with initial value $y(0) = 1$. Taking a step from $t_0 = 0$ to $t_1 = 0.25$ using stepsize $h = 0.25$, we obtain

$$k_1 = f(t_0, y_0)h = 0 \quad \text{and} \quad k_2 = f(t_0 + h, y_0 + k_1)h = -0.125,$$

so that
$$y_1 = y_0 + \tfrac{1}{2}(k_1 + k_2) = 1 - 0.0625 = 0.9375.$$

Continuing with another step from $t_1 = 0.25$ to $t_2 = 0.5$, we obtain

$$k_1 = f(t_1, y_1)h = -0.1099 \quad \text{and} \quad k_2 = f(t_1 + h, y_1 + k_1)h = -0.1712,$$

so that
$$y_2 = y_1 + \tfrac{1}{2}(k_1 + k_2) = 0.9375 - 0.1406 = 0.7969.$$

For comparison, the exact solution for this problem is $y(t) = 1/(1 + t^2)$, and hence the true solution at the integration points is $y(0.25) = 0.9412$ and $y(0.5) = 0.8$.

The best-known Runge-Kutta method is the classical fourth-order scheme

$$y_{k+1} = y_k + \tfrac{1}{6}(k_1 + 2k_2 + 2k_3 + k_4),$$

where
$$k_1 = f(t_k, y_k)h_k,$$

$$k_2 = f(t_k + h_k/2, y_k + k_1/2)h_k,$$

$$k_3 = f(t_k + h_k/2, y_k + k_2/2)h_k,$$

$$k_4 = f(t_k + h_k, y_k + k_3)h_k.$$

This method is analogous to Simpson's rule; indeed it *is* Simpson's rule if f depends only on t. For an illustration of the use of the classical fourth-order Runge-Kutta method for solving a system of ODEs, see Example 10.1.

Runge-Kutta methods have a number of virtues. To proceed to time t_{k+1}, they require no history of the solution prior to time t_k, which makes them *self-starting* at the beginning of the integration, and also makes it easy to change stepsize during the integration. These facts also make Runge-Kutta methods relatively easy to program, which accounts in part for their popularity.

Unfortunately, classical Runge-Kutta methods provide no error estimate on which to base the choice of stepsize. More recently, however, Fehlberg devised a Runge-Kutta method that uses six function evaluations per step to produce both fifth-order and fourth-order estimates of the solution, whose difference provides an estimate for the local error. This approach has led to automatic Runge-Kutta solvers that are effective for many problems but are relatively inefficient for stiff problems or when very high accuracy is required. It is possible, however, to define *implicit* Runge-Kutta methods with superior stability properties that are suitable for solving stiff equations.

9.6.3 Extrapolation Methods

Extrapolation methods are based on the use of a single-step method to integrate the ODE over a given interval, $t_k \leq t \leq t_{k+1}$, using several different stepsizes h_i and yielding results denoted by $Y(h_i)$. This gives a discrete approximation to a function $Y(h)$, where $Y(0) = y(t_{k+1})$. An interpolating polynomial or rational function $\hat{Y}(h)$ is fit to these data, and $\hat{Y}(0)$ is then taken as the approximation to $Y(0)$.

We saw another example of this approach in Richardson extrapolation for numerical differentiation and integration (see Section 8.8). Extrapolation methods are capable of achieving very high accuracy, but they tend to be much less efficient and less flexible than other methods for ODEs, so they are not often used unless extremely high accuracy is required and cost is not a significant factor.

9.6.4 Multistep Methods

Multistep methods use information at more than one previous point to estimate the solution at the next point. For this reason, they are sometimes called *methods with memory*. Linear multistep methods have the form

$$y_{k+1} = \sum_{i=1}^{n} \alpha_i y_{k+1-i} + h \sum_{i=0}^{n} \beta_i f(t_{k+1-i}, y_{k+1-i}).$$

The parameters α_i and β_i are determined by polynomial interpolation. If $\beta_0 = 0$, the method is explicit, but if $\beta_0 \neq 0$, the method is implicit.

EXAMPLE 9.15 DERIVATION OF MULTISTEP METHODS. To illustrate the derivation of multistep methods, we derive an *explicit* two-step method of the form

$$y_{k+1} = \alpha_1 y_k + (\beta_1 y'_k + \beta_2 y'_{k-1})h,$$

where the parameters α_1, β_1, and β_2 are to be determined. Using the method of undetermined coefficients, we will force the formula to be exact for the first three monomials. If $y(t) = 1$, then $y'(t) = 0$, so that we have the equation

$$1 = \alpha_1 \cdot 1 + (\beta_1 \cdot 0 + \beta_2 \cdot 0)h.$$

If $y(t) = t$, then $y'(t) = 1$, so that we have the equation

$$t_{k+1} = \alpha_1 t_k + (\beta_1 \cdot 1 + \beta_2 \cdot 1)h.$$

If $y(t) = t^2$, then $y'(t) = 2t$, so that we have the equation

$$t_{k+1}^2 = \alpha_1 t_k^2 + (\beta_1 \cdot 2t_k + \beta_2 \cdot 2t_{k-1})h.$$

All three of these equations must hold for any values of the t_i, so we make the convenient choice $t_{k-1} = 0$, $h = 1$ (hence $t_k = 1$ and $t_{k+1} = 2$) and solve the resulting 3×3 linear system to obtain the values $\alpha_1 = 1$, $\beta_1 = \frac{3}{2}$, $\beta_2 = -\frac{1}{2}$. Thus, the resulting explicit two-step method is

$$y_{k+1} = y_k + \tfrac{1}{2}(3y'_k - y'_{k-1})h,$$

and by construction it is of order two.

Similarly, we can derive an *implicit* two-step method of the form

$$y_{k+1} = \alpha_1 y_k + (\beta_0 y'_{k+1} + \beta_1 y'_k)h.$$

Again using the method of undetermined coefficients, we force the formula to be exact for the first three monomials, obtaining the three equations

$$1 = \alpha_1 \cdot 1 + (\beta_0 \cdot 0 + \beta_1 \cdot 0)h,$$

$$t_{k+1} = \alpha_1 t_k + (\beta_0 \cdot 1 + \beta_1 \cdot 1)h,$$

$$t_{k+1}^2 = \alpha_1 t_k^2 + (\beta_0 \cdot 2t_{k+1} + \beta_1 \cdot 2t_k)h.$$

Making the convenient choice $t_k = 0$, $h = 1$ (hence, $t_{k+1} = 1$), we solve the resulting 3×3 linear system to obtain the values $\alpha_1 = 1$, $\beta_1 = \frac{1}{2}$, $\beta_2 = \frac{1}{2}$. Thus, the resulting implicit two-step method is

$$y_{k+1} = y_k + \tfrac{1}{2}(y'_{k+1} + y'_k)h,$$

which we recognize as the *trapezoid rule*, and by construction it is of order two. Higher-order multistep methods can be derived in this same manner, forcing the desired formula to be exact for as many monomials as there are parameters to be determined and then solving the resulting system of equations for those parameters.

Alternatively, multistep methods can also be derived by numerical quadrature. For example, since

$$y(t_{k+1}) = y(t_k) + \int_{t_k}^{t_{k+1}} y'(t)\,dt = y(t_k) + \int_{t_k}^{t_{k+1}} f(t, y(t))\,dt,$$

we can take

$$y_{k+1} = y_k + \int_{t_k}^{t_{k+1}} p(t)\,dt,$$

where $p(t)$ is a polynomial interpolating $f(t, y)$ at the points $(t_{k+1-n}, y_{k+1-n}), \ldots, (t_k, y_k)$ for an explicit method of order n, or $(t_{k+2-n}, y_{k+2-n}), \ldots, (t_{k+1}, y_{k+1})$ for an implicit method of order n.

Since multistep methods require several previous solution values and derivative values, how do we get started initially, before we have any past history to use? One strategy is to use a single-step method, which requires no past history, to generate solution values at enough points to begin using a multistep method. Another option is to use a low-order method initially and gradually increase the order as additional solution values become available.

As we saw with single-step methods, implicit multistep methods are usually more accurate and stable than explicit multistep methods, but they require an initial guess to solve the resulting (usually nonlinear) equation for y_{k+1}. A good initial guess is conveniently supplied by an explicit method, so the explicit and implicit methods are used as a *predictor-corrector* pair. One could use the corrector repeatedly (i.e., fixed-point iteration) until some convergence tolerance is met, but doing so may not be worth the expense. So, a fixed number of corrector steps, often only one, may be used instead, giving a *PECE* (predict, evaluate, correct, evaluate) scheme. Although it has no effect on the value of y_{k+1}, the second evaluation of f in a PECE scheme yields an improved value of y'_{k+1} for future use.

Alternatively, the nonlinear equation for y_{k+1} given by an implicit multistep method can be solved by Newton's method or other similar iterative method, again with a good starting guess supplied by the solution at the previous step or by an explicit multistep method. In particular, Newton's method or a close variant of it is essential when using an implicit multistep method designed for stiff ODEs, as fixed-point iteration will fail to converge for reasonable stepsizes.

EXAMPLE 9.16 PREDICTOR-CORRECTOR METHOD. To illustrate the use of a predictor-corrector pair, we use the two multistep methods derived in Example 9.15 to solve the ODE

$$y' = -2ty^2,$$

with initial value $y(0) = 1$. The second-order explicit method requires two starting values, so in addition to the initial value $y_0 = 1$ at $t_0 = 0$ we will also use the value $y_1 = 0.9375$ at $t_1 = 0.25$ obtained using the single-step Heun method in Example 9.14. We can now use the second-order explicit method with stepsize $h = 0.25$ to take a step from $t_1 = 0.25$ to $t_2 = 0.5$, obtaining the *predicted* value

$$\hat{y}_2 = y_1 + \tfrac{1}{2}(3y'_1 - y'_0)h = 0.9375 + 0.5(-1.3184 + 0)0.25 = 0.7727.$$

We *evaluate* f at this predicted value $\hat{y}_2$ to obtain the corresponding derivative value $\hat{y}'_2 = -0.5971$. We can now use these predicted values in the corresponding implicit method (in this case the trapezoid rule) to obtain the *corrected* solution value

$$y_2 = y_1 + \tfrac{1}{2}(y'_2 + y'_1)h = 0.9375 + 0.5(-0.5971 - 0.4395)0.25 = 0.8079.$$

We *evaluate* f again using this new value y_2 to obtain the improved value $y'_2 = -0.6528$, which would be needed in taking further steps. At this point we have completed the PECE procedure for this step. The corrector could be repeated, if desired, until convergence is obtained.

For comparison, the exact solution for this problem is $y(t) = 1/(1 + t^2)$, and hence the true solution at the integration points is $y(0.25) = 0.9412$ and $y(0.5) = 0.8$.

One of the most popular pairs of multistep methods is the explicit fourth-order Adams-Bashforth predictor

$$y_{k+1} = y_k + \tfrac{1}{24}(55y'_k - 59y'_{k-1} + 37y'_{k-2} - 9y'_{k-3})h$$

and the implicit fourth-order Adams-Moulton corrector

$$y_{k+1} = y_k + \tfrac{1}{24}(9y'_{k+1} + 19y'_k - 5y'_{k-1} + y'_{k-2})h.$$

Backward differentiation formulas (BDF), due to Gear, form another important family of implicit multistep methods. BDF methods, typified by the formula

$$y_{k+1} = \tfrac{1}{11}(18y_k - 9y_{k-1} + 2y_{k-2}) + \tfrac{6}{11}y'_{k+1}h,$$

have stability properties that make them particularly effective for solving stiff equations.

The general properties of multistep methods can be summarized as follows:

- They are not self-starting, because several previous solution values are required. Thus, a special starting procedure must be used initially, such as a single-step method, until enough values have been generated to begin using a multistep method of the desired order.
- Changing stepsize is complicated, since the interpolation formulas are most conveniently based on equally spaced intervals for several consecutive points.
- A good local error estimate can be determined from the difference between the predictor and the corrector.
- They are relatively complicated to program.
- Being based on interpolation, they can efficiently provide solution values at output points other than the integration points.
- Implicit methods have a much greater region of stability than explicit methods but must be iterated to convergence to realize this benefit fully (e.g., a PECE scheme is actually explicit, albeit in a somewhat complicated way).
- Although implicit methods are more stable than explicit methods, they are still not necessarily unconditionally stable. Indeed, no multistep method of greater than second order is unconditionally stable, even if it is implicit.
- A properly designed implicit multistep method can be very effective for solving stiff equations.

The stability and accuracy of some of the most popular multistep methods are summarized in Table 9.1, where "stability threshold" indicates the left endpoint of the stability interval for a scalar equation, and "error constant" indicates the coefficient of the h^{p+1} term in the local truncation error, where p is the order of the method. All of these Adams methods have $\alpha_1 = 1$, and $\alpha_i = 0$ for $i > 1$, so we list only the β_i. We observe that the implicit methods are both more stable and more accurate than the corresponding explicit methods of the same order.

TABLE 9.1
Properties of multistep methods

Explicit methods						
Order	β_1	β_2	β_3	β_4	Stability threshold	Error constant
1	1				-2	1/2
2	3/2	$-1/2$			-1	5/12
3	23/12	$-16/12$	5/12		$-6/11$	3/8
4	55/24	$-59/24$	37/24	$-9/24$	$-3/10$	251/720

Implicit methods						
Order	β_1	β_2	β_3	β_4	Stability threshold	Error constant
1	1				$-\infty$	$-1/2$
2	1/2	1/2			$-\infty$	$-1/12$
3	5/12	8/12	$-1/12$		-6	$-1/24$
4	9/24	19/24	$-5/24$	1/24	-3	$-19/720$

9.6.5 Multivalue Methods

As we have seen, changing stepsize is difficult with multistep methods because the past history of the solution is most easily maintained at equally spaced intervals. Like multistep methods, multivalue methods are based on polynomial interpolation, but they avoid many of the implementation difficulties associated with multistep methods.

One of the key ideas motivating multivalue methods is the observation that the interpolating polynomial itself can be evaluated at any point, not just at equally spaced intervals. The equal spacing associated with multistep methods is simply an artifact of the way the methods are represented as a linear combination of successive solution and derivative values with fixed weights.

Another key idea in implementing multivalue methods is choosing the representation of the interpolating polynomial so that its parameters are essentially the values of the solution and one or more of its derivatives at a single point t_k. This approach is analogous to using a Taylor, rather than Lagrange, representation of the polynomial. The solution is advanced in time by a simple transformation of this representation from one point to the next, and changing the stepsize in doing so is easy. Multivalue methods turn out to be mathematically equivalent to multistep methods, but multivalue methods are more convenient and flexible to implement, so most modern software implementations are based on them.

EXAMPLE 9.17 MULTIVALUE METHOD. To make these ideas a bit more concrete, we consider a four-value method for solving an ODE

$$y' = f(t, y).$$

Instead of representing the interpolating polynomial by its value at four different points, we represent it by its value and the values of its first three derivatives at a single point t_k,

$$\mathbf{y}_k = \begin{bmatrix} y_k \\ hy'_k \\ (h^2/2)y''_k \\ (h^3/6)y'''_k \end{bmatrix},$$

where the solution value and derivative values indicated are approximations to those of the true solution. For convenience, the derivatives are scaled to match the coefficients in a Taylor series expansion. By differentiating the Taylor series

$$y(t_k + h) = y(t_k) + hy' + \frac{h^2}{2}y'' + \frac{h^3}{6}y'''_k + \cdots$$

three times, we see that the corresponding values at the next point $t_{k+1} = t_k + h$ are given approximately by the transformation

$$\hat{\mathbf{y}}_{k+1} = B\mathbf{y}_k,$$

where the matrix B is given by

$$B = \begin{bmatrix} 1 & 1 & 1 & 1 \\ 0 & 1 & 2 & 3 \\ 0 & 0 & 1 & 3 \\ 0 & 0 & 0 & 1 \end{bmatrix}.$$

We have not yet used the differential equation, however, so we add a correction term to the foregoing prediction to obtain the final value

$$\mathbf{y}_{k+1} = \hat{\mathbf{y}}_{k+1} + \alpha r,$$

where r is a fixed 4-vector and

$$\alpha = h(f(t_{k+1}, y_{k+1}) - \hat{y}_{k+1}).$$

For consistency, i.e., for the ODE to be satisfied, we must have $r_2 = 1$; but the three remaining components of r can be chosen in various ways, resulting in different methods, analogous to the different choices of parameters in multistep methods. For example, the four-value method with $r = \begin{bmatrix} \frac{3}{8} & 1 & \frac{3}{4} & \frac{1}{6} \end{bmatrix}^T$ is equivalent to the implicit fourth-order Adams-Moulton method given in Section 9.6.4.

We can now see why it is easy to change stepsize with a multivalue method: we need merely rescale the components of $\mathbf{y}_k$ to reflect the new stepsize. Moreover, it is also easy to change the order of the method simply by changing the components of r. These two capabilities, combined with sophisticated tests and strategies for deciding when to change order and stepsize, have led to the development of very powerful and efficient software packages for solving ODEs based on variable-order/variable-step methods. Such routines are analogous to adaptive quadrature routines (see Section 8.4.2) in that they automatically adapt to a given problem, varying the order and stepsize of the integration method as necessary to meet the user-supplied error tolerance in an efficient manner. Such routines often have options for solving either stiff or nonstiff problems, and some even detect stiffness automatically and select an appropriate method accordingly.

The ability to change order easily also obviates the need for special starting procedures. With a variable-order/variable-step method, one can simply start with a first-order method, which requires no additional starting values, and let the automatic order/stepsize selection procedure increase the order as needed for the required accuracy.

9.7 SOFTWARE FOR ODE INITIAL VALUE PROBLEMS

Table 9.2 is a list of some of the software available for numerical solution of initial value problems for ordinary differential equations. Many of these routines have additional variants for special situations, such as root finding or sparse Jacobians. Another important category that we have not discussed is differential-algebraic systems, in which the solution must satisfy a system containing both differential and algebraic equations. The best-known routine for solving such problems is **dassl**, which is available from **netlib**.

Software for solving an ODE $y' = f(t, y)$ typically requires the user to supply the name of a routine that computes the value of the function f for any given values of t and y. Additional input includes the number of equations in the system; the initial values of the independent variable t and the vector y of dependent variables at the start of the integration; the value t_{out} of the independent variable at which the integration is to stop; and absolute or relative error tolerances, or both. Additional input, especially for a stiff ODE solver, may include the name of a routine for computing the Jacobian

TABLE 9.2
Software for ODE initial value problems

Source	Runge-Kutta	Adams	Stiff
FMM	rkf45		
HSL	da02		dc03
IMSL	ivprk	ivpag	ivpag
KMN		sdriv2	sdriv2
MATLAB	ode23/ode45	ode113	ode15s/ode23s
NAG	d02baf	d02caf	d02eaf
NETLIB	dverk	ode	vode/vodpk
NR	odeint		stiff
NUMAL	rke	multistep	gms
ODEPACK		lsode	lsode
SLATEC	derkf	deabm/sdriv1	debdf/sdriv2
TOMS	gerk(#504)		stint(#534)
TOMS	brk45(#669)/rkn(#670)		mebdf(#703)

of f and the name of an array to be used as workspace for storing such matrices. Output typically includes the solution vector y at t_{out}, a status flag indicating any warnings or error conditions, and possibly some measures of the quality and cost of the solution. Usually such software is set up so that it can be called repeatedly, with the new initial t equal to the previous t_{out}, in order to obtain output at desired points across the overall interval of integration.

9.8 HISTORICAL NOTES AND FURTHER READING

Euler proposed his method for initial value problems in 1768. Much of the early impetus for the numerical solution of ordinary differential equations was from celestial mechanics. For example, in 1846 Adams—for whom the classical linear multistep methods are named—finished in a dead heat with Le Verrier in accurately predicting the location at which the planet Neptune would be discovered. Their orbital calculations were based on known but previously unexplained perturbations in the orbit of Uranus.

Runge-Kutta methods were developed independently by Runge and Kutta around 1900. Fehlberg's implementation, which permitted an efficient error estimate, was developed in the 1960s. A practical method based on extrapolation was published by Bulirsch and Stoer in 1966. Gear's method for solving stiff ODEs was published in 1971, along with a very influential computer program **difsub (TOMS #407)** implementing the method. Another influential code for solving ODEs was developed at about the same time by Krogh. Multivalue methods were first proposed by Nordsieck in 1962 to address the implementation difficulties of multistep methods. For the equivalence of multistep and multivalue methods, see Skeel [230].

Recent books on the numerical solution of initial value problems for ODEs include [66, 133, 156, 224]. Earlier textbooks and monographs on this topic include [31, 77, 91, 123, 155, 160, 227]. In addition, see the surveys [32, 58, 92, 111, 226, 228, 238]. Practical advice on using ODE software can be found in [223]. For solving differential-algebraic systems, see [22].

REVIEW QUESTIONS

9.1. True or false: An ODE whose solution curves are unbounded as time increases is necessarily unstable.

9.2. True or false: In the numerical solution of an ODE, the global error grows only if the equation is unstable.

9.3. True or false: In solving an ODE numerically, the roundoff error and the truncation error are independent of each other.

9.4. True or false: In numerically solving an initial value problem for an ODE, the global truncation error is always at least as large as the sum of the local truncation errors.

9.5. True or false: For solving a stable differential equation numerically, an implicit method is always stable.

9.6. True or false: With an unconditionally stable method, one can take arbitrarily large time steps in numerically solving a stable ODE to achieve a given accuracy.

9.7. True or false: Stiff ODEs are always difficult and expensive to solve.

9.8. (*a*) In general, does a differential equation, by itself, determine a unique solution?

(*b*) If so, why, and if not, what additional information must be specified to determine a solution uniquely?

9.9. (*a*) What is meant by a *first-order* ODE?

(*b*) Why are higher-order ODEs usually transformed into equivalent first-order ODEs before solving them numerically?

9.10. (*a*) Describe in words the distinction between a stable ODE and an unstable ODE.

(*b*) What is a mathematical criterion for determining the stability of a *system* of ODEs $y' = f(t, y)$?

(*c*) Can the stability or instability of a system of ODEs change with time?

9.11. Which of the following types of first-order ODEs are stable?

(*a*) An equation whose solution curves converge toward each other

(*b*) An equation whose Jacobian is negative

(*c*) A stiff equation

(*d*) An equation with exponentially decaying solutions

9.12. Classify each of the following ODEs as stable, unstable, or neutrally stable.

(*a*) $y' = y + t$.

(*b*) $y' = y - t$.

(*c*) $y' = t - y$.

(*d*) $y' = 1$.

9.13. How does a typical numerical solution of an ODE differ from an analytical solution?

9.14. (*a*) What is Euler's method for solving an ODE?

(*b*) Show how it is derived.

9.15. Describe in words the difference between the local truncation error and the global truncation error in solving an initial value problem for an ODE numerically.

9.16. Under what condition is the global error in solving an initial value problem for an ODE likely to be smaller than the sum of the local errors at each step?

9.17. In solving an ODE numerically, which is usually more significant, rounding error or truncation error?

9.18. (*a*) Define in words the error amplification factor for one step of a numerical method for solving an initial value problem for an ODE.

(*b*) Does the amplification factor depend only on the equation, only on the method of solution, or on both?

(*c*) What is the value of the amplification factor for one step of Euler's method?

(*d*) What stability region does this imply for Euler's method?

9.19. (*a*) What is the basic difference between an explicit method and an implicit method for solving an ODE numerically?

(*b*) Comparing these two types of methods, list one relative advantage for each.

(*c*) Name a specific example of a method (or family of methods) of each type.

9.20. The use of an implicit method for solving a nonlinear ODE requires the iterative solution of a nonlinear equation. How can one get a good starting guess for this iteration?

9.21. Is it possible for a numerical solution method to be unstable when applied to a stable ODE?

9.22. What does it mean for a numerical ODE method to be of order p?

9.23. (*a*) For solving ODEs, what is the highest-order accuracy that a linear multistep method can have and still be unconditionally stable?
   (*b*) Give an example of a method having these properties (by name or by formula).

9.24. Compare the stability regions (i.e., the stability constraints on the stepsize) for the Euler and backward Euler methods for solving a scalar ODE.

9.25. For the backward Euler method, which factor places a stronger restriction on the choice of stepsize: stability or accuracy?

9.26. Which of the following numerical methods for solving a stable ODE numerically are unconditionally stable?
   (*a*) Euler's method
   (*b*) Backward Euler method
   (*c*) Trapezoid rule

9.27. (*a*) What is meant by a *stiff* ODE?
   (*b*) Why may a stiff ODE be difficult to solve numerically?
   (*c*) What type of method is appropriate for solving stiff ODEs?

9.28. Suppose one is using the backward Euler method to solve a nonlinear ODE numerically. The resulting nonlinear algebraic equation at each step must be solved iteratively. If a fixed number of iterations are performed at each step, is the resulting method unconditionally stable?

9.29. Explain why implicit methods are better than explicit methods for solving stiff systems of ODEs numerically.

9.30. What is the simplest numerical method that is stable for integrating a stiff ODE?

9.31. For solving ODEs numerically, why is it usually impractical to generate methods of very high accuracy by using many terms in a Taylor series expansion?

9.32. In solving an ODE numerically, with which type of method, Runge-Kutta or multistep, is it easier to supply values for the numerical solution at arbitrary output points within each step?

9.33. (*a*) What is the basic difference between a single-step method and a multistep method for solving an ODE numerically?
   (*b*) Comparing these two types of methods, list one relative advantage for each.
   (*c*) Name a specific example of a method (or family of methods) of each type.

9.34. List two advantages and two disadvantages of multistep methods compared with classical Runge-Kutta methods for solving ODEs numerically.

9.35. What is the principal drawback of a Taylor series method compared with a Runge-Kutta method for solving ODEs?

9.36. (*a*) What is the principal advantage of extrapolation methods for solving ODEs numerically?
   (*b*) What are the disadvantages of such methods?

9.37. In using a multistep method to solve an ODE numerically, why might one still need to have a single-step method available?

9.38. Why are multistep methods for solving ODEs numerically often used in predictor-corrector pairs?

9.39. If a predictor-corrector method for solving an ODE is implemented as a PECE scheme, does the second evaluation affect the value obtained for the solution at the point being computed? If so, what is the effect, and if not, then why is the second evaluation done?

9.40. List two reasons why multivalue methods are easier to implement than multistep methods for solving ODEs adaptively with automatic error control.

9.41. For each of the following properties, state which type of ODE method, multistep or classical Runge-Kutta, more accurately fits the description:
   (*a*) Self starting

(b) More efficient in attaining high accuracy

(c) Can be efficient for stiff problems

(d) Easier to program

(e) Easier to change stepsize

(f) Easier to obtain a local error estimate

(g) Easier to produce output at arbitrary intermediate points within each step

9.42. Give two approaches to starting a multistep method initially when past solution history is not yet available.

EXERCISES

9.1. Write each of the following ODEs as an equivalent first-order system of ODEs:

(a) $y'' = t + y + y'$.

(b) $y''' = y'' + ty$.

(c) $y''' = y'' - 2y' + y - t + 1$.

9.2. Write each of the following ODEs as an equivalent first-order system of ODEs:

(a) Van der Pol equation:

$$y'' = y'(1 - y^2) - y.$$

(b) Blasius equation:

$$y''' = -y y''.$$

(c) Newton's Second Law of Motion for two-body problem:

$$y_1'' = -GM y_1/(y_1^2 + y_2^2)^{3/2},$$
$$y_2'' = -GM y_2/(y_1^2 + y_2^2)^{3/2}.$$

9.3. Is the following system of ODEs stable?

$$y_1' = -y_1 + y_2,$$
$$y_2' = -2y_2.$$

Explain your answer.

9.4. Consider the ODE $y' = -5y$ with initial condition $y(0) = 1$. We will solve this ODE numerically using a stepsize of $h = 0.5$.

(a) Is this ODE stable?

(b) Is Euler's method stable for this ODE using this stepsize?

(c) Compute the numerical value for the approximate solution at $t = 0.5$ given by Euler's method.

(d) Is the backward Euler method stable for this ODE using this stepsize?

(e) Compute the numerical value for the approximate solution at $t = 0.5$ given by the backward Euler method.

9.5. With an initial value of $y_0 = 1$ at $t_0 = 0$ and a time step of $h = 1$, compute the approximate solution value y_1 at time $t_1 = 1$ for the ODE $y' = -y$ using each of the following two numerical methods. (Your answers should be numbers, not formulas.)

(a) Euler's method

(b) Backward Euler method

9.6. For the ODE, initial value, and stepsize given in Example 9.10, prove that fixed-point iteration for solving the implicit equation for y_1 is in fact convergent. What is the convergence rate?

9.7. Consider the initial value problem

$$y'' = y$$

for $t \geq 0$, with initial values $y(0) = 1$ and $y'(0) = 2$.

(a) Express this second-order ODE as an equivalent system of two first-order ODEs.

(b) What are the corresponding initial conditions for the system of ODEs in part a?

(c) Is this a stable system of ODEs?

(d) Perform one step of Euler's method for this ODE system using a stepsize of $h = 0.5$.

(e) Is Euler's method stable for this problem using this stepsize?

(f) Is the backward Euler method stable for this problem using this stepsize?

9.8. Consider the initial value problem for the ODE $y' = -y^2$ with the initial condition $y(0) = 1$. We will use the backward Euler method to compute the approximate value of the solution y_1 at time $t_1 = 0.1$ (i.e., take one step using the backward Euler method with stepsize $h = 0.1$ starting from $y_0 = 1$ at $t_0 = 0$). Since the backward Euler method is implicit, and the ODE is nonlinear, we will need to solve a nonlinear algebraic equation for y_1.

(a) Write out that nonlinear algebraic equation for y_1.

(b) Write out the Newton iteration for solving the nonlinear algebraic equation.

(c) Obtain a starting guess for the Newton iteration by using one step of Euler's method for the ODE.

(d) Finally, compute an approximate value for the solution y_1 by using one iteration of Newton's method for the nonlinear algebraic equation.

9.9. For solving an ODE $y' = f(t, y)$ numerically, each of the following methods,

(1) $\quad y_{k+1} = y_k + \frac{1}{2}[f(t_k, y_k)$
$\quad\quad\quad + f(t_{k+1}, y_k + f(t_k, y_k)h)]h,$

(2) $\quad y_{k+1} = y_k + \frac{1}{2}[3f(t_k, y_k)$
$\quad\quad\quad - f(t_{k-1}, y_{k-1})]h,$

(3) $\quad y_{k+1} = y_k + \frac{1}{2}[f(t_k, y_k)$
$\quad\quad\quad + f(t_{k+1}, y_{k+1})]h,$

is of second order, but the methods also have important differences. For each property listed, state which of the three methods has or have the given property.

(a) Single-step method
(b) Implicit method
(c) Self-starting
(d) Unconditionally stable
(e) Runge-Kutta type method

(f) Good for solving a stiff ODE

9.10. Use the linear ODE $y' = \lambda y$ to analyze the accuracy and stability of Heun's method (see Section 9.6.2). In particular, verify that this method is second-order accurate, and describe or plot its stability region in the complex plane.

9.11. The centered difference approximation

$$y' \approx \frac{y_{k+1} - y_{k-1}}{2h}$$

leads to the two-step *leapfrog method*

$$y_{k+1} = y_{k-1} + f(t_k, y_k)2h$$

for solving the ODE $y' = f(t, y)$. Determine the order of accuracy and the stability region of this method.

9.12. Let A be an $n \times n$ matrix. Compare and contrast the behavior of the linear difference equation

$$x_{k+1} = Ax_k$$

with that of the linear differential equation

$$x' = Ax.$$

What is the general solution in each case? In each case, what property of the matrix A would imply that the solution remains bounded for any starting vector x_0? You may assume that the matrix A is diagonalizable.

COMPUTER PROBLEMS

9.1. The populations of two species, a prey denoted by y_1 and predator denoted by y_2, can be modeled by a system of ODEs

$$y_1' = by_1 - cy_1y_2,$$
$$y_2' = -dy_2 + cy_1y_2,$$

due to Lotka and Volterra. The parameters b and d govern the birth rate of prey and death rate of predators, respectively, and the parameter c governs the interaction of the two populations. With the parameter values $b = 1$, $d = 10$, and $c = 1$, and initial conditions $y_1(0) = 0.5$ and $y_2(0) = 1$ (the populations are normalized, and we treat them as continuous variables), use a library routine to solve this system numerically, integrating to $t = 10$. Plot each of the two populations

as a function of time, and on a separate graph plot the trajectory of the point $(y_1(t), y_2(t))$ in the plane as a function of time. The latter is sometimes called a "phase portrait." Give a physical interpretation of the behavior you observe. Can you find nonzero initial populations such that either of the populations eventually becomes extinct?

9.2. The *Kermack-McKendrick model* for the course of an epidemic in a population is given by the system of ODEs

$$y_1' = -cy_1y_2,$$
$$y_2' = cy_1y_2 - dy_2,$$
$$y_3' = dy_2,$$

where y_1 represents susceptibles, y_2 represents infectives in circulation, and y_3 represents infectives removed by isolation, death, or recovery and immunity. The parameters c and d represent the infection rate and removal rate, respectively. Use a library routine to solve this system numerically, with the parameter values $c = 1$ and $d = 5$, and initial values $y_1(0) = 95$, $y_2(0) = 5$, $y_3(0) = 0$. Integrate from $t = 0$ to $t = 1$. Plot each solution component on the same graph as a function of t. As expected with an epidemic, you should see the number of infectives grow at first, then diminish to zero. Experiment with other values for the parameters and initial conditions. Can you find values for which the epidemic does not grow, or for which the entire population is wiped out?

9.3. Suppose that we have three chemical species whose concentrations are denoted by y_1, y_2, and y_3. If the rate of the reaction $y_1 \rightarrow y_2$ is proportional to y_1, and the rate of the reaction $y_2 \rightarrow y_3$ is proportional to y_2, then the concentrations are governed by the system of ODEs

$$y_1' = -k_1 y_1,$$
$$y_2' = k_1 y_1 - k_2 y_2,$$
$$y_3' = k_2 y_2,$$

where k_1 and k_2 are the rate constants for the two reactions.

(*a*) What is the Jacobian matrix for this ODE system, and what are its eigenvalues? If the rate constants are positive, is this system stable? Under what conditions will the system be stiff?

(*b*) Solve the ODE system numerically, assuming initial concentrations $y_1(0) = y_2(0) = y_3(0) = 1$. Take $k_1 = 1$ and experiment with values of k_2 of varying magnitude, specifically, $k_2 = 10$, 100, and 1000. For each value of k_2, solve the system using a Runge-Kutta method, an Adams method, and a method designed for stiff systems, such as a backward differentiation formula. You may use library routines for this purpose, or you may wish to develop your own routines, perhaps using the classical fourth-order Runge-Kutta method, the fourth-order Adams-Bashforth predictor and Adams-Moulton corrector, and the BDF formula given in Section 9.6. If you develop your own codes, a fixed stepsize will suffice for this exercise. If you use library routines, compare the different methods with respect to their efficiency, as measured by function evaluations or execution time, for a given accuracy. If you develop you own codes, compare the different methods with respect to accuracy and stability for a given stepsize. In each instance, integrate the ODE system from $t = 0$ until the solution is approximately in steady state, or until the method is clearly unstable or grossly inefficient.

9.4. Experiment with several different library routines having automatic stepsize selection to solve the ODE

$$y' = -200ty^2$$

numerically. Consider two different initial conditions, $y(0) = 1$ and $y(-3) = 1/901$, and in each case compute the solution until $t = 1$. Monitor the stepsize used by the routines and discuss how and why it changes as the solution progresses. Explain the difference in behavior for the two different initial conditions. Compare the different routines with respect to efficiency for a given accuracy requirement.

9.5. A definite integral $\int_a^b f(t)\, dt$ can be evaluated by solving the equivalent ODE $y'(t) = f(t)$, $a \le t \le b$, with initial condition $y(a) = 0$. The value of the integral is then simply $y(b)$. Use a library ODE solver to evaluate each definite integral in the first several Computer Problems for Chapter 8, and compare its efficiency with that of an adaptive quadrature routine for the same accuracy.

9.6. Homotopy methods for solving systems of nonlinear algebraic equations parameterize the solution space $x(t)$ and then follow a trajectory from an initial guess to the final solution. As one example of this approach, for solving a system of nonlinear equations $f(x) = 0$, where $f: \mathbb{R}^n \rightarrow \mathbb{R}^n$, with initial guess x_0, the following ODE initial value problem is a continuous analogue of Newton's method:

$$x' = -J_f^{-1}(x)f(x), \quad x(0) = x_0,$$

where J_f is the Jacobian matrix of f, and of course the inverse need not be computed explicitly. Use this method to solve the nonlinear system given in Computer Problem 5.13. Starting from the given initial guess, integrate the resulting system of ODEs from $t = 0$ until a steady state is reached. Compare the resulting solution with that obtained by a conventional nonlinear system solver. Plot the trajectory of the components of $x(t)$ from $t = 0$ to the final solution. You may also want to try this technique on some of the other Computer Problems from Chapter 5.

9.7. An important problem in classical mechanics is the motion of two bodies under mutual gravitational attraction. Suppose that a body of mass m is orbiting a second body of much larger mass M, such as the earth orbiting the sun. From Newton's laws of motion and gravitation, the orbital trajectory $(x(t), y(t))$ is described by the system of second-order ODEs

$$x'' = -GMx/r^3,$$

$$y'' = -GMy/r^3,$$

where G is the gravitational constant and $r = (x^2 + y^2)^{1/2}$ is the distance of the orbiting body from the center of mass of the two bodies. For this exercise, we choose units such that $GM = 1$.

  (a) Use a library routine to solve this system of ODEs with the initial conditions

$$x(0) = 1 - e, \qquad y(0) = 0,$$

$$x'(0) = 0 \qquad y'(0) = \sqrt{(1 + e)/(1 - e)},$$

where e is the eccentricity of the resulting elliptical orbit, which has period 2π. Try the values $e = 0$ (which should give a circular orbit), $e = 0.5$, and $e = 0.9$. For each case, solve the ODE for at least one period and obtain output at enough intermediate points to draw a smooth plot of the orbital trajectory. Make separate plots of x versus t, y versus t, and y versus x. Experiment with different error tolerances to see how they affect the cost of the integration and how close the orbit comes to being closed. If you trace the trajectory through several periods, does the orbit tend to wander or remain steady?

  (b) Check your numerical solutions in part a to see how well they conserve the following quantities, which should remain constant:

  Conservation of energy:

$$\frac{(x')^2 + (y')^2}{2} - \frac{1}{r}$$

  Conservation of angular momentum:

$$x\,y' - y\,x'$$

9.8. Consider a restricted form of the three-body problem in which a body of small mass orbits two other bodies with much larger masses, such as an Apollo spacecraft orbiting the earth-moon system. We will use a two-dimensional coordinate system in the plane determined by the three bodies, with the origin at the center of mass of the two larger bodies, and the coordinate

system rotating so that the two larger bodies appear fixed. The coordinate system is shown in the accompanying diagram,

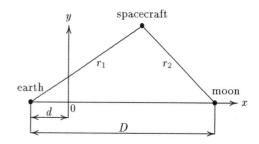

where D is the distance from earth to moon, d is the distance from the center of earth to the center of mass, r_1 is the distance from earth to spacecraft, and r_2 is the distance from moon to spacecraft. The mass of the spacecraft is assumed to be negligible compared with the other masses.

  By using Newton's laws of motion and gravitation, and allowing for the centrifugal and Coriolis forces due to the rotating coordinate system, the motion of the spacecraft is described by the system of second-order ODEs

$$\begin{aligned} x'' = -\,&G\,[M(x + \mu D)/r_1^3 \\ &+ m(x - \mu^* D)/r_2^3] \\ &+ \Omega^2 x + 2\Omega y', \end{aligned}$$

$$\begin{aligned} y'' = -\,&G\,[My/r_1^3 + my/r_2^3] \\ &+ \Omega^2 y - 2\Omega x', \end{aligned}$$

where G is the gravitational constant, M and m are the masses of earth and moon, μ^* and μ are the mass fractions of earth and moon, and Ω is the angular velocity of rotation of the moon about the earth (and hence of the coordinate system). The numerical values of these quantities are given in the following table:

G	6.67259×10^{-11} m^3/(kg $\cdot$ s^2)
M	5.974×10^{24} kg
m	7.348×10^{22} kg
μ^*	$M/(m + M)$
μ	$m/(m + M)$
D	3.844×10^8 m
d	4.669×10^6 m
r_1	$[(x + d)^2 + y^2]^{1/2}$
r_2	$[(D - d - x)^2 + y^2]^{1/2}$
Ω	2.661×10^{-6}/s

Use a library routine to solve this system of ODEs with the initial conditions

$$x(0) = 4.613 \times 10^8, \qquad y(0) = 0,$$

$$x'(0) = 0, \qquad y'(0) = -1074.$$

Plot the resulting solution trajectory $(x(t), y(t))$ in the plane as a function of time. Indicate the positions of earth and moon on the graph. Compute the solution for at least one complete orbit (i.e., until the spacecraft returns to its original location), which is from $t = 0$ until approximately $t = 2.4 \times 10^6$ s. Experiment with various error tolerances to see how much difference they make in whether the orbit is actually closed. Try to monitor the stepsize used by the ODE routine as the integration progresses. When does the stepsize become smaller or larger? How close does the spacecraft come to the surface of earth? (Earth's radius is 6.378×10^6 m, so the center of mass of the earth-moon system is actually *inside* the earth.)

CHAPTER 10

Boundary Value Problems for Ordinary Differential Equations

10.1 BOUNDARY VALUE PROBLEMS

Thus far we have considered only initial value problems for ordinary differential equations. We will now broaden our view to consider boundary value problems. A boundary value problem for a differential equation specifies more than one point at which the solution or its derivatives must have given values. For example, a two-point boundary value problem for a second-order ODE has the form

$$y'' = f(t, y, y'), \quad a \leq t \leq b,$$

with boundary conditions

$$y(a) = \alpha, \qquad y(b) = \beta.$$

An initial value problem for such a second-order equation would have specified both y and y' at a single point, say, t_0. These initial data would have supplied all the information necessary to begin a numerical solution method at t_0, stepping forward to advance the solution in time (or whatever the independent variable might be).

More generally, to single out a particular solution there must as many conditions specified as the order of a scalar ODE, or as the number of components in a first-order system of ODEs. If all the conditions are specified at the *same* point, then we have an initial value problem; otherwise, we have a boundary value problem. For example, a boundary value problem for a system of two first-order ODEs has the form

$$\begin{bmatrix} y_1' \\ y_2' \end{bmatrix} = \begin{bmatrix} f_1(t, y) \\ f_2(t, y) \end{bmatrix}, \quad a \leq t \leq b,$$

with boundary conditions

$$y_1(a) = \alpha, \quad y_2(b) = \beta.$$

The specification of boundary conditions at more than one point in a boundary value problem does not permit as simple a numerical approach as for initial value problems and also can make the existence and uniqueness of a solution more problematic. We will focus on the simplest case, that of two-point boundary problems for second-order ODEs, and we will consider several approaches for solving them numerically. These methods can be generalized to higher-order ODEs, and some of them carry over to partial differential equations as well (see Chapter 11).

10.2 SHOOTING METHOD

The *shooting method* replaces a given boundary value problem with a sequence of initial value problems whose solutions converge to that of the original boundary value problem. In the statement of a two-point boundary value problem for a second-order ODE, we are given the value of $y(a)$. If we also knew the value of $y'(a)$, then we would have an initial value problem that we could solve by one of the methods discussed in Chapter 9. Lacking that information, however, we can try a sequence of increasingly accurate guesses until we find a value for $y'(a)$ such that when we solve the resulting initial value problem, the approximate solution value at $t = b$ matches the desired boundary value, $y(b) = \beta$.

The basic idea of the shooting method is illustrated in Fig. 10.1. Each curve represents a solution of the same second-order ODE, with different values for the initial slope giving different solution curves. All of the solutions start with the given initial value $y(a) = \alpha$, but for only one value of the initial slope does the resulting solution curve hit the desired boundary condition $y(b) = \beta$.

Putting this approach more formally, for a given s, the value at the point b of the solution $y(b)$ to the initial value problem

$$y'' = f(t, y, y'),$$

with initial conditions

$$y(a) = \alpha, \qquad y'(a) = s,$$

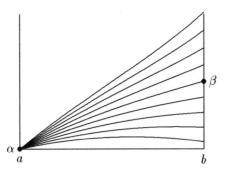

FIGURE 10.1
Shooting method for a two-point boundary value problem.

can be considered as a function of s, say, $g(s)$. Then the boundary value problem becomes the problem of solving the equation $g(s) = \beta$. A one-dimensional zero finder (see Section 5.2) can be used to solve this scalar equation.

EXAMPLE 10.1 SHOOTING METHOD. We illustrate the shooting method by solving the two-point boundary value problem for the second-order ordinary differential equation

$$y'' = 6t, \qquad 0 \le t \le 1,$$

with boundary conditions

$$y(0) = 0 \quad \text{and} \quad y(1) = 1.$$

For each guess for $y'(0)$, we will integrate the ODE using the classical fourth-order Runge-Kutta method to determine how close we come to hitting the desired solution value at $t = 1$. Before doing so, however, we must first transform the second-order ODE into a system of two first-order ODEs

$$\begin{bmatrix} y_1' \\ y_2' \end{bmatrix} = \begin{bmatrix} y_2 \\ 6t \end{bmatrix}.$$

We first try an initial slope of $y'(0) = 1$. Using a stepsize of $h = 0.5$, we first step from $t_0 = 0$ to $t_1 = 0.5$. The classical fourth-order Runge-Kutta method gives the approximate solution value at t_1

$$y^{(1)} = y^{(0)} + \frac{1}{6}(k_1 + 2k_2 + 2k_3 + k_4)$$

$$= \begin{bmatrix} 0 \\ 1 \end{bmatrix} + \frac{1}{6}\left(\begin{bmatrix} 0.5 \\ 0.0 \end{bmatrix} + 2\begin{bmatrix} 0.50 \\ 0.75 \end{bmatrix} + 2\begin{bmatrix} 0.6875 \\ 0.7500 \end{bmatrix} + \begin{bmatrix} 0.875 \\ 1.500 \end{bmatrix} \right) = \begin{bmatrix} 0.625 \\ 1.750 \end{bmatrix}.$$

Next we step from $t_1 = 0.5$ to $t_2 = 1$, obtaining

$$y^{(2)} = \begin{bmatrix} 0.625 \\ 1.750 \end{bmatrix} + \frac{1}{6}\left(\begin{bmatrix} 0.875 \\ 1.500 \end{bmatrix} + 2\begin{bmatrix} 1.25 \\ 2.25 \end{bmatrix} + 2\begin{bmatrix} 1.4375 \\ 2.2500 \end{bmatrix} + \begin{bmatrix} 2.0 \\ 3.0 \end{bmatrix} \right) = \begin{bmatrix} 2.0 \\ 4.0 \end{bmatrix},$$

so we have hit the value $y(1) = 2$ instead of the desired value $y(1) = 1$. We try again, this time with an initial slope of $y'(0) = -1$, obtaining

$$y^{(1)} = \begin{bmatrix} 0 \\ -1 \end{bmatrix} + \frac{1}{6}\left(\begin{bmatrix} -0.5 \\ 0.0 \end{bmatrix} + 2\begin{bmatrix} -0.50 \\ 0.75 \end{bmatrix} + 2\begin{bmatrix} -0.3125 \\ 0.7500 \end{bmatrix} + \begin{bmatrix} -1.25 \\ 1.50 \end{bmatrix} \right) = \begin{bmatrix} -0.375 \\ -0.250 \end{bmatrix}$$

and $\quad y^{(2)} = \begin{bmatrix} -0.375 \\ -0.250 \end{bmatrix} + \frac{1}{6}\left(\begin{bmatrix} -0.125 \\ 1.500 \end{bmatrix} + 2\begin{bmatrix} 0.25 \\ 2.25 \end{bmatrix} + 2\begin{bmatrix} 0.4375 \\ 2.2500 \end{bmatrix} + \begin{bmatrix} 1.0 \\ 3.0 \end{bmatrix} \right) = \begin{bmatrix} 0.0 \\ 2.0 \end{bmatrix},$

so we have hit the value $y(1) = 0$ instead of the desired value $y(1) = 1$. We now have the initial slope bracketed between -1 and 1. We omit the further iterations necessary to identify the correct initial slope, which turns out to be $y'(0) = 0$:

$$y^{(1)} = \begin{bmatrix} 0 \\ 0 \end{bmatrix} + \frac{1}{6}\left(\begin{bmatrix} 0.0 \\ 0.0 \end{bmatrix} + 2\begin{bmatrix} 0.00 \\ 0.75 \end{bmatrix} + 2\begin{bmatrix} 0.1875 \\ 0.7500 \end{bmatrix} + \begin{bmatrix} 0.375 \\ 1.500 \end{bmatrix} \right) = \begin{bmatrix} 0.125 \\ 0.750 \end{bmatrix}$$

and $\quad y^{(2)} = \begin{bmatrix} 0.125 \\ 0.750 \end{bmatrix} + \frac{1}{6}\left(\begin{bmatrix} 0.375 \\ 1.500 \end{bmatrix} + 2\begin{bmatrix} 0.75 \\ 2.25 \end{bmatrix} + 2\begin{bmatrix} 0.9375 \\ 2.2500 \end{bmatrix} + \begin{bmatrix} 1.5 \\ 3.0 \end{bmatrix} \right) = \begin{bmatrix} 1.0 \\ 3.0 \end{bmatrix},$

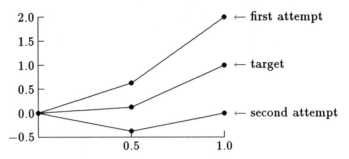

FIGURE 10.2
Shooting method for two-point boundary value problem in
Example 10.1.

so we have indeed hit the target solution value, $y(1) = 1$. These results are illustrated in
Fig. 10.2.

A potential difficulty with the shooting method is that the initial value problem
may be ill-conditioned, perhaps owing to diverging solution curves over part of the
domain, which may make it difficult to hit the desired target. A remedy is provided by
multiple shooting, in which the interval $[a, b]$ is divided into subintervals and shooting
is carried out over each subinterval. Requiring continuity at the internal mesh points
provides the boundary conditions for the individual subproblems. Therefore, multiple
shooting results in a *system* of nonlinear equations to solve rather than just a single
scalar equation.

10.3 SUPERPOSITION METHOD

Another way of replacing boundary value problems with initial value problems is the
superposition method. Consider the homogeneous, linear, second-order ODE

$$y'' = p(t)y + q(t)y', \qquad a \le t \le b,$$

with boundary conditions

$$y(a) = \alpha, \qquad y(b) = \beta.$$

The solution can be expressed as a *superposition* (i.e., linear combination) of two independent solutions, which can be obtained numerically by solving the equation with
each of the two sets of *initial* conditions

$$y(a) = 1, \qquad y'(a) = 0 \qquad \text{and} \qquad y(a) = 0, \qquad y'(a) = 1.$$

This method becomes somewhat more complicated if the equation is inhomogeneous,
and much more complicated if the equation is nonlinear. Moreover, it may be necessary
to use orthogonalization to maintain independence of the solutions computed for the
initial value problems.

10.4 FINITE DIFFERENCE METHOD

Both the shooting and superposition methods convert boundary value problems into initial value problems. We now consider methods that approximate boundary value problems directly by systems of algebraic equations. Finite difference methods convert boundary value problems into systems of algebraic equations by replacing any derivatives that appear with finite difference approximations. For example, to solve the two-point boundary value problem

$$y'' = f(t, y, y'), \qquad a \le t \le b,$$

with boundary conditions

$$y(a) = \alpha, \qquad y(b) = \beta,$$

we first divide the interval $[a, b]$ into n equally spaced subintervals. Let $t_i = a + ih$, $i = 0, 1, \ldots, n$, where $h = (b-a)/n$. We seek an approximation $y_i \approx y(t_i)$ at each of the mesh points t_i. We already have $y_0 = \alpha$ and $y_n = \beta$. We next replace the derivatives with finite difference approximations (see Section 8.7.1), such as

$$y'(t_i) \approx \frac{y_{i+1} - y_{i-1}}{2h} \qquad \text{and} \qquad y''(t_i) \approx \frac{y_{i+1} - 2y_i + y_{i-1}}{h^2},$$

choosing the finite difference formulas so that they have the same order truncation error, in this case $\mathcal{O}(h^2)$, since the accuracy will be limited by the least accurate formula. This replacement yields a system of algebraic equations

$$y_{i+1} - 2y_i + y_{i-1} - h^2 f\left(t_i, y_i, \frac{y_{i+1} - y_{i-1}}{2h}\right) = 0$$

to be solved for the unknowns y_i, $i = 1, \ldots, n - 1$. This system of equations may be linear or nonlinear, depending on whether f is linear or nonlinear in y and y'. In this example, each equation in the system involves only three adjacent unknowns, which means that the matrix of the linear system—or the Jacobian matrix in the nonlinear case—is tridiagonal, thereby saving on both work and storage compared with a general system of equations. Such savings are generally true of finite difference methods: they yield sparse systems because each equation involves only a few variables.

EXAMPLE 10.2 FINITE DIFFERENCE METHOD. We demonstrate the finite difference method by using it to solve the two-point boundary value problem of Example 10.1,

$$y'' = 6t, \qquad 0 \le t \le 1,$$

with boundary conditions

$$y(0) = 0 \qquad \text{and} \qquad y(1) = 1.$$

To illustrate the concepts involved, yet keep computation to a minimum, we will compute an approximate solution at a single mesh point in the interval $[0, 1]$, namely $t = 0.5$. Thus, including the boundary points, we have three mesh points, $t_0 = 0$, $t_1 = 0.5$, and $t_2 = 1$. From the boundary conditions, we know that $y_0 = y(t_0) = 0$ and $y_2 = y(t_2) = 1$, and we seek an approximate solution $y_1 \approx y(t_1)$. Approximating the second derivative by a standard finite difference quotient at the point t_1 gives the equation

$$\frac{y_2 - 2y_1 + y_0}{h^2} = f(t_1, y_1, y_1').$$

Substituting the boundary data, mesh size, and right-hand side for this example, we obtain

$$\frac{1 - 2y_1 + 0}{(0.5)^2} = 6t_1,$$

or

$$4 - 8y_1 = 6(0.5) = 3,$$

so that

$$y(0.5) \approx y_1 = \tfrac{1}{8} = 0.125,$$

which agrees with the approximate solution at $t = 0.5$ that we computed by the shooting method in Example 10.1.

In a practical problem, a much smaller stepsize and many more mesh points would be required to achieve acceptable accuracy, and we would therefore obtain a *system* of equations to solve for the approximate solution values at the mesh points, rather than a single equation as in this example. Nevertheless, this system would still be easy to solve because it would be tridiagonal.

10.5 FINITE ELEMENT METHOD

Another approach to reducing boundary value problems to algebraic systems is the *finite element method*. Finite element methods approximate the solution to a boundary value problem by a linear combination of a finite collection of basis functions ϕ_i, typically piecewise polynomials, which for historical reasons are called "elements." The approximation therefore has the form

$$y(t) \approx u(t) = \sum_{i=1}^{n} x_i \phi_i(t).$$

The coefficients x_i are determined by imposing one of several possible requirements on the residual, which is defined, as usual, to be the difference between the left and right sides of the differential equation. For this reason, these methods are also known as *weighted residual* methods. Each of the three most commonly used criteria leads to a different class of methods:

- *Collocation:* The residual is zero (i.e., the differential equation is satisfied exactly) at n discrete points.
- *Galerkin:* The residual is orthogonal to the space spanned by the basis functions.
- *Rayleigh-Ritz:* The residual is minimized in a weighted least squares sense.

The latter two criteria are often equivalent. It may be helpful in understanding them to recall Fig. 3.2: the true solution to the differential equation does not in general lie in the space spanned by the basis functions, so we seek an approximate solution (i.e., a linear combination of basis functions) such that the residual is minimized, or is orthogonal to the space spanned by the basis functions. Because they are based on an inner product on a function space, these two methods involve the computation of integrals, either analytically or by some quadrature rule.

Each of these three criteria leads to a system of equations to be solved for the coefficients x_i. The system of equations may be linear or nonlinear, depending on whether f is linear or nonlinear. The system will be sparse, and hence require much less work and storage, if the elements are "local," which means that each basis function is zero throughout most of the domain of the problem and that they have little overlap. Typical examples in one dimension are B-splines, such as the piecewise linear "hat" functions (see Section 7.3.4). The resulting sparse matrix of the system, called the *stiffness matrix*, is assembled element by element and is a sum of contributions from each element.

A related family of methods, called *spectral methods*, uses eigenfunctions of the differential operator as basis functions for expanding the approximate solution (e.g., trigonometric series for the second derivative operator). Similar use of other basis functions, such as Legendre or Chebyshev polynomials, leads to a *pseudospectral method*.

EXAMPLE 10.3 COLLOCATION METHOD. We first illustrate the finite element method by using collocation to solve the two-point boundary value problem of Example 10.1,

$$y'' = 6t, \qquad 0 \le t \le 1,$$

with boundary conditions

$$y(0) = 0 \qquad \text{and} \qquad y(1) = 1.$$

With the finite element method, we approximate the solution of the ODE by a function rather than by a table of approximate values. Specifically, using the collocation method, we seek a function $u(t)$ that satisfies the boundary conditions and also satisfies the ODE exactly at a discrete set of mesh points in the interval. Again, for simplicity, we will use only one interior mesh point, namely $t = 0.5$. For illustrative purposes, the function we choose is a quadratic polynomial represented in the monomial basis, so

$$u(t) = x_0 + x_1 t + x_2 t^2.$$

Note that

$$u'(t) = x_1 + 2x_2 t, \qquad \text{and} \qquad u''(t) = 2x_2.$$

In determining the coefficients x_i, we will enforce the boundary conditions at the endpoints of the interval, and the ODE at the point $t = 0.5$. For a general second-order two-point boundary value problem

$$y'' = f(t, y, y'), \qquad a \le t \le b,$$

with boundary conditions

$$y(a) = \alpha \qquad \text{and} \qquad y(b) = \beta,$$

these requirements give the three equations,

$$x_0 + x_1 a + x_2 a^2 = \alpha, \qquad x_0 + x_1 b + x_2 b^2 = \beta, \qquad \text{and} \qquad u''(t) = f(t, u(t), u'(t)).$$

Substituting the data and functions for this example, we obtain the system of three equations

$$x_0 = 0, \qquad x_1 + x_2 = 1, \qquad \text{and} \qquad 2x_2 = 6(0.5) = 3,$$

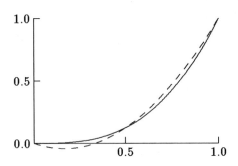

FIGURE 10.3
True solution (solid line) and approximate
solution (dashed line) obtained by collocation.

which has the solution

$$x_0 = 0, \qquad x_1 = -0.5, \qquad x_2 = 1.5.$$

Thus, the approximate solution function is

$$y(t) \approx u(t) = -0.5t + 1.5t^2.$$

At the collocation point, $t = 0.5$, where we forced the function u to satisfy the ODE exactly, we have the approximate solution value

$$y(0.5) \approx u(0.5) = (-0.5)(0.5) + (1.5)(0.25) = 0.125,$$

which agrees with the solution value at $t = 0.5$ that we obtained previously by both the shooting method (Example 10.1) and the finite difference method (Example 10.2).

   In general, these three methods would not produce exactly the same results, but they do so here because of the particular nature of the problem. The analytical solution is easily seen to be $y(t) = t^3$, so that the value $y(0.5) = (0.5)^3 = 0.125$ is in fact exact. We note that the quadratic polynomial produced by the collocation method agrees with the true solution at the three points $t_0 = 0$, $t_1 = 0.5$, and $t_2 = 1$ but does not agree exactly with the true solution at any other points (why?). The approximate and exact solutions are plotted in Fig. 10.3.

EXAMPLE 10.4 GALERKIN METHOD. We further illustrate the concepts involved in the finite element method by again solving the two-point boundary value problem of Example 10.1,

$$y'' = 6t, \qquad 0 \le t \le 1,$$

with boundary conditions

$$y(0) = 0 \qquad \text{and} \qquad y(1) = 1,$$

this time using the Galerkin method with piecewise linear polynomials. We again use the same three mesh points, but now they become the knots in the piecewise linear polynomial approximation. A convenient basis is given by the "hat" functions shown in Fig. 10.4.

   Thus, we seek an approximate solution of the form

$$y(t) \approx u(t) = x_1\phi_1(t) + x_2\phi_2(t) + x_3\phi_3(t).$$

From the boundary conditions, we must have $x_1 = 0$ and $x_3 = 1$. To determine the remaining parameter x_2, we impose the Galerkin condition. Recall that the Galerkin condition requires that the residual be orthogonal to the space spanned by the basis functions and hence to each basis function individually. Recall further (see Section 7.2.4) that the inner product on a function space, and hence the notion of orthogonality, is defined by the integral of the product of the functions. Imposing the Galerkin condition on the interior basis function ϕ_2,

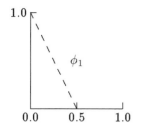
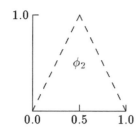
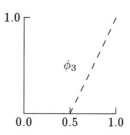

FIGURE 10.4
The "hat" function basis for piecewise linear polynomials.

we therefore obtain

$$\int_0^1 (u''(t) - 6t)\phi_2(t)\, dt = \int_0^1 u''(t)\phi_2(t)\, dt - 6\int_0^1 t\phi_2(t)\, dt = 0.$$

We can evaluate the first of these integrals by parts:

$$\int_0^1 u''(t)\phi_2(t)\, dt = u'(t)\phi_2(t)\Big|_0^1 - \int_0^1 u'(t)\phi_2'(t)\, dt.$$

For the first term, since $\phi_2(0) = \phi_2(1) = 0$, we have $u'(t)\phi_2(t)\Big|_0^1 = 0$. Computing the integral in the second term,

$$\int_0^1 u'(t)\phi_2'(t)\, dt = \int_0^1 \left(\sum_{i=1}^3 x_i \phi_i'(t)\right)\phi_2'(t)\, dt = \sum_{i=1}^3 x_i \int_0^1 \phi_i'(t)\phi_2'(t)\, dt$$

$$= x_1(-1/h) + x_2(2/h) + x_3(-1/h),$$

where $h = \frac{1}{2}$ is the spacing between mesh points. Finally, straightforward evaluation of the other integral gives $6\int_0^1 t\phi_2(t)\, dt = \frac{3}{2}$. Hence, the Galerkin condition gives us the equation

$$-2x_1 + 4x_2 - 2x_3 = -\tfrac{3}{2}.$$

Substituting the known values for x_1 and x_3 then gives $x_2 = \frac{1}{8}$ for the remaining unknown parameter. Thus, the piecewise linear approximate solution is

$$y(t) \approx u(t) = 0.125\phi_2(t) + \phi_3(t),$$

which is plotted in Fig. 10.5 along with the exact solution. We note that $u(0.5) = 0.125$, which again is exact for this particular problem.

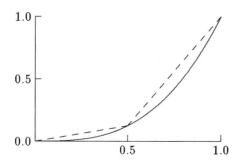

FIGURE 10.5
True solution (solid line) and approximate solution (dashed line) obtained by Galerkin method.

In a more realistic problem, there would be many more interior mesh points and basis functions and correspondingly many parameters to be determined. The resulting system of equations would be much larger, but it would still be sparse, and therefore relatively easy to solve as long as basis functions with localized support, such as the "hat" functions, are used. The resulting approximate solution function would become more accurate as more mesh points are used.

10.6 EIGENVALUE PROBLEMS

A standard eigenvalue problem for a second-order ODE has the form

$$y'' = \lambda f(t, y, y'), \qquad a \leq t \leq b,$$

with boundary conditions

$$y(a) = \alpha, \qquad y(b) = \beta,$$

and we seek not only the solution y but also λ as well. The (possibly complex) scalar λ is called an *eigenvalue* and the solution y an *eigenfunction* for this two-point boundary value problem. More general eigenvalue problems may involve higher-order systems, implicit equations, more general boundary conditions, or nonlinear dependence on λ.

Discretization of an eigenvalue problem for an ODE results in an algebraic eigenvalue problem whose solution approximates that of the original problem. For example, consider the linear two-point boundary value problem

$$y'' = \lambda g(t)y, \qquad a \leq t \leq b,$$

with boundary conditions

$$y(a) = 0, \qquad y(b) = 0.$$

If we introduce discrete mesh points t_i in the interval $[a, b]$, with mesh spacing h, and use a standard finite difference approximation for the second derivative, then we obtain an algebraic system

$$\frac{y_{i+1} - 2y_i + y_{i-1}}{h^2} = \lambda g_i y_i, \qquad i = 1, \ldots, n,$$

where $y_i = y(t_i)$ and $g_i = g(t_i)$, and from the boundary conditions, $y_0 = 0$ and $y_{n+1} = 0$. If $g_i \neq 0$, so that we can divide equation i by g_i for $i = 1, \ldots, n$, then we obtain a standard algebraic eigenvalue problem $Ay = \lambda y$, where A has the tridiagonal form

$$A = \frac{1}{h^2} \begin{bmatrix} -2/g_1 & 1/g_1 & 0 & \cdots & & 0 \\ 1/g_2 & -2/g_2 & 1/g_2 & \ddots & & \vdots \\ 0 & \ddots & \ddots & \ddots & & 0 \\ \vdots & \ddots & & 1/g_{n-1} & -2/g_{n-1} & 1/g_{n-1} \\ 0 & \cdots & & 0 & 1/g_n & -2/g_n \end{bmatrix},$$

which can be solved by the methods discussed in Chapter 4.

TABLE 10.1
Software for ODE boundary value problems

Source	Shooting	Superposition	Finite difference	Collocation	Galerkin
IMSL	bvpms		bvpfd		
HSL			dd02		
NAG	d02haf		d02gaf	d02jaf	
NETLIB	mus		twpbvp		
NR	shoot		solvde		
NUMAL					femlag
SLATEC		bvsup			
TOMS				colsys(#569)	

10.7 SOFTWARE FOR ODE BOUNDARY VALUE PROBLEMS

Table 10.1 is a list of some of the software available for numerical solution of boundary value problems for ordinary differential equations. For a survey of software available for two-point boundary value problems, see [39].

10.8 HISTORICAL NOTES AND FURTHER READING

Classic references on the numerical solution of two-point boundary problems for ODEs are [86, 146]. For an overview of finite difference methods, see the survey [201], and for shooting methods, see [215]. A comprehensive treatment of methods for two-point boundary value problems can be found in [10]. Most books on the finite element method are concerned primarily with partial differential equations, but many of them discuss two-point boundary value problems for ODEs as an introductory illustration; for example, see [17, 20, 140, 247].

REVIEW QUESTIONS

10.1. What specific feature distinguishes a boundary value problem from an initial value problem for a system of ordinary differential equations?

10.2. Explain how a one-dimensional zero finder can be used to solve a two-point boundary value problem for a second-order scalar ordinary differential equation $y'' = f(t, y, y')$ with boundary conditions $y(a) = \alpha$ and $y(b) = \beta$.

10.3. For each type of method listed for solving two-point boundary problems for ODEs, state whether methods of this type convert the boundary problem to one or more initial value problems or to a system of algebraic equations:

(*a*) Finite difference
(*b*) Shooting
(*c*) Finite element
(*d*) Superposition

10.4. List two disadvantages of the superposition method for solving two-point boundary value problems for second-order ODEs.

10.5. For solving a two-point boundary value problem for a *nonlinear* second-order ODE, both the finite difference method and the shooting method are iterative. One of these approximately satisfies the ODE at each iteration, but satisfies the boundary conditions only upon convergence, whereas the other satisfies the boundary conditions at each iteration, but approximately satisfies the ODE only upon convergence. Which is which?

10.6. (*a*) In solving two-point boundary value problems for second-order ODEs, for what type of problem is the multiple shooting method likely to be more effective than the ordinary shooting method?

(*b*) What disadvantage does the multiple shooting method have, compared with the ordinary shooting method?

10.7. When a finite difference method is used to convert a boundary value problem for a differential equation into a system of algebraic equations, what property determines whether the algebraic system will be linear or nonlinear?

10.8. Finite difference and finite element methods for solving boundary value problems convert the original differential equation into a system of algebraic equations. Why does the resulting linear system usually require far less work to solve than the usual $\mathcal{O}(n^3)$ that might be expected?

10.9. Finite difference and finite element methods for solving boundary value problems both require the solution of a system of algebraic equations, but the solutions to the respective algebraic systems differ in their meanings and how they are used.

(*a*) How do the quantities being solved for differ between the two types of methods?

(*b*) How do the resulting approximate solutions to the boundary value problem differ in nature?

10.10. Why is it advantageous if the basis functions used in the finite element method are localized (i.e., each basis function is nonzero on only a small portion of the problem domain)?

10.11. In solving a boundary value problem by a finite element method, what requirement does the collocation method impose on the approximate solution?

10.12. Suppose you are solving a two-point boundary value problem for a linear second-order ODE using the standard second-order centered finite difference approximations to the derivatives. Describe the nonzero pattern of the matrix of the resulting system of linear algebraic equations.

10.13. Suppose you are using the shooting method to solve a two-point boundary value problem for an ODE on an interval $[a, b]$. If the ODE in question is unstable on some portion of the interval, then the resulting sequence of initial value problems may be very sensitive to initial conditions, making it difficult to hit the required boundary condition.

(*a*) How could you cope with such ill-conditioning?

(*b*) How would this affect the nonlinear algebraic equation to be solved?

10.14. In solving a two-point boundary value problem for a second-order ODE numerically, does the approximate solution produced by finite element collocation at a finite set of n discrete points always agree with the exact solution at those n points?

EXERCISES

10.1. Consider the two-point boundary value problem for the second-order ODE

$$y'' = y^3 + t, \qquad a \le t \le b,$$

with boundary conditions

$$y(a) = \alpha, \qquad y(b) = \beta.$$

To use the shooting method to solve this problem, one needs a starting guess for the initial slope $y'(a)$. One way to obtain such a starting guess for the initial slope is, in effect, to do a "preliminary shooting" in which we take a single step of Euler's method with $h = b - a$.

(*a*) Using this approach, write out the resulting algebraic equation for the initial slope.

(*b*) What starting value for the initial slope results from this approach?

10.2. Suppose that the altitude of the trajectory of a projectile is described by the second-order ordinary differential equation $y'' = -4$. Suppose that the projectile is fired from position $t = 0$ and height $y(0) = 1$ and is to strike a target at position $t = 1$, also of height $y(1) = 1$.

(*a*) Solve this boundary value problem by the shooting method:

1. To determine the initial slope at $t = 0$ required to hit the desired target at $t = 1$, use the trapezoid rule with stepsize $h = 1$ to derive a system of two equations for the unknown initial slope $s_0 = y'(0)$ and final slope $s_1 = y'(1)$.

2. What are the resulting values for the initial and final slopes?

3. Using the initial slope just determined and a stepsize of $h = 0.5$, use the trapezoid rule once again to compute the approximate height of the projectile at $t = 0.5$.

(*b*) Solve the same boundary value problem again, this time using a finite difference method with $h = 0.5$. What is the resulting approximate height of the projectile at the point $t = 0.5$?

(*c*) Solve the same boundary value problem once again, this time using collocation at the point $t = 0.5$, together with the boundary values, to determine a quadratic polynomial $u(t)$ approximating the solution. What is the resulting approximate height of the projectile at the point $t = 0.5$?

COMPUTER PROBLEMS

10.1. Solve the two-point boundary value problem

$$y'' = 10y^3 + 3y + t^2, \qquad 0 \le t \le 1,$$

with boundary conditions

$$y(0) = 0, \qquad y(1) = 1,$$

by each of the following methods.

(*a*) *Shooting method.* Use a one-dimensional nonlinear equation solver to find an initial slope $y'(0)$ such that the solution of the resulting initial value problem hits the target value for $y(1)$. Solve each required initial value problem using a library ODE solver or one of your own design. Plot the sequence of solutions you obtain.

(*b*) *Finite difference method.* Divide the given interval $0 \le t \le 1$ into $n + 1$ equal subintervals,

$$0 = t_0 < t_1 < \cdots < t_n < t_{n+1} = 1,$$

with each subinterval of length $h = 1/(n + 1)$. Let y_i, $i = 1, \ldots, n$, represent the approximate solution values at the n interior points. Obtain a system of n algebraic equations for the y_i by replacing the second derivative in the differential equation by the finite difference approximation

$$y_i''(x) \approx \frac{y_{i+1} - 2y_i + y_{i-i}}{h^2},$$

$i = 1, \ldots, n$. Use a library routine or one of your own design, to solve the resulting system of nonlinear equa-

tions. A reasonable starting guess for the nonlinear solver is a straight line between the boundary values. Plot the sequences of solutions you obtain for $n = 1, 3, 7$, and 15.

(*c*) *Collocation method.* Divide the given interval $0 \le t \le 1$ into $n - 1$ equal subintervals,

$$0 = t_1 < t_2 < \cdots < t_{n-1} < t_n = 1,$$

with each subinterval of length $h = 1/(n - 1)$. Take the approximate solution $u(t)$ to be a polynomial of degree $n - 1$. Forcing $u(t)$ to satisfy the boundary conditions at the endpoints and to satisfy the ODE at the $n - 2$ interior points yields a system of n equations that determine the n coefficients of the polynomial $u(t)$. Use a library routine, or one of your own design, to solve this system of nonlinear algebraic equations. The resulting polynomial can then be evaluated at any point in the interval to obtain an approximate solution value at that point. Print the polynomial coefficients and plot the solutions you obtain for $n = 3, 4, 5$, and 6.

10.2. Solve the two-point boundary value problem

$$y'' = -(1 + e^y), \qquad 0 \le t \le 1,$$

with boundary conditions

$$y(0) = 0, \qquad y(1) = 1,$$

using each of the methods in the previous exercise.

10.3. The curve of a hanging rope is described by the system of ODEs

$$y_1' = \cos(y_3),$$

$$y_2' = \sin(y_3),$$

$$y_3' = (\cos(y_3) - \sin(y_3)|\sin(y_3)|)/y_4,$$

$$y_4' = \sin(y_3) - \cos(y_3)|\cos(y_3)|,$$

where $y_1(t)$ and $y_2(t)$ are the horizontal and vertical coordinates of the rope, $y_3(t)$ is the angle between the tangent to the rope and the horizontal axis, $y_4(t)$ is the tension in the rope, and the variable t is the arc length along the rope, with the length of the rope normalized so that $0 \leq t \leq 1$.

(*a*) Use both the shooting and finite difference methods to determine the curve of the rope when the boundary conditions are

$$y(0) = \begin{bmatrix} 0 \\ 0 \\ 0 \\ 1 \end{bmatrix}, \qquad y(1) = \begin{bmatrix} 0.75 \\ 0 \\ 0 \\ 1 \end{bmatrix}.$$

These conditions correspond to a slack rope. Plot the solution curve you obtain for each method.

(*b*) Use both the shooting and finite difference methods to determine the curve of the rope when the boundary conditions are

$$y(0) = \begin{bmatrix} 0 \\ 0 \\ 0 \\ 1 \end{bmatrix}, \qquad y(1) = \begin{bmatrix} 0.85 \\ 0.50 \\ 0 \\ 1 \end{bmatrix}.$$

These conditions correspond to a taut rope. Plot the solution curve you obtain for each method.

10.4. The deflection of a horizontal beam supported at both ends and subjected to axial and transverse loads can be described by the second-order ODE

$$y'' = \lambda(-t^2 - 1)y, \qquad -1 \leq t \leq 1,$$

with boundary conditions

$$y(-1) = 0, \qquad y(1) = 0.$$

The eigenvalues and eigenfunctions for this two-point boundary value problem determine the frequencies and modes of vibration of the beam. Use a finite difference discretization of the ODE to derive an algebraic eigenvalue problem whose eigenvalues and eigenvectors approximate those of the ODE, then compute the eigen-

values and eigenvectors using a library routine (see Section 4.6). Experiment with various mesh sizes and observe how the eigenvalues behave.

10.5. The time-independent *Schrödinger equation* in one dimension,

$$-\psi''(x) + V(x)\psi(x) = E\psi(x),$$

where we have chosen units so that the quantities are dimensionless, describes the wave function ψ of a particle of energy E subject to a potential function V. The square of the wave function, $|\psi(x)|^2$, can be interpreted as the probability of finding the particle at position x.

Assume that the particle is confined to a one-dimensional box, say, the interval $[0, 1]$, within which it can move freely. Thus, the potential is zero within the unit interval and infinite elsewhere. Since there is zero probability of finding the particle outside the box, the wave function must be zero at its boundaries. Thus, we have an eigenvalue problem for the second-order ODE

$$-\psi''(x) = E\psi(x), \qquad 0 \leq x \leq 1,$$

subject to the boundary conditions

$$\psi(0) = 0 \qquad \text{and} \qquad \psi(1) = 0.$$

Note that the discrete eigenvalues E are the only energy levels permitted; this feature gives quantum mechanics its name.

Use a finite difference discretization of the ODE to derive an algebraic eigenvalue problem whose eigenvalues and eigenvectors approximate those of the ODE, then compute the eigenvalues and eigenvectors using a library routine (see Section 4.6). Experiment with various mesh sizes and observe how the eigenvalues behave.

An analytical solution to this problem is easily obtained, which gives the eigenvalues

$$E_k = k^2\pi^2$$

and corresponding eigenfunctions

$$\psi_k(x) = \sin(k\pi x), \qquad k = 1, 2, \ldots.$$

How do your computed eigenvalues and eigenvectors compare with these analytical values as the mesh size of your discretization decreases? Try to characterize the error as a function of the mesh size.

Note that a nonzero potential V would not seriously complicate the numerical solution of the Schrödinger equation, but would generally make an analytical solution much more difficult to obtain.

CHAPTER 11

<hr>

Partial Differential Equations

11.1 PARTIAL DIFFERENTIAL EQUATIONS

We turn now to partial differential equations (PDEs), where many of the numerical techniques we saw for ODEs, both initial and boundary value problems, are also applicable. The situation is more complicated with PDEs, however, because there are additional independent variables, typically one or more space dimensions and possibly a time dimension as well. Additional dimensions significantly increase computational complexity. Problem formulation also becomes more complex than for ODEs, as we can have a pure initial value problem, a pure boundary value problem, or a mixture of the two. Moreover, the equation and boundary data may be defined over an irregular domain in space.

First, we establish some notation. For simplicity, we will deal only with single PDEs (as opposed to systems of several PDEs) with only two independent variables (either two space variables, which we denote by x and y, or one space and one time variable, which we denote by x and t). In a more general setting, there could be any number of dimensions and any number of equations in a coupled system of PDEs. We denote by u the unknown solution function to be determined and its partial derivatives with respect to the independent variables by appropriate subscripts: $u_x = \partial u / \partial x$, $u_{xy} = \partial^2 u / \partial x \partial y$, etc.

11.1.1 Classification of Partial Differential Equations

Partial differential equations are classified by the value of the *discriminant*, $b^2 - 4ac$, in the general linear, two-dimensional, second-order PDE

$$au_{xx} + bu_{xy} + cu_{yy} + du_x + eu_y + fu + g = 0,$$

$$b^2 - 4ac > 0: \quad \text{hyperbolic,}$$

$$b^2 - 4ac = 0: \quad \text{parabolic,}$$

$$b^2 - 4ac < 0: \quad \text{elliptic.}$$

In practice, this classification is not always so clean and simple. If the coefficients are variable, then the type of the equation can vary from one region to another, and if there is more than one equation in a system, each equation can be of a different type. And of course, the problem may be nonlinear or of higher order or dimension. Nevertheless, these terms are often used to describe PDEs even when the meaning is not so precise. Roughly speaking,

- *Hyperbolic* PDEs describe time-dependent physical processes, such as wave motion, that *are not* evolving toward a steady state.
- *Parabolic* PDEs describe time-dependent physical processes, such as the diffusion of heat, that *are* evolving toward a steady state.
- *Elliptic* PDEs describe processes that have already reached a steady state, or equilibrium, and hence are time-independent.

11.2 TIME-DEPENDENT PROBLEMS

Time-dependent PDEs usually involve both initial values and boundary values. For example, the region in which the solution is desired, as well as the initial and boundary conditions that must be specified, are shown for a problem with one space dimension in Fig. 11.1. Two of the most commonly occurring examples of time-dependent PDEs are the heat equation, which is parabolic, and the wave equation, which is hyperbolic.

In one space dimension, the *heat equation* has the form

$$u_t = c u_{xx}, \qquad 0 \le x \le L, \qquad t \ge 0,$$

with given initial and boundary conditions

$$u(0, x) = f(x), \qquad u(t, 0) = \alpha, \qquad u(t, L) = \beta,$$

and c a positive constant. This equation models, for example, the diffusion of heat in a bar of length L whose ends are maintained at temperatures given by the boundary conditions and whose initial temperature distribution is given by the function $f(x)$.

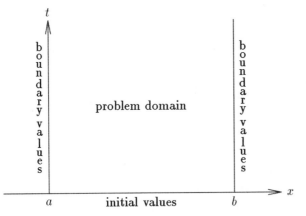

FIGURE 11.1
An initial-boundary value problem for a time-dependent PDE in one space dimension.

The constant c, which governs the rate of diffusion, depends on physical properties of the material, such as its thermal conductivity, specific heat, and density. The solution u to this equation gives the subsequent temperature distribution as a function of both space and time.

In one space dimension, the *wave equation* has the form

$$u_{tt} = cu_{xx}, \qquad 0 \le x \le L, \qquad t \ge 0,$$

with given initial conditions

$$u(0, x) = f(x), \qquad u_t(0, x) = g(x),$$

and boundary conditions

$$u(t, 0) = \alpha, \qquad u(t, L) = \beta,$$

and c a positive constant. This equation models, for example, the vibrations of a violin string of length L whose initial profile and velocity are given by the functions $f(x)$ and $g(x)$, respectively, and whose ends are anchored as given by the boundary conditions. Because it is second-order in time, this equation requires initial conditions for both the solution function and its first derivative with respect to time. It turns out that the solution consists of waves propagating to the left or right with speed $\sqrt{c}$. More generally, this equation describes many types of wave motion, such as the propagation of sound waves in the air or water waves in the ocean.

For both the heat equation and wave equation, we have given only the simplest type of boundary conditions. More complicated boundary conditions may involve derivatives of the solution as well as its values, or combinations of these, or may require that the solution be periodic, for example.

Problems with more space dimensions incur greater computational requirements, both in storage and execution time, but do not introduce significant additional conceptual difficulty, so we will focus on time-dependent problems having a single space dimension. We will also focus on relatively simple model problems, such as the heat and wave equations, rather than attempt a broader treatment of partial differential equations in general. Nevertheless, these model problems illustrate most of the important issues in the numerical solution of PDEs.

11.2.1 Semidiscrete Methods Using Finite Differences

One way to solve a time-dependent PDE is to discretize in space but leave the time variable continuous. This approach results in a system of ODEs, which can then be solved by the methods discussed in Chapter 9. For example, consider the heat equation

$$u_t = cu_{xx}, \qquad 0 \le x \le 1, \qquad t \ge 0,$$

with initial and boundary conditions

$$u(0, x) = f(x), \qquad u(t, 0) = 0, \qquad u(t, 1) = 0.$$

If we replace the derivative u_{xx} with the finite-difference approximation

$$u_{xx} \approx \frac{u(t, x + \Delta x) - 2u(t, x) + u(t, x - \Delta x)}{(\Delta x)^2},$$

where $\Delta x = 1/(n + 1)$, then we get a system of n ODEs

$$y_i'(t) = \frac{c}{(\Delta x)^2}[y_{i+1}(t) - 2y_i(t) + y_{i-1}(t)], \qquad i = 1, \ldots, n,$$

where $y_i(t) \approx u(t, i\Delta x)$. From the boundary conditions, $y_0(t)$ and $y_{n+1}(t)$ are identically zero, and from the initial conditions, $y_i(0) = f(x_i), i = 1, \ldots, n$. We can therefore use an ODE method to solve the initial value problem for this system. This approach is called the *method of lines*. If we think of the solution $u(t, x)$ as a surface over the space-time plane, this method computes cross sections of that surface along a series of lines, each of which is parallel to the time axis and corresponds to one of the discrete spatial mesh points.

The foregoing semidiscrete system can be written in matrix form as

$$y' = \frac{c}{(\Delta x)^2}\begin{bmatrix} -2 & 1 & 0 & \cdots & 0 \\ 1 & -2 & 1 & \ddots & \vdots \\ 0 & 1 & -2 & \ddots & 0 \\ \vdots & \ddots & \ddots & \ddots & 1 \\ 0 & \cdots & 0 & 1 & -2 \end{bmatrix} y = Ay.$$

The Jacobian matrix A of this system has eigenvalues between $-4c/(\Delta x)^2$ and 0, which makes the ODE very stiff as the spatial mesh size Δx becomes small. This stiffness, which is typical of ODEs derived from PDEs in this manner, must be taken into account in choosing an ODE method for solving the semidiscrete system (recall Section 9.5).

11.2.2 Semidiscrete Methods Using Finite Elements

Spatial discretization to convert a PDE into a system of ODEs can also be done by a finite element approach. As we did for two-point boundary problems for ODEs, we approximate the solution by a linear combination of basis functions, except that now the coefficients are time-dependent. Thus, we seek an approximate solution of the form

$$u(t, x) \approx \sum_{j=1}^{n} \alpha_j(t)\phi_j(x),$$

where the $\phi_j(x)$ are the basis function over the spatial domain and the $\alpha_j(t)$ are the time-dependent coefficients. If we use collocation (we could also use Ritz or Galerkin methods), then we substitute this approximation into the PDE and require that the equation be satisfied exactly at a discrete set of points x_i. For the heat equation, for example, this yields a system of ODEs

$$\sum_{j=1}^{n} \alpha_j'(t)\phi_j(x_i) = c\sum_{j=1}^{n} \alpha_j(t)\phi_j''(x_i), \qquad i = 1, \ldots, n,$$

whose solution is the set of coefficient functions $\alpha_j(t)$ that determine the approximate solution to the PDE.

The implicit form of the foregoing system of ODEs is not the explicit form required by standard ODE methods, so we define the $n \times n$ matrices A and B by

$$a_{ij} = \phi_j(x_i), \qquad b_{ij} = \phi_j''(x_i).$$

Assuming the matrix A is nonsingular, we then obtain the system of ODEs

$$\alpha'(t) = cA^{-1}B\alpha(t),$$

which is in a form suitable for solution with standard ODE software (as usual, the matrix A need not be inverted explicitly, but merely used to solve linear systems). We still need an initial condition for the ODE, however, which we can obtain by requiring that the solution satisfy the given initial condition for the PDE at the points x_i. Again, the matrices involved in this method will be sparse if the basis functions are "local," such as B-splines. Alternatively, we could use eigenfunctions of the differential operator (e.g., trigonometric functions for u_{xx}) as basis functions, which would give a spectral method, or other basis functions, such as Legendre or Chebyshev polynomials, which would give a pseudospectral method.

Unlike the finite difference method, the finite element method does not produce approximate values of the solution u directly, but rather it generates a representation of the approximate solution as a linear combination of basis functions. The basis functions depend only on the spatial variable, but the coefficients of the linear combination (given by the solution to the system of ODEs) are time dependent. Thus, for any given time t, the corresponding linear combination of basis functions generates a cross section of the solution surface parallel to the spatial axis.

As with finite difference methods, systems of ODEs arising from semidiscretization of a PDE by finite elements tend to be stiff, which should be taken into account in choosing an ODE method for solving them.

11.2.3 Fully Discrete Methods

Fully discrete methods for PDEs discretize in both time and space dimensions. In a fully discrete finite difference method, we replace the continuous domain of the equation by a discrete mesh of points, we replace the derivatives in the PDE by finite difference approximations, and we seek a numerical solution that is a table of approximate values at the selected points in space and time. In two dimensions (one space and one time), the resulting approximate solution values represent points on the solution surface over the problem domain in the space-time plane. The accuracy of the approximate solution depends on the stepsizes in both space and time.

Replacement of all partial derivatives by finite differences results in a system of algebraic equations for the unknown solution at the discrete set of sample points. This system may be linear or nonlinear, depending on the underlying PDE. With an initial-value problem, the solution is obtained by beginning with the initial values along some boundary of the problem domain and marching forward in time step by step, generating successive rows in the solution table. Such a time-stepping procedure may be explicit or implicit, depending on whether the formula for the solution values at the next time step involves only past information.

We would expect to obtain arbitrarily good accuracy by taking sufficiently small stepsizes in time and space. The two stepsizes cannot always be chosen independently of each other, however. For the approximate solution to converge to the true solution of the PDE as the stepsizes in time and space go to zero, two conditions must be met:

- *Consistency*, which means that the local truncation error goes to zero as the stepsizes go to zero (i.e., the discrete problem approximates the right continuous problem).
- *Stability*, which, as we have seen in other contexts, essentially means that the approximate solution remains bounded.

The *Lax Equivalence Theorem* says that consistency and stability are together necessary and sufficient for convergence. Neither condition alone is sufficient to guarantee convergence.

EXAMPLE 11.1 HEAT EQUATION. As an example of full discretization, consider the heat equation

$$u_t = c u_{xx}, \qquad 0 \leq x \leq 1, \qquad t \geq 0,$$

with initial and boundary conditions

$$u(0, x) = f(x), \qquad u(t, 0) = \alpha, \qquad u(t, 1) = \beta.$$

We let u_j^k denote the approximate solution at $x_j = j\Delta x$ and $t_k = k\Delta t$. If we replace u_t by a forward difference in time and u_{xx} by a centered difference in space, with $\Delta x = 1/(n+1)$, we get the scheme

$$\frac{u_j^{k+1} - u_j^k}{\Delta t} = c \frac{u_{j+1}^k - 2u_j^k + u_{j-1}^k}{(\Delta x)^2}, \qquad j = 1, \ldots, n,$$

or

$$u_j^{k+1} = u_j^k + c \frac{\Delta t}{(\Delta x)^2} (u_{j+1}^k - 2u_j^k + u_{j-1}^k), \qquad j = 1, \ldots, n.$$

The boundary conditions give us $u_0^k = \alpha$ and $u_{n+1}^k = \beta$ for all k, and the initial conditions provide the starting values $u_j^0 = f(x_j)$ for all j, so that we can march the numerical solution forward in time using the difference scheme. In Fig. 11.2a, the pattern of mesh points involved in this scheme is indicated by the lines, with the arrow indicating the mesh point at which the solution is being computed. Such a pattern is called the *stencil* of the given finite difference scheme.

The local truncation error of this scheme is $\mathcal{O}(\Delta t) + \mathcal{O}((\Delta x)^2)$, so we say that the scheme is first-order accurate in time and second-order accurate in space. The local error goes to zero as Δt and Δx go to zero, so the scheme is consistent. To investigate its stability, we note that this fully discrete explicit scheme is simply Euler's method applied to the system of ODEs resulting from the semidiscrete finite-difference method for the heat equation given in Section 11.2.1. There we saw that the Jacobian matrix of the semidiscrete system has eigenvalues between $-4c/(\Delta x)^2$ and 0, and hence the stability region for Euler's method requires that the time step satisfy

$$\Delta t \leq \frac{(\Delta x)^2}{2c}.$$

This restriction on the time step is rather severe and makes this explicit method relatively inefficient compared with implicit methods that we will see shortly.

(*a*) **Explicit method for the heat equation**

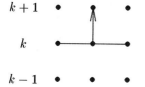

(*b*) **Explicit method for the wave equation**

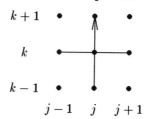

(*c*) **Implicit method for the heat equation**

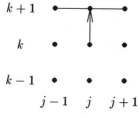

(*d*) **Crank-Nicolson method for the heat equation**

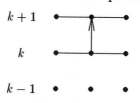

FIGURE 11.2
Stencils of finite difference methods for time-dependent problems.

EXAMPLE 11.2 WAVE EQUATION. As a further illustration of the finite difference approach to full discretization, we now consider the wave equation

$$u_{tt} = cu_{xx}, \qquad 0 \le x \le 1, \qquad t \ge 0,$$

with initial and boundary conditions

$$u(0, x) = f(x), \qquad u_t(0, x) = g(x),$$
$$u(t, 0) = \alpha, \qquad u(t, 1) = \beta.$$

Using centered difference formulas for both u_{tt} and u_{xx} gives the finite difference scheme

$$\frac{u_j^{k+1} - 2u_j^k + u_j^{k-1}}{(\Delta t)^2} = c\frac{u_{j+1}^k - 2u_j^k + u_{j-1}^k}{(\Delta x)^2},$$

or

$$u_j^{k+1} = 2u_j^k - u_j^{k-1} + c\frac{(\Delta t)^2}{(\Delta x)^2}(u_{j+1}^k - 2u_j^k + u_{j-1}^k).$$

The stencil for this scheme is shown in Fig. 11.2*b*. We note that this scheme requires data at two levels in time, which requires additional storage and also means that we need both u_j^0 and u_j^1 to get started. These values can be obtained from the initial conditions

$$u_j^0 = f(x_j), \qquad u_j^1 = f(x_j) + (\Delta t)g(x_j),$$

where in the latter we have used a forward difference approximation to the initial condition $u_t = g(x)$. This scheme is second-order accurate in both space and time, and the stability restriction on the time step is

$$\Delta t \le \frac{\Delta x}{\sqrt{c}},$$

which is much less stringent than that for the scheme we considered for the heat equation.

11.2.4 Implicit Finite Difference Methods

In the finite difference schemes we have considered thus far the values of the approximate solution at the next time level have been given by explicit formulas involving solution values only at previous levels. For ODEs we saw that implicit methods are stable for a much greater range of stepsizes, and the same is true of implicit methods for PDEs.

The explicit method that we considered for the heat equation results from applying Euler's method to the semidiscrete system of ODEs in Section 11.2.1. If instead we apply the backward Euler method to the semidiscrete system, we obtain the implicit finite difference scheme

$$u_j^{k+1} = u_j^k + c\frac{\Delta t}{(\Delta x)^2}(u_{j+1}^{k+1} - 2u_j^{k+1} + u_{j-1}^{k+1}),$$

whose stencil is shown in Fig. 11.2c. This scheme inherits the unconditional stability of the backward Euler method, which means that there is no stability restriction on the relative sizes of Δt and Δx. Accuracy is still a consideration, however, and the fact that this particular method is only first-order accurate in time still limits the time step severely. The simplest unconditionally stable implicit method for the heat equation that is second-order accurate in time is the *Crank-Nicolson method*

$$u_j^{k+1} = u_j^k + c\frac{\Delta t}{2(\Delta x)^2}(u_{j+1}^{k+1} - 2u_j^{k+1} + u_{j-1}^{k+1} + u_{j+1}^k - 2u_j^k + u_{j-1}^k),$$

which results from applying the trapezoid rule to the semidiscrete system of ODEs (or alternatively, by averaging the previous explicit and implicit methods). The stencil for the Crank-Nicolson scheme is shown in Fig. 11.2d.

The much greater stability of implicit finite difference methods enables them to take much larger time steps than are permissible with explicit methods, but they require more work per step because we must solve a system of equations at each step to determine the solution values at the next step. For both the backward Euler and Crank-Nicolson methods for the heat equation in one space dimension, the linear system to be solved at each step is tridiagonal, and thus both the work and the storage required are modest. In higher dimensions the matrix of the linear system does not have such a simple form, but it is still very sparse, with nonzeros in a very regular pattern. We will discuss methods for solving such linear systems in Sections 11.4 and 11.5.

Obviously, many additional finite difference schemes are possible, depending on the particular PDE being solved, the order of accuracy sought, etc. Such schemes are usually custom-tailored to take advantage of the specific features of a given problem.

Finite difference schemes are relatively easy to derive; but analyzing their accuracy, stability, and efficiency can be much more challenging, and consequently they should not be used blindly.

11.2.5 Hyperbolic versus Parabolic Problems

Thus far we have treated all time-dependent problems alike: we simply replaced partial derivatives by finite difference approximations and then considered the accuracy and stability of the resulting scheme for stepping the approximate solution forward in time. A detailed study of the theory of partial differential equations is beyond the scope of this book, but we consider briefly a basic theoretical difference between hyperbolic and parabolic PDEs that has significant implications for practical numerical solution methods.

Consider the following first-order hyperbolic PDE, known as the *one-way wave equation* or *advection equation*:

$$u_t = -cu_x, \qquad t \geq 0,$$

with initial condition

$$u(0, x) = u_0(x), \qquad x \geq 0.$$

It is obvious from the chain rule that a solution is given by

$$u(t, x) = u_0(x - ct).$$

Thus, the initial function u_0 is simply propagated to the right (or to the left if $c < 0$) with velocity c, as depicted in Fig. 11.3.

Note that u_0 need not be smooth or even continuous. This behavior is typical of hyperbolic equations: they propagate steep fronts or shocks (or anything else, including numerical errors) undiminished—for this reason, they are said to be *conservative*. Such behavior can potentially cause difficulties for numerical methods that are predicated on a certain degree of smoothness. In particular, centered finite difference schemes, though desirable for their higher accuracy, often induce unwanted oscillations in the numerical solution to a hyperbolic equation near a sharp front. A useful alternative for the spatial derivatives in such cases is to use one-sided differences whose sample points are on the side from which the front is coming. Such *upwind differencing* biases the approximation toward the passing front, reducing the tendency for unwanted oscillation. Upwind differencing is but the simplest of several approaches to dealing with sharp fronts and discontinuities. Of course, if the initial function is sufficiently smooth, such measures may not be required.

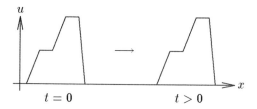

FIGURE 11.3
A solution of the one-way wave equation.

EXAMPLE 11.3 CENTERED VERSUS UPWIND DIFFERENCING FOR A SHARP FRONT. Consider the one-way wave equation

$$u_t = -u_x$$

with initial function u_0 taken to be the step function defined by

$$u_0(x) = \begin{cases} 1 & \text{if } x \leq 0 \\ 0 & \text{if } x > 0 \end{cases}.$$

The discontinuity in u_0, a jump at $x = 0$, will be propagated to the right with time. From the viewpoint of a particular point along the spatial axis, the solution will be 0 until the step function passes by, after which the solution will be 1 (i.e., for a fixed x, the solution will be a step function in t). We should expect finite difference methods to have some trouble following this sharp front.

Figure 11.4 shows the computed solution as a function of t at the point $x = 1$ (i.e., it is a slice of the solution surface parallel to the t axis at the point $x = 1$). The solution on the left was computed using centered spatial differencing of the form

$$u_x \approx \frac{u(t, x + \Delta x) - u(t, x - \Delta x)}{2\Delta x},$$

whereas the solution on the right was computed using upwind spatial differencing of the form

$$u_x \approx \frac{u(t, x) - u(t, x - \Delta x)}{\Delta x}.$$

The centered difference formula is second-order accurate and gives a closer approximation of the sharp front. It overshoots, however, and then goes into an oscillation that is not present in the true solution, which is the step function plotted on the same graph for comparison. The one-sided difference formula is only first-order accurate and captures the sharp front less well, but it is free of the undesirable oscillation exhibited by the centered method, and in this sense it may be a better solution for many purposes. Notice that the one-sided difference uses the adjacent point on the side from which the front is coming. If the front were coming from the opposite direction, we would use the adjacent point on that side (i.e., $x + \Delta x$).

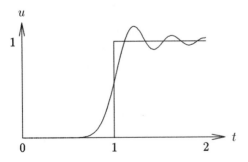 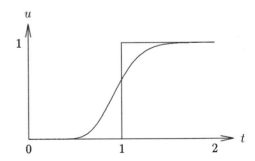

FIGURE 11.4
Approximations to step function solution of one-way wave equation using centered (left) and upwind (right) differencing.

In marked contrast to the behavior just described, parabolic equations are *dissipative*. The solution tends toward a steady state with time, eventually "forgetting" the initial conditions. Any lack of smoothness in the initial conditions, even possible inconsistency in the initial and boundary conditions, is damped out. This behavior makes parabolic equations very "forgiving" and relatively easy to solve numerically, as numerical errors tend to diminish with time (provided a stable method is used). Thus, centered differences tend to work well for parabolic problems, and high-accuracy solutions are relatively easy to obtain.

11.3 TIME-INDEPENDENT PROBLEMS

We now consider time-independent, elliptic PDEs in two space dimensions, such as the *Helmholtz equation*

$$u_{xx} + u_{yy} + \lambda u = f(x, y).$$

Important special cases of this equation include the *Poisson equation* ($\lambda = 0$) and the *Laplace equation* ($\lambda = 0$ and $f = 0$). For simplicity, we consider this equation on the unit square, $0 \leq x \leq 1, 0 \leq y \leq 1$. There are numerous possibilities for the boundary conditions that must be specified along each side of the square:

- *Dirichlet* boundary conditions, sometimes called *essential* boundary conditions, in which the solution u is specified
- *Neumann* boundary conditions, sometimes called *natural* boundary conditions, in which one of the derivatives u_x or u_y is specified
- *Mixed* boundary conditions, in which a combination of solution values and derivative values is specified.

11.3.1 Finite Difference Methods

Finite difference methods for elliptic boundary value problems proceed as we have seen before: we define a discrete mesh of points within the domain of the equation, replace the derivatives in the PDE by finite differences, and seek a numerical solution at each of the mesh points. Unlike time-dependent problems, however, we do not produce the solution gradually by marching forward in time, but rather determine the approximate solution at all of the mesh points simultaneously by solving a single system of algebraic equations.

EXAMPLE 11.4 LAPLACE EQUATION. We illustrate this procedure with a simple example. Consider the Laplace equation on the unit square

$$u_{xx} + u_{yy} = 0,$$

with boundary conditions as shown on the left in Fig. 11.5. We define a discrete mesh in the domain, including boundaries, as shown on the right in Fig. 11.5.

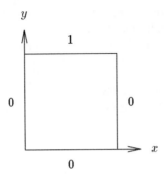 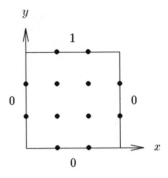

FIGURE 11.5
Boundary conditions (left) and mesh (right) for Laplace equation example.

The interior grid points where we will compute the approximate solution are given by

$$(x_i, y_j) = (ih, jh), \qquad i, j = 1, \ldots, n,$$

where in our example $n = 2$ and $h = 1/(n+1) = \frac{1}{3}$. Next we replace the second derivatives in the equation with the usual centered difference approximation at each interior mesh point to obtain the finite difference equation

$$\frac{u_{i+1,j} - 2u_{i,j} + u_{i-1,j}}{h^2} + \frac{u_{i,j+1} - 2u_{i,j} + u_{i,j-1}}{h^2} = 0,$$

where $u_{i,j}$ is an approximation to the true solution $u(x_i, y_j)$ for $i, j = 1, \ldots, n$, and represents one of the given boundary values if i or j is 0 or $n + 1$. Simplifying and writing out the resulting four equations explicitly, we obtain

$$4u_{1,1} - u_{0,1} - u_{2,1} - u_{1,0} - u_{1,2} = 0,$$

$$4u_{2,1} - u_{1,1} - u_{3,1} - u_{2,0} - u_{2,2} = 0,$$

$$4u_{1,2} - u_{0,2} - u_{2,2} - u_{1,1} - u_{1,3} = 0,$$

$$4u_{2,2} - u_{1,2} - u_{3,2} - u_{2,1} - u_{2,3} = 0.$$

Writing these four equations in matrix form, we have

$$
\begin{bmatrix}
4 & -1 & -1 & 0 \\
-1 & 4 & 0 & -1 \\
-1 & 0 & 4 & -1 \\
0 & -1 & -1 & 4
\end{bmatrix}
\begin{bmatrix}
u_{1,1} \\
u_{2,1} \\
u_{1,2} \\
u_{2,2}
\end{bmatrix}
=
\begin{bmatrix}
u_{0,1} + u_{1,0} \\
u_{3,1} + u_{2,0} \\
u_{0,2} + u_{1,3} \\
u_{3,2} + u_{2,3}
\end{bmatrix}
=
\begin{bmatrix}
0 \\
0 \\
1 \\
1
\end{bmatrix}.
$$

This system of equations can be solved for the unknowns $u_{i,j}$ either by a direct method based on factorization or by an iterative method, yielding the solution

$$
\begin{bmatrix}
u_{1,1} \\
u_{2,1} \\
u_{1,2} \\
u_{2,2}
\end{bmatrix}
=
\begin{bmatrix}
0.125 \\
0.125 \\
0.375 \\
0.375
\end{bmatrix}.
$$

In a practical problem, the mesh size h would be much smaller and the resulting linear system would be much larger than in the preceding example. The matrix would be very sparse, however, since each equation would still involve at most only five of the variables, thereby saving substantially on work and storage. We can be a bit more specific about the nonzero pattern of the matrix of such a linear system. We have already seen in Section 10.4 how this type of finite difference method on a one-dimensional grid yields a tridiagonal system. A rectangular two-dimensional grid can be thought of as a one-dimensional grid of one-dimensional grids. Thus, with a row- or column-wise ordering of the grid points, the corresponding matrix will be *block tridiagonal*, with each nonzero block being tridiagonal or diagonal. Such a pattern is barely evident in the matrix of the previous example, where the blocks are only 2×2; for a slightly larger example, where the pattern is more evident, see Fig. 11.6. This pattern generalizes to a three-dimensional grid, which can be viewed as a one-dimensional grid of two-dimensional grids, so that the matrix would be block tridiagonal, with the nonzero blocks themselves being block tridiagonal, and their subblocks being tridiagonal. Of course, for a less regular grid or mesh, or a more complicated finite difference stencil, the pattern would not be so simple, but sparsity would still prevail owing to the local connectivity among the grid points.

11.3.2 Finite Element Methods

In Section 10.5 we considered finite element methods for solving boundary value problems for ODEs. Finite element methods are also applicable to boundary value problems for PDEs as well. Conceptually, there is no change in going from one dimension to two or three dimensions: the solution is still represented as a linear combination of basis functions, and some criterion (e.g., Galerkin) is applied to derive a system of equations that determines the coefficients of the linear combination.

The main practical difference is that instead of subintervals in one dimension, the elements usually become triangles or rectangles in two dimensions, or tetrahedra or hexahedra in three dimensions. Additional complications can occur, such as dealing with curved boundaries. Basis functions typically used are bilinear or bicubic functions in two dimensions or trilinear or tricubic functions in three dimensions, analogous to the "hat" functions or piecewise cubics in one dimension. Of course, the increase in dimensionality means that the linear system to be solved is much larger, but it is still sparse owing to the local support of the basis functions. Finite element methods for PDEs are extremely flexible and powerful, but a detailed treatment of them is beyond the scope of this book.

11.4 DIRECT METHODS FOR SPARSE LINEAR SYSTEMS

All types of boundary value problems, as well as implicit methods for time-dependent PDEs, give rise to systems of linear algebraic equations to solve. The use of finite difference schemes involving only a few variables each, or the use of localized basis functions in a finite element approach, causes the matrix of the linear system to be sparse. This sparsity can be exploited to reduce the storage and work required for solving the linear system to much less than the $\mathcal{O}(n^2)$ and $\mathcal{O}(n^3)$, respectively, that might be expected in a more naive approach. In this section we briefly consider direct methods for solving large sparse linear systems, and then in the following section we will discuss iterative methods for such systems in somewhat more detail.

11.4.1 Sparse Factorization Methods

Gaussian elimination and its variants such as Cholesky factorization for symmetric positive definite matrices are applicable to solving large sparse systems, but a great deal of care must be exercised to achieve reasonable efficiency in both solution time and storage requirements. The key to this efficiency is to store and operate on only the nonzero entries of the matrix. Thus, special data structures are required rather than the simple two-dimensional arrays that are so natural for storing dense matrices.

For one-dimensional problems, the equations and unknowns can usually be ordered so that the nonzeros are concentrated in a relatively narrow band, which can be stored efficiently in a rectangular two-dimensional array by diagonals. Algorithms are available for reducing the bandwidth, if necessary, by reordering the rows and columns of the matrix. But for problems in two or more dimensions, even the narrowest possible band often contains mostly zeros, and hence any type of two-dimensional array storage would be prohibitively wasteful. In general, sparse systems require data structures in which individual nonzero entries are stored, along with the indices required to identify their locations in the matrix. Explicitly storing the indices not only incurs additional storage overhead but also makes arithmetic operations on the nonzeros less efficient owing to the indirect addressing required to access the operands. Thus, such a representation is worthwhile only if the matrix is sufficiently sparse, which is often the case for very large problems arising from PDEs and many other applications.

When applied to a sparse matrix, LU or Cholesky factorization can be carried out in the usual manner, but taking linear combinations of rows or columns to annihilate unwanted nonzero entries can in turn introduce new nonzeros into locations in the matrix that were initially zero. Such new nonzeros, called *fill*, must then be stored and, depending on their locations, may eventually be annihilated themselves in order to obtain the triangular factors. In any case, the resulting triangular factors can be expected to contain at least as many nonzeros as the original matrix and usually a significant amount of fill as well. The amount of fill incurred is very sensitive to the order in which the rows and columns of the matrix are processed, so one of the central problems in sparse factorization is to reorder the original matrix to limit the amount of fill that the matrix suffers during factorization. Exact minimization of fill turns out to be a very hard combinatorial problem (NP-complete), but heuristic algorithms are available, such as minimum degree and nested dissection, that do a good job of limiting fill for many types of problems. We sketch these algorithms briefly in the following example; see [68, 93] for further details.

EXAMPLE 11.5 SPARSE FACTORIZATION. To illustrate sparse factorization, we consider a matrix arising from a typical two-dimensional elliptic boundary value problem, the Laplace equation on the unit square (see Example 11.4). A 3×3 grid of interior mesh points is shown on the left in Fig. 11.6, with the points, or *nodes,* numbered in a natural, row-wise order. The Laplace equation is then approximated by a system of linear equations using the standard second-order finite difference approximation to the second derivatives. In the diagram, a pair of nodes is connected by a line, or *edge,* if both appear in the same equation in this system. We say that two nodes are *neighbors* if they are connected by an edge.

The nonzero pattern of the 9×9 symmetric positive definite matrix A of this linear system is shown in the center of Fig. 11.6, where a nonzero entry of the matrix is indicated by $\times$ and zero entries are blank. The diagonal entries of the matrix correspond to the nodes in the mesh, and the nonzero off-diagonal entries correspond to the edges in the mesh (i.e., $a_{ij} \neq 0 \Leftrightarrow$ nodes i and j are neighbors). Note that the matrix is banded, but it also has many zero entries inside the band. More specifically, the matrix is block tridiagonal, with each nonzero block being either tridiagonal or diagonal, as expected for a row- or column-wise ordering of a two-dimensional grid. Cholesky factorization of the matrix in this ordering fills in the band almost completely, as shown on the right in Fig. 11.6, where fill entries (new nonzeros) are indicated by $+$. We will see that there are other orderings in which the matrix suffers considerably less fill.

Each step in the factorization process corresponds to the elimination of a node from the mesh. Eliminating a node causes all of its neighboring nodes to become connected to each other. If any such neighbors were not already connected, then *fill* results (i.e., new edges in the mesh and new nonzeros in the matrix). Thus, a good heuristic for limiting fill is to eliminate first those nodes having fewest neighbors. The number of neighbors of a given node is called its *degree,* so this heuristic is known as *minimum degree.* At each step, the minimum degree algorithm selects for elimination a node of smallest degree, breaking ties arbitrarily. After the node has been eliminated, its former neighbors all become connected to each other, so the degrees of some nodes may change. The process is then repeated, with a new node of minimum degree eliminated next, and so on until all nodes have been eliminated. A minimum degree ordering for our example problem is shown in Fig. 11.7, along with the correspondingly permuted matrix and resulting Cholesky factor. Although there is no obvious pattern to the nonzeros in the reordered matrix, the Cholesky factor suffers much less fill than with the band ordering. This difference is much more pronounced

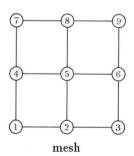

$$
\begin{bmatrix}
\times & \times & & \times & & & & & \\
\times & \times & \times & & \times & & & & \\
& \times & \times & & & \times & & & \\
\times & & & \times & \times & & \times & & \\
& \times & & \times & \times & \times & & \times & \\
& & \times & & \times & \times & & & \times \\
& & & \times & & & \times & \times & \\
& & & & \times & & \times & \times & \times \\
& & & & & \times & & \times & \times
\end{bmatrix}
\qquad
\begin{bmatrix}
\times & & & & & & & & \\
\times & \times & & & & & & & \\
& \times & \times & & & & & & \\
\times & + & + & \times & & & & & \\
& \times & + & \times & \times & & & & \\
& & \times & + & \times & \times & & & \\
& & & \times & + & + & \times & & \\
& & & & \times & + & \times & \times & \\
& & & & & \times & + & \times & \times
\end{bmatrix}
$$

mesh $\qquad\qquad\qquad A \qquad\qquad\qquad\qquad\qquad L$

FIGURE 11.6
Finite difference mesh and nonzero patterns of corresponding sparse matrix A and its Cholesky factor L.

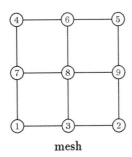 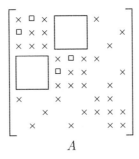 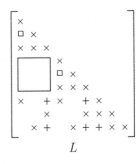

mesh A L

FIGURE 11.7
Finite difference mesh reordered by minimum degree, with nonzero patterns of correspondingly
permuted sparse matrix A and its Cholesky factor L.

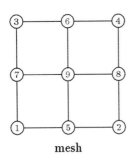 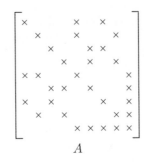 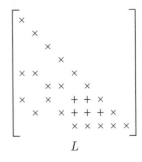

mesh A L

FIGURE 11.8
Finite difference mesh reordered by nested dissection, with nonzero patterns of correspondingly
permuted sparse matrix A and its Cholesky factor L.

in larger problems, and more sophisticated variants of the minimum degree algorithm are
among the most effective general-purpose ordering algorithms known.

Nested dissection is a divide-and-conquer strategy for determining a good ordering to
limit fill in sparse factorization. First, a small set of nodes whose removal splits the mesh
into two pieces of roughly equal size is selected, and these *separator* nodes are numbered
last. Then the process is repeated recursively on each remaining piece of the mesh until
all nodes have been numbered. A nested dissection ordering for our example problem is
shown in Fig. 11.8, along with the correspondingly permuted matrix and resulting Cholesky
factor. Separating the mesh into two pieces means that no node in either piece is connected
to any node in the other, and hence no fill can occur in either piece as a consequence of
the elimination of a node in the other. In other words, dissection induces blocks of zeros in
the matrix (indicated by the squares in Fig. 11.8) that are automatically preserved during
factorization, thereby limiting fill. The recursive nature of the algorithm can be seen in the
hierarchical block structure of the matrix, which would involve many more levels in a larger
problem.

Sparse factorization methods are accurate, reliable, and robust. They are the methods of choice for one-dimensional problems and are usually competitive for two-

dimensional problems, but they can be prohibitively expensive in both work and storage for very large three-dimensional problems. We will see that iterative methods provide a viable alternative in these cases.

11.4.2 Fast Direct Methods

For certain types of PDEs, special techniques can be used to solve the resulting discretized linear system much faster than would be expected. For example, for certain elliptic boundary value problems having constant coefficients and simple boundaries (e.g., the Poisson equation on a rectangular domain), the fast Fourier transform, or FFT (see Chapter 12), can be used to compute the solution to the discrete system very efficiently, provided that the number of mesh points in each dimension is a power of two. This technique is the basis for several "fast Poisson solver" software packages. For a problem with n mesh points, such a fast Poisson solver computes the solution in $\mathcal{O}(n \log_2 n)$ operations, which is nearly optimal since the cost of simply writing the output is $\mathcal{O}(n)$.

Somewhat more generally, for separable elliptic PDEs the method of *cyclic reduction* permits similarly fast solutions. Cyclic reduction is a divide-and-conquer technique in which the even-numbered equations in the systems are solved in terms of the odd-numbered ones, and so on recursively until reaching the bottom of the recursion, where single equations can be solved trivially. This idea obviously works best when the order of the system is a power of two, but it can be adapted to handle systems of arbitrary order. These ideas—FFT and cyclic reduction—can be combined, for example using FFT in one dimension and cyclic reduction in the other. A more subtle combination results in the FACR (Fourier analysis/cyclic reduction) method, which is even faster than either the FFT method or the cyclic reduction method alone. The computational complexity of the FACR method is $\mathcal{O}(n \log \log n)$, which is effectively optimal, since log log is essentially constant for problems of any reasonable size.

11.5 ITERATIVE METHODS FOR LINEAR SYSTEMS

Iterative methods for solving linear systems begin with an initial estimate for the solution and successively improve it until the solution is as accurate as desired. In theory, an infinite number of iterations might be required to converge to the exact solution, but in practice the iteration terminates when some norm of the residual $\|b - Ax\|$, or some other measure of error, is as small as desired.

11.5.1 Stationary Iterative Methods

Perhaps the simplest type of iterative method for solving $Ax = b$ has the form

$$x_{k+1} = Gx_k + c,$$

where the matrix G and vector c are chosen so that a fixed point of the equation $x = Gx + c$ is a solution to $Ax = b$. Such a method is said to be *stationary* if G and c are constant over all iterations.

One way to obtain a suitable matrix G is by a *splitting*, in which the matrix A is written as

$$A = M - N,$$

with M nonsingular. We can then take $G = M^{-1}N$ and $c = M^{-1}b$, so that the iteration scheme becomes

$$x_{k+1} = M^{-1}Nx_k + M^{-1}b,$$

which is implemented as

$$Mx_{k+1} = Nx_k + b$$

(i.e., we solve a linear system with matrix M at each iteration).

Formally, this splitting scheme is a fixed-point iteration with iteration function

$$g(x) = M^{-1}Nx + M^{-1}b,$$

whose Jacobian matrix is

$$G(x) = M^{-1}N.$$

Thus, the iteration scheme is convergent if

$$\rho(G) = \rho(M^{-1}N) < 1,$$

and the smaller the spectral radius, the faster the convergence rate (see Section 5.3.1).

For rapid convergence, we should choose M and N so that $\rho(M^{-1}N)$ is as small as possible. There is a trade-off, however, as the cost per iteration is determined by the cost of solving a linear system with matrix M. As an extreme example, if $M = A$, then the scheme converges in a single iteration (i.e., we have a direct method), but that one iteration may be prohibitively expensive. In practice, M is chosen to approximate A in some sense, but is usually constrained to have some simple form, such as diagonal or triangular, so that the linear system at each iteration is easy to solve.

EXAMPLE 11.6 ITERATIVE REFINEMENT. We have already seen one example of a stationary iterative method, namely, iterative refinement of a solution already computed by Gaussian elimination (see Section 2.4.3). Forward- and back-substitution using the LU factorization in effect provide an approximation, call it B^{-1}, to the inverse of A (i.e., for any right-hand-side vector y, the solution $B^{-1}y$ can be computed by forward- and back-substitution using the LU factors already computed). Iterative refinement then has the form

$$x_{k+1} = x_k + B^{-1}(b - Ax_k),$$

which can be rewritten

$$x_{k+1} = (I - B^{-1}A)x_k + B^{-1}b.$$

Thus, we see that iterative refinement is a stationary iterative method with $G = I - B^{-1}A$ and $c = B^{-1}b$. The scheme therefore converges if $\rho(I - B^{-1}A) < 1$, which should be the case if B^{-1} is a good approximation to A^{-1}, such as the use of forward- and back-substitution with the LU factors obtained by Gaussian elimination with partial pivoting. Indeed, the convergence condition may be satisfied even by a rather loose approximation to the inverse. For example, iterative refinement can sometimes be used to stabilize "fast but risky" algorithms.

11.5.2 Jacobi Method

In the matrix splitting $A = M - N$, the simplest choice for M is diagonal, specifically the diagonal of A. Let D be a diagonal matrix with the same diagonal entries as A, and let L and U be the strict lower and upper triangular portions of A, respectively, so that

$$M = D, \qquad N = -(L + U)$$

gives a splitting of A. If A has no zero diagonal entries, so that D is nonsingular, we obtain the iterative scheme known as the Jacobi method:

$$x^{(k+1)} = D^{-1}(b - (L + U)x^{(k)}).$$

(We use parenthesized superscripts for the iteration index when we need to reserve subscripts to refer to individual components of a vector.) Rewriting this scheme componentwise, we see that, beginning with an initial guess $x^{(0)}$, the Jacobi method computes the next iterate by solving for each component of x in terms of the others:

$$x_i^{(k+1)} = \frac{b_i - \sum_{j \neq i} a_{ij} x_j^{(k)}}{a_{ii}}, \qquad i = 1, \ldots, n.$$

Note that the Jacobi method requires double storage for the vector x because all of the old component values are needed throughout the sweep, and therefore the new component values cannot overwrite them until the sweep has been completed.

To illustrate the use of the Jacobi method, if we apply it to solve the system of finite difference equations for the Laplace equation in Example 11.4, we get

$$u_{i,j}^{(k+1)} = \frac{u_{i-1,j}^{(k)} + u_{i,j-1}^{(k)} + u_{i+1,j}^{(k)} + u_{i,j+1}^{(k)}}{4},$$

which means that each new approximate solution at a given grid point is simply the average of the previous solution components at the four surrounding grid points. In this sense, solving the elliptic problem by an iterative method adds a timelike dimension (analogous to a parabolic problem, in this case the heat equation) in which the initial solution "diffuses" until a steady state is reached at the final solution.

The Jacobi method does not always converge, but it is guaranteed to converge under conditions that are often satisfied in practice (e.g., if the matrix is diagonally dominant by rows). Unfortunately, the convergence rate of the Jacobi method is usually unacceptably slow.

11.5.3 Gauss-Seidel Method

One reason for the slow convergence of the Jacobi method is that it does not make use of the latest information available: new component values are used only after the entire sweep has been completed. The Gauss-Seidel method remedies this drawback by using each new component of the solution as soon as it has been computed:

$$x_i^{(k+1)} = \frac{b_i - \sum_{j<i} a_{ij} x_j^{(k+1)} - \sum_{j>i} a_{ij} x_j^{(k)}}{a_{ii}}, \qquad i = 1, \ldots, n.$$

In the same notation as in Section 11.5.2, the Gauss-Seidel method corresponds to the splitting

$$M = D + L, \qquad N = -U,$$

and can be written in matrix terms as

$$x^{(k+1)} = D^{-1}(b - Lx^{(k+1)} - Ux^{(k)})$$
$$= (D + L)^{-1}(b - Ux^{(k)}).$$

In addition to faster convergence, another benefit of the Gauss-Seidel method is that duplicate storage is not needed for the vector x, since the newly computed component values can overwrite the old ones immediately (a programmer would have invented this method in the first place because of its more natural and convenient implementation). On the other hand, the updating of the unknowns must now be done successively, in contrast to the Jacobi method, in which the unknowns can be updated in any order or even simultaneously. The latter feature may make Jacobi preferable on a parallel computer.

To illustrate the use of the Gauss-Seidel method, if we apply it to solve the system of finite difference equations for the Laplace equation in Example 11.4, we get

$$u_{i,j}^{(k+1)} = \frac{u_{i-1,j}^{(k+1)} + u_{i,j-1}^{(k+1)} + u_{i+1,j}^{(k)} + u_{i,j+1}^{(k)}}{4},$$

assuming that we sweep from left to right and bottom to top in the grid. Thus, we again average the solution values at the four surrounding grid points but always use new component values as soon as they become available rather than waiting until the current iteration has been completed.

The Gauss-Seidel method does not always converge, but it is guaranteed to converge under conditions that are often satisfied in practice and that are somewhat weaker than those for the Jacobi method (e.g., if the matrix is symmetric and positive definite). Although the Gauss-Seidel method converges more rapidly than the Jacobi method, it is often still too slow to be practical.

11.5.4 Successive Over-Relaxation

The convergence rate of the Gauss-Seidel method can be accelerated by a technique called *successive over-relaxation* (SOR), which in effect uses the step to the next Gauss-Seidel iterate as a search direction, but with a fixed search parameter denoted by ω. Starting with $x^{(k)}$, we first compute the next iterate that would be given by Gauss-Seidel, $x_{GS}^{(k+1)}$, then instead take the next iterate to be

$$x^{(k+1)} = x^{(k)} + \omega(x_{GS}^{(k+1)} - x^{(k)}).$$

Equivalently, we can think of this scheme as taking a weighted average of the current iterate and the next Gauss-Seidel iterate:

$$x^{(k+1)} = (1 - \omega)x^{(k)} + \omega x_{GS}^{(k+1)}.$$

In either case, ω is a fixed *relaxation parameter* chosen to accelerate convergence. A value $\omega > 1$ gives *over*-relaxation, whereas $\omega < 1$ gives *under*-relaxation ($\omega = 1$ simply gives the Gauss-Seidel method). We always have $0 < \omega < 2$ (otherwise the method diverges), but choosing a specific value of ω to attain the best possible convergence rate is a difficult problem in general and is the subject of an elaborate theory for special classes of matrices.

In the same notation as in Section 11.5.2, the SOR method corresponds to the splitting

$$M = D + \omega L, \qquad N = (1 - \omega)D - \omega U,$$

and can be written in matrix terms as

$$x^{(k+1)} = x^{(k)} + \omega[D^{-1}(b - Lx^{(k+1)} - Ux^{(k)}) - x^{(k)}]$$
$$= (D + \omega L)^{-1}[(1 - \omega)D - \omega U]x^{(k)} + \omega(D + \omega L)^{-1}b.$$

Like the Gauss-Seidel method, the SOR method makes repeated forward sweeps through the unknowns, updating them successively. A variant of SOR, known as SSOR (symmetric SOR), alternates forward and backward sweeps through the unknowns. SSOR is not necessarily faster than SOR (indeed SSOR is often slower), but it has the theoretical advantage that its iteration matrix, $G = M^{-1}N$, which is too complicated to express here, is similar to a symmetric matrix when A is symmetric (which is not true of the iteration matrix for SOR). For example, this makes SSOR useful as a preconditioner (see Section 11.5.5).

11.5.5 Conjugate Gradient Method

We now turn from stationary iterative methods to methods based on optimization. If A is an $n \times n$ symmetric positive definite matrix, then the quadratic function

$$\phi(x) = \tfrac{1}{2}x^T A x - x^T b$$

attains a minimum precisely when $Ax = b$. Thus, we can apply any of the optimization methods discussed in Section 6.3 to obtain a solution to the corresponding linear system. Recall from Section 6.3 that most multidimensional optimization methods progress from one iteration to the next by performing a one-dimensional search along some search direction s_k, so that

$$x_{k+1} = x_k + \alpha s_k,$$

where α is a search parameter chosen to minimize the objective function $\phi(x_k + \alpha s_k)$ along s_k.

We note some special features of such a quadratic optimization problem. First, the negative gradient is simply the residual vector:

$$-\nabla\phi(x) = b - Ax = r.$$

Second, for any search direction s_k, we need not perform a line search, because the optimal choice for α can be determined analytically. Specifically, the minimum over α occurs when the new residual is orthogonal to the search direction:

$$0 = \frac{d}{d\alpha}\phi(x_{k+1}) = \nabla\phi(x_{k+1})^T \frac{d}{d\alpha}x_{k+1} = (Ax_{k+1} - b)^T\left(\frac{d}{d\alpha}(x_k + \alpha s_k)\right) = -r_{k+1}^T s_k.$$

Since the new residual can be expressed in terms of the old residual and the search direction,

$$r_{k+1} = b - Ax_{k+1} = b - A(x_k + \alpha s_k) = (b - Ax_k) - \alpha As_k = r_k - \alpha As_k,$$

we can thus solve for

$$\alpha = \frac{r_k^T s_k}{s_k^T As_k}.$$

If we take advantage of these properties in the algorithm of Section 6.3.6, we obtain the *conjugate gradient* (CG) method for solving symmetric positive definite linear systems. Starting with an initial guess x_0 and taking $s_0 = r_0 = b - Ax_0$, the following steps are repeated for $k = 0, 1, \ldots$ until convergence:

1. $\alpha_k = r_k^T r_k / s_k^T As_k$.
2. $x_{k+1} = x_k + \alpha_k s_k$.
3. $r_{k+1} = r_k - \alpha_k As_k$.
4. $\beta_{k+1} = r_{k+1}^T r_{k+1} / r_k^T r_k$.
5. $s_{k+1} = r_{k+1} + \beta_{k+1} s_k$.

Each iteration of the algorithm requires only a single matrix-vector multiplication, As_k, plus a small number of inner products. The storage requirements are also very modest, since the vectors x, r, and s can be overwritten.

Although the foregoing algorithm is not terribly difficult to derive, we content ourselves here with the following intuitive motivation. The features noted earlier for the quadratic optimization problem would make it extremely easy to apply the steepest descent method, using the negative gradient—in this case the residual—as search direction at each iteration. Unfortunately, we have already observed that its convergence rate is often very poor owing to repeated searches in the same directions (zigzagging). We could avoid this repetition by orthogonalizing each new search direction against all of the previous ones (see Section 3.4.6), leaving only components in "new" directions, but this would appear to be prohibitively expensive computationally and would also require excessive storage to save all of the search directions. However, if instead of using the standard inner product we make the search directions mutually A-orthogonal (vectors y and z are A-orthogonal if $y^T Az = 0$), or *conjugate*, then it can be shown that the successive A-orthogonal search directions satisfy a three-term recurrence (this is the role played by β in the algorithm). This short recurrence makes the computation very cheap, and, most important, it means that we do not need to save all of the previous gradients, only the most recent two, which makes a huge difference in storage requirements.

In addition to the other special properties already mentioned, it turns out that in the quadratic case the residual at each step is minimal (with respect to the norm induced by A) over the space spanned by the search directions generated so far. Since the search directions are A-orthogonal, and hence linearly independent, this property implies that after at most n steps the solution is exact, because the n search directions must span the whole space. Thus, in theory, the conjugate gradient method is direct, but in practice rounding error causes a loss of orthogonality, which spoils this finite termination property. As a result, the conjugate gradient method is usually used in an iterative manner and halted when the residual, or some other measure of error, is sufficiently small. In practice, the method often converges in far fewer than n iterations. We will consider its convergence rate in Section 11.5.6.

Although it is a significant improvement over steepest descent, the conjugate gradient algorithm can still converge very slowly if the matrix A is ill-conditioned. Convergence can often be substantially accelerated by *preconditioning*, which can be thought of as implicitly multiplying A by M^{-1}, where M is a matrix for which systems of the form $Mz = y$ are easily solved, and whose inverse approximates that of A, so that $M^{-1}A$ is relatively well-conditioned. Technically, to preserve symmetry, we should apply the conjugate gradient algorithm to $L^{-1}AL^{-T}$ instead of $M^{-1}A$, where $M = LL^T$. However, the algorithm can be suitably rearranged so that only M is used and the corresponding matrix L is not required explicitly. The resulting preconditioned conjugate gradient algorithm is given here. Starting with an initial guess x_0 and taking $r_0 = b - Ax_0$ and $s_0 = M^{-1}r_0$, the following steps are repeated for $k = 0, 1, \ldots$ until convergence:

1. $\alpha_k = r_k^T M^{-1} r_k / s_k^T A s_k$.
2. $x_{k+1} = x_k + \alpha_k s_k$.
3. $r_{k+1} = r_k - \alpha_k A s_k$.
4. $\beta_{k+1} = r_{k+1}^T M^{-1} r_{k+1} / r_k^T M^{-1} r_k$.
5. $s_{k+1} = M^{-1} r_{k+1} + \beta_{k+1} s_k$.

Note that in addition to the one matrix-vector multiplication, As_k, per iteration, we must also apply the preconditioner, $M^{-1} r_k$, once per iteration.

The choice of an appropriate preconditioner depends on the usual trade-off between the gain in the convergence rate and the increased cost per iteration that results from applying the preconditioner. Many different choices of preconditioner have been proposed, and this topic is an active area of research. Some of the types of preconditioning most commonly used are:

- *Diagonal* (also called Jacobi): M is taken to be a diagonal matrix with diagonal entries equal to those of A.
- *Block diagonal* (or block Jacobi): If the indices $1, \ldots, n$ are partitioned into mutually disjoint subsets, then $m_{ij} = a_{ij}$ if i and j are in the same subset, and $m_{ij} = 0$ otherwise. Natural choices include partitioning along lines or planes in two- or three-dimensional grids, respectively, or grouping together physical variables that correspond to a common node, as in many finite element problems.
- *SSOR:* Using a matrix splitting of the form $A = L + D + L^T$ as in Section 11.5.1, we can take $M = (D + L)D^{-1}(D + L)^T$, or, introducing the SSOR relaxation parameter ω,

$$M(\omega) = \frac{1}{2 - \omega}\left(\frac{1}{\omega}D + L\right)\left(\frac{1}{\omega}D\right)^{-1}\left(\frac{1}{\omega}D + L\right)^T.$$

With optimal choice of ω, the SSOR preconditioner is capable of reducing the condition number to $\text{cond}(M^{-1}A) = \mathcal{O}(\sqrt{\text{cond}(A)})$, but as usual, obtaining knowledge of this optimal value may be impractical.

- *Incomplete factorization:* Ideally, one would like to solve the linear system directly using the Cholesky factorization $A = LL^T$, but this may incur unacceptable fill (see Section 11.4.1). One may instead compute an approximate factorization $A \approx \hat{L}\hat{L}^T$ that allows little or no fill (e.g., restricting the nonzero entries of $\hat{L}$ to be in the same positions as those of the lower triangle of A), then use $M = \hat{L}\hat{L}^T$ as a preconditioner.
- *Polynomial:* M^{-1} is taken to be a polynomial in A that approximates A^{-1}. One way to obtain a suitable polynomial is to use a fixed number of steps of a stationary iterative method to solve the preconditioning system $Mz_k = r_k$ at each conjugate gradient iteration.
- *Approximate inverse:* M^{-1} is determined by using an optimization algorithm to minimize the residual

$$\|I - AM^{-1}\| \qquad \text{or} \qquad \|I - M^{-1}A\|$$

in some norm, with M restricted to have a prescribed pattern of nonzero entries.

Note that some of these preconditioners require a significant amount of work to form them initially, and this work must also be included in the cost trade-off mentioned earlier. The conjugate gradient method is rarely used without some form of preconditioning. Since diagonal preconditioning requires almost no extra work or storage, at least this much preconditioning is always advisable, and more sophisticated preconditioners are often worthwhile.

The conjugate gradient method is generally applicable only to symmetric positive definite systems. If the matrix A is indefinite or nonsymmetric, then the algorithm may break down both theoretically (e.g., the corresponding optimization problem may not have a minimum) and practically (e.g., the formula for α may fail). The method can be generalized to symmetric indefinite systems, as in the SYMMLQ algorithm of Paige and Saunders [198], for example. The conjugate gradient method cannot be generalized to nonsymmetric systems, however, without sacrificing at least one of the two properties—the short recurrence property and the minimum residual property—that largely account for its effectiveness. Nevertheless, in recent years a number of related algorithms have been formulated for solving nonsymmetric linear systems, including GMRES, QMR, CGS, BiCG, Bi-CGSTAB, and others. These algorithms tend to be significantly less robust or require considerably more storage or work than the conjugate gradient algorithm that inspired them, but in many cases they are still the most effective methods available for solving very large nonsymmetric systems.

EXAMPLE 11.7 ITERATIVE METHODS FOR LINEAR SYSTEMS. We illustrate various iterative methods by using them to solve the 4×4 linear system for the Laplace equation on the unit square in Example 11.4. In each case we take $x^{(0)} = 0$ as starting guess.

The Jacobi method gives the following sequence of iterates for this problem:

k	x_1	x_2	x_3	x_4
0	0.000	0.000	0.000	0.000
1	0.000	0.000	0.250	0.250
2	0.062	0.062	0.312	0.312
3	0.094	0.094	0.344	0.344
4	0.109	0.109	0.359	0.359
5	0.117	0.117	0.367	0.367
6	0.121	0.121	0.371	0.371
7	0.123	0.123	0.373	0.373
8	0.124	0.124	0.374	0.374
9	0.125	0.125	0.375	0.375

As expected, the Gauss-Seidel method converges somewhat faster, giving the following sequence of iterates for this problem:

k	x_1	x_2	x_3	x_4
0	0.000	0.000	0.000	0.000
1	0.000	0.000	0.250	0.312
2	0.062	0.094	0.344	0.359
3	0.109	0.117	0.367	0.371
4	0.121	0.123	0.373	0.374
5	0.124	0.125	0.375	0.375
6	0.125	0.125	0.375	0.375

The optimal acceleration parameter in the SOR method turns out to be $\omega = 1.072$ for this problem, which is so close to 1 that it converges only slightly faster than Gauss-Seidel, giving the following sequence of iterates:

k	x_1	x_2	x_3	x_4
0	0.000	0.000	0.000	0.000
1	0.000	0.000	0.268	0.335
2	0.072	0.108	0.356	0.365
3	0.119	0.121	0.371	0.373
4	0.123	0.124	0.374	0.375
5	0.125	0.125	0.375	0.375

Finally, the conjugate gradient method converges in only two iterations for this problem, giving the following sequence of iterates:

k	x_1	x_2	x_3	x_4
0	0.000	0.000	0.000	0.000
1	0.000	0.000	0.333	0.333
2	0.125	0.125	0.375	0.375

11.5.6 Rate of Convergence

Example 11.7 is too small for the results to be representative of the relative performance of the methods for problems of practical size. Recall from the discussion of convergence rates in Section 5.1.2 that, asymptotically, a linearly convergent sequence with constant C gains $-\log_{10}(C)$ decimal digits per iteration. Thus, the quantity $R = -\log_{10}(\rho(G))$ serves as a useful quantitative measure of the speed of convergence of a stationary iterative method with iteration matrix G. In this context, R is sometimes called the *rate of convergence*, but this term should not be confused with the convergence rate r defined in Section 5.1.2.

If we use the same five-point finite difference approximation as in the previous example for the Laplace equation on the unit square, but with an arbitrary $k \times k$ grid of interior mesh points with mesh size $h = 1/(k + 1)$, then the spectral radius $\rho(G)$ and approximate rate of convergence R for the stationary iterative methods are as shown in Table 11.1. We see that the rates of convergence for Jacobi and Gauss-Seidel are proportional to the square of the mesh size, or equivalently, that the number of iterations per digit of accuracy gained is proportional to the number of mesh points. The constants of proportionality also tell us that Gauss-Seidel is asymptotically twice as fast as Jacobi for this model problem. Optimal SOR, on the other hand, is an order of magnitude faster than either of the other methods, as its rate of convergence is proportional to the mesh size, and hence the number of iterations per digit gained is proportional to the number of mesh points along one side of the grid.

To make these results more concrete, in Table 11.2 are listed the spectral radius and rate of convergence for each method for a range of values of k. We see that the spectral radius is extremely close to 1 for large values of k, and hence all three methods converge very slowly. From the rate of convergence R, we see that for $k = 10$ (a linear system of order 100), Jacobi requires more than 50 iterations to gain a single decimal digit of

TABLE 11.1
Spectral radius and rate of convergence for $k \times k$ grid problem

Method	$\rho(G)$	R
Jacobi	$\cos(\pi h)$	$(\pi^2/\log 10)h^2/2$
Gauss-Seidel	$\cos^2(\pi h)$	$(\pi^2/\log 10)h^2$
Optimal SOR	$(1 - \sin(\pi h))/(1 + \sin(\pi h))$	$(2\pi/\log 10)h$

TABLE 11.2
Spectral radius of iteration matrix and rate of convergence for $k \times k$ grid

k	Jacobi $\rho(G)$	R	Gauss-Seidel $\rho(G)$	R	Optimal SOR $\rho(G)$	R
10	0.9595	0.018	0.9206	0.036	0.5604	0.252
50	0.9981	0.0008	0.9962	0.0016	0.8840	0.0535
100	0.9995	0.0002	0.9990	0.0004	0.9397	0.0270
500	0.99998	0.0000085	0.99996	0.000017	0.98754	0.005447

accuracy, Gauss-Seidel requires more than 25 iterations, and optimal SOR requires about 4 iterations. For $k = 100$ (a linear system of order 10,000), to gain a single decimal digit of accuracy Jacobi requires about 5000 iterations, Gauss-Seidel about 2500, and optimal SOR about 37. Thus, the Jacobi and Gauss-Seidel methods are impractical for a problem of this size, and optimal SOR, though perhaps reasonable for this problem, also becomes prohibitively slow for still larger problems. Moreover, the performance of SOR depends on knowledge of the optimal value for the relaxation parameter ω, which is known analytically for this simple model problem to be $\omega = 2/(1 + \sin(\pi h))$, but which is much harder to determine in general.

The convergence behavior of the nonstationary conjugate gradient method is more complicated, but roughly speaking the error is reduced at each iteration by a factor of

$$\frac{\sqrt{\kappa} - 1}{\sqrt{\kappa} + 1}$$

on average, where

$$\kappa = \text{cond}(A) = \|A\|_2 \cdot \|A^{-1}\|_2 = \frac{\lambda_{\max}(A)}{\lambda_{\min}(A)}.$$

When the matrix A is well-conditioned ($\kappa \approx 1$), convergence is rapid; but if A is very ill-conditioned ($\kappa \gg 1$), then convergence can be arbitrarily slow. For this reason, a preconditioner is usually used with the conjugate gradient method. By doing so, the preconditioned matrix $M^{-1}A$ has a much smaller condition number than A, and hence the convergence rate is greatly improved. The foregoing estimate is conservative, however, and the algorithm may do much better than this. For example, if the matrix A has only m distinct eigenvalues, then theoretically, conjugate gradients converges in at most m iterations. Thus, the detailed convergence behavior depends on all of the spectrum of A, not just on its extreme eigenvalues, and in practice the convergence is often superlinear.

11.5.7 Multigrid Methods

We have seen that stationary iterative methods often have very poor rates of convergence. There are various techniques for accelerating convergence, but these methods generally remain impractical for problems of realistic size. These convergence results are *asymptotic,* however, and such methods may initially make rapid progress before eventually settling into the slow asymptotic phase. In particular, many stationary iterative methods tend to reduce the high-frequency (i.e., oscillatory) components of the error rapidly but reduce the low-frequency (i.e., smooth) components of the error much more slowly, which produces the poor asymptotic rate of convergence (see Computer Problems 11.13 and 12.14 for examples). For this reason, such methods are sometimes called *smoothers.* This observation provides the motivation for *multigrid methods*, which we now outline very briefly.

The notions of smooth or oscillatory components of the error are relative to the mesh on which the solution is defined. In particular, a component that appears smooth on a fine grid may appear oscillatory when sampled on a coarser grid. If we apply a smoother on the coarser grid, then we may make rapid progress in reducing this (now oscillatory) component of the error. After a few iterations of the smoother, the results can then be interpolated back to the fine grid to produce a solution in which the low-frequency components of the error have been reduced. It may then be desirable to use a few more iterations of the smoother on the fine grid to ensure that the high-frequency components of the error are still small. The net result is an approximate solution on the fine grid for which both the high-frequency and low-frequency components of the error are reduced, and then the process can be repeated, if desired, until some convergence criterion is met.

This idea can be extended to multiple levels of grids, so that error components of various frequencies can be reduced rapidly, each at the appropriate level. Transition from a finer grid to a coarser grid involves *restriction* (sometimes called *injection*), whereas transition from a coarser grid to a finer grid involves *interpolation* (sometimes called *prolongation*).

If $\hat{x}$ is an approximate solution to $Ax = b$, with residual $r = b - A\hat{x}$, then the error $e = x - \hat{x}$ satisfies the equation $Ae = r$. Thus, in improving the approximate solution we can work with just this "residual equation" involving the error and the residual, rather than the solution and original right-hand side. One advantage of the residual equation is that zero is a reasonable starting guess for its solution. A two-grid method then takes the following form:

1. On the fine grid, use a few iterations of a smoother to compute an approximate solution $\hat{x}$ for the system $Ax = b$.
2. Compute the residual $r = b - A\hat{x}$.
3. Restrict the residual to the coarse grid.
4. On the coarse grid, use a few iterations of a smoother on the residual equation to obtain a coarse grid approximation to the error.
5. Interpolate the coarse grid correction to the fine grid to obtain an improved approximate solution on the fine grid.
6. Apply a few iterations of a smoother to the corrected solution on the fine grid.

A multigrid method results from recursion in Step 4, that is, the coarse grid correction is itself improved by using a still coarser grid, and so on down to some bottom level. The computations become cheaper as one moves to coarser and coarser grids because the systems become successively smaller. In particular, a direct method may be feasible on the coarsest grid if the system is small enough.

There are many possible strategies for cycling through the various grid levels, the most common of which are depicted schematically in Fig. 11.9. The *V-cycle* starts with the finest grid and goes down through successive levels to the coarsest grid and then back up again to the finest grid. To get more benefit from the coarser grids, where computations are cheaper, the *W-cycle* zigzags among the lower-level grids before moving back up to the finest grid. *Full multigrid* starts at the coarsest level, where a good initial solution is easier to come by (perhaps by direct solution), then bootstraps this solution up through the grid levels, ultimately reaching the finest grid.

By exploiting the strengths of the underlying iterative smoothers and avoiding their weaknesses, multigrid methods are capable of extraordinarily good performance. In particular, at each level the smoother reduces the oscillatory component of the error very

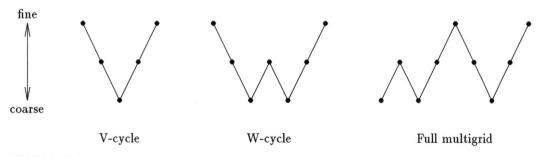

FIGURE 11.9
Cycling schemes for multigrid methods.

rapidly and at a rate that is independent of the mesh size h (since only a few iterations of the smoother, often only one, are performed at each level). Since all components of the error appear oscillatory at some level, it follows that the convergence rate of the entire multigrid scheme should be rapid and independent of the mesh size, which is in stark contrast to the other iterative methods we have considered. Moreover, the cost of an entire cycle of multigrid is only a modest multiple of the cost of a single sweep on the finest grid. As a result, multigrid methods are among the most powerful methods available for solving sparse linear systems arising from PDEs and are capable of converging to within the truncation error of the discretization at a cost comparable to fast direct methods, although the latter are much less broadly applicable.

11.6 COMPARISON OF METHODS

Now that we have examined both direct and iterative methods in some detail, we can summarize their relative advantages and disadvantages for solving linear systems:

- Direct methods require no initial estimate for the solution, but they take no advantage of it if a good estimate happens to be available.
- Direct methods are good at producing high accuracy, but they take no advantage if only low accuracy is needed.
- Iterative methods are often dependent on special properties, such as the matrix being symmetric positive definite, and are subject to very slow convergence for badly conditioned systems. Direct methods are more robust in both senses.
- Iterative methods usually require less work if convergence is rapid but often require the computation or estimation of various parameters or preconditioners to accelerate convergence, which at least partially offsets this advantage.
- Iterative methods do not require explicit storage of the matrix entries and hence are good when the matrix can be produced easily on demand or is most easily implemented as a linear operator.
- Iterative methods are less readily embodied in standard software packages, since the best representation of the matrix is often problem-dependent and "hard-coded" in an application program, whereas direct methods employ more standard storage schemes.

TABLE 11.3

Computational cost of solving elliptic boundary value problems as a function of k, the number of points along each dimension in a regular two- or three-dimensional grid

Method	2-D	3-D
Dense Cholesky	k^6	k^9
Jacobi	$k^4 \log k$	$k^5 \log k$
Gauss-Seidel	$k^4 \log k$	$k^5 \log k$
Band Cholesky	k^4	k^7
Optimal SOR	$k^3 \log k$	$k^4 \log k$
Sparse Cholesky	k^3	k^6
Conjugate gradient	k^3	k^4
Optimal SSOR	$k^{2.5} \log k$	$k^{3.5} \log k$
Preconditioned CG	$k^{2.5}$	$k^{3.5}$
Optimal ADI	$k^2 \log^2 k$	$k^3 \log^2 k$
Cyclic reduction	$k^2 \log k$	$k^3 \log k$
FFT	$k^2 \log k$	$k^3 \log k$
Multigrid V-cycle	$k^2 \log k$	$k^3 \log k$
FACR	$k^2 \log \log k$	$k^3 \log \log k$
Full multigrid	k^2	k^3

To make a more quantitative comparison, Table 11.3 shows the order of magnitude of the computational cost for solving a discretized elliptic boundary value problem in two or three dimensions (2-D or 3-D) by each of the methods we have discussed (and also a few methods that we have not discussed). These results should be taken only as a rough guide, as they depend on several assumptions:

- The discretization is by a finite difference scheme on a regular grid ($k \times k$ in two dimensions, $k \times k \times k$ in three dimensions) with mesh size $h = 1/k$. For the divide-and-conquer methods, k is assumed to be a power of two (and all logarithms are base two).
- The resulting matrix is symmetric, positive definite, and sparse, with a constant number of nonzeros per row and a condition number that is $\mathcal{O}(1/h^2)$.
- For the iterative methods that depend on various parameters, optimal values are known and used in all cases.
- For the band Cholesky method, the bandwidth is $\mathcal{O}(k)$ in two dimensions and $\mathcal{O}(k^2)$ in three dimensions.
- For the sparse Cholesky method, an optimal nested dissection ordering is used.
- For the preconditioned conjugate gradient method, the preconditioner reduces the condition number to $\mathcal{O}(1/h)$.
- The iterative methods are iterated to convergence within the truncation error of the discretization, i.e., until the initial error is reduced by a factor of h^2.

In interpreting these results, several caveats should be kept in mind:

- We have omitted the proportionality constants. In theory these are irrelevant asymptotically, but they may matter a great deal for a specific problem of interest, even quite a large one. Also, the value of the proportionality constant for a given method depends on the specific discretization used.

- The methods listed are not equally applicable. For the Poisson equation on the unit square with the standard five-point difference scheme, for example, all of the foregoing assumptions hold and all of the methods listed are applicable. But for more complicated PDEs, domains, boundary conditions, and discretization schemes, some of the methods listed may not be viable options.
- The methods listed are not equally reliable or robust. Many of the iterative methods depend on judicious choices of parameters or preconditioners that may be difficult to determine in advance, and their performance may degrade significantly with choices that are less than optimal.
- The methods listed are not equally easy to implement—some are relatively straightforward, but others involve complicated algorithms and data structures. Because of such differences, the methods may also vary significantly in the relative speeds with which they perform an equivalent amount of computation.
- In practice the work may depend on implementation details. For example, the cost of multigrid is sensitive to the particular strategy used for cycling through grid levels. The figures given in the table assume the best possible case.
- Computational complexity alone does not necessarily determine the shortest time to a solution. For example, a method with high-order accuracy usually requires more work per grid point than a low-order method but may be able to use far *fewer* grid points to achieve equivalent accuracy.

In Table 11.3 the computational work is stated in terms of the number of grid points per dimension in a regular finite difference grid. In Table 11.4 the equivalent value for the work in terms of n, the order of the matrix, is given for those methods that remain viable choices for finite element discretizations with less regular meshes. The table gives the exponent of n in the dominant term of the cost estimate. These results are applicable to many finite element discretizations and are also consistent with the estimates in Table 11.3 for finite difference discretizations (with $n = k^2$ or $n = k^3$, depending on the dimension of the problem).

In Table 11.3 the methods are listed in decreasing order of cost for two-dimensional problems. Note that the ranking is somewhat different for three-dimensional problems.

TABLE 11.4
Exponent of *n*, the order of the matrix, in the computational cost of solving elliptic boundary value problems in two or three dimensions

Method	2-D	3-D
Dense Cholesky	3	3
Band Cholesky	2	2.33
Sparse Cholesky	1.5	2
Conjugate gradient	1.5	1.33
Preconditioned CG	1.25	1.17
Multigrid	1	1

The reason is that factorization methods suffer a much greater penalty in going from two dimensions to three than do the other methods. Although factorization methods are much less competitive in terms of the work required for three-dimensional problems, they are still useful in some cases because of their greater robustness. This is especially true for nonsymmetric matrices, since iterative methods tend to be significantly less reliable in that case. In addition, methods akin to factorization are often used to compute effective preconditioners.

The tables show that multigrid methods can be optimal, in the sense that the cost of computing the solution is of the same order as the cost of reading the input or writing the output. The FACR method is also optimal for all practical purposes, since $\log \log k$ is effectively constant for any reasonable value of k. The other fast direct methods are almost as effective in practice unless k is very large. Clearly these methods should be seriously considered whenever they are applicable, and good software is available for implementing them. Unfortunately, their robustness and applicability can be quite limited, so these optimal or nearly optimal methods, though they can be quite useful in the right context, are not a panacea, and more conventional methods must often be relied upon in practice.

11.7 SOFTWARE FOR PARTIAL DIFFERENTIAL EQUATIONS

Most of the problem categories we have studied previously are amenable to reasonably efficient solution by general-purpose software. Methods for the numerical solution of partial differential equations, on the other hand, tend to be much more problem-dependent, so that PDEs are most often solved using custom-written software to take maximum advantage of the particular features of a given problem. Nevertheless, some software does exist for a few general classes of problems that occur often in practice. Table 11.5 is a list of some of the software for the numerical solution of PDEs available from major libraries. General problem-solving environments for partial differential equations are also available, including a PDE toolbox for **MATLAB**.

In addition, we list next several individual routines and software packages, many of which are available from **netlib**, for solving various types of PDEs and also for solving sparse linear systems.

TABLE 11.5
Library software for partial differential equations

Source	2-D Poisson	3-D Poisson	Method of lines
IMSL	fps2h	fps3h	molch
NAG	d03eaf	d03faf	d03pcf
NUMAL	richardson		ark/arkmat
SLATEC	hwscrt		

11.7.1 Software for Initial Value Problems

- **CLAWPACK**: 1-D and 2-D hyperbolic systems
- **TOMS**: numerous routines and packages for solving various time-dependent problems in one or two space dimensions, including
  - **pdeone(#494)**: 1-D systems using method of lines
  - **pdecol(#540)**: 1-D systems using collocation
  - **m3rk(#553)**: three-step Runge-Kutta method for parabolic equations
  - **pdetwo(#565)**: 2-D systems using method of lines
  - **bdmg(#621)**: 2-D nonlinear parabolic equations
  - **epdcol(#688)**: 1-D systems using collocation
  - **pdecheb(#690)**: Chebyshev polynomial method for parabolic equations
  - **cwres(#731)**: moving-grid interface for 1-D systems

11.7.2 Software for Boundary Value Problems

- **ELLPACK**: general framework and specific algorithms for solving various elliptic boundary value problems on two- and three-dimensional domains [212]
- **FISHPACK**: fast 2-D Helmholtz solvers using various coordinate systems
- **MGGHAT**: second-order linear elliptic PDEs using finite element method with adaptive mesh refinement and a multigrid solver
- **PLTMG**: elliptic PDEs with grid generation, adaptive mesh refinement, and a multigrid solver [13]
- **TOMS**: numerous routines and packages for solving various elliptic boundary value problems (e.g., Poisson, Helmholtz) in two- or three-dimensional domains, including
  - **gma(#527)**: generalized marching algorithm for elliptic problems
  - **pwscrt(#541)**: fast 2-D Helmholtz solvers using various coordinate systems
  - **fft9(#543)**: fast 2-D Helmholtz solver
  - **helm3d(#572)**: fast 3-D Helmholtz solver
  - **cmmimp(#593)**: fast Helmholtz solver on nonrectangular planar region
  - **gencol(#637)**: collocation method for general 2-D domain
  - **intcol/hermcol(#638)**: collocation method for rectangular domain
  - **hfft(#651)**: high-order fast 3-D Helmholtz solver
  - **serrg2/b2eval(#685)**: separable elliptic equations on rectangular domain
  - **capc/reccn(#732)**: elliptic equations on irregular 2-D domain

11.7.3 Software for Sparse Linear Systems

- **HSL**: **MA** chapter of Harwell subroutine library contains numerous routines for solving sparse linear systems
- **MATLAB**: as of Version 4.0, sparse matrices are supported, including reorderings and factorizations
- **PCGPAK**: preconditioned conjugate gradient methods for linear systems
- **QMRPACK**: quasi-minimal residual methods for nonsymmetric linear systems

- **SLAP**: iterative methods for symmetric and nonsymmetric linear systems
- **SPARSKIT**: iterative methods for sparse linear systems and utilities for manipulating sparse matrices
- **SPARSPAK**: reorderings and factorizations for sparse linear systems and least squares problems
- **SUPERLU**: Gaussian elimination with partial pivoting for sparse linear systems
- **SYMMLQ**: iterative method for symmetric indefinite linear systems
- **TEMPLATES**: iterative methods documented in [15]
- **TOMS**:
  - **gpskca(#582)**: reordering sparse matrices for reduced bandwidth
  - **lsqr(#583)**: iterative method for linear systems and least squares problems
  - **itpack/nspcg(#586)**: stationary and nonstationary iterative methods for symmetric and nonsymmetric linear systems
  - **sblas(#692)**: basic linear algebra subprograms for sparse matrices
  - **jpicc/jpicr(#740)**: incomplete Cholesky factorization preconditioner
- **UMFPACK**: unsymmetric multifrontal method for sparse linear systems
- **YSMP**: Yale Sparse Matrix Package, direct methods for linear systems
- **Y12M**: direct method for sparse linear systems

11.8 HISTORICAL NOTES AND FURTHER READING

The literature on numerical solution of partial differential equations is vast. Two early classics on finite difference methods are [84, 213]. More recent treatments focusing mainly on finite difference methods include [7, 112, 176, 186, 234, 249, 255]. Both finite difference and finite element methods are discussed in [35, 117, 133, 159]. For a detailed discussion of the method of lines, see [219]. For an introduction to finite element methods from a numerical point of view, see [20, 50, 140, 265]. A deeper analysis of the finite element method is given in [247]. A classic engineering text on finite elements is [281]; see also the series [17, 33, 34]. Spectral and pseudospectral methods, though not treated in this book, form another important family of methods for solving differential equations; see [81, 106]. Direct methods for solving sparse linear systems are discussed in detail in [68, 93]. Fast direct methods, which were proposed by Hockney in 1965, are surveyed in [202, 253].

Of the iterative methods we discussed, the Jacobi and Gauss-Seidel methods date from the nineteenth century, whereas the SOR and conjugate gradient methods were both developed around 1950 by Young and by Hestenes and Stiefel, respectively. The conjugate gradient method proved ineffective as a direct method owing to rounding error, so it was temporarily discarded until the early 1970s, when its use as an iterative method was popularized by Reid, Golub, and others (see [102]). For a negative result on the existence of a true analogue of the conjugate gradient method for nonsymmetric systems, see [75]. The multigrid method was popularized in the late 1970s by Brandt and numerous others. Classic references on iterative methods for linear systems are [115, 263, 280]. For more up-to-date treatments of iterative methods, see the surveys [15, 87, 147] or the more comprehensive treatises [12, 114, 194, 218]. For an introduction to multigrid methods, see [24, 139, 271].

REVIEW QUESTIONS

11.1. True or false: For solving a time-dependent partial differential equation, a finite difference method that is both consistent and stable converges to the true solution as the stepsizes in time and in space go to zero.

11.2. True or false: The Gauss-Seidel iterative method for solving a system of linear equations $Ax = b$ always converges.

11.3. True or false: The Gauss-Seidel method is a special case of SOR (successive over-relaxation) for solving a system of linear equations.

11.4. How does a semidiscrete method differ from a fully discrete method for solving a time-dependent partial differential equation?

11.5. (*a*) Explain briefly the method of lines for solving an initial value problem for a time-dependent partial differential equation in one space dimension.

(*b*) How might the method of lines be used to solve a pure boundary value problem for a time-independent PDE in two space dimensions?

11.6. Other than the usual concerns of stability and accuracy, what additional important consideration enters into the choice of a numerical method for solving a system of ODEs arising from semidiscretization of a PDE using the method of lines?

11.7. In using a fully discrete finite difference method for solving a time-dependent partial differential equation with one space dimension, can the sizes of the time step and space step be chosen independently of each other? Why?

11.8. Fully discrete finite difference and finite element methods for solving boundary value problems convert the original differential equation into a system of algebraic equations. Why does the resulting $n \times n$ linear system usually require far less work to solve than the usual $\mathcal{O}(n^3)$ that might be expected?

11.9. Which of the following types of partial differential equations are time-dependent?

(*a*) Elliptic
(*b*) Parabolic
(*c*) Hyperbolic

11.10. Classify each of the following partial differential equations as hyperbolic, parabolic, or elliptic. Also, state whether each equation is time-dependent or time-independent.

(*a*) Laplace equation
(*b*) Wave equation
(*c*) Heat equation
(*d*) Poisson equation

11.11. What is meant by the *stencil* of a finite difference method for solving a PDE numerically?

11.12. The heat equation $u_t = cu_{xx}$ with appropriate initial and boundary conditions can be solved numerically by using a second-order, centered finite difference approximation for u_{xx} and then solving the resulting system of ordinary differential equations in time by some numerical method.

(*a*) On what ODE method in time is the Crank-Nicolson method based?

(*b*) What advantage does the Crank-Nicolson method have over the use of the backward Euler method?

(*c*) What fundamental advantage do both of these methods have over the use of Euler's method?

11.13. In solving the Laplace equation on the unit square using the standard second-order accurate finite difference scheme in both space dimensions, what is the maximum number of unknown solution variables that are involved in any one equation of the resulting linear algebraic system?

11.14. Consider the numerical solution of the heat equation, $u_t = cu_{xx}$, by a fully discrete finite difference method. For the spatial discretization, suppose that we approximate the second derivative by the standard second-order accurate, centered difference formula.

(*a*) Why is Euler's method impractical for the time integration?

(*b*) Name a method for numerically solving the heat equation that is unconditionally stable and second-order accurate in both space and time.

(*c*) On what ODE method is the time integration in this method based?

11.15. Implicit finite difference methods for solving time-dependent PDEs require the solution of a system of equations at each time step. In using the backward

Euler or trapezoid method to solve the heat equation in one space dimension, what is the nonzero pattern of the matrix of the linear system to be solved at each time step?

11.16. (*a*) For a finite difference method for solving a PDE numerically, what is meant by the terms *consistency, stability,* and *convergence?*

(*b*) How does the Lax Equivalence Theorem relate these terms to each other?

11.17. Suppose you are solving the heat equation $u_t = u_{xx}$ by applying an ODE method to solve the semidiscrete system of ODEs resulting from spatial discretization using the standard second-order central difference approximation to the second derivative. Each of the following ODE methods then gives a time-stepping procedure that may or may not be consistent, stable, or convergent. State which of these three properties, if any, apply for each method listed (note that none, one, or more than one of the properties may apply in a given case).

(*a*) Euler's method with $\Delta t = \Delta x$

(*b*) Backward Euler method with $\Delta t = \Delta x$

(*c*) The "zero method," which produces the answer 0 at every time step

11.18. List two advantages and two disadvantages of iterative methods compared with direct methods for solving large sparse systems of linear algebraic equations.

11.19. What principal factor limits the usefulness of direct methods based on matrix factorization for solving very large sparse systems of linear equations?

11.20. What is the computational complexity of a fast Poisson solver for a problem with n mesh points?

11.21. What is meant by *fill* in the factorization of a sparse matrix?

11.22. Explain briefly how the minimum degree algorithm works for reordering a symmetric positive definite sparse matrix to limit fill in its Cholesky factor.

11.23. Explain briefly how the nested dissection algorithm works for reordering a symmetric positive definite sparse matrix to limit fill in its Cholesky factor.

11.24. What is the general form of a stationary iterative method for solving a system of linear equations $Ax = b$?

11.25. (*a*) What is meant by a *splitting* of a matrix A?

(*b*) What form of iterative method for solving a linear system $Ax = b$ results from such a splitting?

(*c*) What condition on the splitting guarantees that the resulting iterative scheme is locally convergent?

(*d*) For the matrix

$$A = \begin{bmatrix} 4 & 1 \\ 1 & 4 \end{bmatrix},$$

what is the splitting for the Jacobi method?

(*e*) For the same matrix as in part *d*, what is the splitting for the Gauss-Seidel method?

11.26. In solving a nonsingular system of linear equations $Ax = b$, what property of the matrix A would *necessarily* cause the Jacobi iterative method to fail outright?

11.27. Which of the following methods for solving a linear system are stationary iterative methods?

(*a*) Jacobi method

(*b*) Steepest descent method

(*c*) Iterative refinement

(*d*) Gauss-Seidel method

(*e*) Conjugate gradient method

(*f*) SOR method

11.28. (*a*) In words (or formulas if you prefer), describe the difference between the Jacobi and Gauss-Seidel iterative methods for solving a system of linear algebraic equations.

(*b*) Which method is more rapidly convergent?

(*c*) Which method requires less storage for the successive approximate solutions?

11.29. Listed below are several properties that may pertain to various methods for solving systems of linear equations. For each of the properties listed, state whether this quality more accurately describes direct or iterative methods:

(*a*) The entries of the matrix are not altered during the computation.

(*b*) A good prior estimate for the solution is helpful.

(*c*) The matrix entries are stored explicitly, using a standard storage scheme such as an array.

(*d*) The work required depends on the conditioning of the problem.

(*e*) Once a given system has been solved, another system with the same matrix but a different right-hand side is easily solved.

(*f*) Acceleration parameters or preconditioners are usually employed.

(*g*) The maximum possible accuracy is relatively easy to attain.

(*h*) "Black box" software is relatively easy to implement.

(*i*) The matrix can be defined implicitly by its action on an arbitrary vector.

(*j*) A factorization of the matrix is usually performed.

(*k*) The amount of work required can often be determined in advance.

11.30. Let A be a nonsingular matrix. Denote the strict lower triangular portion of A by L, the diagonal of A by D, and the strict upper triangle of A by U.

(*a*) Express the Jacobi iteration scheme for solving the linear system $Ax = b$ in terms of L, D, and U.

(*b*) Express the Gauss-Seidel iteration scheme for solving the linear system $Ax = b$ in terms of L, D, and U.

11.31. What are the usual bounds on the relaxation parameter ω in the SOR method?

11.32. Rank the following iterative methods for solving systems of linear equations in order of their usual speed of convergence, from fastest to slowest:

(*a*) Gauss-Seidel

(*b*) Jacobi

(*c*) SOR with optimal relaxation parameter ω

11.33. The conjugate gradient method for solving a symmetric positive definite system of linear equations is in principle a direct method. Why is it used in practice as an iterative method instead?

11.34. What two key features largely account for the effectiveness of the conjugate gradient method for solving large sparse symmetric positive definite linear systems?

11.35. When using the conjugate gradient method to solve a system of linear algebraic equations $Ax = b$, how can you accelerate its convergence rate?

11.36. (*a*) What is meant by *preconditioning* in the conjugate gradient method?

(*b*) List at least two types of preconditioners used with the conjugate gradient method.

11.37. Why are some stationary iterative methods for solving linear systems sometimes called *smoothers?*

11.38. Explain briefly the basic idea of multigrid methods.

11.39. (*a*) Explain the difference between the V-cycle and the W-cycle in multigrid methods.

(*b*) How does *full* multigrid differ from either of these?

11.40. For solving linear systems arising from elliptic boundary value problems, which type of method, iterative or direct, suffers a greater increase in work as the dimension of the problem increases? Why?

11.41. Is any type of method capable of solving linear systems arising from elliptic boundary value problems in time proportional to the number of grid points? If so, name one, and if not, why not?

EXERCISES

11.1. Suppose you are given a general-purpose subroutine for solving initial value problems for systems of n first-order ODEs $y' = f(t, y)$, and this is the only software tool you have available. For each type of problem in parts *a–c* to follow, describe how you could use this routine to solve it. In each case, your answer should address the following points:

    1. What is the function f for the ODE subproblem?

    2. How would you obtain the necessary initial conditions?

    3. What special properties, if any, would the ODE subproblem have that would affect the choice of ODE method?

(*a*) Compute the definite integral

$$\int_a^b g(t)\,dt.$$

(*b*) Solve the two-point boundary value problem

$$y'' = y^2 + t, \qquad 0 \le t \le 1,$$

with boundary conditions

$$y(0) = 0 \quad \text{and} \quad y(1) = 1.$$

(*c*) Solve the heat equation

$$u_t = c u_{xx}, \qquad 0 \le x \le 1, \qquad t \ge 0,$$

with initial condition

$$u(0, x) = g(x)$$

and boundary conditions

$$u(t, 0) = 0, \qquad u(t, 1) = 0.$$

11.2. Consider a finite difference solution of the Poisson equation $u_{xx} + u_{yy} = x + y$ on the unit square using the boundary conditions and mesh points shown in the drawing. Use a second-order accurate, centered finite difference scheme to compute the approximate value of the solution at the center of the square.

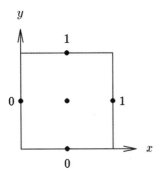

11.3. Give examples to show that neither consistency nor stability alone is sufficient to guarantee convergence of a finite difference scheme for solving a partial differential equation numerically.

11.4. Draw pictures to illustrate the nonzero pattern of the matrix resulting from a finite difference discretization of the Laplace equation on a d-dimensional grid,

with k grid points in each dimension, for $d = 1, 2,$ and 3, as described at the end of Section 11.3.1. Use a value of k that is large enough to show the general pattern clearly. In each case, what are the numerical values of the nonzero entries?

11.5. (*a*) For the matrix of Example 11.5, verify that the nonzero pattern of the Cholesky factor, including fill, is as shown in Figs. 11.6–11.8.

(*b*) Verify that the reorderings given in Figs. 11.7–11.8 are indeed minimum degree and nested dissection orderings, respectively. In each case, write out the permutation matrix P corresponding to the reordering, such that the reordered matrix is given by PAP^T, where A is the matrix in the original natural ordering.

11.6. Prove that the Jacobi iterative method for solving the linear system $Ax = b$ converges if the matrix A is diagonally dominant by rows. (*Hint:* Use the ∞-norm.)

11.7. Prove that the SOR method diverges if ω does not lie in the interval $(0, 2)$.

11.8. Prove that the successive A-orthogonal search directions generated by the conjugate gradient method satisfy a three-term recurrence, so that each new gradient need be orthogonalized only against the previous two.

11.9. Show that the subspace spanned by the first m search directions in the conjugate gradient method is the same as the Krylov subspace generated by the sequence $r_0, Ar_0, A^2r_0, \ldots, A^{m-1}r_0$.

11.10. On the basis of the background facts and motivation outlined in Section 11.5.5, fill in the details of the derivation of the conjugate gradient algorithm stated there. You will probably find it easiest first to derive a straightforward version of the algorithm, then try to improve its efficiency by reducing the number of matrix-vector multiplications and other arithmetic required.

COMPUTER PROBLEMS

11.1. Consider the heat equation

$$u_t = u_{xx}, \qquad 0 \le x \le 1, \qquad t \ge 0,$$

with boundary conditions

$$u(t, 0) = 0, \qquad u(t, 1) = 0,$$

and initial condition

$$u(0, x) = \begin{cases} 2x & \text{if } 0 \le x \le 0.5 \\ 2 - 2x & \text{if } 0.5 \le x \le 1 \end{cases}$$

(a) Using the full discretization given in Example 11.1, with $\Delta x = 0.05$ and $\Delta t = 0.0012$, evolve the solution from $t = 0$ to $t = 0.06$. Plot the solution at the initial time, the final time, and periodically in between (say, every ten time steps or so). If you use interactive graphics, you may prefer to plot the solution at every time step, giving the effect of an animated movie.

(b) Repeat part a, but use a time step of $\Delta t = 0.0013$. Plot the solution in the same manner as before. Can you explain the difference in results?

(c) Solve the same equation again, this time using the implicit method given in Section 11.2.4 based on the backward Euler method. Again use $\Delta x = 0.05$, but try a much larger time step, say, $\Delta t = 0.005$ to advance the solution from $t = 0$ to $t = 0.06$. Plot the solution at each time step. How do the results compare with those in parts a and b? Explain.

(d) Solve the same equation again, this time using the Crank-Nicolson method given in Section 11.2.4. Again use $\Delta x = 0.05$ and $\Delta t = 0.005$ to advance the solution from $t = 0$ to $t = 0.06$. Plot the solution at each time step. How do the results compare with your previous results? Explain.

(e) Form the semidiscrete system for this equation given in Section 11.2.1, using a finite difference spatial discretization with $\Delta x = 0.05$, and use an ODE solver to integrate it from $t = 0$ to $t = 0.06$. Plot the solution as before. How do the results compare with your previous results?

11.2. (a) Use the method of lines and the ODE solver of your choice to solve the heat equation

$$u_t = u_{xx}, \qquad 0 \le x \le 1, \qquad t \ge 0,$$

with Dirichlet boundary conditions

$$u(t, 0) = 0, \qquad u(t, 1) = 0,$$

and initial condition

$$u(0, x) = \sin(\pi x).$$

Integrate from $t = 0$ to $t = 0.1$. Plot the computed solution, preferably as a three-dimensional surface over the (t, x) plane. If you do not have three-dimensional plotting capability, plot the solution as a function of x for a few values of t, including the initial and final times. Determine the maximum error in the computed solution

by comparing with the exact solution

$$u(t, x) = \exp(-\pi^2 t) \sin(\pi x).$$

Experiment with various spatial mesh sizes h, and try to characterize the error as a function of h. On a log-log scale, plot the maximum error as a function of h.

(b) Repeat part a, but this time with Neumann boundary conditions

$$u_x(t, 0) = 0, \qquad u_x(t, 1) = 0,$$

and initial condition

$$u(0, x) = \cos(\pi x),$$

and compare with the exact solution

$$u(t, x) = \exp(-\pi^2 t) \cos(\pi x).$$

11.3. Use the method of lines and the ODE solver of your choice to solve the wave equation

$$u_{tt} = u_{xx}, \qquad 0 \le x \le 1, \qquad t \ge 0,$$

with boundary conditions

$$u(t, 0) = 0, \qquad u(t, 1) = 0,$$

and initial conditions

$$u(0, x) = \sin(\pi x), \qquad u_t(0, x) = 0.$$

Integrate from $t = 0$ to $t = 2$. Plot the computed solution, preferably as a three-dimensional surface over the (t, x) plane. If you do not have three-dimensional plotting capability, plot the solution as a function of x for a few values of t, including the initial and final times. Determine the maximum error in the computed solution by comparing with the exact solution

$$u(t, x) = \cos(\pi t) \sin(\pi x).$$

Note that the solution is periodic with period 2, so the solution should be the same at $t = 0$ and $t = 2$. Is this true for your computed solution? Experiment with various spatial mesh sizes h, and try to characterize the error as a function of h. On a log-log scale, plot the maximum error as a function of h.

11.4. Use the method of lines and the ODE solver of your choice to solve the first-order hyperbolic equation

$$u_t = -u_x, \qquad 0 \le x \le 1, \qquad t \ge 0,$$

with boundary condition

$$u(t, 0) = 1,$$

and initial condition

$$u(0, x) = 0.$$

Integrate from $t = 0$ to $t = 2$, and plot the computed solution, preferably as a three-dimensional surface over the (t, x) plane. If you do not have three-dimensional plotting capability, plot the solution at $x = 1$ as a function of t. Try both one-sided (upwind) and centered finite difference schemes for the spatial discretization. The exact solution is a step function of height 1 moving to the right with velocity 1. Does either difference scheme come close to this ideal? How would you describe the difference between the computed solutions given by the two schemes? Which computed solution is smoother? Which is more accurate?

11.5. Use the method of lines and the ODE solver of your choice to solve the nonlinear *Burgers' equation*

$$u_t = -uu_x + vu_{xx}, \qquad 0 \le x \le 1, \qquad t \ge 0,$$

with boundary conditions

$$u(t, x) = 1/(1 + \exp(x/(2v) - t/(4v)))$$

for $x = 0$ and $x = 1$, and initial condition

$$u(0, x) = 1/(1 + \exp(x/2v)),$$

where v is a scalar parameter representing viscosity. Note that this equation has both a nonlinear convective (hyperbolic) term, $-uu_x$, and a linear diffusion (parabolic) term, vu_{xx}, and the balance between them is determined by the relative value of v.

Integrate from $t = 0$ to $t = 2$, and plot the computed solution, preferably as a three-dimensional surface over the (t, x) plane. If you do not have three-dimensional plotting capability, plot the solution at $x = 1$ as a function of t. Experiment with various values for v, say, $v = 1, 0.5, 0.1$, and 0.01. Try both one-sided (upwind) and centered finite difference schemes for the spatial discretization. Compare your solutions with the exact solution, which is the function used previously to define the boundary conditions. Compare the accuracy and smoothness of the solutions computed by the two schemes as v varies.

11.6. Use the standard five-point finite difference discretization to solve the Poisson equation

$$-u_{xx} - u_{yy} = 2$$

on the L-shaped region in the accompanying diagram, with boundary conditions $u(x, y) = 0$ on all boundaries.

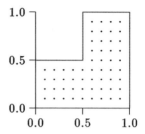

(*a*) Choose a mesh size h (for example, $h = 0.1$ in the diagram) and set up the appropriate matrix and right-hand-side vector. Solve the resulting linear system by a direct method and plot the resulting solution, preferably as a three-dimensional surface over the (x, y) plane. Experiment with various values for the mesh size h and observe the effect on the solution.

(*b*) Repeat part *a*, but this time use the SOR method to solve the linear system. Note that with an iterative method you need not set up the matrix explicitly but can work directly with the approximate solution at each mesh point, updating the values at each iteration. For a given mesh size h, experiment with various values for the SOR parameter ω in the range $0 < \omega < 2$. Can you find an optimal value for ω? Does the optimal ω become larger or smaller as h decreases?

11.7. The time-independent *Schrödinger equation* in two dimensions,

$$-(\psi_{xx}(x, y) + \psi_{yy}(x, y)) + V(x, y)\psi(x, y) = E\psi(x, y),$$

where we have chosen units so that the quantities are dimensionless, describes the wave function ψ of a particle of energy E subject to a potential V. The square of the wave function, $|\psi(x, y)|^2$, can be interpreted as the probability of finding the particle at position (x, y).

Assume that the particle is confined to a two-dimensional box, say, the unit square, within which it can move freely. Thus, the potential is zero within the unit square and infinite elsewhere. Since there is zero probability of finding the particle outside the box, the wave function must be zero at its boundaries. Thus, we have an eigenvalue problem for the elliptic PDE

$$-(\psi_{xx}(x, y) + \psi_{yy}(x, y)) = E\psi(x, y),$$

on the unit square, subject to the boundary condition $\psi(x, y) = 0$ on all boundaries. Note that the discrete eigenvalues E are the only energy levels permitted; this feature gives quantum mechanics its name.

Use a finite difference discretization of the PDE to derive an algebraic eigenvalue problem whose eigenvalues and eigenvectors approximate those of the PDE, then compute the eigenvalues and eigenvectors using a library routine (see Section 4.6). Experiment with various mesh sizes and observe how the eigenvalues behave.

An analytical solution to this problem is easily obtained, which gives the eigenvalues

$$E_{k,j} = (k^2 + j^2)\pi^2$$

and corresponding eigenfunctions

$$\psi_{k,j}(x, y) = \sin(k\pi x)\sin(j\pi y), \qquad k, j = 1, 2, \ldots.$$

How do your computed eigenvalues and eigenvectors compare with these analytical values as the mesh size of your discretization decreases? Try to characterize the error as a function of the mesh size.

Note that a nonzero potential V would not seriously complicate the numerical solution of the Schrödinger equation but would generally make an analytical solution much more difficult to obtain.

11.8. Verify empirically that the Jacobian of the semidiscrete system of ODEs given in Section 11.2.1 has eigenvalues between $-4c/(\Delta x)^2$ and 0. For this exercise, you may take $c = 1$. Experiment with several different mesh sizes Δx. How do the eigenvalues behave as $\Delta x \to 0$?

11.9. Consider the semidiscrete system of ODEs obtained from centered spatial discretization of the one-way wave equation, as in Example 11.3. Examine the stability of Euler's method for this system of ODEs by computing the eigenvalues of its Jacobian matrix. Is there any value for the size of the time step that yields a stable method? Answer the same question for the semidiscrete system obtained from one-sided upwind differencing.

11.10. For the standard five-point approximation to Laplace's equation on a $k \times k$ grid, experiment with various values of the relaxation parameter ω in the SOR method to see how much difference this makes in the spectral radius of the resulting iteration matrix G and the rate of convergence of the algorithm. Draw a plot of $\rho(G)$ as a function of ω for $0 < \omega < 2$. How does the minimum of this curve compare with the theoretical minimum given by

$$\rho(G) = \frac{1 - \sin(\pi h)}{1 + \sin(\pi h)},$$

which occurs for

$$\omega = \frac{2}{1 + \sin(\pi h)},$$

where $h = 1/(k + 1)$? Experiment with various values of k, say, $k = 10, 50, 100$.

11.11. Verify empirically the spectral radius and rate of convergence data given in Tables 11.1 and 11.2.

11.12. Implement the steepest descent and conjugate gradient methods for solving symmetric positive definite linear systems. Compare their performance, both in rate of convergence and in total time required, in solving a representative sample of test problems, both well-conditioned and ill-conditioned. How does the rate of convergence of the conjugate gradient method compare with the theoretical estimate given in Section 11.5.6?

11.13. Implement the Jacobi method for solving the $n \times n$ linear system $Ax = b$, where A is the matrix resulting from a finite difference approximation to the one-dimensional Laplace equation on an interval, with boundary values of zero at the endpoints. Thus, A is tridiagonal with diagonal elements equal to 2 and subdiagonal and superdiagonal elements equal to -1, and x represents the solution values at the interior mesh points. Take $b = 0$, so that the exact solution is $x = 0$, and therefore at any iteration the error is equal to the current value for x.

For the initial starting guess, take

$$x_j = \sin\left(\frac{jk\pi}{n + 1}\right), \qquad j = 1, \ldots, n.$$

For any given value of k, the resulting vector x represents a discrete sample of a sine wave whose frequency depends on k. Thus, by choosing various values for k and then observing the resulting Jacobi iterations, we can determine the relative speeds with which components of the error of various frequencies are damped out.

With $n = 50$, perform this experiment for each value of k, where $k = 1, 5, 10, \ldots, 25$. For each value of k, make a plot of the solution x at the starting value and for each of the first ten iterations of the Jacobi method. For what values of k is the error damped out most rapidly and most slowly? It turns out that frequencies beyond $k = n/2$ (called the Nyquist frequency; see Section 12.1.3), simply repeat the previous frequencies, as you may wish to verify. Do your results suggest that the Jacobi method is a *smoother,* as discussed in

Section 11.5.7? Try the same experiment using a starting value for x with all entries equal to 1. Does the error decay rapidly or slowly, compared with your previous experiments?

11.14. Implement a two-grid version of the multigrid algorithm, as outlined in Section 11.5.7. If recursion is supported in the computing environment you use, you may find it almost as easy to implement multiple grid levels. Test your program on a simple elliptic boundary value problem, such as the Laplace equation in one dimension on the unit interval or in two dimensions on the unit square with given boundary conditions.

11.15. Using the standard five-point discretization of the Laplace equation on a $k \times k$ grid in two dimensions, and systematically varying k, verify empirically as many of the results given in Table 11.3 as you can. Try to determine the approximate proportionality constant for the dominant term in each case.

CHAPTER 12

Fast Fourier Transform

12.1 TRIGONOMETRIC INTERPOLATION

We have already studied interpolation by polynomials, piecewise polynomials, and splines. In dealing with cyclic phenomena, it is often more appropriate and informative to use trigonometric functions, specifically, linear combinations of sines and cosines. A function $x(t)$ is *periodic* if there is some constant $p > 0$ such that $x(t + p) = x(t)$ for all t. The smallest such p for a given function is called the *period* of the function. For example, sine and cosine are both periodic with period 2π.

Representing a periodic function as a linear combination of sines and cosines decomposes the function into its components of various frequencies, much as a prism resolves a light beam into its constituent colors. The resulting coefficients of the trigonometric basis functions tell us what frequencies are present in the function and in what amounts. Moreover, this representation of the function in *frequency space* enables some of the manipulations of the function required in many applications, such as signal processing or solving differential equations, to be done much more efficiently than in the original time domain.

In representing a given function $x(t)$ by a linear combination of sines and cosines, several cases may arise:

- The function $x(t)$ may be defined for all $t \in (-\infty, \infty)$, or it may be defined only on some finite interval.
- The function $x(t)$ may or may not be periodic.
- The function $x(t)$ may be a continuous function whose value is known for any argument t, or its value may be given only at a discrete set of points t_k.

Depending on the particular situation, we may require the continuous Fourier transform (CFT), the Fourier series expansion, or the discrete Fourier transform (DFT) of the function x, all of which will be defined shortly.

In this chapter it will be convenient to use complex exponential notation, which is related to ordinary trigonometric functions by *Euler's identity*,

$$e^{i\theta} = \cos\theta + i\sin\theta,$$

where $i = \sqrt{-1}$. Since

$$e^{-i\theta} = \cos(-\theta) + i\sin(-\theta) = \cos\theta - i\sin\theta,$$

we see that for a cosine wave of frequency k we have

$$\cos(2\pi kt) = \frac{e^{2\pi ikt} + e^{-2\pi ikt}}{2},$$

and similarly for a sine wave of frequency k,

$$\sin(2\pi kt) = i\frac{(e^{-2\pi ikt} - e^{2\pi ikt})}{2},$$

which means that a pure cosine or sine wave of frequency k is equivalent to a sum or difference, respectively, of complex exponentials of half the amplitude and of frequencies k and $-k$.

For a given integer n, we will use the notation

$$w = e^{2\pi i/n}$$

for the primitive nth root of unity. The nth roots of unity are then given by w^k, $k = 0, \ldots, n-1$, and are illustrated for the case $n = 4$ in Fig. 12.1.

12.1.1 Continuous Fourier Transform

If $x(t)$ is defined for all $t \in (-\infty, \infty)$, then we can write

$$x(t) = \int_{-\infty}^{\infty} y(f)e^{-2\pi ift}\, df,$$

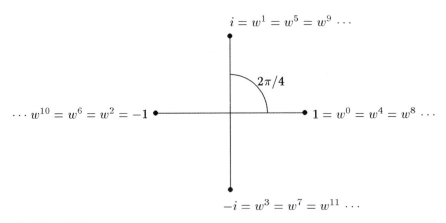

FIGURE 12.1
Roots of unity $w^k = e^{2\pi ik/n}$ in the complex plane for $n = 4$.

where y is the *continuous Fourier transform* (CFT) of x, also known as the *Fourier integral transform*, defined by

$$y(f) = \int_{-\infty}^{\infty} x(t) e^{2\pi i f t}\, dt,$$

assuming the integrals exist. If we think of the variable t as representing time, perhaps in units of seconds, then the variable f represents *frequency*, in units of cycles per second, or Hertz. In the CFT, frequency is a continuous variable, so all possible frequencies are represented. The CFT transforms the function x from the time domain into the frequency domain, and its inverse transforms the function y back into the time domain. The CFT expresses the function $x(t)$ as a "continuous linear combination" (i.e., an integral) of sines and cosines over all possible frequencies.

For simplicity, throughout this chapter we will think of t as representing time, but the same techniques apply to other types of variables as well. For example, if t represented a spatial variable, then f would represent spatial frequency, sometimes called *wave number*, in units of cycles (or waves) per unit distance in space.

12.1.2 Fourier Series

If $x(t)$ is periodic on the interval $[a, b]$, then x can be expanded in a *Fourier series*

$$x(t) = \sum_{m=-\infty}^{\infty} y_m e^{-2\pi i m t/(b-a)},$$

where

$$y_m = \frac{1}{b-a} \int_a^b x(t) e^{2\pi i m t/(b-a)}\, dt.$$

The y_m are known as the *Fourier coefficients* of the function x. Here time is still continuous, but the frequency domain is now discrete, although infinitely many frequencies are represented. Thus, we can view the Fourier series of a periodic function as a linear combination of an infinite number of sines and cosines, but with discrete frequencies.

12.1.3 Discrete Fourier Transform

Suppose $x(t)$ is sampled only at a finite set of equally spaced points $t_k = t_0 + kh$, $k = 0, 1, \ldots, n-1$, and is periodic with period nh. (For convenience, in this chapter we will index sequences and corresponding components of vectors starting from zero rather than one.) Using the notation $x_k = x(t_k)$ and $w = e^{2\pi i/n}$, we then have

$$x_k = \frac{1}{n} \sum_{m=0}^{n-1} y_m w^{-mk}, \qquad k = 0, 1, \ldots, n-1,$$

where

$$y_m = \sum_{k=0}^{n-1} x_k w^{mk}, \qquad m = 0, 1, \ldots, n-1.$$

The sequence $\{y_m\}$ is known as the *discrete Fourier transform* (DFT) of the sequence $\{x_k\}$, and $\{x_k\}$ is the *inverse* DFT of $\{y_m\}$. You may see other formulations in which the minus sign in the exponent is interchanged between the DFT and the inverse DFT, and possibly the scale factor $1/n$ as well (or perhaps $1/\sqrt{n}$ for both). These notational differences have no material effect on the development or usefulness of the DFT.

The DFT can be viewed as trigonometric interpolation of x at n points by a finite linear combination of sines and cosines, with both the time and frequency domains being finite and discrete. The first few basis functions are shown in Fig. 12.2, where the real and imaginary parts (i.e., cosines and sines of various frequencies) are plotted as separate curves. If plotted in three dimensions (the complex plane plus t), each basis function would be a helix, each with a different frequency. The DFT can also be interpreted as a discrete approximation to the CFT or the Fourier series under appropriate conditions.

The DFT of a sequence, even a purely real sequence, is in general complex. This property may seem counterintuitive; but it is in essence only a notational artifact and should not alarm us, as the inverse DFT will get us back into the real domain. How can the inverse DFT of a complex sequence yield a purely real result? Obviously, through cancellation of the imaginary parts. Note that the DFT of a real sequence of length n, though it has a total of $2n$ real and imaginary parts, still contains essentially only n independent pieces of information because the components of the second half of the transformed sequence are complex conjugates of those in the first half. (More precisely, y_k and y_{n-k} are complex conjugates for $k = 1, \ldots, (n/2) - 1$.) This fact can be used to save on storage if the input sequence is known to be real.

The DFT resolves or decomposes an input sequence x into its underlying fundamental frequency components, whose individual contributions are given by the elements of the transformed sequence y. Two components of special interest are y_0, which corresponds to zero frequency (i.e., a constant function), and $y_{n/2}$, which corresponds to the *Nyquist frequency*—the highest frequency representable at the given sampling rate. The component y_0 is sometimes called the DC component, by analogy with

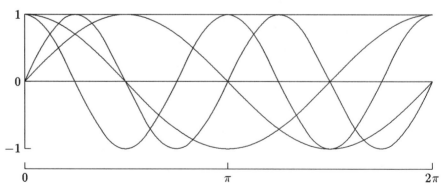

FIGURE 12.2
Basis functions (sines and cosines) for the DFT.

nonoscillating direct electrical current, and its value is simply the sum of the components of x. Because the DFT is periodic in frequency, the components of y beyond the Nyquist frequency correspond to frequencies that are the negatives of those below the Nyquist frequency.

EXAMPLE 12.1 DISCRETE FOURIER TRANSFORM. To illustrate the DFT, we transform two sequences, one chosen randomly, the other chosen to have a definite cyclic character. For the random sequence, we have

$$
x = \begin{bmatrix} 4 \\ 0 \\ 3 \\ 6 \\ 2 \\ 9 \\ 6 \\ 5 \end{bmatrix} \longrightarrow y = \begin{bmatrix} 35 \\ -5.07 - 8.66i \\ -3 - 2i \\ 9.07 - 2.66i \\ -5 \\ 9.07 + 2.66i \\ -3 + 2i \\ -5.07 + 8.66i \end{bmatrix}.
$$

We see that the transformed sequence is complex, but y_0 and y_4 are real, while y_5, y_6, and y_7 are complex conjugates of y_3, y_2, and y_1, respectively, as expected for a real input sequence. There appears to be no discernible pattern to the frequencies present, as expected for a random sequence. And y_0 is indeed equal to the sum of the elements of x.

To illustrate the DFT of a cyclic sequence, we have

$$
x = \begin{bmatrix} 1 \\ -1 \\ 1 \\ -1 \\ 1 \\ -1 \\ 1 \\ -1 \end{bmatrix} \longrightarrow y = \begin{bmatrix} 0 \\ 0 \\ 0 \\ 0 \\ 8 \\ 0 \\ 0 \\ 0 \end{bmatrix}.
$$

This sequence was chosen deliberately to have the highest possible rate of oscillation (between 1 and -1) for this sampling rate. In the transformed sequence we see a nonzero component at the Nyquist frequency (in this case y_4), and no other component is present. Again, y_0 is equal to the sum of the elements of x.

Perhaps you noticed something unusual in definition of the DFT. In performing interpolation, we usually must solve a system of equations to determine the coefficients of the linear combination of basis functions that fits the given data. Consider the case $n = 4$ for the DFT, for example. We need to solve the linear system

$$
\frac{1}{n} \begin{bmatrix} 1 & 1 & 1 & 1 \\ 1 & w^{-1} & w^{-2} & w^{-3} \\ 1 & w^{-2} & w^{-4} & w^{-6} \\ 1 & w^{-3} & w^{-6} & w^{-9} \end{bmatrix} \begin{bmatrix} y_0 \\ y_1 \\ y_2 \\ y_3 \end{bmatrix} = \begin{bmatrix} x_0 \\ x_1 \\ x_2 \\ x_3 \end{bmatrix}
$$

for the y_m given the x_k. We note, however, that

$$\frac{1}{n}\begin{bmatrix} 1 & 1 & 1 & 1 \\ 1 & w^{-1} & w^{-2} & w^{-3} \\ 1 & w^{-2} & w^{-4} & w^{-6} \\ 1 & w^{-3} & w^{-6} & w^{-9} \end{bmatrix}\begin{bmatrix} 1 & 1 & 1 & 1 \\ 1 & w^1 & w^2 & w^3 \\ 1 & w^2 & w^4 & w^6 \\ 1 & w^3 & w^6 & w^9 \end{bmatrix} = \begin{bmatrix} 1 & 0 & 0 & 0 \\ 0 & 1 & 0 & 0 \\ 0 & 0 & 1 & 0 \\ 0 & 0 & 0 & 1 \end{bmatrix}.$$

Since we can write out the inverse of the Vandermonde matrix explicitly, the computation of the DFT is reduced to matrix-vector multiplication, as reflected in the formula given for computing the y_m in terms of the x_k. Hence, we expect the work required to be $\mathcal{O}(n^2)$ arithmetic operations instead of the $\mathcal{O}(n^3)$ that would be required to factor and solve the linear system. With the fast Fourier transform (FFT) algorithm, however, we can do much better still, bringing the work down to $\mathcal{O}(n \log_2 n)$ arithmetic operations, as we will soon see.

12.2 FFT ALGORITHM

By taking advantage of certain symmetries and redundancies in the definition of the DFT, a shortcut algorithm can be developed for evaluating the DFT very efficiently. For illustration, consider the case $n = 4$. From the definition of the DFT we have

$$y_m = \sum_{k=0}^{3} x_k w^{mk}, \qquad m = 0, \ldots, 3.$$

Writing out the four equations in full, we have

$$y_0 = x_0 w^0 + x_1 w^0 + x_2 w^0 + x_3 w^0,$$
$$y_1 = x_0 w^0 + x_1 w^1 + x_2 w^2 + x_3 w^3,$$
$$y_2 = x_0 w^0 + x_1 w^2 + x_2 w^4 + x_3 w^6,$$
$$y_3 = x_0 w^0 + x_1 w^3 + x_2 w^6 + x_3 w^9.$$

Noting from Fig. 12.1 that

$$w^0 = w^4 = 1, \qquad w^2 = w^6 = -1, \qquad w^9 = w^1,$$

and regrouping, we obtain the four equations

$$y_0 = (x_0 + w^0 x_2) + w^0(x_1 + w^0 x_3),$$
$$y_1 = (x_0 - w^0 x_2) + w^1(x_1 - w^0 x_3),$$
$$y_2 = (x_0 + w^0 x_2) + w^2(x_1 + w^0 x_3),$$
$$y_3 = (x_0 - w^0 x_2) + w^3(x_1 - w^0 x_3).$$

We now observe that the transform can be computed with only 8 additions/subtractions and 6 multiplications, instead of the expected $(4 - 1) * 4 = 12$ additions and $4^2 = 16$ multiplications. Actually, even fewer multiplications are required for this small case, since $w^0 = 1$, but we have tried to illustrate how the algorithm works in general. The main point is that computing the DFT of the original 4-point sequence has been reduced to computing the DFT of its two 2-point even and odd subsequences. This property holds in general: the DFT of an n-point sequence can be computed by breaking it into two DFTs of half the length, provided n is even.

Before stating the general FFT algorithm formally, we first consider a complementary development in terms of matrices that yields additional insight. For a given integer n, we define the Fourier matrix F_n by $\{F_n\}_{mk} = w^{mk}$. Thus, for example,

$$F_1 = 1, \qquad F_2 = \begin{bmatrix} 1 & 1 \\ 1 & -1 \end{bmatrix}, \qquad F_4 = \begin{bmatrix} 1 & 1 & 1 & 1 \\ 1 & i & -1 & -i \\ 1 & -1 & 1 & -1 \\ 1 & -i & -1 & i \end{bmatrix}.$$

Let P_4 be the permutation matrix

$$P_4 = \begin{bmatrix} 1 & 0 & 0 & 0 \\ 0 & 0 & 1 & 0 \\ 0 & 1 & 0 & 0 \\ 0 & 0 & 0 & 1 \end{bmatrix},$$

and D_2 be the diagonal matrix

$$D_2 = \begin{bmatrix} 1 & 0 \\ 0 & i \end{bmatrix}.$$

Then we have

$$F_4 P_4 = \left[\begin{array}{cc|cc} 1 & 1 & 1 & 1 \\ 1 & -1 & i & -i \\ \hline 1 & 1 & -1 & -1 \\ 1 & -1 & -i & i \end{array} \right] = \begin{bmatrix} F_2 & D_2 F_2 \\ F_2 & -D_2 F_2 \end{bmatrix},$$

i.e., F_4 can be rearranged so that each block is a diagonally scaled version of F_2. Such a hierarchical splitting can be carried out at each level, provided the number of points is even. In general, P_n is the permutation that groups the even-numbered columns of F_n before the odd-numbered columns, and $D_{n/2} = \mathrm{diag}(1, \ldots, w^{n/2})$. Thus, to apply F_n to a sequence of length n, we need merely apply $F_{n/2}$ to its even and odd subsequences and scale the results, where necessary, by $D_{n/2}$.

This recursive divide-and-conquer approach to computing the DFT is formalized in the following statement of the FFT algorithm, where we assume that n is a power of two:

procedure fft (x, y, n, w)
    if $n = 1$ **then**
        $y[0] = x[0]$
    else
        for $k = 0$ **to** $(n/2) - 1$
            $p[k] = x[2k]$ {split into even and
            $s[k] = x[2k + 1]$ odd subsequences}
        end
        fft $(p, q, n/2, w^2)$
        fft $(s, t, n/2, w^2)$
        for $k = 0$ **to** $n - 1$
            $y[k] = q[k \bmod (n/2)] + w^k t[k \bmod (n/2)]$
        end
    end

We note the following points about the preceding algorithm:

- There are $\log_2 n$ levels of recursion, each of which involves $\mathcal{O}(n)$ arithmetic operations, so the total cost is $\mathcal{O}(n \log_2 n)$. If the weights w^k are precomputed, the total number of *real* floating-point operations required by the FFT algorithm is $5n \log_2 n$, compared with $8n^2$ real floating-point operations for an ordinary complex matrix-vector product.
- For clarity, separate arrays are used for the subsequences, but in fact the transform can be computed in place using no additional storage.
- The input sequence is assumed to be complex. If the input sequence is real, then additional symmetries in the DFT can be exploited to reduce the storage and operation count by half.
- The output sequence is not produced in the natural order. Most FFT routines automatically allow for this by appropriately rearranging either the input or output sequence. This additional step does not affect the overall computational complexity, because the necessary rearrangement (analogous to a sort) also costs $\mathcal{O}(n \log_2 n)$.
- The FFT algorithm can be formulated using iteration rather than recursion, which is often desirable for greater efficiency or when using a programming language that does not support recursion.

Despite its name, the fast Fourier transform is an algorithm, not a transform. It is a particular way (or family of ways) of computing the discrete Fourier transform of a sequence in a very efficient manner. As we have seen, the DFT is defined in terms of a matrix-vector product, whose straightforward evaluation would appear to require $\mathcal{O}(n^2)$ arithmetic operations. Use of the FFT algorithm reduces the work to only $\mathcal{O}(n \log_2 n)$, which makes an enormous practical difference in the time required to transform large sequences, as illustrated in Table 12.1.

Owing to the similar form of the DFT and its inverse (they differ only in the sign of the exponent), the FFT algorithm can also be used to compute the inverse DFT efficiently. This ability to transform back and forth quickly between the time domain and the frequency domain makes it practical to perform any computations or analysis that may be required in whichever domain is more convenient or efficient.

TABLE 12.1
Complexity of FFT algorithm versus matrix-vector multiplication

n	$n \log_2 n$	n^2
64	384	4096
128	896	16384
256	2048	65536
512	4608	262144
1024	10240	1048576

12.2.1 Limitations of the FFT

Although the FFT algorithm has revolutionized many aspects of numerical computation, it is not always applicable or maximally efficient. In particular, the input sequence is assumed to be:

- Equally spaced
- Periodic
- A power of two in length

The first two of these properties follow from the definition of the DFT, whereas the third is required for maximal efficiency of the FFT algorithm. For example, the interpolant given by the DFT, as a linear combination of sines and cosines, will necessarily be periodic, which means that for a sequence of length n, we must have $x_0 = x_n$ or, more generally, $x_k = x_{n+k}$ for any integer k (note that only x_0 through x_{n-1} are actually specified). Thus, some care must be taken in applying the FFT algorithm to produce the most meaningful results as efficiently as possible. For instance, transforming a sequence that is not really periodic or padding a sequence to make its length a power of two may introduce spurious noise and complicate the interpretation of the results.

It is possible to define a "mixed-radix" FFT algorithm that does not require the number of points n to be a power of two. The more general algorithm is still based on divide-and-conquer; the sequence is not necessarily split exactly in half at each level, however, but rather by the smallest prime factor of the remaining sequence length. For example, a sequence of length 45 would be split into three subsequences of length 15, each of which in turn would be split into three subsequences of length five. When a subsequence can be split no further (i.e., when its length is prime), then its transform must be computed by conventional matrix-vector multiplication. The efficiency of such an algorithm depends on whether n is a product of small primes (ideally a power of two, of course). If this is not the case, then much of the computational advantage of the FFT may be lost. For example, if n itself is a prime, then the original sequence cannot be split at all, and the "fast" algorithm then becomes standard $\mathcal{O}(n^2)$ matrix-vector multiplication.

12.3 APPLICATIONS OF DFT

The DFT is often of direct interest itself and is also useful as a computational tool that provides an efficient means for computing other quantities. The DFT is of direct interest in detecting periodicities or cycles in discrete data. Moreover, it can be used to *remove* unwanted periodicities. For example, to remove high-frequency noise from a sequence, one can compute its DFT, set the high-frequency components of the transformed sequence to zero, then compute the inverse DFT of the modified sequence to get back into the original domain.

As another example, weather data often contain two distinct cycles, diurnal and annual. One might want to remove one of these in order to study the other in isolation. Economic data are also often "seasonally adjusted," removing unwanted periodicities to reveal secular trends. Because of such uses, the DFT is of vital importance in many aspects of signal processing, such as digital filtering.

Some computations are simpler or more efficient in the frequency domain than in the time domain. Examples include the discrete circular convolution of two sequences u and v of length n,

$$\{u \star v\}_m = \sum_{k=0}^{n-1} v_k u_{m-k}, \qquad m = 0, 1, \ldots, n-1,$$

and related quantities such as the cross correlation of two sequences or the autocorrelation of a sequence with itself. In each case, the equivalent operation in the frequency domain is simply pointwise multiplication (in some cases with complex conjugation).

For example, convolution is equivalent to multiplication by a *circulant matrix*, and such a matrix is diagonalized by the DFT. Thus, if the convolution z of u and v is given by

$$
\begin{bmatrix} z_0 \\ z_1 \\ \vdots \\ z_{n-2} \\ z_{n-1} \end{bmatrix} =
\begin{bmatrix}
u_0 & u_{n-1} & u_{n-2} & \cdots & u_1 \\
u_1 & u_0 & u_{n-1} & \cdots & u_2 \\
\vdots & \ddots & \ddots & \ddots & \vdots \\
u_{n-2} & \cdots & u_1 & u_0 & u_{n-1} \\
u_{n-1} & \cdots & u_2 & u_1 & u_0
\end{bmatrix}
\begin{bmatrix} v_0 \\ v_1 \\ \vdots \\ v_{n-2} \\ v_{n-1} \end{bmatrix},
$$

then the corresponding transformed sequences $\hat{z}$, $\hat{u}$, and $\hat{v}$ are related by

$$
\begin{bmatrix} \hat{z}_0 \\ \hat{z}_1 \\ \vdots \\ \hat{z}_{n-2} \\ \hat{z}_{n-1} \end{bmatrix} = n
\begin{bmatrix}
\hat{u}_0 & 0 & \cdots & \cdots & 0 \\
0 & \hat{u}_1 & 0 & \cdots & 0 \\
\vdots & \ddots & \ddots & \ddots & \vdots \\
0 & \cdots & 0 & \hat{u}_{n-2} & 0 \\
0 & \cdots & \cdots & 0 & \hat{u}_{n-1}
\end{bmatrix}
\begin{bmatrix} \hat{v}_0 \\ \hat{v}_1 \\ \vdots \\ \hat{v}_{n-2} \\ \hat{v}_{n-1} \end{bmatrix}.
$$

For this reason, when computing the convolution of two sequences it is often advantageous to use the FFT algorithm to compute the DFT of each sequence, compute their pointwise product in the frequency domain, then compute the inverse DFT to get back into the time domain, again via the FFT algorithm.

The FFT algorithm forms the basis for some exceptionally efficient methods for solving certain elliptic boundary value problems, such as Poisson's equation on a regular domain with periodic boundary conditions (see Section 11.4.2). It also provides a similarly efficient approach for implementing spectral or pseudospectral methods for time-dependent partial differential equations with periodic boundary conditions.

12.3.1 Fast Polynomial Multiplication

The FFT algorithm also provides a fast method for some computations that might not at first glance seem related to it. Consider, for example, the problem of multiplying two polynomials $p(t)$ and $q(t)$, whose complexity by straightforward multiplication, using the coefficients of the polynomials, is proportional to the product of their degrees. Suppose that the product polynomial whose coefficients we wish to determine is of degree $n - 1$. A polynomial of degree $n - 1$ is uniquely determined by its values at n distinct points. Moreover, the value of the product polynomial at a particular point t is equal to the product of the factor polynomials at that point, i.e., $(p \cdot q)(t) = p(t)q(t)$. The product polynomial is therefore uniquely determined by the values of the pointwise product of p and q at n distinct points.

Thus, one way to compute the product polynomial is to evaluate p and q at n distinct points, compute their pointwise product, and then obtain the product polynomial by interpolation from these values. Since the pointwise product requires only $\mathcal{O}(n)$ arithmetic operations, the overall efficiency of this method will depend on how efficiently we can evaluate the given polynomials and then interpolate to obtain the product polynomial.

Recall that evaluating a polynomial at a set of points is equivalent to multiplying the vector of its coefficients by a Vandermonde matrix, and interpolation is equivalent to multiplying by the inverse of a Vandermonde matrix. These steps would appear to require at least $\mathcal{O}(n^2)$ arithmetic operations each, but they can be made much more efficient if we choose the evaluation points carefully. In particular, if we choose the nth roots of unity, then the necessary polynomial evaluations and interpolations become simply the DFT and its inverse. For example, if

$$p(t) = \sum_{k=0}^{n-1} x_k t^k,$$

then
$$p(w^m) = \sum_{k=0}^{n-1} x_k (w^m)^k = \sum_{k=0}^{n-1} x_k w^{mk} = y_m.$$

Thus, if the number of points n is a power of two and the FFT algorithm is used in this manner, then the complexity of polynomial multiplication can be reduced to $\mathcal{O}(n \log_2 n)$. Restricting n to be a power of two is not a serious limitation, since we can always consider any polynomial to have degree one less than the next higher power of two by taking the remaining coefficients to be zero. This result may seem to be of largely theoretical interest because the savings are insignificant for polynomial degrees that are likely to occur in practice, but it turns out to be useful in some applications, such as signal processing, and it illustrates how the FFT can crop up in unexpected ways.

12.4 WAVELETS

The sine and cosine functions used in Fourier analysis have many useful features of great practical importance in a wide array of applications, but they are not ideal for all purposes. In particular, these functions are very smooth (infinitely differentiable) and very broad (nonzero almost everywhere on the real line). As a result, they are not very effective for representing functions that change abruptly or have highly localized support. The Gibbs phenomenon in the Fourier representation of a square wave (the "ringing" at the corners) is one manifestation of this.

In response to this shortcoming, there has been intense interest in recent years in a new type of basis functions called *wavelets*. A given wavelet basis is generated from a single function $\phi(x)$, called a *mother wavelet* or *scaling function*, by dilation and translation, i.e., $\phi((x - b)/a)$, where a and b are real numbers with $a \neq 0$. There are many different ways of choosing the mother wavelet. The main issue is the trade-off between smoothness and compactness. A member of one of the most commonly used families of wavelets, due to Daubechies, is illustrated in Fig. 12.3.

Typical choices for the dilation and translation parameters are $a = 2^{-j}$ and $b = k2^j$, where j and k are integers, so that $\phi_{jk}(x) = \phi(2^j x - k)$. If the mother wavelet $\phi(x)$ has sufficiently localized support, then

$$\int \phi_{jk}\phi_{mn} = 0$$

whenever the indices do not both match, i.e., the doubly-indexed basis functions $\phi_{jk}(x)$ are orthogonal. By replicating the mother wavelet at many different scales, it is possible to mimic the behavior of any function at many different scales; this property of wavelets is called *multiresolution*. The Fourier basis functions are localized in frequency, but not in time: small changes in frequency produce changes everywhere in the time domain. Wavelets are localized in both frequency (by dilation) and time (by translation). This localization tends to make the wavelet representation of a given function very sparse.

As with the Fourier transform, there is an analogous discrete wavelet transform, or DWT. The DWT and its inverse can be computed very efficiently by a pyramidal, or

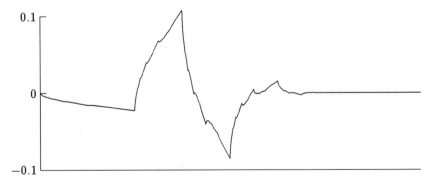

FIGURE 12.3
Daubechies' D_4 mother wavelet.

hierarchical, algorithm. In fact, the sparsity of the wavelet basis makes computation of the DWT even faster than the FFT—it requires only $\mathcal{O}(n)$ work instead of $\mathcal{O}(n \log_2 n)$ for a sequence of length n. Because of their efficiency, both in computation and in compactness of representation, wavelets are playing an increasingly important role in many areas of signal and image processing, such as data compression, noise removal, and computer vision, and are even beginning to be used as basis functions for the solution of differential equations.

12.5 SOFTWARE FOR FFT

Table 12.2 is a list of some of the software available for computing the DFT using the FFT algorithm. Some of the routines compute both the transform and its inverse, whereas others are used as a pair, one for the transform and the other for the inverse. We distinguish between routines that transform only real sequences and those that transform complex sequences. All of the routines listed are for one-dimensional transforms; software is also available for transforms in two dimensions and higher. Software for wavelet transforms is available from **NR** [205] and **TOMS** (#735). There is also a wavelet toolbox available for **MATLAB**. For pointers to additional wavelet software, see [110, 130].

12.6 HISTORICAL NOTES AND FURTHER READING

The work of Fourier on the integral and series that now bear his name dates from the early nineteenth century. The discrete Fourier transform is a more recent invention whose popularity was prompted by the advent of digital computation and communication. Although it had a number of precursors going all the way back to Gauss, the modern form of the FFT algorithm for computing the DFT was discovered by Cooley and Tukey in the mid-1960s. Their version of the algorithm quickly revolutionized many practical computations, including signal processing, convolutions, and time

TABLE 12.2
FFT software

Source	Real DFT	Complex DFT
FFTPACK	rfftf/rfftb	cfftf/cfftb
HSL		ft01
IMSL	fftrf/fftrb	fftcf/fftcb
KMN	ezfftf/ezfftb	cfftf/cfftb
MATLAB	fft/ifft	fft/ifft
NAG	c06eaf/c06faf	c06ecf/c06fcf
NAPACK		fft/ffc
NETLIB	realtr	fft
NR	realft	four1
SLATEC	rfftf1/rfftb1	cfftf1/cfftb1

series analysis. It also inspired the development of fast, divide-and-conquer algorithms for many other computations.

The theory and applications of Fourier analysis, both continuous and discrete, are covered in [185, 266, 267, 269, 270]. An accessible yet comprehensive introduction to the DFT can be found in [25]. For a tutorial overview of FFT algorithms, see the survey in [69]. For a detailed discussion of the FFT and its applications, see [26, 27]. The FFT is elegantly presented from a matrix point of view in [260]. For a brief tutorial introduction to wavelets, see [110, 245]; for a more comprehensive but still readable introduction, see [130, 143].

REVIEW QUESTIONS

12.1. True or false: The fast Fourier transform (FFT) algorithm can compute both the discrete Fourier transform and its inverse with equal efficiency.

12.2. (a) Why is the (continuous or discrete) Fourier transform of a function said to be in the *frequency* domain?

(b) Give two reasons why such a transformation into the frequency domain can be useful.

12.3. For what type of function would trigonometric interpolation be more appropriate than polynomial or piecewise polynomial interpolation?

12.4. For the sine function, $\sin(0) = \sin(\pi)$. Does this mean that the period of the sine function is π? Why?

12.5. List two applications for the discrete Fourier transform (DFT).

12.6. What two assumptions are implicitly made in applying the DFT to a sequence (i.e., what two properties are the data assumed to satisfy)?

12.7. (a) What property must the number of points, n, satisfy for the FFT algorithm to be maximally efficient relative to straightforward evaluation of the DFT by matrix-vector multiplication?

(b) What is the arithmetic complexity of the FFT algorithm in this case?

12.8. The DFT of a sequence of length n can be interpreted as interpolation by a set of n trigonometric basis functions.

(a) Why does computing the DFT *not* require the solution of an $n \times n$ linear system by matrix factorization in order to determine the coefficients of the basis functions?

(b) What is the worst-case computational complexity for computing the DFT? For what values of n is this the case?

(c) What is the best-case computational complexity for computing the DFT? For what values of n is this the case?

(d) Explain briefly the reason for the difference, or the lack of it, between the complexities in parts b and c.

12.9. (a) Why might one consider padding a sequence with zeros, if necessary, to make its length a power of two before computing its DFT via the FFT algorithm?

(b) Why might this *not* be a good idea?

12.10. Explain why the inverse DFT can be computed just as efficiently as the forward DFT using the FFT algorithm.

12.11. Why is the FFT algorithm useful for computing the convolution of two sequences?

12.12. (a) Explain briefly how the FFT algorithm can be used to multiply two polynomials.

(b) How does the computational complexity of this method compare with the conventional approach to polynomial multiplication?

12.13. What advantages do wavelets have over the trigonometric functions used in Fourier analysis?

12.14. What two operations are used to generate a wavelet basis from a single mother wavelet?

12.15. What is the computational complexity of the discrete wavelet transform?

EXERCISES

12.1. Express each of the following trigonometric functions in complex exponential notation.
  (a) $4\cos(2\pi kt)$
  (b) $6\sin(2\pi kt)$

12.2. (a) Assuming that time is measured in seconds, give an expression for a sine wave that oscillates at a frequency of two complete cycles per second.
  (b) What values will you obtain if you sample this function once per second?
  (c) How often would you have to sample to get an accurate value for the true frequency?

12.3. (a) What is the DFT of a pure cosine wave $\cos(t)$ sampled at n equally spaced points on the interval $[0, 2\pi)$?
  (b) What is the DFT of a pure sine wave $\sin(t)$ sampled at n equally spaced points on the interval $[0, 2\pi)$?
  (c) What is the DFT of the sum of the two previous functions sampled at n equally spaced points on the interval $[0, 2\pi)$?

12.4. For a given input sequence x, why is the first component of its DFT, y_0, always equal to the sum of the components of x?

12.5. The Fourier matrix F_n defined by $\{F_n\}_{mk} = w^{mk}$ is obviously symmetric. For what values of n, if any, is F_n Hermitian?

12.6. (a) Show that the matrix $(1/\sqrt{n})F_n$ is unitary, where F_n is the Fourier matrix of order n.
  (b) Using this result, prove the discrete form of Parseval's theorem,

$$\|y\|_2^2 = n\|x\|_2^2,$$

where $y = \text{DFT}(x)$.

12.7. If y is the DFT of a real sequence x of length n, where n is a power of two, show that y_0 and $y_{n/2}$ must be real.

12.8. Verify the operation count given in Section 12.2 for computing the DFT of a sequence of length n, where n is a power of two, using the FFT algorithm.

12.9. If

$$y = \text{DFT}(x),$$

show that

$$x = \frac{1}{n}\overline{\text{DFT}(\bar{y})},$$

where the overbar notation indicates complex conjugation of each element of the sequence. This result implies that a separate routine or option for the inverse DFT is not really needed, although one is often supplied for convenience in many mathematical software libraries.

COMPUTER PROBLEMS

12.1. (a) For each value of m, $m = 1, \ldots, 5$, compute the DFT of the sequence $x_k = \cos(mk\pi)$, $k = 0, \ldots, 7$. Explain your results.
  (b) Draw a plot of the two functions $\cos(\pi t)$ and $\cos(3t)$ over the interval $0 \leq t \leq 7$. Compute the DFT of each of the sequences $x_k = \cos(\pi k)$ and $x_k =$

$\cos(3k)$, $k = 0, \ldots, 7$, and compare the results. Explain why the DFTs can be so different when the functions are so similar.

12.2. Gauss analyzed the orbit of the asteroid Pallas based on the observational data

θ	0	30	60	90
x	408	89	−66	10
θ	120	150	180	210
x	338	807	1238	1511
θ	240	270	300	330
x	1583	1462	1183	804

where θ is the ascension in degrees and x is the declination in minutes.

(a) Fit the given data to the function

$$f(\theta) = a_0 + \sum_{k=1}^{5} [a_k \cos(2\pi k\theta/360) +$$

$$b_k \sin(2\pi k\theta/360)] + a_6 \cos(2\pi 6\theta/360),$$

where a_k, $k = 0, \ldots, 6$, and b_k, $k = 1, \ldots, 5$ are parameters to be determined by the fit. Since there are twelve parameters and twelve data points, the linear system to be solved is square, and the result should interpolate the data. As a matter of historical interest, Gauss performed this computation by a divide-and-conquer method closely related to the FFT algorithm; see [100].

(b) Plot the original data points along with a smooth curve of the function determined by the parameters computed in part a.

(c) Use an FFT routine to compute the DFT y of the sequence x.

(d) What relationship can you determine between the real and imaginary parts of y and the parameters a_k and b_k computed in part a? (*Hint*: You may need to scale by the sequence length or its square root, depending on the particular FFT routine you use.)

12.3. Let x be a random sequence of length n, say, $n = 8$. Use an FFT routine to compute the DFT of x. Now shift the sequence x circularly (i.e., end-around) one place to the right and compute the DFT of the shifted sequence. How do the resulting transformed sequences compare? Take the modulus of each component of each of the two sequences (called the *amplitude spectrum*) and compare them as well. Try other values for the shift distance, again comparing both the transformed sequence and its amplitude spectrum to those of the original unshifted sequence. What conclusion can you draw?

12.4. (a) Let x be the sequence $x_k = 1$, $k = 0, \ldots, n - 1$, where n is *not* a power of two. Let $\hat{x}$ be the same sequence padded with zeros to make its length a power of two (i.e., $\hat{x}_k = 1$, $k = 0, \ldots, n - 1$ and $\hat{x}_k = 0$, $k = n, \ldots, m - 1$, where m is the smallest power of two greater than n). Taking $n = 5$ and $m = 8$, use a mixed-radix FFT routine (i.e., one that allows arbitrary sequence length) to compute the DFT of both x and $\hat{x}$ and compare the results. Do the transformed sequences agree? What can you conclude about padding with zeros in order to make the sequence length a power of two? Try other values for n and m to determine whether your findings are consistent.

(b) Try other sequences (e.g., nonconstant, nonperiodic) for x, and other methods for padding (e.g., linear interpolation between x_n and the replication of x_0) and compare the resulting transformed sequences. Can you find any method for padding that does not alter the transformed sequence?

12.5. Using a mixed-radix FFT routine (i.e., one that allows arbitrary sequence length), measure the elapsed time to compute the DFT of a sequence of length n for $n = 1, 2, 3, \ldots, 1024$ (i.e., for each integer value from 1 to 1024). Plot the resulting execution times as a function of n, using a logarithmic scale for vertical axis. Are the upper and lower envelopes of the resulting data consistent with the theoretical complexity range of $O(n \log_2 n)$ to $O(n^2)$?

12.6. (a) Create two-dimensional plots of the n basis functions for the DFT of length n. On the vertical axis plot the real and imaginary parts of the discrete components of a given basis function (using different colors or dash patterns to distinguish them), and on the horizontal axis plot the index of each component. Although the DFT uses only discrete points, you can connect those points to make continuous curves, which will become smoother as n increases. Try a fairly large value of n to see smooth plots on your screen, but since there will be n separate frames, don't waste paper by printing all of them.

(b) Create three-dimensional plots of the n basis functions for the DFT of length n. On two of the axes plot the real and imaginary parts of the discrete components of a given basis function, and on the third axis plot the index of each component. Connect the points for a given function to make a continuous curve; it will become smoother as n increases. Try a fairly large value of n to see smooth plots on your screen, but again use discretion in making hard copies.

12.7. Use an eigenvalue routine to compute all of the eigenvalues of the scaled DFT matrix $(1/\sqrt{n})F_n$ for $n = 1, 2, 3, \ldots, 16$. How many different eigenvalues do you find? Do you observe any pattern in the multiplicities of the eigenvalues? Try to devise a formula for the multiplicity of each eigenvalue as a function of n and then test it for some values of n not already computed.

12.8. Show empirically that the DFT matrix diagonalizes a circulant matrix by generating a random circulant matrix C of order n and then computing $(1/n)F_n C F_n^H$, which should be diagonal. What does this result imply about the eigenvectors of C? A value of $n = 8$ is reasonable for your experiment, although you may wish to try additional values.

12.9. If your programming environment supports recursion, implement a recursive version of the FFT algorithm, as given in Section 12.2. Compare its performance to a standard (presumably nonrecursive) FFT routine for input sequences of various sizes (powers of two).

12.10. Implement the DFT using standard matrix-vector multiplication by the appropriate Vandermonde matrix. Compare its performance to that of a standard FFT routine for input sequences of various sizes, both powers of two and nonpowers of two (assuming that the standard FFT routine permits a nonpower of two sequence length). In particular, try some fairly large prime values for the input sequence length and compare the performance of the two routines.

12.11. Implement a routine for digital filtering of a sequence. Use an FFT routine to transform into the frequency domain, truncate or otherwise attenuate the frequencies above a given threshold, and then return to the original domain via the inverse transform. Test your routine for some representative noisy signals.

12.12. Implement a routine for computing the convolution of two sequences. Use an FFT routine to transform the sequences, compute the pointwise product of the transformed sequences, and then transform them back into the original domain using the inverse transform.

12.13. Implement a routine for fast polynomial multiplication using the FFT algorithm, as outlined in Section 12.3.1. Test your routine on polynomials of various degrees, both powers of two and nonpowers of two.

12.14. In this exercise we will use the DFT to study properties of iterative methods for solving a system of linear equations. Implement the Jacobi method for solving the $n \times n$ linear system $Ax = b$, where A is the matrix resulting from a finite difference approximation to the one-dimensional Laplace equation on an interval, with boundary values of zero at the endpoints. Thus, A is tridiagonal with diagonal elements equal to 2 and subdiagonal and superdiagonal elements equal to -1; and x represents the solution values at the interior mesh points.

Take $b = 0$, so that the exact solution is $x = 0$, and therefore at any iteration the error is equal to the current value for x. As initial starting value, take all of the entries of x equal to 1. Using a value for n that is a power of two ($n = 64$ is a reasonable choice), perform a few iterations of the Jacobi method, say, 10 or so. After each iteration, use an FFT routine to compute the DFT of the approximate solution vector, $y = \mathbf{DFT}(x)$. Next compute the *power spectrum*, which is a vector whose entries are the elementwise product of y and its complex conjugate. Now plot the first half of the power spectrum vector (i.e., up to the Nyquist frequency), which shows the amount of "energy" present at each frequency. Thus, your plot will show the decay rate of the components of the error of various frequencies. Which frequency components are damped out most rapidly and which most slowly? Do your results suggest that the Jacobi method is a *smoother,* as discussed in Section 11.5.7?

You might find it interesting to repeat this experiment with a two-dimensional problem using a two-dimensional FFT.

CHAPTER 13

Random Numbers and Stochastic Simulation

13.1 STOCHASTIC SIMULATION

We have thus far considered only deterministic numerical methods for solving mathematical problems. An alternative approach, which is often very powerful for certain types of problems, is *stochastic simulation*. A serious study of stochastic simulation methods is beyond the scope of this book, but we will give a brief overview of these methods and the random number generators on which they depend.

Stochastic simulation methods attempt to mimic or replicate the behavior of a system by exploiting randomness to obtain a statistical sample of possible outcomes. Because of the randomness involved, simulation methods are also commonly known in some contexts as Monte Carlo methods. Such methods are useful for studying:

- Nondeterministic (stochastic) processes
- Deterministic systems that are too complicated to model analytically
- Deterministic problems whose high dimensionality makes standard discretizations infeasible (e.g., Monte Carlo integration; see Section 8.5.4)

The two main requirements for using stochastic simulation methods are:

- Knowledge of relevant probability distributions
- A supply of random numbers for making random choices

Knowledge of the relevant probability distributions depends on theoretical or empirical information about the physical system being simulated. As a simple example, in simulating a baseball game the known batting average of a player might determine the probability of his or her getting a hit in a given turn at bat. A more practical example is simulating the diffusion of particles (e.g., neutrons) through a medium (e.g., a shielding material). One must know the "cross section" or "mean free path," which are measures of the probability of a particle collision occurring, and also the probabilities of each possible outcome of a collision. The path of a single particle through the medium is then simulated by a sequence of random choices, each of which is weighted by the appropriate probability. By simulating a large number of such particle trajectories, the probability distribution of the overall results can be approximated, with the accuracy attained depending on the number of trials.

13.2 RANDOMNESS AND RANDOM NUMBERS

The concept of *randomness* is actually somewhat difficult to define. Physical processes that we usually think of as random, such as flipping a coin or tossing dice, are in fact deterministic if we know enough about the equations governing their motion and the appropriate initial conditions. In recent years, the distinction between deterministic and random behavior has become blurred by such concepts as chaotic behavior of dynamical systems. Owing to their extreme sensitivity to initial conditions, the behavior of such systems can be unpredictable in practice even though it is deterministic in principle. For example, detailed weather predictions are impossible beyond approximately two weeks, even though we have a good understanding of the physical processes involved.

One way of characterizing the unpredictability that we associate with randomness is to say that a sequence of numbers is *random* if it has no shorter description than itself. In other words, there is no more economical way to convey the sequence than simply listing its members. Thus, for example, though each of the sequences {1, 2, 3, 4, 5}, {1, 1, 1, 1, 1}, and {4, 1, 5, 3, 2} may be equally likely to occur, only the latter would be considered random. In some cases, even when variables are not really random, such as the arrival times and service times for a queue, they may be so complicated or imprecisely known that they are best treated as random variables, and the study of such systems is often tractable only by stochastic simulation methods.

In addition to unpredictability, another distinguishing characteristic of true randomness is a lack of *repeatability*: one would not expect the same long random sequence of numbers or coin tosses to occur twice. However, lack of repeatability could make testing algorithms or debugging computer programs difficult, if not impossible. Thus, there are advantages to generating random numbers by a repeatable process, but repeatability is a two-edged sword. The statistical significance of a stochastic simulation depends on the independence of the trials, which in turn depends on using different random sequences for each trial. In 1955, before computers were so common, the RAND Corporation published a book entitled *A Million Random Digits*. It was used in selecting random trials for experimental designs and simulations (and perhaps as bedtime reading for insomniacs?). It was soon realized, however, that if everyone always started on page one, then all trials and simulations by all the book's users would depend on the quirks of the same random sequence. This generated much debate on how to select a random starting point in the table of random numbers.

Although random numbers were once supplied by physical processes or tables, they are now produced by computers. Computer algorithms for generating random numbers are in fact deterministic, although the sequence generated may *appear* random in that it exhibits no apparent pattern. However, an algorithm for generating random numbers provides a short description of the sequence it yields, which therefore by definition is not truly random, so such a sequence is more accurately called *pseudorandom*. Although a pseudorandom sequence may appear random, it is in fact quite predictable and reproducible, which is important for debugging simulation programs and verifying results. Moreover, because only finitely many numbers are representable on a computer, any sequence must eventually repeat.

13.3 RANDOM NUMBER GENERATORS

A good random number generator should have as many of the following properties as possible:

- *Random pattern.* It should pass statistical tests of randomness.
- *Long period.* It should go as long as possible before repeating.
- *Efficiency.* It should execute rapidly and require little storage, for many simulations require millions of random numbers.
- *Repeatability.* It should produce the same sequence if started with the same initial conditions.
- *Portability.* It should run on different kinds of computers and be capable of producing the same sequence on each.

It is very difficult to satisfy all of these requirements in a single random number generator. For example, some random number generators in common use produce highly correlated sequences, which may become visually evident when consecutive pairs or triples of members of the sequence are plotted in space. This phenomenon has prompted the remark "random numbers fall mainly in the planes" [172] and can invalidate simulation results obtained using such a generator.

Early attempts at producing random number generators on computers often relied on highly complicated procedures whose very complexity was felt to ensure randomness. An example is the "midsquare" method, which squares each member of the sequence and takes the middle portion of the result as the next member of the sequence. The lack of a theoretical understanding of such methods proved disastrous, and it was soon recognized that simple methods with a well-understood theoretical basis are far preferable.

13.3.1 Congruential Generators

Congruential random number generators have the form

$$x_k = (ax_{k-1} + b) \, (\text{mod} \, M),$$

where a and b are given integers, the starting integer x_0 is known as the *seed*, and the integer M is approximately (often equal to) the largest integer representable on the machine.

The quality of such a generator depends on the choices of a and b, and in any case its period cannot exceed M. It is possible to obtain a reasonably good random number generator using this method, but the values of a and b must be chosen *very* carefully. Many random number generators supplied with computer systems are of the congruential type, and some of them are notoriously poor.

A congruential generator produces random integers between 0 and $M - 1$. In order to produce random floating-point numbers, say uniformly distributed on the interval $[0, 1)$, the random integers must be divided by M (but *not* using integer division!).

13.3.2 Fibonacci Generators

Alternative methods that produce floating-point random numbers on the interval $[0, 1)$ directly are the Fibonacci generators, which generate the new value as a difference, sum, or product of previous values. A typical example is the subtractive generator

$$x_k = x_{k-17} - x_{k-5}.$$

We say that this generator has *lags* of 17 and 5. Not surprisingly, the lags must be chosen carefully to produce a good subtractive generator. Note that such a formula may produce a negative result, in which case the usual remedy is to add 1 to get back into the interval $[0, 1)$.

A Fibonacci generator requires more storage than a congruential generator and also requires a special procedure to get started (analogous to a multistep method for solving an ODE). On the other hand, Fibonacci generators require no division to produce floating-point results, and well-designed Fibonacci generators have very good statistical properties. Another advantage of Fibonacci generators is that they can have a much longer period than congruential generators. The reason for this is that the repetition of a single member of the sequence does not entail that all subsequent members will also repeat in the same order.

13.3.3 Nonuniform Distributions

Thus far we have discussed generating random numbers only from a uniform distribution on the interval $[0, 1)$. If we need a uniform distribution on some other interval $[a, b)$, then we can simply modify the values x_k generated on $[0, 1)$ by the transformation $(b - a)x_k + a$ to obtain random numbers that are uniformly distributed on the desired interval.

A more difficult problem is to sample from nonuniform distributions. If the cumulative distribution function of the desired probability density function is easily invertible, then we can generate random samples with the desired distribution by generating uniform random numbers and inverting them. For example, the exponential distribution with rate λ has the density function

$$f(t) = \lambda e^{-\lambda t}, \qquad t > 0,$$

and cumulative distribution function

$$F(x) = \int_0^x f(t)\,dt = 1 - e^{-\lambda x}.$$

Given $y = F(x)$, we can easily solve for x, obtaining

$$x = -\frac{\log(1 - y)}{\lambda}.$$

Hence, to sample from the exponential distribution, we can take

$$x_k = -\frac{\log(y_k)}{\lambda},$$

where y_k is uniform on $[0, 1)$.

Unfortunately, many important distributions are not easily invertible, and special methods must be employed to generate random numbers efficiently for these distributions. An important example is the generation of random numbers that are normally distributed with a given mean and variance. Some methods for generating normally distributed random numbers are explored in Computer Problem 13.8. Available routines for normal random numbers often assume a mean of 0 and variance of 1. If some other mean μ and variance σ^2 are desired, then each value x_k produced by the routine can be modified by the transformation $\sigma x_k + \mu$ to achieve the desired normal distribution.

13.4 QUASI-RANDOM SEQUENCES

Despite the quest to develop algorithms for generating perfectly random numbers, true randomness is not always a virtue. For some applications, such as Monte Carlo integration, achieving reasonably uniform coverage of the sampled volume can be more important than whether the sample points are truly random. The problem is that random sequences tend to exhibit random clumping (lightning may indeed strike in nearly the same place twice if it is truly random), leading to rather uneven coverage of the sampled volume for a given number of points. At the other extreme, perfectly uniform coverage can be achieved by using a regular grid of sample points, but as we saw in Section 8.5.4, such an approach does not scale well to higher dimensions.

A compromise between these extremes of coverage and randomness is provided by *quasi-random sequences*. Such sequences are in fact not random at all but are carefully constructed to give uniform coverage of the sampled volume while maintaining a reasonably random appearance. By design the points tend to avoid each other, so the clumping associated with true randomness is eliminated. The differences among these three sampling techniques are illustrated in Fig. 13.1. Such quasi-random sequences, also called *low-discrepancy sequences*, are finding increasing use in Monte Carlo integration and other applications, such as optimization by random search, where uniform coverage of the sampled volume is more important than the statistical properties of the sampling procedure.

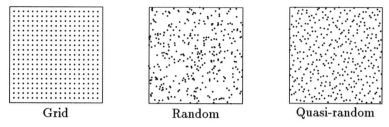

| Grid | Random | Quasi-random |

FIGURE 13.1

Three methods for sampling the unit square using the same number of points.

13.5 SOFTWARE FOR GENERATING RANDOM NUMBERS

Table 13.1 is a list of some of the random number generators available in standard software libraries. Generators are included only for uniform and normal distributions. Some of these sources contain generators for several additional distributions, both continuous and discrete. Software for generating quasi-random sequences is available from **NR** [205] and **TOMS(#647, #659)**. Although stochastic simulation programs can be written in any general-purpose programming language, the particular needs of this field have motivated the development of special-purpose languages and software systems for simulation, including **GPSS**, **Simscript**, **Simula**, and **SLAM**.

13.6 HISTORICAL NOTES AND FURTHER READING

Monte Carlo methods were developed in the 1940s by von Neumann, Ulam, Metropolis, and others, primarily motivated by problems in nuclear physics such as neutron

TABLE 13.1

Software for generating random numbers

Source	Uniform distribution	Normal distribution
FMM	urand	
HSL	fa04	fa05
IMSL	rnunf	rnnof
KMN	uni	rnor
MATLAB	rand	randn
NAG	g05caf	g05ddf
NETLIB	zufall	normalen
NR	ran1/ran2/ran3	gasdev
RANLIB	ranf/genunf	gennor
SLATEC	rand/runif	rgauss
TOMS		grand(#488)/randn(#712)

diffusion. For a brief overview of randomness, random number generators, and simulation, see [107, 191]. For a detailed treatment of stochastic simulation and Monte Carlo methods, see [21, 79, 119, 144, 216, 235]. Congruential random number generators were proposed by Lehmer in the 1950s. Volume 2 of the series by Knuth [150] contains a detailed discussion of random number generators and their analysis. The development of quasi-random sequences dates to the work of Halton and of Sobol' in the 1960s. For a recent review of quasi-random sequences and their applications, see [190].

REVIEW QUESTIONS

13.1. True or false: Stochastic simulation methods are useful only for nondeterministic systems.

13.2. True or false: A very complicated algorithm for generating random numbers tends to be better than a simple one.

13.3. What two requirements are essential for stochastic simulation methods?

13.4. In using stochastic simulation methods, why is repeatability desirable in practice, even if undesirable in theory?

13.5. List at least three desirable properties of a good random number generator.

13.6. What is meant by a *congruential* random number generator?

13.7. What is meant by a *Fibonacci* random number generator?

13.8. List two advantages and two disadvantages of a Fibonacci generator compared with a congruential generator for generating random floating-point numbers uniformly distributed on the interval $[0, 1)$.

13.9. If you have a random number generator for a uniform distribution on $[0, 1)$, how can you use it to generate random numbers uniformly distributed on the interval $[a, b)$ for given real numbers a and b?

13.10. If you have a random number generator for a normal distribution with mean 0 and variance 1, how can you use it to generate random numbers uniformly normally distributed with mean μ and variance σ^2?

13.11. Why are *quasi-random* sequences sometimes more useful than truly random (or pseudorandom) sequences?

EXERCISES

13.1. Consider a congruential random number generator

$$x_k = (ax_{k-1} + b) \pmod{M},$$

with $b = 0$, $M = 8192$, and the seed $x_0 = 1$.

    (*a*) What is the period of this generator if $a = 2$?
    (*b*) What is the period if $a = 125$?
    (*c*) What is the longest possible period, given these values for b, M, and x_0?

13.2. (*a*) Choose a well-structured sport, such as baseball or football, and discuss how you would simulate a typical game. What type of information would be required to perform a fairly detailed and realistic simulation? Where would random choices enter into the simulation?

    (*b*) Would it be feasible to simulate a sport like basketball, soccer, or hockey in this manner? Try to characterize the differences from the previous case.

COMPUTER PROBLEMS

13.1. (*a*) In this exercise we will perform a *chi-square test* of the randomness of the sequence generated by a random number generator. Divide the interval $[0, 1)$ into n equal subintervals. Choose a library routine for generating uniformly distributed random numbers on $[0, 1)$. Generate k random numbers and count the number n_i that fall into each subinterval, $i = 1, \ldots, n$. Compute the chi-square statistic

$$\chi^2 = \sum_{i=1}^{n} \frac{(n_i - k/n)^2}{k/n}.$$

In a table for the chi-square distribution (see [282], for example, or a book on statistics), look up the probability that the chi-square statistic has the value you obtained for $n - 1$ degrees of freedom. Carry out this experiment for $n = 10$ and 20, and for $k = 100, 200, \ldots,$ 1000.

(*b*) Implement your own random number generator, using either the congruential or Fibonacci method, and again perform the chi-square test as outlined in part *a*. Experiment with various choices for the parameters of the generator to see what effect these have on the randomness test. Can you find choices of parameters that produce particularly good or bad results in the randomness test (without being obviously bad, such as having a very short period)?

13.2. Monte Carlo integration requires random sampling of a region in *n*-dimensional space. If the sequence of random numbers one is using exhibits any serial correlation, then the sampling may systematically miss a portion of the region, and may possibly even be confined to a subregion of lower dimension, which would obviously make the estimate for the integral erroneous. One way to detect such serial correlation is to plot pairs or triples of consecutive random numbers in two or three dimensions, so that any nonrandom pattern becomes apparent visually.

(*a*) Use the congruential random number generator

$$x_k = (a x_{k-1} + b)(\text{mod } M),$$

with $a = 125, b = 0, M = 8192$, and the seed $x_0 = 1$, to generate a sequence of random integers, and convert each to a floating-point number f_k on $[0, 1)$ by taking $f_k = x_k/M$. Plot 100 pairs of consecutive members of

the sequence, i.e., $(f_1, f_2), (f_3, f_4), \ldots, (f_{199}, f_{200})$, as points in the unit square. Do you notice any obvious pattern? Make a second plot using 1000 pairs. Now do you notice any obvious pattern?

(*b*) Repeat the previous experiment, but try various values for the parameters a, b, and M. Can you find values that show no obvious pattern when plotted, even when you increase the number of points further?

(*c*) Repeat the same experiment again, this time using a library routine for generating uniform random numbers on $[0, 1)$.

13.3. For each random number generator used in the previous exercise, generate a sequence of n random numbers, where n is a power of two. Use an FFT routine to compute the DFT of each sequence (see Chapter 12). In each case, does the transformed sequence appear to be biased toward any particular frequencies, or does it appear to be "white noise," with all frequencies represented approximately equally? You may need to use a fairly large value of n, say, $n = 1024$, to draw any significant conclusions. How do the results of this "Fourier test" compare with your other tests (i.e., do the same generators fare well or poorly)?

13.4. A sequence of random numbers distributed uniformly on $[0, 1)$ should have mean

$$\mu = \int_0^1 x \, dx = \frac{1}{2}$$

and variance

$$\sigma^2 = \int_0^1 (x - \mu)^2 \, dx = \frac{1}{12},$$

where σ is the standard deviation. Check each of the random number generators used in the previous exercise to see how close they come to these values for a sequence of length 1000. Do all of the generators pass this test?

13.5. (*a*) Suppose that you are given five independent random decimal digits. The possible outcomes can be classified much like poker hands. Show analytically that the probability of each possible outcome is given by the following table:

Hand	Pattern	Probability
Five of a kind	aaaaa	0.0001
Four of a kind	aaaab	0.0045
Full house	aaabb	0.0090
Three of a kind	aaabc	0.0720
Two pairs	aabbc	0.1080
One pair	aabcd	0.5040
Bust	abcde	0.3024

(b) Use a library routine for generating random numbers to determine the probability of each possible outcome by random sampling. Experiment with various numbers of trials. How do your results compare with the analytical results in part a? What is the effect of taking more trials?

(c) The ability to match the correct theoretical distribution of poker hands (called the *poker test*) is sometimes used as a measure of quality of random number generators. Try a poor random number generator from one of the previous exercises and see if it passes this test, for the same number of trials used in part b.

13.6. The *birthday paradox*: Use random trials to determine the smallest number of persons required for the probability to be greater than 0.5 that two persons in a group have the same birthday. Also try to justify your result analytically.

13.7. Use random sampling to determine the probability that the quadratic equation

$$ax^2 + bx + c = 0$$

will have only real roots, if each of its real coefficients a, b, and c is randomly chosen from the interval $[-1, 1]$. Also try to justify your result analytically.

13.8. In this exercise, we will consider three different ways of generating random numbers that are normally distributed with mean 0 and variance 1.

(a) According to the *central limit theorem*, if x_k, $k = 1, \ldots, n$ is a sequence of independent random numbers from a distribution with mean μ and variance σ^2, then as n increases,

$$y = \frac{\sum_{k=1}^{n} x_k - n\mu}{\sigma \sqrt{n}}$$

approaches a normal distribution with mean 0 and variance 1. If the x_k are uniformly distributed on $[0, 1)$, then

$\mu = \frac{1}{2}$ and $\sigma^2 = \frac{1}{12}$, which implies that

$$y = \frac{\sum_{k=1}^{n} x_k - n/2}{\sqrt{n/12}}$$

approaches a normal distribution with mean 0 and variance 1. The choice $n = 12$ makes the foregoing formula particularly simple:

$$y = \sum_{k=1}^{12} x_k - 6,$$

i.e., we just sum up a dozen uniform random numbers and subtract 6, and the result should be approximately normally distributed with mean 0 and variance 1. You might also experiment with other values for n to examine the trade-off between cost and accuracy.

(b) Generate two random numbers x_1 and x_2, uniformly distributed on $[0, 1)$. Then it can be shown that both

$$y_1 = \sin(2\pi x_1)\sqrt{-2\log(x_2)}$$

and
$$y_2 = \cos(2\pi x_1)\sqrt{-2\log(x_2)}$$

are normally distributed with mean 0 and variance 1.

(c) Generate two random numbers x_1 and x_2 uniformly distributed on $[-1, 1)$, and let $r = x_1^2 + x_2^2$. If $r > 1$, reject this pair and generate a new uniform pair x_1 and x_2. If $r \leq 1$, then it can be shown that both

$$y_1 = x_1\sqrt{-2\log(r)/r}$$

and
$$y_2 = x_2\sqrt{-2\log(r)/r}$$

are normally distributed with mean 0 and variance 1.

Implement each of these three methods for generating normally distributed random numbers. To test each routine, generate $n = 1000$ normal random numbers, compute a frequency histogram with bin size $\sigma = 1$, and compare the values obtained with the known values for a true normal distribution: $\ldots, 2.14\%, 13.59\%, 34.13\%, 34.13\%, 13.59\%, 2.14\%, \ldots$. Also compare your results with a histogram similarly obtained using a library routine for generating normally distributed random numbers. You may find it instructive to plot the histograms, perhaps superimposed with a suitably scaled normal density curve. Compare the methods with respect to accuracy and efficiency. You may also wish to experiment with other values for n.

13.9. One of the earliest examples of using randomness to compute a deterministic quantity is the *Buffon needle problem*, in which an approximate value for π

is determined by repeatedly throwing a needle onto a plane surface ruled with equally spaced parallel lines, such as the seams in a hardwood floor. We introduce an (x, y) coordinate system to describe the position of the center of the needle, with the x axis parallel to the lines. Clearly, the probability that the needle intersects a line is independent of x, and depends only on y and the angle θ between the needle and the x axis. For simplicity, assume that the length of the needle, as well as the distance between any two adjacent lines, is 1.

By symmetry, we need be concerned only with values for θ in the interval $[0, \pi/2)$, and for y in the interval $[0, \frac{1}{2})$. To determine the proportion of this rectangle in (θ, y) for which the needle intersects a line, we choose random values for θ and y, uniformly distributed on $[0, \pi/2)$ and $[0, \frac{1}{2})$, respectively. Now a needle with its center at (x, y) will intersect a line precisely when $y \leq \sin(\theta)/2$. Therefore, the probability that the needle will intersect a line is simply the ratio of the area under the curve $\sin(\theta)/2$ over the interval $[0, \pi/2]$ to the total area of the rectangle, which is just $\pi/4$. Thus, the approximate value for π will simply be $2n/m$, where n is the total number of trials and m is the number of trials for which $y \leq \sin(\theta)/2$.

Use a library routine for generating uniform random numbers to implement this method for approximating π. How many trials are required to obtain k correct digits of π, where $k = 1, 2, 3, 4$?

13.10. (*a*) Use the Monte Carlo method to compute the area of a circle of diameter 1 inscribed in the unit square, $0 \leq x, y \leq 1$. Generate a sequence (x_k, y_k) of n pairs of random numbers uniformly distributed on $[0, 1)$, and count the number m falling within the circle. Since the area of the square is 1, the area of the circle should be approximated by m/n. Compare your result with the known area, which is given by $A = \pi r^2 = \pi/4$. Use various values for n, and try to characterize the size of the error as a function of the number of random trials.

(*b*) Use the Monte Carlo method to compute the volume of a sphere of diameter 1 inscribed in the unit cube, $0 \leq x, y, z \leq 1$. Generate a sequence (x_k, y_k, z_k) of n triples of random numbers uniformly distributed on $[0, 1)$, and count the number m falling within the sphere. Since the volume of the cube is 1, the volume of the sphere should be approximated by m/n. Compare your result with the known volume, which is given by $V = 4\pi r^3/3 = \pi/6$. Use various values for n, and try

to characterize the size of the error as a function of the number of random trials.

(*c*) Compare your results for parts *a* and *b* in terms of the accuracy attained as a function of the number of trials. Explain any relationship you may observe.

13.11. Use random trials to simulate the behavior of the Markov chain given in Computer Problem 4.11. For the same transition probabilities and initial state given there, perform m trials, taking k steps for each trial. Experiment with the values for m and k, and compare the resulting probability distribution vectors with the results obtained by the methods in Chapter 4.

13.12. (*a*) Radioactive decay is an inherently nondeterministic process that can be simulated very naturally using the Monte Carlo method. Suppose that the probability of any given atom decaying over a time interval Δt is given by λ, $0 < \lambda < 1$. Then the history of a single atom can be simulated by choosing a sequence of random numbers x_k, $k = 1, \ldots$, uniformly distributed on $[0, 1)$. The atom survives until the first value x_k for which $x_k < \lambda$. Use this approach to simulate an ensemble of n atoms. Make a plot of the number of atoms remaining after k time increments, $k = 1, \ldots, m$. Take $\lambda = 0.1$ and $m = 50$, and try the values $n = 10$, 100, 1000, and 10, 000, making a separate graph for each value of n. How does the value of n affect the smoothness of the resulting curve? Experiment with other values for λ, n, and m to see the range of possible behaviors.

(*b*) We can also develop a continuous, deterministic model of radioactive decay for an ensemble of atoms. The change in the number of atoms Δn over time interval Δt is proportional to the number of atoms present and the length of the time interval. Specifically,

$$\Delta n(t) = -\lambda n(t) \Delta t.$$

In the limit, this gives the ODE

$$n'(t) = -\lambda n(t),$$

whose solution is

$$n(t) = n(0)e^{-\lambda t},$$

the familiar decaying exponential model for radioactivity. For the same values of λ and initial number of atoms n as in part *a*, plot the resulting solution for $t = 1, \ldots, m$ on the same graph with the results from part *a*. How do the two models compare? How is their agreement affected by the initial number of atoms n? Which model do you think is closer to the way nature actually behaves? Why?

13.13. A *random walk* is a sequence of fixed-length steps, each taken in a randomly (and independently) chosen direction. A random walk can be used to model various physical phenomena, such as Brownian motion of small particles suspended in a fluid. In this exercise we will consider only the one-dimensional case in which the walk begins at 0. The walk proceeds by successive steps of unit length, with the direction—positive or negative—chosen randomly with equal probability. Write a program to implement a random walk of n steps, using a uniform random number generator to choose the direction for each step, and compute the distance from the origin at the end of the walk. Run your program for $n = 10$, 100, 1000, and 10,000, averaging the distance from the origin at the end of the walk over several trials for each value of n. Try to characterize the average distance from the origin as a function of n.

13.14. In a two-dimensional random walk, steps are taken randomly on a two-dimensional lattice of points, with the direction—up, down, left, or right—chosen randomly with equal probability. It turns out that such a random walk can be used to solve the Laplace equation. Impose a grid of points on the domain of the equation, including the boundary, then start n trials of a random walk from a given interior grid point, terminating each trial when some boundary point of the domain is hit. The solution at the starting grid point is then given by the average over all the trials of the solution values at the boundary points that were hit.

Implement this two-dimensional random walk approach to solve the Laplace equation, using the same grid and boundary values as in Example 11.4. Compute the solution at each of the interior grid points by averaging over n trials from each point. How many trials are required to obtain results comparable to those in Example 11.4?

Because of the large number of trials required, the random walk method is not competitive with other numerical methods for computing the solution over the entire domain. The random walk method does have the advantage, however, that it can compute the solution at a single point without having to compute it anywhere else, which is in contrast with most other numerical methods. Moreover, the random walk method can easily accommodate very complicated boundaries that may be difficult to deal with using conventional numerical methods.

13.15. A polymer can be modeled as a sequence of n segments (monomers) of fixed length joined by $n - 1$ universal joints, so that each angle between adjacent segments can take any value from 0 to 360 degrees with equal probability.

(*a*) Use a uniform random number generator to implement this model of a polymer in two dimensions. Assume that the units chosen are such that the length of each segment is 1. The $n - 1$ angles θ_k between successive segments should be uniformly distributed on the interval $[0, 2\pi)$. Try several different values for n, say 10, 100, or more if your computer budget allows (real polymers may have thousands of segments). Make several trials for each value of n and compute the average overall length of the polymer (i.e., the distance between the endpoints of the first and last segments in Cartesian coordinates). Try to characterize the average length of the polymer as a function of n. You may find it interesting to draw a picture of the polymer in two dimensions. Note that the result is simply a kind of random walk.

(*b*) Repeat part *a*, but this time in three dimensions. To generate the direction of each new segment, you will probably find it most convenient to use spherical coordinates, with both the azimuth and zenith angles, θ and ϕ, chosen as random numbers uniformly distributed on the interval $[0, 2\pi)$. To draw a picture and compute the length of the polymer, however, you will find it easiest to use three-dimensional Cartesian coordinates. Again, run several trials for each value of n and try to characterize the average length of the polymer as a function of n. Does the increase in dimensionality make a significant difference in the length of the polymer for the same number of segments?

(*c*) The previous model is unrealistic in part because chemical bonds are not universal joints, and they prefer certain bond angles over others. Assume that instead we have swivel joints in three dimensions, with a fixed angle θ and free angle ϕ. Use this new model to simulate polyethylene, which has a favored bond angle of $\theta = 109°$. Again, run several trials for the same values of n and characterize the average length of the polymer as a function of n. Does this model give significantly different results from the previous model? When plotted in three dimensions, do the simulated polymers given by the two models look appreciably different?

13.16. Suppose that neutrons enter one side of a lead shielding wall that is four units thick. Each neutron enters at a random angle and travels a distance of one unit before colliding with a lead nucleus. Such a collision causes the neutron to bounce off in a random direction to travel another unit distance before another collision, and so on. After eight collisions, a given neutron has lost all of its energy and therefore stops. Use Monte Carlo simulation to determine the percentage of neutrons that exit from the other side of the wall. Does it make a significant difference whether the wall is modeled as two-dimensional or three-dimensional?

13.17. Repeat one or more of the preceding exercises using a quasi-random sequence generator (see Section 13.5 for appropriate software) instead of a standard random number generator. Does the quasi-random sequence pass any of the randomness tests given in the first few exercises? Does the quasi-random sequence make a significant difference in accuracy or efficiency for any of your simulation results?

13.18. Evaluate the double integral given in Computer Problem 8.12 using Monte Carlo integration. Try both a standard uniform random number generator and a quasi-random sequence generator and compare their efficiency in attaining a given level of accuracy.

Bibliography

[1] M. Abramowitz and I. A. Stegun. *Handbook of Mathematical Functions*. Dover, New York, 1965.

[2] F. S. Acton. *Numerical Methods That Work*. Math. Assoc. Amer., Washington, DC, 1990. (Reprint of 1970 edition.)

[3] F. S. Acton. *Real Computing Made Real*. Princeton University Press, Princeton, NJ, 1996.

[4] J. H. Ahlberg, E. N. Nilson, and J. L. Walsh. *The Theory of Splines and Their Applications*. Academic, New York, 1967.

[5] G. Alefeld and J. Herzberger. *Introduction to Interval Computations*. Academic, New York, 1983.

[6] E. L. Allgower and K. Georg. *Numerical Continuation Methods*. Springer-Verlag, New York, 1990.

[7] W. F. Ames. *Numerical Methods for Partial Differential Equations*. 3d ed. Academic, New York, 1992.

[8] E. Anderson, Z. Bai, C. Bischof, J. Demmel, J. Dongarra, J. DuCroz, A. Greenbaum, S. Hammarling, A. McKenney, S. Ostrouchov, and D. Sorensen. *LAPACK User's Guide*. 2d ed. SIAM, Philadelphia, PA, 1995.

[9] H. C. Andrews and C. L. Patterson. Outer product expansions and their uses in digital image processing. *Amer. Math. Monthly,* 82:1–13, 1975.

[10] U. M. Ascher, R. M. Mattheij, and R. D. Russell. *Numerical Solution of Boundary Value Problems for Ordinary Differential Equations*. SIAM, Philadelphia, PA, 1995. (reprint of 1988 edition).

[11] K. Atkinson. *Elementary Numerical Analysis*. 2d ed. John Wiley & Sons, New York, 1993.

[12] O. Axelsson. *Iterative Solution Methods*. Cambridge University Press, New York, 1994.

[13] R. E. Bank. *PLTMG: A Software Package for Solving Elliptic Partial Differential Equations*. SIAM, Philadelphia, PA, 1994.

[14] Y. Bard. *Nonlinear Parameter Estimation*. Academic, New York, 1970.

[15] R. Barrett, M. Berry, T. Chan, J. Demmel, J. Donato, J. Dongarra, V. Eijkhout, R. Pozo, C. Romine, and H. van der Vorst. *Templates for the Solution of Linear Systems: Building Blocks for Iterative Methods*. SIAM Publications, Philadelphia, PA, 1994.

[16] R. Bartels, J. Beatty, and B. Barsky. *An Introduction to Splines for Use in Computer Graphics and Geometric Modeling.* Morgan Kaufmann, Los Altos, CA, 1987.

[17] E. B. Becker, G. F. Carey, and J. T. Oden. *Finite Elements: An Introduction.* Prentice Hall, Englewood Cliffs, NJ, 1981. (Texas Finite Element Series, Vol. 1.)

[18] A. Biran and M. Breiner. *MATLAB for Engineers.* Addison-Wesley, Reading, MA, 1995.

[19] Å. Björck. *Numerical Methods for Least Squares Problems.* SIAM, Philadelphia, PA, 1996.

[20] J. F. Botha and G. F. Pinder. *Fundamental Concepts in the Numerical Solution of Partial Differential Equations.* John Wiley & Sons, New York, 1983.

[21] P. Bratley, B. L. Fox, and L. E. Schrage. *A Guide to Simulation.* 2d ed. Springer-Verlag, New York, 1987.

[22] K. E. Brenan, S. L. Campbell, and L. R. Petzold. *Numerical Solution of Initial-Value Problems in Differential-Algebraic Equations.* SIAM, Philadelphia, PA, 1996. (Reprint of 1989 edition.)

[23] R. P. Brent. *Algorithms for Minimization without Derivatives.* Prentice Hall, Englewood Cliffs, NJ, 1973.

[24] W. L. Briggs. *A Multigrid Tutorial.* SIAM, Philadelphia, PA, 1987.

[25] W. L. Briggs and V. E. Henson. *The DFT: An Owner's Manual for the Discrete Fourier Transform.* SIAM, Philadelphia, PA, 1995.

[26] E. O. Brigham. *The Fast Fourier Transform.* Prentice Hall, Englewood Cliffs, NJ, 1974.

[27] E. O. Brigham. *The Fast Fourier Transform and Its Applications.* Prentice Hall, Englewood Cliffs, NJ, 1988.

[28] P. Brinch Hansen. Householder reduction of linear systems. *ACM Computing Surveys,* 24(2):185–194, June 1992.

[29] J. L. Buchanan and P. R. Turner. *Numerical Methods and Analysis.* McGraw-Hill, New York, 1992.

[30] R. L. Burden and J. D. Faires. *Numerical Analysis.* 5th ed. PWS Publishing Co., Boston, 1993.

[31] J. C. Butcher. *The Numerical Analysis of Ordinary Differential Equations.* John Wiley & Sons, New York, 1987.

[32] G. D. Byrne and A. C. Hindmarsh. Stiff ODE solvers: A review of current and coming attractions. *J. Comput. Phys.,* 70:1–62, 1987.

[33] G. F. Carey and J. T. Oden. *Finite Elements: A Second Course.* Prentice Hall, Englewood Cliffs, NJ, 1983. (Texas Finite Element Series, Vol. 2.)

[34] G. F. Carey and J. T. Oden. *Finite Elements: Computational Aspects.* Prentice Hall, Englewood Cliffs, NJ, 1984. (Texas Finite Element Series, Vol. 3.)

[35] M. A. Celia and W. G. Gray. *Numerical Methods for Differential Equations.* Prentice Hall, Englewood Cliffs, NJ, 1992.

[36] F. Chaitin-Chatelin and V. Fraysse. *Lectures on Finite Precision Computations.* SIAM, Philadelphia, PA, 1996.

[37] F. Chatelin. *Eigenvalues of Matrices.* John Wiley & Sons, New York, 1993.

[38] W. Cheney and D. Kincaid. *Numerical Mathematics and Computing.* 3d ed. Brooks/Cole, Pacific Grove, CA, 1994.

[39] B. Childs, M. Scott, J. W. Daniel, E. Denman, and P. Nelson, eds. *Codes for Boundary Value Problems in ODEs.* Springer-Verlag, New York, 1979.

[40] E. Chong and S. Żak. *An Introduction to Optimization.* John Wiley & Sons, New York, 1996.

[41] W. J. Cody. The construction of numerical subroutine libraries. *SIAM Review,* 16:36–46, 1974.

[42] T. F. Coleman and C. Van Loan. *Handbook for Matrix Computations.* SIAM, Philadelphia, PA, 1988.

[43] S. D. Conte and C. de Boor. *Elementary Numerical Analysis.* 3d ed. McGraw-Hill, New York, 1980.

[44] W. R. Cowell, ed. *Sources and Development of Mathematical Software.* Prentice Hall, Englewood Cliffs, NJ, 1984.

[45] R. E. Crandall. *Projects in Scientific Computation.* Springer-Verlag, New York, 1994.

[46] J. K. Cullum and R. A. Willoughby. *Lanczos Algorithms for Large Symmetric Eigenvalue Computations.* Birkhäuser, Boston, 1985.

[47] G. Dahlquist and Å. Björck. *Numerical Methods.* Prentice Hall, Englewood Cliffs, NJ, 1974.

[48] G. B. Dantzig. *Linear Programming and Extensions.* Princeton University Press, Princeton, NJ, 1963.

[49] B. N. Datta. *Numerical Linear Algebra and Applications.* Brooks/Cole, Pacific Grove, CA, 1995.

[50] A. J. Davies. *The Finite Element Method: A First Approach.* Oxford University Press, New York, 1980.

[51] P. J. Davis. *Interpolation and Approximation.* Dover, New York, 1975. (Reprint of 1963 edition.)

[52] P. J. Davis and P. Rabinowitz. *Methods of Numerical Integration.* 2d ed. Academic, New York, 1984.

[53] C. de Boor. *A Practical Guide to Splines.* 2d ed. Springer-Verlag, New York, 1984.

[54] L. M. Delves and J. L. Mohamed. *Computational Methods for Integral Equations.* Cambridge University Press, New York, 1985.

[55] J. W. Demmel, M. T. Heath, and H. A. van der Vorst. Parallel numerical linear algebra. *Acta Numerica,* 2:111–197, 1993.

[56] J. E. Dennis and J. J. Moré. Quasi-Newton methods, motivation and theory. *SIAM Review,* 19:46–89, 1977.

[57] J. E. Dennis and R. B. Schnabel. *Numerical Methods for Unconstrained Optimization and Nonlinear Equations.* SIAM, Philadelphia, PA, 1996. (Reprint of 1983 edition.)

[58] P. Deuflhard. Recent progress in extrapolation methods for ordinary differential equations. *SIAM Review,* 27:505–535, 1985.

[59] P. Deuflhard and A. Hohmann. *Numerical Analysis: A First Course in Scientific Computation.* Walter de Gruyter, New York, 1995.

[60] P. Dierckx. *Curve and Surface Fitting with Splines.* Oxford University Press, New York, 1993.

[61] J. Dongarra, J. DuCroz, I. S. Duff and S. Hammarling. A set of level-3 basic linear algebra subprograms. *ACM Trans. Math. Software,* 16:1–28, 1990.

[62] J. Dongarra, J. DuCroz, S. Hammarling, and R. J. Hanson. An extended set of Fortran basic linear algebra subprograms. *ACM Trans. Math. Software,* 14:1-32, 1988.

[63] J. J. Dongarra, J. R. Bunch, C. B. Moler, and G. W. Stewart. *LINPACK User's Guide.* 2d ed. SIAM, Philadelphia, PA, 1979.

[64] J. J. Dongarra, I. S. Duff, D. C. Sorensen, and H. A. van der Vorst. *Solving Linear Systems on Vector and Shared Memory Computers.* SIAM, Philadelphia, PA, 1990.

[65] J. J. Dongarra, F. G. Gustavson, and A. Karp. Implementing linear algebra algorithms for dense matrices on a vector pipeline machine. *SIAM Review,* 26:91–112, 1984.

[66] J. R. Dormand. *Numerical Methods for Differential Equations.* CRC Press, Boca Raton, FL, 1996.

[67] K. Dowd. *High Performance Computing.* O'Reilly & Associates, Sebastopol, CA, 1993.

[68] I. S. Duff, A. M. Erisman, and J. K. Reid. *Direct Methods for Sparse Matrices.* Oxford University Press, New York, 1986.

[69] P. Duhamel and M. Vetterli. Fast Fourier transforms: A tutorial review and a state of the art. *Signal Processing,* 19:259–299, 1990.

[70] H. Engels. *Numerical Quadrature and Cubature.* Academic, New York, 1980.

[71] D. M. Etter. *Introduction to MATLAB for Engineers and Scientists.* Prentice Hall, Upper Saddle River, NJ, 1996.

[72] D. M. Etter. *Engineering Problem Solving with MATLAB.* 2d ed. Prentice Hall, Upper Saddle River, NJ, 1997.

[73] D. J. Evans, ed. *Software for Numerical Mathematics.* Academic, New York, 1974.

[74] G. Evans. *Practical Numerical Integration.* John Wiley & Sons, New York, 1993.

[75] V. Faber and T. Manteuffel. Necessary and sufficient conditions for the existence of a conjugate gradient method. *SIAM J. Numer. Anal.,* 21:315–339, 1984.

[76] R. W. Farebrother. *Linear Least Squares Computations.* Marcel Dekker, New York, 1987.

[77] S. O. Fatunla. *Numerical Methods for Initial Value Problems in Ordinary Differential Equations.* Academic, New York, 1988.

[78] A. V. Fiacco and G. P. McCormick. *Nonlinear Programming: Sequential Unconstrained Minimization Techniques.* SIAM, Philadelphia, PA, 1990. (Reprint of 1968 edition.)

[79] G. S. Fishman. *Monte Carlo: Concepts, Algorithms, and Applications.* Springer-Verlag, New York, 1996.

[80] R. Fletcher. *Practical Methods of Optimization.* 2d ed. John Wiley & Sons, New York, 1987.

[81] B. Fornberg. *A Practical Guide to Pseudospectral Methods.* Cambridge University Press, New York, 1996.

[82] G. E. Forsythe, M. A. Malcolm, and C. B. Moler. *Computer Methods for Mathematical Computations.* Prentice Hall, Englewood Cliffs, NJ, 1977.

[83] G. E. Forsythe and C. B. Moler. *Computer Solution of Linear Algebraic Systems.* Prentice Hall, Englewood Cliffs, NJ, 1967.

[84] G. E. Forsythe and W. R. Wasow. *Finite Difference Methods for Partial Differential Equations.* John Wiley & Sons, New York, 1960.

[85] L. Fosdick, E. Jessup, C. Schauble, and G. Domik. *An Introduction to High-Performance Scientific Computing.* The MIT Press, Cambridge, MA, 1995.

[86] L. Fox. *The Numerical Solution of Two-Point Boundary Problems.* Dover, New York, 1990. (Reprint of 1957 edition.)

[87] R. W. Freund, G. H. Golub, and N. M. Nachtigal. Iterative solution of linear systems. *Acta Numerica,* 1:57–100, 1992.

[88] F. N. Fritsch and R. E. Carlson. Monotone piecewise cubic interpolation. *SIAM J. Numer. Anal.,* 17:238–246, 1980.

[89] W. Gander and J. Hřebiček. *Solving Problems in Scientific Computing Using Maple and MATLAB.* 2d ed. Springer-Verlag, New York, 1995.

[90] B. S. Garbow, J. M. Boyle, J. J. Dongarra, and C. B. Moler. *Matrix Eigensystem Routines: EISPACK Guide Extension.* Springer-Verlag, New York, 1972.

[91] C. W. Gear. *Numerical Initial Value Problems in Ordinary Differential Equations.* Prentice Hall, Englewood Cliffs, NJ, 1971.

[92] C. W. Gear. Numerical solution of ordinary differential equations: Is there anything left to do? *SIAM Review,* 23:10–24, 1981.

[93] A. George and J. W.-H. Liu. *Computer Solution of Large Sparse Positive Definite Systems.* Prentice Hall, Englewood Cliffs, NJ, 1981.

[94] C. F. Gerald and P. O. Wheatley. *Applied Numerical Analysis.* 5th ed. Addison-Wesley, Reading, MA, 1994.

[95] P. E. Gill, W. Murray, and M. H. Wright. *Practical Optimization.* Academic, New York, 1981.

[96] P. E. Gill, W. Murray, and M. H. Wright. *Numerical Linear Algebra and Optimization,* Vol. 1. Addison-Wesley, Reading, MA, 1991.

[97] D. Goldberg. What every computer scientist should know about floating-point arithmetic. *ACM Computing Surveys,* 18(1):5–48, March 1991.

[98] D. Goldfarb. Algorithms for unconstrained optimization: A review of recent developments. In W. Gautschi, ed. *Mathematics of Computation 1943–1993: A Half Century of Computational Mathematics.* Vol. 48 of *Proc. Symp. Appl. Math.*, pages 33–48. Amer. Math. Soc., 1993.

[99] D. Goldfarb and M. J. Todd. Linear programming. In G. Nemhauser et al., eds. *Optimization,* pages 73–170. North-Holland, New York, 1989.

[100] H. H. Goldstine. *A History of Numerical Analysis from the 16th through the 19th Century.* Springer-Verlag, New York, 1977.

[101] G. H. Golub. Numerical methods for solving linear least squares problems. *Numer. Math.,* 7:206–216, 1965.

[102] G. H. Golub and D. P. O'Leary. Some history of the conjugate gradient and Lanczos methods. *SIAM Review,* 31:50–102, 1989.

[103] G. H. Golub and J. M. Ortega. *Scientific Computing and Differential Equations.* 2d ed. Academic, New York, 1992.

[104] G. H. Golub and C. F. Van Loan. *Matrix Computations.* 3d ed. The Johns Hopkins University Press, Baltimore, MD, 1996.

[105] G. H. Golub and J. H. Welsch. Calculation of Gauss quadrature rules. *Math. Comp.,* 23:221–230, 1969.

[106] D. Gottlieb and S. A. Orszag. *Numerical Analysis of Spectral Methods.* SIAM, Philadelphia, PA, 1977.

[107] H. Gould and J. Tobochnik. *An Introduction to Computer Simulation Methods.* 2d ed. Addison-Wesley, Reading, MA, 1996.

[108] A. R. Gourlay and G. A. Watson. *Computational Methods for Matrix Eigenproblems.* John Wiley & Sons, New York, 1973.

[109] T. A. Grandine. *The Numerical Methods Programming Projects Book.* Oxford University Press, New York, 1990.

[110] A. Graps. An introduction to wavelets. *IEEE Comput. Sci. Engr.,* 2(2):50–61, 1995.

[111] G. K. Gupta, R. Sacks-Davis, and P. E. Tischer. A review of recent developments in solving ODEs. *ACM Computing Surveys,* 17:5–47, 1985.

[112] B. Gustafsson, H.-O. Kreiss, and J. Oliger. *Time Dependent Problems and Difference Methods*. John Wiley & Sons, New York, 1995.

[113] S. Haber. Numerical evaluation of multiple integrals. *SIAM Review,* 12:481–526, 1970.

[114] W. Hackbusch. *Iterative Solution of Large Sparse Systems of Equations*. Springer-Verlag, New York, 1994.

[115] L. A. Hageman and D. M. Young. *Applied Iterative Methods*. Academic, New York, 1981.

[116] W. Hager. *Applied Numerical Linear Algebra*. Prentice Hall, Englewood Cliffs, NJ, 1988.

[117] C. A. Hall and T. A. Porsching. *Numerical Analysis of Partial Differential Equations*. Prentice Hall, Englewood Cliffs, NJ, 1990.

[118] G. Hämmerlin and K.-H. Hoffmann. *Numerical Mathematics*. Springer-Verlag, New York, 1991. (Translation of 1989 German edition.)

[119] J. M. Hammersley and D. C. Handscomb. *Monte Carlo Methods*. Chapman and Hall, New York, 1965.

[120] D. Hanselman and B. Littlefield. *Mastering MATLAB*. Prentice Hall, Upper Saddle River, NJ, 1996.

[121] P. C. Hansen. Regularization tools: A MATLAB package for analysis and solution of discrete ill-posed problems. *Numerical Algorithms,* 6:1–35, 1994.

[122] M. A. Hennell and L. M. Delves, eds. *Production and Assessment of Numerical Software*. Academic, New York, 1980.

[123] P. Henrici. *Discrete Variable Methods in Ordinary Differential Equations*. John Wiley & Sons, New York, 1962.

[124] N. J. Higham. A survey of condition number estimation for triangular matrices. *SIAM Review,* 29:575–596, 1987.

[125] N. J. Higham. A survey of componentwise perturbation theory in numerical linear algebra. In W. Gautschi, ed. *Mathematics of Computation 1943–1993: A Half Century of Computational Mathematics*. Vol. 48 of *Proc. Symp. Appl. Math.,* pages 49–77. Amer. Math. Soc., 1993.

[126] N. J. Higham. *Accuracy and Stability of Numerical Algorithms*. SIAM, Philadelphia, PA, 1996.

[127] D. R. Hill. *Experiments in Computational Matrix Algebra*. Random House, New York, 1988.

[128] T. Hopkins and C. Phillips. *Numerical Methods in Practice*. Addison-Wesley, Reading, MA, 1988.

[129] A. S. Householder. *The Numerical Treatment of a Single Nonlinear Equation*. McGraw-Hill, New York, 1970.

[130] B. B. Hubbard. *The World According to Wavelets*. A K Peters, Ltd., Wellesley, MA, 1996.

[131] IEEE. IEEE standard 754-1985 for binary floating-point arithmetic. *SIGPLAN Notices,* 22(2):9–25, 1987. (See also *IEEE Computer,* March 1981.)

[132] E. Isaacson and H. B. Keller. *Analysis of Numerical Methods*. Dover, New York, 1994. (Reprint of 1966 edition.)

[133] A. Iserles. *A First Course in the Numerical Analysis of Differential Equations*. Cambridge University Press, New York, 1996.

[134] D. Jacobs, ed. *Numerical Software: Needs and Availability*. Academic, New York, 1978.

[135] P. Jarratt and D. Nudds. The use of rational functions in the iterative solution of equations on a digital computer. *Computer J.,* 8:62–65, 1965.

[136] M. A. Jenkins and J. F. Traub. Zeros of a complex polynomial. *Comm. ACM,* 15:97–99, 1972.

[137] M. A. Jenkins and J. F. Traub. Zeros of a real polynomial. *ACM Trans. Math. Software,* 1:178–189, 1975.

[138] A. Jennings and J. J. McKeown. *Matrix Computation.* 2d ed. John Wiley & Sons, New York, 1992.

[139] D. C. Jespersen. Multigrid methods for partial differential equations. In G. H. Golub, ed. *Studies in Numerical Analysis,* pages 270–318. Math. Assoc. Amer., Washington, DC, 1984.

[140] C. Johnson. *Numerical Solution of Partial Differential Equations by the Finite Element Method.* Cambridge University Press, New York, 1987.

[141] D. C. Joyce. Survey of extrapolation processes in numerical analysis. *SIAM Review,* 13:435–488, 1971.

[142] D. Kahaner, C. Moler, and S. Nash. *Numerical Methods and Software.* Prentice Hall, Englewood Cliffs, NJ, 1989.

[143] G. Kaiser. *A Friendly Guide to Wavelets.* Birkhäuser, Boston, 1994.

[144] M. H. Kalos and P. A. Whitlock. *Monte Carlo Methods.* John Wiley & Sons, New York, 1986.

[145] W. J. Kaufmann and L. L. Smarr. *Supercomputing and the Transformation of Science.* Scientific American Library, New York, 1993.

[146] H. B. Keller. *Numerical Methods for Two-Point Boundary-Value Problems.* Dover, New York, 1992. (Reprint of 1968 edition.)

[147] C. T. Kelley. *Iterative Methods for Linear and Nonlinear Equations.* SIAM, Philadelphia, PA, 1995.

[148] W. J. Kennedy and J. E. Gentle. *Statistical Computing.* Marcel Dekker, New York, 1980.

[149] D. Kincaid and W. Cheney. *Numerical Analysis.* 2d ed. Brooks/Cole, Pacific Grove, CA, 1996.

[150] D. E. Knuth. *The Art of Computer Programming: Seminumerical Algorithms,* Vol. 2. Addison-Wesley, Reading, MA, 1969.

[151] N. Köckler. *Numerical Methods and Scientific Computing.* Oxford University Press, New York, 1994.

[152] I. Koren. *Computer Arithmetic Algorithms.* Prentice Hall, Englewood Cliffs, NJ, 1993.

[153] A. R. Krommer and C. W. Ueberhuber. *Computational Integration.* SIAM, Philadelphia, PA, 1996.

[154] P. K. Kythe. *Boundary Element Methods.* CRC Press, Boca Raton, FL, 1995.

[155] J. D. Lambert. *Computational Methods in Ordinary Differential Systems.* John Wiley & Sons, New York, 1973.

[156] J. D. Lambert. *Numerical Methods for Ordinary Differential Systems.* John Wiley & Sons, New York, 1991.

[157] R. H. Landau. *A Project Approach to Computational Physical Science.* John Wiley & Sons, New York, 1997.

[158] R. H. Landau and P. J. Fink. *A Scientist's and Engineer's Guide to Workstations and Supercomputers.* John Wiley & Sons, New York, 1993.

[159] L. Lapidus and G. F. Pinder. *Numerical Solution of Partial Differential Equations in Science and Engineering.* John Wiley & Sons, New York, 1982.

[160] L. Lapidus and J. Seinfeld. *Numerical Solution of Ordinary Differential Equations.* Academic, New York, 1971.

[161] F. M. Larkin. Root-finding by fitting rational functions. *Math. Comp.,* 35:803–816, 1980.

[162] H. T. Lau. *A Numerical Library in C for Scientists and Engineers.* CRC Press, Boca Raton, FL, 1995.

[163] C. L. Lawson and R. J. Hanson. *Solving Least Squares Problems.* SIAM, Philadelphia, PA, 1995. (Updated reprint of 1974 edition.)

[164] C. L. Lawson, R. J. Hanson, D. R. Kincaid, and F. T. Krogh. Basic linear algebra subprograms for FORTRAN usage. *ACM Trans. Math. Software.,* 5:308–325, 1979.

[165] G. Lindfield and J. Penny. *Numerical Methods Using MATLAB.* Ellis Horwood, New York, 1995.

[166] D. W. Lozier and F. W. J. Olver. Numerical evaluation of special functions. In W. Gautschi, ed. *Mathematics of Computation 1943–1993: A Half Century of Computational Mathematics.* Vol. 48 of *Proc. Symp. Appl. Math.*, pages 79–125. Amer. Math. Soc., 1993.

[167] D. G. Luenberger. *Linear and Nonlinear Programming.* 2d ed. Addison-Wesley, Reading, MA, 1984.

[168] J. N. Lyness. When not to use an automatic quadrature routine. *SIAM Review,* 25:63–88, 1983.

[169] J. N. Lyness and R. Cools. A survey of numerical cubature over triangles. In W. Gautschi, ed. *Mathematics of Computation 1943–1993: A Half Century of Computational Mathematics.* Vol. 48 of *Proc. Symp. Appl. Math.*, pages 127–150. Amer. Math. Soc., 1993.

[170] J. N. Lyness and J. J. Kaganove. Comments on the nature of automatic quadrature routines. *ACM Trans. Math. Software,* 2:65–81, 1976.

[171] A. R. Magid. *Applied Matrix Models.* John Wiley & Sons, New York, 1985.

[172] G. Marsaglia. Random numbers fall mainly in the planes. *Proc. Nat. Acad. Sci.,* USA, 61:25–28, 1968.

[173] J. H. Mathews. *Numerical Methods.* 2d ed. Prentice Hall, Englewood Cliffs, NJ, 1992.

[174] W. Miller. *The Engineering of Numerical Software.* Prentice Hall, Englewood Cliffs, NJ, 1984.

[175] W. Miller and C. Wrathall. *Software for Roundoff Analysis of Matrix Algorithms.* Academic, New York, 1980.

[176] A. R. Mitchell and D. F. Griffiths. *The Finite Difference Method in Partial Differential Equations.* John Wiley & Sons, New York, 1980.

[177] C. B. Moler. Matrix computations with Fortran and paging. *Comm. ACM.,* 15:268–270, 1972.

[178] C. B. Moler and D. Morrison. Singular value analysis of cryptograms. *Amer. Math. Monthly,* 90:78–87, 1983.

[179] C. B. Moler and C. F. Van Loan. Nineteen dubious ways to compute the exponential of a matrix. *SIAM Review,* 20:801–836, 1978.

[180] R. E. Moore. *Methods and Applications of Interval Analysis.* SIAM, Philadelphia, PA, 1979.

[181] J. J. Moré. The Levenberg-Marquardt algorithm: Implementation and theory. In G. A. Watson, ed. *Numerical Analysis,* pages 105–116. Springer-Verlag, New York, 1977.

[182] J. J. Moré, B. S. Garbow, and K. E. Hillstrom. User guide for MINPACK-1. Technical Report ANL-80-74, Argonne National Laboratory, Argonne, IL, 1980.

[183] J. J. Moré and D. C. Sorensen. Newton's method. In G. H. Golub, ed. *Studies in Numerical Analysis,* pages 29–82. Math. Assoc. Amer., Washington, DC 1984.

[184] J. J. Moré and Stephen J. Wright. *Optimization Software Guide.* SIAM, Philadelphia, PA, 1993.

[185] N. Morrison. *Introduction to Fourier Analysis.* John Wiley & Sons, New York, 1994.

[186] K. W. Morton and D. F. Mayers. *Numerical Solution of Partial Differential Equations.* Cambridge University Press, New York, 1994.

[187] S. Nakamura. *Numerical Analysis and Graphic Visualization with MATLAB.* Prentice Hall, Upper Saddle River, NJ, 1996.

[188] S. G. Nash, ed. *A History of Scientific Computing.* ACM Press, New York, 1990.

[189] S. G. Nash and A. Sofer. *Linear and Nonlinear Programming.* McGraw-Hill, New York, 1996.

[190] H. Niederreiter. *Random Number Generation and Quasi- Monte Carlo Methods.* SIAM, Philadelphia, PA, 1992.

[191] J. Nievergelt, J. C. Farrar, and E. M. Reingold. *Computer Approaches to Mathematical Problems.* Prentice Hall, Englewood Cliffs, NJ, 1974.

[192] J. Nocedal. Theory of algorithms for unconstrained optimization. *Acta Numerica,* 1:199–242, 1992.

[193] A. R. Omondi. *Computer Arithmetic Systems.* Prentice Hall, Englewood Cliffs, NJ, 1994.

[194] J. M. Ortega. *Introduction to Parallel and Vector Solution of Linear Systems.* Plenum, New York, 1988.

[195] J. M. Ortega. *Numerical Analysis: A Second Course.* SIAM, Philadelphia, PA, 1990. (Reprint of 1972 edition.)

[196] J. M. Ortega and W. C. Rheinboldt. *Iterative Solution of Nonlinear Equations in Several Variables.* Academic, New York, 1970.

[197] A. M. Ostrowski. *Solution of Equations and Systems of Equations.* 2d ed. Academic, New York, 1966.

[198] C. C. Paige and M. A. Saunders. Solution of sparse indefinite systems of linear equations. *SIAM J. Numer. Anal.,* 12:617–629, 1975.

[199] B. N. Parlett. *The Symmetric Eigenvalue Problem.* Prentice Hall, Englewood Cliffs, NJ, 1980.

[200] E. Part-Enander, A. Sjoberg, B. Melin, and P. Isaksson. *MATLAB Handbook.* Addison-Wesley, Reading, MA, 1996.

[201] V. Pereyra. Finite difference solution of boundary value problems in ordinary differential equations. In G. H. Golub, ed. *Studies in Numerical Analysis,* pages 243–269. Math. Assoc. Amer., Washington, DC, 1984.

[202] M. Pickering. *An Introduction to Fast Fourier Transform Methods for Partial Differential Equations, with Applications.* John Wiley & Sons, New York, 1986.

[203] R. Piessens, E. deDoncker Kapenga, C. Uberhuber, and D. Kahaner. *QUADPACK: A Subroutine Package for Automatic Integration.* Springer-Verlag, New York, 1983.

[204] R. Pratap. *Getting Started with MATLAB.* Saunders College Publishing, Fort Worth, TX, 1995.

[205] W. H. Press, S. A. Teukolsky, W. T. Vetterling, and B. P. Flannery. *Numerical Recipes.* 2d ed. Cambridge University Press, New York, 1992.

[206] D. Redfern and C. Campbell. *The MATLAB Handbook.* Springer-Verlag, New York, 1996.

[207] C. H. Reinsch. Smoothing by spline functions. *Numer. Math.,* 10:177–183, 1967.

[208] C. H. Reinsch. Smoothing by spline functions II. *Numer. Math.,* 16:451–454, 1971.

[209] J. R. Rice, ed. *Mathematical Software.* Academic, New York, 1971.

[210] J. R. Rice, ed. *Mathematical Software III.* Academic, New York, 1977.

[211] J. R. Rice. *Numerical Methods, Software, and Analysis.* 2d ed. Academic, New York, 1993.

[212] J. R. Rice and R. F. Boisvert. *Solving Elliptic Problems Using ELLPACK.* Springer-Verlag, New York, 1985.

[213] R. Richtmyer and K. W. Morton. *Difference Methods for Initial-Value Problems.* 2d ed. John Wiley & Sons, New York, 1967.

[214] G. F. Roach. *Green's Functions.* 2d ed. Cambridge University Press, New York, 1982.

[215] S. Roberts and J. Shipman. *Two-Point Boundary Value Problems: Shooting Methods.* Elsevier, New York, 1972.

[216] R. Rubinstein. *Simulation and the Monte Carlo Method.* John Wiley & Sons, New York, 1981.

[217] Y. Saad. *Numerical Methods for Large Eigenvalue Problems.* John Wiley & Sons, New York, 1992.

[218] Y. Saad. *Iterative Methods for Sparse Linear Systems.* PWS Publishing Co., Boston, 1996.

[219] W. E. Schiesser. *The Numerical Method of Lines Integration of Partial Differential Equations.* Academic, New York, 1991.

[220] R. B. Schnabel, J. E. Koontz, and B. E. Weiss. A modular system of algorithms for unconstrained minimization. *ACM Trans. Math. Software,* 11:419–440, 1985.

[221] L. L. Schumaker. *Spline Functions.* John Wiley & Sons, New York, 1981.

[222] H. R. Schwarz. *Numerical Analysis: A Comprehensive Introduction.* John Wiley & Sons, New York, 1989.

[223] L. F. Shampine. What everyone solving differential equations numerically should know. In I. Gladwell and D. K. Sayers, eds. *Computational Techniques for Ordinary Differential Equations,* pages 1–17. Academic, New York, 1980.

[224] L. F. Shampine. *Numerical Solution of Ordinary Differential Equations.* Chapman and Hall, New York, 1994.

[225] L. F. Shampine and R. C. Allen. *Numerical Computing: An Introduction.* W. B. Saunders, Philadelphia, PA, 1973.

[226] L. F. Shampine and C. W. Gear. A user's view of solving stiff ordinary differential equations. *SIAM Review,* 21:1–17, 1979.

[227] L. F. Shampine and M. K. Gordon. *Computer Solution of Ordinary Differential Equations.* W. H. Freeman, San Francisco, 1975.

[228] L. F. Shampine, H. A. Watts, and S. M. Davenport. Solving nonstiff ordinary differential equations—the state of the art. *SIAM Review,* 18:376–411, 1976.

[229] K. Sigmon. *MATLAB Primer.* 4th ed. CRC Press, Boca Raton, FL, 1994.

[230] R. D. Skeel. Equivalent forms of multistep methods. *Math. Comp.,* 33:1229–1250, 1979.

[231] R. D. Skeel and J. B. Keiper. *Elementary Numerical Computing with Mathematica.* McGraw-Hill, New York, 1993.

[232] I. H. Sloan and S. Joe. *Lattice Methods for Multiple Integration.* Oxford University Press, New York, 1994.

[233] B. T. Smith, J. M. Boyle, Y. Ikebe, V. C. Klema, and C. B. Moler. *Matrix Eigensystem Routines: EISPACK Guide.* 2d ed. Springer-Verlag, New York, 1970.

[234] G. D. Smith. *Numerical Solution of Partial Differential Equations.* 3d ed. Oxford University Press, New York, 1985.

[235] I. M. Sobol'. *A Primer for the Monte Carlo Method.* CRC Press, Boca Raton, FL, 1994.

[236] H. Späth. *One Dimensional Spline Interpolation Algorithms.* A K Peters, Ltd., Wellesley, MA, 1995.

[237] P. H. Sterbenz. *Floating-Point Computation.* Prentice Hall, Englewood Cliffs, NJ, 1974.

[238] H. J. Stetter. Initial value problems for ordinary differential equations: Development of ideas, techniques, and implementation. In W. Gautschi, ed. *Mathematics of Computation 1943–1993: A Half Century of Computational Mathematics.* Vol. 48 of *Proc. Symp. Appl. Math.,* pages 205–224. Amer. Math. Soc., 1993.

[239] G. W. Stewart. *Introduction to Matrix Computations.* Academic, New York, 1973.

[240] G. W. Stewart. *Afternotes on Numerical Analysis.* SIAM, Philadelphia, PA, 1996.

[241] G. W. Stewart and T. G. Sun. *Matrix Perturbation Theory.* Academic, New York, 1990.

[242] J. Stoer and R. Bulirsch. *Introduction to Numerical Analysis.* 2d ed. Springer-Verlag, New York, 1993.

[243] G. Strang. *Introduction to Applied Mathematics.* Wellesley-Cambridge Press, Wellesley, MA, 1986.

[244] G. Strang. *Linear Algebra and Its Applications.* 3d ed. W. B. Saunders, New York, 1988.

[245] G. Strang. Wavelets. *Amer. Scientist,* 82:250–255, 1992.

[246] G. Strang. *Introduction to Linear Algebra.* Wellesley-Cambridge Press, Wellesley, MA, 1993.

[247] G. Strang and G. Fix. *An Analysis of the Finite Element Method.* Prentice Hall, Englewood Cliffs, NJ, 1973.

[248] V. Strassen. Gaussian elimination is not optimal. *Numer. Math.,* 13:354–356, 1969.

[249] J. C. Strikwerda. *Finite Difference Schemes and Partial Differential Equations.* Chapman and Hall, New York, 1989.

[250] A. H. Stroud. *Approximate Calculation of Multiple Integrals.* Prentice Hall, Englewood Cliffs, NJ, 1972.

[251] A. H. Stroud and D. Secrest. *Gaussian Quadrature Formulas.* Prentice Hall, Englewood Cliffs, NJ, 1966.

[252] W. H. Swann. Direct search methods. In W. Murray, ed. *Numerical Methods for Unconstrained Optimization,* pages 13–28. Academic, New York 1972.

[253] P. N. Swarztrauber. Fast Poisson solvers. In G. H. Golub, ed. *Studies in Numerical Analysis,* pages 319–370. Math. Assoc. Amer., Washington, DC, 1984.

[254] R. A. Thisted. *Elements of Statistical Computing.* Chapman and Hall, New York, 1988.

[255] J. W. Thomas. *Numerical Partial Differential Equations,* Vol. 1. Springer-Verlag, New York, 1995.

[256] J. F. Traub. *Iterative Methods for the Solution of Equations.* Prentice Hall, Englewood Cliffs, NJ, 1964.

[257] L. N. Trefethen. Three mysteries of Gaussian elimination. *SIGNUM Newsletter,* 20(4):2–5, 1985.

[258] L. N. Trefethen and D. Bau. *Numerical Linear Algebra.* SIAM, Philadelphia, PA, 1997.

[259] S. Van Huffel and J. Vandewalle. *The Total Least Squares Problem.* SIAM, Philadelphia, PA, 1991.

[260] C. F. Van Loan. *Computational Frameworks for the Fast Fourier Transform.* SIAM, Philadelphia, PA, 1992.

[261] C. F. Van Loan. *An Introduction to Computational Science and Mathematics.* Jones and Bartlett, Sudbury, MA, 1996.

[262] C. F. Van Loan. *Introduction to Scientific Computing.* Prentice Hall, Upper Saddle River, NJ, 1997.

[263] R. S. Varga. *Matrix Iterative Analysis.* Prentice Hall, Englewood Cliffs, NJ, 1962.

[264] S. A. Vavasis. Gaussian elimination with pivoting is P-complete. *SIAM J. Disc. Math.,* 2:413-423, 1989.

[265] R. Wait and A. R. Mitchell. *Finite Element Analysis and Applications.* John Wiley & Sons, New York, 1985.

[266] J. S. Walker. *Fourier Analysis.* Oxford University Press, New York, 1988.

[267] J. S. Walker. *Fast Fourier Transforms.* 2d ed. CRC Press, Boca Raton, FL, 1996.

[268] D. S. Watkins. *Fundamentals of Matrix Computations.* John Wiley & Sons, New York, 1991.

[269] H. J. Weaver. *Applications of Discrete and Continuous Fourier Analysis.* John Wiley & Sons, New York, 1983.

[270] H. J. Weaver. *Theory of Discrete and Continuous Fourier Analysis.* John Wiley & Sons, New York, 1989.

[271] P. Wesseling. *An Introduction to Multigrid Methods.* John Wiley & Sons, New York, 1992.

[272] D. J. Wilde. *Optimum Seeking Methods.* Prentice Hall, Englewood Cliffs, NJ, 1964.

[273] J. H. Wilkinson. Error analysis of direct methods of matrix inversion. *J. ACM,* 8:281–330, 1961.

[274] J. H. Wilkinson. *Rounding Errors in Algebraic Processes.* Prentice Hall, Englewood Cliffs, NJ, 1963.

[275] J. H. Wilkinson. *The Algebraic Eigenvalue Problem.* Oxford University Press, New York, 1965.

[276] J. H. Wilkinson and C. Reinsch, eds. *Handbook for Automatic Computation, Linear Algebra,* Vol. 2. Springer-Verlag, New York, 1971.

[277] G. M. Wing. *A Primer on Integral Equations of the First Kind.* SIAM, Philadelphia, PA, 1991.

[278] M. H. Wright. Interior methods for constrained optimization. *Acta Numerica,* 1:341–407, 1992.

[279] M. H. Wright and S. Glassman. Fortran subroutines to solve linear least squares problems and compute the complete orthogonal factorization. Technical Report SOL-78-8, Systems Optimization Laboratory, Stanford University, Stanford, CA, April 1978.

[280] D. M. Young. *Iterative Solution of Large Linear Systems.* Academic, New York, 1971.

[281] O. C. Zienkiewicz and R. L. Taylor. *The Finite Element Method.* 4th ed. McGraw-Hill, New York, 1989.

[282] D. Zwillinger, ed. *Standard Mathematical Tables and Formulae.* 30th ed. CRC Press, Boca Raton, FL, 1996.

Index